Come, Let Us Reason Together

Come, Let Us Reason Together

A Life of John Wood Oman

Fleur S. Houston

☙PICKWICK *Publications* · Eugene, Oregon

COME, LET US REASON TOGETHER
A Life of John Wood Oman

Copyright © 2024 Fleur S. Houston. All rights reserved. Except for brief quotations in critical publications or reviews, no part of this book may be reproduced in any manner without prior written permission from the publisher. Write: Permissions, Wipf and Stock Publishers, 199 W. 8th Ave., Suite 3, Eugene, OR 97401.

Pickwick Publications
An Imprint of Wipf and Stock Publishers
199 W. 8th Ave., Suite 3
Eugene, OR 97401

www.wipfandstock.com

PAPERBACK ISBN: 978-1-6667-7551-8
HARDCOVER ISBN: 978-1-6667-7552-5
EBOOK ISBN: 978-1-6667-7553-2

Cataloguing-in-Publication data:

Names: Houston, Fleur S. [author].

Title: Come, let us reason together : a life of John Wood Oman / Fleur S. Houston.

Description: Eugene, OR: Pickwick Publications, 2024 | Includes bibliographical references and index.

Identifiers: ISBN 978-1-6667-7551-8 (paperback) | ISBN 978-1-6667-7552-5 (hardcover) | ISBN 978-1-6667-7553-2 (ebook)

Subjects: LCSH: Oman, John, 1860–1939. | Oman, John, 1860–1939—Biography. | Church history. | Theologians—Scotland. | Presbyterian Church.

Classification: BX9225 H68 2024 (paperback) | BX9225 (ebook)

VERSION NUMBER 01/16/24

To Walter

Contents

Preface | xi
Acknowledgments | xv
Abbreviations | xvii

1   Orkney | 1
     Parents | 2
     John Oman: Schoolboy | 13
     Siblings | 14
     The UP Church, Stromness | 18
     Geographical Environment | 26

2   Edinburgh | 34
     The University of Edinburgh | 34
     Studies | 36
     Students | 38
     The Edinburgh University United Presbyterian Students' Society | 42
     Oman's Friends | 48
     The Professors | 52
     Professors in the Honors Class | 55
     The Edinburgh University Philosophical Society | 63
     Graduation | 66

3   A Turning Point | 67
     The Case of William Robertson Smith | 68
     The Call | 73
     The United Presbyterian Church Divinity Hall | 80
     Practical Work | 93
     Theological Debate | 99

4   Germany | 101
        First Impressions | 102
        Erlangen | 107
        Heidelberg | 114
        Professors | 117

5   Ministry | 124
        Probationer | 124
        Pastoral Ministry | 132
        The Presbyterian Church of England | 137
        Clayport Street Church, Alnwick | 143
        Marriage | 150

6   Early Literary Works | 154
        On Religion: Speeches to Its Cultured Despisers | 154
        Vision and Authority | 158
        Academic Recognition | 167
        The Problem of Faith and Freedom in the Last Two Centuries | 168

7   Alnwick | 184
        Ecumenical Collaboration | 184
        The Education Bill | 186
        Chairs | 197
        A Visit to America | 202
        Call to Westminster College | 212

8   Westminster College Cambridge | 215
        Senatus | 217
        The College Course | 221
        College Devotional Life | 228
        Workers | 231
        "A Bad Book" | 235
        "A Stranger of the Dispersion" | 237
        The Glasgow Chair | 239

9   War | 241
        The First Months | 241
        War and Peace | 243
        The War and Its Issues | 246
        Westminster Students and the YMCA | 259
        National Service | 262

CONTENTS

    Oman and the YMCA | 264
    "Human Freedom" and "War" | 268
    Grace and Personality | 273
    The Army and Religion | 288
    Birmingham | 290

10 A New Age | 301
    Church Reunion | 301
    Westminster College After the War | 306
    The New Principal | 307
    Unity in Diversity | 309
    The World Alliance for Promoting International
        Friendship Through the Churches | 311
    A Visit to the Ruhr and the Rhineland | 314
    Promotion of International Christian Fellowship | 323
    Christianity in a New Age | 324

11 Moderator | 333
    Moderator | 333
    The Natural and the Supernatural | 338
    Poetic Intelligence | 348
    Further Pursuits | 354

12 Last Years | 361
    Germany 1934 | 361
    Germany 1935 | 368
    Retirement | 370
    Honest Religion | 374

13 "A Truly Prophetic Word" | 379

Bibliography | 389
Index of Subjects | 403
Index of Names | 409

Preface

This book originates in a painting. A portrait in a college dining room. Obviously executed by a consummate artist. The treatment of the subject was unusual. I wondered. It originates also in a book entitled *Grace and Personality*, an account of faith and love and freedom, which I read in 2004. But when I inquired further about John Oman, the subject of the portrait, the author of the book, I was told that, apart from his publications, there was very little primary source material. So I set out to find some.

Files slowly accumulated. Holidays in Orkney and Northumberland and meetings in Cambridge enabled work in archives. I gave short conference papers on Oman. But other priorities intervened and it wasn't until the pandemic lockdowns and their associated periods of social isolation that I had the space and time to begin to write this long-deferred biography.

I have tried to recount some of the events and imaginings that inspired Oman's thinking and made him who he was, using available sources as faithfully as possible. This did seem initially to present a major problem; most of his personal papers, including more than a hundred poems, were allegedly destroyed after his death on his own request. But the deficit has been supplied to an extent by material culled from nineteen different archives, large and small, in Britain, Sweden, Germany, the US, and Canada. The enterprise has sometimes felt like a giant jigsaw puzzle, and I have been aware of the constant need to guard against making erroneous assumptions.

On the grounds that such a narrative has to be embedded in a setting, and in line with Oman's theological emphasis on the importance of context, I have attempted throughout to evoke the richness and complexity of time and place.

Where possible, I have left him to speak for himself. Oman tells stories wonderfully well, often with a keen sense of humour; these cannot be made more concise without losing their impact. His two major published works,

Grace and Personality, with its theological acuity, and *The Natural and the Supernatural*, with its dynamic strata of profundity, defy too ready a summary. And elsewhere, as in *Honest Religion*, there is a particularly personal resonance in his address to the reader.

Oman uses non-inclusive language in line with the custom of his time and I have made no attempt to alter it or to comment on it. Capitalization of references to the divine is also reproduced from the texts—though interestingly this is not a feature of *The Natural and the Supernatural*.

I wish to acknowledge with gratitude the courteous permission of William Riviere as representative of the artist's estate to publish his uncle's portrait of John Oman. The image is reproduced with the permission of Westminster College Cambridge. And I am grateful too for the editor's permission to use two articles which were published in earlier versions in the *Journal of the United Reformed Church History Society*.

Thanks are due also to the trustees of the Marquis Fund for a generous grant toward costs of publication.

The thrill of working in archives has been enhanced by the pleasure of collaborating with archivists who have engaged enthusiastically with my research and made helpful suggestions. Among these, particular thanks are due to Margaret Thompson and Helen Weller of Westminster College Cambridge; David Martin of the Orkney archives, Kirkwall; archivists of the Evangelisches Zentralarchiv, Berlin; and the Edinburgh Centre for Research Collections, Edinburgh University Library.

It would be invidious to name all those with whom I have conversed to my profit on various aspects of this work, but I would like to single out the following: William Leslie Alexander, Charles Bailey, Martin Ballard, Stephen Bevans, David Thompson, Alan Witton. I recall with pleasure long conversations with Christa Kessler about the "missing manuscript" and the keen interest which drove her to find catalogues from the Leipzig Book Fair in the British Library; and I recall too the readiness with which Camilla Veitch accepted to translate from Swedish into English the report of Oman's adventures in the Ruhr and the Rhineland. I also acknowledge with gratitude the gift from his son of a beautiful edition of the poetry of Percy Hawkridge and the loan of her unpublished doctoral thesis from Daphne Hampson.

This research began to take shape in Orkney. I have happy remembrance of the hospitality extended to myself and Walter, my husband, by Peter and Kathleen Leith, neither of whom to my regret has lived to see the fruits of our collaboration. And I wish too to express appreciation to Patricia Long for a delightful shared journey of discovery, in anticipation of the day when there will be a plaque in St Magnus Cathedral to commemorate one of Orkney's most distinguished sons.

Finally, I wish to express a particular indebtedness to Clyde Binfield, who read and commented on the first eight chapters. From the outset he gave me grounds to think that this project was worthwhile and generously encouraged me to proceed.

The task of copy-editing a book like this, with extensive footnotes and references sometimes in German, and a sizeable bibliography, is not to be underestimated. And so I acknowledge with considerable appreciation the generous assistance of my daughter Amy, who copyedited two chapters at a particularly busy time in her life, and Walter, who set aside his own work to copyedit the remaining chapters, the references and bibliography, and save me from inexactitude. To him with love and acknowledgment of shared enterprise this book is dedicated.

Fleur S. Houston
Macclesfield, 2 August 2023

Acknowledgments

I am grateful to the editor of the *Journal of the United Reformed Church History Society* for his kind permission to reproduce the following articles in part or in whole:

> "In the Open Country of Action and Enquiry: John Oman and the Great War." *Journal of the United Reformed Church History Society*, vol. 9, no. 1, November 2012.
>
> "A Visit to the Prisons of the Ruhr and the Rhineland." *Journal of the United Reformed Church History Society*, vol. 9, no. 6, May 2015.

I acknowledge with appreciation William Riviere's permission on behalf of the artist's estate to publish the portrait of John Oman by Hugh Riviere. The image is reproduced with the permission of Westminster College Cambridge.

Abbreviations

CO	Conscientious Objector
COPEC	Conference on Christian Politics, Economics and Citizenship
ET	*Expository Times*
FC	Free Church
FOR	Fellowship of Reconciliation
HTR	*Harvard Theological Review*
JTS	*Journal of Theological Studies*
JURCHS	*Journal of the United Reformed Church History Society*
PCE	Presbyterian Church of England
RAMC	Royal Army Medical Corps
SCM	Student Christian Movement
SJT	*Scottish Journal of Theology*
UDC	Union of Democratic Control
UF	United Free (Church)
UP	United Presbyterian (Church)
URC	United Reformed Church
WCC	World Council of Churches
YMCA	Young Men's Christian Association

1

Orkney

THE PORTRAIT ABOVE THE fireplace in the dining room of Westminster College, Cambridge, is arresting. The subject, three-quarters length, adopts a casual stance, his strong hands thrust into the pockets of his dark slightly rumpled suit. He is wearing a teaching gown, and a deep clerical collar marks him out as a minister of religion. He gives an impression of being keenly engaged in discussion, and of enjoying the moment to the full. His head is upright and turned slightly to the left. The features are spare, and the neat grey beard and sparkling eyes convey a sense of poise and alertness. The background is luminous but plain: there are none of the customary accoutrements of his profession, there is nothing here to distract attention from the expressiveness of the face or the personality that is revealed.[1]

The subject of this remarkable portrait is John Wood Oman, at the time principal of the college and professor of systematic theology and apologetics. It was commissioned in 1933 to mark his year as moderator of the Presbyterian Church of England; and it was executed by Hugh Goldwin Riviere, the most notable portrait painter of his generation. Riviere's own opinion was that this was "the best portrait I shall ever paint."[2] There was an immediate rapport between the artist and his subject. On 9 April 1933, Riviere wrote: "[Oman] stayed with me and we had some wonderful talks. He is a remarkable personality and a man of the very widest interests

---

1. Nathaniel Micklem describes it as "one of the most speaking likenesses I have ever seen." *The Box and the Puppets*, 133.

2. Hugh G. Riviere to Roy Whitehorn, 26 April 1934, Westminster College archives.

possible. We both enjoyed his visit very much and I think I have turned out one of my best bits of work."[3]

Two months later, Norman Robinson, chair of the college committee, comments: "It is very interesting to see what Riviere says about the Principal. . . . I thought the portrait admirable. . . . The second time I looked at it, I felt that, if instead of the dog-collar and clericals, it had been oilskins or a fisherman's jersey, he might have been an Orkney fisherman with a tiller in his hand. Everyone I spoke to seemed delighted with it, and Riviere himself seems to feel he has really got here."[4]

Fanciful though Robinson's perception may be, it gives pause for thought. What if any is the connection between Oman the cosmopolitan intellectual, professor, and pastor, and the sea captain's son from Orkney? Oman himself always possessed a strong sense of the formative power of place. He observed about Immanuel Kant: "Kant's philosophy . . . is not proved right or wrong by any fact about his life. But the infusion of Scottish blood and the home of a poor and pious saddler did something to make him a different man, and, therefore, a different thinker, from what he would have been had it been Italian blood and the home of a wealthy and worldly nobleman."[5] So what was it about Oman's early years in Orkney that made him distinctive in later life as a person and as a thinker? What were the formative influences that were brought to bear on him in his childhood?

John Wood Oman was born on 23 July 1860 in the farm of Biggings, in the parish of Stenness, Orkney, the third child and second son of Isabella Irvine Rendall, aged thirty-three, and her husband, Simon Rust Oman, forty-three. But the baby's birth was more than a mere biological event. He had an inheritance from the past which gave his life meaning before he was consciously aware of it.[6]

Parents

Mother

His mother, Isabella, was a dressmaker by profession. Before her marriage, she shared a house in Main Street, Stromness, with her unmarried aunt, Ann, who was a bonnet-maker, and it is highly likely that Oman's lifelong esteem of skilled workmanship may originate at least in part in his family

3. Postcard to Roy Whitehorn, Westminster College archives.
4. Letter to Roy Whitehorn, 16 June 1933, Westminster College archives.
5. Oman, *Natural*, 352.
6. Oman, *Natural*, 267–68.

associations with Stromness coopers, straw-plaiters, and stocking-knitters. Isabella's father, Magnus Rendall, like his father before him, was a master cooper, servicing a thriving seasonal economy based on the herring industry. Her mother, Isabella Wood, was, before marriage, a schoolmistress,[7] typically teaching local girls the arts of "reading, knitting stockings, and sewing white seam,"[8] and her aunt, Ann, was engaged in straw-plaiting.

The name John Wood came down in Isabella's family, John Wood Oman, as he was proud to state, being the fourth to bear the name. His maternal great-grandfather, John Wood (1764–1815), appears to have been conservative even by the standards of the time. He "was about the last man in Stromness to wear a long waistcoat and silver buckles to his shoes and was a strong supporter of the parish minister and all things established."[9] His son, the second John Wood (1789–1834), was said to be more dismissive of the parish minister. He "made Mr Clouston's stale productions more stale by repeating them, when well out of his father's ears, word for word well garnished with portentous coughs." He was a teacher, who "taught the youth of Stromness with such a strong hand that it is said he could send an offender with one cuff from the far side of the room into the fireplace."[10] The third John Wood (1820–67), his son and Oman's uncle, was like many others in the family a master mariner.

From the above, we may surmise that Isabella's family heard sermons regularly in the Established Church. When at the age of twenty-six, on 24 May 1853, she married Simon Oman, then a master mariner in Stromness, the ceremony was conducted by the parish minister, the Reverend David Ramsay. We know very little about her as a person but Oman makes one allusion, while minister of Clayport, to her piety. After a lively and whimsical account of a train conversation on a winter's evening with a light-weight boxing champion, he concludes: "My mother's prayer I felt had been answered in my case as prayers often are, later on. I had been helpfully profited, my mind having been intellectually stimulated and my heart socially advantaged and even my soul spiritually expanded. I too have had a look over the dividing wall and have felt that if now, as long ago, the childlike spirit finds easily the Kingdom of Heaven the prize-fighter probably enters before the 'good sort of chap.'"[11] In an undated photograph, possibly taken

---

7. In the 1861 census, the widowed Isabella is earning a living as a "stocking knitter."
8. Sinclair, *Statistical Account*, 16:453: Stromness, County of Orkney.
9. Oman, *Orkneys*.
10. Oman, *Orkneys*.
11. "Tommy Colligan, Light Weight—an interview," unpublished manuscript, Westminster College archives.

around 1881, she is comfortably seated, a matriarch in her Sunday best, surrounded by all her children, and flanked by Captain Oman and her sister, Jane.[12] She looks directly at the camera, with a sweet unselfconscious smile.

Father

Of the Oman side of the family, we know rather more. The family tree could be traced to the fifteenth century, when the King of France had a bodyguard of Scots archers, famed for their courage and loyalty.[13] These, for a contemporary eyewitness, "were real giants for the shortest of them stood nine hands high." They wore as uniform "rich coats of fine white cloth, with a guard of silver bullion an handful broad."[14] Amongst them, in the 1469 muster rolls, there are several distinctive Orkney names, amongst whom Jehan Omon. And from him, three Stenness households of Oman or Omand or Omond claimed descent, all distantly related to one another.[15]

In the mid-eighteenth century, Helen Omand of Bigswell gave birth to a son out of wedlock, and named him John.[16] John went on to marry Mary Halcro in 1771, and inherited through her the farm of Biggings. Their fourth child, James, and his wife, Margaret Sclater from Orphir, made their home in a smallholding of three acres at Bridge of Waith. This was a very small property at a time when "there were more children than the fields could hold."[17]

And so James and Margaret's eldest son, Simon Rust Oman, like thousands of young men from Orkney in the nineteenth century, sailed to the Davis Strait in search of whales.[18] About his father's experiences as a whaler, Oman remains silent. But we know from other sources that this was an occupation mired in whale oil, blubber, and blood,[19] and extremely peril-

---

12. Jane, four years younger than Isabella, married a master mariner, John Flett Wood, who died in 1867 at the age of forty-seven.

13. Forbes-Leith, *Scots Men-At-Arms*, 1:56.

14. Clouston, *Orkney and the Archer Guards*.

15. The Omands of Bigswell, who kept their small estate at a time when these were being absorbed by larger ones, Omond of Savedale who had been there for ten or twelve generations and Oman of Biggings. The different spellings are variants of the same name.

16. Was she "the daughter of one of the elders" who was "dealt with in private" by the Kirk Session in a roadside alehouse at Knockhall? See Leith and Leonard, *Kirk and Parish*, 7.

17. Brown, *Orkney Tapestry*, 42.

18. Obituary, *Orcadian*, 31 July 1897, 5.

19. See *Hampshire Telegraph*, 16 July 1892.

ous. There were few years when vessels and crew were not lost.[20] Herman Melville's novel *Moby-Dick*, published in 1851, and hailed as a classic account of whaling in the mid-nineteenth century, depicts the brutality and violence that can arise between men under those circumstances, and gives a remarkable picture of the ongoing remorseless struggle between men and the sea. More recently the way in which the sea threatens to exact its revenge upon humanity is captured in the wordlessly immersive documentary *Leviathan*,[21] shot off the coast of New Bedford, the "whaling city" of New England, where Melville's fictional ship, the *Pequod*, is said to have given chase to the great white whale. We react viscerally as the crash and thunder of the waves shuts out the stars, we hear the screeching chains and winches, we see the fish leaping and the gulls wheeling vertiginously. We are left in no illusion about the challenges involved. But men from Orkney, according to John Franklin, whose vessels watered in Stromness on their way to the Arctic, would rise to the challenge with bravery and endurance.[22] They were accustomed to pitting their energies against the sea. With the mighty outpouring of water between the Atlantic and the North Sea and the intermittent ferocity of the gales in the Pentland Firth, the Orkney waters were amongst the most dangerous in the world and shipwrecks were frequent occurrences.[23]

"By industry, application, and dint of perseverance" Simon Oman graduated from whaling to be a shipmaster in Stromness.[24] This was a highly responsible professional position. As master of a merchant coastal vessel, he had to prove his ability to sail in command of an oceangoing ship, and was responsible for its safe and efficient operation. When he inherited the farm of Biggings from his parents on or soon after his marriage in 1853, "he devoted his natural abilities to the management of matters which were more parochial,"[25] combining these in the mid 1860s with the duties of captain of the mail-boat which plied between Stromness and Scrabster.

---

20. See the account in the *Morning Post*, 20 September 1847, of the destruction of the *Bon Accord* and the *Alfred* in the Davis Straits, and the notification in *Pall Mall Gazette*, 7 November 1892, of a steam whaler crushed by icebergs with thirty-five lives lost.

21. By Véréna Paravel and Lucien Castaing-Taylor, 2013.

22. Oman, *Orkneys*.

23. The wreck of the *Albion* off Graemsay on 1 January 1866 led to the launching of the first Orkney lifeboat the following year.

24. *Orkney Herald*, 4 August 1897, 5.

25. Obituary, *Orcadian*, 31 July 1897.

Udaller

Captain Oman, described in his obituary in the *Orcadian* as a "much respected, shrewd, honest, calculating, and highly intelligent man," now applied himself systematically to acquiring and improving land. Land tenure in Orkney was subject to Norse law,[26] according to which Simon was a udaller, a freeholder who held his land by absolute right.[27] He held that land inalienably for himself and his heirs and thus enjoyed a sense of freedom and independence.[28] According to the Mutual Disposition and Settlement of 10 January 1887, Simon held three portions of inherited udal land, itemized in his will:[29] "All and hail nine settings malt mailing udal land under the house of Clicking acquired by my father James Oman"; "all and hail my two meils four settings mailing under the house of Biggings sometime possessed by John Miller tenant and now by myself"; and "all and hail my eight settings mailing formerly under the house of Tongue now under Luath sometime laboured by my father, then William Isbister and now by myself." This accumulated udal land was to go to Isabella in her lifetime and thereafter was settled on James as eldest son and his "heirs and assignees whomsoever heritably and irredeemably." In addition, on 14 November 1856, a disposition in his favor was granted by David Balfour Esq of Balfour and Trenabie, of the lands of Fea (nine and a half acres), and Simon "acquired absolute right by assignation" to a further eleven and three quarter acres "part of the allotted commonty of Stenness." Finally, on 13 April 1869 Simon "acquired by absolute right by assignation in [his] favour" the lands of Foulmires and pertinents.

When Simon acquired these lands, they were not necessarily well maintained. In the mid-nineteenth century, farming was, as John Oman testifies, "of the most primitive character."[30] The Statistical Account of 1845

---

26. This had been the case since 1471 when the Orkneys were annexed to the Scottish Crown and land tenure continued to be governed by Norse law. The prevailing opinion of Scottish lawyers today is that entitlement under udal law represents a survival of customary land tenure within the prevailing body of Scots law.

27. Jones, "Notions of Udal Law"; Sutherland, *Against the Wind*, 30.

28. By the time Simon died in 1897, his eldest son, James, had settled in Madagascar, but he continued to be listed in the land register as proprietor of Biggings, Clatkins, Foulmire and Brecks until 1922, his brother Simon being listed as proxy. According to family tradition, James married and raised a family in Madagascar. In law, these would have had prior claim to the land. Even so, as the eldest of Simon Rust Oman's surviving children, it was John who inherited the property in 1922 following James's death on 22 November 1921, and maintained Biggings with the help of a tenant farmer for the rest of his life. On John's death, ownership of Biggings passed to his eldest daughter, Isabella, who sold it around 1952 to the sitting tenant.

29. Orkney Archives, Kirkwall.

30. Oman, *Orkneys*.

shows little or no improvement since the first Account in 1795.[31] Although the best land in the vicinity of the Kirk of Stenness was cultivated, rotation of crops between bear and oats ensured that it was never allowed to remain fallow and the ensuing crops were of poor quality. Animals were not enclosed; lambs were carried off by ravens and eagles, farmers set their dogs on the wild sheep and starving cows, and small swine rooted up any available grass. By 1861, however, Biggings was already a reasonably sized farm of sixty acres. Over the next ten years, it more than doubled in size: it is listed in the 1871 census as a farm of 150 acres, of which ninety are arable; the household includes a dairy maid, a house maid and a farm servant; and, significantly, small ancillary cottages are home to a pauper, an egg merchant, and a knitter.

Ten years later, Biggings is described as "a large and handsome farm house with a garden and offices attached,"[32] and along with the egg merchant, the census for 1881 records a farm manager and an apprentice. By then it appears that animals were maintained over the winter and the land fertilized: in a codicil to his will, dated 8 May 1894, Simon assigns straw and fodder on the farm along with a threshing mill to "James Oman and his aforesaids," with provision for all disponees to buy the turnips and manure. Captain Oman has proved to be an astute entrepreneur, a skilled farmer, and a person of status.[33]

It is evident too that he was generous towards those who were less fortunate. He took good care to ensure that his widowed sister-in-law, Jane Rendall or Wood, lived out her life in security in Stromness; and on his daughter Margaret's death[34] he made provision for "the maintenance, education and upbringing of such of Margaret's children as may require the same" or to "establish any of them in business" or otherwise. He was described as a "kind, liberal, warm-hearted neighbour," and the author of his obituary writes: "the widow, the orphan, the old and afflicted, will miss a bountiful and generous friend indeed."[35]

31. Sinclair, *Statistical Account*, vol. 14 (1795) 125–38 (Firth and Stenness); *New Statistical Account*, vol. 16, 520–22 (Firth and Stenness).

32. Ordnance Survey Name Books—*Orkney*.

33. He was very far from the image of the dour crofter "needing to know how to plough a stony field" (Bevans, *John Oman*, 6) or the "humble farmer" evoked by Yandall Woodfin (Woodfin, *John Wood Oman*, 3). Following his death, the *Orkney Herald* of 11 May 1898 describes the farm of Biggings as "135 acres or thereby of land, mostly arable."

34. Margaret Slater Oman died of heart disease in 1896 in hospital in Stromness at the age of thirty-eight. She left a husband, Charles Robertson, and seven children, the youngest of whom, Isabella, was then two years old.

35. *Orcadian*, 31 July 1897; *Orkney Herald*, 4 August, 1897.

Influence on His Son

Captain Oman was described in the United Free Church Record as "a fine type of the old Norse UDALLER or landlord."[36] The writer makes an implicit comparison with John Oman, whose "great influence over his students" was said to be "due not merely to his learning and ability, but still more to the strength and simplicity of his character, and his genuineness and honesty." In acknowledging his father's influence, John paid him a graceful tribute in dedicating his Kerr lectures, published in 1906 under the title *The Problem of Faith and Freedom in the Last Two Centuries*,[37] "to the memory of my father, a scholar only of life and action, but my best teacher." The dedication is evocative; it conveys esteem, affection and filial piety. But might it also indicate a more specific influence? Over the course of nine lectures, Oman had introduced students at the Glasgow United Free College to "the ultimate problem of at least the last two centuries," that is, "the relation of Faith and Freedom, the problem of how Faith is to be absolute and Freedom absolute, yet both one."[38] Might some of Oman's thought on these subjects have been stimulated, not just by "really great books,"[39] but also, more personally, by the influence of his father? If so, in what might that consist?

We may note here that there is a certain resonance between the wording of Oman's dedication and his observations about the influence of the father of Immanuel Kant upon the great philosopher.[40] It was the influence of his father, a harness-maker, that shaped Kant's ability to "look for the freedom and dignity of man in deeper matters than intellectual attainments or any kind of outward situation."

Was Oman's suspicion of creeds and confessional formulae inherited at least in part from his father? A leitmotiv of *The Problem of Faith and Freedom* is that creeds and confessions are potentially an authoritarian barrier to true faith. In his introductory lecture, Oman argues that "we have, in no right sense, either revelation or faith, so long as any human voice comes between us and God. The idea that an outward infallible authority is necessary for faith, presupposes that the revelation of God is a thing wholly foreign to us. That means, in the last issue, an unspiritual trust, for ultimately our belief must come to rest on the material guarantee."[41]

---

36. *United Free Church Record*, June 1922.
37. Oman, *Faith and Freedom*.
38. Oman, *Faith and Freedom*, 4.
39. Oman, *Faith and Freedom*, 27.
40. Oman, *Faith and Freedom*, 170. Oman returns to this theme in Oman, *Natural and Supernatural*, 267–68.
41. Oman, *Problem*, 23.

This distrust of human formulas was very much in the spirit of the Secession.[42] From 1799, when Burgher seceders, spiritual descendants of Ebenezer Erskine, disclaimed "compulsory measures in religion," to 1806 when Anti-Burgher Seceders declared that "no human composure ... can be supposed to contain a full and comprehensive view of divine truth," the Westminster Confession was held to be subordinate to its ultimate authority, holy scripture.[43] While we know nothing about Simon Oman's personal approach to Church affairs, we do know that in 1878, during the ministry of Mr. Kirkwood, he was called to the eldership of Victoria Street United Presbyterian Church, Stromness, but declined office following interview by the Session. The Session minutes laconically record that "[the elders elect] appeared one by one before the Session who dealt with them one by one as to their soundness of piety and soundness in the faith and principles of the Church, and also their acceptance of the call addressed to them by the congregation. Messrs. John Craigie and Simon Oman declined."[44] The most usual reason for this was an inability on grounds of conscience to accept the confessional Standards, the Westminster Confession and the Longer and Shorter Catechism. Elders of the United Presbyterian (UP) Church were required to subscribe to the Westminster Confession as a detailed statement of the Church's doctrine. So too were ministers,[45] and it has been suggested that the prospect of signing up to this seventeenth-century Calvinist manifesto might have been a factor in the leaching of able theological students from the theological hall.[46] Given his strength of character and his liberal-mindedness, Captain Oman may have had scruples about subscription to the Westminster Confession in its entirety. If so, he would not have been alone. Even as he declined the call to eldership, concerns around the theological adequacy of the Confession were coming to a head in the UP Church.[47] But there we must leave the matter for the moment.

42. For details, see below, 18–20.

43. Cheyne, "Bible and Confession," 26.

44. Session Minutes, Victoria Street United Presbyterian Church, OCR 30/3, 15 November 1878.

45. Robert Balmer waited for two years before being licensed in 1812 by the Associate Presbytery of Edinburgh on the grounds that he "could not wholly admit the formula which he would be required to subscribe as a licentiate" (Chambers and Thomson, eds., *Biographical Dictionary*). When John Cairns was licensed in 1845, he hesitated to sign till after a lengthy discussion with the Presbytery (MacEwan, *John Cairns*, 212–13, 226).

46. Cairns, *Autobiography*, 125. It had long been obvious that chapter 23 of the Westminster Confession, "Of the Civil Magistrate," was not applicable to a church of the Secession.

47. Drummond and Bulloch, *Church in Late Victorian Scotland*, 35.

Schools

In this short detour, we have temporarily neglected an important aspect of Captain Oman's achievement. He knew the value of education. The writer of his obituary in the *Orcadian* indicates that he "manifested great zeal for the cause of education, and did all in his power to advance whatever tended to the comfort of pupils and teachers, and encouraged progress in every well-directed effort. Prior to the Education Act of 1872, he was one of three pioneers of education who praiseworthily built a good and commodious school, and diligently and successfully laboured to make it a success."[48]

The need for a school to serve the children who lived at the western side of Stenness had been felt for some time. The two existing denominational schools presented difficulties. Stenness Parish School, shared by the parishes of Firth and Stenness, was situated at Stymilders, about three miles from Biggings, on what was the main road between Kirkwall and Stromness. The location was already unsatisfactory: some children would have had to travel quite a distance to get to school in all weathers. And matters were not improved when in 1860 a new road was opened, bypassing Stymilders. The Free Church, established in Stenness in 1843, had set up its own school at Braeside, not far from Savedale. In 1860, the schoolmaster, Philip Corner from Orphir, "was considered to be such a good teacher that several scholars from neighbouring parishes attended his school, Mrs Corner giving them board and lodgings. . . . The average attendance [was] estimated at forty, a considerable number for those days when attendance was not compulsory and there was no transport to school."[49] In 1863, "Captain Omond [sic] of the Royal Mail" gave a prize and his eight-year old son James won one. The following year, the *Orkney Herald* reported on further successful examinations and noted that the pupils received instruction in "Latin and Euclid." In 1865 the *Orkney Herald* reported "the superior character of the teaching given at this school, and to congratulate the inhabitants in possessing so faithful and diligent a teacher as Mr Corner." However, there appears to have been some difficulty over the headmaster's stipend. The minister of Firth, the Reverend William Smith, reported in 1867 that an offer from the Education Committee of the Church of Scotland to pay a salary of £25 "if the buildings were handed over free of charge for ten years to the Education Committee," had been refused by the trustees of the Free Church buildings.[50] And Philip Corner and his family subsequently moved to Rendall,

---

48. Obituary, *Orcadian*, 31 July 1897.
49. Leith and Leonard, *Kirk and Parish*, 17.
50. *Orkney Herald*, March 1867.

where he became head of the "Madras Society School"[51] and inspector of the poor. He would have moved about the time that John started at the Braeside school, winning a prize in the junior division in October 1867, as did his sister Isabella, while Margaret won a prize in the senior division.

However, the days of the Braeside school were numbered and in January 1868, only three months after John Oman won his first prize, a Madras School was founded on non-denominational principles and serving Stenness only.[52] The school was to be run according to the "Madras System of Education" as devised by Dr. Andrew Bell of St Andrews and Madras (1753–1831). Key to this was the notion of mutual tuition where older children mentored the younger ones, and the absence of corporal punishment. The idea of a learning environment where "the pupil was free to speak as the teacher, and anyhow by the contact of mind with mind"[53] was central to Oman's own teaching method in his Cambridge years and regarded even then as something of an innovation.

Preparations for the new school had got off to a good start the previous year, with hearty assurances of goodwill from David Balfour Esq of Balfour, who promised to double the subscriptions made by tenants in the parish and provide "firing" for use of a teacher. Captain Oman began the subscription list with £10 and made a free grant of two acres of land from his property as a site for the building, with ground for the use of the teacher. The Reverend William Smith of Firth assured those present that promoters were members of all religious denominations in the parish who were "desirous to provide a good school and teacher for the benefit of every family who chose to avail themselves of the privilege."

The *Orkney Herald*[54] reported that "considerable difficulties had been met with by the Committee in prosecuting their object, but they had now happily been surmounted. Upwards of £94 had been raised in the district and this, with a grant of £50 from the Bell fund, had built the present commodious and substantial schoolhouse along with a dwelling house for the teacher. A grant of £25 a year had been received from the Educational Committee of the Church of Scotland; so that along with the Government grant and the school fees, they would be able to provide for the comfortable maintenance of their teacher."[55]

51. Existing records do not reveal which of the two Madras Schools came first.

52. Gregor Lamb, *Sib Folk News*, 78 (June 2016); Alastair MacDonald, *Sib Folk News*, 79 (September 2016).

53. Oman, *Concerning the Ministry*, 156.

54. 7 January 1868.

55. This was James Morrison's first situation as a teacher, aged twenty. He recorded almost daily in the school log book (Orkney Archives), "lessons according to time-table,

The school opened with a soirée of tea and fruit attended by 200 persons on 2 January 1868. Fifteen pupils enrolled immediately, and enrolment continued over the next few months. While the school log-book does not record the names of these pupils, it may be anticipated, given the fact that their father was a trustee, that Oman children, at least Margaret, ten, and Isabella, six, were amongst them.[56] It is possible that John, who was eight, was also enrolled, although he was to embark that year on his nine years of further education in Stromness.

The examiners visited the school in February 1870, and gave a glowing report, congratulating "the teacher, the trustees, and the parents, on the great success of this school, it being certainly one of the best which has fallen to their lot to examine."[57]

In 1873, when the School Board of the parish of Firth and Stenness was elected according to the terms of the Education (Scotland) Act 1872, Captain Oman was elected chair of trustees, a post which he held for the next nineteen years. The Madras School was now to serve as the Public School on condition that it remained where it currently stood.[58] However, by 1890, both school and schoolhouse were in need of repair. On 22 August 1890 it was decided "not to repair the old school but to build a new school mid-way between Germiston and Ireland, measured by the public road."[59] Oman's protest against the proposed move was registered and the reply from Colonel Balfour, on learning that the proposed new building would be on his land, was "left to lie on the table." Two years later, Captain Simon Oman's resignation from the Board due to ill health was accepted with regret.

---

the children made the usual progress." There was continuing enrolment over the next few months.

56. The school roll only begins in 1875, but we may assume that the trustees had a vested interest.

57. *Orkney Herald*, 27 March 1870.

58. In the minutes of the next meeting, held on 17 October 1873, it appears that a problem had occurred with the transfer. It transpired that no decision could be made by the Trustees without the agreement of the minister of the parish and that, owing to the state of his health, it could not be got; so the transfer was deferred.

59. These were the extremities of the parish. The School Board minutes of 7 July 1893 confirm that the new buildings were finished according to the plan and specification and that the Board would accept the building from the contractor. They also confirm that the old school buildings were sold by public roup (auction)on 7 March 1894 to Mr Omand of Savedale, Stenness.

John Oman: Schoolboy

On 2 February 1875, Magnus Spence became headmaster of the Firth and Stenness Public School at the age of 22, and that same year the names of the two youngest Oman children, Simon, 11, and Thomas, 8, are recorded in the register. John Oman later alludes to Spence as "my old friend,"[60] and the enquiring teenager would have had much in common with the scholarly young teacher.[61]

But although the school provided an excellent basic education, it was not intended to prepare for university entrance. And from 1868, John was regularly steering an Orkney yole[62] across the Bay of Ireland to Stromness, where he attended a "private school" with the Robertson boys[63] from a neighboring farm.[64] When, allegedly, neighbors expressed concern at a child undertaking such a dangerous crossing, Simon is said to have expressed utter confidence in the boy's ability to handle the boat.[65] His tutor, from family recollection, lived in the Double Houses at Ness.[66] It is more than likely that this was Alexander Riddoch, listed in the 1871 census as a sixty-year-old widowed Free Church minister with three young children and a servant.[67] The oldest child, Alexander, was born in Stenness. Mr. Riddoch had been in Stenness for around twenty years but his ministry there had come to grief. His wife died leaving him with small children, and to provide a mother for the children he secretly married his servant-girl. Although this was arguably legal under Scots law, the presbytery charged him with fornication

---

60. Oman, *Orkneys*.

61. Spence maintained, first in Stenness and later at Deerness, the weather station which had been serviced daily for fifty-eight years since 1827 by the Reverend Charles Clouston. In 1893 he published an article on "The Standing Stones and Maeshowe of Stenness," and in 1914, his major work, *Flora Orcadensis*, which remains an authoritative guide to wild flowers in Orkney.

62. A boat of Nordic design and rigged for sailing, the yole was heavier than a dinghy, sharp at both ends like a whaler, suitable for more open water and heavier seas—the Bay of Ireland is open to the Atlantic.

63. The Robertsons rode on horseback six miles from Lyking in Sandwick to Stromness with a farm hand to take the horses back.

64. In October 1877, Oman's matriculation certificate from Edinburgh University testifies that for the previous nine years he had attended a "private school" in Stromness.

65. Family communication. It is possible that John may have been accompanied by James who in 1868 would have been thirteen; it would have required skill and experience rather than physical strength to steer a yole across the Bay of Ireland.

66. Six houses back to back with their own pier, built by the redoubtable business woman, Christian Robertson.

67. I am indebted to Patricia Long for this identification. See also Leith and Leonard, *Kirk and Parish*, 16n62.

and deposed him from the ministry. Feelings ran high in the congregation, some of whom left and went elsewhere, and Mr. Riddoch himself moved to Rendall and then to Stromness. It is almost certain that the tutoring arrangement served the dual purpose of giving John a solid grounding for university education and helping Mr. Riddoch to make a living.

Details of John's education in Stromness are sparse, but we do know that he received at least the rudiments of a classical education. He reflects "my only regret is that the time I spent was not better directed, for the little I did plough through gave me my first idea of literature, increased my power to enjoy it, if not to write it, and gave the bleak but very important knowledge that most of our thoughts had been thought not only before us but before our age, and that there were great men before our modern Agamemnons."[68] From his earliest days, "a problem was a provocation."[69] He was a voracious reader. He later recalls that: "My career as an Apologist began by reading Tom Paine's Age of Reason at fourteen; and my business in life has led me to read many worse books since then: and there may be ground for dubiety about the result. Yet I hope I have never taken . . . the ideas of the materialists like the faith of the prophets."[70] However, John's tutor attempted to discourage his parents from their ambition to send him to Edinburgh University to study medicine;[71] he saw no promise "to justify such an effort"; the boy was a "dreamer."[72] Up to the age of fifteen, as he says of himself, "my chief ambitions [were] to sail a boat in a gale and ride a horse bare-backed."[73] But his parents clearly had confidence in their son's mental capabilities. With their support, John Oman went to university and his dreams led to a distinctive career, not as a doctor, but as a theologian and philosopher.

Siblings

Biggings must have been a hive of activity in 1860 when John was born. His elder brother James was five in 1860, and Margaret two. There were two ploughmen, from Hoy and Stenness, a dairymaid from Stromness, and a domestic servant, a ten-year old girl from Stenness who would doubtless have helped Isabella with the children. And before much longer

68. Oman, *Concerning the Ministry*, 166.
69. Alexander, "Memoir of the author," xvii.
70. Oman, *Concerning the Ministry*, 139.
71. Healey, *Religion and Reality*, 158.
72. Family communication.
73. Oman, *Concerning the Ministry*, 32.

John was to have three further siblings: Isabella (born 1862) Simon (1864) and Thomas (1867).

On 16 November 1876, when she was nineteen, his sister Margaret married at Biggings a neighboring farmer, Charles Robertson of Upper Hobbister. They were wed by Thomas Kirkwood "after Banns according to the forms of the UP Church of Scotland,"[74] and John was one of two witnesses.

Like many of their contemporaries, James, Isabella, Simon, and Thomas were all engaged in trade in various ways.

The Orkney that Oman knew as a child was cosmopolitan. Before the whaling industry took off, farmers' sons traditionally found employment in fur-trading in Hudson's Bay or as seamen in the British merchant service. Each year, Hudson Bay Company ships visited Stromness where James Login supplied drink to the sea captains and water to the ships. As they waited for wind, they engaged men for the "Nor'-Wast" to trade with the indigenous peoples of west and north Canada. They exchanged a variety of goods including blankets in pink wool with black stripes for the beaver pelts used for waterproof felt hats. Cut off from family and friends, many took indigenous "country wives" and sent their children back to Orkney to live with relatives.[75] Metis children of Inuit or Cree ancestry were Oman's contemporaries. Some traders remained, some returned with considerable sums of money to settle as farmers or tradesmen at home. They brought back souvenirs: knife sheaths, or beautifully embroidered moccasins in beaver and moosehide. In Oman's boyhood, the exotic was almost commonplace.

Those who were employed in the merchant service also left their mark on the wider community when they returned with stories of far-flung places. Memories are still alive of a teacher in Stromness who had a hook, his hand having been bitten off by a shark. Oman recalls how "there were two at most three farmers who had not visited foreign shores in our immediate neighbourhood. One had traded in all the ports of the British Isles and the North of Europe, another was still Captain of an East Indiaman, another had prospected, traded and navigated in Australia. The result was a wonderful freshness and openness of mind. With that went a certain distinction of manner, which I think to some extent characterises the poorest and an extraordinary self-possession."[76]

---

74. Statutory Registers of Marriages, 1876, 017/11.

75. In the Stromness museum there are accounts of Peter Borwick of Caperhouse; William "Huskie" Saunders of Stromness; the Well sisters of Stronsay; and Elizabeth and William Flett from the Red River.

76. Oman, *Orkneys*.

James Oman

His elder brother James was typical. He was at home in Biggings in 1871, aged sixteen, listed in the census as "farmer's son," and may have gone to sea after that: he does not appear in any subsequent statutory records. A family photograph, possibly taken around 1881, shows him to be a strong, well-built man, with a direct gaze. By 1888, he appears to be well-established in Madagascar. In his father's obituary, he is described as "a successful business man in Madagascar."[77] According to one of the family, there was a story that he started the first ferry service between Madagascar and Africa; he seems to have been important as there were photographs of him in the platform party on important occasions.[78] It is in fact probable that he founded the firm of Oman in Natal, which was contracted to carry mail from Toliara on the south-west coast of Madagascar to Durban, where it could be forwarded to European destinations or to Antananarivo.[79] In November 1893, a Norwegian missionary, Gotfred Petersen, arrived in Nosy Ve, an island off the south-west coast of Madagascar. On this island there were merchants, French, German, Austrian, English, Swedish, Norwegian, who had fled the mainland because of raids from robbers. The Swedes and Norwegians were employed by the English. He writes: "Especially with the latter ones we took refuge. In particular I must mention one James Oman, who often had been a good refuge for the missionaries in Fiherenana."[80] Traders depended for their success on the ability to relate well to their trading partners, and the ensuing diplomatic skills would have stood James in good stead in difficult political situations. He died on 2 November 1921 and is buried in Morondava. The consular record of his death certifies that he was a trader.

Isabella

John Oman's younger siblings were also engaged in commerce. Isabella (1862–1947) described variously as "a dear sweet lady" or, when she visited Cambridge after the second world war, as "a screaming racist,"[81] married at the age of forty-seven the son of a near neighbor, James Moir Irvine, a grocer in Galashiels. The couple emigrated to Somerset West, South Africa, where James Irvine had business interests. Three of Isabella's nieces and

---

77. *Orcadian*, 31 July 1897, 5.
78. Personal family communication.
79. Campbell, *Economic History*, 268 and n112.
80. Petersen, *Seks år*, 92–93 (41 in pdf).
81. Personal family communications.

nephews, Margaret's children, also emigrated to South Africa: one of them, John, developed a fruit farm and began to market Co-operative Outspan.

Simon and Thomas

Oman's younger brothers, Simon (1864–1935), and Thomas (1867–1932), also made a career in commerce. Up to the first world war, the Langland Steam Navigation Company ran a regular boat service between Orkney, Liverpool and Manchester, calling at small places on the way that had no other connection with the outside world. This was how Simon, followed by Thomas,[82] found employment in Manchester as representatives for a grocery wholesaler, an Orcadian with family connections, whose main products were cheese, butter, bacon and eggs.

The brothers each married and made their homes in Manchester, where they were members of Grosvenor Square "Scottish" Presbyterian Church.[83] They were remembered with affection and esteem. Simon was, like his father, "a big and kindly" man, whose horticultural expertise was legendary. His married life was dogged with tragedy.[84] Thomas was the epitome of "brotherliness, love and unselfishness."[85] He radiated good will "by the fireside, amidst the distractions of the busy streets, in the Session House, or on the City Football Ground." He served for 26 years as Session Clerk of Grosvenor Square and "made it his business to know the people . . . without a shade of difference to suggest that some were important and some unimportant. . . . He did more than anyone to make the congregation a Christian household. . . . As a friend we think of Mr Oman as he was, a big man, big-natured, generous-minded, slow of speech and movement, but full of wisdom and goodness. He had kept, as long as I was in Grosvenor Square,

---

82. Thomas had gone to school at George Watson's, Edinburgh, when John was at university there, but had to abandon any hopes he may have had of going to university when he had an accident on the Salisbury Crags from which he suffered long-lasting effects.

83. A significant preaching station of the Presbyterian Church of England, in Lower Ormond Street. It was founded in 1844 by those expelled from St Peter's Square Presbyterian church. Following bomb damage, it was closed in 1940, and merged with Withington Presbyterian Church.

84. His wife died at a relatively young age of cancer; their little daughter drowned while playing in a park with her nursemaid; their son, George, a gifted graduate of Manchester University, died at the age of twenty-nine following a leg amputation. Simon went to South Africa after his wife's death to help Isabella wind up her late husband's estate, was involved in a car crash, and died of his injuries.

85. Tribute by Professor John S. B. Stopford, in Grosvenor Square, *Faithful as David*, 11.

his sense of fun, and his zest in a good game."[86] And the Reverend George D. Walker, who conducted his funeral service there in 1932, added: "It was . . . just what he so plainly was, that took away my fears in considering the call. I knew that in partnership with him I should be safe."[87]

The Biggings family appears to have been close-knit and affectionate. But because of a paucity of material, we can only guess at the family relationships. This may be partly because they were taken for granted or it may reflect a more profound reaction to events such as Margaret's premature death. In the context of a conversation with students in the Westminster Principal's Lodge many years later, Oman writes revealingly: "You may feel that . . . the deeper any experiences you have may be, the less you can talk about them. Even with your most intimate friends you are reserved about intimate things of your spirits. . . . My whole generation had something of this reserve, and perhaps I was one of the worst of them."[88]

The UP Church, Stromness

Oman had a distinctive political and spiritual heritage in the United Presbyterian Church, the fruits of which may be traced throughout his adult life. Although, as we have seen, his parents were married by the minister of the parish church, it is not long before evidence emerges of Simon and Isabella's allegiance to the UP congregation which assembled in the Meeting House in Stromness, where their first three children were baptized.

The young John Oman was familiar with family accounts[89] of how he was related through a branch of the Halcro family to brothers Ralph (1685–1752) and Ebenezer (1680–1754) Erskine, leaders of the original Secession from the Church of Scotland.[90] At a time when congregations were exhorted to respect "heroes of the faith," he is likely to have been well aware of Ebenezer's egalitarianism, force of character and reputation for acting on principle with honesty and courage. He would have learnt of his ancestor's uncompromising stances on two neuralgic issues. The first was doctrinal. A book entitled *The Marrow of Modern Divinity*[91] was repudiated by the

---

86. Tribute by the Reverend Joseph D. M. Rorke, in Grosvenor Square, *Faithful as David*, 8–9.

87. In Grosvenor Square, *Faithful as David*, 10.

88. Oman, *Concerning the Ministry*, 146.

89. Peter Leith, personal communication.

90. Ralph and Ebenezer were sons of the Reverend Henry Erskine by his second wife, Margaret Halcro (1647–1725) from Orkney.

91. See McCrie, *Marrow*; Lachman, *Marrow Controversy*.

General Assembly of the Church of Scotland in 1722 on the grounds of alleged antinomianism and universalism. Erskine, a firm believer in the free offer of grace to all, challenged the Assembly's decision and was rebuked. The second issue was a matter of polity. In 1731 the General Assembly ruled that, when a patron did not exert his right to present a minister to a congregation, selection would be restricted to the landowner and elders of the parish even where this would lead to the forced settlement of ministers on unwilling parishioners. The trigger for Ebenezer's suspension and subsequent deposition was his uncompromising sermon the following year at the Synod of Perth and Stirling, where he fulminated, "I can find no warrant from the Word of God to confer the spiritual privileges of his house upon the rich rather than the poor; whereas, by this Act, the man with the gold ring and gay clothing is preferred unto the man with the vile raiment and poor attire."[92]

Others followed Erskine out of the Established Church and the newly founded Associate Church grew rapidly until 1747, when it split following disagreement over the civic oath required of the burgesses of Edinburgh, Glasgow and Perth. This required the burgesses to pledge to "oppose papistry" and to support "true Protestant religion presently professed within this realm and authorised by the laws thereof." Many members of the Associate Church resisted the implied support of the Established Church and were designated "anti-burghers."

The Stromness congregation was "New Licht Anti-Burgher."[93] That is, it stemmed from that section of the Secession Church which condemned the swearing of the Burgess Oath as sinful and inconsistent with the Covenant and Secession Testimony, and refused additionally to recognize the authority of the civil magistrate in ecclesiastical affairs. But on 15 March 1819, the Stromness session "cordially approved" the proposed union with the New Licht Burghers.

The Secession Church represented more than a radical approach to ecclesiastical and political events, it also embodied, and particularly so in Orkney, a profound spiritual awakening. In Kirkwall, the Secession Church called its first minister, Mr. Broadfoot, in 1798. Faced with the stale sermons

92. Middleton, *Ralph Erskine*.

93. In 1820 the New Licht sections of the Anti-Burgher and Burgher Synods united, followed in 1847 by their union with the Relief Synod to become the United Presbyterian Church of Scotland. There were few doctrinal differences with the Free Church of Scotland, but there were differences of opinion as to the relationship between church and state. Fruitless negotiations took place between 1863 and 1873. Advances were made in 1896, which led to union on October 31 1900, and the birth of the United Free Church of Scotland. For further detail see Sell, "Living in the Half-Lights."

of the parish minister in Stromness, around thirty people from Stenness and Stromness, including one elder, Mr. Peter Skethway, a surgeon of Stromness, regularly walked to Kirkwall and back on a Sunday, a distance of fifteen miles each way, to worship God and hear the gospel preached. Their commitment was obvious, but the distance was too great for their families. So money was raised by several congregations towards building a place of worship in Stromness.[94] Many local people supplemented gifts of money with free labor: "even the poorer women among them are said to have helped by carrying on their backs the materials used in the building."[95] The building was opened for public worship on 7 December 1806. With the grant of disjunction from the Kirkwall congregation, the congregation called its first minister, the Reverend Andrew Wylie, on 16 March 1809. Numbers grew rapidly despite some "disapproval of having any tunes introduced in the Congregation that are of a quick, giddy, and light manner in their performance, and that have so many repeats in them"[96] The choice of an "Englishman" (a Mr. Hunter from Kirkwall) as precentor only fueled this indignation! But the session appears to have dealt with the matter wisely, and Oman writes[97] of Mr. Wylie's pastoral skills with empathy and appreciation. "He began his work amid all the evils which accompanied the French wars, when Dissent and treason were regarded as very much the same thing, when there was a very rough element in the town, and feeling was very bitter. In spite of this, he not only built up a large congregation, but I remember being told of how the worst women in the town, and the war had done a good deal to make them worse than they were, mourned his loss. The people who were young when he died, and old when I knew them, still bore his image very tenderly in the depth of their hearts." Three years after Mr. Wylie's untimely death, a call was issued to Rev. William Stobbs, who was to serve for thirty-four years from 1829 to his death in 1863.

The congregation had now outgrown the old meeting-house. "The building was a small and inelegant structure, with a gallery around three sides of it. It was not completely floored; but the pews, which were narrow and uncomfortable, had boards or planks for the feet of the worshippers to rest upon. It was artificially lighted by candles, placed in wooden candelabra hung from the ceiling; and some anxiety was experienced in evading the melted tallow which fell from them. The number of worshippers at this time, also, was larger than at any subsequent period in the history of the

---

94. Small, *History of the Congregations*, 2:491.
95. *Victoria Street*, 4.
96. *Victoria Street*, 12.
97. Oman, "Reminiscences," 32.

congregation, the membership being 498 according to the Statistical Return made to the Presbytery in 1852, and remaining at nearly the same figures down to the year 1862."[98]

This was the church where the infant John Wood Oman was brought by his parents for baptism on 26 August 1860.[99] Like his elder siblings, James on 13 May 1855 and Margaret on 6 June 1858, John was baptized by William Stobbs, minister of the church. Mr. Stobbs died when John was three years old, but he made a lasting impression on the congregation. Oman affirms that "of Mr Stobbs I heard more than of any other person in the world."[100] His portrait, which Oman saw in many people's houses, made him a reality: an "old-fashioned portrait . . . with white hair standing up, and something both of the potentate and the parent in his face." He pursued his vocation with zeal. He catechized the whole congregation, and would surely have visited the family in Biggings. "And when he came to visit, there was no small talk as in this degenerate age, but Bible questions and catechism, and all the children were arranged before him with simply an appalling wealth of theological knowledge in their small heads." Besides the Sunday school which he superintended and in which he taught, he held large weekly Bible classes for young men and women, whom he visited at work, and, if they were not already having religious instruction, induced them to attend. He also saw to it that the Session kept a watchful eye on the conduct of members. There may have been some austerity, but as Oman writes "when one thinks of the Stromness of those days, with its harbour solid with storm-stayed vessels, and its many public houses full of sailors, the dancing and amusements upon which the Session frowned did perhaps lead to dangers requiring stern measures."[101]

---

98. *Victoria Street*, 20. In August 1860 the newly created management committee held a meeting, at which they agreed to "procure a plan for the rebuilding or enlarging the present place of worship, church and session house." The decision having been made to build a new church, work began in June 1862. The minutes of a meeting held in February 1862 state that "it should be left to the managers to fix upon the site for the new building on whatever portion of the ground belonging to the church they deem most expedient." (Minutes of the UP Congregation, Stromness, Orkney Archives.) There is also mention of money recouped from the sale of wood removed during the removal of the old building (*Victoria Street*, 21). Victoria Street UP Church opened for public worship on 28 June 1863 (*Victoria Street*, 20).

99. The Baptismal Register of the United Presbyterian Congregation of Stromness.

100. Oman, "Reminiscences," 33.

101. Oman, "Reminiscences," 33.

There was, however, "mingled . . . with the awe a very sincere regard and even affection for a minister who did watch for souls as one who must give an account."[102]

The Oman family, along with others from Stenness, walked in all weathers to church services in Stromness; by the bridge, a distance of around three miles. All the news of the parish was distilled on the way to church. Oman observes dryly: "On a Sunday in the old days, a sturdy people trudged along the roads, wet or dry. Here and there a patriarch bestrode a pony. The first innovation was a cart with a liberal allowance of straw. . . . Some epicurean person puts springs to his cart, and then the way was open for dogcarts and even pony phaetons, and now it is rumoured that walking is becoming a lost art."[103]

Two years after Mr. Stobbs's death, Mr. James Nesbit was called to Stromness where he ministered during Oman's formative years, from the age of five to fourteen, but without seemingly making any significant impact. Oman's recollections of his ministry are unclear. "The part of the history which seems strange to me is not the old part, but the time of Mr. Nesbit's ministry. I have some kind of memory of disturbed thoughts about the use of a gown, of some dissatisfaction about an innovation in shaving, and of a lengthy series of discourses on the Heroes of the Faith."[104] There is no sense of personal relationship here nor of any imaginative appeal, nor indeed of that empathy which Oman, when a minister himself in 1906, expressed towards Mr. Wylie and Mr. Stobbs.

The next minister, however, was another matter. On 20 July 1876, just before Oman's sixteenth birthday, Mr. Thomas Crauford Kirkwood, Probationer, was ordained and entered into ministry in Stromness. Though Mr. Kirkwood's ministry there only lasted four years, it was fruitful. The membership of the church rapidly increased; he was, it was said, "an able preacher and greatly beloved by his people."[105] But it was Mr. Kirkwood's work with young people that had most immediate impact on the teenage Oman and his peers. For the minister himself "the work among the young folks was . . . a perennial joy. The fine Bible Classes and Sabbath Schools in the town and country, and the district services in Kirbuster, Ireland and Outertown were most encouraging. Everywhere ready helpers lightened and enriched the work. Some of them I meet occasionally occupying responsible and often lucrative posts in the cities of the south, or in the US, or Greater Britain

---

102. Oman, "Reminiscences," 33–34.
103. Oman, "Reminiscences," 38.
104. Oman, "Reminiscences," 32.
105. *Victoria Street*, 24.

beyond the sea. Names such as Dr John Gunn, Edinburgh, Dr John Oman, Alnwick, Dr James Rossie, Bathgate, Mr Wm Inkster, Aberdeen, and the Corrigalls and Sinclairs and others in Glasgow and Edinburgh are but a few of these, even in my time, whose distinguished course reflect credit on their fatherland and mother-church."[106]

The effect of Mr. Kirkwood's ability to relate to the "young folks" should not be underestimated. Oman affirms: "Mr Kirkwood, with his human ways, his interest in rich and poor, great and small, especially in us boys, upset all our traditional notions about ministers. Even his preaching was not the exercise of keeping one's attention and not looking at the clock it ought to have been. The prayer-meeting became a small congregation, and when he held a meeting in the country there ceased to be any denominations."[107]

As Oman was not given to eulogizing, Mr. Kirkwood must have had considerable ministerial talent. Although he left Stromness for Kelso in 1880, he was to keep in touch with Oman, and on 19 December 1889 he attended his ordination and induction to Clayport Church, Alnwick. During the soirée and public meeting in Alnwick Corn Exchange that followed, Mr. Kirkwood gave "a few very human remarks." He had, he said, "the honour of being (Oman's) minister and the minister of his family in the north for a period of four years. He saw that Oman was taking a deep interest in religious work but never thought he would come up into the ministry."[108] In this Mr. Kirkwood appeared to underestimate not only his personal influence on the young man but also the glimpses he afforded into a style of ministry that attracted because of its humanity.

When he returned to "the north" to speak at the centenary celebrations of Victoria Street UF Church, Mr. Kirkwood recalled "the large and reverent audiences at worship, from week to week and through all kinds of weather. . . . It indicated a people that truly sought after the Lord, and were ready to hear the gospel."[109] To substantiate this, he continues: "A couple who came from a long distance told me that, when prevented from attendance, they read and pondered the Confession of Faith and the Larger and Shorter Catechism. They realised the chief end of man; and such study put iron and strength into their thought and life." The communion seasons were particularly memorable. Mr. Kirkwood recalls that "the services extended from Saturday to Monday. From the manse windows the groups from the country could be seen approaching, like the tribes going up to Jerusalem.

106. *Victoria Street*, 68–69.
107. Oman, "Reminiscences," 34.
108. *Alnwick and County Gazette*, Saturday, 21 December 1889.
109. *Victoria Street*, 64–65.

The hospitable homes in the town, as in ancient Jerusalem, were in many cases at the service of friends from the country districts."

He signaled the "excellence of the congregational singing," led by "that worthy and buoyant veteran, Robert Clouston, and his loyal and hearty choir" which "gave tone and life to the other parts of our worship."[110]

Mr. Kirkwood was impressed too by "the intelligence and striking attention of the audience. There seemed to be no restlessness and few if any sleepers. The people had come to worship God reverently and earnestly." While some of this attentiveness may be attributed to Mr. Kirkwood's skills as a preacher, he notes that "in Stromness and in Orkney generally the worshippers were a reading people. They knew their Bibles. They were in touch with the most distant parts of the world through their seafaring relations. Their homes were adorned with curios and other treasures from all lands. They brought their best to the sanctuary."[111] Spiritual zeal was allied to systematic liberality. The weekly offerings and the special collections bore witness to this, in particular the special offerings for Home and Foreign Missions after the December communion.

In particular Mr. Kirkwood treasured the fellowship he enjoyed with "devout and prayerful" elders. There were "blessed prayer meetings" on Wednesday nights, attended by around two hundred people, in which the elders always took part.[112] Oman too held these elders in high regard.

> No institution, I believe, was ever served with more faithfulness, ability, and weight of character than the old Presbyterian church by the eldership, and the old Stromness Session ranked high even in that honourable body. We heard them called by their Christian names like the prophets and apostles. I can see them yet as they stood by the plate, mostly clad in that smooth black cloth which was the accepted adornment of all grave and reverent persons. I remember their faces as well as I remember the face of the clock, though I was only allowed a furtive glance in passing, and I have studied the clock an hour and ten minutes at a time while our reverend neighbour was under the illusion that he was instilling the word into us.[113]

From a distance of thirty years, Oman looked back on those who, like him and his family, sat in the pews.

---

110. *Victoria Street*, 65–66. The "band" which had been so strongly objected to in the days of Mr. Wylie, was now an institution.

111. *Victoria Street*, 66.

112. *Victoria Street*, 68.

113. Oman, "Reminiscences," 35.

But when my thoughts go back, it is not always, perhaps not usually, to the officials. . . . In the early days, it was only the male members who decided things. But the highest and most beautiful life of the church seems to me to have been enshrined not in the men, but in the women. When people talk of the severity of Presbyterian religion, I always think of the old ladies, perhaps especially of the old maiden ladies, in the UP Kirk in Stromness. Am I mistaken when I think I remember being taken as a small boy in a kilt, possibly in a frock, to see the Misses Skethway, who, I suppose, would be daughters of that first elder? Surely they lived up a close, and were very gracious old gentlewomen. It comes back to me like a scent of clover across the sea, and it must be a true impression. When I went from home the first time, Miss Hourston gave me her book of poems.[114] Alas! They have been lost in my many peregrinations, but I still retain some memory of the multiplication tables which she drilled into me.[115]

Oman comments further in his memoir on the sincere piety and strong Christian character of the members. "They were mostly reserved in utterance regarding the deepest things, the things they felt most. They had a dignity derived from the sense of being God's children, and even the fine manners which came from living always in God's sight. The Secession no doubt had its narrowness and its hardness, but the religion which produced them was rooted in the love of God."[116]

From childhood onwards John Oman imbibed the ethos of the United Presbyterian Church. While the following chapters will trace in greater detail its influence upon his life and thought we may single out at this point a reverent engagement in worship, a zeal for the word of God, an egalitarian awareness of the fellowship of all the saints, and a perception of God's loving grace, available for all. There is a recognition that ordained ministers are called to faithful preaching and pastoral attentiveness, with an emphasis on outreach and on the spiritual nurture of young people. And as a heritage of the Secession, the understanding of the church as "a religious, a Divine society, not to be identified with the civil society, and yet with a national significance on better justification than mere recognition by the State."[117] The basis of true catholicity is where "each one sees the same reality, drinks of

---

114. Mr. Kirkwood refers to receiving on ordination "a beautiful and touching manuscript written for the occasion by your local poetess, the sainted Cecilia Hourston. I treasure it still." *Victoria Street*, 64.

115. Oman, "Reminiscences," 36–37.

116. Oman, "Reminiscences," 37.

117. Oman, *Church and Divine Order*, 303.

the same spirit and gladly accepts as his own the same Divine rule" instead of seeing it "by fixed creed, uniform organisation, and even by an ordering of recognised duties."[118] As we shall see, this attitude is at the core of Oman's approach to ecumenism.

Geographical Environment

From an early age, Oman's environment stirred his reflective mind.[119] The Biggings farmhouse faced the Hoy hills, rising above the Bay of Ireland in a vast expanse of sky. "When you are in Orkney," Oman reminisced some years later, you will "see land and water intermingled, the sea a perfect azure and the hills every shade from brilliant green to dark brown and purple, and gaze without interruption from horizon to horizon and watch the changing shadows cast by the brilliant white light and breathe the vast air."[120] In these surroundings of great natural beauty, the child pondered questions such as these: What am I? What sort of universe is this in which I find myself? What is time? What is space? With Oman's distinctive ability to enter into the mind of the child he once was, we have in *The Natural and the Supernatural* a vivid impression of the boy's mental processes as seen through the lens of the subsequent professor of philosophy. We find these references particularly in part II of the book, where he deals with "knowing and knowledge" and by extensive quotation, I leave these passages to speak for themselves, as commentary on his mind as a child. In chapter 8 he discusses awareness and apprehension, distinguishing these from comprehension and explanation. "We can recall a time," he writes, "when we lived in a continuous, lively awareness, with apprehension only as a bright light always moving across its field, without ever keeping one object long in the foreground and when comprehending and explaining did not trouble us."[121] This is typical, he suggests, of a child's perceiving. And he continues:

> Unfortunately, the only experience available for the purpose is one's own. But an average sort of child, living under the conditions in which man has developed his powers of perception, with nature's work much in evidence around him and man's little, often alone under the open sky, and about as much on the sea as on the land, among simple stay-at-home people and some far-travelled folk and wandering gypsies, is at least as near the

118. Oman, *Paradox*, 277.
119. Alexander, "Memoir of the Author."
120. Oman, *Orkneys*.
121. Oman, *Natural*, 123.

conditions in which man's perception developed as this Western modern world affords.[122]

He writes further:

> The most noticeable feature of my own earliest view of the world is how minutely, definitely, decisively everything in it was individual. My language being an advanced Aryan tongue, I had abstract terms, and no doubt made some use of them. But they were luxuries and not necessaries. That to their owner a flock was only sheep, which he did not know one from another, seemed to show an incredible blindness. The birds were too numerous and rapid and changing for personal acquaintance, but a flock of them was an object by itself, with its qualities of flight and grouping; and when birds were nearer and few enough for separate attention, they were always particular living creatures, each with some singularity of colour or form or behaviour. Life of every kind fascinated: and there was a different quality of apprehension of it which is lost when interests are in another direction and classification has to be used to save the trouble of individual apprehension.[123]

Such a person in adult life "will not readily believe that later ideas, regulated by what we comprehend and explain, are a better means of perceiving the whole of reality than his earlier simple apprehension and awareness."[124] The most striking exercise of this apprehension and awareness

> was an astonishing rapidity, sureness and penetration in directly apprehending other minds. Later experience, though it has added something of intellectual and moral judgment, has added little or nothing to this kind of aesthetic knowledge, which is more certain and often more just. Moreover, only as we carry this kind of knowledge with us from our youth, has any other kind of knowing our fellow real insight. As I recall it, the judgement was independent both of approval and of liking. Personal feelings indeed rather interfered, one's own relatives being taken for granted. But the idiosyncrasies of a gypsy who, on his wife's testimony, was to be five score his next birthday ever since I could remember, though I understood his character of very mixed shades of grey downwards, no more troubled me than when I read of Falstaff today. I had just the same artistic interest

122. Oman, *Natural*, 133.
123. Oman, *Natural and Supernatural*, 133–34.
124. Oman, *Natural and Supernatural*, 134.

in what might be called a consistent character of inconsistencies. With this mind Shakespeare saw Falstaff, and with this in mind we read of him, though perhaps, if we met him in the flesh, our adult reflexions would have nothing but disapproval.[125]

> Along with this detailed, concrete, individual apprehension went a general awareness, from the peculiar qualities of which the sustained interest in apprehending everything in it individually was derived While my apprehensions of the countryside continually varied with sunshine and shadow, day and night, summer and winter, my general awareness of it was neither of a changing scene, nor of the aspect I preferred, nor was it of an average impression or a composite picture, but of something one in all its moods and aspects, much like awareness of a friend. From this, and not from pleasure or pain given by the separate objects themselves, the insatiable thirst for apprehending everything in its individuality came.[126]

It may of course be argued that when children reach adulthood and attain "the time of reflexion" they will recognize that the only possible motives for such interest are subjective pleasure and pain, but Oman disputes this.

> This is to settle a question of experience by a general conclusion of comprehension, which is precisely what is here being challenged. As a matter of fact, we boys knew perfectly well when people shrank from looking at anything, say blood, because the sight pained them. Our seniors did absurd things and they might if they liked, but in boys we regarded this as highly reprehensible.
> Nor was it different with action. For daring, large liberty of conduct was allowed, but, for mere subjective pleasure, none. No language would have expressed our opinion of a boy who consciously and habitually made this his motive, could we have conceived such a person to exist. And at any age is not desire of pleasure or fear of pain a morbid and reflective and even artificial motive?[127]

Rising out of this state of awareness, Oman as a child had "a very early and insistent and dominant obsession with infinity. . . . It expressed itself in time and space. . . . Strictly perhaps it was not an idea at all, not being

---

125. Oman, *Natural and Supernatural*, 134.
126. Oman, *Natural and Supernatural*, 135.
127. Oman, *Natural and Supernatural*, 136.

an experience of something, but a form of experiencing everything."[128] He gives a graphic illustration of this.

> To the very long sight of one who constantly looked from horizon to horizon, the depth of the sky was overwhelmingly impressive, and was the first object I think ever to hold my attention immovably. It compelled me to think of travelling on and on for ever and ever without being any nearer the end. Thus though space was, as it were, the illustration, the real impressiveness was in time: and perhaps time is always what gives the impressive quality. Through this first came the idea that I was alone. I had been to church. I think the preacher had been expressing the absolute difference between good and evil under the material forms of heaven and hell. I went down to the edge of the water alone, and stood, a very small child, with the full tide at my feet. Along the smooth waters of the sound a path of sunshine carried the eye out to the open sea. It flashed on me that, if I dropped in and floated out, with endless sea around, I should be alone for ever and ever.[129]

"The result was a consciousness of myself which set me thinking, yet not about myself. Instead it caused doubt about whether the world I saw was in the least like the world other people saw. . . . Theoretically," he continues,

> no very small boy should have any such notions: nor would he, if they were problems of comprehending and explaining. But the contention here is that they rise up spontaneously from the form of our awareness. This is what gives them their extraordinarily intense character, quite different from our later days when, by understanding and explaining, we have reduced time and space from fascinations to formulas. . . . [The child's] discernment of himself is one side of the whole aesthetic nature of his early awareness: and its peculiar quality, which leads to questions about the soul, is the feeling of something of the same absolute quality in himself as that which he feels in the sense of time and space. Through both he perceives how utterly he is alone.[130]

The young Oman's imagination was also stirred by the neolithic monuments that were all around. In Stenness there are two stone circles, the Stones of Stenness with two outlying stone pillars, and the more sizeable Ring of Brodgar, which, with the great chambered cairn of Maeshowe, are

128. Oman, *Natural and Supernatural*, 136.
129. Oman, *Natural and Supernatural*, 136–37.
130. Oman, *Natural*, 137.

all linked to the coastal settlement of Skara Brae by a neolithic low road. Not far from Biggings, the Stones of Stenness stand on a promontory on the south bank of the stream which joins the sea loch of Stenness with the freshwater loch of Harray. Magnus Spence, head of the Parish School, was the first to prove "by the most convincing argument of measurements and observations of the heavens that the whole is united in one system."[131] There were many theories of origin. "One maintains it is the monument of a great victory, a kind of Trafalgar Square, his successor will have it a burial place, a kind of Westminster Abbey, a third will have it a place of religious worship or at least of religious ceremonial, a kind of Pictish St Peter's." And Oman continues: "All are equally dogmatic and equally contemptible of other views. Personally I rather hold to the last view." But irrespective of antiquarian concerns, the place had the power to stir a child's imagination. In a review of Rudolph Otto's *The Idea of the Holy*, Oman illustrates his critique with this recollection:

> When a boy of fourteen or thereabouts, I was riding through the Standing Stones of Stenness on a winter afternoon when dusk was settling into darkness. They stand on the top of a lone narrow neck of land between two lochs. The close-cropped heather crackled under my horse's feet, the loch on the right was still shining under the glow of sunset and the loch on the left was dark almost to blackness, and cross a bay the gravestones in the churchyard stood white and clear over it. The circle of stones had a look of ancient giants against the grey sky, and the gaping mounds which had been opened stood shadowy and apart. A more numinous scene at a more numinous hour, could not be found on earth. And the feeling which suddenly struck me is not inaptly described as the *mysterium tremendum et fascinans*. But at the same moment it struck my old horse at least as vehemently as myself. He threw up his head, snorted, set his feet, trembled, and finally bolted at a rate I should have thought impossible for his old bones.[132]

And Oman was left to ponder the question: Was that peculiar eerie feeling religious? Was it religion or merely superstition? He was later to develop a response to these questions in his investigation of the relation of the natural and the supernatural, which will be dealt with in a subsequent chapter. (Below, 338–48.)

---

131. Oman, *Orkneys*. Associations with the solstice have become respectable with the excavations of the Ness of Brodgar.
132. Oman, review of Otto, *Idea of the Holy*, 282.

The Sea

The sea was Oman's environment and seafaring, part of his inheritance. He perceived that exposure to the sea in all its moods gave rise to a certain distinctive approach to life, underlying which was a Calvinist perception of the sovereignty of God. This was certainly in tune with UP thinking and it is not unlikely that he spoke of these things with his father from time to time. What can be said is that he used this awareness effectively up to his last published work. In *Honest Religion*, he writes: "Extreme Calvinism I never came across, for I knew it only among a race who, whether for thought or action, divided humanity into men who went to sea and muffs who stayed at home, and for whom the sovereignty of God meant the assurance of being able to face all storms, and seek no harbour of refuge."[133]

For the seafarer, this assurance gave rise to a sense of peace. In 1917, when Europe was being torn apart by the ravages of the first world war, Oman wrote in *Grace and Personality*: "There is a security upon the ocean never to be won by hugging the shore. . . . With the solemn splendour of the stars in our hearts and their far travelling light upon our way, we can unite an ever increasing endeavour with an ever deepening peace, in a way foreign to every form of moral imperative."[134] And he concludes with the observation, "every peace-maker is a fighter . . . yet he is not a peace-maker merely by fighting even in the cause of truth and righteousness. To make peace we must ourselves possess it."[135]

He perceived that a constant awareness of the risk of death was conducive to a strong belief in divine providence: "There is little else can give a man courage and calm in face of an Atlantic roller when the only thing seen in the dark night is the hissing foam at the top, except faith in him who holds the winds and the waves in his right hand."[136] It is in this context that we may see Oman's evocation of an old fisherman whose face used to haunt him when he was a boy. "It was like the reflection of the azure heavens from placid ocean depths. Yet it was said that absolute calm was only seen on it when the cloud-rack and the spin-drift began to meet.[137] Nor did anyone doubt that the source of it was a more intense realisation at such a time of the God who holds the waters in the hollow of His hand."[138] Oman then alludes

---

133. Oman, *Honest Religion*, 165.
134. Oman, *Grace and Personality*, 85–86.
135. Oman, *Grace and Personality*, 91.
136. Oman, *Orkneys*.
137. These are signs of a rising storm.
138. "The Peacemaker and the Peaceable," in *Paradox*, 155–67; here, 162.

to an occasion when this fisherman, whose name was John, was caught in an Atlantic storm in an open boat, with his young inexperienced son and a "fellow craftsman" for crew. He describes elsewhere what ensued.[139]

> John himself was a Plymouth brother, really a very good man. Peter whom he sometimes took with him, was a notorious character, a most skilful fisherman but a very thirsty person. Out on the broad Atlantic a storm broke upon them. Peter wrought hard till night descended. Then fear unmanned him. The situation was described by John's wife. "The poy was at the sail and our John was at the steer, but poor Peter was no use at all, at all, but was sitting in the pottom of the poat, crying upon his Maker. And no wonder, for our John was going to glory, but poor Peter was just going to meet his old friend the Tevil."

The event clearly made a profound impression upon Oman and had an important place in his quest for a theology that was adequate to the times. He comments in a sermon published in 1921:

> It is not given to all, or to anyone at all times, to have a peace which works by knowledge and foresight and skill. In that boat there was also another kind of peace, without which it would never have reached harbour. While the other man was helpless, because he looked only on the tumult of the sea, the child was able to do what was needed, because he was conscious of little save his father's face, from which he read what was required of him and received the quietness and strength necessary for the doing of it. Why it was done he might not know; that it must be done he accepted from a wisdom beyond his own.... When troubles "roar like the roaring of the sea, and the light is darkened in the heavens, and counsel perishes from the wise," the only wisdom available is to stand in our place and look up into the face of the Great Steersman of the world's barque, who alone knows its course and its port.[140]

In his informal talks to his students published on his retirement, he draws on his own experience as pilot of a ship to illustrate the relationship between changing convictions and ultimate truth.

> If you are growing, [your convictions] will change, possibly towards what may seem a quite opposite direction. Yet, like tacking with a changing wind, it should be plain that the port you

---

139. Oman, *Orkneys*.
140. Oman, "The Peacemaker and the Peaceable," in Oman, *Paradox*, 155-67; here 163.

are making for is still the same. Throughout there should be the deeper consistency of seeking only to know God's truth and following only His purpose. Moreover, while you may, as you go on, have to correct some points in your bearings, this goal is not anywhere on the wide horizon, but there will be the further consistency that you are still advancing in a course that is never far from the same direction. Your compasses may need to be corrected, yet you still know that the Pole Star is the true North.[141]

And so when at the age of seventeen, John Wood Oman entered Edinburgh University, it was "with a well-stored mind, with anything but an insular intellectual outlook and more important still, with his native gift of original thought unimpaired."[142]

---

141. Oman, *Concerning the Ministry*, 87.
142. Alexander, "Memoir of the author," xvii.

2

Edinburgh

The University of Edinburgh

IN OCTOBER 1877 JOHN Oman, who described himself retrospectively as "a raw lad from the ends of the earth," with a "vast responsiveness to the intellectual environment"[1] entered the University of Edinburgh. Edinburgh was known as the "Athens of the North." Its setting was distinctive. Dominated at one end by the Salisbury Crags and at the other by the castle mound, the Royal Mile led from the medieval palace of Holyroodhouse past the closes and turrets of the Old Town to Playfair's elegant Georgian New Town, adorned with pillars, porticos and pilasters. In the glory days of the Scottish Enlightenment, it was a hotbed of genius, the home of famed artists, writers, poets, philosophers. As he walked across the New Town from his lodgings, and on up the Mound to the university, Oman imbibed the atmosphere of David Hume, whose *Treatise of Human Nature* gave rise to what was arguably the greatest philosophical and theological revolution since Bacon and Luther, and Hume's distinguished friend and colleague, Adam Smith, who had first expounded in his public lectures his philosophy of economics as "the simple system of natural liberty."

The University of Edinburgh was undergoing significant development and organizational change. Alexander Campbell Fraser, Oman's Professor of Logic and Metaphysics, writes in his *Biographia Philosophica* that

---

1. Oman, "Method," 82.

the European fame of the undeveloped university rested on the eminence of the professors in two preceding centuries, in mathematics, metaphysics and medicine: and on the occasional emergence of a literary, scientific or political celebrity from the ranks of its alumni. . . . Nevertheless, with the advance of the nineteenth century, there were symptoms of decline, aggravated by a chronic war between the professors and the Council of the city; probably too by the ecclesiastical war in Scotland which preceded and followed the convulsion of 1843.[2]

The immediate consequence of the Disruption was a dramatic fall in student numbers. Yet longer term it was to serve the Scottish Universities well. Fraser comments:

> The prospect of "a great Free University,"[3] supported by the claim of a large portion of the Scottish people now outside the Established Church, as well as the intellectual value of an open field from which to choose professors, produced the Act of Parliament which in 1853 relaxed the tests that had hitherto bound the chairs to the Established Church, and opened them to the intellect of the world. Popular interest in the universities accordingly revived; there was an organised movement for reform, in which James Lorimer[4] was a leader; and the memorable Act of 1858,[5] which made Lord Advocate Inglis the greatest benefactor of the Town's College since its foundation in the days of James VI, was brought into operation in the four following years.[6]

In Fraser's eyes,

> the life of the university, unprecedentedly active in the thirty years which followed the legislation of Inglis, owed much of its vigour and charm to the personality of Sir David Brewster and of Sir Alexander Grant, who successively presided as Principals. . . . Almost a million of money was poured into its coffers, from voluntary gifts as well as grants by Parliament. New buildings,

---

2. Fraser, *Biographia*, 208-9. The reference is to the Disruption. Bitter conflict within the Established Church of Scotland over relations between church and state led in 1843 to schism and the formation of the Free Church of Scotland.

3. This was the vision behind the formation of New College, which failed to become more than a school of Divinity.

4. Regius professor of Law (1862-90), distinguished political philosopher, whose application of natural law to international relations was widely influential in Europe.

5. Universities (Scotland) Act 1858.

6. Fraser, *Biographia*, 209-10.

which doubled the accommodation for study, fellowships and scholarships to encourage original research, and the new professorships, tutorships, and examinerships, were a magnificent testimony to the place which the University had taken in public regard, and to the wise policy of the Principal, whose administration fitly culminated in 1884, in the Tercentenary Festival, organised and directed by him, which attracted to Edinburgh scholars and philosophers from the chief seats of learning in the world, in a congregation unprecedented in Britain.[7]

Nearly 200 guests were invited from universities and learned bodies from other parts of the world, over 140 honorary degrees were awarded to distinguished scientists, scholars, clergy and other public figures, and Edinburgh University was promoted as a beacon of international academic cooperation, freedom of thought and the harmonious relationship of religion and science.

It was during this buoyant period of the University's life, that, in October 1877, the seventeen-year-old John Wood Oman matriculated as a student. He signed the *Sponsio Academica*, the solemn oath in Latin[8] taken by all matriculating students in the four ancient Scottish Universities, committing himself to "the pursuit of true piety before everything else," to be "sedulous in the usual studies of an academic course as befits a well brought up young man," and for the duration of that course of study to be obedient to all his teachers, and not to be "an instigator or participant in any rebellion or riot either secretly or openly"; he undertook, for the rest of his life, to "regard the university itself with an attitude of thankfulness and good will." And so, having received his matriculation certificate, with 934 other new students in the Faculty of Arts, John Oman was launched into his university career.

Studies

Although the norm for the honors MA degree was four years, it was not unusual for a student to take five years to complete the course. The reasons

---

7. Fraser, *Biographia*, 213–17.

8. Ego Academiae Edinburgenae Discipulus sincere ac sancte promitto quod et syngrapha hac mea in perpetuum testatum cupio, mihi ante omnia cordi ac curae futurum verae pietatis studium; me etiam in assuetis academici curriculi studiis sedulum fore, ut adolescentulum bene institutum decet; et quamdiu in illo curriculo permansero praeceptoribus omnibus morigerum memet praestiturum, nec ullius dissidii aut tumultus clam palamve vel auctorem vel participem futurum, et per reliquam vitam Academiam ipsam grato et benevolo animo prosecuturum, idque omnibus officiis pro facultate mea et occasione data testaturum esse.

for this varied: it may have been impossible for him to keep the four statutory winter sessions, there may have been financial constraints, or he may have wished to study additional subjects. We may only speculate as to why Oman's course took five years. But there may be a pointer to this in the fact that, in the session 1881 to 1882, he won third place in the Advanced class for "Private study of the Ethics of Kant's metaphysics (special examination)." James Seth, who also took five years to work for the degree, wrote that "for the sake of the special advantages offered in Mental Philosophy, I supplemented the usual curriculum of undergraduate study by a special course in that department."[9] And Oman may well have done the same. At all events, his timetable was well filled. There were two class sessions in each year, the winter session, from October to April, and the summer session, following a three week break, from May to July. Apart from the summer and spring vacations there was little opportunity to return to Orkney. He had a day's holiday on Good Friday and, as a special concession to Arts students, another on the second Monday in February, with a two-week Christmas recess, but the exigencies of travel in the winter and the extra likelihood of storms in the Pentland Firth would have made returning home an uncertain prospect. Any initial feelings of unfamiliarity with his new surroundings would have been countered by the fact that his landlord, Alexander Corner, a tailor and clothier, and his wife, Jane, were both Orcadians from Orphir,[10] and his fellow lodger, John W. Slater, was a student in Theology from Kirkwall, two years older than himself and a fellow member of the University UP Society. The house, at 9 St Bernard's Row, was a brisk thirty minutes' walk from the University.

It seems to have been taken for granted at the time, both by himself and his parents, that Oman would study medicine,[11] and this would appear to be confirmed by his matriculation certificate, which informs us that he had no previous medical education. As a prospective medical student, he was required first to follow the standard Arts course with further specialization leading to an honors MA degree. This involved a course of study in three departments: Classical Literature (i.e., Latin and Greek); Philosophy (Logic and Metaphysics, Moral Philosophy (ethics), and Rhetoric and English

---

9. Letter of application for the chair of Logic and Metaphysics, the University of Toronto, in *Testimonials in favour of James Seth M.A. Edinburgh, candidate for the chair of Logic and Metaphysic in the University of Toronto* (Legare Street Press, creative media, 9 September 2021).

10. There may indeed have been closer connections: Alexander was four years younger than Philip Corner, headmaster of the Free Church school in Stenness, who also hailed from Orphir. (Above, 10.)

11. Below, 67.

Literature); Mathematics and Natural Philosophy (physics).[12] Although as a prospective honors student, Oman did not have to sit the exams for the Ordinary degree, attendance at lectures was compulsory, and checked by roll calls, and he would have had to procure a certificate of attendance from the relevant professor before he was allowed to graduate.[13] No certificate of attendance was given to any student without evidence that the student had duly returned all books borrowed from the library!

The move to the final year of study for an honors degree was exhilarating. Oman writes of himself as a fourth-year student, "one remembers how life was one vast intellectual problem, how the imagination responded with warmth to all that kindled it, how traditional opinion was in abeyance, and how the critical spirit dominated all and had no timidity in pronouncing judgment on men and things." Soberly he continues: "If experience has done nothing else, it has taught me that life has many sides and that the best-considered judgments are full of error."[14] He went on to sit the examinations for the honors degree in Logic, Metaphysics and Moral Philosophy, graduating in 1882 with high distinction in the class of Metaphysics (senior), a second prize award (Bruce of Grangehill and Falkland prize), and a first class honors degree in Philosophy.[15]

Students

By today's standards, the students were young; they were on average aged between fifteen and seventeen when they matriculated, and the *Sponsio Academica* assumes that the university was *in loco parentis*. They came from all over Scotland and not a few from further afield. The University Calendar lists students from Cairo, Canada, The Cape, England, India, New Zealand and the West Indies. Of Oman's closest friends, Adam Cleghorn Welch was the son of a UP missionary in Jamaica, and George William Alexander came from Nova Scotia. Most of them would have left home for the first time. There were few opportunities for social life. J. M. Barrie, who was contemporary with Oman as a student, comments soberly that "there are

---

12. *Alphabetical List.*

13. Oman would have had to certify that he had attended classes for four Winter sessions, including attendance for not less than two sessions at classes in Humanity (Latin), Greek, and Mathematics respectively and attendance for not less than one session at classes of Logic and Metaphysics, Moral Philosophy and Natural Philosophy, as well as the class of Rhetoric and English Literature.

14. Calderwood, *Henry Calderwood*, 389.

15. Calendar 1882–1883.

tragedies in a college course . . . some, alas! forget their mother. There are men—I know it—who go mad from loneliness; and medalists have ere now crept home to die."[16] In his presidential address to the Edinburgh University UP student society, Oman refers to "the hectic cough and consumption look which makes its friends tremble."[17] Weakened by inadequate diet and overwork, it was not unknown for high-achieving students to succumb to tuberculosis and almost certain death.[18]

Such circumstances were mitigated to some extent by the interest taken by individual professors in their students, often supported by generous hospitality. Barrie records how the Professor of Greek, John Stuart Blackie, "one of the most genial of men," who will "show you to your room himself, talking six languages," invited students to breakfast, lively affairs, with "the eggs being served in tureens."[19] Blackie would also direct students to befriend one another: "two students were told to talk about Paulo-post futures in the cool of the evening, and to read their Greek testament and to go to the pantomime."[20]

The interest taken in his students by Henry Calderwood, Professor of Moral Philosophy, was legendary. James Seth, a former student of the class of 1878, recalls that "Professor Calderwood's evening parties were among the pleasantest social features of a University life which possessed too few features of the kind, and among the most delightful memories of the moral philosophy class."[21] Charles Douglas, the professor's assistant, comments further: Calderwood

> was keenly aware of the strain which circumstances impose on many men in the peculiar conditions of Scottish University life. He knew how severely poverty often presses on those who are perhaps finding their difficult way to great careers. He knew how greatly such hardship is aggravated by the solitary brooding to which the Scottish student so easily falls a victim, and he spared no effort to alleviate the difficulties of his pupils. His efforts to bring them together at his house in friendly social intercourse,

---

16. Barrie, *Edinburgh Eleven*, 96.
17. Westminster College Archives, WT1/12/15.
18. Neil M. MacLean gives a dramatic account of the death of Robert MacLeod, aged 21, in *Life at a Northern University*, 316–28. In 1866, at the age of 19, George Robertson Smith returned home to the manse of Keig crowned with university prizes and honors from the University of Aberdeen, only to die shortly afterwards (Maier, *William Robertson Smith*, 50–53).
19. Barrie, *Edinburgh Eleven*, 31.
20. Barrie, *Edinburgh Eleven*, 31.
21. Calderwood, *Henry Calderwood*, 180.

his interest in every University society, his easy personal kindness—all helped to endear him to his pupils.[22]

And Barrie elaborates: Calderwood had "such an exceptional interest in his students that he asks every one of them to his house. This is but one of many things that makes him generally popular, he also invites his ladies' class to meet them. The lady whom you take down to supper suggests Proposition 41 as a nice thing to talk about, and asks what you think of the metaphysics of ethics." Barrie concludes: "Professor Calderwood sees the ladies into the cabs himself. It is the only thing I ever heard against him."[23] Calderwood vigorously promoted the higher education of women. He promoted the Edinburgh University Certificate in Arts for women, which from 1874 was granted to those students who had passed university exams in three or more subjects up to MA standard. When the Universities (Scotland) Act of 1892 enabled women students to graduate, Calderwood was among the first to urge Edinburgh to avail itself of this opportunity.

Communication in the lecture theatre was both verbal and non-verbal. The students seem to have been boisterous and engaged in a good deal of horseplay, and much of the time this seems to have been accepted by the professors in a spirit of good humor. Students would express approval by stamping their feet; and if they did not understand the lecturer, foot-scraping was the accepted sign of disapproval. Professor Blackie, at the end of session, would annually recite an ode of his own composition, in honor of the occasion. "At critical moments," Barrie writes, "a student in the back benches would accompany him on a penny trumpet."[24] Peter Guthrie Tait, Professor of Natural Philosophy, and a celebrated mathematical physicist, was a "superb demonstrator." Yet even he was not above juvenile behavior. Barrie records: "I have seen a man fall back in alarm under Tait's eyes, though there were a dozen benches between them. These eyes could be as merry as a boy's, though, as when he turned a tube of water on students who would insist on crowding too near an experiment, for Tait's was the humour of high spirits."[25] However, when George Chrystal moved from St Andrew's in 1879 to take up the chair of Mathematics in Edinburgh, "he rooted up the humours of the class-room as a dentist draws teeth . . . horse-play fled before the Differential Calculus in spectacles."[26] "Fourth year men" were maturer in behavior than those in the Ordinary classes; as Oman puts it, "there is,

22. Calderwood, *Henry Calderwood*, 185–86.
23. Barrie, *Edinburgh Eleven*, 45.
24. Barrie, *Edinburgh Eleven*, 34.
25. Barrie, *Edinburgh Eleven*, 50.
26. Barrie, *Edinburgh Eleven*, 73.

in manner and thought, at least half a life time between a first-year's man and a fourth."[27] And distinctively, "perfect discipline prevailed in Professor Calderwood's classroom." This may be attributed to Calderwood's "individual knowledge of his students" and to "the obvious moral earnestness of the man."[28] Seth elaborates: "In his relation to his class there was something very human, as in the rule of a wise and kindly father, and a subtle influence for good, which the most careless student could not escape. The most important educative influence was the personality of the Professor, and it was a unique and commanding personality."[29]

A large part of this was his capacity to be "a student among students." His students responded to this attitude. In his contribution to Calderwood's biography, Oman recalls: "Most of them were serious and thoughtful, hasty in judgment, but ever ready to correct it on wider knowledge; and they were free from all considerations except desire to know the truth. Professor Calderwood stood up before them as one of themselves with the same aim."[30] And he continues:

> We all knew his opinions, not only on ethical, but religious subjects, and we were all ready enough to distrust men who seemed to be committed to traditional opinions and policies, but no man ever doubted that Professor Calderwood thought and acted according to the best light he was able to see. What all respected in him was his fundamental conviction that no opinion, no creed, no policy, should ever fear truth. To that conviction he was loyal in thought and action, and he ever assumed that every one of us would abhor any attempt to build our lives on any lie, however well sanctioned by custom or buttressed by profit. This was a matter not requiring any deep philosophy to understand, and in consequence, no professor was more honoured by the rank and file of his class.[31]

Around 150 to 200 students passed through Calderwood's class every year and yet he had a remarkable ability to recognize faces and remember names even after the passage of years. He was aware that most of his students would follow professional careers "settled in every village in Scotland and scattered through the length and breadth of the world," and would end each class "with an earnest word about professional ideals . . . about the doctor's

---

27. Calderwood, *Henry Calderwood*, 391.
28. Calderwood, *Henry Calderwood*, 179.
29. Calderwood, *Henry Calderwood*, 179.
30. Calderwood, *Henry Calderwood*, 391.
31. Calderwood, *Henry Calderwood*, 391.

healing art, the lawyer's care of justice, the teacher's training of the mind, the minister of religion's care for sacred things." This was, Oman notes, "a vast opportunity. One thing he was resolved upon, that he would do what in him lay to aid in providing the supreme requirement for every office of responsibility, the unbending sense of duty."[32]

James Seth recalls how Calderwood's ability to relate to his students personally enhanced his reputation as a lecturer: he and his contemporaries "entered the class with a definite expectation of the Professor and his work."[33] Calderwood's women students "often expressed their indebtedness to him for the high tone and the helpfulness of the teaching he gave."[34]

As if recognizing that such lectures needed to be supplemented with something more interpersonal, Calderwood devoted two hours in the week to oral examination and discussion with the students of prescribed portions of the *Hand-Book of Moral Philosophy* which he himself had written. Oman records how "the class was transformed into a debating society, but always with the utmost propriety and order. He enjoyed the conflict with young minds. . . . Again, we were not always satisfied, but our minds were stimulated and the professor never came out of this situation, so impossible for most men, without having gained in our respect."[35] In the advanced class, "the contact of mind with mind was of the highest value; and few left it without a profounder regard for the Professor; and this was a better mood for the young philosopher than entire acquiescence in every utterance of his teacher. Professor Calderwood's whole attitude said: 'I neither expect nor desire entire agreement with all I say, but I look for honest investigation, calm judgment, and high principle.'" And Oman continues, "He generally received what he asked, with abundant difference of opinion into the bargain."[36]

The Edinburgh University United Presbyterian Students' Society

Calderwood's concern for student welfare was reflected also in his patronage of student societies. Recognizing that there were few opportunities for students to explore common interests together outside the classroom, "he

---

32. Calderwood, *Henry Calderwood*, 394.
33. Calderwood, *Henry Calderwood*, 178.
34. Calderwood, *Henry Calderwood*, 233.
35. Calderwood, *Henry Calderwood*, 393.
36. Calderwood, *Henry Calderwood*, 394.

felt strongly that the banding together for good purpose, of students of the University, deserved every support from the Professors."[37]

On 24 November 1877, the UP Students' Missionary Society amalgamated with the UP Students' Temperance Society to form the Edinburgh University UP Students' Society, with Professor Calderwood as its honorary President.[38] The Society met weekly at seven o'clock on a Saturday evening from November to March with a ten-day interlude over Christmas. These meetings provided students with an opportunity to fraternize with others of a similar religious background. They also promoted skills in interpersonal relationships, in public speaking and in debate. And the intermittent magazine nights fostered an atmosphere of relaxed sociability.

John Oman was co-president of the society between 1880 and 1881.[39] The first meeting of the session was convened on 13 November in Professor Kerr's classroom in Castle Terrace. But those present quickly realized the inconvenience of having to end by nine o'clock and by the following week, arrangements had been made to meet in Principal Cairns's room where they might remain till ten o'clock. The downside of this arrangement was that it was found impossible to hold the monthly "tea meetings" and it was resolved, with stoical regret, to discontinue these. However, by 4 December, members were discussing "the propriety of renewing the tea service at Magazine meetings," and having ascertained that the overwhelming majority of members found this desirable, they accepted Mr. Swanson's offer to make tea on Magazine nights at a charge of 8d (old pence) a head. The following week tea was served without any evident difficulties!

Attendance at meetings from 1880 to 1881 ranged from eight to twenty-three with three meetings being deemed non-quorate. But the four Magazine nights were consistently popular. The formula was simple. The meeting was constituted by prayer, tea was served, an installment of a serial story was read, and "the Meeting was further entertained by numerous songs and recitations from the members." On other occasions, there was a varied syllabus of essays and debates. Some of the debates were on religious or ecclesiological subjects: "Should an atheist be admitted to the House of Lords?"; "Should the Church of Scotland be disestablished?"; "Ought instrumental music to be introduced into churches?"[40] Others were more

---

37. Calderwood, *Henry Calderwood*, 200.

38. This and subsequent details of the Society are to be found in the Minute Book of the University of Edinburgh UP Students Society 1877–91. University of Edinburgh New College Collections AA3.7.

39. No record of membership exists, but Oman is likely to have been a member of the committee between 1879 and 1880, and to have joined the society in 1878–79.

40. Calderwood proposed a motion, which was carried, in the UP Synod of 1872 to allow the use of musical instruments in worship. Calderwood, *Henry Calderwood*, 256.

ethical in nature: "Is it wrong for an unprotected maid to hang a man's hat in the lobby in order to inspire a salutary terror in callers?"; "Should tobacco be banned and the pipes shattered about the ears of those who idly idolize so base a weed?" Others had a political emphasis: "Is party feeling a sufficient reason for supporting parliamentary questions?" "Should the Rt Hon W. E. Gladstone retire from the Chancellorship of the Exchequer?"[41] "Was the execution of Charles I justifiable?" And some debates were on literary subjects. On 10 January 1881, an essay was read on "The Character of Lear," which was then critiqued and discussed; and on 5 March, those present pondered the question "Is Hamlet's madness real?"

On 17 March, however, the following question was discussed: "Should debates and essays on Religious Subjects be introduced more prominently into the work of the Society?" To judge by the fact that there were six votes in favor and two against, with several abstentions, was there perhaps a sense that there had been a disproportionate number of debates and essays on non-religious subjects during Oman's tenure of office?

And yet one cannot but wonder whether in this varied syllabus, Oman and his committee had not shown themselves to be discerning. It could be argued that the combination of religion, ethics and literature is a valuable preparation for public life. Whereas a discussion of religious matters on their own could be conducive to habits of certainty or dogmatism, which was obviously, from his presidential address, already a concern of Oman's, the cultivation of ethical imagination teaches a sense of responsibility and a judgment of consequences; the realization that there are social as well as personal consequences in allowing this action or preventing that one. And the case could be made that a study of literature, particularly the works of Shakespeare, mitigates the use of cliché and fixity of meaning and enriches human understanding.

Oman's lifelong friend, George Alexander, describes him at this time as a "dreamy, shy youth who addressed fellow-students of his own Church with such diffidence, and at whom we were apt to smile until we found he was always worth listening to."[42] This may be illustrated by Oman's retiring speech to the Society, delivered in November 1881 at the end of his presidential year,[43] which gives an evocative glimpse into his own attitudes and those of his contemporaries to the stressful demands of student life.

He addresses the question:

---

41. Between 1880 and 1882 Gladstone held the offices of Prime Minister and Chancellor of the Exchequer (finance minister) concurrently.

42. "Memoir of the Author," in Oman, *Honest Religion*, xv.

43. Unpublished MS, Westminster College Archives, WT1/12/15.

> What is the exact use of this society? Why in the nature of things has it any rational claim to existence? or why on Saturday nights should I have to drag my weary and reluctant limbs to keep its somewhat feeble pulse abeating are the vexed questions which this now somewhat venerable society has called up many and many a time.

He expresses some sympathy with the objections of his fellow students. First of all, there is the need to work. "In this workaday world of ours in which examinations ride us with sharpened spurs and jagged bits," the society may be considered to be "an interruption to one's labours. But," he continues, "though we were sent into this world to do our work honestly and well we were never meant to be beasts of burden."

Burning the midnight oil, being "cribbed, cabined and confined," leads to indigestion and bad temper. Under such circumstances a student may well ask himself:

> Why should not I for one day at least lead the life of an ordinary mortal? If I have the good luck to have a maiden aunt why should not I for once in a week at least have the pleasure of drinking tea with real cream not chalk in it. Why, if I have a few bright faced cousins should I not one day out of seven enjoy their smiles? and what day I pray you is left for these and a hundred other things I could mention come Saturday?

"My dear Sir," Oman continues with a light touch of irony, "being entirely ignorant of such temptations I cannot appreciate them . . . mine is a virtue of necessity in such matters which gives me no moral vantage ground wherefrom to look down on you."

Then, in a neat twist, he continues:

> But there is still another student and it is with him that we have mainly to do. The student who is doing his very best to improve himself, not merely in the way of his studies but all round, who is striving not merely to make himself a scholar but a man, and who has come to the conclusion that even after he can repeat by rote all the Greek verbs, irregular and defective . . . and spout Hegel in his dreams he is not already perfect.

This man may be weighing up whether or not to continue to attend the UP Society. Does this society not encourage "sect prejudices and UP dogmas"? Oman refutes this briskly: "If there is anything that this society does it is to terrify the life out of such narrow-mindedness. The air of this society is not the rank hot unwholesome air that nourishes such weeds."

And he observes: "The atmosphere here is rather bracing, sufficiently warmed by friendliness to save it from being chilly, yet with quite enough of the healthy frost of criticism in it to save it from being enervating.... We are not such a very narrow sect after all." The members do, however, need to be wary of being "too much of one mind [and] apt to fall into similar ruts of thought and feeling." A possible remedy, he suggests, is to join an additional society.[44]

The second charge is weightier: "as a debating society it is of little or no use." The speeches, Oman alleges, are not long, but often tedious, "of no very elegant form yet of even worse matter." The speaker "does not speak, he talks. The whole air and tone of the society is against good speaking."[45] "Now gentlemen," he continues robustly, "these things ought not so to be." Indicating that "the Society has a good effect upon a man, physically, intellectually, and morally," he states rather dismissively that most students "are apparently very much above such mundane considerations as their bodies ... unremitting grinding, insufficient exercise, and late hours surely point in this direction. But let me tell you," he warns, "that in a puny undeveloped, half-dying body you will never do much in this world, more especially in the way of public speaking."

After citing a few examples of sturdy well-built orators, he concludes: "Even Demosthenes, great orator intellectually as he was, could make no impression till he overcame his physical defects." And almost as if he were speaking to himself, he adds, "Go thou and do likewise."[46] As to intellectual rigor, "readiness and cleanness of thought and expression are no mean attainment, and this undoubtedly [the society] furnishes."

Then, revealingly, he continues:

> The improvement which it affords to our moral nature which to me of all others seems most important is in the most unaccountable manner usually passed over. The great benefit which accrues to oneself personally from it is acquiring command over oneself and this surely is no small acquisition. It is a ... ludicrous spectacle to see a poor wretch while on his feet loose [sic] all command over himself, gaze wildly round, grip the nearest

---

44. During the session 1881–82, Oman joined the Edinburgh University Philosophical Society, serving as a member of the committee the following year and as co-president between 1883 and 1884.

45. This resonates with his remarks to students in *Concerning the Ministry* (below, 109–18).

46. Oman may have had a speech impediment of some sort as a young man. George Alexander writes of his "great thinking [which] strove with limitations of oral expression" ("Memoir of the Author," in Oman, *Honest Religion*, xvi).

object with the grip of despair, mutter some wretched nonsense and then sit down with a feeling of desolation and degradation as if the waves of hell were passing over him.

And he continues briskly:

> If you do not wish to form the subject of another interesting story of nonsense and breakdown learn in time. . . . But this habit of self-control once learned will help you not merely to face your fellow mortals, but to control yourselves in all circumstances to decide firmly to act quickly and give you at least the ability to do right if you have the grace in you to do it.

Then Oman moves on from the individual member to the society itself. It "might by the united action of its members be the nursing mother of great men and nations." But first of all there has to be

> a renovation in the whole spirit of the society. There must be no . . . thinking of work, still less must there be no half-done work. The society must really rise to the dignity in which its censure will be feared. . . . Friendliness is all very well and will, I hope, always exist, but when friendliness generates carelessness and when carelessness is the order of the day, be assured that friendliness is scarcely on the right tack. Unless this is made a working society and a striving society, it fulfils no useful function on this earth. . . . But it cannot be made this save by an entire renovation of spirit, and it is at this point that reform must begin. . . . It somehow wants an animating purpose, a moving force, to set in motion its but [sic] no means feeble machinery, and the impetus can only be well given if every member puts his whole strength to the wheel.

And with an eye to its future well-being, he affirms that "a much more careful diagnosis of the diseases of the society than I have been able to offer would be very desirable."

Handing over the chair to his successor, he brings his hearers back to the present: "It is now my very pleasant duty to welcome you back to the walks of science and of literature" and concludes with his hopes that the "society and especially the magazine meetings will have charms of sufficient power and sweetness to counterbalance the softer allurements of cream and cousins."

In language and style, this is a consummate deliverance by a literate young person. There are signs here of moral authority, combined with human sympathy, a distinctive sense of humor, and a clear-sighted vision for the future of the society along with a readiness to point out its defects, in a way which might not have endeared him to all his hearers. Oman raises here topics to which he will return in later life when, as a professor himself, he gives advice to theological students, or addresses ecclesiological matters either in writing or in the councils of the church. As we shall see, the man who was affectionately regarded by his students as the "prophet of Westminster" was not slow to point to the need for reform in the church which he served so faithfully, and "it cannot be said that he never had to face opposition."[47]

In an environment where there were few opportunities for socializing, the UP Students Society fostered a familiar camaraderie between UP students. Oman's closest friends, George William Alexander and Adam Cleghorn Welch, were both members between 1881 and 1883.[48] Although there is no reference to Benjamin R. H. Mein in the Minute Books of the Society, George Alexander refers to him as being in 1883 "ever one of [Oman's] closest friends."[49] They were to pursue different career paths, Alexander in educational administration, Welch in ministry and scholarship, and Mein in the ministry of the local church, reflecting distinctive emphases in Oman's own life and career. And the four men were to remain in personal contact for the rest of their lives.

Oman's Friends

George William Alexander (1864–1941)

Frank Ballard, Oman's son-in-law, comments that "Oman and Alexander were fellow-students in Edinburgh and the friendship then formed never waned. Never, I imagine, was a major decision made in the life of either without the knowledge of the other. Readers of Oman's books will know how often he was indebted to his friend for help in reading manuscripts and proofs."[50] While other friends may have been entrusted with a book or a chapter of a book, Alexander proofread in their entirety seven of Oman's major published works[51] in addition to Adam Welch's *Anselm and his Work*, 1901.

47. Alexander, "Memoir of the Author," xv.
48. See Minute Book of the Edinburgh University United Presbyterian Students' Society. University of Edinburgh New College collections, AA3.7.1.
49. Alexander, "Memoir of the Author," xviii.
50. In his introduction to Oman, *Honest Religion*, xi–xiv, here xiii–xiv.
51. Schleiermacher, *On Religion: Speeches to Its Cultured Despisers*, trans. John Oman, 1893; *Vision and Authority*, 1902; *Faith and Freedom*, 1906; *The Church and Divine Order*, 1911; *Grace and Personality*, 1917; *The Natural and the Supernatural*, 1931; *Honest Religion*, 1941.

A mutual respect and lifelong personal regard emerges from Alexander's "memoir of the author," which prefixes the posthumous edition of various addresses that Oman gave in Cambridge.[52] Alexander writes feelingly of "a friend to whom I have owed so much," and comments: "His friendship once given was never withdrawn: differences there might be, but at the worst there could be agreement to differ." He shared Oman's general theological outlook and his wide interest in education. Born in 1864 in Halifax, Nova Scotia, Alexander graduated MA in 1883 and launched into a career in educational administration. As clerk to the Glasgow School Board, he came to be known as a champion of the education of girls and women.[53] In 1907 Alexander was elected clerk to the Edinburgh Board.[54] Two years later, he was Assistant Secretary to the Scotch Education Department in Whitehall, living in Earls Court, Kensington, with his wife Phoebe.[55] In 1918, however, Phoebe died aged fifty, and with the relocation of the Department (now renamed the Scottish Education Department) to Edinburgh, Alexander returned to Scotland.

We may briefly single out two areas of subsequent involvement which are sure to have been of keen interest to his friend, although no letters between them survive. Described as "a gentleman of the very highest educational experience and attainments,"[56] he assisted the commission on primary education in Ireland, chaired by the Catholic Irish peer Lord Killanin, and the commission for intermediate education which met under the chairmanship of the Right Honorable T. F. Molony, Lord Chief Justice of Ireland. Given his own resistance to the Education Act 1902 in England, Oman will have followed his friend's involvement in Irish education with particular interest. The proposals of the Commissions, issued in March 1919, were bitterly controversial: local school committees would be established to deal with the many problems identified, costs would be met by a local rate, and there was to be an elaborate salary scale for teachers.[57] Catholic bishops were opposed to educational reform under British auspices, and alleged that Irish people were being forced to finance with their own money a moral perversion of their own children.[58] Again, seven years later, Alexander was in Cam-

---

52. Oman, *Honest Religion*, xv–xxv.
53. McDermid, "Gender," 255.
54. "Scotland from our own correspondent," *Otago Witness*, November 1907, 27.
55. He married Phoebe Emily Buckmaster in Kingston, Surrey, in 1892.
56. *Hansard*, 9 May 1919.
57. Titley, *Schooling in Ireland*, 55.
58. Debates were lost in the confusion of the Irish war of independence, and the new era began with primary and secondary schools largely under the control of the Roman Catholic Church.

bridge, one of two representatives of the Scottish Education Department at the Imperial Education Conference (Advisory Committee)[59] under the presidency of Lord Balfour. This was "to advise on Empire education," and brought together High Commissioners and Agents-General of the Overseas governments, with representatives of the India Office, the Colonial Office, the Board of Education, and the Scottish Education Department.

George Alexander was amongst the mourners at Oman's funeral service at St Columba's Church, Cambridge, in May 1939, when he is listed in the *Cambridge Daily News* as "family."

Adam Cleghorn Welch (1864–1943)

The general lines of Adam Welch's career trajectory were similar to Oman's. Welch was born in Goshen, Jamaica, the son of a UP missionary and his wife. On graduating from Edinburgh University in 1883, he entered the UP Hall to study for the ministry. He served congregations at Waterbeck (1887–92), Helensburgh (1892–1902) and Claremont, Glasgow (1902–13). He became known as a preacher and a distinguished scholar. In 1913, he was appointed to the chair of Hebrew and OT exegesis at New College, Edinburgh where he proved himself to be an outstanding critic of the school of Wellhausen, and on his retirement in 1934, he was elected President of the Society for Old Testament Study.

He and Oman proofread and critiqued one another's works. In 1906, he helped "put through the Press" Oman's Kerr lectures at the University of Glasgow, published as *Faith and Freedom*; and six years later, Oman repaid the compliment: when Welch in his turn published Kerr lectures on *The Religion of Israel under the Kingdom*, he acknowledged his "indebtedness . . . to Professor J. W. Oman, DD, and Rev. B. R. H. Mein, MA, for their careful reading of the proofs, and for their suggestive and sympathetic criticism of the line of argument." In 1931, Welch read "the Old Testament part" of *The Natural and the Supernatural*.

Both men were awarded the BD of the University of Edinburgh in 1886; both were recognized by the British Academy in 1938. Oman was elected to the Fellowship of the Academy that July, and under its auspices Welch delivered that year the Schweich Lectures on Biblical Archaeology on "The Work of the Chronicler." Only the ill-health "which prevented

---

59. See *Hansard*, 24 February 1927; the conference was first constituted in 1912, with two chairs, George Adam Smith and J. G. Adami.

[Oman] from travelling and attending meetings of the Academy, and eventually caused his death on 17 May 1939"[60] prevented him from attending his friend's lectures.

Benjamin R. H. Mein (1864–1949)

Mein was born in Roxburgh Barns Farm House. His mother, Margaret, was the daughter of Henry Renton, a distinguished minister of the UP church in Kelso and a former moderator of the Synod.[61] His grandfather's books, which he had inherited, many of them having previously belonged to "Fisher one of the Secession Fathers," were a tangible reminder of his ecclesiastical roots.[62] Graduating MA from Edinburgh University in 1883, he entered the UP Hall and, with Oman, was to spend a summer session in Erlangen. Ordained to the ministry of the Presbyterian Church of England on 13 September 1888, he was inducted to the charge of Thropton in Northumberland, where he was to serve for the next fifteen years. His Coquetdale flock were delighted with their new minister, who "was a young man with a quiet, retiring manner"; but he told racy anecdotes of his student days and showed "a quaint humour."[63] At his death it was minuted that "his work was marked by a gentleness and earnestness of devoted service of the Master." They also appear to have been attached to his wife, Mary Molina Mein, whose father had been an "operatic singer" and who herself had a beautiful singing voice.[64]

Within a year, Oman and he were colleagues in Northumberland. When Oman was also ordained to the ministry of the Presbyterian Church of England, and inducted to Clayport church in Alnwick, Mein was one of those appointed by the Northumberland Presbytery to lay on hands and Alexander records: "It helped [Oman] greatly to have his old friend so near and to have his guidance while yet a stranger to the Presbytery, to both its members and its ways of working."[65]

60. Tennant, "John Wood Oman."
61. See Small. *History of the Congregations*, 2:264–65.
62. Letter from Benjamin Mein to Mr. Shaw, 30 October 1922, Westminster College archives.
63. Ward, *The First Two Hundred Years*.
64. Two stained glass windows, designed by Stanley Scott, were installed in the church between 1950 and 1954 to celebrate Mein's ministry: one featuring him in the guise of St Paulinus baptizing at Holystone, and the other depicting his wife as St Cecilia, holding a harp. They may be seen by appointment with the Coquetdale Music Trust.
65. "Memoir of the Author," in Oman, *Honest Religion*, xx.

It appears that neither Benjamin nor Mary Molina enjoyed good health and the congregation released them for six months in 1898 to recuperate in South Africa. Their home-coming was cause for celebration and they were presented with a silver tea service.[66] However, on November 4 1903 the Presbytery of Northumberland recorded[67] "that Mr Mein . . . had decided to accept the offer of the charge of the services at Algiers for the winter in connection with the UF Church of Scotland and that as he did not deem it right and wise even if permitted by the Presbytery to be absent from the oversight of the congregation so soon again he had resolved to resign his charge."

As we shall see, Mein and Oman were to collaborate once again and in a very different context, when in 1911 Mein took charge of a church extension project at Erdington, Birmingham, with which Oman had been closely involved since its inception the previous year. Although the project was prospering, Mein resigned in 1915, leaving Oman and various Westminster students to fill the breach.

In 1902, along with George Alexander, Mein proofread *Vision and Authority*, and in 1931 the "later part" of *The Natural and the Supernatural*. In 1912, he collaborated with Oman in proofreading *The Religion of Israel under the Kingdom* by Adam Welch, and in 1941, as a final token of friendship, he proofread with George Alexander Oman's last published work, the posthumous *Honest Religion*.

The Professors

The Arts professors at the time were distinguished scholars. Two of those whom Oman sat under in his first three years were influential in different respects.

Professor Peter Guthrie Tait (1831–1901)

The professor of Natural Philosophy was Peter Guthrie Tait, an alumnus of the University of Edinburgh and of Peterhouse, Cambridge, where he graduated as senior wrangler[68] in 1852. After two further years as a fellow and college lecturer, he was appointed professor of mathematics in Queen's University, Belfast, returning to his alma mater to take up the chair of Natural Philosophy in 1860. His initial specialism was in the study of quaternions, on which

---

66. Dixon, *Upper Coquetdale*.
67. Minutes of the Presbytery of Northumberland, 4 November, 1903, 219.
68. The candidate gaining top marks in mathematics in the final exam.

he published two textbooks, but it was his later work on thermodynamics in cooperation with Sir William Thomson, later Lord Kelvin, and James Clerk Maxwell, that was to give rise to popular controversy. This investigation into the various forms of energy and their relationship with one another became associated with theories that challenged traditional Christian concepts of cosmology and anthropology. "In general," as Bernhard Maier observes,[69] "these theories were highly critical not only of traditional Christianity, but also of all forms of idealism and speculative nature philosophy, contrasting traditional vitalism with mechanistic theories which intended to explain all natural phenomena by physical forces, assuming a continuity in which matter, energy, life and perhaps even consciousness could be regarded as manifestations of one and the same principle." The search for a single unifying principle of reality emphasized a materialistic perspective which was often taken to undermine Christianity. "Thus," Maier continues, "any young theologian with an interest in the natural sciences must have regarded a sound knowledge of the most recent advances in physics as a useful prerequisite to combating theories which were taken to undermine Christianity."[70] Maier is referring obliquely here to William Robertson Smith who, for the two years he spent from 1868 as Tait's laboratory assistant in Edinburgh, combined his divinity studies with the teaching of physics, but the remark would surely apply also to John Oman who studied under Tait seven years later. In future years Oman's interest in apologetics led him to return to these issues, most notably in *The Natural and the Supernatural*, 338–48.

Professor David Mather Masson (1822–1907)

In Scotland, though not in England, the study of philosophy was bound up with the study of literature, and poetry in particular.[71] Oman wrote poems, none of which have survived;[72] and in a memorable chapter in *The Natural and the Supernatural* on "Awareness and Apprehension"[73] he extols the innate gifts of the poet and the child who perceive reality by sensory apprehension rather than in terms of abstract principles. A number of the foremost Scottish Idealist philosophers were also men of literature: Edward Caird wrote on Wordsworth and Carlyle, and Henry Jones followed suit

69. Maier, *Robertson Smith*, 68.
70. Maier, *Robertson Smith*, 69.
71. See Ker, "Philosophy of Art."
72. Around one hundred poems were destroyed after his death. See Bevans, *John Oman*, 124n66.
73. Oman, *Natural and Supernatural*, 120–43.

with books on Browning, Scott, Tennyson, Browning, and Shakespeare.[74] And English literature was an essential component of the MA curriculum in the University of Edinburgh. Oman's professor of Rhetoric and English Literature, rhetoric here being understood in the Aristotelian sense as the art of persuasion, was David Masson, an enthusiastic friend and admirer of Thomas Carlyle.[75] Masson earned scholarly acclaim for his Life of Milton in six volumes (1858–80) and his three volume Library edition of Milton's Poetical Works (1874). He was credited with being J. M. Barrie's literary mentor[76] and it may be no exaggeration to deduce that the enthusiasm with which Oman refers in his published work to Milton, Browning, Coleridge, Carlyle, and Shakespeare was fostered by Masson.

The professor's classroom style was memorable: lectures were reinforced by dramatic illustration. Barrie writes that

> Masson always comes to my memory first knocking nails into his desk. . . . He said that the Danes scattered over England, taking such a hold as a nail takes when it is driven into wood. For the moment, he saw his desk turned into England; he whirled an invisible hammer in the air, and down it came on the desk with a crash. No one who has sat under Masson can forget how the Danes nailed themselves upon England.[77]

To conclude, "he masters a subject by letting it master him; for though his critical reputation is built on honesty, it is his enthusiasm that makes his work warm with life."[78] Oman too was impressed with Masson's flights of imagination and gives a further example:

> My old professor of English used to picture Ben Jonson in conversation as like a Spanish galleon, and Shakespeare playing round him like an English frigate. In spite of his ready wit, Shakespeare may not have felt bound to reject a telling hit because it was somewhere in his writings. But he would, I think, be trying to forget that he had ever put pen to paper, while the illustrious Ben would, probably, be always trying to recall the wise and witty sayings he had laboriously manufactured at his desk. Possibly, however, he carried it off like the professor himself, who, though the description had been given from a way-worn

---

74. David Boucher, ed., *The Scottish Idealists*, 3–4.

75. Masson was also a resolute supporter of the campaign for women's higher education.

76. Dunbar, *Barrie*, 37–41.

77. Barrie, *Edinburgh Eleven*, 16.

78. Barrie, *Edinburgh Eleven*, 17.

manuscript with verbal exactness to many generations of students, always managed to deliver it as though it had occurred to him at the moment, because, somehow, he could convince himself that it had.[79]

Many years later, Oman was to quote this example to students for the ministry at Westminster College as an instance of "the spontaneity which is an essential of interesting human intercourse."[80]

Professors in the Honors Class

Although the classes for the Ordinary MA were often large and it was not uncommon for the professors to employ an assistant, usually for a term of two years, a regular junior academic staff did not yet exist and the smaller fourth year Honors classes were invariably taken by the professors themselves. These tended to make a deep personal impression on their students. In Oman's case, this may be instanced by Henry Calderwood and Alexander Campbell Fraser, his professors respectively in Moral Philosophy and Logic and Metaphysics.

Professor Henry Calderwood (1830–97)

The "power to meet the questions of the day" is the particular province of Moral Philosophy. "A special grandeur belongs to moral philosophy,—a science which treats of right and wrong; of individual character and of conduct; of social interests and obligations; and, above all, of man's relation to eternity and to God."[81] This was the sphere of influence exercised for twenty-nine years among the students of Edinburgh University by Henry Calderwood. They knew and respected him for his commitment to the church, for his engagement in social issues and for his dedicated teaching of moral philosophy. His commitment led to a bond with many of his students who "knew that they were in contact with one who simply and sincerely shared with them the faith in which they had been trained, and who ungrudgingly and unreservedly lived under its inspiration. It was natural that they should look with peculiar confidence to his treatment of a subject which, more perhaps

---

79. Oman, *Concerning the Ministry*, 181.
80. Oman, *Concerning the Ministry*, 181.
81. Calderwood, *Henry Calderwood*, 170.

than any other in their academic course, might seem to bear a close relation to their religious beliefs."[82]

Henry Calderwood was an ordained minister of the UP Church to which he remained profoundly committed. The move in 1868 from the pulpit of Greyfriars church in Glasgow to the professor's chair in Edinburgh appears to have caused no change in his sense of vocation. While his dedication to the welfare of his students was exemplary, he continued to take a full part in Presbytery and Synod affairs, led services in local churches, and served as an elder in his local church for twenty-seven years: "to many a home and heart under the shadow of trial, his visits were like beams of summer sunshine, carrying with them comfort and sustaining."[83] As a token of the esteem in which he was held, he was elected Moderator of the Presbytery Synod in 1880. He also supported wholeheartedly the work of Moody and Sankey when they came to Edinburgh in 1873 and took a lively interest ten years later in the evangelistic campaign amongst students led by Henry Drummond. Calderwood's son comments: "How much the success of this movement which far exceeded anything that took place in any other university, was due to the sympathetic interest of the Edinburgh professors, it is impossible to say; but it was at least a striking coincidence that an unusual proportion of them were in thorough sympathy with such work."[84]

Like many members of the UP Church, Calderwood was involved in social reform. The first chair of the Edinburgh School Board, he promoted educational improvements, he was an indefatigable campaigner for Temperance, for women's suffrage and for the right of women to university education. Although he had been a Liberal all his life, he split with Gladstone at the time of the Home Rule Bill and campaigned on behalf of the Liberal Unionists up and down the country from the Borders to Orkney.[85]

Although Calderwood was to mellow in his later years to such a degree that the earlier "warrior" could barely be recognized, Oman remembered him from his own student days as having "little chiaroscuro either in his thought or his action." In his attitude to philosophy, Calderwood had long since made his position clear. In his first and most famous book, *The Philosophy of the Infinite*, he had, as a twenty-four-year-old student, entered the lists against Sir William Hamilton, his former professor of Logic and Metaphysics, who was then at the height of his professional career. In the courteous correspondence that ensued, Calderwood's religious earnestness

---

82. Calderwood, *Henry Calderwood*, 183; recollection by Mr Charles Douglas.
83. Calderwood, *Henry Calderwood*, 399.
84. Calderwood, *Henry Calderwood*, 397.
85. McKimmon, "Secession," 378.

is apparent. Both he and Hamilton recognize that the terms "Absolute" and "Infinite" may be translated "God." But while Hamilton believes that God as infinite may be the object of faith, but not of knowledge, Calderwood strenuously contests this.[86] As he saw it, as we come to know the universe, we align our thoughts with those of God.

He returns to the theme in his inaugural lecture in 1868. "There can be nothing but gain if the philosophy of the country be distinguished by a religious spirit. The philosophic spirit, in its high and noble sense, reverence for truth, is indeed identical with the religious spirit, reverence for God."[87] After indicating what he felt to be the necessarily close connection between philosophy and religion, he went on to describe the impact of "the Scottish philosophy."

> It sprang up under the necessity which the nation felt for delivering itself from the disorder and uncertainty which a philosophical scepticism showed itself competent to bring about with the materials afforded by an empirical philosophy. The dangers which threatened were, on the one hand, an intellectual scepticism; on the other, a utilitarian system of morals: on the one hand, the loss of the real in the phenomenal; on the other, the loss of an immutable morality in a higher or lower type of utility. The success of the Scottish philosophy in averting these dangers, has been acknowledged by competent witnesses, and has its own lasting testimony in the abiding faith of the nation.[88]

The development of Scottish philosophy along Idealist lines was in many respects alien to the Scottish philosophy that went before. Whereas Sir William Hamilton accommodated the influences of Kant and Hegel,[89] Calderwood did not. In 1881, Calderwood's thirteenth session in the Chair, as Oman called to mind, "he was often driven to dire straits in defending [his conclusions] by general and philosophical reasons."[90] But the professor's own views on the relation between philosophy, religion and ethics remained unaltered.

> His sole ideal of the moral man was a man who applied clear principles with unbiased judgment to life and action, while his well-regulated sentiments sat ever ready, like judges, to carry

---

86. Calderwood, *Henry Calderwood*, 18.
87. Calderwood, *Henry Calderwood*, 166.
88. Calderwood, *Henry Calderwood*, 167.
89. For an account of the themes and shifts of Scottish Idealist philosophy, see Boucher, *Scottish Idealists*, 1–22.
90. Calderwood, *Henry Calderwood*, 392.

out the verdict. And he had the best reason for this conception, seeing that he actually followed it—his whole nature being ever a court of justice in perpetual session.[91]

Oman sums up Calderwood's "whole thought" in this question: "How is man to be made to see with the divine insight which is in him, and realise in his own action the eternal decrees?"[92]

Calderwood's approach to philosophy may not have given intellectual satisfaction to all of his students, and Oman records how

> the best students especially saw that this analysis left the supremely difficult question of how the faculties ever came to be together, the supremely difficult question of their unity and harmony untouched, and a great deal besides; but none went away without some confirmation of moral principle, and none went away with the notion that life could be well spent in spinning cobwebs of the brain. No man could afterwards avoid facing the question whether or not there were behind this visible garment of the Deity, eternal, vital, immutable principles; and if he rejected the position, he did it with his eyes open.[93]

The reference to "eternal, immutable principles" raises questions of sound doctrine and right belief. Calderwood "stood by all the old positions, and in particular, was strongly attached to the evangelical view of the Atonement.... He thought that the man who did not set forth the atoning death of Christ as the ground for the forgiveness of sin had no Gospel to preach, and should not be an accredited teacher of the United Presbyterian Church."[94]

However, distinctively, he also held that faith should keep abreast of cultural change. Persuaded that "a wider knowledge must lead to a wider faith"[95] he applied himself to study anatomy, physiology, and biology, and published three books on the relation of science and religion.[96] He was also open-minded about matters which some took to be central to the Faith. He had no problem in accepting the views of W. Robertson Smith about the authorship of the Pentateuch, for he was convinced "that these did not

91. Calderwood, *Henry Calderwood*, 393.
92. Calderwood, *Henry Calderwood*, 393.
93. Calderwood, *Henry Calderwood*, 393.
94. Calderwood, *Henry Calderwood*, 274. The reference is to the Reverend David Macrae of Gourock, who, in the Synod of 1879, had denounced the doctrine of eternal punishment as set out in the Westminster Confession of Faith in favor of some form of universal restoration.
95. Calderwood, *Henry Calderwood*, 260.
96. McKimmon, "Secession," 379.

touch the real question of inspiration or the abiding influence of the Word of God. On one occasion, after hearing the arguments with regard to the later authorship of the latter part of the book of Isaiah, and after examining certain portions of the text, he at once said: 'There is no doubt that Isaiah never wrote these words,' although, up to that time, he had accepted the traditional view."[97] The remarkable ability to divest himself of the old and accept what is new sprang, according to Charles Douglas, "from his love of truth, and the strong faith in God that enabled him to believe that all new light, from whatsoever quarter it came, would, in the end, make ever clearer the revealed will of God."[98]

The implications are that as a student Oman was one of those who saw intellectual difficulties in the professor's stance on philosophical matters, but there can be no doubt that Calderwood, with his integrity, his engagement with social issues, his devotion to his ministerial calling, and his principled pursuit of truth, was influential.

Professor Alexander Campbell Fraser (1819–1914)

Barrie notes whimsically that "Calderwood and Fraser had both their followings. The moral philosophers wore an air of certainty, for they knew that if they stuck to Calderwood he would pull them through. You cannot lose yourself in the back garden. But the metaphysicians had their doubts. Fraser led them into strange places."[99]

Fraser had followed his father in 1843 into the Free Church of Scotland and was ordained to its ministry the following year. After three years' service as assistant minister at Cramond, he was appointed to the chair of logic at New College before succeeding Sir William Hamilton as Professor of Logic and Metaphysics in the University of Edinburgh in 1856.[100] Fraser had deep sympathy with the Scottish philosophical tradition, and was seen as a link between Thomas Reid's Common Sense school of thought and the empirical schools of philosophers, notably Berkeley and Locke, on whom he wrote extensively.

He was indebted both to Reid and to Kant, particularly in his persuasion that what is not subject to limitation cannot be known by human

---

97. Calderwood, *Henry Calderwood*, 275.
98. Calderwood, *Henry Calderwood*, 275.
99. Barrie, *Edinburgh Eleven*, 63.
100. The appointment had not been uncontroversial. The other competitor was James Frederick Ferrier, professor of Moral Philosophy and Political Economy at the University of St Andrews, who vigorously refuted Reid's Common Sense.

minds. And he attempted to find a mediating philosophy between the skeptical empiricism of Hume, Mill, and their followers, and the claims of Hegelian absolute idealists. "In this way," he writes, "I found myself on a *Via Media*, repelled alike from an agnostic science wholly ignorant of God, and from a gnostic science which implied Omniscience."[101] In his memoir he picks up the view he had expressed earlier in his Edinburgh Gifford lectures[102] that, while the physical and moral universe was essentially reasonable, it was not fully knowable by the human intellect.[103] Writing of "The Omniscience of God who knows all things past, present and to come, and to whom the thoughts of all men's hearts always lie open,"[104] he suggests that "in religion the complex constitution of man—emotional, active and intelligent—is found in ultimate practical relation to the Power universally at work, the *Mens Divina agitans molem*, the Spirit that animates the universe. In metaphysic, intellect in man tries to express in thought our ultimate relation to the Supreme Reality."[105]

It was said that Professor Fraser's "contribution to philosophy came more from stimulating his students to pursue the subject with emotion than by making any novel claims himself."[106] He had an outstanding teaching ability and was hugely influential. Many of his students were to achieve eminence in philosophy. He records in his memoir that

> the classroom ... has sent not a few professors and books of philosophy into the world, in the latter decades of the nineteenth century. It has given two professors of philosophy to Edinburgh, two to Glasgow, three to Aberdeen, two to St Andrew's; one to Oxford, and another to Cambridge; besides a still larger number to American universities, and to colleges in India and Japan and Australia. Others are distinguished in Parliament, or on the judicial bench, and in the Church.[107]

In action in the classroom, Fraser was perceived to be "rather a hazardous cure for weak intellects. Young men whose anchor had been certainty of themselves went into that class floating buoyantly on the sea of facts, and came out all adrift—on the sea of theory—in an open boat—rudderless—one

---

101. Fraser, *Biographia*, 186.
102. Published as *Philosophy of Theism* (1895–97).
103. In this he was following the thought of Sir William Hamilton, whom he had succeeded in 1856.
104. Fraser, *Biographia*, 202.
105. Fraser, *Biographia*, 204.
106. https://www.giffordlectures.org/lecturers/alexander-campbell-fraser.
107. Fraser, *Biographia*, 206.

oar—the boat scuttled. How could they think there was any chance for them when the Professor was not even sure of himself?" Barrie evokes the spectacle of him

> rising in a daze from his chair and putting his hands through his hair. "Do I exist," he said thoughtfully, "strictly so-called?" The students (if it was at the beginning of the session) looked a little startled. This was a matter that had not previously disturbed them. Still, if the Professor was in doubt, there must be something in it. He began to argue it out, and an uncomfortable silence held the room in awe. If he did not exist, the chance were that they did not exist either. It was thus a personal question. The Professor glanced round slowly for an illustration. "Am I a table?" A pained look travelled over the class. Was it just possible that they were all tables?[108]

Fraser leaves an attractive account of the development of his thinking and his approach to teaching in his *Biographia Philosophica*. Of one thing he was clear—he had no intention of teaching philosophy "dogmatically from a book, instead of being thought out by the student for himself, aided by the intellectual stimulus of the university." His lectures were intended "for those who were learning in the classroom to think for themselves." He continues:

> In philosophy I had still to confess myself "a seeker." Perhaps the thought in the lectures and my solitary thought were kept too much apart. Perhaps I ought to have admitted the main current, some of which was finding occasional exit in essays and annotations, more fully into speech. I might in this way have engaged the undergraduates in a greater degree as helpful fellow-thinkers. On the other hand, the final problems which lay in the heart of my literary work seemed hardly appropriate for those who came to college to begin to think. They still needed to have "the mist and veil of words" removed, their sense of logical consistency made more acute, and themselves made more awake to the difference between probability and fancy in estimating evidence. One remembered that the path of human life was strewed with fallacies and sophisms, and that these were apt to be multiplied on the part of the path frequented by abstract thinkers. The duty of the teacher in these circumstances was first of all to prepare the young philosophers to encounter fallacy and sophism, by analysing valid reasoning.[109]

---

108. Barrie, *Edinburgh Eleven*, 64.
109. Fraser, *Biographia*, 198.

Fraser's course would have refined and developed Oman's ability to think logically and systematically. "Logic," as Fraser put it, "was of course the elementary logic which proposes scientific forms for the unabridged expression of reasoning, deductive and inductive; lessons in definition and method; and criteria for testing interpretation of nature in daily life and in physical science—not logic, in the high Hegelian or even Kantian meaning, concerned with the ultimate categories of thought. It bore more immediately on opening life than that."[110]

Truth itself was at stake. Before they were in a position to wrestle with Kant and Hegel, students had to learn to expose and dissect the concrete fallacies that stem from syllogism. "Logic studied in this spirit and with this practical aim warns the student of the aptness of men unconsciously to produce fallacies in the guise of valid reasoning." But while this approach secures a consistency between conclusions and their premises, "it provides no final warrant for the truth of the premises themselves. Premises are concluded from preceding premises and so on, in an infinite regress." This exposes "an accumulation of error and fallacy."[111] Fraser continues:

> On what must human reasonings all rest at last? Why is the pathway to ultimate reality obstructed by an accumulation of error and fallacy? Lectures and exercises on the practice of reasoning naturally raised those questions. They led us onwards from formulas of syllogism . . . to a reflective study of the spiritual constitution of the human reason—in a word, from Logic to Psychology; and through this to Metaphysics or ultimate philosophy, and analysis of religion.[112]

For Professor Fraser, philosophical education entailed giving his students scope "to test the authority" in order to think out their final intellectual position for themselves. He writes:

> So in 1865 I opened separate lectures for any so disposed. In the following quarter of a century more than 400 students entered in this class. In those lectures I avoided final system, and unfolded some of the great philosophies of the past, destructive and constructive; in the faith that human thinkers differ, not totally, but in the degree of their approach to the perfect philosophy that is fully reached by none. The history of metaphysics is in much like the history of poetry or art; yet the collisions of metaphysicians represent gradual advancement on the whole. And now

---

110. Fraser, *Biographia*, 199.
111. Fraser, *Biographia*, 200.
112. Fraser, *Biographia*, 200.

the young aspirants, by going into the river, and "moving up and down in its depths and shallows" each bestirring himself as he best could, were able in the end to discover something.

And Fraser concludes dryly: "This attempt to educate independent thinkers was not unsuccessful."[113]

The Edinburgh University Philosophical Society

This aim was bolstered by the weekly meetings of the Edinburgh University Philosophical Society, of which several key members were to make important contributions to philosophical thought in later years. Robert Adamson, R. B. Haldane, D. G. Ritchie, W. R. Sorley, all former students of Fraser and Calderwood, were already beginning to forge distinguished careers when Oman became a member of the society in the session 1881-82. He was elected to the committee the following year, when James Seth[114] was president, and succeeded Seth as a president of the society for the year 1883-84.

It was a heady time for the "young metaphysicians." Exposure to the teaching of philosophy in German universities was leading them to reassess trends in Scottish philosophy in the light not only of Kant's critical and moral philosophy but also of Hegel.[115] Overall the program of essays and debates in the society meetings reflects this engagement.[116] According to the 1882-83 syllabus, members debated such questions as: Is a philosophy of religion possible? Has the belief in immortality a practical influence on life? Is a philosophy of history possible? Can Positivism be justified philosophically? Is conscience a product of experience? Is the Hamiltonian doctrine of the infinite satisfactory? Can the belief in personal identity be accounted for as the product of experience? Is Kant's ethical system consistent with his intellectual? On 10 January 1883, the Society was addressed on "The Value of Ideals" by William Wallace, professor of Moral Philosophy in the University

113. Fraser, *Biographia*, 205.

114. James Seth joined the Society in 1879-80. On graduation he undertook the full course training for the ministry of the Free Church at New College; after studying philosophy at Leipzig, Jena, and Berlin, he accepted a two year appointment in 1883, following his brother as assistant to Alexander Campbell Fraser. There followed professorships in Dalhousie College, Brown University, and Cornell University, from where he returned to Edinburgh in 1898 to take up the chair of Moral Philosophy on the death of Henry Calderwood, a post which he held for the next twenty-six years.

115. For a fuller account, see the introduction to Fergusson, ed., *Scottish Philosophical Theology*, 11-19, and the introduction to Boucher, ed., *Scottish Idealists*, 1-22.

116. See Records of the Edinburgh University Philosophical Society, Centre for Research Collections, EUA GD23, University of Edinburgh.

of Oxford,[117] who had furthered the understanding in the English-speaking world of certain German philosophers, notably Kant and Hegel, some of whose works he had translated into English. And on 7 November 1883, Oman delivered an essay to the society on "Perfection the ethical end." While no trace of this essay is to be found, the reference to Kant is unmistakable.

That same year, James Seth's elder brother, Andrew Seth,[118] a previous president of the society between 1877 and 1878, co-edited with R. B. Haldane *Essays in Philosophical Criticism*, in which various prominent contemporary British philosophers engaged critically with Kant and Hegel. Edward Caird's preface is itself a landmark event: in describing the approach of the authors, it seeks to forestall misunderstandings about the method adopted, and sets out a future agenda for British Idealist philosophy. Inasmuch as Oman will subsequently engage with some of these ideas, Caird's preface is summarized in some detail.[119]

Caird starts by explaining his brief: to explore the degree to which the contributors to the book share "a common purpose or tendency." He concludes that where there is agreement, this is not to do with "an intention to advocate any special philosophical theory," but "an agreement as to the direction in which inquiry may most fruitfully be presented." However, he continues, "Such an agreement is consistent with great and even vital differences. For any idea that has a principle of growth in it . . . is certain, as it develops, to produce wide divergences and even to call forth much antagonism and conflict between its supporters." Ideas that have "given rise to the most far-reaching controversy" have been the most fruitful both in religion and in philosophy. These differences are not insuperable. So long as "the differences are due to the various development of one way of thinking in different minds . . . they may be expected ultimately to be overcome by the same spiritual energy which has produced it."

In contrast, "a doctrine that passes unchanged from hand to hand, is by that very fact shown to have exhausted its inherent force."

There is general agreement by the authors of the various chapters in the book "that the line of investigation which philosophy must follow . . . is that

117. Members of the society were on occasion also addressed by Mr. Balfour, Sir Alexander Grant, Professors Henry Sidgwick, Knight, Bosanquet, and Jones. Fraser, *Biographia*, 204.

118. Having graduated from Edinburgh University with first class honors in classics and philosophy in 1878, he spent the following two years studying in Berlin, Jena, and Göttingen, and returned to Edinburgh as Alexander Campbell Fraser's class assistant between 1880 and 1883. In 1891, following professorships in Cardiff and St Andrews, Andrew Seth was to succeed Fraser as professor of Logic, Rhetoric, and Metaphysics at Edinburgh University.

119. Seth and Haldane, *Philosophical Criticism*.

which was opened up by Kant and for the successful prosecution of which no one has done so much as Hegel."[120] Yet Caird cautions against claims to be the disciple of a particular philosopher; this is inconsistent with the belief "that the history of philosophy is a living development," and he elaborates:

> The work of Kant and Hegel, like the work of earlier philosophers, can have no speculative value except for those who are able critically to reproduce it . . . and each reproduction, again, is not possible except for those who are impelled by the very teaching they have received to give it a fresh expression and a new application . . . the liberal importation of Kant and Hegel into another country and time would not be possible if it were desirable, or desirable if it were possible.[121]

Historical and geographical context are all important. "The mere change of time and place, if there were nothing more, implies new questions and a new attitude of mind in those whom the writer addresses, which would make a bare reproduction unmeaning." This is especially so in an era when there have been dramatic developments in science, in social and religious life, when "anyone who writes about philosophy must have his work judged, not by its relation to the intellectual wants of a past generation, but by its power to meet the wants of the present time." Readers are not interested in what a philosopher owes to his predecessors. "For them the only question of interest is, whether in the writer they have immediately to deal with, there is a living source of light which is original in the sense that, whatever may be its history, it carries its evidence in itself. And this evidence must lie in its power to meet the questions of the day, and in the form in which they arise in that day."[122]

As W. J. Mander has shown,[123] Idealist thought continued to be influential long after the emergence of new schools of thinking and provided a counter-current to language and logic-based styles of philosophy. Ironically, given the emphasis on contextuality in Caird's Preface, it was external events, notably the First World War, rather than philosophical arguments, that ultimately contributed to the demise of Idealist thought. Oman remarks in his

---

120. In a graceful tribute to T. H. Green, to whose memory the book is dedicated, Caird comments: "For while in the main, he accepted Hegel's criticism of Kant, and held also that something like Hegel's idealism must be the result of the development of Kantian principles rightly understood, he yet regarded the actual Hegelian system with a certain suspicion as something too ambitious, or at least, premature." Seth and Haldane, *Philosophical Criticism*, 5.

121. Seth and Haldane, *Philosophical Criticism*, 2.

122. Seth and Haldane, *Philosophical Criticism*, 3.

123. Mander, *British Idealism*.

preface to *Grace and Personality* in 1917 that "the fact that such sorrow and wickedness could happen in the world, became the crucible in which my whole view of the world had to be tested."[124] He concludes that "the main intention seems to have stood the test in a way impossible, not only for a merely sentimental faith in a beneficent Deity, but also for any doctrine that starts from the Absolute, whether as the absolute process of Reason or as the absolute divine Sovereignty." We will examine the degree to which his view of the world stood the test in a later chapter. (Below, 273–88.)

For the moment, we may discern in the young Oman an increasing engagement with philosophy, and with the thought of Kant in particular. His move from the UP Society to the Philosophical Society in 1881 may indicate a sense of constraint with what he described as a tendency towards "ruts of thought and feeling" and a desire for greater freedom of thought.

Graduation

When in 1882 John Oman graduated in the crowded Assembly Hall decked out in robes from James Middlemass & Co, there were as yet no indications of an imminent decision to change career. On graduation, he was awarded two university scholarships in Philosophy. The Rhind scholarship was tenable for two years and appeared to assume a further period of university study. Oman was also awarded the Gray scholarship, tenable for up to two years. Once the Senatus was satisfied that there were no suitable candidates by the name of Gray, or who came from the parishes of Midcalder or Kirknewton, this was awarded to "the most distinguished candidates for the Degree in Arts, alternating among the Honors departments." There was however, a further stipulation which may throw some light on Oman's career aspirations. The successful candidate had to be a recent graduate of the university, seeking to pursue further studies in medicine, theology or law.[125] As Oman had no professed desire at this stage to pursue a career in law or in theology, one has to conclude that he was still, in 1882, contemplating a career in medicine.

---

124. Oman, *Grace and Personality*, vi.
125. See University of Edinburgh, Calendar, 1882–83.

3

A Turning Point

THE YEAR 1882 WAS a turning-point in Oman's life. Having graduated from the University of Edinburgh with a distinguished degree in Philosophy, boundless intellectual curiosity, and a scholarship which would enable him to pursue further studies in medicine, he resigned the scholarship[1] and offered himself as a candidate through the Presbytery of Orkney for the ministry of the United Presbyterian Church. The minutes of the Presbytery meeting on 28 August 1882 state that "the Clerk acting on the request of Mr Woodside[2] moved that Mr John W. Oman MA be certified to Theological Committee for admission to the Hall. He further stated that as Mr Oman had to go south last week he had met and conversed with him about motives etc and was satisfied that the Presbytery should agree to the motion. The Presbytery agreed to the motion and hereby certifies Mr John Wood Oman MA for admission to the Hall."[3]

Tantalizingly, no further content is provided for the "motives etc." although, in a rare glimpse into his friend's piety, George Alexander testifies that "no-one can deny that 'the deep things of God' were his first interest and that he had the highest ideal of his calling."[4] His father was, it was said, "quite

---

1. In favor of Robert Allerdine, MA, who held it for one year. See the University of Edinburgh, Calendar, 1882–83.

2. Rev. David Woodside, minister of Victoria Street UP Church, Stromness, 1881–85.

3. OCR/FC/1/4: Synodical Minutes of Orkney United Associate Presbytery, U.P., 1880–84.

4. Alexander, "Memoir of the Author," xxv.

opposed to this"[5] while the minister of his teenage years, Mr. Kirkwood, reported candidly at Oman's ordination soirée in 1889 that in those days "he saw that Oman was taking a deep interest in religious work but never thought he would come into the ministry."[6] We may not know the precise reasons for these reactions, but Oman's later allusion to "the most fatal of all objections to the calling" to ministry is suggestive: "Suppose one starts as a boy, how is he to know what he will believe at thirty? It may be as well to make the admission that it is not a good calling in which to settle on one's lees—economically, socially, intellectually, spiritually."[7] At the very least, a parent might urge caution.[8] Oman was, however, also aware that "there is neither joy nor true success in any profession without gifts for it and interest in it.... To enter the medical profession mainly with a commercial mind is to run the risk of finding a task which will be a laborious and dull drudgery to the person himself and a very mechanical business in the distress of other people."[9] He had not to date shown any particular interest in medicine. While significantly, as he was subsequently to acknowledge to his Cambridge students, he "did not want to be a minister, but somehow could not escape,"[10] he articulates in *The Problem of Faith and Freedom* "the responsibility of personal freedom, as when a young person has to reject the authority of a parent under the constraint of a higher authority in his own heart."[11]

The Case of William Robertson Smith

He leaves us in no doubt as to what prompted this calling to his life's work. He refers explicitly on several occasions to the impact upon him of the "Robertson Smith case" which was "shaking the land"[12] during his student career at Edinburgh University. The heresy trial of Professor William Robertson Smith held the attention of the nation like no other such trial before or after. Oscillating over five years from one ecclesiastical court to another,

---

5. Conversation recorded in Bevans, *John Oman*, 121n28; Isabella Ballard, on dedication of communion chairs in Victoria Street UF Church, *Orcadian*, October 1960.

6. *Alnwick and County Gazette*, Saturday, 21 December 1889.

7. Oman, "Ministry of the Nonconformist Churches," 129.

8. Robert Rainy's father urged delay when his teenage son, fired with enthusiasm for the Disruption, decided to abandon a prospective career in medicine for the ministry of the Free Church. Simpson, *Principal Rainy*, 85–87.

9. Oman, "Ministry of the Nonconformist Churches," 127.

10. Oman, *Concerning the Ministry*, 32.

11. Oman, *Faith and Freedom*, 20.

12. Oman, "Method in Theology," 82.

it culminated on 24 May 1881 with Smith being deprived of his chair of Hebrew and Old Testament Exegesis in the Free Church Hall, Aberdeen, on the grounds that it was "no longer safe or advantageous for the Church that Professor Smith should continue to teach in one of her colleges."[13] His teaching was not condemned and he retained his ministerial status.

We may well ask why this particular case, involving a professor of the Free Church, had such a singularly dramatic effect on Oman. He gives an explicit account of his immediate reactions in his first book, *Vision and Authority* (1902), where he suggests that at the time his perceptions were "by way of intuition" rather than "based on grounds of reason," and in "Method in Theology," his inaugural address as principal of Westminster College in 1923, where he offers a more mature and polished reflection.

It would seem that the scholarly issues at stake were not his primary concern. In his inaugural address, Oman alludes to the Robertson Smith affair with these words: "I had no notion, in those days, of ever being interested in theology, and my ignorance of the matters in dispute was profound."[14] It would be easy to over-interpret this statement. Although Oman's student days were marked by an increasing engagement with philosophy as a discipline, this introduced him to the disputes between idealism and realism, located in the long Scottish tradition of metaphysical debate, which were of considerable theological significance. The ethos of the UP church in which he had been raised was theological, and in and out of class he regularly discussed religious, moral and ethical matters with fellow students. But theology was not at this stage his primary enterprise, and up to 1882 he had no intention of pursuing it professionally.

Biblical "Higher Criticism"

The "matters in dispute" about which Oman professed such ignorance were stimulated by higher criticism, described as "the last great controversy of the nineteenth century, and which nearly rent the Free Church in twain, [but] never made itself felt in the United Presbyterian."[15] This was not, as David Woodside suggests, because of indifference: "Their ministers watched keenly the movement, as it developed in the Free Church, with varying degrees of sympathy, and, on the part of some, but not many, with a distinctly hostile attitude. The United Presbyterian Church, however, produced no man

---

13. Black and Chrystal, *William Robertson Smith*, 426.
14. Oman, "Method in Theology," 82–83.
15. Woodside, *Soul of a Scottish Church*, 280.

who brought the subject into prominence."[16] There was no equivalent in the UP church either of Andrew Bruce Davidson (1831–1902), described by Patrick Carnegie Simpson as "the glory of New College,"[17] where he taught Old Testament criticism, or of his distinguished student, William Robertson Smith.

The fact that Oman was largely ignorant about these matters in his student days is, then, scarcely surprising, especially as the UP Church had over the years come to the understanding that a faithful reading of the Bible was quite compatible with historical criticism; views had evolved gradually since the early days of the Secession. In 1879 its position was set out in Article seven of the Declaratory Act, which states "that, in accordance with the practice hitherto observed in this Church, liberty of opinion is allowed on such points in the Standards, not entering into the substance of the faith, as the interpretation of the 'six days' in the Mosaic account of the creation: the Church guarding against the abuse of this liberty to the injury of its unity and peace."[18] Implicitly, in the eyes of the UP Church, interpretation of the "six days" did not "enter into the substance of the faith." A person might hold firmly to a belief in the inspiration of Scripture while entertaining emerging scholarly views about the authority, dates and unity of the Biblical books. There is no need to look far for an example of this attitude. We have seen the profound influence upon his students of Henry Calderwood, Oman's Professor of Moral Philosophy in Edinburgh University. His personal piety was beyond question but as we have noted[19] he had no problems in accepting the views of William Robertson Smith about the authorship of the Pentateuch.

We have every reason to suppose that this chimed with Oman's own approach.[20] In March 1900 he contributed to a series of articles commissioned by the United Presbyterian Magazine on the topic "Is Christian faith helped or hindered by the Higher Criticism?" with a "temperately expressed and well phrased contribution, though lacking the decisiveness of the paper on the same subject from the pen of the Reverend A. C. Welch, BD, Helensburgh."[21] Six years later, in *The Problem of Faith and Freedom in the Past Two Centuries*, he makes his position clear: "With this witness of the Church [of the saints] and this evidence of faith, why should we fear any investigation into

16. Woodside, *Soul of a Scottish Church*, 280.
17. Simpson, *Recollections*, 32.
18. Drummond and Bulloch, *Church in late Victorian Scotland*, 37.
19. See chapter 2.
20. Oman, *Vision and Authority*, 71.
21. *Ardrossan and Saltcoats Herald*, Friday, 16 March 1900.

Scripture? Why should anyone fear for a book in which he finds words for his inmost thoughts, songs for his joy, utterances for his hidden griefs, pleadings for his shame and feebleness? Faith and Scripture are reciprocal, the Word feeding Faith and Faith witnessing to the Word. This proves that, for all who seek truth with humble spirits, it is an unquestioned guide, but it does not prove that it is a book to be in all points unquestioned."[22]

This appears generally to have been the attitude of most members of the UP Church,[23] and although in the Free Church a vocal minority of people felt that faith was threatened by the new scholarship, leading Free Churchmen such as Professor A. B. Davidson and Professor James Candlish[24] openly adopted an attitude of "believing criticism."[25] To quote George Adam Smith,[26] "those who, with Professor Robertson Smith instigated the [critical study of the Scriptures in Scotland] were some of the devoutest men in the Church. . . . These men believed that Christ's promise of the Holy Spirit for the education of his Church was being fulfilled not less in the critical than in the experimental use of the Bible; they defended criticism on the highest grounds of faith in God and loyalty to Christ."[27]

The Free Church, however, had not recovered from the bitter controversy that raged between 1867 and 1873 between supporters and opponents of union with the UP Church, and conservative Calvinists were restive following the success of the travelling revivalists D. L. Moody and I. D. Sankey in 1873–74. Further, as Bernhard Maier points out, the identity of the Free Church was shaken by the repeal of the Patronage Act in 1874.[28] The cumulative unrest fueled the passions which were to focus on one of its most brilliant scholars. From its inception in 1843, the Free Church had

22. Oman, *Problem of Faith and Freedom*, 285.

23. In 1890, UP Presbyteries received complaints from students that "little heed was paid to current controversies, especially those which bear on the authorship and authority of the books of the Bible." MacEwen, *Life and Letters*, 756.

24. A. B. Davidson was Smith's professor of Hebrew Language and OT Exegesis at New College. In 1862, he published a Commentary on Job which raised questions as to how divine authorship might be reconciled with the disparate nature of the documents. Candlish is described as "a teacher of undoubted orthodoxy, a most spiritual preacher . . . a man of courage and the most perfect justice." Smith, *Henry Drummond*, 129.

25. Smith, *Answer to the Libel*, 27–63.

26. Smith, *Henry Drummond*, 129.

27. After the union of the two churches in 1900, discussion of historical criticism was considerably more measured than it had been in previous debates. When George Adam Smith was himself brought before the bar of the UF General Assembly in 1902, the case was dismissed, Principal Rainy's motion to that effect being supported by that champion of orthodoxy, Professor James Orr.

28. Maier, *Robertson Smith*, 151.

upheld confessional orthodoxy and the plenary and verbal inspiration of Scripture; but Smith represented a new climate of thought which for many seemed to threaten the church's traditional understanding of Scripture. Higher criticism seemed to strike at the very heart of their faith; it appeared to challenge a cherished heritage of biblical inspiration according to which the Bible was universally recognized as the "supreme rule of faith and life," the *Holy* Bible. Those who felt threatened were not slow to point to the malign influence of "the paper parcels from Germany."[29] The image is striking, but, as Maier indicates, misleading.[30] German culture and scholarship had for some years been percolating through the Scottish churches. It was the custom for divinity students to spent the summer term in German universities.[31] Smith himself had fond memories of his sessions in Bonn and Heidelberg: he appreciated the distinction made between revelation and the Bible[32] in the writings of Heinrich Ewald and Richard Rothe, and was to address Albrecht Ritschl, to his perplexity, as the "*Urvater* (ultimate ancestor) of the Aberdeen heresy."[33] He had little time for those representatives of the conservative wing of the Free Church, such as the Reverend Alexander McCraw of Kilbogie, who wrote to the *Scotsman*, on 1 June 1877, referring to "Germany, the fountain of all poisons, where these vain young men get themselves spoiled, who wish to be wiser than their fathers."[34]

It is worth recalling in this context that Oman was to spend summer months at the Universities of Erlangen (1883) and Heidelberg (1885) and spoke fluent German, which was subsequently to stand him in good stead. For the moment, given the incursion of German philosophy into the philosophical syllabus of the University of Edinburgh and his personal engagement with the thought of Kant in particular, he would have regarded it as axiomatic that this transnational currency of scholarship could give insight into fresh truths.

---

29. Black and Chrystal, *Robertson Smith*, 401, quoting an anonymous pamphlet of 1881. The author is thought to be the Reverend John Kennedy, Dingwall. See Black and Chrystal, *Robertson Smith*, 400n2.

30. Maier, *Robertson Smith*, 86.

31. In the 1840s this followed the interest in German thought stimulated by Sir William Hamilton in Secession students. Early "landlouping students of divinity" included John Ker and John Cairns who "paved the way for the time, not so far distant, when Wellhausen, Ritschl, Herrmann and Harnack would be household words in the manses of the land." Cheyne, *Studies*, 1999, 27.

32. Robertson Smith, *Lectures and Essays*, 123.

33. Letter to Ritschl, 9 February 1877, cited by Rogerson, *Bible and Criticism*, 79. Smith also sustained a long correspondence with Julius Wellhausen.

34. Rogerson, *Bible and Criticism*, 58.

The Call

Oman makes it clear that when he read Smith's speeches and when on one occasion he heard him speak, he experienced an intellectual, emotional and spiritual awakening, which he interpreted as a call to the ordained ministry of the church. The call, as he was subsequently to specify, consisted typically of three stages: first the awareness of his "own peculiar gifts, and, second, by the special service needed of him by his generation," the final stage being the discernment of the requisite spiritual gifts by the congregation. "Only so does it rightly call him and impose this task upon him. And, for himself, he is not a candidate for their suffrage, and is not honoured by it or required to be grateful and submissive for it, but is through them called of God and responsible to Him."[35] For Oman in 1882, the third stage is still some years ahead, but for the moment it appears that Robertson Smith and the circumstances surrounding his removal from his teaching post aroused a strong awareness of the special service that was needed of him by God. About forty-one years later, as newly elected principal of Westminster College, he was to revisit this kairos moment. "I read [Smith's] speeches," he says, "and on one occasion, heard him. I seemed to find the same kind of knowledge as was making the world a place for me of incessant discovery and the same passion for reality as seemed at the moment life's supreme concern."[36]

Smith appealed to his audiences at an intellectual, emotional and spiritual level. In his powerful sincerity, he was intensely charismatic, as is evident from the eye-witness accounts of his speeches given by P. Carnegie Simpson.[37] On hearing him in Glasgow in 1878, Simpson writes: "It was difficult to avoid being carried away by the combined religious unction and dialectic dash of this brilliant pleader who so feared God and so disregarded man—dead or living."[38] The same could be said of the two subsequent Edinburgh Assemblies in 1880, where Smith "set a noble seal upon a great victory"[39] and in May 1881, when for the last time before being deprived of his post, Smith delivered a sustained defense of his position, lasting more than an hour.

While one cannot exclude the possibility that Oman heard Smith speak at one of these assemblies, it is more likely that he was galvanized by one of the popular lectures which Smith delivered to large audiences in

---

35. Oman, "Ministry of the Nonconformist Churches," 128.
36. Oman, "Method in Theology," 82.
37. Simpson, *Principal Rainy*, 306–403.
38. Simpson, *Principal Rainy*, 338.
39. Simpson, *Principal Rainy*, 374.

Edinburgh and Glasgow between 10 January and 1 April, 1881, which were published in monograph form in the beginning of May as *The Old Testament and the Jewish Church*. One thing that Oman would have found attractive about Smith's exposition was an emphasis on the unity of experience. He would have identified "the methods of science, philosophy and historical enquiry"[40] which he himself had been cultivating over his university career: different intellectual disciplines, all ultimately concerned with the same quest for truth. For the rest of his life, Oman was to continue to see all forms of intellectual endeavor as an interrelated part of the same developing world order,[41] summed up axiomatically in the opening words of *The Natural and the Supernatural*: "Seeing that the world is one and our experience of it 'one universe of discourse,' there is no ultimate separateness either in what we study or how we study it."[42]

Furthermore, he perceived this claim for the unity of intellectual enquiry to be ultimately religious: the meaning of life was ultimately revealed in the unity of God. In *Vision and Authority*, he argues: "To fear the intellect is to lack faith, for it is to divide life, to divide the soul, to divide the dominion of God, to divide God himself." Where that is the case, religion "lacks the sense of reality. It ceases to be a victory over the world. It loses virility and becomes sentimental. . . . No true knowledge can be anything but helpful to true religion; and when we think otherwise, either the religion or the knowledge is false. If God is one, all His truth is one."[43]

He elaborates on this in his inaugural address. "We must go as far as we can in understanding the world, because the better we interpret things as they are, the better we may see the higher world to be realized through them. Yet philosophy is only, as it were, the grammar of experience. Religion alone reaches out to what eye hath not seen and ear not heard, as it were to life's poetry and prophecy."[44]

This is the "kind of knowledge" that Oman would have found in Smith. In both men, the "passion for reality" was profoundly theological. Despite Smith's aim in his lectures "to present a continuous argument, resting at every point on valid historical evidence,"[45] he made it clear from the outset that his stance was that of a theologian, and a Calvinist one at that. He made large claims for the working of divine providence and for the inner

---

40. Oman, "Method in Theology," 84.
41. Oman, "The Sphere of Religion."
42. Oman, *Natural and Supernatural*, 2.
43. Oman, *Vision and Authority*, 70–71.
44. Oman, "Method in Theology," 90.
45. Smith, *Old Testament*, vi.

workings of the Holy Spirit.[46] Critical studies were ancillary. Oman would have warmed to Smith's distinctive combination of evangelical faith and scientific scholarship and would have identified in him the passionate religious integrity of a fellow traveler in the search for truth.

Smith's speeches and lectures leave the reader in little doubt that he saw his task as prophetic.[47] He had already maintained in 1872 that "the Old Testament prophets . . . did in Israel precisely the work that ministers of the Gospel must do now,"[48] and in *The Prophets of Israel and Their Place in History*,[49] he writes: "The place of the prophet is in a religious crisis where the ordinary interpretation of acknowledged principles breaks down, where it is necessary to go back, not to received doctrine, but to Jehovah himself."

For Smith, the prophet was the figure for a crisis, not a mere interpreter of the Torah or a predictor of messianic hopes. Prophets were represented as proponents of the laws of universal morality to be perfected by the revelation of God's will brought by Jesus.[50] This is not the place to engage further with Smith's construction but simply to point to the similarity between his image of prophets and the image he projected of himself. For Oman too, an appropriation of the prophetic was integral to his ministerial calling, although over the years he may have come to differ from Smith in details of interpretation. In *Vision and Authority*, which he described as "the outcome of long years of reading and thinking"[51] on the Robertson Smith controversy, he writes of the role and task of the prophet.[52] A significant final chapter of *The Natural and the Supernatural* is devoted to the subject, and in his posthumous publication, *Honest Religion*, he writes succinctly about the significance of a prophetic call to ministry:

> All progress has been by those called and endowed for it; and the significance of Israel for the knowledge of God and of His rule no doubt meant special gifts and experiences of special persons. Yet prophecy is not exalted, ecstatic, individual manifestations, but is an interpretation of experience for all to verify by insight and consecration. Nor is there any finality ever offered except ceaseless loyalty to the inexhaustible Divine purpose. Hence the honest people to whom it still commends itself are those who believe

46. Maier, *Robertson Smith*, 189.
47. Maier, *Robertson Smith*, 163.
48. Smith, *Lectures and Essays*, 231.
49. Smith, *Prophets of Israel*, 82.
50. Carroll, "Biblical Prophets as Apologists."
51. Oman, *Vision and Authority*, 2nd ed., 9.
52. Oman, *Vision and Authority*, 73–78.

wholly in the eternal expansion of truth, seek with perfect heart the beauty of holiness, hunger and thirst after righteousness and humbly and faithfully follow the highest God has given them to know. Religion speaks of faith, not courage, but faith is just inspired courage to follow the beckoning of the highest.[53]

In that "inspired courage to follow the beckoning of the highest" we begin to see the glimmering of Oman's call to ministry, a call which was given content by service to the church. What that service might involve was brought home to Oman by the controversy aroused in the Free Church by Robertson Smith. To his mind, the reactions of "religious people" highlighted the fallibility of the Church, a trend towards complacency and disregard of truth.

He states in his inaugural address that he was disturbed to hear "people declare that, even if all [Smith] said were true, regard for useful tradition and the ecclesiastical amenities should have kept him from saying it."[54] To his mind, the very idea that "religious people are more concerned about what is correct than about what is true" was "the greatest of all hindrances to religious appeal."[55] Not only was this inimical to the mission of the church, but, as he perceived it, playing for safety was the antithesis of venturing with God into the unknown.

This was typified by a lawyer whom he knew to be "a really good man as well as a most devout elder of the Free Church."[56] Oman was shocked—the term is his—to hear this person say: "Granting . . . that Robertson Smith is right, if it is truth, it is dangerous truth, and he has no right, as a professor of the Church, to upset the Church by declaring it." Oman continues:

> I hope I have not since weakened in my loyalty to truth, but in those days I thought intellectual truth the one worthy pursuit in life; and this suggested that the Church was not interested in it. Had I been then intending the ministry, probably I should have been put off it, but this affected me somewhat as a call to my life's work. . . . I was left no option between facing the search for a truth, which would shine in its own light in face of all inquiry, and complete skepticism.[57]

---

53. Oman, *Honest Religion*, 71.
54. Oman, "Method in Theology," 83.
55. Oman, "Method in Theology," 83.
56. Oman, *Vision and Authority*, 2nd ed., 9.
57. Oman, *Vision and Authority*, 2nd ed., 12–13.

The paradoxical nature of this decision was recognized by T. W. Manson, Oman's distinguished former student and erstwhile junior colleague, who wrote in his introduction to the eighth edition of *Vision and Authority* that "numbers of men, and among them some of the ablest, found it impossible to reconcile the theology that was offered to them with the philosophic and scientific and historical learning they already possessed; and so they abandoned the theological course."[58] Oman, however, was one of those who "felt the difficulty acutely, but determined to grapple with it in the faith that, however painful and costly the struggle might be, the ultimate gain would far outweigh the loss."[59]

His determination was fueled by the attitude of church leaders in the Robertson Smith case. He was outraged by

> the manifest ignorance of the judges which entitles them to no opinion at all on the matter under decision; but the far more serious cause is that they do not even appear to desire to know. In my own case my trouble was not in the least that the judges were not critics and philosophers, even though all my interest at the time was in history and thought, but that, as I then understood the business, they were so far from being seekers after truth, that, as we said, they would not have recognized it if they had met it in their porridge. . . . The impression may have been all wrong, but my point is that ecclesiastical persons, in particular, should give diligent and constant care not to suffer it, by any mistake, to be made of young and inquiring minds, because it will probably, as in my case, never be obliterated as long as life lasts.[60]

Making due allowance for the possibility of a young man's bias, he observes elegantly that in his opinion the ecclesiastical leaders were "more exercised about unanimity than veracity," commenting to his hearers in 1923 that "this may be a prejudice, but it is a prejudice which there has been too little care to avoid creating. I confess to sharing it a little and my excuse is that it was stamped on my mind at the most impressionable time of my life." He continues: "My impression from it all may, very likely, have been hasty, crude, ill-informed, but that does not make it less typical, because the need is just to take heed not to offend one of the little ones whose chief knowledge

---

58. Oman, *Vision and Authority*, 8th ed., 1–2.
59. Oman, *Vision and Authority*, 8th ed., 2.
60. "Method in Theology," 83–84.

about theology consists in thinking that no obligation is so sacred as to seek truth with all our hearts and to manifest it with all our powers."[61]

Oman's first book, *Vision and Authority*, was an "inquiry into the foundations on which all Churches rest,"[62] an "honest record"[63] of that search for truth. As is suggested by the title and the subtitle, *The Throne of St. Peter*, the realization that truth might be obscured by an exercise of external authority was for Oman a major aspect of the Robertson Smith affair.

He comments incisively: "of all undivine ways of opposing inquiry, none is worse than to resist it by a narrow and mechanical conception of the Church and by an unspiritual appeal to its visible authority."[64] Instead, truth is to be pursued in "the forbearance and the patience of love. This does not set assertion against assertion but meets inquiry by inquiry. Instead of denouncing inquiry as the sin of rebellion, it urges more patience, more humility, and more charity . . . by no other way can there be entrance into life's deepest meaning."[65]

In order to appreciate the significance of this, it is worth rehearsing briefly the decision of the 1881 Free Church General Assembly. In the long-term interests of the Free Church, Principal Robert Rainy wanted to avoid an outright condemnation of biblical criticism.[66] But he was equally determined to avoid what he perceived to be a real risk of schism[67] and felt that the only way of doing so was to deprive Smith of his chair. Attitudes were polarized by the stances taken by Smith and Rainy. In personality, they jarred. Rainy saw Smith as "an impossibility"[68] in that he was "utterly unable to realize that very many Christian men could not help preferring tradition to truth, and found it difficult to do anything with a prophet but stone

---

61. Oman, "Method in Theology," 83.

62. Oman, *Vision and Authority*, vii.

63. Oman, *Vision and Authority*, 2nd ed., 10.

64. Oman, *Vision and Authority*, 247. He returns to this theme throughout his work. See, e.g., Oman, *Vision and Authority*, 1902, 92–97; Oman, *Problem of Faith and Freedom*, 1906, 417–18; Oman, *Church and Divine Order*, 1911, 307–33; Oman, "Why I Am Not a Catholic," 1931, 230–56.

65. Oman, *Vision and Authority*, 247.

66. In 1874, Rainy treated questions of Biblical Criticism in his Cunningham lectures "with the care of a bomb disposal unit" (Drummond and Bulloch, *Church in Late Victorian Scotland*, 7) and in 1878, he gave a course of lectures at the London college of the PCE on "The Bible and Criticism," in which he mounted a guarded defense of biblical criticism (Drummond and Bulloch, *Church in Late Victorian Scotland*, 66).

67. He may have been over-anxious. See Drummond and Bulloch, *Church in Late Victorian Scotland*, 78.

68. Simpson, *Principal Rainy*, 1:360.

him."[69] As his biographers indicate, Smith was uncompromising and displayed a "remarkable blend of self-confidence, obstinacy, sense of mission and pugnacity which friend and foe alike found difficult to handle."[70] Rainy, on the other hand, was the Church statesman, he "evaded a plain answer. He condemned Smith not for lack of truth but for lack of tact."[71] This condemnation was achieved at the General Assembly of 1881, by 423 votes to 245, following Rainy's compromise with hardline factions, and the arguably illegitimate invention of the Assembly's "reserve power." This was felt by many to be "an unconstitutional act of 'mob-law,'"[72] described by Smith as "an act of violence and without a legal decision being obtained from the General Assembly of the Church on questions which certainly cannot be permanently disposed of until they have been exhaustively considered in their relation to the doctrine of the Protestant Churches on the one hand, and to the laws of scientific inquiry and the evidence of historical fact upon the other."[73] In Smith's eyes this was justified by the argument "by which despotism has always been supported . . . that the State must always have the power to prevent the State from suffering ill."[74] So, in 1881, the Free Church General Assembly upheld freedom of scholarship in its refusal to condemn historical criticism but it also abused its own powers by throwing Smith to the wolves. Rainy's biographer concludes soberly that Smith was "not only the protagonist but also the martyr of criticism in an orthodox and evangelical Church."[75]

Although, as Oman suggests with hindsight, he was at the time young and passionate and with strong views that may have been crude and uninformed, it was this complex and tragic affair that led him to articulate a calling "to help men to true beliefs, high aspirations and right loyalties."[76] He could scarcely have envisaged how this would take shape but calling the saints to pursue truth was to be the bed-rock of his future ministry. With hindsight, Oman had this to say:

---

69. "Robertson Smith. Aberdeen Centenary Celebrations, Professor Raven's Oration," *Scotsman*, 9 November 1946.

70. Maier, *Robertson Smith*, 159.

71. Drummond and Bulloch, *Church in Late Victorian Scotland*, 77.

72. Simpson, *Principal Rainy*, 1:397; Drummond and Bulloch, *Church in Late Victorian Scotland*, 78; Black and Chrystal, *Robertson Smith*, 429.

73. Smith, *Prophets of Israel*, v–vi.

74. Smith, *Prophets of Israel*, 435.

75. Simpson, *Principal Rainy*, 1:402.

76. Oman, "Ministry of the Nonconformist Churches," 130.

> Like all human institutions, [Nonconformity] too has its defects, yet there is nothing else in our midst which serves man's highest needs quite as faithfully, and it well deserves that a man give his best thought and fullest consecration to be a teacher and a leader in the midst of it; and if he has a message and an inspiration, nothing else will give him the same backing. If with open mind and courage he seek truth and stand for righteousness, he will not in this service need other motive, or feel he lacks regard, or grow weary in well-doing.[77]

The United Presbyterian Church Divinity Hall

And so in 1882, at the age of twenty-two, Oman enrolled as a student of the UP Hall. For the next three years, he took a full share[78] in its life and work and in two respects this was to prove particularly influential. On the one hand, he was exposed to the personal influence of Dr. John Cairns and Dr. John Ker, and "the struggle to make truth more pure and more living"[79] was honed by "practical work" amongst the inhabitants of an industrial area between the Union Canal and the Caledonian Railway. Again, his theological horizons were expanded, his linguistic skills extended and his cultural experience enriched by the sessions he spent as a student in Erlangen in 1883 and Heidelberg in 1885, with a further three months in Neuchâtel to improve his French.

In order to understand more fully the context in which Oman now found himself, it is worth rehearsing at this point something of the recent history of the Hall. In 1878, following a Synod decision two years before, the Hall had moved from its premises at 5 Queen Street to a newly acquired building in Castle Terrace, large enough to accommodate the Synod and Theological Hall. The decision had been taken "with extraordinary unanimity on the part of the Church, although the restructuring of the course to accommodate six professors who were released from pastoral charge meant an additional cost of several thousands a year,"[80] a considerable financial

---

77. Oman, "Ministry of the Nonconformist Churches," 130. Cf Oman, *Concerning the Ministry*, 14.

78. As stated by Mr. Kirkwood, at the ordination soirée in Alnwick. *Alnwick and County Gazette*, Saturday, 21 December 1889.

79. MacEwen, *Life and Letters*, 746.

80. Woodside, *Soul of a Scottish Church*, 135. The building cost £50,000, and each professor was to receive £700 annually. The church raised a large capital sum and used the interest to help towards payment of the extra costs, the remainder coming from free-will offerings of the congregations.

outlay for a voluntarist church, especially one that was weakened in 1876 by the leaching of its 110 congregations in England who united with the English Presbyterian church to form the Presbyterian Church of England (PCE).[81] Coming hard on the heels of failed union negotiations with the Free Church in 1873, it was a bold commitment to the future. John Cairns comments in his biography of Principal Cairns that:

> During the ten years' negotiations for Union a considerable number of pressing reforms in the United Presbyterian Church were held back for fear of hampering the negotiations, and because it was felt that such matters might well be postponed to be dealt with in a United Church. But, when the negotiations were broken off, the United Presbyterians, having recovered their liberty of action, at once began to set their house in order. One of the first matters thus to be taken up was the question of Theological Education.[82]

In this, the decision to move premises was significant. Number 5, as it was known, was in the heart of Edinburgh's New Town, adjacent to the recently opened Philosophical Institution. The handsome eighteenth-century house had been purchased by the United Secession Church in anticipation of the union with the Relief Church (above, 19) and extended in 1847 by the addition of a sumptuous Hall[83] designed by Dick Peddie. It was a self-confident assertion by the newly formed UP church that its theological training was on a par with the intellectual and cultural ethos of the Athens of the North.

In moving to its new premises in Castle Terrace, however, the UP was making a statement that it was also moving with the times. The grand building at the foot of the Castle Mound, a splendid example of Victorian High Gothic, had been constructed as a theatre the year before to a design by Frederick Thomas Pilkington. But it had been a financial loss, and was sold to the UP church for a third of its building cost. The new Hall was situated not far from the university, and within walking distance from New College. But, significantly, it was not far either from the industrial heart of nineteenth-century Edinburgh. A stone's throw away, on Lothian Road, there was a goods yard, where freight trains were marshalled, keeping those

---

81. Cairns, *Principal Cairns*, 98.

82. Cairns, *Principal Cairns*, 119.

83. Now a BBC studio, the building's "principal glory is Dick Peddie's Synod Hall cube within Greek cross and stairs in each corner, proscenium arch, anthemion frieze, panelled coved ceiling supporting two tiered lantern and galleries to side and rear" (https://portal.historicenvironment.scot/designation/LB29532).

who lived nearby awake at night and belching out smoke on the environs. Nearby too was the Port Hopetoun basin, the terminus of the Union Canal which transported minerals from the mines and quarries of Lanarkshire to Edinburgh. In the other direction, there was the Grassmarket, whose turnpike stairways and crow-stepped gables concealed a level of poverty and deprivation that was described by the anonymous author of *Slum Life in Edinburgh* as "a scandal to civilisation, not to mention our much vaunted Modern Athens."[84]

The move to Castle Terrace conveyed the message that the intellectual standards of the Hall were to be maintained while students were to be prepared to face the challenges of ministry in a rapidly changing industrial society.

In keeping with these aims there was a radical re-modelling of teaching.

The six-week sessions (per year!) of the Old Hall were replaced by a five-monthly session lasting from November to April which brought its successor more into line with the Universities and Free Church colleges. Other factors may have been operative. Synod might have been concerned about allegations that, despite the quality of their instruction, "the students came to regard the six or seven weeks in the capital of Scotland as more or less of a holiday."[85] Woodside adds: "They spent much of their time on the roof of the Old Queen Street Hall, enjoying the sunshine of a warm Autumn day and sharpening their wits upon one another." And there may also have been those who shared the view of Peter Landreth that "the inadequacy of all the teaching and training that were likely to be received by a student from his attendance at the Divinity Hall for a succession of short sessions was glaringly evident. The Hall left him alone, and had nothing whatever to do with him, for more than ten consecutive months in each year; and though the instructions, which the Hall period of less than two months poured into and over his intellect . . . provided intellectual as well as theological culture, yet the ten months of entire and continuous Hall inaction must have tended to reduce him to mental sterility."[86] By 1892, however, the Synod came to the sober opinion that the church "had been fully as well served by the old system as by the new."[87]

In his enthusiasm for the new system, Landreth fails to give credit here to the thorough course of reading and instruction that had been carried out by the Presbyteries throughout previous years. Woodside elaborates:

84. T.B.M., *Slum Life in Edinburgh*; first printed as articles in the *Weekly Scotsman*.
85. Woodside, *Soul of a Scottish Church*, 135.
86. Landreth, *UP Divinity Hall*, 296.
87. Woodside, *Soul of a Scottish Church*, 139.

Not a few of the ministers appointed by Presbyteries to examine the students were thorough martinets and determined that the youth of the Church should be thoroughly equipped. They prescribed large portions of Greek and Hebrew, considerable portions of books on theology and Church History, and at the same time, required written sermons, lectures, and exercises. It was a rule that the students had to deliver one or more of these without notes before the Presbytery, and to many sensitive students this ordeal was worse than the terrors of death.[88]

Although many Presbyteries abandoned this régime in 1876, it appears that the Presbytery of Orkney was not among them. Between 1882 and 1885, it gave Oman "intersessional exercises," and in 1885, he had to give satisfaction in the following "exercises for trial: Personal Religion; Theology—Regeneration; Lecture—Romans 12:1-2; Homily—John 8:31-32; Popular Sermon—1 Timothy 1:15; Exegesis and address—1 Corinthians 2:9-11; Thesis: Is God knowable?"[89] It would appear that Oman acquitted himself satisfactorily, for in 1886, he was transferred to Edinburgh Presbytery "with a note of his trials for licence."[90]

The remodeling of the Hall in 1878 brought a further significant change. Whereas up to then, the professors, all serving ministers, had combined their lecture programs with their pastorates, the introduction of the long winter session made this impossible and they were disjoined from pastoral charge in order to focus on the work of the Hall. There were new appointments: David Duff, who taught Church History, Robert Johnstone, New Testament and Exegesis, and James Paterson, Hebrew and Old Testament literature, but Oman does not record his indebtedness or lack of it to their teaching.[91] It is quite another matter, however, with the remaining two: Dr. John Cairns (1818-92), who taught Systematic Theology and Apologetics, and Dr. John Ker (1819-86), who was appointed in 1876 to the new chair of Pastoral Theology. While we have little evidence of the content of Cairns's lectures, we may note in passing, in the light of Oman's subsequent engagement with Schleiermacher, the enthusiasm for

---

88. Woodside, *Soul of a Scottish Church*, 137. James Brown gives a graphic description of the harsh treatment of a student by the Presbytery of Edinburgh in *Life of a Scottish Probationer*, 77.

89. There is no reference here to the Old Testament, possibly reflecting a personal bias on the part of his assessors.

90. Synodical Minutes of Orkney, United Associate Presbytery, UP, OCR 1/5, 106, 11, 68, quoted in McKimmon, *John Oman*.

91. Although he acquitted himself sufficiently well in these subjects to be awarded the Edinburgh BD in 1886.

the German theologian—philosopher shown by both Professors. John Ker wrote admiringly of Schleiermacher's "Ciceronian eloquence";[92] and John Cairns records of his uncle that "through life he had a deep reverence for Neander, whom he regarded, with perhaps premature enthusiasm, as the man who shared with Schleiermacher the honour of restoring Germany to a believing theology."[93] The personal influence of Ker and Cairns was profound and the "practical work" which they facilitated was greatly influential. From them, Oman learned that "matters of conducting services, pastoral duties etc. are no doubt important, but they must be learned from experience in the world."[94]

What this involved will now be charted in some detail.

Preaching: John Ker

Ker was regarded as one of the most distinguished preachers of his generation and his influence on Oman is not hard to trace. When on 1 November 1906 Oman dedicated a new organ chamber in Clayport Church Alnwick in Ker's memory, the memorial tablet read: "Varied learning, poetic fancy, human sympathies, spiritual insight, made a great preacher and teacher."[95]

His sermons marked "the type of United Presbyterian preaching at its best. . . . Nothing is thought to be alien to the pulpit that affects man's life and character."[96] It was a kind of extraordinarily elevated conversation."[97] He would write out his sermons in detail, memorize them and then deliver them without a note, so that they seemed to come from the heart. In the pulpit as in the lecture theatre, he held his audience spellbound. His sermons, it was said, read[98] almost as well as they delivered. Woodside testifies that

> while there is a certain evangelistic appeal in them, it is by no means prominent. It is there in the spirit rather than in the letter. Still, these sermons leave you in no doubt as to where the

---

92. Ker, *History of Preaching*, 302.

93. Cairns, *Principal Cairns*, 56. Neander was a pupil of Schleiermacher, whose thinking he followed. At the age of 25, Cairns had attended in Berlin Neander's lectures on *Dogmatik* and *Sittenlehre*.

94. Oman, *Systematic Theology*, introduction, 2.

95. *Presbyterian Messenger*, December 1906. John Ker was one of Oman's predecessors at Clayport.

96. Woodside, *Soul of a Scottish Church*, 161.

97. Woodside, *Soul of a Scottish Church*, 161.

98. He published two volumes of sermons, the first went into 14 editions and was, according to Woodside, "decidedly the better." *Soul of a Scottish Church*, 162.

preacher stands. There is constantly set before the hearer by implication, if not directly, the great choice of Life and Death, of Blessing and Cursing. He too, like Ebenezer Erskine, appealed to his hearers to choose well, for their choice was brief and yet endless. Yet there are no hysterics.

The feeling was always well under control: "It merely brought into relief what had been practised in the United Presbyterian Church from the first."[99] The UP church placed great emphasis on keeping alive the Secession tradition of evangelical preaching. Woodside relates that

> all the preachers, of course, were not Ralph Erskines, and there were periods when conflicts as to Predestination and Freewill, the Limited or Universal nature of the Atonement, and such like, took a great deal of real vitality out of preaching. But the United Presbyterian ministry, as a whole, recognized that they were there to lead men to the deeper decisions of life, and to set before them the great facts of eternal life, judgment and the world to come.[100]

For many years "read" sermons were frowned upon. "Even when the students were preaching before a handful of members of Presbytery they were required by the law of the Church to deliver their discourse. The aim was that the preachers of the church should prove themselves to be in possession of a message, and able, through God's help, to bring men from darkness to light."[101] This required care in preparation and delivery. Some, like Ker, "mandated," committed their sermons to memory prior to delivery, an effort which may in his case have contributed towards his regular nervous breakdowns. Others spoke from brief notes which, from Oman's experience, enabled more direct communication with their hearers. "Speaking from a manuscript, whether read or remembered, is like following the turnpike; speaking from few notes or none is like keeping your eye on the goal and taking the hedges and ditches as they come and as best you can. They are not merely different practices, but involve different attitudes of mind."[102]

For Oman, preaching was always one of the most significant aspects of ministry, and he was to devote a large part of his energy to developing the qualities and skills he considered desirable in a preacher. In his informal,

---

99. Woodside, *Soul of a Scottish* Church, 163.
100. Woodside, *Soul of a Scottish* Church, 150.
101. Woodside, *Soul of a Scottish* Church, 150.
102. Oman, *Concerning the Ministry*, 189.

often humorous *causeries* in the Westminster Lodge he instances his own early experiences as a painfully self-conscious tyro:

> Public speaking is neither my foible nor my forte.... I may be pardoned for thinking that my native defects were increased by the painful consciousness of my voice forced upon me when beginning. As I was obviously in need of help, the advice of my friends was frequent and free; and I learned too late that it was uniformly mistaken. I was told to speak up when I should have been told to speak more quietly and let weight and force out of my lungs, instead of applying twice the force necessary, to the ruining of my vocal chords [*sic*]. I was told to keep my lungs full when my fault was in keeping them bang full all the time and not emptying them, with the result of making breathing self-conscious and spasmodic. I was urged to be livelier, whereas I ought to have been told to be more deliberate. But the worst was that it gave me the distressing sense that preaching was a business of impressive exhibition, not a self-forgetting task of persuasion.[103]

In reacting against "impressive exhibition" Oman embodied a tension between two strands within the UP church. For the descendants of the Secession, "the gospel was to be set forth in all its native majesty . . . any attempt to make it palatable to man's heart by fine writing or by 'purple passages' could only thwart the main purpose of preaching,"[104] a style which, Woodside observes, attracted churchgoers rather than "the indifferent." Preachers in the Relief tradition, on the other hand, "never despised ornament or finish."

Oman's disdain for what T. W. Manson described as "all *ad captandum* arts" had profound theological resonance. His dislike of coercion disinclined him to overpower his hearers with rhetoric. In his rigorous search for truth that could be lived he was utterly committed to "honest religion," and he was, as Manson knew, "completely in earnest in the search."[105] A minister had to work continually at improving his preaching, for this was "the special manifestation of the truth to which he was especially called."[106]

A brief examination of Oman's own sermons illustrates the process. There are the published sermons, those which he himself carefully prepared for publication for a wider audience in 1921,[107] and those which were pub-

---

103. Oman, *Concerning the Ministry*, 110.
104. Woodside, *Soul of a Scottish Church*, 151.
105. In Oman, *Vision and Authority*, 8th ed., 1.
106. Oman, *Concerning the Ministry*, 57.
107. Oman, *Paradox*.

lished after his death, "carefully selected and altered" by Dr. R. H. Strachan and Dr. H. H. Farmer.[108] At their best, they reveal Oman's exegetical ability, his hermeneutical skill and an imaginative grasp of everyday illustration. They are "pithy and graphic."[109] In the best tradition of the UP church, he challenges his hearers, often unflinchingly, to an authentic religious life. And then there are the manuscripts. Tightly packed in Stone's "universal" portfolios, pages held together with a pin, some written in ink, some in typescript, usually on pages from a ruled exercise book. These date from 1888 when Oman was still an assistant at St James's church, Paisley, till 1905, towards the end of his time in Alnwick, and they achieve something the published sermons cannot. They give an impression of the preacher at work, with the hearer in view as much as the reader, and as they do, they reveal Oman's steady application to improving his preaching. The earliest sermons are systematically presented and solemnly labored. But as he becomes more confident, his style becomes more "conversational," he includes vivid imaginative illustrations and analogies from everyday life. His language is simple and accessible. Stressed words and phrases are underlined in red pencil and there are frequent alterations in ink where he revised a sermon, possibly for subsequent use in another place. While most of these are written out in full, some of the last sermons are set out in note form as aide-mémoires. Then even these cease. This fluency was hard won. Referring to his early attempts to preach, he writes:

> You cannot have less natural gift for free speech than I had, nor possibly receive less encouragement to try. One friend said, "It is no use. Your written word seldom lacks character, your spoken word has none." Another said, "What on earth took you today? I heard your voice certainly, but not one word that was yours." I saw that if I continued to write every word I had to utter, the writing would soon be as much without character as the speaking. Wherefore, though it tried the long-suffering of the audience and distressed myself, I persisted.[110]

He encourages his hearers.

> If you write with any degree of care, you may find yourself helpless without your manuscript, but if you have clearly before you where you hope to arrive, and use notes only to indicate the turnings and perhaps the concrete word you want when you are in danger of diverging into abstractions, you will get

108. Oman, *Honest Religion*.
109. Hood, "God's All-Conquering Love," 150.
110. Oman, *Concerning the Ministry*, 190.

along without stumbling, and the fewer notes, even to none, the smoother the passage.[111]

From personal experience, he knew the value of "the incalculable effect that may come from hearing, and therefore from preaching which truly makes men hear."[112]

A rare insight into Oman's preaching style in 1907 is provided in a detailed and observant account of a sermon preached in the Grosvenor Road Presbyterian Church, Highbury. "H.M." writes:

> It is not often that the London Presbyterians have an opportunity of hearing this Northumbrian preacher. He is seldom tempted from the Border town where he has seen "visions" and speaks with "authority." Probably outside Presbyterianism and a select company of theological students his name will be comparatively unknown. Yet he is one of the great educative forces of the denomination. . . . Professor Oman[113] is in the prime of life with the air and cast of a student. So far as I could see he used no manuscript, but spoke out of the fulness of a well-stored mind. His style is conversational . . . he made no attempt at oratorical display but rather held himself in check. One wished at times that he would let himself go and forget the professor in the preacher. His voice is metallic and carrying. Though he spoke with the utmost ease he was heard in every part of the large church. He indulged in few gestures, and these were appropriate and suggestive.[114]

There is nothing here to confirm the legend that Oman was a poor preacher, and as Adam Hood demonstrates[115] this may in part have been an over-interpretation of Oman's self-deprecating remarks to his students.[116] But legends die hard, and William Wright, a member for the final eighteen months of Oman's ministry at Clayport Church, Alnwick, was stung in 1962 to hear a rumor circulating among students that Oman had been a failure as a minister:

> I earnestly trust to dispel that impression, and at the same time repay the great debt I owe to him for his help and guidance in the early days of my Christian life. Let me say at once that

---

111. Oman, *Concerning the Ministry*, 191.

112. Oman, *Concerning the Ministry*, 159.

113. He had the previous month been appointed to the Chair of Systematic Theology at Westminster College, Cambridge.

114. *London Daily News*, Monday, 3 June 1907.

115. Hood, "God's All-Conquering Love," 143–46.

116. For example: Healey, *Religion and Reality*, 10; Bevans, *John Oman*, 12.

throughout my long life I have been fortunate to sit under many able and gifted men, but none made such a deep and lasting impression on my mind and heart as he.[117]

Wright's description of Oman's preaching style in 1902 reinforces H.M.'s account.

> He did not possess the popular gifts of eloquence and gesture; but his voice, which in later years was heard imperfectly, at that time was heard with ease, and his simple gestures, used merely to emphasize, had no hint of display. My most vivid memories of him are in his pulpit and Bible-class work. He had a high concept of the value of public worship. . . . Even now, across those sixty years, I can recall his quiet tense voice reading, say, the letters of St Paul, so impressive and so moving that it seemed as though the apostle himself was speaking. . . . Those who knew him through his writings only, wonder how he succeeded in getting his thoughts across to an average congregation. Admittedly his books are difficult, but that could not be said of his sermons. . . . I have in my possession two volumes of his sermons, and these provide a very fair sample of his customary preaching, and they are as applicable today as when they were written.[118]

Personal Influence: John Cairns

Cairns's personality was an undeniable influence on Oman during his years in the UP Hall. In an affectionate tribute following Cairns's death in 1892, Oman gives a vivid evocation of the impact his former principal made upon himself and his fellow students.[119] "Whatever the cause may be," he writes, "the fact remains that a great man has departed, for myself I would say the greatest man I have ever met." Oman elaborates. Cairns's great learning went hand in hand with great humility. Students were overawed by his ability to "learn a new modern language just as a recreation." In Holland he addressed conference delegates in Dutch, at the Evangelical Alliance Conference in Copenhagen he made a speech in Danish. In ancient languages his prowess was formidable.[120] He had "an easy familiarity" with Greek literature both

---

117. Cited in Healey, *Religion and Reality*, 150.
118. Healey, *Religion and Reality*, 151.
119. "Dr Cairns by one of his old students." MS, Westminster College archives, n.d. The hand and style are unmistakably Oman's.
120. He made himself familiar with Assyrian grammar, and decided during a meeting of Synod to learn Arabic, so that he could read the Qur'an and pray for Muslims in their own language.

sacred and secular. "I have never made a special study of oriental languages, gentlemen," he would say, "Hebrew in my day was very imperfectly taught." Then he would shut his eyes and quote from his Hebrew Bible by the page. "And he was not mocking us," Oman assures his reader, "he was genuinely apologizing for his inferior knowledge." Alluding to the encyclopedic nature of Cairns's erudition, Oman continues:

> But some utilitarian will be asking what was the use of all this learning. If occasionally it rather hampered him rather than forwarded him in his lecturing, if out of it all he only produced one book of any consequence, might he not have been as well without it. Perhaps they will not be satisfied if we say that such large contact with life produced one truly humble man at least and helped year by year to give a little of that same Christian space of humility to thirty or forty students very well satisfied with themselves not to speak of casual influence upon others.

His idiosyncrasies contributed to the affectionate regard in which he was held. His laugh was "like a mountain enjoying an earthquake"; he enjoyed skimming stones on the water at the sea-shore; "every morning he came down for his class like a boy late for school"; "a waving motion of his right hand was necessary to him in speaking whether in the class-room or at the tea-table"; while he would "lose himself" in music, his singing was "a most disconsolate performance." His devotion to duty was absolute, making his classroom preparation almost too conscientious. Oman indicates that "there was some truth in the saying that 'if Cairns had to write an article on how to blow the nose he would have to read all the fathers through in the original to see what they had to say on the subject.'"

But if his regular lectures were "not quite from the stand-point of most of [his students], their real influence showed itself in the great reverence that grew day by day for a great and wise and unconscious soul and in the humility that did spring up in contemplating it in one's all too shallow heart."

At a prayer meeting for departing missionaries, Oman records that "when Dr Cairns rose we felt a higher spirit among us. There was felicity of expression, strong feeling and sympathy, all that we look for in one who leads prayer but there was something else, something of a man whose ordinary life is in the infinite not the finite. And therein in one word was his true greatness. He ever felt the infinite around him and lay perpetually like a child upon its bosom."[121]

121. See also the testimonies of the Reverend John Smith and Thomas Kirkup (MacEwen, *Life and Letters*, 558–60 and 560–62); Woodside, *Soul of a Scottish Church*, 163: "We lived in an old-world community crammed with mediocrities, and the

There is more here than personal appreciation; there is an awareness that in his herculean pursuit of learning Cairns was striving towards that ultimate divine truth which in his personal piety he glimpsed and which he quite unselfconsciously reflected to those around. Oman describes him simply as a "truly great and good man whose mere presence in the world was a benediction."

Evangelism

We may detect in Oman's affectionate regard for his principal an esteem for his sincerity, which Oman saw as fundamental to the quest for truth. That sincerity found expression in Cairns' evangelistic activity. His successor as minister in Berwick, the Reverend John Smith, observed of his friend that

> he was chiefly filled with the joy of bringing men to personal decision for Christ. His humility in taking the lowest place at evangelistic gatherings, his deference to those who were greatly his inferiors, because of their one talent of earnest evangelistic preaching, his holy urgency of pleading with men for God, and his beautiful insensibility to what others might think, intensified the charm of his character.[122]

Cairns' example would have given Oman a first-hand opportunity to reflect upon contemporary evangelistic practice, in the wake of one of the most distinctive features of nineteenth-century religious life, the revival inspired by Moody and Sankey, with its special emphasis upon personal salvation.[123] Cairns had attended the great revival meeting in Newcastle in 1873, and while initially he was uncomfortable with Moody's unconventional approach, he was before long impressed by the simple, dynamic message of grace and the whole-hearted emotional appeal.[124] He saw that there was a quickening of church life across denominational boundaries, bringing permanent change to many people's lives who were on the fringes of the church.[125] Moody's preaching was homely and vivid. He knew his Bible and he had a clear perception of human nature. He brought the sense of God's love and grace to all, without any need to qualify that with a Calvinistic

---

colossal personality gripped our imagination and hearts. His commanding intellect controlled our thoughts, and his quenchless imperial faith and pure exalted character dominated our lives."

122. MacEwen, *Life and Letters*, 602.
123. Bebbington, *Evangelicalism in Modern Britain*.
124. MacEwen, *Life and Letters*, 575.
125. Drummond and Bulloch, *Church in Late Victorian Scotland*, 15.

doctrine of election, and he called for decision. And when Cairns saw that the revivals were responding to a widely felt spiritual need, he spoke, along with Henry Calderwood and other "respected leaders of religion," "from the evangelists' platforms, helped in the enquiry rooms and instructed the young converts.... On all sides the fire spread."[126]

An ability to relate easily to people of different stations in life helped. Cairns' biographer records that "one good lady, who made it her business to read to the poorer class of tailors in their workshops, tells how she asked him to address a small gathering, and how willingly he went, in the busiest time of the session, to speak to twenty coatless, shoeless men just risen from 'the boards.' She and they were deeply touched by the friendly warmth of the address which he gave."[127]

For Oman, to observe Cairns in action was a memorable experience. He recalls one occasion during the great International Exhibition of Industry, Science and Art in Edinburgh when between 6 May and 30 October 1886, halls and galleries specially constructed for the occasion were filled with the wonders of the Victorian age, and Cairns kept 4,000 to 5,000 visitors listening with rapt attention to a lengthy historical vindication of the doctrine of justification by faith. His style of delivery was idiosyncratic, his message, utterly sincere. Oman writes:

> When he rose his face had the look of a simple rather embarrassed countryman. He hung his shoulders in a kind of apology for being there at all. At first his sentences had a somewhat Germanic structure.... Gradually his hand began to move slowly to and fro at first then with a strange backward jerk. As it finally settled into a regular rhythmic motion like a sower casting seed, his sentences compacted themselves into a fine stateliness and point and his figure was standing out clear in his firm strength of muscle with his head thrown back. Unhesitatingly he found his way through fact and argument and appeal till at the end when he closed with a motion like one drawing water from an eastern well the audience had forgotten all about his motions and himself and everything but the subject he had been speaking of.

---

126. Smith, *Henry Drummond*, 56.
127. MacEwen, *Life and Letters*, 712.

Practical Work

An appreciation of evangelism was accompanied by a recognition of the value of Home Mission work for future ministers and missionaries. Cairns and Ker actively encouraged students to engage in this during the session, in an awareness "of the hardening and secularising influence of the systematic study of the doctrines and literature of religion, and he regarded actual participation in Christian work, even amidst lectures and examinations, as the best counteractive."[128]

They organized a system of placements for the students during the summer months, when those who were not spending the semester at a continental university would gain practical experience as missionaries or assistants to ministers in different parts of the country.[129]

We may note in passing that Oman appeared to have spent "several months" with a friend either in 1881 or 1882, from early summer, before the tourist season got under way, in a Northumberland fishing village, "five miles away [from] an old castle on a headland."[130] The only evidence of this is a lively paper delivered some years later to an Edinburgh audience of Scots Presbyterians with Liberal sympathies, where with an ironic sense of humor, he gives free rein to his sense of the ridiculous and lampoons the Northumberland vicar.[131] In Oman's view, this man is clearly inferior to the "missionary in the Presbyterian church," who is "a scholar and a gentleman." The episode may be dated with reasonable accuracy from the musings of local Tories that "Lord Beaconsfield had been a very great man," and that, "as the Liberals had just got into power, the country was fast going to the dogs."[132] And it would have enabled Oman to acquire some practical experience of mission work prior to his entrance to the UP Hall.

Both professors gave active encouragement to the UP Divinity Hall Missionary Society, which, according to Woodside,[133] "carried on Home

---

128. MacEwen, *Life and Letters*, 643.

129. At the same time, the two colleagues undertook semi-episcopal tours to visit remote congregations in difficulties (MacEwen, *Life and Letters*, 713). When in 1882 illness forced Ker again and again to suspend his work at the Hall, Cairns, with the help of Henry Calderwood, carried on the Practical Training course (MacEwen, *Life and Letters*, 715).

130. Beadnell is a possible candidate.

131. "A few months in a Northumbrian fishing village," MS, n.d., Westminster College archives.

132. While one cannot be too precise about the date, Disraeli, created Earl of Beaconsfield in 1876, resigned as Prime Minister on 21 April 1880 and died on 19 April 1881. Gladstone's second Liberal government lasted from 1880–885.

133. Woodside, *Soul of a Scottish Church*, 102.

and Foreign Mission work up till 1900. It maintained a Home Mission in the slums of Edinburgh, in which the students themselves took a large part in the work of visiting and preaching; and every year sent out its members, two by two, amongst the congregations to plead for the support of their Home Mission scheme as well as for some definite Foreign Mission enterprise—selected generally from outside the denomination." Exposure to Edinburgh slums would have driven home to the students the human cost of abject deprivation in poor housing conditions. The author of *Slum Life in Edinburgh* suggests that "those persons whose knowledge of slum life has been derived from sources other than actual contact with it, cannot summon before their imagination any accurate representation of existence there."[134] The book paints a grim picture of human misery: families where the breadwinner had occasional employment lived out a cheerless existence in filthy one-room dwellings, with wretched furnishings, rented weekly; children were beaten, neglected, starved and driven on to the streets. Others, further down the poverty scale, lived in furnished lodgings at the mercy of rapacious landlords, or in common lodging houses, with a total lack of privacy, while many others, destitute and dissolute, drowned their sorrows in whisky or methylated spirits.

The oldest parts of Edinburgh had become so vile that in the eyes of the City Corporation the only solution appeared to be to tear them down and start again. Slum clearance was seen as an environmental improvement measure, but as the Corporation had no authority to rebuild, redevelopment was left to entrepreneurs and philanthropists.

However, Woodside's statement that Oman and his contemporaries "visited and preached" in the "slums" of Edinburgh may need to be nuanced. Oman affirms, in an address given to "plead the scheme" on behalf of the Student Missionary Society, that the Home Mission work of the Hall was "carried on in North Merchiston Edinburgh."[135] Between 1930 and 1960, the tenements in Fountainbridge/North Merchiston were found to have degenerated into some of the worst slums in Edinburgh, but this was not necessarily yet the case in 1882, when there was high employment in the area. It was an area just over a mile south-west of Castle Terrace, where land was cheap, bordered by the Union Canal to the south and the Edinburgh to Glasgow railway line to the north and bisected by the Caledonian railway line. As these stimulated associated industries, breweries, distilleries and iron works, the population of the area was growing rapidly. This had also since 1856 been home to two of Edinburgh's major industries, the North British

---

134. T.B.M., *Slum Life in Edinburgh*.
135. MS, Westminster College archives, n.d.

Rubber Company which produced galoshes and Wellington boots on twenty acres of land by the canal, and opposite, the gigantic MacEwan's brewery.

The industrial heart of North Merchiston with its blocks of tenements was bounded distinctively by "colony" developments, built as houses for artisans. To the north, by Haymarket station, was the small Dalry colony built in 1868–70 to accommodate skilled employees of the Caledonian railway. Further south were North Merchiston Park and Shandon, both completed in 1883, and the larger Shaftesbury Park colony where work began in 1883 where before there was open farmland.[136]

The chief architect and engineer of the developments was James Gowans,[137] whose campaign for "light and air" to bring relief from the worst effects of industrial pollution was a major factor in the construction of these colony type houses, each consisting of two flats, with front doors on opposite sides of the building, and a garden each. The beehive plaques on the walls indicate that they were constructed by the Edinburgh Co-operative Building Company, founded by seven Edinburgh stonemasons to enable workers on modest but regular incomes to be rehoused in better homes. This was a radical experiment in home ownership based on principles of mutuality and participation.

The success of suburban developments such as the colonies was seen by the members of the Royal Commission on the Housing of the Working Classes when they met in Edinburgh in 1885 to justify a faith in private enterprise, without undermining the moral fiber of the artisan residents but they recognized too that it failed to address the needs of those at the end of the chain, classified, with dubious morality, as the "undeserving poor." As was recognized at the time, the colony developments did not provide an answer to the fundamental dilemma of urban planning—how could renewal attempts truly benefit the residents of the area to be renewed? If slums were cleared, what happened to the very poor who could not afford commercial rents?[138] Faced with apparent municipal indifference to the fate of those who could not or would not help themselves, the efforts of the churches were uncoordinated. The author of *Slum Life in Edinburgh* observes sagely: "It is time to have done with this guerrilla warfare, to abandon this irresponsible skirmishing, and to attack the evil with united front. Not till then shall

---

136. Ordinance Survey large scale Scottish town plans, 1847–95, National Library of Scotland.

137. He had invested in the construction of the New Theatre and incurred heavy losses when it was sold to the UP church. From 1875 to 1888, his office, known as the "Pineapple tenement," was at 31 Castle Terrace.

138. In April 1885, the question was raised by the Royal Commission. See Smith, "Rehousing/Relocation Issue," 100.

we see any appreciable amelioration in the conditions of life in the slums of Edinburgh."

UP Mission in North Merchiston

As to the ecclesiastical context of the student mission, it is worth noting that the two existing UP churches in the area, as Voluntarist congregations, had found they had fallen on stony ground. In 1882, the UP congregation in Slateford village, south of Merchiston, "was not meeting the requirements of the district," "the soil was confessedly hard, and progress did not come up to expectation."[139] Then, in June 1881, a church was opened in Gilmore Place Merchiston to accommodate members of a struggling mission church in the Vennel, Grassmarket, which the Presbytery could no longer support.[140] The Grassmarket, according to Small, was "overwrought"; there was a "working man's church" in the center and a Free Church only a little way from each extremity. But for many members of the UP congregation, the move to their new home was "too far," some withdrew in the desire to escape "money burdens," and the congregation was further depleted by disputes over the use of communion wine and various other "wearisome struggles."[141] Nevertheless, the UP Presbytery felt that, in view of the recent population explosion in North Merchiston, "a preaching station might be opened without injury to existing interests."[142] And it is now possible to define the area covered by Oman and his friends a little more exactly. Small informs us that on 7 February 1882, "a preaching station was opened in this area by Dr. John Ker with the sanction of Edinburgh Presbytery."[143] The Students' Missionary Society had, we are told, been active in the area for some time and they had erected an Iron Church[144] with sittings for 300 people, in Yeaman Place, just

139. Small, *History of the Congregation*, 1:616.

140. The property was sold to the Salvation Army. The UP Vennel Mission may be contrasted with the more successful independent Grassmarket Mission established by James Fairbairn in 1886 which supported families with children and the homeless with food and clothing as well as services and talks.

141. Small, *History of the Congregations*, 1:486-88.

142. Small, *History of the Congregations*, 1:489. In 1876 the Church of Scotland had set up an Iron Church in Angle Park Terrace, between the industrial area and the colonies to the south. When the Iron Church was removed, it was superseded in December 1883 by St Michael's Church whose tower, 41 meters high, was a landmark for the colonies in Slateford Road.

143. Small, *History of the Congregations*, 1:492.

144. This was a simple prefabricated chapel in riveted corrugated iron with optional add-ons such as a porch or a tower, which could be transported easily to a new site when money was raised to construct a stone building.

north of the Union Canal. This was in the industrial area. The smell of malt would remind the students of the proximity of McEwan's brewery, and this would at certain times of day have competed with the stench of rubber from the North British Rubber Company factory; and when the wind was in the wrong direction, they would know that the municipal manure depot was in the vicinity.

Undeterred, on 27 March 1883 the students were servicing a congregation with a membership of 34, and the following year, management was handed over by the students to the congregation. In October 1884, they were assessed by the Presbytery to be in a position to call a minister and on 26 February 1885, the Reverend John Pollock was inducted.[145] From then on, there was a discernible trajectory from a mission oriented Tin Church in an industrial area to a settled preaching station in a distinctive mature township. While the "mission room" was to remain on the site in Yeaman Place, on 3 November 1887 the church moved to its own hall in Polwarth Gardens,[146] south of the canal, where the elegant villas with servants' quarters, traditional flatted terraces and two to three story tenements left few opportunities for development. But this is to anticipate. For the moment it suffices to note that Oman's involvement with the project was in its early stages between 1882 and 1885.

He justified his appeal to an unspecified church congregation on behalf of the Students' Missionary Society by the facts: "1) that the students are here receiving a most valuable part of their education—a practical training which will afterwards be of advantage to the Church at large, and 2) that really good substantial work which is being done. Our special mission is to the soulless and indifferent, those whose Church going is a mere name if even that, and the result is such as to call for thankfulness and gratitude."[147]

We may infer that Oman intended the reference to the "soulless and indifferent" as an allusion to the inhabitants of the tenements and colonies, and the "really good substantial work" as personal evangelism, and we may see in this student missionary address the direct influence of Cairns and Ker. Personal evangelism is the primary concern. While it is inadvisable to

---

145. Small, *History of the Congregations*, 1:492–93.

146. Small, *History of the Congregations*, 1:492–93. The hall was opened by Principal Cairns, and in May 1892, Mrs. William Nairn, John Ker's sister, donated £6000 in his memory for a commodious building with sittings for a thousand worshippers," designed by David Robertson, chief architect of the UP Church. At the close of 1899 the John Ker Memorial Church had 785 members and we may only speculate as to how many of them lived north of the canal.

147. Address by Oman as a student representative of the Hall Missionary Society; MS, Westminster College archives, n.d.

attach too much weight to one document, nonetheless it is worth noting that there is no indication here of a desire to apply Christian ethics to social problems. As Bebbington indicates, while "Evangelical activism carried over into social concern as an end in itself, there was a diffidence among many Evangelicals about certain aspects of relief work."[148]

Oman was not, however, silent on the matter. In a society which still lacked a state welfare system the churches were the most obvious source of help, and the philanthropic efforts of local congregations were supplemented by the societies which redistributed wealth to those who were most in need. But about one thing Oman was clear: charity could have pernicious effects. If a poor man was able to work he should help himself rather than rely on charity.

> Among the poorer classes too, Presbyterianism—indeed all dissent—has to struggle against the multitudinous charities of the church, charities which I believe are pernicious to every one of them. Charities which help those who can help themselves. Charities which foster in the working man the thought that he is the poor man, which destroy that feeling of independence which would make a true man scorn to receive help so long as he had a copper in his purse or a flexible muscle in his body.[149]

This was entirely compatible with the thinking that inspired the colonies, as shared by many radicals within the Edinburgh Liberal party, and notably by the prominent Free Church minister, James Begg (1808–83), scourge of William Robertson Smith. Workers, Begg felt, should be able to club together their savings from not visiting public houses to buy land outside the town center and pool their building skills. While wholeheartedly agreeing with the need for a healthier environment Begg was firmly opposed to any intervention in support of the working classes that might undermine individual responsibility and lead to the working classes becoming dependent.[150]

Oman leaves no indication at this stage as to his views about what should happen to the very poor who no longer had a copper in their purse, those most likely to be found in the tenements rather than the colonies, those who were widely perceived to be "undeserving."

---

148. Bebbington, *Evangelicalism in Modern Britain*, 121.
149. "A few months in a Northumbrian fishing village." See n132.
150. Smith, "Rehousing/Relocation Issue."

Theological Debate

It was a measure of Oman's expressed interest in theology that he attached high importance to theological debate. The main opportunity for this was the UP Students' Theological Society, but this was not, he claimed, "in a healthy state," and in an address to the Society, he challenges his hearers to consider why. Although he is of course speaking to the converted, he makes his own views clear in two significant respects. First, he considers it axiomatic that the cut and thrust of debate is essential to furthering theological truth. However

> there are men who have been studying for five, six, seven years met together in one institution and yet have not sufficient interest in intellectual and moral questions to drive them together to talk about them. The reply, of course, is that there is so much public instruction that really quiet reading in one's lodgings is more beneficial. . . . It may be admitted at once that we are too much lectured, but a society such as this supplies an element that is lacking in lectures. There is and ought to be reaction as well as action. There is the opportunity of refusing as well as swallowing.

And secondly, he defiantly challenges his hearers to reflect on the importance for their future ministry of discussing theological issues:

> Gentlemen say they get nothing from coming to the society. The statement betrays an utter want of comprehension of the meaning of such a society, an utter want of sympathy with its purpose, which means an utter want of sympathy with your object in being here, and I do not hesitate to say, an utter unfitness for your object in life, which is to be a teacher of others. . . . We all feel this work we are interested in, we feel it in the missionary society, we manifest it in all practical matters; how is it that on questions of theology and literature, questions which would naturally be considered of supreme importance to us as theological students we show no desire to sharpen our minds by contact with others. There can only be one answer, we have no interest in them. . . . It is . . . the want of the desire to know for knowing's sake; the want of what for lack of a better term we may call "sweetness and light."[151]

While we do not know how Oman's fellow students reacted to this trenchant criticism, and we may note in passing a similarity of tone to the

---

151. Undated MS, Westminster College Archives.

speech he gave in 1881 to the Edinburgh University UP Students' Society, (above, 44-48) we do know that this protégé of Fraser and Calderwood was determined to "sharpen his mind by contact with others," and had ample opportunity to do so during the summer terms he spent on the continent.

4

Germany

OMAN SPENT THE SUMMER term of 1883 under the auspices of the UP Hall at Erlangen University, followed in 1885 by four months in Heidelberg and around two and a half months in Neuchâtel, a rich experience of student life on the continent which had an obvious and far-reaching influence. "My original purpose being study," he writes, "involved some knowledge of the languages, and some intercourse with the people. In addition I voyaged as fancy prompted or funds allowed."[1] Although the "letters to his home" alluded to by George Alexander[2] cannot be traced, Oman gives a lively account of his experiences in two unpublished essays: "Reminiscences of Continental Travel" and "Notes on German Student Life." These are undated, and the intended readership is unclear, but here Oman reveals a keenly observed sense of the distinctiveness of his new environment. Determined to improve his linguistic skills, he engages in conversation with friends and strangers, with impoverished students and wealthy counts, and with landlady and professor alike. He enjoys the company of theological students, and expresses undisguised admiration for Martin Luther's brave stance for truth and freedom. Everywhere he goes, and particularly in Switzerland, he betrays a profound susceptibility to natural beauty. And in lectures and discussions he was exposed to debates on matters which were exercising some of the foremost contemporary German theologians.[3]

1. Oman, "Reminiscences of Continental Travel."
2. Alexander, "Memoir of the Author," xviii.
3. He was well grounded in German theology by John Cairns, who, in his own

Why Erlangen? Although shrill voices at the time of the Robertson Smith affair claimed that Germany was a hotbed of liberal theology, the evidence suggests that many Scottish students sought out faculties or professors who were thought to share their evangelical beliefs,[4] and Erlangen attracted students from the UP Hall. What became known as the "Erlangen School" of theology had its roots in the Lutheran Pietist revival, and emerged as a protest against the Prussian monarchy's heavy promotion of a united Protestant church. However, not all the theologians of this school were ultra-Conservative neo-Lutherans, and the "land-louping students of theology"[5] from Edinburgh were exposed to fresh ways of balancing their evangelical inheritance with an awareness of historical contextuality. "What cannot be questioned," Oman affirms,

> is the existence in this Lutheran theology of the vitality of a new religious life, making it dissatisfied with a merely contemplative and artistically expansive type of freedom. It insists that to be in God we must be of God after the practical fashion of living above our world and above ourselves. It sees that a religion which merely interprets God by the world, is helpless in the day of our calamity, that unless we find a religion which interprets the world by God, we have no power to bear us up, that unless we have faith and not merely induction, our hope will vanish in the day we most need it.[6]

First Impressions

"You can only go properly abroad once," Oman writes, "and to do so effectively you should not be too long out of your teens."[7] And so it was that, with a working knowledge of German, he set off for Erlangen in 1883 with Benjamin Mein and another fellow student at the UP Hall, James Gardner, about whose premature death he was later to speak so affectingly.[8]

Wanderjahr, read "Jacobi, Schleiermacher, Ranke, with the chief dogmatic systems of the old Rationalist, Straussian and Orthodox Schools" (MacEwen, *Life and Letters*, 159).

4. Statham, "Landlouping Students of Divinity," 42–67.

5. Cairns to Wilson, 30 October 1843, in MacEwen, *Life and Letters*, 152. Adam Cleghorn Welch spent the summer of 1885 at Erlangen.

6. Oman, *Faith and Freedom*, 347.

7. Oman, "Reminiscences of Continental Travel."

8. "He told me that of his recovery there was no hope and for himself scarcely even a desire. Then seeing me so sad and unable to answer him, he began to speak pleasantly of a summer we had spent together. But he added with apparent distress. How sorry I

The young travelers embarked in high spirits on a three-day journey by sea to Cuxhaven.[9] The crossing was rough: "We were then sitting under the shadow of the deckhouse, late on a Sunday afternoon, attempting to sing hymns, a foot or two of water washing across the lower deck under our feet, and a vivid sun sinking over a vast black wilderness of heaving waters. I was sick, one of my friends was afraid, and the other both sick and afraid."[10] When they arrived, they succeeded in buying a railway timetable for sixpence, and, having fortified themselves with a cup of coffee and "little hard baked white rolls and fresh butter," set off by train for a hectic schedule of voracious tourism. Oman's youthful thrill at being exposed to new places, people, language, and culture, "the freshness, the amazing foreignness of everything"[11] is obvious from his "Reminiscences of Continental Travel." From Hamburg, where they spent a day, they travelled on to Berlin. There, after a very full day of sightseeing on foot, Oman declares: "Finally there is, I know not where, a huge opera house, where we sat celestially half in a waking half in a sleeping dream and heard Tannhäuser."[12] The next morning, they "did" Potsdam where Oman still remembered "details like the felt slippers we had to put on to cross the long Sahara of polished floor in the Crown Prince's palace, and the great terraces that led up to Frederick the Great's palace of Sans Souci." At midday, they were off to Wittenberg where they called a halt. "We had had our lesson and learned that man drinks better out of a cup than a water butt, and ever after 'hastened with leisure.'" Oman's imagination was seized by the Luther associations: the Castle Church where he was alleged to have nailed his theses to the door, the transept where he and Melanchthon were buried, the little pulpit from which he set Germany afire, the monastery where he lived, with "his plain oak writing table [and]

---

am for having studied so little German. It seemed strange. There will surely be a sweeter and even more universal language in heaven. What would be the use of German of all things in the world. Besides it was so strange for him to speak of regret for not having studied who lay there dying just because he had wasted his candle by burning it too feverishly. But now I see the matter in another light. There was no man who studied for prizes or for worldly success but for the sake of truth and the praise of God and death had nothing to do with quenching his student's zeal." (Oman, sermon on Rom 2:29, Clayport, 6 July 1890, MS Westminster College archives.)

9. They are likely to have set off from Leith.
10. Oman, "Reminiscences of Continental Travel."
11. Oman, "Reminiscences of Continental Travel."
12. Oman, "Reminiscences of Continental Travel."
The performance of this tale of a wanderer seeking redemption by love may have been intended to mark Wagner's death on 13 February 1883.

the double chair for himself and his lord Kate."[13] "No-one," he writes, "who knows anything of the sixteenth century could visit Wittenberg unmoved."[14]

Luther Anniversary Celebrations

We may now pause briefly to note the significance of the fact that this year, 1883, was the 400th anniversary of Luther's birth, marked by celebrations in towns and cities in Germany and in the United Kingdom. Oman records a memorable occasion on 8 August, when the friends attended the students' Luther Festival at Erfurt and Eisenach. At Erfurt, they watched from the terrace of the cathedral as a great procession of students and town guilds enacted the entry into Worms, "one of the most genuinely picturesque incidents in history. Here in Erfurt, Luther studied at the university, here he resolved to be a monk after his student friend had been struck dead at his side by lightening [sic], and in the Augustinian monastery in the church of which we attended service, he tried, as he himself said, as hard as any man could, to go to heaven by monkery."[15] In Eisenach, where Luther went to school, and "sang for his bread in the street," the friends "toiled up to the Wartburg," the great castle where Luther took refuge after escaping from Worms, and where he laboriously worked on his translation of the Bible into German. "Being worsted in conflict with Hebrew constructions,[16] he saw the visible devil and stood up to him, as he had ever done to his invisible embodiment, flinging at him the only weapon at his disposal his inkbottle. The marks are usually pointed out on the wall." It was, Oman recollected, a "sombre rainy day, with great masses of shadow moving slowly across the dark olive billows of the pine forest," which "fitted in with Luther's mood at that time of his highest anxiety." Then there were speeches in large halls, and concerts in big gardens, but—for Oman the culmination—"the most

13. Oman, "Reminiscences of Continental Travel."

14. Oman, "Reminiscences of Continental Travel." Oman conveys his considered opinion of Luther as a person in a book review in 1923. "Though without any form of panegyric, the result is an impression of Luther's real greatness, far greater than is ever made by any of the pious pictures of the orthodox biographies, with all their paeans of adoration. He is flesh and blood, he is inconsistent, he does not prove himself a great theologian, he fails to maintain his ideal when in contact with the actual, but one does not admire the person who would fail to see . . . a true man of deep religious insight, breadth of human nature, massiveness of mind, with utter sincerity and courage." Oman, review of *La Liberté Chrétienne*, 212.

15. Oman, "Reminiscences of Continental Travel."

16. While he may have resumed work on his translation of the Old Testament at some point, his major achievement in the Wartburg was to translate the books of the New Testament from Greek into German.

impressive thing of all, the greatest . . . performance I have ever heard, was some three thousand students singing 'A Safe Stronghold my God is Still.'"[17] He comments further: "That is the true German national anthem, the noblest in any language."

Oman alludes obliquely here to the fact that the anniversary of Luther's birth, notionally 10 November, was as much a national as a religious festival, "a site where the German national idea was articulated and fiercely debated."[18] A mere twelve years since the end of the Franco-Prussian War, when Germany had become a nation-state for the first time in its history, the 1883 anniversary saw Luther transformed into a thirteenth apostle, conflated Protestantism with German national identity, and reinforced the marginalization of many loyal subjects of the emperor, who, being Roman Catholics, were more inclined to mourn than to celebrate.[19] This confessionally exclusive manifestation of German identity reinforced antagonisms that had led, in 1871, to the establishment of a *kleindeutsch* (Little German) Empire, where the German states were unified under Prussia, with Austria excluded, and the hostile measures of *Kulturkampf* which targeted Roman Catholics.[20] Although the legislation proved unworkable, the impression was reinforced that Roman Catholics were alien to Germany.[21]

The Emperor himself was cautious, absenting himself in September from the Luther festival in Wittenberg to watch military maneuvers. But he sent a friendly greeting which was delivered by the Crown Prince, praying that the festival "may be blessed to the awakening and deepening of Protestant good morals, and the confirming of peace in our Church."[22]

On his return to Edinburgh, Oman had an opportunity to attend commemorations of a less overtly political nature. On 31 October 1883, the

---

17. Oman, "Reminiscences of Continental Travel." On the way to the festival, they visited the castle of Coburg, where Luther wrote the hymn.

18. Landry, "Luther Memory," 215.

19. Landry, "German National Idea."

20. This was an attempt by Otto von Bismarck, Chancellor both of Prussia and the Reich, to subject the Roman Catholic Church to state control: seminaries were closed, religious orders, notably Jesuits, were abolished, civil marriage was made compulsory, there was to be no Roman Catholic education in schools, church property was confiscated, and thousands of Roman Catholic clergy, who opposed these measures, were arrested or went into exile. Jews were likewise seen by many to be non-citizens. In 1880, the Prussian Court Pastor, Adolf Stoecker, and Heinrich von Treitschke launched an Antisemitic Petition which was signed by a quarter of a million Germans, asking for severely restrictive measures to be imposed on Jews. This was quashed by the Crown Prince.

21. Landry, "German National Idea," 294.

22. *The Times*, 14 September 1883.

winter session of the UP hall was opened by John Cairns with a lecture "to a large audience in the Synod Hall" on the theme of "Luther's translation of the Bible." We are informed that "the lecturer thought the Bible in Luther's hand looked like a divine book, although the translation was by no means free from fault."[23] Over the anniversary weekend, "a large number of meetings and special services were held in Protestant churches" in Edinburgh, where "the main meeting on Saturday evening was addressed by Professors Cairns, Calderwood and [D]uff."[24] These professors in the UP tradition were persuaded, not only of Luther's significance in Reformation history, but also of the unsuitability of too close a relationship between church and state. As early as 1844, on the first of many visits to Germany, Cairns wrote from Berlin:

> The present central powers have resolved to support the Throne by forming a strong Church party, for which purpose the Evangelical section of the many-coloured Prussian Church has been selected. Its most orthodox and symbolical leaders are inflamed with an unhappy zeal . . . and the cause of pure Christianity, if it does not actually degrade itself by a secondary preaching of divine right, affords colour to the reproach that pietism, to gratify its own intolerance, is willing to become the slave of despotism. Would that the Church would stand fast in the liberty wherewith Christ has made her free! But Church independence and toleration as understood and practised in Scotland are here unknown.[25]

In 1883 Protestantism was seen as the servant of the state, and Luther was being hailed as the pioneer par excellence of the German nation. Long afterwards, Oman recalled

> that the German Church was the most submissively Erastian form of Christianity that has ever appeared in all the ages, and that, as the Government saw to the appointment of all its superintendents and many of its ministers, any revolt would have been looked upon as a desecration of the holy of holies. Except the Junkers, there were no greater Imperialists than the Prussian ministers; and imperial order to the others was the untouchable

---

23. *Dundee Courier*, 2 November 1883.

24. *Tavistock Gazette*, 16 November 1883. Special services were held on the Sunday in various cities in Britain. In London, a crowded meeting in Exeter Hall was chaired by Lord Shaftesbury in front of a reproduction of the Cranach portrait of Luther framed by a laurel wreath. Shaftesbury spoke in quasi messianic terms of Luther as the "special servant of God who delivered us from intolerable thraldom," and a telegram of goodwill was sent to the Emperor of Germany from "the Protestants of England."

25. Cairns to Wilson, 9 March 1844, in MacEwen, *Life and Letters*, 167.

ark of the covenant. The mere suggestion of discussing it was at once silenced as an impiety.[26]

Oman would read coverage of the "great national festival" in Germany in the British press. At Eisleben, according to the correspondent of the *Daily News*,[27] the occasion was marked by a pealing of church bells the previous evening, flowers, garlands, a display of the escutcheons of all the Luther towns, triumphal arches, a sermon in St Andrew's church preached by Court chaplain Frommel on Luke 1:66–80, the unveiling of a great bronze statue of the Reformer "consecrated by court chaplain Koegel," and a lavishly costumed historical pageant with 200 horses. Among the 30,000 visitors were many government officials and clergy.

From his first published work, *Vision and Authority*, onwards, Oman never wavered in his belief in the spiritual freedom of the church. The book was, he wrote, "the outcome of long years of reading and thinking on a situation which was the more challenging for still having something of newness."[28] As we have seen, the immediate spur to Oman's thinking here was the Robertson Smith affair, but it is undeniable that his experiences in Germany of military, national, and ecclesiastical authority, once digested, were also to have profound implications for his future work.

Erlangen

In following Oman's Luther pilgrimage, we temporarily left the three friends in Wittenberg, from where they proceeded on their way to Erlangen by an "old steam kettle." The trio appear to have travelled third class, which was relatively inexpensive: to travel fourth class, without any seats, ever remained one of Oman's "unsatisfied ambitions."[29] On arrival, they made their way to Friedrichstrasse where their lodgings were "conspicuous as the shabbiest house in an extremely respectable street."[30] "You could do fairly well," Oman observes, "for £4 a session." You are required to provide "your own firewood and light" and you dine out like most German students. You pay extra for "brushing your clothes and boots." Nailing his visiting card to the door of his room, he entered. There was no carpet, he observed, but the floor was carefully scrubbed. "The chairs bear marks of conflict. Our room

26. Oman, "Germany: Fifty Years Apart," III.
27. *Tavistock Gazette*, 16 November 1883.
28. Oman, *Vision and Authority*, 2nd ed., 11.
29. Oman, "German Student Life."
30. Oman, "Germany: Fifty Years Apart," I.

in Erlangen was a perfect Greenwich hospital of maimed veterans although they seemed sound to the inexperienced eye. There is a standing desk and a sitting desk, a sofa made by the joiner across the way, both commodious and comfortable, a table and a tile above."[31] On Oman's arrival, Frau Memmert, his landlady, delivered a document to the police authorities stating his name, age, and standing, and he was now ready to matriculate as a student of the university, passing "from the care of the usual magister to the university authorities. Henceforward whatsoever misdeed you may commit you will not be arrested if you quietly allow the police to take down your name and address from your matriculation card."[32]

Matriculation at Erlangen was, he comments, "an event to be remembered" in contrast to Heidelberg: red tape was further complicated by the students' linguistic ignorance. "Thereafter the pro-rector said something about obeying the laws, which laws we knew not but we promised faithfully, bowed profoundly and came away." When they had received their matriculation certificates in Latin, and paid fifteen shillings, they "stood before the world veritable German students."[33] They were then free to enroll in their classes. There were four faculties—Philosophy, Theology, Arts, and Medicine—and the faculty of Philosophy included all history, science, language, and literature. As distinct from the system in Scotland, the student specializes from the outset. "Not only does he begin his professional studies at once but he carries them on in any way that pleases him. When he goes to a university, he does not ask which classes would come [next] in order but which professors would be most profitable. Consequently the man of one session may sit down with the man of six and the only thing necessary is that the requisite classes should have been taken before he presents himself for examination."[34] The German student can study under all the great professors in Germany if he wishes. In faculties other than medicine, "there is simply no escape from the incapacity of the professor and very little help even from him in specialising."[35] In Oman's view, this could not be attributed

---

31. Oman, "German Student Life." Oman adds: "The bed is an oblong box made also by the neighbouring joiner. . . . It may be the finest resting place you ever reposed on or it may be a place of torture. . . . I learned gradually not to stretch myself and in the swelteringly hot weather did not wish to wrap myself in a thick feather bed which is the usual covering under which the German student sleeps."

32. Oman, "German Student Life."

33. Oman, "German Student Life." So they remained until they "ex-matriculated" when on payment of a fee they received a document certifying their good conduct and attendance upon classes.

34. Oman, "German Student Life."

35. Oman, "German Student Life."

to lack of money. "There is plenty of money if it were right distributed. Very much better work could be done by professors who did not have £2000 a year."[36] "In Germany," he relates,

> you will find a man of world-wide renown living up three flights of stairs.[37] Prof. Frank in Erlangen, a man known all over Germany[38] when he invited us to what was called in the invitation a quite simple supper had just roast veal, lettuce, beer and cigars and no servant was visible and when anything was wanted Miss Frank rose for it. The furniture though simple, was tasteful and there was nothing lacking to true refinement. Probably Frank would have an income of from £200 to £300.[39]

After outlining with some skepticism the system of appointing professors by habilitation, Oman concedes that "it is only fair to say that German professors as a rule seriously and honestly face the difficulties of their subjects."

The classes in Theology, he informs us, varied in size from 130 to nine; an inept teacher was usually left to lecture to empty benches. Oman comments that "it must be hard for the poor professor, but one can hardly doubt that this stern application of the law of the survival of the fittest is employed with advantage for the rest of the human race."[40] Professor Frank was clearly one of the fittest. The following description by Oman of the lecture room deserves to be quoted at length both for its intrinsic interest and for its evocative description of his determination to follow Frank's train of thought.

> You shall go with me to my first lecture in Frank's classroom in Erlangen. You have time to see that the room is rather dingy when the conversation is hushed and a white haired ruddy close shaven man of reverent aspect enters. Immediately all the students rise to their feet. The professor bows and as he takes his place behind his desk the students again seat themselves. All German professors so far as I saw stand while lecturing. Each student is provided with pen and ink and several hefts of paper which he carries in a little case called a mappe and in a moment

---

36. Oman, "German Student Life."
37. From 1882 to 1894, Frank lived at Hauptstrasse 13, Erlangen.
38. The commemorative plaque outside his house certifies that he was a *Kgl. Geheimrat*; a privy councilor of the king (presumably Ludwig II of Bavaria, the "fairytale king" who was declared insane in 1886). Even if the title was purely honorific, it indicates formal recognition.
See the "Gedenktafel für Franz Hermann Reinhold Frank am Haus Hauptstrasse 13 in Erlangen." (Wikimedia Commons).
39. Oman, "German Student Life."
40. Oman, "German Student Life."

they are all busy writing as the professor dictates. The paragraph being ended the lecturer expounds it more fully either by reading more rapidly or more generally before talking without book. Though you are a novice at German you will begin to detect certain phrases. Prof. Frank's habitual expression is "*absolut nicht meine Herren*" and as he utters it he bends his forefinger gracefully over his nose. The intricacy of paragraph within paragraph would annihilate anything but a German brain. First there is the largest set which one called Roms I, II etc. The next in order is small i. Capital A follows and small a closes the procession. Occasionally it takes all the skill of professor and students to be quite sure there is no mistake. Hitherto you have made a determined effort to follow, but gradually your fondest resolve cannot hold you to it, and you find yourself counting how many words are in each sentence. Even that becomes too hard work and you get your watch out and time the sentences. At the end you are rewarded by recognising two words which mean "have had" with which most sentences end. It then dawns upon you that a good many Germans are almost as inattentive as you. And thereafter your conscience does not trouble you when your ears retire from business and your eyes begin. Do not be ashamed of yourself, for many a long day after this, you will be as helpless amidst the involutions of Frank's slow stately sentences as Laocoon in the encircling folds of the sea-serpent.[41]

At the end of the lecture, the students stand, the lecturer bows and leaves, caps are donned and there is a fifteen-minute pause before the next lecture. "In the sultry summer days the perpetual succession of classes hour after hour in one room rather exhausts the already overheated atmosphere" but "when we were done we could push out into the lovely garden over which the various buildings which composed the university were scattered somewhat promiscuously."[42]

Students

Oman records how he plunged confidently into conversation in German with fellow travelers and fellow students. In a light-hearted account of his linguistic pitfalls, he advises his reader to "hold on undismayed though the grammar quake under your feet like a bog or genders trip you up like fallen branches, resolute to attain somehow if not by stately procession up

41. Oman, "German Student Life."
42. Oman, "German Student Life."

the front avenue then anyhow by some back door."[43] "The enjoyment," he continues, "is largely in the sense of danger. After a whole day of it—three lectures, let us say, then a general discussion at dinner, then a long walk with two or three friends to the nearest place where good coffee is to be obtained, ending up with a deep discussion of theological subjects towards midnight, and you go home as satisfied as if you had walked forty miles and sleep like a navvy."[44]

The students he knew in Erlangen came chiefly from the Baltic region. "At bottom, . . . simple good-hearted fellow(s) . . . unworldly and though perhaps not much given to church-going . . . not without a strong element of piety. High metaphysics are rather out of fashion and Darwin and Herbert Spencer are the divinities of the present German Olympus."

The swords that hung on the classroom pegs were a reminder that many were training for the army. Looking back on his experiences fifty years later, Oman wrote:

> The first Emperor still ruled, and Bismarck was more than the power behind the throne. The Franco-Prussian War was only some dozen years away. No student, and few others, questioned that serving in the army was not merely patriotic, but the highest form of altruism, the absence of which proved us to be an individualistic and undisciplined people. Serving in the army was one of the most frequent subjects of conversation, and students in uniform during their year of training, were our constant companions.[45]

Once qualified, they served as underofficers, the second military grade. In his account of "German Student Life" Oman elaborates:

> Many of them are very far from rich . . . while the loss of a year must count for something. However they do not seem unwilling to serve and they are all mad on the glory of Germany especially the Prussians. There is still a strong dislike of Prussia especially in the smaller states. . . . But professional men have a fear of offending the government and students as a rule speak with much reserve on political matters.

---

43. Oman, "Reminiscences of Continental Travel."
44. Oman, "Reminiscences of Continental Travel."
45. Oman, "Germany: Fifty Years Apart," II.

Verein

Almost every student belonged to some kind of club, members of different clubs being distinguished by their caps. These ranged from the frugal Verein which met for "fellowship and study," to the very select and expensive, where members wore velvet jackets and long boots. "The theological Verein," according to George Alexander, "welcomed the Scottish students to guest membership and contributed not a little to the educational value of the term."[46] That that contribution was indeed considerable is clear from Oman's account of its activities, educational, social, and cultural. Members met daily in the Black Bear for dinner at 12:30, "not too soon," he observes drily, "if you breakfasted at 6 on a cup of coffee and two small rolls." On Tuesday at 7:30 they gathered in the Verein room of a local pub, under threat of a fine for non-attendance, to expound the Book of Galatians, and on Friday they convened for a debate. The person who opened debate had to post his thesis before Thursday afternoon. The thesis was then rigorously debated and a vote taken; then for the final hour and a half, Greek texts and commentaries gave way to song books and beer glasses, and the German students showed themselves to be "right vivacious and noisy."[47] On Saturdays they would often walk the twelve miles or so to Nuremberg or take "a friendly saunter" to the neighboring villages where they would sing and play skittles together. In the midsummer holidays it was not unusual for members of the Verein to go away for several days together, and the English-speaking students split up for the benefit of their German. "If you wish to travel economically and see everything," Oman recommends, "join a band of German students. My three days walking tour cost me eleven shillings. Now and again we were reduced to eggs and schinken in which case I always was satisfied with eggs but there was usually plenty of good milk and at least we dined royally. Our tour was in the Franconian Switzerland, a stretch of Dolomite country lying about twelve miles from Erlangen. The fantastic rocks rise up in sharp peaks through the trees, a road winds along the narrow valley, the eminences are crowned with ruined castles." The walkers pass crucifixes and shrines to Mary.

> One village is a famous place of pilgrimage[48] and the Franciscan monks go about it in brown cloaks and hoods and rope belts and bare feet as they did in England 400 years ago. The great sight is the Sophia cave. The vast chambers have strange galleries

---

46. Alexander, "Memoir of the Author," xviii.
47. Oman, "German Student Life."
48. Goessweinstein.

enabling you to walk almost along the roof with fluted pillars of stalactites through which the light shines. . . . No-one could fail to be impressed but the German student has a peculiar impressibility . . . and here we saw the other side of our beer drinking, song-singing friends.[49]

To begin with, they marched in instinctive accord with the German military training. Oman comments:

> You will naturally start in step with the rest of the company but after you have thoroughly wearied yourself it begins to dawn upon you that it is a manner of walking entirely unnatural to you. The German has his satchel between his shoulders, his head back, his chest out, his body upright and he uses a short military step. Example is strong but habit becomes stronger and before long you discover you are not walking five miles but only three. . . . By next evening you are a pedestrian hero.

Duels

The military ethos also accounted for another aspect of German student life which was particularly foreign to the experience of the Edinburgh students: the practice of dueling. "Doubtless," Oman writes, "it would soon die were it not for the spirit of defiance, a mixture of high animal spirits and vanity which make a certain class of students imagine that to be once at least in the university prison is needful for their manhood. But the chief cause is the military spirit in the country and the military code of honour which the system of serving in the army maintains."

However, the theological Verein actively prohibited its members from engaging in a duel. "The information that there have been six duels in the yard of the little inn at the end of the bridge which crosses the Regnitz and that there were still three to come off was too tempting however and as soon as dinner is over away we go. . . . Our German friends show considerable trepidation and will not enter the hospital with us so we go alone." There they find four or five men being treated for wounds, and watch as two fresh warriors are equipped for the fray. Oman stayed for the first two fights.

> Nothing but the ridiculous nature of the proceedings struck me, though I have lost a night's sleep after seeing such a small operation as a tonsil cut out.[50] We meant to be off at once but an

---

49. Oman, "German Student Life."
50. Perhaps a further counter-indication to a medical career.

American German friend took us captive. Why, the next was an offence duel. There had been nothing greater of the season. So stay we must and stay we did. The one warrior was the captain of the Bavarian corps, the most hacked and hewed man in all Erlangen with the left side of his face from temple to chin like a beef steak, the other was a little first year's man with a face smooth as when his mother dandled him on her knee. The sword play was excellent, the self-possession of the little man magnificent. It was no longer a farce. However perverted it was undoubtedly a display of skill, courage and endurance. The big Bavarian had already two cuts and was breathing heavily while the little man had only a pin scratch and was calm as a judge when the cry of Gendarme was heard. In two minutes the wounded and accoutrements were well on their way to Erlangen. The Gendarme came, looked as if he had no desire to find and then sat down and ordered a glass of beer to wet his dry German whistle.[51]

While Oman's curiosity appeared to have been satisfied by the first two matches which aroused in him scorn, pity, and a sense of the ridiculous, he found himself increasingly fascinated by the third duel. Though he had never given any evidence of military zeal, he was captivated by the bravery and skill of the combatants, and there is an unspoken sense of regret when the intrusion of the police brought proceedings to an abrupt end. He did not, however, attend any further duels in Heidelberg.

Heidelberg

On 6 July 1885, Oman matriculated at Heidelberg University, along with some 1,500 students, a significant minority of whom came from Scotland.[52] For the next four months, he "inhabited two small rooms in the third story" of an old house on the banks of the Neckar, built of wooden frames and sun-dried brick.[53] Oman observes: "Whenever I am cold I think of that room about four o'clock in a July afternoon." He was clearly not the first Edinburgh student to lodge there. His landlady was "the widow of a cabinet-maker and undertaker," who had been the butt of student pranks in Heidelberg and the subject of stories that were "often retold by the ingenuous

---

51. Oman, "German student life."

52. From 1837 to 1914, the Scots made up 25.5 percent of all the students in Heidelberg who gave a British or Irish address. See Maier, *Robertson Smith*, 91.

53. Oman, "Reminiscences of Continental Travel."

youth of Edinburgh University."[54] By now, Oman was fluent in German, and he was able to engage her in conversation about politics. She "could tell a tale and she was a politician besides and disliked Bismarck and the Prussians in a body." After a duel, "she used to bring the shirts for my inspection, while she enlarged on the folly of such customs. At such times she was full of moral reflections and pious contemplations, and though I don't think she ever went to church all the four months I was under her roof, I believe they were genuine. At least they were fresh and racy."

In Heidelberg, Oman was reminded of the pervasiveness of the military system. In front of the house was the *Exerzierplatz*, "from which I used to hear the word of command every day and almost all day long."[55] Reminiscing about this fifty years later, he wrote: "Every self-respecting town had a barracks for training soldiers, and before cock-crow you were wakened by multitudes of stoutly shod feet marching past, and the place echoed at other times with the word of command and the stamp of the *Potzdammer Schritt* (goose-step)."[56]

Looking back later on his experiences, he comments that "only the public, ever present spectacle of the army could nourish in the younger Germans the militaristic mind which possessed their seniors. It entered into everything, even theology. A prominent theologian like Hermann argued for God as the supreme drill sergeant."[57]

His fellow lodger was "a kind of Hungarian count," and the following anecdote deserves to be quoted both for its biographical interest and as an example of Oman's ironic style. He tells how the Antal von Latzko stopped him in the street one day.

> He is a member of a small and indeed select club composed mostly of law students, but of a somewhat freer nature than the *Burschenschaft*. He is lugubrious. "You have never visited me and I have been so lonely." On sympathetic inquiry into his calamities, I found that he has got nine days in the carcer for pulling down a shop sign. I ask how he is walking at large in this way and learn that he is out for his class. In the evening I call but the Antal von Latzko is having supper out with his club. Next time I go in the afternoon and am more fortunate. The Antal von Latzko and a fellow prisoner are entertaining their friends. Strawberry bole . . . was being ladled out. . . . After a

---

54. Oman, "Reminiscences of Continental Travel."
55. Oman, "Germany, Fifty Years Apart," I.
56. Oman, "Germany, Fifty Years Apart," II.
57. Oman, "Germany, Fifty Years Apart," II.

most hospitable reception I am seated on the right hand of the chairman whom I find to be a most interesting and intelligent fellow. After a little the servant maid appeared to say that the noise, which certainly was considerable, was against prison regulations.[58]

With a Canadian friend, whom he refers to as "Jones," he set off by train and Rhine steamer to continue his homage to Luther with a visit to Worms. The day was sultry, and the pair were thirsty, so "Luther and all the kings and queens of the time of the Niebelungen and the quarrels of Chriemhild and Brunhild and all the rest had to be postponed to the carnal necessity of getting something to drink." Refreshed, they imagine "the appearance of the brave monk who would enter Worms though it contained as many devils as tiles on the houses, and that great assembly with emperor and cardinal and prince and bishop and the little monk with his resolute answer, 'Here I take my stand, I can do no otherwise. God help me.'"[59] On another occasion, he concluded his pilgrimage with a visit to Marburg castle, the site of "Luther's conference with Zwingli which ended the hopes of a united Reformation, when in place of argument, he took a chalk and wrote in Latin on the table, 'This is my body.'"[60]

The Poet's World

From his early days as a member of the Edinburgh University UP students' society onwards, Oman maintained steadfastly that religion was impoverished when "its world is not sufficiently the poet's world, but one seen too much with eyes bleared and blinkered by theory."[61] One of the attractions of Heidelberg appears to have been its natural setting. Week after week, Oman would climb the hill behind the town, with the great alluvial plain of the Rhine at his feet, and "wander round [the castle] and find ever fresh beauty and interest. . . . It is beautiful in the fresh morning light, beautiful also in the sleepy afternoons, beautiful in the dark nights when it is illuminated with various coloured lights, but its perfection is under a full moon when the music is floating up from the town."

From Heidelberg, Oman travelled on to Neuchâtel, where he remained for about two and a half months to improve his French. Although

58. Oman, "German Student Life."
59. Oman, "Reminiscences of Continental Travel."
60. Oman, "Reminiscences of Continental Travel."
61. Oman, *Natural and Supernatural*, 147.

information about his stay is sparse, his abiding impression of Switzerland was of mountains of incomparable grandeur. After four hours of hard climbing to the summit of the Weissenstein, he writes, "all at once I saw the mountains, first the great mass of the Bernese hills, then far above them, great white clouds half way up the sky, the snow mountains. From my feet the whole earth seemed to be tilted right up to heaven. . . . That is the first view of Switzerland, and perhaps the greatest." The next picture he evokes is "the chain of the Alps at sunset as seen from the shore of the lake" at Neuchâtel. For a fortnight, "the mountains would never once be visible. Then some afternoon perhaps, you saw the whole chain from Titlis to Mount Blanc shining more white and glistening than polished silver, like the battlements of heaven. Thus it continued till the sun began to touch the top of the Jura behind the town, when the faintest blush showed in the silver, which deepened as the sun sank till the whole range stood a great mass of burnished gold." Then there is the view from the top of the Rigi, which he climbed with a friend who was a refugee from Bulgarian atrocity; "the grouping of the white peaks, great white shoulders huddled together like enormous sheep crowding through a gateway," while, down below, "the lake of Lucerne winds round the foot of the hill a deep peaceful blue." And the final picture is "not the greatest, but the solemnest." Alone, he climbed up into the long valley which runs from Meiringen to Grindelwald, along the foot of the snow mountains. Having been caught out by the dark, he stopped "in the moonlight under the Wellhorn for I have never seen anything in nature more sublime and solemn."[62]

Professors

This seems a suitable point to make a pause and take a closer look at those German scholars who may be regarded as influencing Oman's thinking over these years.[63] Typically, given his lively interest in art and literature, he supplemented his core curriculum in Erlangen with lectures on Church architecture by Albert Hauck (1845–1918),[64] and, in Heidelberg, by lectures on German literature by Karl Bartsch (1832–88), and on Goethe's *Faust* by Kuno Fischer (1824–1907).[65] Goethe's distinctive emphasis on grace will

62. Oman, "Reminiscences of Continental Travel."
63. Alexander, "Memoir of the Author," xviii.
64. These may have stimulated the keen interest he displayed in his travels in the architecture not only of churches and cathedrals, but also of villages and towns, with a strong preference for the medieval over the modern.
65. Fischer occupied the chair of "Philosophy and the history of modern German literature."

have engaged Oman's imagination, especially as it was only four years since the UP Synod found the Reverend David MacRae guilty of heresy[66] on the grounds of his dissent from the dogma of everlasting torment. Otherwise, Oman's program of study introduced him to the different perspectives and gradations of opinion that were then a distinctive feature of German academic theology. He attended lectures in Erlangen by Franz Hermann Reinhold von Frank (1827-94), the doyen of Erlangen Systematicians. He also attended lectures by Theodor Zahn (1838-1933), whose work on the New Testament was marked by an intense theological conservatism,[67] and by Gustav Class (1836-1908), who, as professor of philosophy, boldly attempted to combine certain concepts of Schleiermacher and Hegel.[68] In Heidelberg, according to George Alexander, Oman appears to have attended lectures chiefly in Biblical Studies, by Adalbert Merx (1838-1909), a notable Syriac scholar,[69] who lectured on the Psalms, and by Adolf Hausrath (1837-1909), who lectured on the New Testament.[70] "With the death of Richard Rothe (1799-1867), the contribution of theological-philosophical systematics in Heidelberg ceased for decades. In the rise of the important School of Albrecht Ritschl from Göttingen in the last third of the nineteenth century, the Heidelberg faculty hardly participated. On the contrary, it turned now entirely towards history."[71] A disciple of the Tübingen school,[72] Hausrath had

---

66. Cairns had swayed Synod with his argument that a doctrine of Universal Restoration was incompatible with the doctrine of grace. MacEwen, *Life and Letters*, 676-77.

67. His conclusion that the Gospel of John was written by the apostle himself and that the New Testament canon was datable to the first century placed him out of sympathy with historical-critical research and its exponents. Nonetheless, he was nominated three times for the Nobel Prize for literature, in 1902, 1904 and 1908.

68. See Class, *Ideale und Güter*.

69. In view of Oman's subsequent Cambridge career, it is of interest to note that Merx was to devote much of his later research to the Sinaitic Palimpsest discovered in 1892 by the distinguished Cambridge scholar, Agnes Smith Lewis.

70. The historical romances which Hausrath published under the pseudonym George Taylor are dull and ideological. In 1901, he would publish a biography of Heinrich von Treitschke who had died five years before, depicting Treitschke as an Achilles or young Siegfried, who "retained the . . . joy and sunshine of eternal youth." An impassioned apostle of violence and race hatred, Treitschke advocated an authoritarian power politics, with the state as the center of the lives of its citizens. Hausrath's biography would doubtless contribute to making Germany receptive to National Socialism.

71. Hinz, *Aus der Geschichte*, 151.

72. Following Ferdinand Christian Baur (1792-1860), who rigorously applied Hegel's theory of dialectic to the development of the early Church, arguing that second-century Christianity represented a "catholic" synthesis of Jewish (Petrine) and Gentile (Pauline) Christianity. By the 1840s this theory was losing ground to historical analysis.

written a biography of D. F. Strauss,[73] and we may assume that *Das Leben Jesu*[74] would have figured on the syllabus. While it is probable that Oman had already read the work, which was the bête noire of Scottish theologians in the mid-nineteenth century, leaving many a childhood evangelical faith in tatters,[75] his desire "to speak the gospel to the seekers and the tremblers of their fretful age"[76] would have led him to sympathize with any attempt to confront the challenges of industrial society and aggressive naturalism and to seek Christ anew in the Gospels. He would have seen from his term in Erlangen how Albrecht Ritschl's three-volume *Rechtfertigung und Versöhnung* (The Christian Doctrine of Justification and Reconciliation) had put the work of Christ back on the agenda of German Protestant theology.

The immediate impact of these scholars upon Oman is hard to gauge, given the lack of any surviving letters, but we may deduce from his authoritative overview of German, French and English theology, *The Problem of Faith and Freedom in the last two centuries*,[77] that Frank introduced him to later interpretations of Schleiermacher and, as a critical partner, to Albrecht Ritschl (1822–89),[78] each of whom would affect Oman's theological thinking profoundly. Accordingly, a brief sketch of Frank's thinking will follow.

Professor Frank taught Church History and Systematic Theology in Erlangen from 1857, and was largely influenced by his mentor Johann von Hofmann (1810–77), who was widely read in Scotland and "drew scores of international students to Erlangen."[79] "Frank," Oman writes, "considers Hofmann the greatest theologian since Schleiermacher, and if intellectual resource and originality are the tests, his opinion is not indefensible."[80] He records that Hofmann, though confessionally a conservative Lutheran,

> had no intention of restoring the past undefended and unchanged. While acknowledging that his religious life was deeply rooted in the existing religious institutions, he maintained an attitude of

73. Hausrath, *David Friedrich Strauss*.

74. Strauss, *Leben Jesu*. It was described by the Earl of Shaftesbury as "the most pestilential book ever vomited out of the jaws of hell."

75. Robert Rainy and A. B. Bruce were each profoundly unsettled as students.

76. Statham, "Dogma and History," 172.

77. Below, 168–83.

78. Frank published *Über die kirchliche Bedeutung der Theologie Albrecht Ritschls* (On the ecclesial importance of Albrecht Ritschl's theology) in 1888, and *Zur theologie Albrecht Ritschls* (On the theology of Albrecht Ritschl) (3rd ed., 1891).

79. Statham, "Dogma and History,"

80. Oman, *Faith and Freedom*, 344. Karl Barth considered Hofmann to be the greatest conservative Protestant theologian of the nineteenth century (Barth, *Protestant Theology*, 610, 608).

> freedom towards them as much as any liberal theologian. The only regard for the past he cared for was to maintain the growing life and thought of the Church that had nurtured him.[81]

Hofmann's theology is based on "the freedom which comes from a new relation to God."[82] A living faith stems from the experienced fact of being united with Christ as Lord and Redeemer. But this is far from pietistic subjectivism. Oman elaborates: though "all real conviction is in this way from within, yet it is no real conviction unless it rest on something without. The true revelation of God is history."[83] And this revelation in history is unfolded in Scripture. For Hofmann, Scripture was to be understood both as world history and as salvation history with Christ at the center. It is future oriented "because it sees into the inner meaning of events and finds the creative beginnings of the Kingdom of God. It is, therefore, not to be regarded as a repository of texts, but as an organism to be brought to bear as a whole upon the whole system of truth."[84] We may note in passing here that this has implications for biblical interpretation; Hofmann's hermeneutical reflections, based on Schleiermacher, were to influence Heidegger, Gadamer, and Paul Ricoeur.

Oman concludes, approvingly: "We find a wonderful unity of history and truth, so that the essential thing in history, which is the unfolding of sonship to God, repeats itself in the heart of man just as it was first wrought by God." History is given meaning and unity by viewing it from the end, not the beginning; the end is already given in Jesus. So there is a future, eschatological dimension. "But history is also fulfilment, and Christ stands at the centre as the . . . beginning of its fulfilment. . . . His obedience, which endured the assaults of evil . . . made a new order of things possible; and He founded the new society which is God's witness to the peoples, to carry out this new order."

All this is grounded in divine love, the cause of God's free decision to realize a new humanity in Jesus, thereby reconciling the world to himself. Through God's grace, world history is then seen as part of salvation history.

As Statham has shown, Hofmann's theological method "took seriously the Protestant religious experience of sin and grace. He intended the resolutely historical understanding of revelation at the heart of his version of salvation history to secure the old Protestant esteem for Scripture's unique revelatory function and normative authority in Christ."[85]

---

81. Oman, *Faith and Freedom*, 344.
82. Oman, *Faith and Freedom*, 345.
83. Oman, *Faith and Freedom*, 345.
84. Oman, *Faith and Freedom*, 346.
85. Statham, "Dogma and History," 135.

These two emphases, subjective regeneration and salvation history, were the pillars of the system of Frank, who mainly "work[ed] with Hofmann's suggestions."[86] He adopted an apologetic approach to systematic theology,[87] with the aim of making faith secure, and sought to integrate Schleiermacher within traditional orthodoxy.[88]

Although Oman felt that Frank's systematic analysis "may be open to question," nonetheless he acknowledged the "vitality of a new religious life" which "insists that to be in God we must be of God after the practical fashion of living above our world and above ourselves." This is "the summit of experience, with all the soul has won from the past and all it experiences in the present and all it anticipates from the future."[89]

However, Oman parted company with Frank over his interpretation of justification. For Frank, God's love was "only one of many equal attributes and the Kingdom only one of many ends."[90] In his eyes, justice should not be subordinated to love nor should justification be considered merely in reference to the kingdom of God. Oman takes issue with this.

> The belief that love is supreme in God is, moreover, necessary for our freedom on the one hand and for any sure estimate of what is divine on the other, while the equality of justice with love is not necessary for maintaining that solemn sense of the majesty of the moral order which made it for Kant the supreme object of reverence.[91]

Here, Oman shows congruity with the system of Albrecht Ritschl, who regarded love as "God's supreme attribute and His Kingdom as His personal end."[92] In Ritschl's eyes, Frank's notion of an absolute God was "a metaphysical idol," incompatible with a Christian conception of a living, personal, loving God.[93] So to Ritschl we now turn.

There is no indication that Oman met or heard Ritschl lecture, but during his months as a student in Erlangen and Heidelberg, Ritschl was

---

86. Oman, *Faith and Freedom*, 347.

87. In his *System der Christlichen Gewissheit*, 1870–873 (System of Christian certainty) and his *System der Christlichen Wahrheit* 1878–80 (System of Christian truth), followed by *System der Christlichen Sittlichkeit* 1884–1887 (System of Christian morality), each title consisting of two volumes.

88. Oman, *Faith and Freedom*, 347.

89. Oman, *Faith and Freedom*, 348.

90. Oman, *Faith and Freedom*, 390.

91. Oman, *Faith and Freedom*, 391.

92. Oman, *Faith and Freedom*, 390.

93. Oman, *Faith and Freedom*, 363.

making a profound impression on German thought, as professor of Systematic Theology in Göttingen.

> He was a child of the Union of the Lutheran and Reformed Churches, a vigorous defender of the Protestantism that went with it, and a trenchant critic of the High Lutheran assumption of being the only true Church. The true Church exists, he held, wherever the Christian moral life is set up through faith in Christ.[94]

One of Ritschl's deepest convictions is that we possess authentic faith only as we are living it out in the activities of obedience. For Ritschl, as for Kant, the kingdom was understood as the exercise of the moral life in society, identified in individual religious experience, and in the gradual realization on earth of an ideal society. This led him to challenge Hofmann for making subjective experience the foundation of the truths of theology, on the grounds that such individualism was not social; theology had to have community and be saved from individualism by turning to its historical source, the spiritual movement founded by Jesus Christ, whom Ritschl interpreted as a world-affirming teacher of universal love. While Ritschl was charged with bringing the Christian faith too close to the modern world,[95] his ethical interpretation of the gospel, and his understanding that faith in God was related to a moral duty to serve other human beings, had a significant impact in Scotland and would "appeal strongly to the activist and progressive temper of the age."[96]

On 10 November 1883, shortly after Oman's return to Edinburgh, Ritschl delivered a widely publicized address at the University of Göttingen, which made a significant contribution to the wider nineteenth-century debate on Luther and modernity.[97] In demonstrating that Luther's interpretation of Christian faith was a culturally significant force in contemporary society, Ritschl refused to endorse either exaggerated claims about Luther, or anti-Luther diatribes, but placed a strong emphasis on the world as part of God's plan.[98] The cosmopolitan, Enlightenment overtones of his discourse militated against any identification with the *Volk*. This speech widened the

---

94. Oman, *Faith and Freedom*, 353.

95. Karl Barth described Ritschl dismissively as "the very epitome of the national-liberal bourgeois in the age of Bismarck." Barth, *Protestant Theology*, 642. James Orr was vociferously opposed to Ritschl's claim that religious and theoretical knowledge are mutually exclusive: Scorgie, *Call for Continuity*, 55–78.

96. Drummond and Bulloch, *Church in Late Victorian Scotland*, 179.

97. Svenson, "Theology for the Bildungsbürgertum," 205, 221–27.

98. Spencer, *Kulturprotestantismus*, 519–49.

rift between himself and his ultra-conservative colleague, Professor Paul Lagarde,[99] who saw Luther as an "insignificant sectarian" who undermined true German culture and hindered the German people from becoming a vehicle of divine revelation.

Oman believed that the shape of conversation with other voices was constantly changing, and that conclusions reached were always provisional.[100] He knew that "one of the greatest and most difficult labours is to carry on the work of our predecessors without being burdened by it, and to inherit it without being fettered."[101] Even though he engaged with Ritschl's thinking, notably in *Grace and Personality*, and drew extensively on *Rechtfertigung und Versöhnung* in his lectures on theology to students at Westminster College, he recognized that

> Ritschl, no more than any of his successors, has spoken the final word. His method, nevertheless, sums up the result of this long discussion in a way not to be ignored ... we must accept the very thing which to so many has been the chief rock of offence. We must recognise not only the right but the duty of untrammelled investigation laid upon us by personal freedom in God.[102]

99. Lagarde was a distinguished orientalist and a rabid anti-Semite.
100. Oman, *Natural and Supernatural*, 117.
101. Oman, *Office of the Ministry*.
102. Oman, *Faith and Freedom*, 395.

5

Ministry

Probationer

ON WEDNESDAY, 21 APRIL 1886, the Edinburgh University Spring graduation ceremony was held with "a large attendance of students and friends"[1] in the Synod Hall, Castle Terrace. Eighteen graduands were awarded the BD degree, amongst them John Wood Oman, MA. That same year, he was transferred from the Presbytery of Orkney to Edinburgh Presbytery "with a note of his trials for licence,"[2] and placed on the UP list of probationers. So began a period of transition marking the final testing stage of his call to ministry. As a probationer, his role was clearly defined. He was "authorized to preach, but not to dispense the sacraments . . . the title 'Reverend' is only given to him by courtesy and never in official documents; he wears the pulpit gown, but not the bands."[3] Oman was now in the hands of a small committee who allocated vacant churches to candidates, usually several candidates being introduced to the same pastorate at the same time.[4] Dr. James Brown suggests in his *Life of a Scottish Probationer* that "there is an air of romance about the wandering life to which the UP probationer is at once

1. *Glasgow Herald*, 22 April 1886.
2. Synodical Minutes of Orkney, United Associate Presbytery, UP, OCR 1/5, 11 and 68.
3. Brown, *Life of a Scottish Probationer*, 79.
4. *Paisley and Renfrewshire Gazette*, 10 September 1887, records that five candidates had been proposed for a vacancy at Johnstone, and that the votes counted were: 13, 127, 4, 17, 18.

introduced. He is sent east and west, north and south, at the bidding of the committee. He sees new cities, and unexplored districts of country become familiar to him. He has large opportunities of acquainting himself with various men and various manners."[5] But the understanding was always that the office was temporary; that this itinerancy would come to an end when the probationer accepted a call from a local congregation. The practice was that, after the licentiate had preached "with a view" on two Sundays, the congregation would decide whether or not to issue a call to ministry. But those who were licensed to preach often had to wait several years before receiving a call to a pastorate, and this would prove a severe test of their vocation.[6] David S. Cairns, nephew of John Cairns, was licensed in 1892, but was then unsuccessful in sixteen vacancies before he was finally called in 1895 to the UP church in Ayton.[7] Oman likewise had to wait almost four years for a call to be issued. It is probable that, like Cairns, he would have felt that "it was rather an anxious and depressing experience. . . . And it may have been wholesome but it was extremely unpleasant to be found wanting by so many congregations of worthy people."[8]

Various factors contributed to such delays. In his autobiography, Cairns indicates that "for probationers it was rather a bare period," suggesting that the number of students at the UP Hall in those years was "above the average owing to the remaining influence of Moody's second visit to Scotland which . . . left a very deep mark on the lives of many young people."[9] Adam Hood draws on UP Synod records to show how during Oman's time at the UP Hall there were so many students in ministerial training that it would have been difficult for them all to find a vacant pastorate.[10] He further indicates how, from 1880 on, the UP Church was exploring the possibility of deploying an increasing number of students in the Presbyterian Church of England.[11]

---

5. Brown, *Life of a Scottish Probationer*, 83.

6. Brown recalls how the Reverend James Smith Candlish (1835–97), from 1872 professor of Systematic Theology at the Free Church College, Glasgow, and a doughty defender of William Robertson Smith, "nearly lost heart before a sphere of work was found for him." *Life of a Scottish Probationer*, 174.

7. David [S.] Cairns, *Autobiography*, 12.

8. David [S.] Cairns, *Autobiography*, 153.

9. David [S.] Cairns, *Autobiography*, 123.

10. In 1883, out of 123 students in the UP Hall, 114 were training for the ministry. Hood, "God's All-Conquering Love," 144.

11. There was a close relationship between the two traditions. In 1876 the UP had given up 110 congregations which united with the English Presbyterian Church to form the PCE. (See above, 81.)

And in 1888, perhaps as a way of easing the situation, the Hall professors petitioned Synod to allow probationers to take up assistantships.[12]

In his classic account of the "life of a Scottish probationer," James Brown points to one further drawback in the system: "it inevitably leads congregations to judge of men too exclusively by their pulpit gifts. Inquiries into scholarly attainments and general ability are not so common as in the other churches. There is not the same opportunity for men of high culture, who lack to some extent the power of effective utterance, attaining a position where their gifts can be used for the general good of the church."[13]

As we have seen, Oman's achievement as a preacher was hard won. "During these months," Alexander writes, "[Oman] preached in a number of vacant churches in Scotland, but his lack of what is known as a 'good delivery' did not make up for the oft recognised quality of his sermons."[14] He contrasts the confidence and authority with which his friend later came to address "men of all churches, less in Scotland than in England, where lines are more sharply drawn," with these early critical years when "great thinking strove with limitations of oral expression, in circumstances where the value of the latter could not be despised and, as far as his chosen profession was concerned, narrowly escaped defeat."[15] We do not know whether, like many another "under the influence of 'hope deferred,' he was looking about for some other avenue of usefulness."[16]

Makerstoun

But we do know that Oman had two appointments over this intervening period, very different in character from one another. In that they will have contributed to his ministerial formation, it is worth examining them more closely. For a few months in 1887, he was put in charge of a recently founded UP preaching station in Makerstoun, a rural estate village about four miles south-west of Kelso, by the rich fishing stretches of the river Tweed. In 1881 the population was 361 and falling steadily; with few exceptions, most lived in farm houses or workmen's cottages, in relative poverty.[17] There was a

---

12. Hood, "God's All-Conquering Love," 144.
13. Brown, *Life of a Scottish Probationer*, 82.
14. Alexander, "Memoir of the Author," xix.
15. Alexander, "Memoir of the Author," xvi.
16. Tait, *Two Centuries*, 241.
17. The Established Presbytery of Kelso was scornful of their "declared inability, through the poverty of the parish, to prosecute their case" (*Edinburgh Evening News*, 8 July 1886).

public school, a parish church and cemetery and a Free Church built and endowed by the landowner, Miss Maria Georgina Scott Makdougall [sic]. Miss Makdougall had inherited the estate five years after her baptism in Dublin Street Baptist Church, Kelso, and we are told that "the duties and responsibilities of her position as a Christian believer became one of the guiding principles of her new life. In the twenty-seven years that followed,[18] Bible Study, extraordinary liberality, gracious hospitality, and temperance enterprise received Christian interpretation."[19] She kept a close eye on the spiritual well-being of her estate workers and their families, for whom she built a Gospel Hall attached to the House, serviced by "preachers from far and near." The house steward "ran a psalmody class and frequently gave the exhortation. Believers from among the families in the estate were baptised in the river Tweed . . . [which] received the contents of the wine cellar."[20]

All was not at ease, however, in this small Border village. A viciously orchestrated campaign to get rid of the young minister of the Established Church, the Reverend Philip Bainbridge, had come to a head in 1886. Unsubstantiated rumors of his "habitual drunkenness" took hold easily in a small population imbued by their landowner with the virtues of temperance. Many people stopped attending Sunday services, the Kirk Session resigned and Sunday School and Bible class were suspended. A libel was issued by Frederick Galloway, teacher at Makerstoun public school and erstwhile session clerk, and Bainbridge was condemned by the Presbytery of Kelso. However, protesting his innocence, he appealed to General Assembly where cogent testimony in his support was given amongst others by Mr. Dobbie, the Free Church minister, the local doctor, and Bainbridge's sister-in-law, who affirmed significantly that as a Yorkshireman "he speaks with an English accent and in a manner . . . not familiar . . . to agricultural workers here. He speaks at all times rather slowly."[21] The General Assembly, convening as court, overturned the verdict of the Presbytery and absolved Bainbridge of all charges.

Those who had left the Parish Church then held a meeting in Makerstoun public school "for the purpose of considering the advisability of forming a preaching station in the parish, under the auspices of the UP Presbytery of Kelso."[22] While the Established Presbytery of Kelso made

18. She died on 14 May 1890 at the age of 86.
19. Little, "Baptist Church, Kelso."
20. Little, "Baptist Church, Kelso."
21. McIntosh, *Presbytery of Makerstoun*, 197.
22. *Edinburgh Evening News*, 12 June 1886. The link with the UP was already well established. By 1836, a "considerable number of communicants" at Kelso (Burgher) church came from Makerstoun (Small, *History of the Congregations*, 2, 264).

disapproving "remarks" about the seceders, the UP Presbytery approved their "spirit and zeal" and agreed to "take all necessary steps in securing a stated supply of services and the organisation of a Sabbath school in the district."[23] In consequence a UP preaching station was opened in 1886 in the public school, the fourth place of worship in the small community.

This is the enterprise to which Oman was sent the following year. It was a challenging situation, given the implacable behavior of the seceders towards their previous minister, their indignation at being thwarted by General Assembly and the fact that Mr. Bainbridge remained minister of the parish church. There is no indication that Oman had a designated mentor, although Alexander tells us that he was able to "renew association" with Thomas Kirkwood, his former minister in Stromness, who now ministered in Kelso.[24] There were, however, compensations. It was during these few months that Oman began a friendship with David S. Cairns of the manse of Stichill, "which," as Cairns writes, "to my great profit lasted till his death more than half a century later in the fulness of his years."[25] The fact that Oman lodged in Kelso and regularly "had to walk to and fro for his services"[26] would not have presented any problems to someone who was accustomed to walking long distances. But in Makerstoun he had to relate on a short-term basis to a recently formed UP congregation in need of reconciliation, with little scope for mission in a small population already served by three other churches. "He was not sorry" Alexander tells us,[27] "when his time there came to an end."

Paisley

Oman's second appointment was another matter entirely. It began in October 1887, when he moved to Paisley to assist Dr. James Brown, minister of St James's Church. Alexander testifies that "in Oman he found a man after his own heart and Oman always looked back happily on his time in Paisley." It enriched his pastoral experience and gave him the opportunity to learn from "one of the leading men in the Church, a man of great charm, [with] a

23. *Edinburgh Evening News*, 16 June 1886. For the leading role played by the UP church in "promoting temperance sentiment," see Woodside, *Soul of a Scottish Church*, 219–22.

24. The UP church had recently been rebuilt with a substantial disbursement by Mrs. Renton Mein, daughter of the late minister and mother of Benjamin Mein. It was opened by Principal Cairns on 29 October 1886.

25. Cairns, *Autobiography*, 79.

26. Alexander, "Memoir of the Author," xix.

27. Alexander, "Memoir of the Author," xix.

large and attached congregation."[28] It would appear that one of Oman's first commissions there was to assist Dr. Brown in making preparations for a week of special evangelistic services led by the five Synod Evangelistic Deputies, and on 30 October he and Dr. Brown together conducted the Sabbath evening meeting which brought the week's events to a close.[29]

When the church's missioner, David Duff, left in November for "an appointment in Helensburgh,"[30] Oman succeeded him immediately and for the next two years, he was placed in charge of the St James's Mission.[31] He earned his stipend.[32] The Directors reported in 1888 that "Mr Oman . . . has shown himself to be an able and indefatigable worker. [He] has been untiring in his devotion to our interests in the district and nothing has been awanting, on his part, to make the work of the Mission successful, and a blessing to those for whom it is especially intended."[33] Activities of the mission included a Sabbath school with 150 registered scholars, and an average attendance of 94, held every Sunday morning at 10:00 in the Church Hall, a Sabbath evening meeting, with increasing numbers of young men, enlivened by a choir of boys and girls from the morning school, and a Mothers' Meeting conducted by "ladies," where "attendance has not been so encouraging as it might have been." In his "Missionary's Report,"[34] Oman also refers to his "visiting among the non-church going" where he was aided by "a number of ladies, who distribute among the people of the district a monthly tract." Aware of the fact that those new to churchgoing needed encouragement, he states: "It would greatly encourage the work if some additional visitors could be found who would not only call for the people, but attend the meeting along with them." And he concludes: "Progress is slow, but on the whole it is progress, which, considering the nature of the work, is matter for gratitude." There follows a robust challenge to the church, not without an element of rebuke:

> Meantime it must be confessed that to undo the indifference of a lifetime is not an easy matter for common mortals. If churches

28. Alexander, "Memoir of the Author," xix.

29. St James's United Presbyterian Church, Reports for year ended 31 March 1888.

30. In 1891, having "turned aside from the probationer life to the educational profession," he edited a volume of his late father's lectures on the *History of the Christian Church During the First Centuries*. Small, *History of the Congregations*, 1, 237.

31. Established on 28 October 1885, with the appointment of David Duff as missionary.

32. £25.00 a quarter. St James's United Presbyterian Church, Reports for the year ended 31 March 1888.

33. St James's UP Church, Reports for the year ended 31 March 1888.

34. St James's UP Church, Reports for the year ended 31 March 1888, 26.

sit with their hands folded for generations they have no right to expect to make up for lost time by one day's work, especially if it be one of by no means superhuman exertion. Considering, therefore, how little of "a pull together" our work has been, we have rather reason to thank God for its success than to grumble at the small result. The Sabbath School especially is prosperous, and through it the rest is ultimately to be attained. If we, the professedly Christian people, had but Christ's spirit of humility and love towards which the poor and sinful naturally seek, we should have less reason to complain against buildings and the other external machinery. Till then these are comfortable reasons which, being to some extent valid, may be allowed to stand.

There are indeed indications elsewhere in the reports, both by the directors of the missions and the minister, of a sense of complacency in the congregation in its attitude to the missionary work. While we cannot exclude the possibility that some were suffering from buildings fatigue—it was only four years since their new church was opened—we may wonder whether the generous philanthropic disbursements made by Sir Peter Coats, the thread magnate, and the practical involvement of his family in the work[35] may have diminished a sense of general responsibility.

Oman's Missionary's Report is his first known published writing. Whereas, in keeping with the genre, the other church reports are factual, objective, and largely dispassionate, the tone of Oman's report is different. There is an abrupt directness in his challenge to the members of St James. And a desire to rouse the Church to an awareness of the urgent need to respond to the needs of those outside its walls was to be a distinctive feature of his future ministry.

The church clearly bore Oman no ill-will for his directness. On the contrary, he was much appreciated. Not only did he sustain the work of the mission but for nine months, it also fell to him to sustain the everyday ministry of the church. Dr. Brown testified at the ordination dinner in Alnwick to the fact that, in Paisley,

---

35. Coats was "a pillar in the congregation." Generous in his philanthropy, he had gifted most of the £29,000 required to build the handsome new church, with sittings for 1,100 worshippers. Designed by Hippolyte Blanc, in early French Gothic style, it was opened by Principal Cairns on 1 March 1884. In 1888, Peter Coats junior was treasurer of Wallneuk Mission, to the north of Paisley, the older of the two St James missions, where he and his brother George were both directors. Archibald Coats was one of the Church managers and joint vice-president of the Missionary Society, and Mrs. George Coats was a collector.

he [Mr. Oman] had had a great deal more work put upon him than he bargained to do, on account of an unfortunate illness which he [the speaker] had, and which lasted for nine months, and kept him entirely away from duty. With unwearied perseverance, he did the whole of the work, and the result of his doing so much work and doing it so heartily was that when he returned he found that he had thoroughly established himself in the confidence of a pretty large congregation.[36]

Mr. George Knox, elder, spoke on the same occasion of how "during the protracted illness of Dr Brown, it had been their privilege to benefit by the teaching of Mr Oman's richly stored mind and which was a happy blending of culture, spirituality and human sympathy. Many had not failed to recognise that power which had been earnest, thoughtful and wide." It was reported of his farewell meeting in Paisley in December 1889, that his "popularity and well proven ability were testified to by the large congregation which had assembled on the previous night to listen to his parting discourse, which was both able and eloquent. Mr Oman had many friends in their midst."[37]

Dr. Brown also saw "the large turn-out" on this occasion as "indicative of the esteem and respect in which Mr Oman was held by the congregation. . . . In his visitation and mission work from house to house . . . he showed an unwearied devotion to duty which could not fail to win the admiration of all. His kindness and attention to the poor, the sick and the dying, would long be remembered by those whose privilege it had been to enjoy them."[38] Of Oman's preaching, Dr. Brown said, "I have seldom heard a young man who was so much a 'young' man in his pulpit appearance as Mr Oman has proved himself to be." In token of "friendship and indebtedness," Oman was then presented with handsome gifts from the congregation: a gold watch and "a standard work on German theology in sixteen volumes,"[39] which he himself had chosen, as well as three volumes of Bishop Lightfoot's commentaries,[40] from his colleagues in the Mission Sabbath School. In response, Oman said that

36. *Alnwick Guardian*, 21 December 1889.
37. *Paisley and Renfrewshire Gazette*, 21 December 1889.
38. *Paisley and Renfrewshire Gazette*, 21 December 1889.
39. I am unable to identify such a standard work in 16 volumes, and the *Alnwick Guardian*, 21 December 1889, specifies, possibly more convincingly: "sixteen volumes of theological works."
40. J. B. Lightfoot, *Paul's Epistle to the Galatians* (1865), *Philippians* (1868), *Colossians and Philemon* (1875), which demonstrate the first-century origin of the New Testament and demolish the Tübingen School of biblical criticism.

despite the many fair prospects of future success so graphically described by Dr Brown and Mr Knox, the present occasion looked like the crowning point of his life. It had been a special privilege to be with Dr Brown in his time of adversity as well as prosperity, and he would always look back upon these two years as two of the most fruitful years of his life.[41]

Oman's calling had been shaped and nurtured by the experience of ministry in a congregation where he was loved and appreciated. He worked with a senior colleague whom he admired, and with whose pastoral, evangelistic and teaching ministry he had much in common. He had proved himself, to quote Dr. Brown, "a most capable and indefatigable worker, who has the power not only of working himself, but of inducing others to work with him, and whose power as a preacher is warmly appreciated by many."[42]

Pastoral Ministry

Call, Ordination and Induction

To put the events about to be chronicled into perspective we need now to turn to Clayport Church, Alnwick, Northumberland, where at the annual congregational meeting held on Monday, 28 January 1889, a statement from the minister, the Reverend William Limont, was read by the clerk.[43] As Limont had already intimated to the session, "after long and serious consideration the time had come when from failing health and long service[44] he now found himself unable to continue the sole care of the congregation and that he wished to ask the congregation for a colleague and successor." In the interests of his successor, he would relinquish his stipend, while retaining free use of the manse and the garden. This request was granted unanimously by the congregation and Presbytery who "expressed themselves very kindly towards Mr Limont." It was agreed to "apply for supply of preachers for a month, to pay £1/10/- per Sabbath inclusive of railway fare" and "to enquire

---

41. *Alnwick and County Gazette*, Saturday, 21 December, 1889.

42. St James United Presbyterian Church, Reports for the year ended March 1888, Pastoral Letter.

43. UPC Clayport Street, Alnwick, minutes of session (see bibliography).

44. This had been Mr. Limont's sole charge. Ordained and inducted as successor to Dr. John Ker, to Clayport Church (then UP) on 23 December 1851, he now felt unable to preach and visit regularly.

after suitable accommodation for the preachers with the rate of board and lodging including washing."[45]

On 23 February 1889, the *Alnwick Guardian* announced that candidates for the vacancy would be heard on the next and following Sundays. On 16 April 1889, it is recorded that after 5 May, when the current supply of preachers ended "they would apply . . . to the UP for a supply."[46] On 2 July, they decided to "go on hearing candidates" and to hold a congregational meeting in August to see if the congregation was "ready to go forward to a moderation in a call."[47] On 30 September, Mr. James Frater, clerk of the adjoined congregational meeting, reported that "the congregation is ready to apply to the Presbytery for a moderation in a call to one to be a colleague and successor to the present minister."[48] From then on, the matter was relatively expeditious. The Presbytery having agreed, a meeting was called for the evening of Monday, 14 October.[49] Those entitled to vote sat in the body of the church and others in the balcony, while the Reverend W. Rogerson of Warkworth conducted proceedings. The congregation had heard a number of preachers over the previous six months, three of whom were then nominated from the floor of the meeting and seconded. These included John Oman who was nominated by Luke Scott, the session clerk, and seconded by Alderman Robertson. By a show of hands, Oman received fifty-six votes, Mr. E. H. E. Franks, fifteen, and Mr. John Forsyth, forty-four. Franks having been eliminated, Oman then received fifty-eight votes and Forsyth, fifty-seven. On Mr. Rogerson expressing the hope that those in the minority would assent, a large majority of hands were raised and the call to Mr. John W. Oman, MA, BD, to be colleague and successor to the Reverend William Limont was signed then and the following Sunday by 124 members with the concurrence of twenty-seven adherents.[50]

A deputation from Clayport attended the next Presbytery meeting on 1 November 1889, which after some discussion, unanimously decided to sanction the call, and during the meeting a telegram arrived from Oman to state that if the call were sustained, he would accept it. One final hurdle remained: "the trials for ordination." At the next meeting of the Presbytery, at Morpeth on 3 December, we are told that "Mr John Oman MA BD delivered

---

45. UPC Clayport Street, Alnwick, minutes of session.
46. UPC Clayport Street, Alnwick, minutes of session.
47. UPC Clayport Street, Alnwick, minutes of session.
48. UPC Clayport Street, Alnwick, minutes of session.
49. The following account is based on the *Alnwick Guardian*, 19 October 1889.
50. Oman would tell, against himself, that he was called "by a majority of 1." MacArthur, *Setting up Signs*, 21.

trial discourses and was examined in Hebrew, Greek, Church History, and Theology, after which these exercises were sustained."[51] The way was now clear for Oman to be ordained and inducted on Thursday afternoon, 19 December 1889, as colleague and successor to the Reverend William Limont, minister of Clayport Church, Alnwick.

He was supported by a "numerous congregation." Amongst the guests were two former ministers of Stromness, Thomas Kirkwood from Kelso and David Woodside from Woodlands, Glasgow; James Brown, from St James's Paisley, and David Hall from Mossvale, Paisley;[52] and amongst the contingent from the Northumberland Presbytery, "it was a special pleasure" to have his long-standing friend, Benjamin Mein, who had been ordained at Thropton the previous year (above, 51–52). George Alexander, who also was present, remarked how "it helped [Oman] greatly to have his old friend so near and to have his guidance while yet a stranger to the Presbytery, to both its members and its ways of working."[53] But perhaps most notable of all was the fact that Simon and Isabella Oman, his parents, had braved the rigors of the Pentland Firth in winter to attend, "as well as some other of his relations," who, Mr. Kirkwood suggested, "no doubt were glad at seeing that the good hand of God had brought their son and brother to this place."[54]

Before proceedings began, the Reverend William Rogerson "read the usual notice from the Presbytery to the members of the Congregation that if any of them had any objection to the character or doctrine of Mr Oman, they should at once repair to the vestry, where the Presbytery were met."[55] No objections having been raised, the Reverend Mr. Conway of Wooler preached "an eloquent sermon" on 1 Corinthians 1:22–23. The "steps taken" were stated, and the "questions of the Formula" were put to Oman by the moderator, who then offered the ordination prayer with laying on of hands. This was followed by the "shaking of hand by each member of Presbytery and welcome to the ministry of the church."[56] Then the moderator gave the charge to "the newly made minister with a few words of earnest counsel bearing upon his life and work. The Rev. A. H. Drysdale then addressed the congregation on submission to their new pastor, beseeching them to

---

51. *Alnwick and County Gazette*, 7 December 1889.

52. The congregation was the product of the missionary efforts of St James's to a destitute part of Paisley. Hall, its second minister, was ordained on 7 June 1887 (Small, *History of the Congregations*, 2, 528).

53. Alexander, "Memoir of the Author," xx.

54. *Alnwick and County Gazette*, 21 December 1889.

55. *Alnwick Guardian*, 21 December 1889.

56. *Alnwick and County Gazette*, 21 December 1889. The quotations following in this and the next paragraph are from the same source.

give him opportunities and encouragement to make himself a thoroughly equipped occupier of his post. At the conclusion of the service, most of the members of the congregation filed past the foot of the pulpit and shook hands with the Reverend John Wood Oman."

Afterwards, we are told, "a splendid repast was held at the White Swan Hotel for all ministers, friends and relatives and guests from Alnwick" presided over by William Limont. Dr. Brown gave the chief toast, to the newly ordained minister. "He said the intimate acquaintance of more than two years with Mr Oman as a colleague entitled him to bear testimony to his worth. He referred to the esteem in which he was held by the congregation at Paisley. He spoke of Mr Oman as a man of high culture and great moral worth, and hinted that his abilities might soon call him to more important spheres than Clayport Church, Alnwick." In response, Oman "made reference to the pleasure of his association with Dr Brown, and the value of the training he had received under him." At six o'clock, around 750 people sat down to "an enjoyable afternoon tea" in the Corn Exchange, after which all the ministers went to the platform with Mr. Limont in the chair, to hear "anthems and pieces of sacred music" sung by the combined choirs of St James, Pottergate, known as the "English Presbyterian church," and Clayport. In offering his congratulations, Mr. Kirkwood gave "a few very human remarks" about the new minister: "He had watched his career through the Divinity Hall up to the present night and could bear testimony to the unvaried dignity and courtesy Mr Oman had shown all through and likewise to his brilliant talents as well as to his common sense.... He felt sure that when Mr Oman was in the pulpit he would give them solid and truthful sermons."

On behalf of "the ladies of the congregation," Mr. Balmbra, manager of the savings bank and a staunch member of Clayport, then presented Oman with a preaching gown. In responding, Oman

> said it was a symbol of the teacher, not as was generally supposed of the preacher. It had long been worn by those who set themselves to expound the truth. It was worn in some sense by the prophets of old, but he believed their gown was not made exactly of that material—it was supposed to have been made out of goat's skin.[57]

Oman went on to appraise his new situation with realism and in unusually personal terms. The *Alnwick and County Gazette* reports:

> Mr Oman said Mr Limont was strong enough to follow his own way, and he acknowledged that he was right himself in following

---

57. *Alnwick Guardian*, 21 December 1889.

his sometimes; but he was sure they would agree though their individuality might lead them in very different directions. He hoped they would always give him that encouragement and sympathy that would be necessary and not be too hard on his feelings, for they were many. He also trusted they would always think he was doing what he could though perhaps not what he should like (applause).[58]

Amongst the speakers who followed, David Woodside said that "he thought a man growing up in the midst of such surroundings would not be half a man unless he had a character and force of will that belonged to those scenes among which their friend was reared."[59] The remark was nuanced. Woodside might have been alerting those who had ears to hear to traits of character which were delineated by Dr. Brown after his sermon the following Sunday morning. He had chosen as his text the description of John the Baptist in John 1:23, "The voice of one crying in the wilderness," which he followed by an introduction of Oman to the congregation that was so discerning that it merits extensive quotation. After speaking of Oman's years of training, Brown continued:

> He comes to you, therefore, thoroughly educated, a man qualified by hard intellectual training to grapple with the questions which in those days of unrest are pressing for solution. He comes to you as no novice, but has learned how to apply his learning and the power of thought which he has acquired in his studies to the actual every-day needs of simple men and women struggling in the battle of life and face to face with the realities of eternity. This is not a place for exaggerated praise or for the complimentary words that it is pleasant to speak of a young man entering on his work. I do not speak of Mr Oman's talents and learning—they will gradually unfold themselves to you as the years go on. All I wish to testify is that he is a real man, who never, as far as my experience goes, speaks a word he does not believe and feel, and who never shrinks from speaking any words that it is his duty to speak because it may offend some hearers. He is a man of independent mind, sees with his own eyes, and elucidates the truth for himself. He does not belong to any of the schools of theology, either orthodox or heterodox, he is a seeker after truth, and if you accept his guidance he will be a helper to your faith. He is in a word a "voice" and not an echo. I take this to be his distinctive character, and therefore I augur

---

58. *Alnwick and County Gazette*, 21 December 1889.
59. *Alnwick and County Gazette*, 21 December 1889.

for him a successful ministry in this place that has a record of many faithful ministries written upon its annals. I commend him to you. I wish you to bear with him. A man who is a "voice" and not an echo is often apt to speak rough words that may be misunderstood, that may give offence. I ask you to bear with him and to understand that he speaks from the heart and in the name of his Master. When you have had experience of him you will learn to know that his words are loving words, and that he is a guide whom you may safely and wisely follow.[60]

In the evening, "a large congregation listened with rapt attention" as Oman preached "a powerful sermon" on the text "O house of Jacob, come ye and let us walk in the light of the Lord" (Isa 2:5) and he was launched into his ministerial career.

The Presbyterian Church of England

He was now a minister, not of the UP as he might at one time have envisaged but of the Presbyterian Church of England (PCE), a union, ratified in 1876, between the Presbyterian Church in England and the English Synod of the United Presbyterian Church, thereby bringing together in England and in one church former members of the Free Church of Scotland and the United Presbyterian church. As Buick Knox states, "in its membership, its ministry and government, and in its practice the Presbyterian Church of England was an amalgam of many strains of Scottish Presbyterianism and even after 1876 this was the predominant mark of its life."[61]

Insofar as this was to impact on Oman's approach to ministry, a brief indication of its origin and development might be useful. The Presbyterian Church *in* England was formed in 1842 when a number of Presbyterian churches in towns and cities in England, consisting largely of immigrants from Scotland, formed themselves into an autonomous body that initially looked to the Church of Scotland. However, after the Disruption the following year, strong sympathy with the Free Church led to a distancing from the Church of Scotland and the forming of links with the Free Church.[62] There were also a significant number of former Secession churches in England, which, with

---

60. *Alnwick Guardian*, 30 December 1889.

61. Knox, "Relationship," 66.

62. When the Presbyterian Church in England founded its college in London in 1844, it looked initially to the Free Church for its professors.

the coming into being of the UP church in 1847, were some of its strongest congregations, many within Presbyteries that straddled the Border.[63]

Overtures for union between these bodies were well received over subsequent years but they were overshadowed by protracted and inconclusive attempts in Scotland to unite the Free Church and the UP church. In 1871 it was decided at the UP English synod in Birmingham that "delays in Scotland should not be allowed to hold up union indefinitely" and "to inform the United Presbyterian General Synod that the English synod wanted an immediate union in England and that the General Synod should take the administrative steps necessary to facilitate such a union."[64]

The union was finally declared in 1876 thanks to the "Christian prudence and conspicuous ability"[65] of the Reverend J. Oswald Dykes,[66] minister of Regents Park PCE, who was chair of the negotiating committee and a former member of the Free Church of Scotland, and Professor John Cairns, who, before moving to Edinburgh in 1867, was minister of the former Secession church in Berwick,[67] and a leading ecumenical statesman.

To put this into perspective, a quick sketch will follow of the approach of the PCE to areas which proved divisive north of the Border: Establishment and the voluntary principle, and subscription to the Westminster Confession.

Church and State

The PCE had to contain within itself different attitudes to the relationship between church and State. Whereas in Scotland the Free Church was generally in favour of a national church so long as it was open to reform, the UP argued for freedom of conscience, repudiated the notion of a national church and maintained that the church should receive no financial support from the government.[68] However, as Buick Knox states, "in England this was not a live issue for Presbyterians. The Presbyterian Church in England had to be a voluntary society, living within the law of the land, entitled to

63. There were four UP Presbyteries in England: London, Lancashire, Newcastle and Carlisle (Knox, "Relationship," 57).

64. Knox, "Relationship," 63.

65. Knox, "Relationship," 60.

66. Chris Statter, "Managing the Disruptions." In 1888, Dykes was called to the Barbour Chair of Divinity and Principal of the English Presbyterian College in London, which, in 1899, relocated to Cambridge as Westminster College.

67. In 1859 the old meeting-house in Golden Square was abandoned for a stately gothic church in Wallace Green.

68. Drummond and Bulloch, *Church in Late Victorian Scotland*, 81.

no special privileges, and depending on the generosity of its members. The synod made passing references to the state but these were sympathetic gestures to the Free Church rather than practical politics in England. Practical necessity brought the Presbyterian Church in England closer to that other family of presbyterian churches to be found in cities and towns in England, namely the United Presbyterian Church."[69] The general attitude of the PCE appears to have been that, while a proper establishment of the church by the state was desirable, its absence was not an insuperable obstacle to union.

However, such compromise solutions often leave unresolved issues to surface as occasion arises: as we shall see, Oman's stance for freedom of conscience while minister of Clayport Street Church brought him to infringe the law and attracted some fierce criticism within the councils of the PCE.

The Westminster Confession: Subscription

One of the most immediate issues Oman had to face as he prepared for his ordination concerned the Formula of subscription to the Westminster Confession. There had been widespread agitation in the Presbyterian churches about this for several years. While reasons varied, it was felt by many that the truths of the gospel about the sovereign power of God's grace did not receive the same emphasis in the Confession as in the Bible. Benjamin Warfield comments: "When the formula of acceptance is such that no-one signs without some mental reservation, some soon learn to sign without reference to mental reservation, and gross heterodoxy becomes gradually safe, because there is no-one so wholly without sin that his conscience permits him to cast the first stone."[70] Alexander affirms of Oman, "it was not in him to take vows lightly."[71] So how was he able to assent with good conscience to "The questions of the Formula" on 19 December 1889?

To begin to address that question, we need to return to the UP General Synod of 22 July 1879. Two ministers, Fergus Ferguson and David MacRae, were impeached for heresy, having attracted widespread publicity for their respective challenges to the clauses in the Confession about limited atonement and eternal punishment. Ferguson was able to satisfy the Synod as to his orthodoxy, and was sent back to his flock duly admonished, whereas MacRae, who was more intransigent, was deposed from the ministry by a reluctant Synod. In reaching each of these decisions the gathering was swayed by the eloquence of Henry Calderwood. Favorably disposed

69. Knox, "Relationship," 56.
70. Warfield, "Presbyterian Churches and the Westminster Confession."
71. Alexander, "Memoir of the author," xxi.

towards Ferguson, Calderwood denounced MacRae, on the grounds "that the man who did not set forth the atoning death of Christ as the ground for the forgiveness of sin had no Gospel to preach, and should not be an accredited teacher of the United Presbyterian Church."[72] John Cairns, chair of the Committee, likewise found that MacRae's theories were incompatible with the doctrines of grace.

That same Synod took the radical decision to pass a Declaratory Act[73] glossing the Confession for catechetical purposes in seven key areas.[74]

Cairns clarified the situation: "We propose nothing in the way of repeal or abrogation or recall of the Standards. We only propose what will explain them and free them from difficulty, and also put them in such a position as will grant liberty here and there which was not formally allowed, though generally believed to be acted upon."[75] He made it plain that Calvinism in its scholastic form was not an end in itself. The Secession Church had already shown itself to be in accord with the Synod of Dort in emphasizing the universality of God's love, and Cairns recognized that the mind of the UP Church was now closer to "the evangelical Arminianism of our own times . . . which is so favorably represented by the Methodists."[76] However, though he affirmed that "the sense of grace bestowed upon the unworthy is the living pulse of all working and joyful Christianity,"[77] he remained loyal to the Calvinist roots of his church and defended the special covenant relations of the Atonement.[78]

The UP Act concluded with this clause:

---

72. Above, 58, 118.

73. With the lead of the UP Church of Scotland, Presbyterian Churches in different continents followed suit. In Scotland, after much agonizing, the Free Church authorized new forms of subscription in 1892, which were modified in 1894, and in 1905 the Church of Scotland cautiously modified its subscription to the Westminster Confession, which remained its "principal standard." In the Basis of Union (1929) these prior Declaratory Acts were incorporated into the doctrinal standards of the Established Church.

74. The doctrines of redemption, of election to eternal life, of total depravity, of salvation, as well as the authority of the Civil Magistrate, the voluntary principle, and the authority of the Standards.

75. MacEwen, *Life and Letters*, 668.

76. MacEwen, *Life and Letters*, 668.

77. MacEwen, *Life and Letters*, 669.

78. The issue had led to a major crisis in the United Secession Church in 1841 when James Morison questioned whether the doctrine of election could express the fullness of God's love. The ensuing "Atonement Controversy" led to his dismissal from the ministry of the church. See McKimmon, "The Secession and United Presbyterian Churches."

> In accordance with the practice hitherto observed in this Church, liberty of opinion is allowed on such points in the Standards, not entering into the substance of the faith, as the interpretation of the "six days" in the Mosaic account of the creation: the Church guarding against the abuse of this liberty to the injury of its unity and peace.[79]

The statement is noteworthy. In its deliberate vagueness, it allows for liberty of opinion, on matters which do not "enter into the substance of the faith," such as, for example, biblical criticism, so long as such liberty does not injure the church.[80]

This was a remarkable achievement, the first attempt in the history of Presbyterianism to review the relation of the Westminster Standards to the actual belief of the nineteenth century and, thanks largely to John Cairns' skilled chairmanship, "it was made and carried through without acrimony, party feeling, or schism."[81]

With the Free Church, however, there was an intensity of feeling that surpassed anything in the UP. The Highland Presbyteries were bitterly opposed to a similar Declaratory Act passed by the FC General Assembly in 1892, as "destroying the integrity of the Confession of Faith," and disputed the proposal to alter the Questions and Formula to bring the commitment of ordinands and office-bearers into line with the provisions of the Declaratory Act.[82] A secession of malcontents the following year led to the formation of the Free Presbyterian Church of Scotland.

Against this background in Scotland, the PCE was also, from 1883 on, "busily engaged in considering its relations to (the Westminster Confession)"[83] and a Declaratory Statement was approved in 1886. The intention, according to J. Oswald Dykes, was

> not of necessity to supersede the Westminster confession as the standard of orthodox teaching from the pulpit, yet for sundry other practical uses, as, for example, the clear presentation to the public of the Church's exact doctrinal teaching, or for the

---

79. Drummond & Bulloch, *Church in late Victorian Scotland*, 36–37.

80. This clause finds an echo in the "Statement of the Nature, Faith and Order of the United Reformed Church," 1972.

81. MacEwen, *Life and Letters*, 675. While the vote was unanimous, some of those who had wanted the Westminster Confession to be totally rewritten, like A. E. Garvie, were to leave the UP Church for the Congregational Union of Scotland.

82. Hamilton, *Erosion of Orthodoxy*, 192.

83. Warfield, "Presbyterian Churches and the Westminster Confession."

indoctrination of catechumens, or even for an intelligent profession of their faith by ruling elders and deacons.[84]

However, given the large number of former Free Church personnel in the PCE, and a possible reluctance to risk the recently achieved union falling apart so soon, the Statement was set aside and the PCE did not pursue the idea of a Declaratory Act. In 1890, however, The Twenty-Four Articles of the Faith were approved unanimously.[85] Strongly trinitarian, these had a pronounced emphasis on grace as "offer of forgiveness and eternal life to all."

Oman makes his personal attitude clear in one of his Sunday evening lectures at Clayport.[86]

> Interpreted as a historical document, interpreted according to the circumstances which gave it birth, the Confession is a very wonderful document and even a very liberal document. Even the passage on elect infants, properly read was a great step in advance. "Elect infants," it says, "are regenerated and saved by Christ through the Spirit who worketh when and where that he pleaseth." More could not be said except on a doctrine of universal restoration. . . . It was a great advance to put behind this mystery, instead of the rules of the Church, the merely mechanical and accidental distinction of being baptised or non-baptised, the gracious Spirit of God working "when and where and how he pleases."

In contrast with the medieval church which "consigned everyone outside its pale to perdition, . . . the authors of the Confession allow that persons outside the Christian faith may be subjects of God's grace in ways we cannot understand." Oman's ministry was colored by a belief in a comprehensive gospel, his preaching by an apologetic rather than a dogmatic emphasis, and his theology by the grace of God. One of his most acclaimed works, *Grace and Personality*, was "a Christian valuation of men and means, souls and things" hammered out in the "sorrow and wickedness" of the First World War,[87] and his moderatorial address to the General Assembly of the

---

84. J. O. Dykes, quoted in Warfield, "Presbyterian Churches and the Westminster Confession," 646.

85. The idea of a Declaratory Act was revived in the 1940s, but it was rapidly concluded that the best course was to draft a new Declaration of Faith, approved with difficulty in 1956.

86. MS Westminster College Archives, n.d., but from internal evidence, probably August or September 1904.

87. Oman, *Grace and Personality*, preface.

Presbyterian Church of England in June 1931 was on the theme of *The Westminster Confession*.

Clayport Street Church, Alnwick

We turn now from the collective personality of the denomination to the personality and mind-set of an individual congregation.

When Oman's ministry in Alnwick began, Alexander confirms, "he was already of ripe experience and his natural interest in all sorts and conditions of men made his new life easy to him."[88] Alnwick was a small medieval market town, dominated by the gothic castle of the Duke of Northumberland. The old market square was bounded by eighteenth- and nineteenth-century houses, some with carriage entrances, and shops. There was an air of sober prosperity. J. Lesslie Newbigin,[89] a senior manager of Clayport Street church, and secretary of the Alnwick Missionary Society for over forty years, had traded in a chemist and druggist shop in Narrowgate since the 1850s, and many other tradesmen, among them a bookseller, a watchmaker, an ironmonger, a tailor, a cabinet maker, a butcher, a fishmonger, a grocer, a draper, a jeweler, were fellow members of Clayport church, as well as a painter, an inn-keeper, a farmer, a laborer and a shepherd. From about 1893, these included also a doctor of medicine, a clerk, a reporter, a lawyer and an editor.[90] Some prominent members of the church were well-known Freemasons.[91]

The church building, described by Nikolaus Pevsner as having "two embattled polygonal towers like a gatehouse and a recessed centre with lancet windows and a gable,"[92] was built during the ministry of John Ker, subsequently Oman's tutor in pastoral theology at the UP Hall, and it succeeded the former Green Batt meeting house.[93] Ker's years there (1845–49) were

88. Alexander, "Memoir of the Author," xx.

89. Father of Lesslie Newbigin, manager and elder of Clayport church, and grandfather of J. E. Lesslie Newbigin, Bishop of the Church of South India and minister of the United Reformed Church.

90. Green Batt/Clayport Baptism Register, Northumberland Archives UR/P28/1/1/1/1.

91. In May 1897, Oman took the funeral of Mr. John Bell, Mr. Limont's son-in-law, and "an ardent Freemason," and in March 1905, that of Mr. W. M. Robertson, "an office-bearer for many years" and Past Master of Alnwick Lodge. (*Alnwick and County Gazette*, 22 May 1897; 18 March 1905.)

92. Pevsner and Richmond, *Buildings of England*, 67.

93. The congregation received notice from the Duke of Northumberland that the lease of the land would not be renewed as the plot was required for the new Anglican church of St Paul. (Straker, *St James' United Reformed Church*, 24.)

short but memorable,[94] not least because of his tireless efforts to help the living and the dying during the 1849 cholera epidemic which claimed 136 lives in a month, mostly in the Yards, the overcrowded tenements of Pottergate.[95] Mr. Limont was ordained to the "office of the ministry of oversight of the United Presbyterian congregation" in 1851[96] and exercised a vigorous ministry "associated with many philanthropic causes"[97] until his failing health led to the appointment of Oman as his colleague and successor. Of this Mr. Limont was to write on his retirement to Edinburgh nine years later:

> Our united experience has justified the step that was then taken. Whilst I have been increasingly incapacitated for rendering active service, all the duties of the pastoral office have been undertaken and performed by my colleague the Rev. John Wood Oman BD of whose qualifications and energy you have had ample proof.

Alexander remarked that Oman's "congregation was his first care" and that "if it was not long before he began his literary work, that brought no neglect of his people." And so, deferring for the moment an examination of Oman's literary achievements during his ministry in Northumberland, his engagement with Clayport will now be charted in some detail.

Pastoral Engagement

The session minutes had already indicated a need for administrative reform. At the meeting when Mr. Limont asked for a colleague, he "took the roll home with a view to revise and correct it," stating at a subsequent meeting "that he had examined the roll which he found in a very confused state but after a good amount of time and trouble he had got it into better order."[98]

---

94. In 1902 it was decided to put up a tablet in his memory to the west of the pulpit, and one to Limont to the east. In 1906 a new organ chamber in the church was dedicated in Ker's memory by Oman.

95. A local doctor successfully campaigned to introduce a piped water supply in 1858, and in 1890, a pink Italianate granite and sandstone water fountain, in Bondgate Within, connected to the mains water supply, was presented to the town by Alderman Adam Robertson, a leading Freemason and treasurer of Clayport church.

96. Session Minutes 1827–53. Northumberland Archives UR/P28/2/1/2/1.

97. Straker, *St James' United Reformed Church*, 29.

98. Session Minutes 1853–97. Northumberland archives, UR/P28/2/1/2/2. Where no other reference is given in the following paragraphs, it can be assumed to be, according to the date, either to this volume or to the following one: Session Minutes 1898–1923, Northumberland archives, UR/P28/2/1/2/3.

The Minutes of Session also record a move by the elders to exercise their traditional prerogative of moral and spiritual discipline. On 8 April 1891, for instance, "it was agreed that certain members of the congregation who had not lately been attending Church be waited upon by the elders." Before long, we find Oman being invited to "wait upon" backsliders.[99] On 5 June 1892, "in the case of Mr. Thomas Milne it was agreed that Mr. Oman see him and report," and on 19 June "a meeting was called to consider a matter concerning a member of the congregation. It was decided that Mr Oman draw up a minute of the meeting." On 29 January 1894, "it was agreed that Mr Oman see George Elliott and others about their attendance." On 12 March 1899 "Mr Oman stated that he had seen Mr Lough on the subject of his inconsistency as a member of the church and he had to report Mr Lough's resignation as a manager in the congregation which the Session agreed to accept." On 20 March 1904, "The case of Thomas and Elizabeth [Dell] who was [sic] guilty of incontinence was considered when Mr Oman together with Mr J. Goodfellow and Mr Douglas were appointed to speak with them and report." The visit impressed on Thomas and Elizabeth "the greatness of their sin, and admonished them as to their future life." Elizabeth applied for membership of the church.

Visiting people in their homes afforded an opportunity for deeper awareness of their needs and Oman fostered closer pastoral engagement of the elders with church members. On 8 April 1898, "after deliberation, it was decided that the congregation be divided into districts." On 1 May 1898 the clerk produced a list, dividing the congregation into eight districts "according to the number of working elders." In addition "the attendance of elders at the church doors was considered" and agreed in pairs and on a rota basis.

Liturgical reform was also in the air. At the first session meeting of 1890, Oman was immediately plunged into consideration of the consequences of the resignation the previous October of the precentor, Mr. Bell. It was decided to "return to the system of having a paid leader of the Psalmody." But despite adverts being placed annually, no suitable applicant was found, and the work continued with the help of dedicated volunteers, notably Mr. Balmbra as precentor/choir master and Miss Nellie Robertson as accompanist until 4 November 1906 when Mr. Balmbra resigned the office of precentor "in view of a pipe organ shortly to be introduced to the

---

99. In a sermon on 1 Timothy he writes: "It is a very unfortunate thing when the minister who is the teacher and should always move among the people with a spirit of mildness has to deal with these matters." Unpublished MS, assigned to 1891, Westminster College archives.

church."[100] In 1907 "after a good deal of negotiations" it was agreed to appoint Mr. Gifford as organist and choir master on a trial basis of one year.

There was also the matter of hymnbooks. *Church Praise*,[101] published in 1882 and authorized by the Synod of the PCE, was ripe for revision. There was, however, another contender from north of the Border. In 1891, reflecting a widespread dissatisfaction of Scottish congregations with their limited range of praise following the campaign of Moody and Sankey, the Free Church of Scotland made an initial overture to the Church of Scotland Psalmody Committee and the following year, the UP accepted an invitation to collaborate in producing a draft hymnal.[102] When published in 1898, *Church Hymnary* was adopted for use by all three churches. At Clayport, in 1903, "a conference was held on the relative difference between *Church Praise* and the *Church Hymnary*"[103] and it was finally decided in January 1904 to adopt *Church Hymnary* which was designed to be used along with the Psalter. With the session's decision "that nothing be done in haste," it would appear that this considerable step was uncontentious.

However, despite Oman's best efforts, his desire that children be baptized during a public act of worship rather than at home[104] where there were no compelling pastoral reasons why this should be the case, was not realized. On 10 July 1891, "Mr Oman received an application from Mr Matheson (fishmonger) to have his child baptized at his own home. After consideration it was resolved that Mr Oman comply with the request on Sabbath afternoon." Subsequently, however, similar requests from Mr C. Turnbull, 18 March 1894, Mr George Green, 16 September 1894, and Mr A. Robertson, 2 February 1902, to have a child baptized in their own house were agreed on condition the Baptism be announced from the Pulpit. And on 3 July 1903,

> The subject of Baptisms were [sic] brought before the session for consideration by the Moderator.[105] More especially the desire

---

100. "[A] new organ of the best class of pipe organs" was opened on 28 November 1906 by Mr. Storey of Tyneside, who "gave an organ recital to a large congregation."

101. Published under the auspices of the PCE by James Nisbet & Co., London, rev. ed. 1908.

102. Drummond and Bulloch, *Church in Late Victorian Scotland*, 309.

103. Session Minutes 1898–1923. The PCE was involved in the preparation of the second edition of Church Hymnary (1927) which was then authorized for use in its congregations.

104. Records of Baptisms at Green Batt are patchy, and until 1810 largely unsigned, but many of those recorded by the Reverend D. Paterson, minister of the congregation between 1806 and 1843, are designated "at home."

105. The minister in his role as chair of the session.

of the parents to avoid the public ordinance. After conference, the Session considered the desirability of making an appeal to the members and adherents of the congregation on the subject. It was however thought best to leave the matter over to be considered again.

The elders were clearly unwilling to grasp the nettle and we must assume that Oman exercised discretion in not pursuing the issue further.

In other matters, he appears to have been more assertive. On 12 March 1893 after morning service "Mr Oman brought forward a proposition to the effect that the communion be dispersed four times in the year instead of three times as at present. After conversation it was agreed that it be held about Easter, July, October and Christmas." On 4 April 1890, the elders were told that Oman had applications for admission to membership from five young people. "Mr Oman stated that he wished to make a change in the admission of candidates for the first time. He would prefer that they be admitted publicly in the congregation. Agreed that this have a trial and if found not suitable to be discontinued." Over the years, the practice was affirmed, the church increased in membership and such was Oman's evident popularity that several people transferred their allegiance to Clayport from St James, Pottergate.

Realizing that the young people had to be encouraged socially to foster integration, the elders agreed, on 19 November 1899, "to take steps at once to the formation of a fellowship society," and that "the inaugural meeting should take the form of a social evening." Mr. Oman was invited "to make some arrangements to the means of conducting the society." On 3 December the elders accepted with some misgiving Oman's decision "that the Young People be left much to themselves in the arrangements of the social gathering," and were relieved when on 11 March 1900 Mr. Balmbra reported on the first meeting of the Young Men's Fellowship Society. There had been a good attendance and "fair promise of usefulness to the church." "Mr Oman also stated that the Young Woman's [sic] Society was now formed and he had occupied the chair at the first meeting."

We had already marked Oman's zeal to reach those who had no connection with the church, whether in Edinburgh or Paisley. That this concern was undiminished is evinced by the Session Minutes of 8 February 1893, when "an arrangement was agreed to that Mr Oman should see some of the Ladies of the congregation to form a committee of visitations with the desire to gather in those who attend no place of worship."

The bland language of the Session Minutes conveys the detail of congregational life in a small-town church emerging from a period of stagnation with an elderly and increasingly frail minister to face the challenge of change with a young and dynamic assistant. Despite implications that this was not always easy either for the church or for Oman, his ministry was enabled by a strong pastoral bond. True to his belief that church life had to be rooted in context, he fostered relations with the wider community and, as we shall see, sustained a fruitful collaboration with local colleagues in other denominations.

Public Engagement

Accounts in the local press illustrate that the church was well integrated socially into the life of the town. Its annual soirées attracted around 400 people.[106] The one described by the *Morpeth Herald* on 17 February 1900 was typical. Notwithstanding the inclemency of the weather, there was a large gathering of the congregation and their friends, including members from nearly every denomination in the town. An excellent tea was provided and served by ladies of the congregation. Then, following a brief introduction by Oman, three ministers from nearby churches "gave bright and interesting addresses. The choir sang several anthems very effectively . . . and solos were tastefully rendered." It was generally agreed to have been "a really enjoyable and interesting re-union."

The public Sunday evening lectures which Oman delivered over the winter months in Clayport were much appreciated. They were said to "have appealed to the reading and thinking part of the community as few lectures do."[107] In 1894, it was reported that

> large audiences have been attracted at Alnwick to the Sunday evening lectures on the Bible by the Rev John Oman BD. The course is now almost finished, there being only . . . another one to come. Though the lectures may not in the common acceptance of the word be termed "popular," including, as they did a great deal of thought and discernment as well as much literary skill, they have, perhaps, been the best attempt ever made in that town to deal, from the platform, with a subject of a Biblical nature.[108]

Whereas most public lectures by contemporary ministers in Alnwick were travelogues, Oman also engaged his hearers on topics such as "Our Lord's teaching concerning the Kingdom," "The Visible Church," "The

106. *Morpeth Herald*, 19 December 1891.
107. *Orkney Herald*, 22 May 1907.
108. *Newcastle Journal*, 15 January 1894.

Catholic Idea," "The Reformation," "Calvinism," and "Scripture." On 6 February 1897, the *Gazette* advertised his lectures on "A Presbyterian" adding that "Mr Oman's pleasant and scholarly manner has always been admired and we may be sure that this lecture will prove as instructive as his predecessors [sic]."[109] However, not all his lectures were equally dispassionate. His eloquent lecture on the "Free Church case," delivered after the decision by the House of Lords in August 1904 to vest the property of the UF Church in the Free Presbyterian Church of Scotland was clearly written in a spirit of high indignation.[110]

His eagerness to promote public education was also reflected in his enthusiastic support of the *Chautauqua Scientific and Literary Society* which had been set up in 1887 by the "rising generation [of Clayport church] and with a view to promoting the moral and intellectual improvement of its members." Named after a holiday resort in New York state, the Alnwick branch, it was reported, "has taken root and is flourishing."[111] Meetings were held fortnightly throughout the winter months in Clayport and a magazine was produced, edited by Miss Newbigin. Some of the papers were, in the opinion of the reporter, "evidence of considerable literary taste."[112]

A few weeks after Oman's ordination, he gave "a series of readings from Browning" to members and friends of the Society. It was reported that

> Mr Oman succeeded in investing the extracts he read with new life and, in giving a deeper meaning to the characters and incidents depicted by the poet than the ordinary reader would be able to ... showed unmistakably that he was a thorough student of the great master mind who has (just) passed away from us. ... While admitting there were many difficulties to encounter in the study of Browning and that in all probability he would never be a popular poet, he strongly urged the study of his works not only for their literary merits but on account of the noble lessons the poet strove to teach.[113]

In October that year (1890), following the suggestion that there might be a French class, Oman's offer to take this on as teacher was received with enthusiasm and it was decided to hold the French class for an hour before the ordinary meeting of the Society.[114] From the regular newspaper re-

109. *Alnwick and County Gazette*, 6 February 1897.
110. MS, Westminster College archives, dated in pencil, 17 October 1904.
111. *Alnwick and County Gazette*, 11 May 1889.
112. *Alnwick and County Gazette*, 7 December 1889.
113. *Alnwick and County Gazette*, 1 March 1890.
114. *Alnwick and County Gazette*, 4 October 1890.

ports, the Society continued to flourish, with songs, "toothsome cakes" and lectures on a range of topics, from the "Kailyaird School" to "Parsifal, with notes on Wagner and Bayreuth"[115] and on 18 December, that year, a paper by Mr. William Stephenson (Alnwick) on "A Living Wage."

Marriage

On 21 February 1897, Clayport celebrated its Jubilee with services in the morning and afternoon and a soirée in the Corn Exchange the next day.[116] Oman preached on 1 Kings 2: 2–3, exhorting his hearers, in remembering those who had done great things in the past, to be strong and earnestly perform the duties that lay before them. "The whole of the services" we are informed, "were exceedingly bright and hearty."[117] At the soirée, the mood was light-hearted. The Reverend W. Rogerson spoke first.

> He too had been associated in terms of close intimacy with their junior minister, Mr Oman. (applause). He dare say they perhaps had not always been in harmony, but Mr Oman was an exceedingly straight-forward man and was always ready to take part in a debate in which he differed from any other person (laughter). There had been no breaking up of the close and friendly relations that had existed between him and their minister.

The Reverend R. McNair gave a vote of thanks. He had been associated closely with Oman for seven years and regarded him as a friend. "He did not know that he ever saw Mr Oman look more radiant than he did that night (laughter) perhaps he came under Mr Williamson's first head, that of hopefulness—all possible success and joy in the future (applause)."[118] The occasion for Oman's radiance was revealed when on 1 June his marriage with Mary Hannah Blair was solemnized in Jesmond Presbyterian Church, Newcastle. The officiating ministers were the Reverend Hugh Falconer, minister of Jesmond, assisted by the Reverend Richard Leitch, of College Road Presbyterian Church, Newcastle, who had been moderator of General Assembly two years before. Simon Oman, John's brother (above, 17), was best man[119] and Jeanie Robertson, his niece, one of the bridesmaids. The

---

115. *Alnwick and County Gazette*, 30 October 1897.
116. *Alnwick and County Gazette*, 27 February 1897.
117. *Alnwick and County Gazette*, 27 February 1897.
118. *Alnwick and County Gazette*, 27 February 1897.
119. Oman was to officiate at Simon's wedding to Isobel Traynor on 12 June 1901 at Grosvenor Square Presbyterian Church, Manchester.

large number of guests attended a reception afterwards at Mary's home, 2 Fernwood Road, Jesmond, and the couple left in the afternoon for a honeymoon in the Lake District.

They were presented on July 19 with handsome presents from the church, a piano from the congregation and a clock from the Sunday School teachers and the Bible Class, both gifts purchased from prestigious Alnwick shops. Mr. J. L. Newbigin and Mr. J. C. Akeroyd, who made the presentations, "made allusions to the high esteem in which Mr Oman is held, and spoke of the unanimity and good feeling which had always existed between them during the time Mr Oman had been with them. They wished him all success, and hoped that he and Mrs Oman would be long spared to work among them. The Rev. Mr Oman suitably returned thanks, after which the evening was pleasantly wiled [sic] away."

On July 24, Captain Simon Oman died at Biggings of heart disease, and three days later, Oman registered his father's death in person in Stenness. Though he was to return to Orkney on several occasions over the following years, his most intimate family connections with Stenness were now severed.[120]

No record survives as to how John and Mary met, but the Blair family had close connections with Alnwick through Hunter Blair, Mary's father, and her uncle, Henry Hunter Blair. Hunter's mother Ann[121] and all her siblings had been baptized in Green Batt Meeting House. As a child Hunter lived with his widowed grandmother, Mary Hunter, in St Michael's Place, and until her death in 1854, he worked as a "draper's apprentice" in the town.[122]

Henry Hunter Blair was an Alnwick institution. He had a bookshop in Market Place which in addition to books and stationery, sold concertinas and violins to provide "entertainment on winter evenings." He served on numerous Boards and committees in the town, he was sword-bearer for the Northumberland Provincial Grand Lodge[123] and served until 1871[124] as session clerk of St James's Presbyterian church. He bought the *Alnwick Mercury*

---

120. His mother, Isabella, had died in 1894, followed by Margaret, his elder sister and Jeanie Robertson's mother, in 1896. Although, on 23 March 1899, he witnessed in Stromness the marriage of his sister Isabella to James Irvine of Johannesburg, they were to settle in South Africa (above, 16.)

121. Baptized on 30 April 1797. She was to die shortly after Hunter's birth.

122. In 1860 Hunter went to live in Morpeth, where his father, Peter, was a bookseller and printer. On his father's death the following year, Hunter's step-mother, Ann, then aged 68, took over the business and Hunter moved to Newcastle.

123. *Shields Daily News*, 29 September 1876.

124. There appears to have been some dissension, giving rise to his resignation from St James and transfer of membership, along with Dr. Candlish, a fellow elder, with a large practice in Alnwick, to Lisburn Street Presbyterian Church.

in 1859 and ran it as a successful concern until it merged with the *Alnwick and County Gazette* in 1884. From 1882, the purchase of "two splendid machines" enabled his Minerva printing works to "execute book binding in all its branches." Although he died in 1887, the business continued under the same name and there are continuing references in local press over the next years to "Mr Hunter Blair." As Henry's only son died at the age of five in 1860, it looks as if the business may have been vested either in Hunter, who by 1887 was well established as a shoe manufacturer in Newcastle[125] or in his son Henry Hunter Blair, Mary's brother, also domiciled in Newcastle.[126] In either case, regular business trips would have been required. Henry's widow, Ann, continued to live in Alnwick along with her daughter Henrietta and it is likely that the two families exchanged visits from time to time. And a good quality bookshop with a stock of stationery, pencils and notebooks, would have been a magnet for Clayport's minister.

An additional opportunity for contact between Oman and the Blairs was provided by the Berwickshire Naturalists' Club, The objective of the Club was "to investigate the natural history and antiquities of Berwickshire"[127] and neighborhood, and it met five times a year for lectures on natural history or archaeology, excursions to sites of historic importance, and dinners. When Oman was admitted into membership in 1892[128] he would have ample occasion to meet fellow members with common interests, notably Mary's eldest brother, Charles Henry Hunter Blair, MA, DLitt, FSA, who, in addition to following in the family business as a shoe manufacturer, distinguished himself in historical and antiquarian research.

As Mr. Limont was still resident in the manse, John and Mary had to find suitable accommodation.[129] On 8 February 1897, John had signed a tenancy agreement for accommodation in Bondgate Within. This was, however, annulled a month later, presumably because something more suitable for a family home had become available. And there we must leave the matter,

---

125. One of the founders of the boot and shoe manufacturing firm of S. and C. W. Dixon and Company, in 1863 he married Hannah Mary, daughter of Charles Dixon. The *Presbyterian Handbook 1915–1916* states that "he was a magistrate, and closely identified with the philanthropic and religious work of the city." He served for many years as elder of Blackett Street Presbyterian Church until he joined the newly formed Presbyterian congregation at Jesmond.

126. In the 1881 census, aged 16, he is described as a "merchant's clerk"; in 1891 as a "ship owner"; in 1901, as a "steam ship owner." In 1911, he is "branch manager of a paint manufacturing company."

127. *Berwickshire News and General Advertiser*, Tuesday, 5 July 1881.

128. *Berwickshire News and General Advertiser*, Tuesday, 18 October 1892.

129. Since coming to Alnwick, Oman had taken up lodgings, along with a local school teacher, at The Willows, 164 St Michael's Place, run by a widow, Mary Douglas.

except to note that on 10 June 1899 Mr. Limont informed the Clayport elders of his intention to "remove from Alnwick as my place of residence. . . . I trust that the change may conduce to the welfare and usefulness of my successor and the prosperity of the congregation."[130] And when a few weeks after that, Mr. Limont retired to Edinburgh with his wife, John and Mary Oman were free to move with their daughter Isabella, then a toddler,[131] into the manse in Percy Terrace.

Although there are many testimonies to Oman's conscientious attentiveness to his congregation, and to "the strong bond of affection and trust between himself and the humblest of his flock,"[132] he was soon to embark on the literary work which was to gain him wider prominence. A tribute in the *Orkney Herald* affirms that "it is doubtful if any congregation of the size of Clayport Church has ever enjoyed for so long a period the ministry of so eminent a scholar" and the writer continues: "Although a frequent contributor to the UP Church magazine in Scotland, Dr Oman was some years in our midst before he gave to the world at large evidence of his literary ability"[133] During these years, his library had continued to expand. In 1892, at the monthly prayer meeting of the congregation, he was presented by Mrs. Adam Robertson "in a neat and graceful manner" with "a handsomely bound edition of the Revised Bible and a selection of valuable English and German works," gifted by the ladies of the church, using the surplus of the collection for his preaching gown. "I trust," he responded, "by means of these materials to do something that will be more worthy of your attention than anything I have done before in my life. Thanking you sincerely for the gift, I would simply conclude by saying that I trust to show you my gratitude in a better way by using them well."[134]

Tangible evidence of this soon emerged.

130. Minutes of Session, June 1899.

131. Isabella Gertrude Oman was born on 17 April, 1898, to be followed by Mary Blair Oman on 24 November 1899, and Jean Wood Oman, born 12 August 1904. A fourth daughter, Helen Dixon Oman, was born in Cambridge in 1908.

132. Straker, *St James' United Reformed Church Alnwick*.

133. *Orkney Herald*, 22 May 1907.

134. *Orkney Herald*, 2 March, 1892.

6

Early Literary Works

DURING OMAN'S ALNWICK YEARS, he produced his first major literary works, which drew him to the attention of a wider public and earned him an international reputation.

On Religion: Speeches to Its Cultured Despisers

Oman recorded that "I did Schleiermacher during the first years I was in Alnwick from sheer loneliness."[1] With the encouragement of Professor Calderwood, he whiled away the long evenings in his lodgings on a translation of Friedrich Schleiermacher's *Reden über die Religion—On Religion: Speeches to Its Cultured Despisers*, to which he added a substantial literary and biographical introduction, with an additional index. Published in 1893, his work was of such quality that it is still widely used.[2] It won Oman instant scholarly recognition and in August 1893, the offer of a chair at Chicago Theological Seminary, which he refused after some soul-searching.

Although it had been almost a hundred years since the *Reden* was first published in Germany, it had remained untranslated into English. However, translation is not the only way in which a person's thought can transfer from

---

1. Healey records that this letter of 1935 "came into my hands." *Religion and Reality*, 159. It has since disappeared.

2. It is regrettable that Oman's Introduction was omitted in the reprint published by Westminster John Knox Press in 1994. The subsequent translation of the third edition by Terrence N. Tice in 1969 seems to have made little impact.

one living culture to another, and Schleiermacher was not unknown in Britain. He visited London briefly in 1828,[3] and in the decades after his death in 1834, his thought was absorbed and transmitted by "land-louping students of divinity"[4] who read German. His preaching ability too was widely recognized.[5] However, sustained conservative criticism of his *Critical Essay on the Gospel of St Luke* set back the British reception of Schleiermacher for many years,[6] and fueled the widespread distrust of German theologians which exploded into a furor with the publication in 1860 of *Essays and Reviews*.[7] As the century progressed, however, there was an increase in translations into English of German works of theology and ethics.[8] By 1890, there had been six translations of Schleiermacher,[9] leaving only two major works outstanding, his large systematic treatise, *The Christian Faith*[10] and the *Speeches on Religion to Its Cultured Despisers*. Oman opted for the *Speeches*. Here is how he subsequently explained his choice: "No doubt his *Glaubenslehre* or *Doctrine of Faith*, a book which, it has been said, taught theologians what was meant by systematic thinking, is both more complete and more mature. But the *Speeches* had the deep and lasting influence which a book can only have when it is borne on the crest of a great movement. . . . Moreover, the author continued to attract and add to the work during a good part of his life, a process which added little to its lucidity but a great deal to its interest."[11]

As Oman knew, translation involved self-discipline. "The first requirement," he told his Westminster students, "is to have your loins girt and your lamp burning, to concentrate, and that on a clearly-seen purpose."[12] One

3. Ellis, "Schleiermacher in Britain."

4. MacEwen, *Life and Letters*, 150.

5. John Ker refers to Schleiermacher's "Ciceronian eloquence" in his *History of Preaching*, 302.

6. Schleiermacher, *Gospel of St Luke*. In this he addresses the matter of the priority of the Synoptic Gospels. See Ellis, "Schleiermacher in Britain," 423. From 1825 on, there was a preference for English translations of conservative biblical theologians such as Neander.

7. Two of the distinguished essayists were tried for heresy in the Court of Arches and, though they were acquitted on appeal in 1864, the book was condemned by both Houses of the Church of England Church Assembly.

8. Lincicum, "Fighting Germans."

9. Schleiermacher, *Gospel of St Luke* (1825); "Schleiermacher's Religious Views" (extracts from Schleiermacher presented in translation) (1849); "Select Letters by Schleiermacher" (1849); Schleiermacher, *Brief Outline* (1850); Schleiermacher, *Christmas Eve* (1890); *Schleiermacher: Selected Sermons* (1890).

10. Schleiermacher, *The Christian Faith*.

11. Oman, *Rationalism and Romanticism*.

12. Oman, *Concerning the Ministry*, 184.

had then to adopt a sound method: choosing equivalent words from the dictionary would not do; nor would "the easy device of paraphrasing."[13] Schleiermacher's own advice was to "leave the writer alone as much as possible and move the reader toward the writer,"[14] giving a sense of what it would be like if the reader had grown up speaking that language even if that allowed certain marks of foreignness in word choice and syntax to remain.[15] This required linguistic skill as well as an ability to understand the author's thought: "every human being is . . . in the power of the language he speaks; he and his whole thinking are a product of it. He cannot, with complete certainty, think anything that lies outside the limits of [this] language."[16] To judge by the success of his translation, Oman had this skill in abundance.

In insisting that *Reden* should be translated *Speeches*, not *Discourses*, he shows sensitivity to different registers of language.

> The religious man, being in touch with the Infinite, deeply feels the need of confirming and completing himself by fellowship with others. To utter his deepest feelings is an inward and maybe an overwhelming necessity. But in doing so, he cannot fall into the light tone of common conversation. On this the highest subject with which language has to deal, all fulness and splendour of human speech should be expended. When poetic skill is wanting, religion can only be expressed and communicated rhetorically, in all power and skill of speech . . . enthusiastic, flowing, intense, rhetorical—in deliberate contrast to the dull level of expository prose, the cherished medium of Rationalism.[17]

In the light of this, it is perhaps surprising that Oman chose to translate the third edition of the *Reden*, published in 1821.[18] After all, as he acknowledged, "it is not the book which made the first deep impression."[19] It was in many respects a different text from the first edition of 1799[20] published anonymously by Schleiermacher, who was at the time the Reformed chaplain at the Charité hospital in Berlin. This first edition alone,

---

13. Oman, *Concerning the Ministry*, 184.
14. Schleiermacher, "On the Different Methods of Translating," 42.
15. Bernofsky, "Schleiermacher's Translation Theory," 176.
16. Schleiermacher, "On the Different Methods of Translating," 38.
17. Oman, *Rationalism and Romanticism*.
18. Oman, "Schleiermacher," 404.
19. Oman, *Faith and Freedom*, 210.
20. This was translated by Richard Crouter in 1988: Schleiermacher, *On Religion* (1st ed.). Crouter's was the first translation to benefit from the *Kritische Gesamtausgabe*, here vol 1.2, 1984.

Oman suggests, could "be properly described as the religious programme of Romanticism."[21] Was he perhaps influenced in his decision by Schleiermacher's progressive changes of emphasis? Whereas in 1799, Schleiermacher laid himself open to charges of pantheism in his eagerness "to show that religion is not mere doctrines and moralities," but rather the "artistic sense applied to the Universe,"[22] by 1806 when the second edition was published, he was a theological professor in Halle and the question of the relationship of religion to moral conduct had become more urgent.[23]

Furthermore, the third edition of the *Speeches* incorporated extensive "Explanations." These were not so much an exposition of the text as an attempt to harmonize the earlier editions with the later one and bring it into line with the *Glaubenslehre* (*The Christian Faith*), which had been published shortly before, and Oman may have felt that, in choosing to translate the third edition, he was also introducing an English-speaking audience to Schleiermacher's magnum opus.

We may note in passing that there are emphases in the second and third editions of the *Speeches* to which Oman was to return. There is Schleiermacher's understanding of God's plan of love and wisdom for the world; the emphasis on truth and freedom, realized in Christ through the church; the visibility of the church as a "fellowship in pursuit of righteousness";[24] and a particular conception of the individual, whose prophetic vocation is firmly grounded in universal truth and morality.[25]

On a personal level, Oman will have discerned in Schleiermacher a fellow traveler of an earlier age; each exhibited the distinctive piety of the traditions that nurtured them; both were scholar-preachers; both asked radical questions about the nature and authority of the church; both saw the urgent need to relate religion to those who found it alien. In Schleiermacher Oman found a theologian who "preached with a prophetic voice" and was regarded as an agitator for reform in church and state.[26] And he

21. Oman, *Faith and Freedom*, 212. It is a weakness of Healey's analysis that he does not distinguish between the first and subsequent editions of the *Reden* (*Religion and Reality*, 14–23).

22. Although Ritschl was to criticize Schleiermacher as mystical, pantheistic and unethical, he too insisted on the experiential nature of religious knowledge. See Oman, *Faith and Freedom*, 359–60.

23. Oman, *Faith and Freedom*, 211.

24. Schleiermacher, *On Religion*, 242.

25. Schleiermacher, *On Religion*, xxiii.

26. Schleiermacher believed that Protestantism with its basis on truth and freedom was threatened by the vassal status of Prussia following Napoleon's decisive victory at Jena on 14 October 1806, and in the *Dreifältigkeit* church in Berlin he "preached with a prophetic voice, showing the spiritual purpose and the spiritual claims of such a time."

appreciated the value of Schleiermacher's thought as a stimulus for future theologians. "Schleiermacher," he wrote, "never did escape from the merely artistic outlook of Romanticism. But if he is to be corrected, it will have to be by beginning more seriously with what he has done and facing more thoroughly the questions he tried to answer."[27] This was to be Oman's agenda for the foreseeable future.

Vision and Authority

Vision and Authority, published in March 1902, was, Oman wrote, "the product of long years of reading and thinking" prompted initially by his scandalized perception that in the Robertson Smith affair, the church and its theology were more concerned with unanimity than veracity. He was then, as he wrote, "left with no option between facing the search for a truth, which would shine in its own light in face of all inquiry, and complete scepticism." Insofar as this book was "an honest record of that search,"[28] it was also designed to help readers interpret their own experiences of the moral, intellectual, and spiritual challenges of the day. As Charles Taylor discerns, a breach had been knocked in Victorian religion by a powerful alternative morality. "It was not some supposedly logical incompatibility between science and faith but this imperious moral demand not to believe which led many Victorians to feel that they had to abandon, however sorrowfully, the faith of their ancestors."[29] Oman writes: "The supreme difficulty has been the shaking of the foundations, so that no one seems quite sure what things that cannot be shaken remain. All authority has been questioned, and moral as well as intellectual confusion has doubtless ensued."[30] Yet without "some sense of the dignity of man, some perception of the higher uses of life, some inward conscience of right, some outward vision of truth ... our path is into darkness."[31] In order to speak with conviction, the Church had to recover a sense of the true authority on which it was founded.[32]

Where blame seemed to him to be due he spoke out, and for a newspaper article was severely censured by the government." Schleiermacher, *On Religion*, xlviii.

27. Oman, "Schleiermacher," 404.
28. Oman, *Vision and Authority*, 2nd ed., 9–10.
29. Taylor, *Sources of the Self*, 406.
30. Oman, *Vision and Authority*, 2nd ed., 1.
31. Oman, *Vision and Authority*, 2nd ed., 3.
32. The publisher's fear that the original title, *The Throne of St Peter*, might be misinterpreted as Protestant polemic led to its being demoted in favor of the present title, which Oman felt could also be misleading. (Oman, *Vision and Authority*, 2nd ed., 8.)

Hugh Sinclair records advice from a friend, "'Read that book and you'll feel you've knocked up against something.' I read the book, and among many impressions it made upon me, the sense of having 'knocked up against something' remained dominant."[33] It was apparently unusual at the time to find "so much solid and fearless thought packed into a single book"[34] geared to a popular readership, but the author was an experienced minister accustomed to addressing "ordinary people, who read little but what our parish minister at home said he had come to in his old age—God's book and the Devil's, The Bible and a certain newspaper."[35] As T. W. Manson recognized, "it has something to say to every man about human dignity and human freedom and about the only Rock on which these things can be founded. . . . Above all it is a book for Churches and church people—ecclesiastical leaders or ordinary lay-folk. For them it is essentially a message of hope and encouragement. It compels them to look beyond institutions that may be challenged, to the things that know neither decay nor defeat, the grace of the Lord Jesus Christ and the love of God and the fellowship of the Holy Spirit."[36]

In its style, it was for Herbert Farmer "in some ways the most attractive of his books."[37] There are signs of homiletical skill; the language is non-technical, Oman accumulates questions for rhetorical effect, he identifies himself with his readers by using 'we' and 'us'; he illustrates what he says by vivid examples from everyday life, and every so often, we glimpse an outraged social conscience. Sometimes, illustrations take on a life of their own, as when he evokes the roughly hewn wooden chair of the apostle transmogrified into the bejeweled throne of St Peter. In order to be "relevant to the needs of the time," he emphasized, "religious thinking ought to face the ordinary religious life; and it ought, as far as possible, to be expressed in ordinary language. Otherwise it is apt to be up in the air and end in abstraction." His efforts were rewarded. A writer to the *British Weekly* affirms that "I do not know of any book which can help more at the present time, by which a man may find his bearings."[38] And a correspondent from "a tiny hamlet in the heart of Dorset," referring to "Professor Oman's delightful book" says that "we read and re-read it before breakfast in the mornings,

---

33. Sinclair, "Living Voices," 429–30.
34. Sinclair, "Living Voices," 429–30.
35. Oman, *Vision and Authority*, 2nd ed., 10.
36. Oman, *Vision and Authority*, 8th ed., 6.
37. Farmer, "Theologians of Our Time," 132–35.
38. *British Weekly*, 31 May 1928 (B. Grey Griffith, Baptist Missionary Society).

and are finding it to be 'a feast of fat things' indeed."[39] It won grudging approval from Professor Norman Kemp Smith to whom it was lent by a retired minister: "It contains much admirable matter," he wrote to Friedrich von Hügel, "but strangely combined with a stupidly eloquent style—at the same time frequently surprisingly good, eg p.36 on Christ's regarding the child as the exemplar, not because of its supposed plasticity but because of its eagerness and earnestness, qualities I am much impressed by in my gay little daughter."[40]

The author was not writing a Summa, but exploring progressively over four sections, each divided into short chapters, what it might mean for individuals and the Church to exercise an authority that comes from God.

Book 1. The Internal Authority

In this first section, we find examples of Oman's vividly evocative style at its best.[41] However, as he himself recognized,[42] the opening three chapters are not generally an easy read and in the revision of the text for the second edition in 1928, he recast them. The material in his original Introduction is largely incorporated into the first chapter, some material dropped and some transposed.[43] With hindsight, he acknowledged that in 1902, he "had rather seen things by way of intuition than based them on grounds of reason." And he commented drily, "Since then I hope I have made some progress in the latter task, but I have found little of the intuition to alter. Much of what is here said is not as new as when it first appeared, but it still seems to me as true, and as relevant to the needs of the time."[44]

The thrust of this section is that the authority of the Church derives from the "internal authority" of the individual seeker after truth who keeps a spiritual vision fresh, chiefly through prayer, in association with the many

---

39. *British Weekly*, 13 December 1928 (Emmeline Atkinson, Compton Valence Rectory).

40. Smith to von Hügel, 8 March 1920, Papers of Friedrich von Hügel, University of St Andrews Special Collections, ms 2993. Smith, then Professor of Logic and Metaphysics at the University of Edinburgh, was noted for his work on Kant and Hume.

41. See particularly chapter 4, "Man's Heritage," and chapter 5, "The Essential Attitude."

42. Oman, *Vision and Authority*, 5–6. Ian MacLaren described the first chapters as "rather stiff reading." (*Orkney Herald*, 22 May 1907.)

43. The original chapter 3, headed "Psychological Analysis," which he judged to be "worse than irrelevant," is dropped entirely and replaced by "The Great and the Small." Oman, *Vision and Authority*, 2nd ed., 6.

44. Oman, *Vision and Authority*, 2nd ed., 11.

such individuals who make up a community. In similar vein Oman writes in his article on "Individualism,"[45] published the same year as his Kerr lectures: "Whatever institution . . . we may submit to, we can only belong to the true Church by first of all having 'salt in ourselves' (Mk 9.50) by being of the truth and hearing Christ's voice (Jn 18.17) . . . the possession of such a personal relation to truth is a common bond of more power than any external tie; and . . . the visible organization is only vital and useful as it expresses this union."

Book Two: The External Authority

In the light of this, "the old external dogmatic attitude of the Church" with its emphasis on infallibility, whether of leadership or scripture, "cannot be maintained."[46] That is not to say, however, that the Church does not have authority. The true authority of the Church "from which we have received so much and by which we have been so largely fashioned,"[47] is ultimately derived from Christ, "a teacher who speaks directly to man's sense of truth, his deepest feelings, his highest conception of the uses of life,"[48] and it is exercised through successive generations of apostles and prophets.

This is an authority "not of office, but of insight and of love . . . [and this] is the actual foundation upon which the Church in all the ages has been truly built."[49] The authority of apostolic succession so defined is the only credible basis for "the one Church, the catholic, the true," a perception which Oman sees to be highly significant for discussions of church unity.[50]

The final chapter in this section, on "Discerning the Body of Christ," was said by Ian MacLaren to be "one of the most lucid statements of the subject I have ever read."[51] The Body of Christ, Oman maintains, is discerned not in authoritarianism, but in the respect of his followers for one another in ordinary life. "It means discriminating in the woman old and poor, in threadbare gown and old-fashioned bonnet, the beauty of holiness and the dignity of Christ's gentleness, and being able to treat her in every relation

---

45. Oman, "Individualism." One of three articles, "Individual," "Individualism," "Individuality," which Oman contributed to Hastings, ed., *Dictionary of Christ and the Gospels*.

46. Oman, *Vision and Authority*, 88, 174.

47. Oman, *Vision and Authority*, 85.

48. Oman, *Vision and Authority*, 186. There are echoes here of Schleiermacher.

49. Oman, *Vision and Authority*, 128.

50. Oman, *Vision and Authority*, 138–44 and 151–58.

51. *Orkney Herald*, 22 May 1907.

of life as the guest who has been honoured to sit at Christ's right hand."[52] And, in a recapitulation of one of Oman's favorite parables, it is revealed supremely in the patient love of the father who waits non-judgmentally for the return of his prodigal son.

The gospel, Oman suggests, enables a person to find God and himself at the same time: the relation of the individual to God is as child to a loving Father. This does not diminish the distinctiveness of the individual; it is of the essence of God's love to allow individuals to work out their own destiny. They are free to make mistakes. But the love of God is at work and with that comes awareness of the grace of God.[53]

With this authority of insight and love, we are "set free with the liberty of the children of God. . . . Were this condition perfectly fulfilled, the authority without and the authority within would be in perfect agreement, and we should have the final assurance of truth, the final assurance of His authority Who made the world in wisdom and the spirit of man after His own image and Who appointed both history and experience as His witnesses. Only through this agreement can we attain to freedom; and only thus can we know the God who would win and not compel us to His obedience."[54]

Book Three: The Church's Creed

Unsurprisingly, Oman makes it clear that doctrines of an infallible Church and an infallible Bible are untenable. While "truth is presented exactly in the form which the humble, reverent and obedient soul can receive,"[55] as Christ "speaks straight to the heart and to experience,"[56] his followers learn from one another in a common search for truth; they are both learners and teachers. This takes effort, but "instead of mourning that a hasty assent is no longer easy to command, we should rather rejoice in the perplexities which compel to a more brotherly regard to our own limitations and our neighbour's duties. Let us be grateful for the perplexities that keep us in a measure in the course in which truth ought to be sought; whereby, if our present possession may seem small and insecure, the reversion of our true inheritance will not only be surer but of ampler promise."[57] Jesus did not after all "secure infallible accuracy" by writing an autobiography or a

52. Oman, *Vision and Authority*, 161.
53. Oman, "Individual," in *Dictionary of Christ and the Gospels*.
54. Oman, *Vision and Authority*, 168.
55. Oman, *Vision and Authority*, 178.
56. Oman, *Vision and Authority*, 181.
57. Oman, *Vision and Authority*, 184.

"compendium of theology," he "entrusted His life and His teachings to the souls that knew Him and loved Him."[58] And while "the person of Jesus is ever itself the corner stone of all testimony regarding Him ... the evidence which is valid from age to age goes back to it, not through the void, but through the peace and joy and holiness it has wrought in the souls of men."[59]

Oman is careful to draw a line between a personal experience of religious truth and personal opinion and he illustrates that with veiled allusion to the ecclesiastical furor which had propelled him into the ministry.

> The judgment of a prince of the Church is as much a private interpretation as the judgment of a commentator, with the further danger of being the fruit of more bias and less inquiry. Nor may we escape the same result by falling back upon the councils, for what is the vote of a council but a mass of private interpretations, if it has the dignity of being an interpretation at all and not a mere echo of party cries.... An interpretation warped by personal bias, tradition, formalism, prejudice, self-interest, is private, however many be agreed in it. On the other hand, indifferent to party, one solitary thinker may stand, and his interpretation may not be private, because it rests on the universal grounds of truth and holiness, because it is the fruit of a large and loving perception of God's gentle and patient method, and of a large and loving anticipation of the wide Kingdom of God.[60]

Oman sees the "great certainties of the Church's Creed,"[61] the incarnation, atonement, grace, eternal life, as revealing God's truth in human experience through Jesus "who manifests the Father ... by a life among common men."[62] This involves, not a once and for all statement of absolute truth, but a slow unfolding of the truth. And so "the Church of the Saints will be equal to the high task of preserving and applying all the essential doctrines of the faith. The spiritual inheritance she has received she will hand on, not diminished by the wear and stress of time, but enriched by man's varied experience and tested by helping at least to solve the problems of every age."[63]

---

58. Oman, *Vision and Authority*, 187.
59. Oman, *Vision and Authority*, 91.
60. Oman, *Vision and Authority*, 203.
61. Oman, *Vision and Authority*, 211.
62. Oman, *Vision and Authority*, 228.
63. Oman, *Vision and Authority*, 248.

Book Four: The Church's Organization

The church, which is the communion of saints, the Body of Christ, is also a human institution, prone to failure. It has to learn to repent, to see the Cross as the hallmark of discipleship, to learn "from her Lord how to fail, how to make failure her last and greatest appeal, how to fail, not in discouragement, much less in indifference, but in faith and hope and love."[64] This is what Oman describes strikingly as "the sacrament of failure." In repentance and in faith the human community is reshaped by love.

In his theology of grace, Oman is developing the link made by Schleiermacher between faith and morality. Freedom cannot be realized by an autonomous individual divorced from the world around but only on the basis of a commitment to God and one's neighbor. Not only does this perspective introduce a new religious order; it "brings in its train a new political, social, and even material order.... It is in freedom of self-restraint, regard for others, submission to the guidance of love, in short it is fitness for our place in God's final order."[65]

Although there is an eschatological element here, there are also political and economic implications for the present day; and Oman's earlier exposure to life in the tenements and colonies of North Merchiston had left him well aware of the widening gap between rich and poor in an industrial society.[66] "What kind of possession of the earth is that," he writes, "which must forget the poverty that hides its head in squalid dens where aching limbs shiver under scanty rags, which casts its children on the street to live by their too precocious wits, and must suffer its daughters to become a prey, not of passion, but of hunger?"[67] He was also aware that there were philanthropic individuals with a strong conviction of Christian stewardship who saw and acted upon opportunities to alleviate such distress. In a sermon preached in June 1907 at Grosvenor Road Presbyterian Church, Highbury,[68] he invites his hearers to reflect on what made Barnabas "a good man." Barnabas, we are told, was large-hearted and generous with his money, and "he was not content with one act of generosity." Faced with the continuing plight of the poor Christians in Jerusalem, he "had an abidingly generous spirit."

64. Oman, *Vision and Authority*, 306.

65. Oman, *Vision and Authority*, 2nd ed., 333.

66. The church could not be satisfied with "twelve millionaires dining at one end of London and finding the cultivated globe too small to please their palates, and at the other a million and a half of their fellow creatures not knowing whether they will have any dinner at all." Oman, "Individualism."

67. Oman, *Vision and Authority*, 26.

68. *London Daily News*, 3 June 1907.

Oman contrasts this with the "more negative idea of goodness" prevalent among some of his contemporaries: "going perhaps regularly to the church, and behaving respectably in our homes; but never having any call upon our hearts and upon our lives which insists on bearing much and doing much and accomplishing much." But, he states sternly, religious life is not "a cut flower decoration," it is rooted in the example of Jesus Christ, "it is the large demands of a generous heart, inspired by the example and power of Him who gave all He had for mankind, it is that that is of efficacy in the world." Through the power of the Spirit, God works "the most extraordinary changes in the most unlikely cases." And this is rooted in God's gracious love.

For the church, the issue of social reform was not clear-cut. As Charles Taylor indicates,[69] there was a complex relationship between Christian and secularized moral forces. Calvinist roots between godliness and social transformation had always involved a strong emphasis on practical charity, but in realizing that Christianity could be revived by "practical benevolence," Christian faith had to some extent been redefined. Difficulties arose in the church between reformers and those who were more cautious and conservative. Some held that too great an identification with social reform could lead to the error of seeking salvation in works, while a hyper-Augustinian view came to be accepted that a dedication to secular reform sat uneasily with Christian faith.[70]

Given that many of those most committed to the cause were feeling compelled to abandon orthodox Christianity,[71] there was, as Oman had perceived, an urgent need for an apologetic response. He explores the issue rhetorically, questioning the

> axiom that the first duty of the Church is by large, easy, comprehensive methods of charity, organisation, and, if need be, legislation to turn the world into a place of universal well-being. Is it not, men confidently ask, the Church's duty to fight the oppressions which rob men of the due reward of their toil, to control the ignorance which wastes their resources, to encourage regulations which lead to more effective combination? Should she withhold her hand from the task of sanitation? Should she not even take her share in providing recreation? Should not her aim be to introduce into the whole realm of material things a beneficent era of Christian supervision and control?

69. Taylor, *Sources of the Self*, 401.

70. Taylor, *Sources of the Self*, 400.

71. Uncertainty as to how much emphasis the Church was to place on social reform was leading many people to turn to secular humanitarian institutions. Raven, "Social Justice."

Yet the Master chose another way . . ."[72]

Implicit in what Oman says here is a critique of Protestant exceptionalism whereby the church was understood to have a unique mission to transform the world.[73] He notes astutely how moral action is often limited by a restricted imagination which implicitly renders much suffering invisible.[74]

> Especially among those who commit their thoughts to writing, the tendency is to measure all things by the desires of the civilised inhabitant of the temperate zone, generally according to the standard of the upper middle class. Hence their chief perplexities are poverty, ill-health, and the temptations which spring from outward situations. Were the world theirs they would have all incomes princely, all houses palatial, all heads hard and all pillows soft. . . . Were it granted, they would transform society into a beneficent club, housing mankind in the Mall, with Kent in front for a garden and the Trossachs behind for a pleasure ground. . . . God's thoughts, however, may not be as our thoughts.[75]

In challenging the church to transcend the limits of its bourgeois aspirations, Oman is also calling it to lay stronger demands upon itself than had previously been the case. In his view, it could only address social issues worthily if animated by Christian faith and love, and inspired by the power of the Cross. In doing so, it served God's kingdom. "The Kingdom of the Crucified is an everlasting dominion, because it is the eternal order which is freedom and the eternal bond which is love. Of this order is the Church which is ever being built."[76] And it is by these standards that it is judged.[77]

These passages evoke Oman's passionate social and evangelistic concerns and his keen awareness of the risk that the Church might betray its calling. They also illustrate perhaps more than any other section of the book, its "sermonic" thrust.

This approach is well described by a reviewer:

> Dr Oman stands, and has always stood, for the conception of religion which makes it not a system of philosophy, a code of laws,

---

72. Oman, *Vision and Authority*, 314.
73. This had roots in Calvinism, in the doctrines of predestination and divine providence.
74. Taylor, *Sources of the Self*, 398.
75. Oman, *Vision and Authority*, 2nd ed., 222; cf. 1st ed., 214.
76. Oman, *Vision and Authority*, 337.
77. This view was echoed by Forsyth, *Principle of Authority*, 8.

or an esoteric doctrine, but the reaction of men to God in the daily discipline and tasks of common life. Simplicity and loyalty, personal fidelity and righteousness in the market place, are to him the infallible marks of true religion, and undefiled. Above all, he is tuned to the heroic note. His message is concerning the great venture and adventure of faith, the hold on God that grows firmest where life's contradictions are greatest, the certainty that feeds on doubt.

And Hugh Sinclair concludes: "The good folk of Alnwick are to be congratulated on having so virile and modern a thinker in their pulpit, and Mr Oman is to be congratulated and thanked for giving to the thinking world so strong and reasonable a book on one of the most important subjects within the range of religion."[78]

Academic Recognition

On 16 December 1902, the *Orkney Herald* reported that the Reverend John Oman "has been appointed to succeed Professor Martin of Edinburgh, as lecturer at Westminster College, Cambridge. The lectureship was quite recently founded. Professor Martin lectures in May 1903, and Mr Oman in 1904." These lectures, which were delivered in April 1904 and entitled "Some inherited problems of theology,"[79] were a "first outline" of the set of lectures which Oman was to give in Glasgow in January 1906. For he had also been appointed as Kerr lecturer by the UF Church of Scotland from November 1903 to November 1906. Although Oman was, as he acknowledges wryly, a "stranger of the Dispersion in England,"[80] the Kerr trustees stipulate that "appointments . . . may also from time to time, at the discretion of the Committee, be made from among eminent members of the Ministry of any of the Nonconformist Churches of Great Britain and Ireland, America and the Colonies, or of the Protestant Evangelical Churches of the Continent."[81] These appointments gave him occasion to establish friendly relations with Principal Dykes, his colleagues and students in Cambridge, and Principal Lindsay and colleagues in Glasgow. They were a clear recognition of Oman's academic ability.

---

78. Sinclair, "Living Voices," 430.
79. Carruthers, *Digest of the Proceedings*, 275.
80. Oman, *Faith and Freedom*, viii.
81. Oman, *Faith and Freedom*, xi. Oman was the sixth Kerr lecturer and the first from outside Scotland: Oman, *Faith and Freedom*, 144.

So too was the award of the degree of doctor of philosophy[82] by the University of Edinburgh on 13 March 1904 for a thesis entitled "Rationalism and Romanticism: A Study of Kant's *Religion within the Limits of Reason Alone* and Schleiermacher's *Speeches on Religion*." "The degree (says the *British Weekly*) is not an honorary one, but has been won by strenuous scholarly work."[83] Though this thesis was never published, the text was substantially incorporated in Oman's fourth and fifth Kerr lectures.[84]

The Problem of Faith and Freedom in the Last Two Centuries[85]

James Denney, Professor of New Testament language and literature in the Free Church College, Glasgow, described how Oman

> delivered these lectures in our College here, and I thought them exceedingly good. I think so still, though the exposition of his ideas is sometimes cumbered a little by unnecessary information, and sometimes by indifference and a kind of inarticulateness in himself. For those who can digest this kind of matter, however, it is a very appetising book, and the more you know of the people he writes about, the more highly you think of it.[86]

Once more Oman engages in what he described as "a cross-country steeplechase after truth,"[87] continuing the quest he had embarked on in *Vision and Authority*. But whereas *Vision and Authority* was designed to bring a message of hope and encouragement to thoughtful churchgoers in general, *Faith and Freedom* is based on nine lectures with an audience composed largely of theological students. Within this framework Oman engages critically with the thinking of selected theologians over the previous 200 years, enabling his readers to glimpse his own thinking in the process. In his first chapter, he establishes his rationale and his method, as he proposes to address "the ultimate problem" for theology over at least the previous two

---

82. This was a relatively new degree at Edinburgh, referred to severally as DPhil or PhD.

83. *Orkney Herald*, 13 March 1904.

84. Oman, *Faith and Freedom*, 137–237.

85. The Kerr lectures were intended for the "promotion of scientific theology," and had to be published at the lecturer's own expense within a year of delivery. Oman, *Faith and Freedom*, was the result.

86. Letter from James Denney, Glasgow, 8 December 1906, Westminster College archives.

87. Quoted in Healey, *Religion and Reality*, 42.

centuries, "the relation of Faith and Freedom, the problem of how Faith is to be absolute and Freedom absolute, yet both one."[88] Acknowledging the considerable scope of the subject, he takes as axiomatic Luther's view that the freedom of the children of God was the "only ultimate basis of a true faith and a stable spiritual order" and that such freedom was futile apart from God. But radical questions remained. Should religious faith be firmly fixed in the traditions of the past, steadfastly unchanging through personal, cultural or sociopolitical changes? Or should it engage in ongoing enquiry, in informed and responsible freedom? Are faith and freedom irreconcilably opposed to one another? In tackling such subjects, Oman was, as he suggested, not "afraid of the battle!"[89]

The method adopted is ambitious. It recalls the agenda of British Idealist philosophy.[90] Drawing on theologians from France, England and Germany who each illuminate aspects of the problem in their own way, Oman makes it clear that he has "no account of uniform progress" to offer[91] and that

> to summarise in such a way as to degenerate into a catalogue of names and books would be a futile and depressing waste of time. . . . The real interest is to see a man's attitude towards the great elemental truths, to see what interest preponderates for him, and from what point of view he regards the world. It is not, as in the physical sciences, an account of adding one discovery to another, but of an advance in conscious grasp of the whole bearings of the problem through the continual pressure upon it of thought and living interest. This feeling of life is the difficult and the important thing to retain. But as the thinkers reflect the movement, certain great books reflect the thinkers, and these I propose to make the centre of my exposition. The result ought to be to preserve more living interest than would otherwise be possible; and, at all events the method has the merit of introducing you to really great books, a literature of first importance for your studies.[92]

---

88. Oman, *Faith and Freedom*, 4.
89. Oman, *Faith and Freedom*, 4.
90. See above, 64. Caird in Seth and Haldane, *Philosophical Criticism*.
91. Oman, *Faith and Freedom*, 4.
92. Oman, *Faith and Freedom*, 26–27.

Lecture II "Jesuitism and Pascal's *Pensées*"

The authors of these "great books" come from different historical and geographical contexts and different church traditions, enabling new questions and a new attitude of mind in their successors. For the first of these, Blaise Pascal, Oman's admiration is transparent. He writes that the *Pensées* bears "the stamp of spiritual genius Its intuition of truth is so immediate that it never can be a relic of dead controversies, but must always remain an enduring utterance of the human heart."[93] It "threw [Pascal] back on a living experience of the grace of Christ." Oman saw this as a primary theological intuition; he expresses little sympathy with the Jesuit exaltation of the church[94] or the belief that we are justified only "when Christ's righteousness, working through the Church, produces our righteousness." He affirms that "it is Christ, not the Church, that is the last court of appeal; and it is not the Christ of the Church, but the Christ of living faith and of the Gospels, the Christ who is God's answer to the enigma of life. Towards Him the heart goes out and finds its emancipation; and that is the note which makes the *Pensées* of such high significance for our inquiry."[95] Revealingly, Oman states that Pascal "never lapses into a mere intellectual discussion, but always speaks from a faith that is backed by his whole heart's devotion. He . . . is always a man speaking of man's highest concern."[96]

Oman's admiration for the *Pensées* did not obscure his perception that Pascal's brave attempt to achieve theological reconciliation between the temporal and the eternal had not entirely succeeded. The issue of the human being "touching the clod with one hand and the eternal laws of truth and righteousness with the other" presents a problem that "becomes at once of amazing difficulty and of amazing importance."[97]

Oman concludes revealingly that "we have in Pascal something of the right attitude, however much we may fail to find the ultimate solution. We have a sense that religion seeks not the submission of the mind but the homage of the heart."[98]

---

93. Oman, *Faith and Freedom*, 62.
94. Oman, *Faith and Freedom*, 40.
95. Oman, *Faith and Freedom*, 70.
96. Oman, *Faith and Freedom*, 66.
97. Oman, *Faith and Freedom*, 76.
98. Oman, *Faith and Freedom*, 77.

Lecture III "English Deism and Butler's *Analogy*"

In England, Joseph Butler too had realized the limitations of the intellect where matters of faith were concerned. At a time when Newton's theory of universal gravitation seemed to prove that the world was governed by one simple mathematical order, Butler was arguing in his *Analogy of Religion* that observation of the natural world revealed it to be full of mysteries and he concluded on that basis that the teaching of Christianity about the mystery of Revelation was probably true.[99]

He also maintained like Pascal that "a practical faith,"[100] not mathematical demonstration, was the only true guide for life. Specifically, he recognized that guidance by conscience was the "real key to the meaning of life."[101] For conscience involved not merely an absence of restraint but also a "high and solemn and vast responsibility."[102]

Yet although Oman clearly saw the emphasis on conscience as helpful in the work of reconciliation between faith and freedom, he also noted that Butler's view of grace was deficient. Butler saw God as "somewhat less than a Father, having in Him always something of the household disciplinarian. In this," Oman writes, "Butler comes short of the glorious liberty of the children of God."[103]

Lecture IV "Rationalism and Kant's *Religion Within the Bounds of Reason Alone*"

It is already obvious that Oman saw that the way to achieve reconciliation was not by a closed system but by a straightforward openness to truth. Professor John Macleod comments perceptively that he had "at one point a high respect for Rationalism, in so far as Rationalism meant respect for the spirit of enquiry, willingness to be open to the voice of the actual, humility to wait for reality's witness."[104] From his student days at Edinburgh University to his recent doctoral research, Oman had come to see Kant as the "crowning

---

99. Oman points to the "remarkable likeness ... between Pascal's Wager" and Butler's doctrine of probability. Oman, *Faith and Freedom*, 425.

100. Oman, *Faith and Freedom*, 24.

101. Oman, *Faith and Freedom*, 129.

102. Oman, *Faith and Freedom*, 123. Oman comments on the surprising neglect in Germany of the significance of Butler's doctrine of conscience. Oman, *Faith and Freedom*, 426–27.

103. Oman, *Faith and Freedom*, 134.

104. MacLeod, "John Oman as Theologian," 349.

product of the 18th century," who offered "a great lesson in the faith which believes that the way to counter balance defects and complete truth, is to continue to press forward."[105] He portrays Kant as a "confident rationalist" who saw the springs of moral and immoral action in the freedom of the will. He evolved an "austere and profound scheme of morals" which was a reaction against the "shallow optimistic views of human nature and the shallow utilitarian views of human duty"[106] prevalent in his day. The supernatural has no place in his scheme, nor does he expect a work of grace to do what we must do ourselves. Yet, as Oman indicates, "No one has a deeper sense of man's failure to rise at any time to the just demand, to be holy as our Father in Heaven is holy, of the need of a blessed assurance of perseverance in good, and above all of the difficulty of being delivered from a guilt already incurred. . . . In spite of the emphasis he puts on freedom, he cannot make men free, but only makes more evident the need of a higher power than mere resolute purpose to raise him to the glorious liberty of the children of God."[107] In short, Kant displays "remarkable insight into the deep meaning of Christian doctrines in which a shallow age had found nothing but absurdities."

Jesus, for Kant, was "a teacher who taught publicly a pure, penetrating, simple religion in face of a burdensome ecclesiastical faith,"[108] and he saw the function of the Church as being to forward the moral order of the kingdom of God.

In both these views Oman found "a sufficient amount of truth to be worthy of our consideration" albeit with the acknowledgement that this "is not a religion that came to seek and to save the lost."[109]

Lecture V "Romanticism and Schleiermacher's *Speeches on Religion*"

The "law of reason" had its limitations; "It enjoined man to be moral, but did not show what he was to be moral about; it asserted the dignity of the individual, but did not show in what form of individuality this dignity was to display itself; it asserted freedom, but it was freedom in a vacuum not a world."[110] Kant's ethical thinking was broader than this; but there was no place for feelings. Oman saw that the work of Schleiermacher was an

---

105. Oman, "Rationalism and Romanticism," 28.
106. Oman, *Faith and Freedom*, 188.
107. Oman, *Faith and Freedom*, 182.
108. Oman, *Faith and Freedom*, 182.
109. Oman, "Rationalism and Romanticism," 25.
110. Oman, *Faith and Freedom*, 196.

essential corrective; it was rooted in what it meant to be fully human. And he resumes: "the conception of religion as rooted in primary intuitions has proved itself truer that the criticism which reduces all religion to intellectual and abstract conceptions.... With many the cry has been 'Back to Kant' but they always mean by way of Schleiermacher."[111] While "Kant's is the only secure way in the end.... Without vision, few do great things in life" and "to him who is willing in the sweat of his brow to define it by the great experiment of life, it is neither hazardous nor useless."[112]

Lecture VI "The Revolution and Newman's *Apologia*"

"Pressure of thought" did not invariably advance the quest. Newman is one instance. Despite the fact that here was "the greatest special pleader who ever used the English speech,"[113] and that the *Apologia pro Vita Sua* was a "narrative written from within with full sympathy and unrivalled subtlety of presentation,"[114] Oman finds it ultimately to be a "supreme repudiation of the task of uniting freedom and faith in a bond of mutual interaction and common support."[115]

This could partly be explained by the contemporary historical context. The *Apologia* "palpitates with the horror of the Revolution."[116] The sense that true freedom could only exist in an ordered world led Newman to the "closely compacted dogmatic and hierarchical system"[117] of the Church of Rome, a magnifier for the "pale, faint, distant Apostolic Christianity."[118] In maintaining that "Christianity comes as a divine institution, whole, objective, infallible," Newman had come to the view that the essence of all religion was authority and obedience.[119]

---

111. Oman, "Rationalism and Romanticism," 49.

112. Oman, *Faith and Freedom*, 196.

113. Oman, *Faith and Freedom*, 287. The *Apologia* was a superbly crafted response to a scurrilous public attack by Charles Kingsley.

114. Oman, *Faith and Freedom*, 196, 258.

115. Oman, *Faith and Freedom*, 274.

116. Oman, *Faith and Freedom*, 258.

117. Oman, *Faith and Freedom*, 289.

118. Oman, *Faith and Freedom*, 265.

119. Newman's teaching on infallibility had a complex history; whereas in the *Apologia* he defended vigorously the necessity of an infallible teaching authority, in his Anglican days, he had regarded infallibility as the fundamental flaw in the Roman Catholic system, and as a Roman Catholic he opposed the movement to declare the infallibility of the Pope.

With an authority vested with infallibility, the Church of Rome had the power to control reason and suppress intellectual effort. In Newman's experience, humility was required, but Oman perceived such a conception of humility as "perverted." As he put it, "true humility must surely be submission to God, and, therefore, acceptance of God's task; submission to truth, and, therefore, diligence in investigation. But to Newman true humility might be mere intellectual surrender."[120]

Oman was clear that such an exercise of authority is inimical to religious freedom.

> What is the worth of God's long patience and all the infinite device of His providence, if infallibility goes by office, and the end of all our search is not the light of the souls that love truth and the liberty of the souls that obey it, but the reception at the hands of another of a body of doctrine, and the performance at the direction of another of a body of ritual? How much grander and truer to reality, how much more satisfying . . . to all our instincts of harmony and completeness, to conceive the Christian faith, not as an infallible body of doctrine, guarded by an infallible body of men, but a new power of vitality which enters the world, partakes of its evil, and again rejects it, at times by violent commotion. . . . Revolution may as gloriously reveal providence as death reveal immortality.[121]

Newman, however, "can dream of no meeting-place for those who love truth anywhere between the anarchy of individual notions and the rigidity of dogmas received from without."[122] And Oman concludes that "this inability to see any spiritual truth except at his own ecclesiastical angle must be accepted in Newman once for all . . ."[123]

Lecture VII "The Theory of Development and Baur's *First Three Centuries*"

Newman justified his view that the Church of Rome was the legitimate successor of the Church of the Apostles by asserting that "to live is to change, and, manifestly, the changes which come by growth are inevitable and

---

120. Oman, *Faith and Freedom*, 282.
121. Oman, *Faith and Freedom*, 271.
122. Oman, *Faith and Freedom*, 286.
123. Oman, *Faith and Freedom*, 287.

legitimate."[124] And he saw no contradiction between this and his belief that "truth, to be true, must have one form and one expression, absolutely true and proving all else to be false."[125]

Oman perceived that there were traces of Hegel in all this, and that his influence was even more marked in the Tübingen school of Theology under the leadership of Ferdinand Christian Baur. The scheme to reconcile opposites by thesis, antithesis and synthesis, "became a rack on which to torture the facts of history into the required shape."[126] The reference was to the study of Christian origins. Baur concluded from the frequent contradictions in the gospel narratives that Christianity was a reconciliation of the bitter antagonisms that existed between the factions led by Peter and Paul, and that the Catholic Church was a reconciliation of the opposing views which prevailed at the end of the second century. Oman was unconvinced. "Apart altogether from the question of whether the facts justify this scheme, Baur . . . cannot obscure the fact that it is a great departure from the freedom of the Apostle of the Gentiles."[127] Nor does it give any explanation of "the unique Personality by whom so many have pierced their way through a world of sin and suffering to a buoyant and glad hope, a radiant Kingdom of God."[128] By 1853, when Baur's *Church History of the First Three Centuries* appeared, his theory was vigorously contested by Albrecht Ritschl in particular. Oman comments: "the interest of the work is in the mode of trying and not in the measure of success. From the first it was a forlorn hope."[129]

In contrast to Baur, from whom he had learned the scope of the problems associated with the rise of the early Church, Ritschl "does not deal with bloodless categories but with living men, and . . . sees that the supreme concern is the Person of Christ."[130] Over the next ten pages, Oman outlines the ways in which freedom and legalism are intertwined in Ritschl's account of Scripture and the church, concluding that "so long as we remember that the purpose of these things is to enable us to pass beyond them, the New Testament will ever continue to raise two questions with increasing emphasis—the significance of Christ for this freedom, on the one hand, and the necessity of striving after the life of freedom, if we would realise our relation to Him, on the other. If Christ has this practical value, the Scriptures derive

124. Oman, *Faith and Freedom*, 287.
125. Oman, *Faith and Freedom*, 286.
126. Oman, *Faith and Freedom*, 294.
127. Oman, *Faith and Freedom*, 310.
128. Oman, *Faith and Freedom*, 314.
129. Oman, *Faith and Freedom*, 302.
130. Oman, *Faith and Freedom*, 314.

their significance from Him, and not from any conclusions regarding their accuracy or authorship."[131] The Scriptures of the Old and New Testaments may be distinguished from the patristic writings, "as the literature of our goal of freedom in God. The practical test of it is whether, against the world without and within, it can afford ground for maintaining the glorious liberty of the children of God."

Lecture VIII "The Theology of Experience and Ritschl's *Justification and Reconciliation*"

Oman sums up his investigations of Newman and Baur with this remark: "Through all this discussion one result has become clear. Christianity has no means left to it whereby to compel consent from the outside. There is no sound doctrine of Scripture which can overbear us; and just as little is there any sound doctrine of the Church. What power the Scripture and the Church have a right to exercise presupposes faith. They cannot therefore be the foundation upon which faith is built."[132] It cannot be a matter of finding peace in the world, but requires peace in spite of the world."[133] And that, Oman suggests, requires reconciliation with oneself and with God.

And so he looks at the significant work on the Atonement by Campbell, Maurice, Mozley, Dale. While ultimately finding their arguments "unconvincing," he praises their "willingness to recognise the fragmentary nature of human knowledge and to allow a due place to all the fragments, they insist on the living issues of life's tasks, on the necessity of doing them with what light we have, and they do not soar into abstractions either about man or about God."[134]

This "fidelity to life, this regard for the hints and half lights of experience," however, is often at the cost of "fundamental principles."[135] The same could not be said of contemporary German theologians whom Oman surveys briefly before turning to Albrecht Ritschl who, in his magisterial work on the *Christian Doctrine of Justification and Reconciliation*, "sought a reconciliation between historical Christianity and the modern mind, which should do justice to both and subordinate neither"[136]

---

131. Oman, *Faith and Freedom*, 323.
132. Oman, *Faith and Freedom*, 327.
133. Oman, *Faith and Freedom*, 329.
134. Oman, *Faith and Freedom*, 337.
135. Oman, *Faith and Freedom*, 338.
136. Oman, *Faith and Freedom*, 357.

Ritschl was teaching in Göttingen in 1883, while Oman was a student in Erlangen, and while there is no indication that Oman ever heard him lecture, he was introduced to his thought by Professor Frank, who was not uncritical.[137] Recalling how Ritschl had come to react against the Hegelian philosophy that undergirded the thought of Baur and the Tübingen School, Oman writes: "He had gone into the spider's parlour of the absolute Philosophy, the web of its dialectic had been woven round his limbs, a religion of mere ideas had threatened to suck the life-blood from a religion of active and burden-bearing faith."[138] As he recoiled from this, Ritschl developed a view of the true church as the community of saints, invisible but real, to which God reveals himself in Christ. His aim was to make this church "as objective a basis of faith as a visible church with organisation, creed and authoritative Scripture."[139] Here and in what follows, Oman engages creatively with Ritschl's thought. We are made members of the church in the freedom given by reconciliation. Freedom for Ritschl was personal. This was the basis of the worth of every individual, it required a distinction not only between a person and the world but also between a person and God. He conceives of God's grace as exalting but not obliterating human personality, whose responsibility it is to introduce moral order and unity into life. This is achieved not through intellect as in Kant, nor by feeling as in Schleiermacher, but by will, God's will and ours, insofar as we are willing to do God's will. In consequence, "the person who is reconciled to God is reconciled to two things—to those among whom he is to seek God's purpose, and to the life wherein he is to seek it. Wherefore he ranges himself in the community, and not above it; and he exercises his freedom in life, and not apart from it."[140]

Lecture IX "Method and Results"

Herbert Farmer commented on the concluding chapter of *The Problem of Faith and Freedom in the Last Two Centuries* as being "a further example of . . . the theological and philosophical penetration of Oman's thought . . . which on the basis of a critical estimate of Ritschl anticipates a number of the main issues which have occupied the thought of theologians since the date of its publication (1906)."[141] While recognizing that "Ritschl, no more

---

137. Oman, *Faith and Freedom*, 361, 390.
138. Oman, *Faith and Freedom*, 355.
139. Oman, *Faith and Freedom*, 354.
140. Oman, *Faith and Freedom*, 378.
141. Farmer, "Theologians of Our Time."

than any of his successors, has spoken the final word,"[142] Oman states that "his method, nevertheless, sums up the result of this long discussion in a way not to be ignored.... We must recognise not only the right but the duty of untrammelled investigation, under the sense of the obligation laid upon us by personal freedom in God."[143] Accordingly, in this final chapter, Oman reveals his own thoughts.

A method which works by freedom will always be "slow and irregular, full of failure, apparently having more of man in it than of God, but we shall see that nothing else has in it any spiritual promise. One requirement it must wait for—the faith which works by love, for by it alone can God enter a life in freedom."[144] In Oman's eyes, the way out of "the great intellectual morass" of the previous two hundred years is divine grace.

Oman saw, as Ritschl had not, that God's love is necessarily linked to God's power. "When God undertakes to work with freedom, He undertakes to bear and forbear, and the method of Christ becomes the revelation of a higher Omnipotence. Power becomes love, and gains in power by being love. Power can only rule by iron law, love can rule with the freedom of God's children; power can only create a vast plaything, love can create a Kingdom of God."[145]

Such love, for Oman, is God's supreme attribute.[146] This is

> necessary for our freedom on the one hand and for any sure estimate of what is Divine on the other, while the equality of justice with love is not necessary for maintaining that solemn sense of the majesty of the moral order which made it for Kant the supreme order of reverence. The conviction that God is supremely and wholly and exclusively love should not, if we think with Ritschl that it is a love which cherishes man's freedom, make us less able to consider with Butler, "what it is for us creatures, moral agents, presumptuously to introduce that confusion and misery into the Kingdom of God which mankind have in fact introduced." Wherefore... Christ, if He is to have for us the full worth of Godhead, must have something of cosmic as well as

---

142. Oman came to realize that Ritschl's "greatest weakness is where he seems strongest. His ethic never escapes pharisaic righteousness." *Journal of Theological Studies*, vol. 28, 189.

143. Oman, *Faith and Freedom*, 395.

144. Oman, *Faith and Freedom*, 416.

145. Oman, *Faith and Freedom*, 416.

146. This was contested by Frank who held that love was only one of many equal attributes; for him, justice must never be subordinated to love. Oman, *Faith and Freedom*, 390.

individual significance, a relation to the restitution of the moral order as well as of the erring person.[147]

While brainstorming the lecture on Ritschl, Oman wrote a letter to Cairns which reveals the way his own thinking was developing.

> The fundamental misunderstanding of Ritschl I take to be, that his affirmation of the primacy of will is misunderstood. It is only primary in the sense that reason is in Hegel, feeling in Schl. It is the point where we touch bottom. In this I take him to be right. His theory of religion explains the phenomenon. Schleiermacher's doesn't. Fundamentally also I think he is right about what he takes to be mysticism. But what I want to be at in my conclusion is, that we reach another mysticism. The mysteries of the intellect we must either solve or leave alone. The mysteries of the will we must live on the top of. The final result is that freedom is the only spiritual thing. What a man can maintain his freedom with has the echo of the eternal in it. Regulation after all is only material. Necessary like body to spirit but a corpse when the spirit dies. I dimly see rise out of this position of putting freedom first and faith afterwards a doctrine of revelation, a basis for critical principles, a doctrine of the person of Christ, a doctrine of God on the side of what I may call his microscopic infinity—in short a way out of the great intellectual morass of the last two centuries. Do you see any light in that sketch?[148]

He continues: "I am also coming to put more stress on Kant's autonomy of the will. It again was the first great assertion of the microscopic against the telescopic infinity of the XVIIIth cent. And I incline to read Butler more through his sermons. But we must take the consequences which is to go the whole hog on freedom."

An emphasis on freedom had been a distinctive feature of western society since the Enlightenment. Yet it had been defined by a variety of beliefs that were not always coherent.[149] Where freedom is understood merely as absence of restraint, there is no conception of the virtues of love and generosity that make it valuable.[150] But Oman's account of the glorious liberty of the children of God requires moral and spiritual intuitions, personal

---

147. Oman, *Faith and Freedom*, 391.

148. John Oman to D. S. Cairns, Alnwick, 20 November (no year), Papers of D. S. Cairns 1893–1906, University of Aberdeen, Special Libraries and Archives.

149. Isaiah Berlin reduces these to negative and positive freedom. Berlin, "Two Concepts of Liberty."

150. Fleur Houston, "Freedom as Authorization."

responsibility and love of truth, respect for others and questions about what constitutes a meaningful life. This is the basis for an enlightened society.

His view of freedom is inseparable from his ethics. He argues that "if . . . freedom is a genuine act of choice, and if the sense of right is a guide to the eternal and the ultimate meaning of things, history becomes the record of man's advance towards God's purpose, and has a significance not measured by space and time. The ideals and purposes of individual men have an absolute worth which societies, institutions and cultures cannot in themselves provide."[151]

Now Oman faces directly the question: how can we be morally independent as well as dependent on God? Conscience he sees as key. In that we are self-determined by the self-direction of an educated conscience, we make free choices between preference and duty. "If God's law is directly announced to man, if the Almighty has condescended to ask from each child of His willing and conscious concurrence and to tolerate refusal . . . a new measure of greatness has appeared in the world. . . . If freedom is not mere arbitrary action, but is a real possibility of choice between the Eternal Will and our present pleasure, conscience must be fundamental and cannot be combined with any equal authority."[152] Issues of morality arise. "With real freedom of choice, there must be that interaction between ourselves and the world which requires faith both in a free agency in ourselves, and in a free agency behind the world . . . right morality and true religion must be in entire accord."[153]

Oman is careful to point out that religion is not the same as morality. Religious faith involves feeling and thought as well as will, united in one vision, groping forward towards the truth. And so he addresses the radical question, raised by Schleiermacher, which he was to explore further in *The Natural and the Supernatural:* Is there any absolute difference between Christianity and other religions? And he concludes with the judgment that insofar as it is identified with the institutional church, "Christianity is only one among many phases of temporal things" but "if it trusts to nothing in the last issue except reconciliation and grace; if it will be satisfied with nothing less than a relation to God in which we shall be wholly free intellectually and morally, it must belong to the absolute, the eternal order."[154] There can be no kind of understanding of the church apart from Christ, who "remains

---

151. Oman, *Faith and Freedom*, 409. He elucidates this further in "The Judgment of Worth," appendix 3, in Oman, *Faith and Freedom*, 428-33.

152. Oman, *Faith and Freedom*, 398.

153. Oman, *Faith and Freedom*, 4.

154. Oman, *Faith and Freedom*, 412.

for every religious soul not of relative but of absolute significance. And the reason is that in Him we find the perfect freedom which could only be sustained by the perfect relation to God."[155]

Christ reveals the power of God's gracious love through the Church. And as the Church is called to serve the kingdom of God, it has a responsibility "to call men into the glorious liberty of God's children, always demanding of them a higher, more personal faith, and a more inward, more personal obedience, than she has any right to demand of them for herself."[156] We may note in passing how Oman is slipping here from the language of autonomous individuality to that of personhood, of relationship, a theme which will be a central strand of *Grace and Personality*.[157]

But is there not a risk that the scandal of the gospel may be bowdlerized into quiescent piety? What is the relationship between worldly and spiritual order and power? The question which Oman had already raised in *Vision and Authority* continues to exercise him.[158] In an appendix to *Faith and Freedom*,[159] where he expands with passion on "this appalling state of society," professing himself "sick of that individualism whose Kingdom of Heaven is in Park Lane with a Gehenna only a few streets away," he asks what relevance this might have to his previous conclusion that as freedom advances the institutional will give way to the individual. He concludes that "the power which upholds the system is not a defective government. It is the commonness of the belief that a man's life consists in the abundance of the things he possesses." And the situation cannot be remedied "until man's true life, his worth as an individual and the sphere in which he finds scope for his individuality, is found in the things which the State must cease to regulate. Then it may be possible for men to enjoy the fruits of the earth as much in common as they now breathe the air of heaven."[160] Ultimately, he

---

155. Oman, *Faith and Freedom*, 413.

156. Oman, *Faith and Freedom*, 418. In Oman, "Individual," he writes: "Insofar as the institution serves this Kingdom of God, this kingdom of souls, whose only authority is God the Father as revealed in the Son, and whose only rule is love, it is to be honoured; but it must ever be prepared to be judged by that standard."

157. Oman, *Grace and Personality*.

158. It would be raised acutely by Karl Barth in his exposure of the way German Christians were using Luther's doctrine of the state to endorse National Socialism.

159. "Freedom and Socialism," in Oman, *Faith and Freedom*, 434–36. It is interesting to note similar reactions by W. B. Selbie in the sermon he delivered at the monthly "people's service," Emmanuel Congregational Church, Cambridge, following the 1906 General Election when the number of Labour MPs rose from 2 to 29. See https://lostcambridge.wordpress.com/2021/01/14/rev-william-boothby-selbie-of-emmanuel-congregational-church-the-labour-movement/.

160. He develops further the relationship of individualism to socialism and the

concludes, "the issue will not be decided by movements but by men." And he adds: "Perhaps the crisis through which the Church is passing is not in the last issue intellectual at all. The thing that may prove whether Christ is a reality or not may be the attitude of His followers to the things of this world."

Conclusions

As Oman takes stock of his survey of the theological achievements of the previous two centuries, he asks: "in view of the magnitude of the task, have we any right to be discouraged by the result? We have not, it is true, wrung any absolute secret from the universe, we have not yet made a secure synthesis of all knowledge, we have not been able to finish off the lessons of history with the fine point of a formula, but we have attained a deeper sense of the meaning of freedom in so great a world and of its significance as a basis for our spiritual hopes."[161]

These lectures apply the principles of Caird's Preface[162] to the fundamental question of philosophical theology and the resulting book is strikingly original in its method. Through exploration of selected works by seven great thinkers over the previous two hundred years, Oman demonstrates how each one, despite differences of opinion from the others, contains a sufficient amount of truth for a succeeding generation, working in a different context, to give it fresh expression and a new application. This is a method that works with freedom, and philosophy, so conceived, is a living development. The book is open-ended. Although Oman finds Ritschl to be the most important link between past and present, he sees that neither

---

methods of the gospel in "Individualism," 817–18. Oman's interest in socialism was doubtless stimulated by the work of Thomas Kirkup (1844–1912), "from whom," Cairns wrote, "of all modern authorities upon the social question, I have learned most." (Cairns, *Christianity in the Modern World*, viii). Kirkup's *History of Socialism* went into five editions: 1892, 1900, 1906, 1909, 1913. With its scholarly grasp of continental socialism, this was the standard text for those interested in socialist thought and was widely read outside Britain. Kirkup was impressed by Marx's political economy: "the most complete presentation of socialism that has ever been offered to the world." But he was also critical of the increasing dominance of Marxist thought within continental socialism. He saw "the work of Marx" as "an arbitrary and artificial attempt to force his formulas on the facts of history" and characterized by an "absoluteness, abstractness, and deficient sense of reality." Oman would have agreed with this and with Kirkup's ethical critique of capitalism in *An Inquiry into Socialism*, (1887, 1888, 1907). Kirkup believed that "the dominant factor in history will always be the moral one" and further that "without a great moral advance socialism may be regarded as impracticable." (Noel Thompson, "Thomas Kirkup.)

161. Oman, *Faith and Freedom*, 400.

162. Above, 64.

he nor his successors has spoken the last word. "When God undertakes to work with freedom, . . . the method of Christ becomes the revelation of a higher Omnipotence. Power becomes love, and gains in power by being love. Power can only rule by iron law, love can rule with the freedom of God's children; power can only create a vast plaything, love can create a Kingdom of God."[163] In arguing that human freedom is nourished by God's grace, Oman is preparing the way for one of his greatest books, *Grace and Personality*.[164]

---

163. Oman, *Faith and* Freedom, 416.
164. Below, 273–88.

7

Alnwick

Ecumenical Collaboration

IN EXPLORING OMAN'S LITERARY work, we have temporarily set aside other aspects of his Alnwick years, to which we now return.

As Mr. Limont had foretold, Oman took part conscientiously in the work of the Northumberland Presbytery. The *Morpeth Herald* records his involvement in discussions and debates, the interest he took in Church extension projects and his activities as Presbytery Moderator in 1902. And although he was, as Alexander suggests, "no ecclesiastic,"[1] he displayed a readiness to collaborate with colleagues in other church traditions on religious and social issues. On the day of his ordination Oman had expressed pleasure at seeing representatives of other churches present. "He looked forward to a great deal of intercourse and fellowship with the other brethren in that place; and he hoped they would all work together in unity and love."[2]

An immediate locus of ecumenical cooperation appears to have been the Alnwick Ragged School,[3] which was the only undenominational school in the town. Luke Scott, Clayport's session clerk, and Adam Robertson, treasurer, served on the committee, and given Oman's interest in education, his

---

1. Alexander, "Memoir of the author," xxi.
2. *Alnwick Guardian*, 21 December 1889.
3. The Victoria Infants' School in Lisburn Street, founded in 1838, was reformed in 1854 as the Ragged School, one of several independent charity schools in Britain, which taught destitute children to read and write and which were gradually absorbed into the new Board Schools following the 1870 Education Act (in England).

own involvement was scarcely surprising. Although the teachers "laboured diligently and conscientiously" and "every care was taken of [the children's] moral and religious training,"[4] the reports of the inspectors were not satisfactory, attendance fluctuated, and in 1890, government grants were withheld. Despite this, it was reported at the annual public meeting in the Town Hall the following year, that thanks to the generosity of the subscribers, 78 scholars had received free education, with donations of clogs, clothing, and cocoa tokens, and a balance was recorded of £7 3s. 5d. Comment was made that there was now "a stronger claim on the voluntary efforts of philanthropists and those who looked to the welfare of the town," and that "as a whole the reports of the committee made on their regular visits to the school were of far more importance than the report of any Government Inspector. (Applause)." Oman moved the adoption of the forty-third Annual Report and financial statement, seconded by the minister of the Congregational Church, Rev. W. H. Chesson, who made the telling point that "now the poor man's child had a right to education as well as the rich man's child."[5] The element of defiance in the speeches has a political edge and there is no need to look far for reasons. The involvement with the Ragged School may have tallied with the dawning realization amongst Nonconformists that in order to address the problems of society, philanthropy was not enough. As attitudes were beginning to change, the charitable efforts that were made by interdenominational bodies such as the Ragged School Union were not felt to be sufficient in the face of a deepened sense of responsibility for the welfare of people living in intolerable conditions.[6] And in the case of the Alnwick Ragged School, developments may also be seen against the background of national education reforms.

On the eve of the 1892 General Election, Oman made it clear that while he had opinions on political matters, he had no intention of engaging in party politics in the pulpit. He had this to say: "Perhaps you will regard me as rash to make a General Election the occasion for such a discourse. It is my first opportunity and perhaps I shall be wiser next time. . . . While I have my political opinions and will give you them as a private citizen if you wish . . . I have never been concerned to make proselytes to them and certainly the last place I would think of using for such a purpose would be the pulpit.

4. *Alnwick Guardian*, 28 March 1891.

5. *Alnwick Guardian*, 28 March 1891. Two years later, a meeting of subscribers was held under the chairmanship of C. B. P. Bosanquet of Rock Hall. The school was to be renamed the Industrial School; the two teachers were to be dismissed; a sub-committee for technical education was appointed and the teaching of religion made more prominent. *Morpeth Herald and Reporter*, 8 April 1893.

6. Bebbington, *The Nonconformist Conscience*, 38.

Probably most of you are yet ignorant of what side I would take and trust you will not be made any wiser today. I have no desire to influence your vote . . ." He places emphasis here on personal attitudes rather than on issues, declaring that "we can all do something to make this a great occasion full of great thoughts and memorable for wise and considerate feeling or we can help to degrade it by sottish animal stupidity and envy and all uncharitableness."[7] But his chosen text, "Open the gates, so that the righteous nation that keeps faith may enter in," could evoke a partisan perspective, and it is not long before he takes a very public stance on successive government measures to reform the education system.

The Education Bill

To appreciate the significance of Oman's involvement, we need to take a closer look at these developments. Most Nonconformists had come to support Forster's Education Act of 1870, largely because Section 14 of the Act, the Cowper-Temple clause, allayed their concerns that their children might be taught Anglican doctrine, by providing that the teaching of religion in the new state Board schools would be non-denominational and parents would be allowed to withdraw children from religious instruction in these schools if they so desired. But the matter was by no means settled. Amongst other things, the financial situation of voluntary schools had to be resolved given the declaration by the Church of England that its schools were feeling "intolerable strain." Political and religious considerations permeated debates. When, in 1895, the massive rout of Liberals in the General Election resulted in the election of a new Conservative-Liberal Unionist coalition government under the leadership of Lord Salisbury, it gave immediate priority to a comprehensive overhaul of the education system. Few questioned the need for this, but the proposed repeal of the Cowper-Temple clause nearly brought down the government.[8] In 1896 the Bill was attacked with ferocity by Nonconformists in and out of Parliament, and although it was approved at second reading after five nights of heated debate, it was then swamped by amendments at Committee stage and withdrawn. Six years later, similar legislation, in the name of A. J. Balfour, was approved in the teeth of the same raging opposition. With a new system of secondary schools, Board Schools were abolished, County and Borough Councils were made the Local Education Authority for all schools, rate payers were to subsidize Anglican or

---

7. Sermon preached in Clayport, n.d., on Isaiah 26:1–2, Westminster College archives.

8. Daglish, "Planning the Education Bill of 1896."

Roman Catholic instruction, irrespective of their religious beliefs, and Nonconformists were up in arms.

Oman spelt out his personal attitude to the Education Bill 1896 in a vehement, even intemperate letter to the *Orkney Herald* where he announces his intention "to vote with all [his] heart against the present government, because a more retrograde and brazenly party and sectarian measure than this bill has not been offered to the country since it became in any sense constitutional."[9] Voluntary schools[10] had to be explained to a Scottish readership as National Schools mostly affiliated to the Episcopal Church, where teachers were required to be confirmed in the Church of England and "the English Prayer Book is much more faithfully taught than the Bible." Worse, because school attendance was compulsory, "children have to be sent to be taught things of which their parents do not approve, and in which they have no voice." Given "the present Romanising tendency in the Church of England . . . doctrines are taught our children which we regard as worst superstition, as that sacraments administered by a Church clergyman are essential to salvation, and that no Dissenter can be a holy man." While the "Education Bill of 1870 suffered this system to continue . . . it was tolerated in the hope that things would gradually right themselves, by Board Schools gradually ousting the sectarian schools. This has been taking place." However, following pleas from the Church of England for financial assistance, the "sectarian" voluntary schools were now to be supported not only by taxes, but also from the rates. "If we were chastised with whips before, we shall have absolutely no redress now if we are chastised with scorpions." Not that this is accompanied by any improvement in education. According to Oman, "the instruction is not only sectarian, it is also inferior . . . without provision for non-episcopal teachers." As for the teaching of religion, "The whole religious plea is the vilest cant. It is not the teaching of religion at all that is at stake, but the power of the church clergyman. For their own sakes we wish to have them out of this false position of lording it over God's heritage, that they may no longer be the proud priests of a great organisation, but the humble ministers of Jesus Christ." And he concludes, "The question of today is the old question of civil and religious liberty against classes who have made privilege their God." There is an unmistakable note of aggrieved hostility here towards the status of the Established church.

In England, the newly constituted National Free Church Council, described by Bebbington as "one of the most significant pressure groups for

---

9. *Orkney Herald*, 3 June 1896.

10. Effectively the Church of England now stood for the voluntary principle in education.

political engagement in Edwardian England,"[11] quickly became the vehicle for passionate protest against the Education Bill. In Alnwick as elsewhere, there had been moves towards Free Church solidarity. On Oman's initiative, a meeting was held in 1897 to consider the desirability of forming a Free Church Council for the District, and existing cordial relations were formalized. The *Alnwick & County Gazette* reported on the meeting:[12] "The Rev J. W. Oman presided. In the course of a few remarks, the chairman expressed his hearty sympathy with the principles of a Free Church Federation." The Reverend W. Glover, of Heaton, "secretary of the Federation in the northern counties, . . . pointed out that while the attitude of the Free Church Councils towards the established Church was not one of aggressive hostility, it might be their duty to act on the defensive with regard to their principles and interests, as occasion arose." "It was agreed that the object of the Council be to promote co-operation in questions religious, social, civic and educational."

Occasion arose five years later. In May 1902, in St James' Hall, London, Rev. John Monro Gibson,[13] minister of St John's Wood Presbyterian Church, addressed around 1,100 delegates of Free Church Councils in England and Wales, calling on the House of Lords to reject the Education Bill. Having outlined the requirements of the Free Churches, he concluded: "And now that we have been forced into battle, we shall not cease from the conflict until these hopes of justice and of national well-being have been all secured."[14] That same month, at a special meeting of the Alnwick Free Church Council in the Zion Lecture Hall, "the opposition of members to the Education Bill was strongly expressed" and the following resolution was passed unanimously: "That this council, representative of the Evangelical Free Churches of Alnwick, condemns the Education Bill now before Parliament as an entire reversal of the leading principles of the settlement of 1870, and as a violation of public justice, seeing that it destroys the direct popular management and the unsectarian character of schools wholly maintained by the ratepayers; and further indignantly protests against the bill because it compels Nonconformists to pay rates and taxes to schools whose teaching is repugnant to their conscience; perpetuates the unjust subjection of a State-paid teaching profession to sectarian tests, thus closing a large majority of the

---

11. Bebbington, *Nonconformist Conscience*, 62.

12. 6 February 1897.

13. Moderator of the PCE 1891; President of the National Council of Free Churches 1897. In 1902 he was convenor of the PCE Instruction of Youth Committee.

14. *Presbyterian Messenger*, May 1902. Gibson's views would have resonated with staff and students of Westminster College Cambridge, who, in line with the city of Cambridge, took a vigorous stance against the Bill (*Presbyterian Messenger*).

possible appointments against Nonconformist teachers otherwise eligible, and threatens to extend the sectarian training college system and further, because it would certainly lead to the multiplication of sectarian schools, and though it may seem to [permit the] provision of undenominational schools under the local authority, the conditions attached to the permission are so difficult as to render it illusory, and hence the bill would completely fail to redress the injustice from which the Free Churches have suffered too long; and we, therefore, pledge ourselves to use every right means to secure the defeat of the bill."[15]

Fired with crusading zeal, on 30 May the Council convened a public meeting in the Alnwick Corn Exchange to discuss the Education proposals with two prominent Liberal MPs, Sir Edward Grey, for the Northumberland Berwick Division, and Dr. Macnamara, North Camberwell. The following resolution, moved by George Elliott and seconded by John Oman, was carried with three dissentients: "This meeting holds that the state, having rightly made education compulsory, is not free to leave it under sectarian management,[16] but is bound, if it is not to be oppressive to the liberty of its subjects, to provide in every place schools, guaranteed, so far as public management can guarantee them, against teaching and influence contrary to the conscientious convictions of the parents. Wherefore it opposes the present Bill, and demands a measure establishing a general system both of elementary and secondary education under effective public control."[17] This meeting is noteworthy. It provides evidence of alignment between the Alnwick Free Churches and the Liberal Party, of an emphasis by Oman on freedom of conscience and of his increasing engagement with the protest.

While protestors could argue that their motives were religious, because based in conscience, nonetheless the question may be asked whether conscience was a product of other factors as well as religion, whether it was possible to induce individual men and women to follow their conscience in a particular direction, or whether such conscientious opposition could be organized.[18] While not wishing to deny the integrity of those who were opposed to the Bill on grounds of conscience, one may wonder about the extent to which they were being manipulated.[19] The editor of the *British Weekly*, William Robertson Nicoll, knowing he could count on the active

15. *Morpeth Herald*, 10 May 1902.
16. The reference is to the Church of England.
17. *Morpeth Herald*, 7 June 1902.
18. Munson, *Nonconformists*, 267.

19. There were parallel happenings nationwide. For an account of events in a Baptist church in Coventry, see Binfield, *Pastors and People*, 119–38; Munson, *Nonconformists*, 275.

support of the network of local Free Church Councils, was already urging his readers to campaign against the education rate, drawing on the old tradition of "persecution for conscience's sake."[20] On 31 July 1902, he issued a call to arms in the words of the Pilgrim's Progress, "Set Down my Name Sir." The sole resistance was to be refusal to pay the education rates. A national Passive Resistance Committee was formed[21] and when on 18 December 1902 the Bill received royal assent, a coordinated campaign of civil disobedience began in anticipation of the first wave of rate demands in June.

Passive Resistance

In Alnwick, Oman was at the forefront of the campaign. On 8 June 1903, it was reported in the *Times* that "at Alnwick petty sessions on Saturday Councillor J. W. Thompson, cabinet maker, the Rev. John Oman, minister of Clayport Presbyterian Church, the Rev. J. E. S. Otty,[22] and the Rev. E. H. Oliver,[23] all of Alnwick, were summoned at the instance of the overseers of the parish of Alnwick[24] for refusing to pay the education rate of 3d in the pound." It appears that the overseers had instructed a barrister, Mr. Joel of Newcastle, to prosecute.[25] Accusing the men of seeking martyrdom, he produced evidence that they had not paid the education rate. "Mr Oman complained of the overseers having gone to the unnecessary expense of employing a barrister against them," and Mr. Joel warned them "that they might lose their franchise if they did not pay their rates." The defendants were called in turn. "Mr Oman had nothing to say, except that he had a conscientious objection to the rate being imposed. An order was made for £1.15s."[26] The news flashed across the country in newspapers, national and local. Some opinion columns were scathing, particularly in the Tory press. The *Maryport Advertiser* heaped scorn on the "shoddy martyrs of 1903 who

---

20. Munson, *Nonconformists*, 253.

21. After a "full and frank exchange" on 1 December, the Free Church Council General Committee felt it was not expedient to organize a No Rate campaign. Munson, *Nonconformists*, 262.

22. John Elgar Sugden Otty MA (Glasgow) (1870–1961); minister of Alnwick Congregational Church 1901–5.

23. Ernest Henry Oliver, b. 1874, minister of Methodist New Connexion, Alnwick (1902–5).

24. The overseers of the (civil) parish were the traditional administrators of the Poor Law, who levied the poor rate; the education rate became part of their responsibilities also.

25. *Northern Daily Telegraph*, 8 June 1903.

26. *The Times*, 8 June 1903.

call themselves passive resisters" and cast aspersions on Oman, implicitly the ringleader.[27] Events then proceeded following a recognized pattern: distress warrants were issued and on 24 June "goods appraised to the value of the amounts due were taken from the houses of each and conveyed to the Century Hall where they await a sale by auction. The seizure was kept almost secret, and few people were aware that it was taking place."[28] Distrained items included an oak revolving chair from Mr. Thomson's house, a walnut Canterbury from Mr. Oliver's, twelve volumes[29] of Silvester Horne's *History of the Free Churches* from Mr. Otty's, and two walnut easy chairs in leather from Mr. Oman's. At the sale a few days later, the auctioneer, Mr. Henderson, "asked that there might not be any demonstration by the company while he was offering the goods for sale, and in respect to his wishes there was none, although the police were within call should any emergency arise." Attendance was orderly, unlike the occasion two years previously when goods belonging to the anti-vaccinationists were being sold in Wirksworth, and the violence was such that "sixty policemen were unable to keep order."[30] While the other items were bought by their owners, "the two chairs belonging to Mr Oman were sold to Mrs Horne and Mr Henderson for 17s 6d and 14s respectively."[31]

Respectability was a virtue in Nonconformist circles: it was unnerving for ministers to be accused of misdemeanor in court and humiliating to see their belongings removed by bailiffs for public auction. Some faced imprisonment. This was, as Munson observes,[32] "a form of middle-class martyrdom," and many had no doubt that they were witnessing for Christ. The communion sermons which Oman preached in Clayport in July and October 1903 resonate with the intensity of his personal experiences.[33] Following the pre-communion service on 3 July where Mr. Otty preached on Matthew 6:10: "Thy will be done," Oman preached at the morning communion service on 5 July on the text: "For I through the law am dead to the law that I might live unto God" (Gal 2:19); and that evening, on Isaiah 40:1: "Comfort ye, comfort ye my people saith the Lord." At the October pre-communion service, Oman preached from Luke 3:4: "The voice of one

---

27. *Maryport Advertiser*, 13 June 1903.
28. *Alnwick and County Gazette*, 27 June 1903.
29. Perhaps "copies" rather than "volumes" as reported?
30. *Manchester Courier and Lancashire General Advertiser*, 8 June 1903.
31. *Alnwick and County Gazette*, 11 July 1903.
32. Munson, *Nonconformists*, 267.
33. United Presbyterian Church Clayport Street Alnwick, minutes of session (1898–1923).

crying in the wilderness, prepare ye the way of the Lord, and make his path straight," and at the communion service on 4 October he preached from Matthew 6:38: "My soul is exceeding sorrowful even unto Death. Tarry ye here and watch with me."

Between these two communion seasons, Oman addressed two large public meetings. In August, at an "indignation meeting"[34] in Alnwick Town Hall, convened by the four protesters, he gave a "powerful indictment" of the Education Act and all that it stood for to an "enthusiastic" audience. "Our action in refusing willingly to pay a rate is one so inconsistent with our usual behavior as loyal citizens, that we have felt it right to give our fellow townsmen an opportunity of hearing our reasons."[35] His primary emphasis now is political.

> I have voted hitherto not for party but for what I took to be principle. But one must recognize that only the ancient party of privilege could have passed this measure by foreclosing debate, and thereby making mockery of representative government. All the more reason to scorn Mr Balfour's suggestion that passive resistance "is not the right political game," and that what we ought to do is to get a majority in the Commons and reverse the Act.

His second reason is "local circumstance." He professes himself "bitterly disappointed" in the County Council. But, after all, "what should one expect from a body consisting of one party whose leader proclaims that religious teaching should be a matter of possessing land?" Returning to the issue in hand, "I am asked to contribute a considerable sum each year to the Church of England School, and . . . to the Roman Catholic School. . . . Am I to pay for inculcating the crude material idea of the mass?" In summary, "the whole thing is a fraud and a delusion (applause) and . . . the whole pretence of an equivalent in control for your money is an unqualified humbug." Pointing to the difference between rates and taxes, he concludes that: "there is a limit to human endurance. Even the worm will ultimately turn."

That brings him to his third reason for refusal: "on the general principles of freedom. . . . No ordered freedom could stand on the methods by which this Bill was passed." He instances with vigor the wrong that compels your children to be taught "that your creed is wrong, your church a sect, your ordination irregular, your sacraments schismatic" and says that "it is on this policy of passive resistance that all ordered freedom has been built . . . on the day that minorities cease to set limits to their coercion, on the day

---

34. Bebbington, *Nonconformist Conscience*, 17.
35. All quotations from this speech are from the *Orkney Herald*, 5 August 1903.

they will no more suffer for their convictions, on the day majorities think they can ride over everybody's rights and everybody's conscience, on that day majority rule will end, and give way . . . to the easier rule of an autocrat." Christianity

> alone has been able to inspire men with the self-sacrifice upon which freedom alone can rest. Unless there are some few at least who will not sell their birthright for any mess of potage, who value justice above goods and liberty above life, no community will long remain free. I do not claim that we are doing anything very heroic. By collecting our chairs, we have still enough to sit down upon. . . . But we are quiet people, some of us here harmless creatures, studious people, all of us lovers of peace, and none of us people who would take up this attitude without strong compulsion of conscience.

This brings him finally to religious grounds for refusal. "It is the capital article in my creed, that religion never was forwarded, never yet was anything but wronged and misrepresented by any association with injustice." And so he concludes:

> An education permeated by the spirit of religion in the community is a supreme good, religion under the control of ecclesiastical persons for the ends of a particular church is a curse. . . . There is only one way of forwarding religion, believe me, and that is to follow justice and truth with all our heart, and that, whether we are mistaken or not, that is what we, who cannot concur in this Act, believe we are doing (loud applause).

It is likely that Oman's passionate protest was fueled by indignation at the fact that his old friend, Benjamin Mein, minister of Thropton, had been "deliberately passed by" by the "already notorious Northumberland Education Committee"[36] in favor of "the incumbent of the Thropton Episcopalian Church," despite the fact that Presbyterianism was strong in the district and Mein had served on the School Board for fifteen years.[37]

Oman was by now firmly associated with the Liberal Party which seemed to most Nonconformists to offer the only prospect of repeal of the Education Act. In early September 1903, he appeared on the platform party at a by-election meeting in Crail, alongside the Liberal candidate for the St Andrew's Burghs, Captain Edward Charles Ellice. Identified as a "passive

---

36. *Presbyterian Messenger*, September 1903, 228.
37. *Presbyterian Messenger*, November 1903, 284.

resister, who has had his effects distrained for the cause," Oman "delivered a speech condemnatory of the English Education Act."[38]

He was to be sued for nonpayment of the rates and his goods distrained on at least two other occasions, on 19 March 1904 and 4 March 1905[39] when the original four protesters were joined by James Hume, gentleman, Elizabeth Hume, stationer, James McMillan Scott and William Percy, drapers.[40] In 1905, Mr. Thompson, by then a magistrate, left the Bench in order to answer the charges.[41] I find no further references to the Alnwick Passive Resisters, but by 1906 the movement nationally was beginning to lose momentum. The Liberal victory in the polls in January had to be a major factor, although hopes that this would presage an educational settlement were short-lived. The Free Church Councils had begun to feel that a focus on politics had contributed to a sapping of religious vitality and detracted from local evangelism. And in 1905, both Mr. Otty and Mr. Oliver had left Alnwick.

Reactions by the Church

Members of Clayport church were clearly proud of the stance of their minister. At the social evening which marked Oman's move to Cambridge, the Reverend William Rogerson said that he

> had acquitted himself as to win the respect of the entire community. Whatever his opinions had been they had been the result of careful and prayerful thought. He had ever been ready to stand up to any truths or principles which had commended themselves to his conscience, without fear or favor, and with an earnest desire to discharge his duties faithfully in the community in which he lived.[42]

The wider councils of the PCE, however, were more ambivalent. On 9 June 1903, there was a long and lively discussion about passive resistance

---

38. *Dundee Courier*, 11 September 1903. Captain Ellice gained the seat from the Liberal Unionists by a small majority.

39. *Morpeth Herald*, 26 March 1904, and *Berwick Advertiser*, 10 March 1905.

40. Percy, Scott, and Hume had previously had their goods auctioned on 16 September 1903, when the overseers failed to find a local licensed auctioneer willing to conduct the sale. The assistant overseer, Mr. Elias Gibson, was clearly embarrassed at having to officiate and thanked them effusively for attending. *Morpeth Herald*, 19 September 1903.

41. *Berwick Advertiser*, 10 March 1905.

42. "The Departure of Dr Oman from Alnwick," *Alnwick Guardian*, 28 September 1907.

at a meeting of the Newcastle Presbytery. The Reverend J. Rorke of Heaton brought this motion: "Insomuch as the Education Act of 1902 inflicts a grievous wrong upon the rights and liberties of Free Churchmen in England, this Presbytery expresses its sympathy with those ministers, office-bearers, and members within its bounds, and also with all Free Churchmen, who feel constrained on grounds of conscience to adopt a policy of passive resistance to that portion of the rates which is levied on behalf of sectarian education."[43] Faced with attempts by the Presbytery to defer debate, the Reverend J. A. Hutton asked the Presbytery "to support him in a vote of sympathy to one of their own brethren, who, in a contiguous place, had already suffered under this Act. He desired them to pass a vote of sympathy with the Reverend John Oman who had had to stand in public the insolent references of men to this behavior." Despite being declared "out of order," Mr. Hutton persisted, proposing that "in addition to voting upon this particular matter of passive resistance—it is only a brotherly act—we send a vote of sympathy to the minister of Clayport, Alnwick." This was met with a stern rebuke by the Reverend Richard Leitch: "We are a spiritual Court, organized to discuss matters pertaining directly to the Lord Jesus Christ, and the discussion must not degenerate into a semi-political discussion. I strongly object to attending a conference that sympathizes with people who defy the law of England as it stands today." If we recall that Leitch was one of the two ministers who had officiated at John and Mary's wedding, the tone of his words is painfully condemnatory.

It is noteworthy that the Reverend J. Rorke of Heaton was instrumental that year in establishing the PCE Passive Resistance Association, which he served as co-secretary with the Reverend J. R. Gillies of Hampstead. This issued clear advice about procedure to those who were resisting on grounds of conscience. However, although National PCE Synods between 1902 and 1905 protested against the injustices of the Education Act, they refused to bind themselves to the Passive Resistance movement, believing that to be a matter for individual conscience.

In 1902, a resolution was carried condemning the Bill, which was then before Parliament, for its "intolerable injustice" and its "interference with the rights of conscience." The terms were to be sent to Balfour and Campbell-Bannerman[44] and in the event of the Bill going to Committee, amendments were to be pressed.[45] The following year, a motion was carried to appoint a special committee to monitor the progress of the Education

---

43. *Sunderland Daily Echo and Shipping Gazette*, 10 June 1903.
44. Leader of the opposition Liberal Party.
45. Carruthers, *Digest*, 605–7.

Bill for London[46] with the rider that "the Synod declines to make any pronouncements on the Education Bill, on the ground that any pronouncement on what is a political question is outside its function as a Church of Christ." The ensuing debate on Passive Resistance concluded with this resolution: "That the Synod, whilst it regards the question as one to be determined by the individual conscience, and does not see its way to pronounce any judgment on the policy of Passive Resistance, recognizes the grave injustice of the Education Act, and the invasion of the rights of conscience involved in the teaching of sectarian dogmas out of public funds, and fully sympathizes with such of its Ministers and people as feel constrained by conscience to adopt that policy."[47] However, the matter remained divisive and when in 1904 the Synod reaffirmed its sympathy "with such of its Ministers and people as feel constrained by conscience to adopt the policy known as Passive Resistance," thirty members dissented.

Effects on Oman's Personal Life

It is intriguing to note that George Alexander gives no hint of these developments in his *Memoir* which is in other respects so faithful an account of Oman's life. And yet he cannot have been unaware of his friend's stance. Frank Ballard suggests that "never was a major decision made in the life of either without the knowledge of the other."[48] Was this perhaps an issue over which the two friends had an "agreement to differ"?[49]

For Oman, the Passive Resistance campaign was of greater significance than the distraint of his fine walnut armchairs. There is a sense in which Oman's thinking and his experience were harmonizing and shading into one another. As he stood in the dock, pleading freedom of conscience, did he feel a sense of kinship with the prophet "who was true to the individuality God had given him" even if that pitted him against "both the State and the people"?[50]

As we have seen, the intense engagement with protest against the Education Act coincided with a concentrated period of lecture preparation and the publication of *The Problem of Faith and Freedom*. And all this was

---

46. The government was proposing to apply to London the principles embodied in the Act of 1902.

47. Carruthers, *Digest*, 607–9.

48. Alexander, "Memoir of the Author," xiii.

49. Alexander, "Memoir of the Author," xxv. Alexander was at the time clerk to the Glasgow School Board.

50. Oman, "Individual."

against the background of vigorous building activity at Clayport and the fundraising it necessitated. "I am growing tired," Oman confessed to Cairns, "and this last straw of building has almost broken the camel's back."[51]

For eleven years, the Clayport Street session minutes[52] had recorded discussions about Church alterations. These got off to a good start[53] but with a congregational deficit that had reached £92 in 1901, remaining plans had been put into abeyance.[54] Offers of practical help were received over the next few years and on December 24 1905 the session met to "consider what steps should be taken until the work of the church was so far advanced as to enable the congregation to meet there for divine service." The session met in the manse or in the house of John Balmbra, the session clerk; on January 14 1906, the pre-communion service was held in "Zion Congregation's church hall" and the sabbath communion in the Town Hall. The vestry was enlarged, and a minister's room added. On November 1, the clerk reported on the opening of the new organ chamber, dedicated to the memory of the Revd. John Ker, and "a new organ of the best class of Pipe organs" was installed. On November 28, Mr. Storey of Tyneside "gave an organ recital to a large congregation."

Chairs

On 30 November 1906, Oman wrote to Cairns, "As soon as I get myself pulled together and surmount the ecclesiastical distractions which have beset me, I shall return your books."[55] Having exercised a conscientious pastoral ministry in Alnwick for seventeen years, Oman's calling to teach theology was being redefined. Already in 1893 he had informed the Clayport Session that he had received an offer from the Congregational Theological Seminary of Chicago to become Professor of Systematic Theology. He was clearly tempted. He told the elders that "he had the matter under

---

51. John Oman to D. S. Cairns, Alnwick, November 20, Papers of D. S. Cairns, University of Aberdeen Special Libraries and Archives.

52. UPC Clayport Street Alnwick minutes of session.

53. In January 1895, plans for "reseating and other alterations" were submitted and approved by the congregation with "substantial subscriptions to justify the members in proceeding at once with the work." On April 28, "arrangements were made to reopen the church the next Lord's Day for special services" and on May 13, we learn that the cost of alterations to the church was £400. By 21 October 1896, however, the total cost of improvements had risen to £495. 4.1. Session minutes 1853–1897.

54. Session minutes 1898–1923.

55. John Oman to D. S. Cairns, Alnwick, 30 November 1906, Papers of D. S. Cairns, University of Aberdeen, Special Libraries and Archives.

consideration and hoped to be able to announce his decision in the course of a few weeks... the Session agreed to leave the matter in Mr Oman's hands and express the hope that he might be divinely guided in this matter."[56] Only five days later, the elders received a letter from Scone, Perth, confirming Oman's decision "not to accept the invitation to Chicago." He continues: "In point of inclination I always preferred the thought of remaining in Alnwick and I have now resolved the matter of duty also and feel that I go away on my holidays[57] with a much lighter mind. I can only ask you to continue to me the same sympathy and forbearance that you have always given me and I could wish that we should all be stirred up to oppose more actively the indifference of our town."[58] The elders decided to minute "their cordial satisfaction with the decision at which Mr Oman had arrived and their hope that this incident in the history of the congregation may be over-ruled by God for the good of the congregation and the advancement of the Kingdom of Christ."[59] Although he was subsequently invited to deliver a series of lectures in Chicago, he declined.[60]

However, between 1904 and 1906, it was becoming increasingly clear that the minister of Clayport was "marked out for important professorial work."[61] On 9 April 1904, he graduated as doctor of philosophy in the McEwan Hall, Edinburgh. On 13 April, he was nominated by the Presbytery of Orkney amongst others for the chair of Systematic Theology in Edinburgh following the resignation of Professor Laidlaw on grounds of ill health. The election took place the following month at the UF General Assembly. It attracted keen interest, with a "full attendance of members of the House, while there was also a large gathering of the general public, chiefly ladies, in the galleries."[62] There were three candidates, one of whom, Dr. Forrest, minister of North Morningside, Edinburgh, withdrew on consideration that it had been only one year since his induction. That left Hugh R. Macintosh from Aberdeen and John W. Oman from Alnwick. Oman's candidature was impressive. There were letters in support from Professor Seth (Edinburgh), Principal Oswald Dykes (Cambridge) and Principal Fairbairn (Oxford). He was proposed by Mr. John Cowan, an elder in Edinburgh, who assured his

---

56. 15 August 1893. Session minutes 1853–1897.

57. He was "on a visit to his native islands." *Orkney Herald*, 6 September 1893.

58. Minutes of session 1853–97, 20 August 1893.

59. Minutes of session 1853–97, 20 August 1893.

60. See the *Courier*, Saturday, 28 May 1904. James Denney subsequently accepted to deliver these lectures in 1894. They were to be the substance of his book *Studies in Theology*.

61. *Orkney Herald*, 22 May 1907.

62. *Scotsman*, Saturday, 28 May 1904.

hearers that "in Dr Oman he proposed a man because he was a man, and sitting in the pews as he [Mr Cowan] did, he thought they in the pews had some idea of the kind of man who ought to be in a Theological chair."[63] Cowan had known Oman from the time he first came to Edinburgh as a student, when they both attended a Young Man's fellowship and had followed his career ever since. Revealingly he continued: Oman "was the possessor of the great gift of imagination, with a vigorous and clear intellect. His was a master mind that expressed itself in beautiful language . . ." He added that Oman "was a man of great physical and mental strength, large-hearted, and he would be a 'persona grata' among students, influencing them and leading them to the highest flights of thought."[64] According to the reporter from the *Courier*, however, "the speech of the day was certainly Mr Welch's."[65] In seconding Oman's nomination, Adam Welch "introduced many of us to a new star and he effected the transference of several votes to his nominee."[66] Oman however was at a disadvantage in being previously unknown to most of those present, and by a show of hands, the chair went to Macintosh.

In May 1905, he was nominated by the UF Presbytery of Orkney and others for the chair of Dogmatic Theology at the UF church college in Aberdeen, vacated on the death of Professor Salmond on 22 April. However the Aberdeen UF Presbytery decided for financial reasons to opt for a year's delay in filling the post, the work being spread in the meantime among the existing four professors.[67]

The UF college in Glasgow appeared to be laboring under similar constraints. In April 1906 Oman was again among those nominated by various Presbyteries for the Chair of Practical Training and Ethics. But at the meeting of the Kirkcaldy UF Presbytery, a motion was unanimously agreed that "under the present uncertain state of the church with regard to its colleges, that no more life interests should be created." And in proposing the motion, the Reverend Mr. Elder commented that "it was quite within the bounds of possibility that the Aberdeen College might be given over on request to the legal Free church, and in that case, they would have a number of

---

63. *Scotsman*, Saturday, 28 May 1904.
64. *Edinburgh Evening News*, Friday, 27 May 1904.
65. *Courier*, Saturday, 28 May 1904.
66. *Courier*, Saturday, 28 May 1904.
67. In 1907 D. S. Cairns was appointed to the chair of Dogmatics and Apologetics, and in 1923 he was appointed principal. Following the church reunion of 1929, Christ's College became a college of the Church of Scotland, and when the college integrated with the University of Aberdeen, Cairns was appointed Professor of Christian Dogmatics.

superfluous Professors. They should make a temporary arrangement with regard to Glasgow college."[68]

The Free Church Case

To put this briefly into perspective, a catastrophe had hit the UF church within four years of its formation in 1900, when the UP church and the majority of members of the Free Church of Scotland had united. In 1904, a claim was made to the whole property of the Free Church by the small number of members[69] of the Free Church who had dissented from the Union. The claim was dismissed by four senior Scottish judges, but an appeal to the House of Lords as the supreme court (at that time) of the UK was sustained on the second hearing. The law was simple enough: the property of the Free Church was held in trust according to the principles of its constitution. Therefore it should be taken from those who had departed from these principles and given to those who adhered to them. But the matters under dispute were not primarily legal, and these were the questions the Lords had to adjudicate: had the union with the UPC infringed FC principles around Establishment? What was the bearing of the Calvinist doctrine of Predestination on the evangelical offer of the gospel?[70] The legal Free Church refused arbitration and seized church property. UF ministers and their families were evicted and the consequent outrage led to the establishment of a Royal Commission and the intervention of Parliament. The judgment of the Lords was reversed, the church's liberty vindicated and the property restored to its original possessors.[71]

While Oman's reactions to his aborted candidacy for the Aberdeen and Glasgow chairs cannot be ascertained, he gave a passionate account to an Alnwick audience of what became known as the Free Church case. Reflecting on the lawsuit, he expressed outrage at the decision of the House of Lords "that you shall not take the Creed as a historical document but as a prospectus of a company to be interpreted and applied in literal detail," and

---

68. Saturday, 7 April 1906, *Fifeshire Advertiser*. The vacancy, caused by the death of the Reverend Dr. Alexander Hislop, was ultimately filled in 1910 by the Reverend A. B. Macaulay, who had been teaching there for the previous two sessions.

69. "Around thirty ministers, nearly all from the remote Highlands, with their flocks and adherents" (Simpson, *Principal Rainy*, 300). For a careful analysis of this affair, see Simpson, *Principal Rainy*, 300–467.

70. In passing the Declaratory Act of 1892, General Assembly had claimed authority to determine which parts of the Westminster Confession entered into the substance of the Reformed faith, and qualified it accordingly. (Above, 140n73).

71. The UF Church re-entered New College on 1 January 1907.

he added: "This hard, literal construction no thoughtful person would think of putting upon the confession." Yet Presbyterians in England had often been dissuaded by legal considerations from doing "some things we ought to do," and he concluded: "Liberty of interpretation is all very well, but an express statement of the liberties we take is far better—honester and truer in every respect."[72] Oman also feared an adverse effect on church union negotiations between Congregationalists and Evangelicals and among the different Methodist affiliations. For the Christian church, "it is a vast calamity." And not least, "It exposes every movement to the mercy of cranks. Not merely do our creeds and documents commit us, but our generous understandings as well." Yet, he believes, "good will come, and is coming out of it. The Union has been cemented in a most wonderful way. As it was said lately, Principal Rainy has had too much honour over the Union. Its true author is the Lord Chancellor. . . . For us all there is a great warning against relying upon outward securities and a great need to aim at a higher trust, a great lesson in the knowledge that only the unseen and eternal abides."

We may only speculate as to why in 1906 Oman turned down the offer of a chair from Ormond College, Melbourne which had become vacant on the death of the first incumbent, Professor Murdoch MacDonald. But had he accepted, he would have been plunged immediately into further controversy between Church and State, with the vigorous Rationalist campaign against initiatives to install a divinity degree at the University of Melbourne. Following the failure of an initial attempt in 1905, allegiances were complex and members of Ormond were divided.[73]

From the above, we may deduce that the issues of freedom which were preoccupying Oman as he prepared his Kerr lectures were of more than academic importance. His engagement in passive resistance to the Education Act highlighted the significance of personal conscience in matters of Church and State and raised the question as to whether individuals should be free in certain circumstances to resist the law of the land. While the Free Church Act also raised matters of conscience, this time for the Church, it illustrated the fact that Parliament could overturn decisions of the House of Lords when justice and freedom were at stake.

---

72. Unpublished MS, Westminster College archives, penciled date 17 October 1904.

73. In 1910, a compromise was achieved whereby degrees were to be awarded through the appropriate college and, following a stormy passage, the Melbourne College of Divinity Bill won government assent. Biddington, "Rationalism and the University of Melbourne."

A Visit to America

The year 1907 appears as a time of transition. After the publication of *The Problem of Faith and Freedom*, Oman sought "relief from German abstractions by a spell at Hebrew."[74] On 10 January he sent George Adam Smith a closely argued paper which he had previously written on the chronology of the Kings of Israel and Judah, with the comment that he had "looked over the subject again."[75] Was this anything more than mental relaxation? It may be suggestive that on 13 January Oman preached at the communion service on the text: "Hereafter I will not talk much with you: for the prince of this world cometh, and hath nothing in me" (John 14:30), and after the sacrament gave an address entitled "Waiting on the Lord." Had all these overtures about professorships over a relatively short period of time been unsettling? Was he aware of a further call which he found tempting?

The following Thursday, 17 January, he informed the elders that he had been invited to give a course of lectures at Auburn Theological Seminary, NY State, which he would like to accept. Because this would entail a two months' leave of absence he would want to ensure that they had a good locum tenens. He also informed them that, the previous July, he had turned down the offer of a chair in Theology at Auburn "which he had not seen his way to accept," and that no appointment had as yet been made. Having received the "cordial and unanimous" agreement of the Session and Managers, with the assurance of their pride in his achievements, Oman's imminent departure was announced by John Balmbra in crusading terms to the congregation after morning service. "No truer, more experienced or better equipped Knight of the Cross rode forth to do battle for his Lord. Their hearts went out to him and their prayers would follow him, because they believed in the faith he held with such steadfastness and freedom and for which he was so strenuous a fighter." A social gathering was held on 28 January to wish him godspeed and two days later, he set off aboard the White Star liner *RMS Baltic* for New York.

His passage was booked at last minute; he sent on the minimum fare and "asked for as good a cabin as they had left over." As there were few travelers, he had a "sumptuous cabin all to [himself] with two port holes, three electric lights, a wardrobe and hooks enough to have hung up the clothes of a village." And he added: "There is much to be said for a winter crossing."[76]

74. John Oman to George Adam Smith, 10 January 1907, Alnwick, Northumberland. University of Edinburgh, New College Library.

75. John Oman to George Adam Smith, 10 January 1907, Alnwick, Northumberland. University of Edinburgh, New College Library.

76. Oman, "Visit to America."

The week was relaxing. "Nothing troubled me," he wrote, "but the change of the hour."[77] He reveled in the luxury of the ship, and its huge size: even a NW gale could not make it roll. Despite five days of very rough weather, time passed agreeably: "we read light literature, gazed out upon the heaving sea with its green and white flashing though the slaty blue, and studied fellow passengers and dreamt vaguely of the vastness of things." One of his fellow passengers was Dr. John Watson, who was something of a legend in the PCE.[78] Watson too was embarking on a lecture and preaching tour in America. They are likely to have dined together at the captain's table.[79] Watson remarks on the "pleasant companionship"—there were several others at the table whom he knew or who knew him, and he and his wife had "little parties after dinner" in their sitting room while the gale raged outside.[80] Given Watson's regard for Oman, it is highly likely that he was among them.[81] The two men shared future prospects. Before setting off from Liverpool, Watson had accepted nomination for the principalship of Westminster College, Cambridge as successor to J. Oswald Dykes, and Oman was probably aware that he was being actively considered as a candidate for Dykes's chair of Systematic Theology.[82]

When they arrived at Sandy Hook, it was piercingly cold, and "the water was grey with broken ice and looked like a road paved with cobbled stones." But with its paddle boats, ferries, and huge liners, "a more magnificent harbour, spacious, safe, deep, could not be conceived." With a declaration that he "was possessed of 850 dollars, was not an anarchist[83] or a

---

77. Oman, "Visit to America."

78. Under the pseudonym "Ian MacLaren" he published a popular collection of short stories, *Beside the Bonnie Brier Bush*, which topped the best-seller charts in the US in 1895. Along with other stories of Scottish rural life, he also published religious non-fiction either under his pseudonym or his own name. He was a vigorous preacher, and while minister of Sefton Park, Liverpool, he raised £16,000 in five weeks towards the costs of the move of Westminster College from London to Cambridge in 1899.

79. Oman quotes Watson as saying to him one day: "Man, are you not tired of the humbug of thinking of what you are to eat." Oman, "Visit to America."

80. Nicoll, "Ian MacLaren," 364.

81. "Ian MacLaren's" appreciative review of *Vision and Authority* in the *Alnwick Guardian* was accompanied by a private letter to the editor, saying that "burdened as he was by work, only the high opinion which he held of Dr Oman constrained him to undertake the task." *Orkney Herald*, 22 May 1907.

82. On 12 April Oman was welcomed back at a social gathering of the Clayport congregation, during which Mr. Balmbra remarked that "there seemed to be no doubt that the call to Westminster College would be of a good unanimous character."

83. President MacKinley had been assassinated by an anarchist six years before.

polygamist and that [he] was a British citizen intending only to travel for a little in the States," Oman's visit to America began.

His account of his travels[84] is engaging. One could cite for example his detailed description of New York with its grid-plan, skyscrapers,[85] and clubs,[86] and his acute perception of the immense wealth of Broadway. He also gives brief descriptions of Boston, Albany, and Buffalo. Particularly memorable are his accounts of two long train journeys where he articulates the vivid impression made upon him by the countryside covered in snow. The first journey was on the sleeper train from New York to Buffalo via the Hudson and Mohawk valleys.[87] "From the first streaks of daylight," he watched the changing landscape, as the train proceeded along the river basin, and passed along the streets of towns, clanging a bell. "At dawn the skyline showed against the frosty sky sharp as the edge of a saw. Then a soft flush of violet pink spread over the horizon and presently the sun came up with a rush, bright and hot and large."

The second journey he describes is the return from Princeton to Buffalo by way of the Lehigh Valley. Once the train had crossed the Delaware, "then you begin climbing the slope of its tributary the Lehigh. Hour after hour we wound up the stream passing at first two or three large manufacturing towns and then coming to sheer forest and wilderness without a glimpse of human habitation. At the summit was a view to take one's breath away": the great wooded plateau, ridges of hills fading away into the distance, and "the spacious winding valley of the N. Susquehanna." Then onwards to the Great Lakes where he glimpsed Erie and Ontario before stopping off at Niagara "to see the cataract and the falls in the moonlight."

Next morning Dr. Stewart, principal of Auburn seminary, joined him for a visit to the falls by daylight and the following extract illustrates further Oman's sensibility to nature and his creative imagination:

---

84. Oman, "Visit to America," which is likely to be the substance of the talk he gave in Clayport on his return.

85. Oman stayed in a hotel in a skyscraper and remarked: "I was low down but I could hear the wind whistling round over head as if I were at sea and the bed vibrated quite visibly in the gusts."

86. An invitation to an "Anglo-American dinner" occasioned Oman's visit to the Century Club, at 7 West 43rd Street, near Fifth Avenue, Manhattan. Here, in "the most famous and among the least gorgeous of New York clubs," he met some distinguished men and narrowly missed Mark Twain. In early February, possibly on the same occasion, John Watson recorded a similar "lunch with literary men" at the Century Club. Nicoll, *"Ian MacLaren,"* 365.

87. He may have got off at Syracuse. This was his first experience of the American sleeper. The jolting, the noise, the heat kept him awake for most of the night.

The gorge is wide and one does not take in its width, and a fall of 130 feet like a small Swiss cascade coming down 700 or 800 feet amid fantastic rocks and clinging trees with the gleam of a white snow peak overhead. But slowly an impression of overwhelming force gains on you. As you pass up the Canadian side you see more clearly the whole scene. Then you descend into the gorge and look up at the cataract. We crossed the river on the ice and I climbed the slope and stood right in face of the American fall with the rush of water spraying my face and the sound ringing in my ears. I measured my whole length descending but that was of no account in the circumstances. Standing in the middle on the seamed and broken ice I realised for the first time the width of the gorge and that it was the current of a river that swept under your feet and not an arm of the sea and that it has carried water for untold ages from the farthest North East slopes of the Rockies to the Atlantic, a river draining half a continent.

In the gorge, "the impression of resistless might is, I think, greater than in the falls themselves." He woke again and again during the night "struggling in the grip of the swirling waters as they make their last swift rush ... and clash together in one Titanic embrace."

However, whatever may be inferred from Oman's immigration declaration, the primary purpose of his visit was to give lectures. By the end of his visit to America, he had preached and lectured thirty-one times.[88] We know that sixteen of these lecturing engagements were at Auburn Theological Seminary, where he also preached at least once, on 18 February,[89] and a further four in nearby Syracuse University. He also preached at Princeton, lectured at Yale "and other places," occasioning visits to Harvard, Buffalo, Rochester and Boston, where an old friend from Edinburgh University days showed him Longfellow's house. On one Sunday alone, he preached three times in New York. In Buffalo, at a dinner of the Presbyterian Union at the First Presbyterian Church on The Circle, which he attended along with Dr. Stewart, he spoke on "the religious situation in England" which was found to be "very complex and very perplexing." Perhaps judiciously, he "said very little" about Mr. Campbell's Atonement theology, but elucidated the Education Bill.[90]

88. Press cutting dated 12 April 1907 inserted with session minutes, describing the church social gathering to welcome Oman home.

89. On "Barnabas, a good man." Calendar, Auburn Seminary Record.

90. Oman, who in the *British Weekly* had replied to Campbell "in the light of modern scholarship," "admitted that Mr Campbell has a large following." *Buffalo Express*, Wednesday morning, 27 February 1907.

Lectures in America

The Problem of Faith and Freedom

The focus of his visit, however, was the invitation from Auburn seminary to be lecturer-in-residence in theology. It was reported[91] that it was "a great pleasure to have Dr Oman, during his stay, rooming in Morgan Hall, and sharing our common life at the Silliman Club House." From 12 February, over five weeks, Oman gave two courses, the first consisting of twelve lectures on "The Problem of Faith and Freedom," morning and afternoon, four a week. "Special attention," it was observed, "was given to the epoch-making books on the problem," from the *Pensées* of Pascal to Ritschl's *Justification and Reconciliation*.[92] These were almost certainly the nine Kerr lectures, resurrected and adjusted to accommodate the three additional lectures. And the second course, of four evening lectures from 19 February, was entitled "The Foundations of Belief." "These lectures," the President recorded, "were open to all of the students and were attended by larger numbers and were received with more interest and enthusiasm than has been the case for a long while with extra curriculum lectures. Dr Oman's profound scholarship, his luminous style, his keen appreciation of the living problems in theology contributed largely to give these lectures the highest value. His work was warmly appreciated and his visit will not soon be forgotten."[93]

At short notice, it would appear, plans were made for the second set of lectures to be repeated at Syracuse University. On 15 February, Oman gave apologies for having to leave early a banquet arranged by the Presbyterian Union in Park Presbyterian Church, Syracuse because he had a train to catch, and the following day it was announced that he might come to Syracuse to deliver a course of lectures.[94] Arrangements were made by Professor Ismur J. Peritz, and tickets for a course of four lectures in the Syracuse University Assembly Hall on "The Foundations of Belief" were advertised. "Dr Oman," it was said, "is regarded as a scholar of wide learning and a clear thinker."[95] It was additionally noted that "the Ministerial Association of Syracuse has expressed itself as in favor of the course, which is expected to have more than ordinary interest at the present time."[96]

---

91. Seminary Annals, *Auburn Seminary Record*, 10 March 1907.
92. Seminary Annals, *Auburn Seminary Record*, 10 March 1907.
93. The President's Annual Report, *Auburn Seminary Record*, 10 March 1907.
94. *Post-Standard*, Syracuse, NY, Saturday morning, 16 February 1907. These were held on 27 February, and 2, 5 and 6 March.
95. *Post-Standard*, Syracuse, NY, Saturday morning, 23 February 1907.
96. *Post-Standard*, Syracuse, NY, Saturday morning, 23 February 1907.

To put this remark into context, it is worth recalling that Auburn seminary had for many years been the focus of theological battles over the authority of the Bible and the Westminster Confession. A brief indication of the development of this might be useful. In 1837, the General Assembly of the Presbyterian Church had summarily condemned without due process four Synods in NY State[97] for alleged doctrinal errors which were judged to be irreconcilable with membership of the Presbyterian church. A convention of the excluded bodies met at Auburn under the presidency of the Professor of Christian Theology and produced what became known as the *Auburn Declaration*. This was not a new Confession of Faith, but a commentary on the Westminster Confession. Opposition from what was known as the "Old Church" hardened. But ironically, when reconciliation between the two bodies was achieved in 1868, the *Declaration* was declared by the Assembly to be an orthodox interpretation of Scripture and the Westminster Confession. And by the beginning of the twentieth century, Auburn, with its famous defense of freedom, was regarded as the center of theological enquiry.[98]

To quote President Stewart: "The agitation about and among the seminaries is making increasingly evident the peculiar strength of this seminary. . . . The strength of our position is not merely geographical. Our ideals are also an element of our strength. . . . We have a place and a mission, never more so than now."[99]

The Foundations of Belief

Oman's lectures on *The Foundations of Belief* were in tune with this ethos and demonstrated that the issues he raised in *Vision and Authority* were still topical in the American context. The first, "The questioning of the old

---

Oman commented appreciatively on the strong ecumenical links he observed: "I had ministers at my lectures from the Episcopalian to the Unitarian. Both usually belong to the ministers' meeting." Oman, "A Visit to America."

97. The Synods of Western Reserve, Utica, Geneva and Genesee.

98. For a detailed account, see Adams, *Auburn Theological Seminary*. In his Annual Report (*Auburn Seminary Record*, 10 March 1907), the President affirmed that during the second term, he "conducted a weekly quiz with the Middle Class in the Westminster Confession of Faith." In the battles over the authority of the Bible of early 1920s, Auburn was once more at the center of controversy. "The Auburn Manifesto" of 1924 countered the efforts of those who campaigned to impose a single interpretation of Scripture over others, which had led to the resignation of Henry Fosdick from his charge in 1923.

99. President's Annual Report. There was also an Auburn tradition of involvement in social movements: members of the faculty had campaigned against slavery, advocated women's suffrage and pressed for reforms to help the poor.

authorities and the authority of the church," drew an estimated two hundred people to explore the fallibility of the church as a human organization and the importance of the church for belief. The standard of the real church, they were told, "is to live in purity and love, making the kingdom of God the environment of our life."[100] His second lecture on "The authority of the Scripture" revealed how the real value of the Bible had been enhanced by rejecting the doctrine of scriptural inerrancy.[101] Much interest in Oman's third address, on "The authority of Christ" was awakened by the Syracuse *Post-Standard*'s "rather sensational" report of his previous lecture, and it was "much more largely attended by people from outside the seminary than previous lectures have been."[102] On this occasion Oman's preaching skills stood him in particularly good stead, for he "was obliged to present his discourse without notes, his grip containing the manuscript and other belongings having been stolen from the train on which he left Jersey City on Saturday evening last. Dr Oman hopes that the railroad company will be able to locate the stolen property."[103] It was affirmed that he was "at no great disadvantage in having to give material 'from his own head.'"[104] While the *Post-Standard* carried the controversial headline "Asserts Christ was limited in knowledge,"[105] the report in the *Auburn Semi-Weekly Journal* is credibly nuanced. Having made the point that "the brotherhood and the saving power of Jesus Christ were made perfect only by giving up the old idea of the omniscience of the human Jesus" and that Jesus was "intellectually a part of his age," Oman affirmed that he "chose the human and hence imperfect way of transmitting his revelation." Jesus "did not leave a single word in writing"; the gospels were in general "written by the second generation of Christians for the second generation of Christians." The reporter sums up as follows: "In what way is Jesus then an authority in religion? It is not primarily by being a perfect teacher in theology. He is an authority because, in the midst of sufferings, weaknesses and struggles, He Himself was perfectly the subject of religion. He showed perfect fidelity through every trial that might shake Him. He not merely shows us about the Father, He shows us the Father. It is this that lifts the authority of Christ above all other authorities."

100. *Post-Standard*, Syracuse, NY, Thursday morning, 28 February 1907.

101. *Auburn Semi-Weekly Journal*, 8 March 1907.

102. *Auburn Semi-Weekly Journal*, 8 March 1907.

103. *Auburn Citizen*, Wednesday, 6 March 1907. The *Auburn Semi-Weekly Journal*, 8 March 1907, reported the same event as follows: "While Dr Oman was watching the beauties of New York from the ferry-boat on Saturday, some-one else was watching his bag. However, as Dr Oman put it, they got chiefly sermons."

104. *Auburn Semi-Weekly Journal*, 8 March 1907.

105. *Post-Standard*, Syracuse, NY, Wednesday morning, 4 March 1907.

The last and fourth address on the "Authority of experience" was delivered in the afternoon of Wednesday, 6 March, in the Assembly Hall, Syracuse. At the close, the speaker said he would be glad to answer any questions. These had a sharp edge. "'What I would like to know,' said a man near the front, 'is whether Christ was divine or not.'

"'I have tried to convey the impression,' was the answer, 'that he was divine but accepted human limitations to better carry on his work.'

"'Was he a member of the Trinity or not?' persisted the questioner. 'I am not here to be questioned as to my theology,' said Dr Oman.

"'It doesn't make any difference what you are here for,' said the inquisitor, 'I am glad you have left us a personal God anyway, you have taken away almost everything else.'

"'If there are mistakes in the Bible, how can we trust it?' was the question of an elderly woman. 'What I want is something to go by. I can't study these things as scholars do.' The speaker explained that it was the spirit of the Bible that was true and that the Bible was not necessarily a text to be followed literally as a guide to right conduct. Rev Guy B. Galligher asked the speaker if he had said that Christ was a product of his age, and Dr. Oman replied that he had said that Christ was of his age, which was different from saying that he was a product of his age."[106]

When the lecture was repeated at 8:00 that evening in the Willard Memorial chapel[107] of Auburn Seminary, it attracted "quite a houseful." The gist of Oman's thinking, conveyed by the *Auburn Citizen*, mirrored the thrust of *The Problem of Faith and Freedom*:

> No man can be free in a merely mechanical world, a spiritual world is necessary. A spiritual world would be inexplicable without an infinite being, God. . . . God did not create the world, and then let it loose to run out its course as a machine, but God has been in the world and manifested himself in history. Faith in this God is as vital as faith in the world. . . . The relation between the Infinite and the finite is just what is beyond our comprehension. In the end we shall have to affirm the omnipotent God and man's freedom as well. No theory can reconcile perfect responsibility with perfect freedom, but what a theory cannot do intellectually, love can do practically. There are some things which man's finite mind cannot understand and still remain finite. . . . Conscience is like revelation—both human and divine. When a man says this is right and I will follow it out through

---

106. *Auburn Citizen*, Thursday, 7 March 1907.

107. The interior was uniquely designed and crafted entirely by the Tiffany workshop.

life and death, no matter what the consequences—we feel that this man has come to something absolute and eternal. . . . Life is real, sometimes it is terrible. Yet, if we choose the right, we cannot believe that God will over-ride our efforts. God does not reconcile the world through power, but love. . . . It is love that conquers the world. . . . We test our feelings and experiences by the relation they bear to will and freedom, not on any theory of their origin. . . . It isn't God's purpose to help us, for that would be an easy thing for him, but his purpose is to help us help ourselves.[108]

Oman received a large ovation.

Church and World

Oman's prior experience of the social effects in Britain of rapid industrial expansion and the outrage he expressed in *The Problem of Faith and Freedom* about the widening gap between the rich and the poor sensitized him to "the vastness of the problem" in the States. He spoke with people of conscience, mostly professors and ministers, who were struggling to understand their Christian responsibilities in a situation where rapid industrial development had given rise to unprecedented wealth and unimaginable poverty. He perceived that "the overwhelming material prosperity of the last ten years ha[d] created an immense mass of newly rich people who have boundless resources and no responsibilities and who create in a great many more the desire to climb by the same ladder." Immigrants, students,[109] workers, all appeared to "think the pursuit of money an adequate end of life . . . and . . . judged by the newspapers public morality [was] not high"[110]

He discerned in the Americans he met a greater sharpness of distinction between the Church and the world than in England. "Good men . . . very strongly realise that nothing can be done without the truth while at the same time they are very conscious of the need of all the strength of conviction and of organisation which the Church can attain. One cannot but admire their faith and courage both in intellectual and in practical matters." And

---

108. *Auburn Citizen*, Thursday, 7 March 1907.

109. He observed that "the universities are flooded with young men, but the ablest of the students go not into the professions, but into manufacture and the handling of finance."

110. "A Visit to America." This raised questions about the limits of free speech. "The newspapers all indulge in accusations which would best end either in an action for libel against the paper or an action for swindling against the official, and I found the best type of men ready to admit that, as things are, this freedom of comment was necessary."

he continues: "These men are beginning to realise that they must concern themselves more with the public life of the nation. . . . President Woodrow Wilson of Princeton made just before I left a most wise and discriminating political deliverance. President Elliott of Harvard has done more than any man alive to rescue education from the political scramble."[111]

In this context, it is suggestive that Oman gave an address on "Ritschl and his school" in the chapel of Rockefeller Hall, Rochester Theological Seminary on the evening of Monday, 11 March.[112] There was a strong conceptual link between Ritschl and the Social Gospel movement and it is not too fanciful to imagine that Walter Rauschenbusch, who was then professor of Church History at Rochester, was in Oman's audience. The book which catapulted him into prominence as the most important exponent of the Social Gospel in America, *Christianity and the Social Crisis*, was published that year, giving a compelling portrait of the current troubled circumstances, and a theological vision of social justice which called for faithful witness and transformative engagement by the Church.

While further information about Oman's lecture remains elusive, a subsequent *JTS* review which he wrote on *Ritschlianism* may be indicative.[113] Following an outline of various misunderstandings of Ritschl's position, he sets the record straight. In sum, Ritschl's strength was in "ethical religion." The fundamental question about Christ was not an "intellectual scheme but what Jesus meant for the souls that trusted in him";[114] hence the prior significance of the Epistles over the Gospels. History was "a real struggle for ideals, a real battle in which there were genuine defeats and victories. Through this conflict . . . men reach up to God. They find themselves small and weak, yet with both the burden and promise of freedom; while, opposed to them is a world vast and powerful, yet subject to necessity." The world "is the means whereby our freedom is to be won, and God's end in us fulfilled."[115] Jesus forms his followers into "a society which shall at once work for the Kingdom, and also enjoy the blessings of it."[116]

---

111. "A Visit to America."
112. *Rochester Democrat and Chronicle*, Saturday, 9 March 1907.
113. Oman, "Ritschlianism."
114. Oman, "Ritschlianism," 472.
115. Oman, "Ritschlianism," 473.
116. Oman, "Ritschlianism," 473.

Return

Oman says little about the return journey on a much smaller and by inference less grand ship, the RMS Majestic. Built for speed, one of the "greyhounds of the Atlantic," it "rolled copiously with a sea on the aft quarter and finally when the wind settled on her side, took a list." There were few passengers, but with sixty firemen and forty-two coal shifters, it "arrived on even keel in a flat calm and a thick fog in the Mersey."[117]

He was home by 30 March and it was reported that "it was a sincere pleasure to Dr Oman's many friends to see how well he [was] looking after his voyage and his somewhat arduous labours lecturing and preaching in America." On 12 April, Clayport held a social gathering to welcome him back and it was clear from John Balmbra's speech that the nomination to Westminster College was by now an open secret. "There seemed to be no doubt," he felt, that "the call would be of a good unanimous character. If he were called there, he had no doubt that he would add strength to their church in a way that otherwise, working in a small community, he would be unable to do. . . . He would ever remain in their hearts, for he occupied a place in their affections which could never be removed, though distance might separate them." With a round of applause, Oman expressed confidence in the fact that he "could go away and lecture and that Mr Borland[118] could take it up and carry it on and he never be missed." After an account by Oman of his experiences, Borland was presented by the Bible class with Ruskin's works and a copy of *The Problem of Faith and Freedom*. He said in reply, presciently, that he felt that Oman had originality still waiting to break out, and "that the best of [his] work had yet to come."

Call to Westminster College

On 9 May, Oman was called by the PCE Synod to the Barbour chair of Theology at Westminster College.[119] Arrangements were made for Clayport. He

---

117. "A Visit to America."

118. Alexander Borland, b. 1885, educated Glasgow university, had further assistantships at Montrose, Perth and Arbroath, before ordination at Kirkcaldy in 1910. He was described as "a forthright speaker, and writer on many ecclesiastical matters" (*Glasgow Herald*, 24 January 1967).

119. Oman's proposers were the Reverend James Christie, minister of Warwick Road Church, Carlisle and the Reverend Hugh Falconer, who had officiated at Oman's marriage to Mary in 1897 and was a member of the Synod College Committee. Of the three nominees, D. S. Cairns was withdrawn at his own request. The ballot showed 402 votes for Oman and 101 for Rev. Patrick Carnegie Simpson, of Renfield Church, Glasgow. Oman was then unanimously called to the chair. Carruthers, *Digest of Proceedings*, 147.

would finish in June but continue to preach in July, letting the manse in August to a supply preacher. On 6 August, members of the Northumberland Presbytery "all spoke in feeling and eulogistic terms" of the loss they were to sustain and presented Oman with "two handsome silver candlesticks, with inscription."[120] The pastoral charge was declared vacant.[121] On 22 September, "although far from well, being just recovered from a trying operation," Oman preached eloquently "and with considerable energy" to a full church with many present from outside the congregation, on the words "But this thing I do, forgetting these things which are behind, and reaching forth unto these things which are before,"[122] and so took leave of his congregation. At the farewell social three days later, he was presented by the congregation with a solid silver tea and coffee service, and Mary with "a valuable brooch"; while the Bible Class, Fellowship Meeting and Sunday School teachers gave him "twenty-one volumes of Scott's, and six of Thackeray's works." John Balmbra alluded to the "harmony and cordiality" which had marked the seventeen years of Oman's ministry among them, and after appraising the reputation of his publications, he said:

> He had so acquitted himself as to win the respect of the entire community. Whatever his opinions had been they had been the result of careful and prayerful thought. He had ever been ready to stand up for any truths or principles which had commended themselves to his conscience, without fear or favour and with an earnest desire to discharge his duties faithfully in the community in which he lived. . . . He was sure Dr. Oman carried with him not only the respect, but the affection of all who knew him.

And he continued:

> They, as a congregation, knew . . . what a grasp he had had of the life of ordinary mortals face to face with life's difficulties and tasks. Dr. Oman, as a preacher, had been both fresh and forceful. He had always maintained their intense interest when he had been preaching to them, and it had been a marvel to many of them, who had known him in the weekly and other meetings, how he could be so prodigal of material which many men would have kept for state occasions. . . . His preaching always had Love

---

120. *Morpeth Herald*, Saturday, 10 August 1907.

121. The Reverend W. Rogerson was appointed interim moderator, and on 19 December the Reverend A. C. Don accepted a call to Clayport with stipend of £200, the manse and four Sundays off a year. Session minutes 1898–1923, 19 December 1907.

122. Philippians 3:13. For the full text of the sermon, see *Alnwick Guardian*, "The Departure of Dr. Oman from Alnwick," 28 September 1907.

> as its source . . . and they had recognised time and again that he had constrained them by love to follow in the footsteps of our Lord.

In reply, Oman acknowledged that to leave Alnwick was a wrench. In thanking them for the tea service, he foresaw that it would be well used in giving hospitality to students in Cambridge. It would not be possible to do visiting there as they had done in Alnwick, but "quite indescribable, and overwhelming influences met a student in a university town—mostly good but some bad and it was no small matter to him to have someone who took an interest in him, some home he could go to; some place where he knew he would be welcome."[123] Commenting on the task that lay ahead for himself, Oman said "he did not take it up with a light heart. He did not go from here to Cambridge with a feeling he was only going there to conquer. . . . On the other hand, from the beginning of his student days, he had had a deep interest in the great questions of the faith. It had been an age, as they all knew, in which every young man who came to think for himself found himself in great perplexity, an age when great issues were at stake in belief and practice. Out of the welter that dismayed a great many people, he had the utmost faith that something new and great was growing up."[124] And so, with the statutory votes of thanks, the singing of Psalm 121 and the benediction, Oman's ministry in Alnwick came to an end.

---

123. Perhaps he was thinking of the hospitality he himself enjoyed as a young student in Edinburgh from Professor Calderwood.

124. *Alnwick Guardian*, "The Departure of Dr. Oman from Alnwick," 28 September 1907.

8

Westminster College Cambridge

In 1907, Westminster College was fast acquiring a reputation for outstanding theological scholarship. Given the uphill struggle of the previous decades this could not have been foreseen. In 1842, on the formation of the Presbyterian Church in England, the Synod had decided that provision had to be made for the training of its future ministers. The Presbyterian College[1] in London was the result. Its efforts to survive are described by Buick Knox as "a record of idealism, perseverance and generosity, all maintained with remarkable constancy amid financial crisis and fluctuating numbers."[2] The abolition of religious tests[3] opened the door for the college to move from London to Cambridge and the possibility was raised at the Synod of 1873 though not pursued. But the thought once planted did not go away and the emergence in Cambridge of a small Presbyterian congregation revived latent aspirations.[4] At a measured Synod debate on 29 April 1895, the decision was finally taken to come to Cambridge. The vote was close with most of the Presbyteries almost equally split.[5] Fears were rife. There were concerns that

---

1. The subsequent change of name on moving to Cambridge was "as a link with seventeenth century Presbyterianism and with the Westminster confession and catechisms." Knox, *Westminster College*, 20.

2. Knox, *Westminster College*, 1–12.

3. In 1871 the Universities Tests Act enabled non-Anglicans to become full members of Oxford, Cambridge and Durham universities.

4. Cornick, "Cambridge and Reluctant Dissent," 123–43.

5. 222 votes for Cambridge, 209 against. That evening, opponents of the move withdrew their opposition. For a summary of the arguments, see Knox, *Westminster College*, 12–16.

students would be contaminated by Anglican ritualism and fears that they would be so immersed in the academic environment that they would lose the common touch. However, the matter was clinched by the offer of land purchased from St John's College by the distinguished scholars and loyal Presbyterians, Dr. Agnes Smith Lewis and her sister, Dr. Margaret Dunlop Gibson, together with a generous contribution towards building costs and the promise of future endowment.[6]

It was obvious that a new site was needed; the lease on Queen's Square, London would end in 1918. The choice was, as John Watson argued, "between Cambridge with the gift of a site, or the uncertainty of a London suburb."[7] The newly constituted College Building Committee wasted no time, and at its first meeting listed the various rooms that would be required and invited "a number of architects to furnish plans in competition and to offer a premium of 200 Guineas for those adjudged the best and of 100 Guineas for those second in merit, the Committee, however, not binding the Church to accept of necessity the plans of any of the competitors. The Committee further resolved that the sum of £20,000 be named as covering the entire cost of the Building."[8] It was soon evident, however, that this sum was inadequate "for the erection of a worthy building,"[9] and the total required rose to £40,000. Anonymized submissions were assessed by John MacVicar Anderson, who had recently retired as president of the RIBA, and the design by Henry Hare was selected.[10] Thanks to John Watson's whirlwind money-raising campaign, the college was able to open on 17 October 1899 free of debt.[11]

Eight years later, almost to the day,[12] Oman was inducted to the Barbour chair of Systematic Theology at a service held in St Columba's Church Cambridge, along with the Reverend Charles Archibald Anderson Scott

6. Their portraits hang in the hall of Westminster College. At a time when academic learning was seen as the province of men, they were at the forefront of Biblical and Semitic scholarship, acclaimed in particular for the discovery and interpretation of a rare fourth-century Sinai palimpsest with the gospels in Syriac underwritten, and the discovery of a fragment of *Ecclesiasticus* in Hebrew. With a common background in the UPC, they appointed Oman their executor.

7. Cornick, "Cambridge and Reluctant Dissent," 138.

8. Minutes of the College Buildings Committee, 19 July 1895, Westminster College Archives.

9. Knox, *Westminster College*, 17.

10. Minutes of the College Buildings Committee, 27 March 1896, Westminster College Archives. Second prize was awarded to Messrs. Seth-Smith and Fenning.

11. On 27 September 1905, the Senatus extended "a hearty welcome [to the authorities of Cheshunt College] on the removal of their own foundation to Cambridge."

12. On 10 October 1907 at 5:00 p.m.

who had been called to the newly endowed Dunn chair of New Testament.[13] The charge was preached by the Reverend John Monro Gibson,[14] acting Principal, and before adjourning for dinner in the college, "the new professors . . . took their seats as members of the senatus."[15]

Senatus

Although Oman had no links with the former college in Queen's Square, he had already a sense of connection with his new colleagues. He would have approved of the vigorous stance of the College against the Education Bill in 1902,[16] and his delivery of the Westminster lectures two years later enabled more personal contact. That same year, when he was shortlisted for the chair of Systematic Theology at New College, Edinburgh, Principal Oswald Dykes was one of his referees, along with Principal Fairbairn of Mansfield College and Professor Seth. And there were subsequently opportunities for conversation about college life with John Watson, during the voyage to America. News of Watson's death in the States while the 1907 Synod was in session came as a considerable shock to the church and it was decided not to appoint a principal for a further year. Then the Reverend John Skinner was unanimously elected.[17]

John Skinner

There was mutual friendship and understanding between Skinner and Oman. Both were scholar ministers with a Scots evangelical background. Skinner had served with distinction as professor of Old Testament and Apologetics from 1890, for the first nine years in London and then in Cambridge. His first book, the *Book of the Prophet Isaiah*, was published in 1906, and his magisterial commentary on Genesis four years later.[18] He and Oman had similar attitudes to the church and in his preface to *The Church and the*

---

13. The professorship in NT studies had been in abeyance since 1886.

14. Described as "the unmitred archbishop of the church" (*Presbyterian Messenger* 1915, 194), Gibson was minister of St John's Wood Presbyterian Church and chaired the College Committee.

15. Senatus minutes, 10 October 1907, Westminster College archives.

16. *Presbyterian Messenger*, May 1902.

17. *Presbyterian Messenger*, 1908, 197.

18. When the University of Oxford first opened divinity degrees to non-Anglicans, Skinner was the first nonconformist to receive the DD in June 1920, along with W. B. Selbie, principal of Mansfield college.

Divine Order Oman records his indebtedness "to many discussions with my colleague, Principal Skinner."[19] The two men had a strong awareness of the need for the Church to "be found among the poor more readily than among the rich"[20] and both urged upon Westminster students the importance of Church extension work.[21]

For the students, while Oman was "the prophet of Westminster," Skinner was "the saint."[22] On Skinner's death in 1925, the Board of Studies recorded that his "far-seeing wisdom, his ripe experience and his sympathetic understanding of students, gave him a position of unique authority on the Board. In the familiar intimacy of our own counsels, his clear vision and unerring judgment were of peculiar value, and his self-effacing brotherliness made co-operation with him always a privilege and a joy. We give God unfeigned thanks for a man so pure-hearted and so full of Christian grace."[23]

John Gibb

John Gibb, was like Skinner, ordained in the Free Church of Scotland and, although said to be "generally a rather reserved man,"[24] he appears to have been a genial colleague.[25] He too had moved to Cambridge in 1899 with the Presbyterian College where he had taught New Testament Exegesis and patristic literature for the previous twenty-two years. The endowment of the Dunn chair in 1907 relieved him of teaching New Testament, and he was able till his retirement in 1913 to focus on patristic Church History. Although learned, he published no books, allegedly because he was "averse to the intense discipline of literary production,"[26] and he took little part in the public work of the church.

---

19. Oman, *Church and Divine Order*, viii.

20. Oman, *Church and Divine Order*, 328.

21. Typically, in 1908, when Trinity Church, Camden, with a small, impoverished congregation and an unsafe building, was threatened with closure, Skinner, supported by Oman, urged upon a reluctant Presbytery the need to maintain a church there and before long, Oman succeeded him as moderator of session.

22. Robson, *Our Professors*, 15.

23. Minutes of Board of Studies, 7 May 1925, Westminster College archives.

24. Knox, "John Gibb," 329.

25. Knox, "John Gibb," 328–37.

26. Knox, "John Gibb," 330.

Patrick Carnegie Simpson

This could scarcely be said of his successor, Patrick Carnegie Simpson, minister of Egremont PCE in Wallasey.[27] His *Life of Principal Rainy* is still an important source for the Robertson Smith affair, the negotiations that led to the formation of the UF Church in 1900, and the Free Church case four years later. He was to prove himself "a great ecclesiastical statesman,"[28] not only in dedicated engagement with the work of the PCE Synod and the General Assembly (as the Synod was named from 1921) but also in the formation of the Free Church Federal Council and in the energy which he devoted to the abortive discussions between the Church of England and the Free Churches. Randall Davidson regarded him as a "trusted and effective exponent of the Reformed position."[29] Simpson's personality was very different from Oman's. "He and I," Simpson recollected, "had differing points of view . . . but I always had for his work the highest respect; and the more I knew him, the deeper was my regard for the man. . . . I remember Skinner once saying that he could hardly bring together four men more different than himself, Oman, Scott and me. Yet we lived in entire harmony, and, indeed, a college would be a poor place if all its professors had been cast in the same mould."[30]

Charles Archibald Anderson Scott

Anderson Scott, previously Minister of St John's Presbyterian Church, Kensington, was the first professor in the College's history to be English-born and a Cambridge graduate. He actively fostered relationships between the College and the University. In 1909 and 1912, he was a member of the Special Board for Theology, then, following the historic decision by the University to follow Oxford in opening the degrees of BD and DD to non-Anglicans, he was appointed to the Divinity Degree Syndicate on the Regulations for Admission to Degrees in Divinity.[31] He soon made his mark as a distinguished scholar.[32] He gave lectures to the Faculty on "Paulinism"

---

27. In 1914, he was elected by 258 votes to 187 over Anderson Scott, who thus remained in the chair of NT studies. He had in 1907 candidated unsuccessfully for the Barbour chair in Systematics.

28. Elmslie, *Westminster College*, 24.

29. Knox, *Westminster College*, 26.

30. Simpson, *Recollections*, 66.

31. Thompson, "Oman and the University," 79.

32. In 1912 Scott received an honorary DD from Aberdeen University; and in 1920, he received the DD under regulation from Cambridge University. As was noted with

in 1910-11, and in 1929 he was the first non-Anglican appointed by the University to deliver the Hulsean lectures. His relationship with Oman was warm. He paid tribute to his colleague in the General Assembly of 1922: "It has been said that the more you disagree with him, the more you like him; that is probably why I like him so much."[33]

John Oman: Honors

As for Oman, his scholarly reputation continued to grow rapidly. In December 1907, he was nominated for the DD of the University of St Andrews by Alexander Lawson, professor of theology and Dean of the Faculty of Arts. Lawson spoke in glowing terms of Oman's career trajectory and his publications, singling out his translation of the Reden "with its scholarly and vigorous introduction marked by both breadth and acuteness," and *Faith and Freedom* as showing him to be "a philosophical and theological thinker and truly original as well as a man who has read very widely . . . all the most outstanding works in theology and philosophy in Britain, France and Germany."[34] However, the University decided not to confer any DD degrees that year and although six were awarded in 1908, Oman was not a candidate.[35] In 1910, the University of Edinburgh awarded him the DD, as "a theological thinker of a massive and original type."[36] He was appointed by the University of Cambridge[37] as lecturer in Comparative Religion from 1913 to 1922, and in 1928, until 1932, Stanton lecturer in the Philosophy of Religion. The University of Oxford conferred on him the DD in 1928, Jesus College Cambridge elected him to an honorary fellowship when he retired, celebrating the occasion with champagne glasses at the High Table,[38] and in 1938 he was made a Fellow of the British Academy. He served for many years

---

pride by the Presbytery of London North (*Minutes*, 8 June 1920), he was the first nonconformist minister to do so since 1662. His works on St Paul, published in the 1930s, were highly regarded.

33. Knox, *Westminster College*, 28.

34. Muniments of the University of St Andrews, UYUY7, Sec. 2, 1907-8.

35. Minutes of Senatus meetings, 18 January 1908, 8 February 1908. Muniments of the University of St Andrews. Lacking further evidence, speculation as to the reasons for this are futile.

36. *Orkney Herald*, 13 July 1910.

37. Having been made a member of Queens' College in 1908, he was given an honorary MA in March 1909 along with Dr. Owen Charles Whitehouse, Principal of Cheshunt College, this being the only way at the time to recognise those not educated at Cambridge as members of the University. Thompson, "Oman and the University," 80.

38. *Annual Report*, St John's College, Cambridge, 1935.

on the Board of the Faculty of Divinity and on the Degree Committee, and it was recorded that "members of the Faculty who learned from his wisdom and enjoyed his friendship cherish their memory of him as among the most original minds that have contributed to theological studies in recent times."[39]

The College Course

To see Oman's impact upon the college in perspective, his contribution to the course has now to be charted in some detail.

Apart from the addition of a fourth chair in New Testament in 1907 the college syllabus appeared to have changed very little following its translation to Cambridge. On 1 June 1908, the first occasion when Skinner presided over a Senatus meeting as Principal, the lecture list was discussed and provisionally agreed. In the first year, there were to be five lectures a week in Hebrew and the Old Testament, five in Greek and the New Testament, and two each on Apologetics and early Church History, in each of the terms. Mr. Scott was to conduct a sermon class with the first year. The second and third years combined for one lecture on the Old Testament, four on the New Testament, three on Church History, four on Dogmatics, and one on Pastoral Theology. There were statutory classes for all students in elocution.[40]

Oman was quick to realize the value of the most recent developments in the teaching of elocution. Remembering perhaps his own early struggles with preaching technique, he wrote in the *Presbyterian Messenger*, "We never made a greater mistake from the point of view of effective public speaking than when for years we allowed our men to be trained in the model of the stage."[41] The style of speaking once promoted in the college might have been fashionable, but it was mannered, and Oman emphasizes the advantages of the more natural method advocated by the new teacher of elocution, Dr. Henry Harper Hulbert.[42] With a vocation to "deliver the Church from a calculated and stagey form of speaking," Hulbert expected every student "to spend a short time every day reading aloud a short passage from Scripture . . . till he captures, not only the meaning, but the spirit, the feeling, the inspiration." For Hulbert, "the voice . . . is only irresistible when it is the organ

---

39. Cited in Oman, *Honest Religion*, xxx.
40. Minutes of Senatus, 1 June 1908, Westminster College archives,
41. John Oman, "Elocution in the College," *Presbyterian Messenger*, July 1935, 200.
42. Hulbert, a member of the Royal College of Surgeons, whose specialty was the throat, devised a "natural" system of teaching voice production which was based on his experience of physical training. From 1908 to 1914, when he joined the RAMC, he taught with Elsie Fogarty at the Central School of Speech Training and Dramatic Arts in the Albert Hall.

of the spirit." The impact on sermon delivery was pronounced. As Oman put it, "eloquent recitation from a rather turgid MS" is replaced by "animated elevated conversation." As a departure from a previous emphasis on voice, diction and gesture, this development was radical. And it was in line with Oman's commitment to sincerity, integrity and truth.

This somewhat austere regime was fleshed out fourteen years later when the Special Correspondent of the *Presbyterian Messenger* spent a day at the college. On the surface, little seemed to have changed, although prayers were now at 8:45, after a lavish breakfast of porridge, sausages and fish. Devotions were led by Skinner, featuring Paul's exhortation to Timothy to stir up the gift that was in him, and included a prayer for the meetings of the Free Church Council. "There was a full class-room at nine o'clock for Dr Oman," whose lecture on faith "proved to be an exercise of rare spiritual refreshment. Fortunate indeed are the men who learn their business from such teachers." The journalist noted that "all the lectures stressed the paramount importance of sincerity" commenting that "the world is in sore need of honesty, and the hunger for it among those who think is a great passion. If only those who complain about compromise and camouflage in the Church could have heard these men speaking—some of them would have decided on the spot to enter the ministry." After some free time to enjoy the beauties of the Backs, the opportunity arose to hear Oman give the last of his series of lectures on the Philosophy of Religion in the Divinity School, on "Immortality." "Incisive, though not unkind, reference to Spiritualism did not come as a surprise," the reporter remarked, "for by this time one had realised that all Westminster teaching is fully alive to the questions that interest modern England." At a meeting of the Student Council he learned that the college had recently "gained a decisive victory" at football over Mansfield College; and the work of the day was rounded off with sermon class in the library where a student preached on the Golden Calf, "followed by crisp and valuable comments from all four professors."[43]

However, concerns about the adequacy of the core curriculum continued to emerge and Oman made his views clear in the memorandum which he submitted in 1918 to the Assembly Sub-Committee on Ministry.[44] All four disciplines were taught in the spirit of an open-ended pursuit of theological truth—"we have four professors of theology, not one." As to the popular view that Hebrew and Greek occupied a disproportionate time in the curriculum, Oman echoed Skinner's vigorous defense of Hebrew in

---

43. *Presbyterian Messenger*, May 1921, 101–2.

44. Moderator's Committee, Sub-Committee on Ministry, Memorandum by Rev. Professor John Oman D.D., Typescript, Westminster College Archives, n.d.

particular: "the usual question is, what time is spent on it, whereas the important question is, how is it studied? Is it as a linguistic exercise or as the sole key to the mind which lies behind not only the Old Testament but the New?"[45] Some people thought that other subjects should be added. However this is to "ask for what any decently trained minister should be able to supply for himself."

Oman drew comparison with the American colleges which he had visited, where there was a large number of options and practical subjects. "The matter interested me at that time," Oman wrote "and I had an entirely open mind"; but "the almost unanimous opinion, even from those who taught the subjects, was that such spreading out of study was a mistake. The strongest opinion I had from President Wilson[46]—'Stick at all costs to your four central subjects. Our method means utterly superficial knowledge, which leaves a man in a year preaching out of the last book he read or the newspapers ... with disastrous results.'"

Oman's experience as a teacher had taught him "the enormous difference between knowing a subject and knowing about it . . . between what men have seen and what they have been told." His experience with soldiers during the War had shown him "the enormous gain afforded by our type of training in dealing with ordinary people and their religious difficulties. The men who had it never needed to stand off or fear to take the button off their foil. With the growth of education and greater social equality our system will have a chance of coming to its own even in England."

He contested the opinion expressed in the *Presbyterian Messenger* by the Reverend James Fraser that the training of ministers was "too academic," and insufficiently "in accord with the genius of Christ."[47] Even if "many people of different kinds approved" of these opinions, Oman insisted that "all we can do is to teach men the importance of a first-hand knowledge and independence of judgment in face of any situation that may arise. No doubt one feels safer on life's ocean with a cork-jacket of rules and other people's examples. But, if you want to swim, you must risk a header into it naked: and getting the cork-jacket off may be as dangerous as it is difficult."

---

45. Skinner, *Observations*. The ensuing report of the Committee confined itself to suggesting that the Senatus make alternative arrangements for Biblical instruction for any student whose linguistic capability was inadequate. *Reports to the Synod of the Presbyterian Church of England*, 1920.

46. Of Princeton University.

47. *Presbyterian Messenger*, "Are We Too Academic?," May, June, July 1932. For Oman's letter, see *Presbyterian Messenger*, June 1932, 56.

He was however fundamentally in agreement with Fraser about the value of pastoral placements.[48] He observed that, when he moved with the rump of the college to Birmingham towards the end of the First World War, "many, even of modest gifts became astonishingly good preachers and pastors" although "we had the pressure of a very great need and the stimulus of a very terrible time."[49] Hinting at the "necessary physical and mental energy" he himself had expended in accompanying them, he concludes that "the experience of trying to revive struggling causes, on their own, with someone to beard the lions occasionally, enabled men far better to cut their wisdom teeth than assistantships in large and prosperous churches."

He references initiatives which had begun before the war and which might be revived, notably "such work as we used to do at Kentish Town"; implicitly the reference is to the support given by the college to Trinity Church Camden. Oman concludes: "Some contact with Mr Fraser's work would be far more instructive and inspiring for students than pottering away on their own at a mission."[50]

Mutual relations had to be maintained between the college and the wider church. The practice might be revived of inviting "a regular relay of visiting ministers from all over the church; for one of our chief dangers is that we are apt to be withdrawn from the church and the church from us." But it was also imperative to broaden the interests of students beyond Church affairs. Pointing to the danger of "becoming a mere Seminary," Oman suggests that this might be avoided by asking "specialists to speak to members of the college on their own subjects and particularly on social and educational questions."

And there was a more immediate way in which student horizons might be broadened. A bare month after his arrival, "Professor Oman drew the attention of the [College] committee to the fact that the rooms at Westminster were not fully occupied and expressed the opinion that it would help both the College and the Committee's finance if [they] could encourage

---

48. Fraser's suggestion of a "term's work with a professor in a different situation from Cambridge" resonated with Oman's own experience in Birmingham, although it would, Oman writes ruefully, require "a pretty tough professor."

49. Moderator's Committee, Sub-Committee on Ministry, Memorandum by Rev. Professor John Oman DD, Typescript, Westminster College Archives, n.d.

50. In early 1914 the Reverend James Fraser, minister at Bexhill on Sea, was encouraged by Oman to accept a call from Trinity, Camden. Inducted in April 1914 for a fixed term of three years, he was to remain there for 36 years, showing "committed concerns for peace and justice in both industrial and international affairs." Elliott, *Trinity Camden*, chapter 4. https://www.trinity-camden-urc.org.uk/a-brief-history-chapter-4. (See below, 232.)

private students to take up residence at Westminster College."[51] This was accepted and a tradition began which over the years enabled interconnection between Westminster students and lodgers to the mutual benefit of both, so much so that by 1924, "the Principal reported that our College was now being approached with a view to becoming a recognised place of residence for university students."[52]

All these measures reflected Oman's "deep interest in education as something much greater than mere instruction."[53] While he believed implicitly in the duty to cultivate rigorous standards of thought, he also perceived that creative gifts were to be nourished as a vital contribution to ministry. His personal appreciation of the arts and literature has already been noted. And he articulates this in a letter which he wrote from sick-bed to Allan G. Wyon to acknowledge receipt of a photograph of one of his sculptures. Alluding to Wyon's ordination as priest in the Church of England in 1933, he says: "It is when I think of this and still more of Skinner's[54] that I rather grudge you even to the ministry. During a time when art was in danger of being prostituted to violence, you gave your message of peace: and in no sphere can you do more." And Oman concludes: "Though it is my job to train men in a certain way, and though I believe in it as the routine method, I have always urged a greater and freer recognition of special calls, special gifts, and special experiences. Anyhow the great matter is to have good news of God, a gospel, and it will get itself delivered somehow."[55]

Lectures

Oman spent four terms out of six on the systematic "presentation of Christianity in relation to reality and life" which seemed "both the only convincing apologetic and the only really religious ethic."[56] The remaining two terms

51. With the bursar's approval, it was unanimously agreed that the termly charge for such lodgers be reduced from £25 to £15. Minutes of the College Committee, 20 November 1907. The College was governed by the PCE National Synod, which exercised its authority through the College Committee.

52. Minutes of the Board of Studies, 29 October 1924.

53. Cited by H. H. Farmer in Oman, *Honest Religion*, xxx.

54. In c. 1931 Wyon sculpted the bust of Skinner, displayed in Westminster College. Amongst other works, he executed distinctive war memorials, among others the Hinckley war memorial (1921–22); and the representation of St Michael in The Quarry, Shrewsbury (1922–23).

55. John Oman to Allan G. Wyon, The Lodge Westminster College, September 16 n.d., possibly 1933. Cambridge University Library (Add. 7651) WYON 12/4/80.

56. Moderator's Committee, Sub-Committee on Ministry, Memorandum by Rev.

were devoted to apologetics with a view to meeting difficulties in the minds of students and giving them a perspective from which to face current difficulties of belief. Typically, he kept his teaching up to date with his own reading. In his early years, he said, his focus had been on encouraging students to read "Butler, Otto and Ward," but this had gradually given way to a "more positive line," taking into account the history of religions, the psychology of religion, and its metaphysics.

While these lectures were never published, we do have detailed notes typed from shorthand by D. M. Niccol, a student of the College between 1919 and 1922.[57] Here, Oman formulates an orderly and coherent account of the Christian faith, asking ultimate questions about the world while fostering a continuing search for truth. His aim is "not merely . . . the clearing up of perplexities about Biblical facts" but enabling "people to believe that the spiritual world in which Jesus and God work really exists today."

God in relation to the world and man is followed by an extensive section on *Jesus Christ and the Doctrine of Reconciliation* where he addresses the theories of Strauss and Schweitzer on the historical Jesus, of Ritschl on the offices of Christ, and the doctrine of sin. He reflects on *Our relation to the Church's creeds* through the writings of Paul, John and Peter; interrogates von Hügel and the Tübingen School on the self-consciousness of Jesus and explores various contemporary theories about the kingdom of God. His lectures on apologetics handle questions around the Holy Spirit in the world, the sacraments of Baptism and the Lord's Supper, and the role of the church community. And there follows an extensive sequence of questions around "the Holy Spirit in relation to man," which deal with aspects of salvation and faith. The concluding lectures offer commentary on our "sphere of service," the relationship between "a State Church and the Kingdom of God"—a topic which acquired particular significance post war—Christian character, eternal life and "Last Things." He reveals a growing interest in apocalyptic.

We may detect in these lectures maxims which featured in *Vision and Authority* and *Faith and Freedom*. Students must "take care," for "a great deal of religious discussion is purely assertion. Intellectual honesty is all important. One can only be free in the truth." And, drawing on Schleiermacher, he advises the student from time to time to review theological study "in connection with the whole of life." To identify Systematic Theology with dogmatics is inadequate—there has to be "some system of the scope and meaning and application of the Christian faith," which would include also ethics and apologetics. Even so, three major questions may be asked: "Is

---

Professor John Oman DD, Typescript, Westminster College Archives, n.d.

57. Westminster College Archives.

there any room for religion? This is not a question of argument but of whole attitude to life . . . some theologians say that the answer is of faith not reason. But it is not right to divide into compartments like this. We must use philosophical as well as spiritual insight." Then, secondly, "What is religion? . . . If we try to get a general idea we don't get a picture of any real individual Christian." And finally, "What are the meaning and relationship of the great historical religions?" Already we can see here the development of fresh germs of thought that would bear fruit in *The Natural and the Supernatural*.

Teaching Method

Oman reflected in *Concerning the Ministry* that "as a teacher I have never got beyond doing my best for each person as occasion offers."[58] And in the Senatus report to the Synod in 1910, he clarifies that. Though lectures had to be given, he hoped that "his view is only taught in such a way as will help each student to find his own." And so, possibly recalling his own early experience as a student of Calderwood and Fraser, he got students in some classes to present papers "on the subjects dealt with in his lectures and this was one way of preparing them for their life work of teaching truth: 'Even when as frequently happened the result was somewhat less than illumination, it accomplished the profitable end of showing that such a task is not as easy as it at first appears.'"[59]

This initiative was a new development in the history of the College and many students will have benefited, but Oman knew that not all were able to follow his thinking: "That I leave many in a pretty dark penumbra I am well aware, but I trust they at least see on which side the light lies and on which the darkness." J. W. Johnston was one such. At his ordination as minister of Buckna Presbyterian church, Antrim, he "made no claim to be a scholar, as he was not the type out of which scholars are made. He had always been too much interested in the practical application of his work to make a scholar, but at the same time he had been indebted to many eminent scholars, men who had made an impression on him and gave him impressions which he would always be grateful for and without which he could not carry on." Of the three whom he singled out, one was "Dr John Oman, a man of great power of mind and character who had his respect at all times whether he agreed with him or not."[60] Lesslie Newbigin found Oman's lectures "obscure to the point of opacity, but his writings and, above all, his occasional

58. Oman, *Concerning the Ministry*, 33.
59. Senatus Minutes, 1910, Westminster College Archives.
60. *Ballymena Weekly Telegraph*, 24 August 1929.

utterances in chapel, were full of profound insight." When he criticized a sermon in sermon class, "he could be devastating; but when he went on to say how he would have expounded the text, he would produce gems of exposition that I could never forget."[61]

Oman's capacity for caustic criticism on occasion was also noted by a colleague on the Board of the Faculty of Divinity, who wrote that Oman's "shrewdness and humour, and his dislike of sham or pretentious work could make him a severe critic where severity was deserved; but his judgement was always generous in its recognition of good work and of promise, especially in the young student."[62]

"Sham" and insincerity for Oman were much the same. They involved an evasion of truth and a deficit in integrity. He knew himself called to seek truth with all his powers and could be sharply dismissive of those who showed signs of the "unlit lamp and ungirt loin." Yet, as Henry Farmer observed, "Oman's austerity had a deep, if reserved, sympathy at its heart, as many of his students have learned from experience, and the only thing he really required of the not too bright student was that he should use such powers as he had to their fullest pitch. . . . It was because Oman's sincerity was integrally bound up with his reverence for God and his understanding of his purpose in the world, that he was able to send forth many students deeply changed by their sojourn at Westminster college."[63]

College Devotional Life

In following Oman's subject matter and his teaching method, we have temporarily neglected aspects of the college life, devotional, spiritual, pastoral, where he had an important contribution to make.

The life of the college was sustained by a regular diet of worship. The professors and tutor took their turn with students in conducting daily prayer and Sunday morning and evening services. From 1907 on, a communion service was held "on a week-day as near the end of the Easter Term as might be convenient."[64] Skills were also imparted in leading worship; on Friday evening, "student discourses" were examined and reported on. It regularly

---

61. Newbigin, *Unfinished Agenda*, 31. In "Assembly Proceedings," 4 May 1923, we read that Oman's moderatorial address was "studded with phrases which, even when read apart from their context, show Dr Oman's gift for terse and paradoxical expression at its best, that gift which makes his writings so fascinating to follow, though sometimes hard to understand." *Presbyterian Messenger.*

62. Quoted by Farmer in Oman, *Honest Religion*, xxx.

63. In Oman, *Honest Religion*, xxvii.

64. Senatus minutes, 25 November 1907.

fell to Oman to examine the homily and the "topical lecture and sermon" was taken by all professors in rotation.

Personal spirituality, understood as "the struggle to find and keep a steady discipline of prayer, meditation and contemplation," was, according to Lesslie Newbigin, "ignored."[65] While such matters may have been considered a private affair between a person and God, there were in fact informal opportunities for discussion. Oman's familiar, conversational "Saturday Talks" with students which he describes as a "sort of *hors d'oeuvre* to the whole curriculum" were reconstituted as *Concerning the Ministry*,[66] a book which has been described as a spiritual classic.[67] The *Aberdeen Press and Journal* enthused: "There isn't a Christian with any sort of hankerings after an 'interior' life who will not profit here."[68] Recognizing that faith needs regular nourishment, Oman advocates "the good habit of methodical application," to include "exercises like family worship and your own praying with your Father in secret." When reading the Bible, the student should on occasion "lay aside the scholar and become the simple Christian." Otherwise, while some devotional literature may be helpful, "the parched spirit may more readily go to the poets than to any of them for the water of life."[69] On Sundays, he concludes, "you worship with your congregation, and do not merely conduct services for them, and preach to your own souls as much at least as to other people's."[70]

The quality of Oman's pastoral interaction is well attested. In his short Memoir of his friend, George Alexander evoked the warm personal relationships between Oman and his students: "To be with him on a Sunday and find his students dropping in for tea or a smoke was to realize a relationship a classroom by itself could never give. And it was here, if I may say so, that Mrs Oman came into her kingdom. Her interest in the men was natural and unaffected. They could talk to her freely and her memory was of the order to call forth some kindly recollection of a student years after, if his name cropped up."[71] The silver teapot from Clayport was well used. Roy Whitehorn had warm memories of Sunday lunch with the Oman family

65. Newbigin, *Unfinished Agenda*, 32. This was his experience in 1933, contrasting with his previous experience with the SCM.

66. Oman, *Concerning the Ministry*.

67. This includes material from addresses given at Dunblane to ministers of the Church of Scotland and the United Free Church and published as a pamphlet at their request (Oman, *Office of the Ministry*).

68. 15 April 1936.

69. Oman, *Concerning the Ministry*, 28.

70. Oman, *Concerning the Ministry*, 29.

71. Alexander, "Memoir of the Author," xxii.

after church,[72] and he "recalled in particular a tea-party at the Omans' when [he and Connie] first had hopes of becoming engaged."[73] EWP recalled how they would sit round the study fire to the small hours—"some of us know too how kindly and patiently he would listen to our difficulties and how wisely he would advise and guide us." He evoked also the "lighter side of things. Dr Oman's humorous stories and parlour games" and the "homely and friendly atmosphere" created by Mrs. Oman.[74]

In two respects in particular Oman's influence on his students would impact on the wider life of the church. He created

> an interest in philosophy which the men of a past generation have largely lacked as students of divinity. It was quite a common thing for the student or young minister to disparage the philosophical side of theology in true Ritschlian or Pragmatist fashion, greatly to the delight of the man in the pew, who has always suspected philosophy of being a distinct waste of time. Today such an attitude is an anachronism and it is largely due to Dr Oman's influence.[75]

And then again:

> From the start he flung the whole weight of his personality on the side of that ministerial ideal which Principal Skinner has so powerfully impressed upon the life of Westminster—an ideal which has inspired Westminster men not only to be willing to take hard and unpromising charges, but to be "keen" on it, as representing the highest honour a minister of Jesus Christ can covet. He has always deprecated a conception of our Church's function which reduces her to little more than an association of private chapels for the use of pleasant suburban communities with Presbyterian leanings, and has helped to inspire his students with the conviction that unless her ministers realise that they have a sacred apostolate to our great unchurched city and country populations, the Church is dead, even while she seems most alive.[76]

---

72. Whitehorn, *Roy Whitehorn*, 4.

73. Whitehorn, *Roy Whitehorn*, 37. Oman was to preach the charge at his ordination as a minister in the Presbytery of London North, 10 October 1923.

74. EWP, "Appreciation of Dr Oman: The New Principal," *Presbyterian Messenger*, July 1922, 154–55.

75. Sinclair, "Living Voices."

76. Sinclair, "Living Voices."

Workers

Outwith the college, Oman exercised his profession with "workers," students and other lay people, much of it on an ecumenical basis. Experience in Alnwick with the Chautauqua movement had introduced him to non-denominational courses of directed reading and study to serve the educational needs of adults in full-time employment. So it is unsurprising to find him giving a series of lectures for the Free Church Correspondence College on the Doctrine of Sin in November and December 1908, at St John's Wood Presbyterian Church. The college was founded by a group of ministers to "help the many workers in the Free Churches" for whom training in a residential college was out of reach. Lectures covered the core academic subjects for ministerial formation with additional pedagogical guidance for Sunday School teachers; and students were also coached "for several of the Free Church denominational colleges as well as for the Baptist and Congregational Union examinations." The College, the secretary said, was "not a money-making institution . . . and at best can only cover its working expenses."[77] Following the principle of mediated tutor-student interaction, this was the ancestor of today's distance learning programs.

The intensity of his calling to present the cause for Christianity to as wide a constituency as possible is seen in his attempt to galvanize D. S. Cairns on hearing that his friend had refused the invitation to give the Christian Evidence lectures[78] in Cambridge, pleading with him to change his mind. "It is essential that we should be represented by someone who has largely overcome the prejudices of the student beforehand. As a simple matter of fact, you alone have. You could be sure of an audience and I know of no other non-Anglican who could. Nor am I quite indifferent to the fact that you are a Presbyterian, and to the desire to see this historic monument initiated by one of us. We have done more than any other body to bring it about: Skinner was the first non-Anglican president of the Theological Society and Scott the first non-Anglican member of the Theological Board. . . . Now I am not going to say a word about anything else not even to ask how you are, lest it should seem that I write about anything else . . . but I continue to think this an appeal you can hardly set aside. Besides it is wholly amazing how little persuasively religion is presented here to any open and

---

77. *London Daily News*, 26 November 1908.

78. The Christian Evidence Society, founded in 1870, was an early example of ecumenical collaboration, tending to attract moderate or evangelical churchmen, Anglican and Free Church. Faced with the danger of unbelief, church dividing matters seemed less important.

inquiring mind."[79] Cairns was persuaded, and four lectures were given "in the spring of 1913."[80]

Oman received regular invitations to preach from 1907 onward in a variety of Presbyterian churches in England and Scotland. This gave him an opportunity to engage with his hearers from the pulpit and frequently also in discussion afterwards. In December 1912, for example, after the evening service at Clapton, he undertook "to conduct the 'conference' . . . when any man or woman who finds difficulties in religious belief whether agnostic or atheist, Jew or Christian, will be welcomed, and have a free opportunity of asking questions and stating opinions."[81]

His persuasion that the Church had a special missionary obligation to engage with the poor and vulnerable was influential. During his years as principal, "he travelled about among the congregations, [and] had been enabled to see some of the difficulties which his outgoing students had tackled in obedience to his teaching, 'Don't seek soft jobs.'"[82] He was in particular demand for the ordinations of those students who were to exercise ministry in challenging situations: men like James Scott,[83] called in 1908 to Bermondsey, which was said to be "so rough that the policemen walked in pairs," and David Anderson, called to Trinity, Camden in October, 1909. Oman could claim credit with Skinner for having saved the Camden church. It had served the neighborhood from 1869 when the first services of worship were held to cater for the navvies building the railway in the squalid surroundings of the railway arches on St Pancras Road, but in 1908 it faced closure by the Presbytery. But Oman and Skinner argued persuasively that the working man should not be deserted, and with the generous assistance of Hampstead and Frognal congregations, and Anderson's acceptance of a call, they were able to set the congregation on a more stable footing.[84]

Amongst the archive materials in Westminster College, there is an undated manuscript charge to a minister and congregation in just such a situation. Here Oman addresses aspects of ministry, the Church, and its mission that we find elsewhere in his published work.[85] Eschewing the customary

---

79. Oman to Cairns, 20 February 1913, Papers of D. S. Cairns, Special collections, Aberdeen University,

80. Cairns, *David Cairns*, 19. These were the substance of the lectures he gave to the troops in France in 1916, published in 1918 with the title *The Reasonableness of the Christian Faith*, with an epilogue which restated the argument under war conditions.

81. Unidentified newspaper clipping, Westminster College Archives.

82. "The Assembly—Day to Day," *Presbyterian Messenger*, May 1932, 34.

83. He was to be one of Oman's chaplains as Assembly Moderator in 1931.

84. Elliott, *Trinity Camden*, https://www.trinity-camden-urc.org.uk/a-brief-history.

85. E.g., in *The Office of the Ministry* and *Concerning the Ministry*.

emphasis on "practical matters," Oman reminds the ordinand of the need for his ministry to be fed by study of the Scriptures.[86] "No other study gives such freshness to your teaching or such inexhaustible variety." In preaching, he is exhorted to be spontaneous, and diligent in preparation. Spontaneity is sustained by "being in a position to speak to people you know and who . . . have been able to know you." The work to which the ordinand has been called is "of exceptional difficulty and exceptional importance."

He expands accordingly: "Our experiment here I feel is nothing short of a crisis in the life of our whole church. The question of whether the gospel can be preached to the poor is not a question about our preaching but *the* question.[87] For John . . . the convincing argument that Jesus was he who should come, was that unto the poor good news is preached. . . . If it is only for people insofar as they are well off or have a certain amount of education, then quite clearly it is for something else in man than his immortal soul and speaks in some other voice than God's to whom these things are nothing." He reiterates trenchantly his view that "the whole church mission method is moved by condescension." It is "largely a business of taking the mote out of our brother's eye" without taking note of "the beam which is in our own eye, that beam of self-satisfaction with ourselves because we are privileged people. . . . Till we see what a mockery of God's mercy our whole self-esteem is, the gospel, as Christ taught it, will have no meaning for us." We have "nothing in the end to fall back on but God's unmerited pardon and grace. That gospel can surely be preached anywhere."

This is more important than any increase in numbers. "Do not then," he advises, "set your heart . . . on mere visible success. It may be God's will to try our faith, the Church's faith still further. We only know that this is the right thing to do."

> Freedom from anxiety in your work ought to be your greatest contribution to the life of this neighbourhood. Strictly speaking the problem in this district is not poverty. It is anxiety. It is the uncertainty which crushes. Are you merely to enter into this scramble to get your share of members? . . . On the contrary surely your gospel is a gospel of calm and peace, and you will only commend it by being a man in whom the spirit of peace reigns, a man who . . . takes the real things to be the unseen not the seen. . . . The harassed multitudes of London want men like that more than the ablest organisers.

86. Cf. "The Exposition of the Word," in Oman, *A Dialogue with God*, 145–52: esp. 146.

87. The church's obligation to the poor and vulnerable is a motif of *Vision and Authority* and *The Problem of Faith and Freedom*.

Oman acknowledged his own lack of experience of such work, but even if he had views as to how it should be done, he wouldn't speak of them, "for the very essence of the right way of accomplishing it is not to start with a preconceived scheme, but to expect that God will open a great door and effectual, and to be prepared to enter in any way he makes plain to you. The only thing quite certain about it is that it must be a frank and friendly and human way, a way not of reforming men, but of finding in God's children a responsive echo to God's voice in your own soul."

Turning to the people, he asks "Why have we been so eager to keep this an independent congregation and not a mission dependent on some wealthier congregation? Probably you will always have to receive of the church's temporal things, but if you are independent in the right way, they will be no more than your due, because like the church at Jerusalem you will have given of your spiritual things." Reminding them nonetheless to make such financial contribution as they can, he continues: "But you have to give more than that. You have to give your attendance upon worship even at the cost of inconvenience, remembering that the fellowship of the church which is the secret of its power will miss something every time you are absent.

Then you must contribute your time and your thought to the work of the church, to singing with melody not only in your voices but in your hearts, and above all to teaching the young remembering that no-one can speak to them like those who live among them and know their speech and their ways of thinking."

He urges them to "contribute to the peace and unity of the church by forebearance and gentleness and kind speech and brotherliness. Sometimes that is the hardest and most necessary task of all."

"Your greatest contribution," he concludes, "will not be anything you do, but the peace of God which passes all understanding in your hearts and lives. The awful thing in our national life is not the number who are poor, but the number who are without hope in the world. . . . You will first gather to your fellowship the broken-hearted, the fallen, the lost, but the healing power of your gospel will travel far beyond anything that will ever be gathered into your fellowship."

Here we have a view of Christian life and truth which regards living faith in Christ as all-sufficient mediator of God's grace, both for the individual and the Church. It is catholic and evangelical.

"A Bad Book"

"I never wrote a book by conscious purpose but one, and it was bad, even for me. The others just came somehow and insisted on being written."[88] The book in question was *The Church and the Divine Order*[89] which "grew out of an article written to order."[90] His writing here is self-conscious, and lacks crispness, the thinking is often condensed and the sentences long and propositional, lacking the light and shade of metaphor and allusion to which one has become accustomed. Unusually for Oman, the personal impact of what he writes is lessened by reference to sources. The reviewer for the Hibbert Journal considered Oman's view of the church to be too ideal: "sublime enough, perhaps to stimulate further developments, and true enough to be a guide and stimulus to superior souls, but probably in the present state of existence, impractical for average human nature, and that, after all, forms the great mass of the material with which the Church has to deal."[91]

However, it would be unwise to dismiss the book too quickly for it is possible to see "the history of men's thoughts regarding the church,"[92] the ostensible subject of the book, as secondary to his main interest, the significance of church, Jesus, and the kingdom of God for a contemporary society marked by increasing inequality of wealth.

The Preface begins provocatively: "This whole discussion will appear to many a pure anachronism. When we are in the throes of deciding whether our society is to rest on individual competition or legal socialism, what does it matter, they ask, whether men belong to one Church or many or none at all?"[93] He begins where he left off at the end of *Faith and Freedom*, with socialism. He sees socialism and "individual competition" alike as "organized force." "The long, weary struggle of history has no meaning, if force, however organised, can conserve man's highest interests. The only hope of socialism lies in teaching men that their economic position, and all the outward good force could conserve, are subordinate interests. With that, a time might come when food and raiment were as much common property as water and air." "Organised individualism," when divorced from solidarity and the "grace and joy of life itself" is no better. Each of these need to be subordinated to a "higher order of love and freedom." Served by a prophetic

---

88. Oman, *Concerning the Ministry*, 33.
89. Oman, *Church*.
90. Healey, *Religion and Reality*, 160n7.
91. David Frew, review of Oman, *Church*, in *Hibbert Journal* 7 (1911–12), 629.
92. Oman, *Church*, viii.
93. Oman, *Church*, v.

remnant,[94] "all forms of social order must be saved, whether individualistic or collective. In some order of love and freedom, that is in some kind of Church, the historical struggle of mankind must be gathered up, and, if it is not being served by the present Churches, then a supreme effort should be made to recall them to their true task. . . . They all contain elements of self-sacrifice not found elsewhere; and except by self-sacrifice no social salvation will ever be won."[95]

But before the church can serve as the primary navigational aid to society, familiar hindrances must be addressed: "the basis of the Church is freedom, not authority, individual faith, not organised constraint, prophetic hope, not priestly tradition."[96] And again,

> Congregations of wealthy persons are gathered in one place and of poor in another, and worse still, the rich condescend to the poor in congregational missions, and the prosperous business man . . . is established on power in too many congregations . . . a dominant respectability turns Christianity into a Phariseeism whose whole moral standard is negative . . . the consequence is a loss of any deep passion either for reality or for justice.[97]

Oman is clear that "an enormous wealth resting on over thirty per cent. of abjectly poor, would seem more of a denial of God than Judea under the foreign yoke."[98] For the church, what was needed is "some kind of apocalyptic outlook, some sense that life is not good in itself, but only good when we overcome it through faith in a rule which God Himself will introduce."[99]

In linking different churches to changing views of God and salvation in history, Oman is indicating ways in which the denominations, faced with numerous social and economic questions, might relate to one another and to the contemporary world and so realize their apocalyptic identity. He conjures up an image of people who "lay themselves open to the Spirit of God. . . . They have small concern with the might of evil . . . for God Himself assures to them the kingdoms of this world and the glory of them. God's rule being the environment of their spirits, they need not to strive or cry, but simply to live as if the kingdom of God were already come for the earth as it has come for themselves. This temper has not failed. It has not been

---

94. See below, 329-30, 366.
95. Oman, *Church*, vii.
96. Oman, *Church*, 290.
97. Oman, *Church*, 294.
98. Oman, *Church*, 39.
99. Oman, *Church*, 39.

tried."[100] This might be described as the high point of Oman's quietism. God is personal, present to the human spirit. The church must always point away from itself to God. As it experiences righteousness, peace and joy in the Holy Spirit, it heralds the coming cosmic renewal and final sanctification of the world.[101] A prophetic ideal of the church is proclaimed, although there is little indication as to how this might be realized. Within three years this view will be tested.

"A Stranger of the Dispersion"[102]

Oman had always envisaged that one day he would return to Scotland. He had close personal friends north of the border and he had sustained links with the North in other ways. These took different forms. After his father's death, he maintained Biggings with a sitting tenant for the rest of his life and made return visits as circumstances permitted. On these visits, he was in demand as a local dignitary. When Stromness school closed for the summer holidays, Oman presented books given by the Board as attendance prizes;[103] he chaired a bazaar in Mr. Terras's store at North End Stromness in aid of the organ fund of the Free Church,[104] he opened a flower show at Stromness.[105]

Until he moved further south to Cambridge, he addressed meetings of the Edinburgh University Orkney and Shetland Association. In 1904, he "expressed great pleasure to be present at such a representative meeting of his fellow-countrymen. Such a thing, he said, did not exist in his time but he was delighted to see it in existence now, and wished the Association every prosperity. He then gave an interesting and entertaining lecture on 'Student Life in Germany.' The subject was naturally agreeable to the Association and the lecture was keenly relished by the audience."[106] Two years later, as Hon. President of the Society, he gave "a most fascinating lecture on 'some qualities of a good book,'" foremost among which was "absolute truth in expression, in thought and in feeling." This was followed by "imagination."[107]

100. Oman, *Church*, 332.

101. See below, 332.

102. A self-description during the centenary celebrations of Victoria Street UFC, Stromness, 29 August 1906. (Above, 21–25.)

103. *Orkney Herald*, 17 July 1901.

104. *Orkney Herald*, 7 September, 1910.

105. *Orkney Herald*, 28 August 1912.

106. *Orkney Herald*, 21 December 1904.

107. *Orkney Herald*, 5 February 1906. He maintained his links with the Society; he was present at the annual meeting in the Caledonian Hotel Edinburgh on 8 February 1922. *Orkney Herald*, 20 February 1922.

That same year he also presided at the annual reunion of around 400 islanders in the Berkley hall, St Andrew's Halls, Glasgow. In a "hearty welcome," the chair observed that Oman was "rapidly coming to the front as a thinker and man of letters and the islanders are always ready to recognise merit among their fellow-countrymen, no matter what sphere of activity it shows itself." And the reporter commented: "Not a few quaint old stories did he tell the audience in the course of a speech bristling with bright flashes of humour."[108]

On Oman's move to Cambridge in 1907, he became a member of the Viking Club. This had originated[109] as a social and literary society for those from Orkney and Shetland who lived in London, but it soon became caught up in the Victorian Viking revival. It was reconstituted in 1894 as the Viking Club or Orkney, Shetland and Northern Society to include all who were interested in Norsemen and the history of the north, coordinating an "invisible college" of old north enthusiasts. Oman's old friend Magnus Spence, former head of the Public School in Stenness, was active in the Society and Oman's brother Simon and his cousin Thomas Leask were also subscribers. Mocked initially for its esoteric titles by the Pall Mall Gazette with the headline, "Vikings drink tea,"[110] it was soon to achieve a reputation for scholarship rather than conviviality and brought together prominent scholars in the literature, life and scientific world of the north. Many of the records were destroyed in the war, but Oman is marked in the 1913 Year Book as subscriber to "Old-Lore series only" rather than to the *Saga Book* (the Journal) and other proceedings, suggesting that his main interest was in Orkney rather than in wider aspects of the Society's activities. The First World War curtailed activities seriously; and the old northern unity of scholars and lay persons in Britain and all over Europe was shattered.[111] In 1924 when records resume Oman's name is not recorded.[112] The north however, maintained its power to attract and when anonymous friends on his retirement presented himself and Mary with tickets for a two week cruise to the fjords of Norway, all expenses paid, he commented afterwards that he had never

---

108. *Orcadian*, 15 December 1906.

109. *The Saga-Book of the Viking Club*, vol. 1, pt. 1, 1892, "Social and Literary Branch of the Orkney and Shetland Society of London."

110. *Pall Mall Gazette*, 15 January 1894.

111. Wawn, *Vikings*, 369.

112. I acknowledge with gratitude the assistance of Dr. Alison Finlay, editor of the Saga-Book and Professor of Medieval and Icelandic Literature, Birkbeck College, London.

been in a country where he "felt quite so much at home with so little sense of being among a foreign people as in Norway."[113]

The Glasgow Chair

In 1914 Oman was faced with a crux. Was this the time? Rumors were circulating in January that "the name of Professor Oman D.D. of Westminster College, Cambridge is being mentioned in connection with the vacancy in Glasgow UF college caused by the death of Professor Orr D.D."[114] The Glasgow chair was prestigious. In contrast with his Edinburgh candidature in 1904, Oman was now well known in Scotland's Presbyteries. His reputation as a scholar and as a teacher was well established and he had served Westminster College with commitment for the previous seven years.

The rumors were sufficiently credible to cause alarm. On 17 February 1914, Dr. R. C. Gillie, convenor of the Westminster College Committee, circulated widely a letter agreed by the fifty members of the Committee, representative of the PCE Presbyteries, requesting the recipient to sign an "enclosed communication" to Oman, appealing to him to "give no encouragement to such a proposal as his removal from Cambridge would inflict a serious blow both on the college and the church."[115]

By March, he had been nominated by several Scottish Presbyteries. The Birmingham Presbytery was quick to express dismay; and on 5 March, the Reverend J. R. Gillies moved the adoption of a resolution by the Presbytery of London North, expressing

> deep concern at the possibility of Prof Oman D.D. being called to a theological chair in Glasgow, and the Presbytery's earnest hope that he would see his way to set aside any proposal, however tempting, which might issue in his separation from a church where he is so highly honoured and beloved, and to whose welfare and progress he seems at the present time to be indispensable. The resolution stated that a new and higher ideal of personal devotion and ministerial efficiency is at work in the Church, and that this can be traced largely to Dr Oman's influence over the younger ministers. The resolution was seconded

---

113. A letter which cannot be traced, quoted in Healey, *Religion and Reality*, 159n15.
114. Press cutting, unattributed, 25 December 1913, scrap-book, Westminster College archives.
115. 17 February 1914, Westminster College archives.

by Dr Voelcker and was at once carried by a standing vote. A copy was ordered to be sent to Dr Oman.[116]

Oman did not respond immediately. But on 4 April, he addressed a meeting of the London Presbytery North. After "thanking the Presbytery for the kindly terms of its resolution passed at the last meeting, expressing the hope that he would discourage the efforts that were being made to secure his services for Scotland, [he] stated that he had been led to see that it was his duty meanwhile to live and labour in England, where the great religious problems of the day are centred. His statement was received with much satisfaction."[117] While we can only guess at the personal cost of Oman's decision, which effectively closed the door on any further opportunity to return to Scotland, we must assume that the high estimation of his achievement in ministry rendered the call to remain in England the more effectual.

No-one could have guessed from any of this that Britain was on the verge of one of the defining episodes of modern history; or that with the outbreak of the First World War in a matter of months, Oman was about to embark on an unprecedented new phase of ministry.

---

116. Press cutting, unattributed, scrap-book, Westminster College archives.
117. Press cutting, unattributed, scrap-book, Westminster College archives.

9

War

The First Months

On 18 June 1914, Commemoration Day at Westminster College was celebrated with "the most brilliant weather." The gardens looked "as gay and brilliant as ever." Ladies in long white dresses and large hats mingled with men in suits and gowns. Oman was relaxed and genial and the lecture on "the Crisis of the Church" given by Professor Paterson from Edinburgh University was "the great event of the day."[1]

Within ten days, the assassination of Austria's Archduke was to trigger the First World War[2] and the college faced radical upheaval. Although the Principal reported in September that "he had received applications for admission by ten regular students,"[3] by October, nearly all the students in residence had volunteered for work with the YMCA in the Bedford camp, Dr. Joseph Sinnreich, a student of the college and an Austrian citizen, was interned near Wakefield, and Herbert Farmer had chosen as a pacifist to work at a farm near Histon.[4] By November "several of the undergraduate students had asked, and received, permission to defer their courses in order

---

1. *Presbyterian Messenger*, August 1914.

2. 1 August, Germany declared war on Russia; 4 August, Britain declared war on Germany; 12 August, Britain and France declared war on Austria-Hungary.

3. Minutes of Senatus, 29 September 1914.

4. Minutes of the College Committee, 26 October 1914. It is likely that this was under the auspices of the Chivers family, who were farmers and jam manufacturers in Histon and strict Baptists.

that they may serve in the army during the period of the war,"[5] and from 21 December to 15 January 1915, 141 to 125 soldiers were billeted in the college,[6] with the beginning of Lent term postponed until 19 January. As casualties began to arrive at the First Eastern Hospital in Cambridge, Oman provided the services of a Presbyterian minister.[7] The *Presbyterian Messenger* reported with approval how "except for an absence in France of some months in summer," Oman and the Reverend W. A. Leslie Elmslie "have been continuously at work almost since the hospital was opened" thereby freeing up R. H. Strahan, minister of St Columba's Church, for "work at the two isolation hospitals and among the cadets."[8] It was also reported that "Westminster College is more and more known among the cadets as a centre of hospitality. Within the walls of the Lodge, every Thursday evening, a number of our Presbyterians from Great Britain, Canada, Australia, and New Zealand, are gathered together on the invitation of the Principal and professors." This was in line with Cambridge colleges who through engagement with the young trainees, "took on a fresh lease of life. . . . The kindness of senior members of the University, whether in entertaining, in lecturing, or in acting as cicerones, and the generosity of the Union Society did much to make the cadets feel themselves an integral part of the community."[9]

Oman also began to pay regular visits to prisons and internment camps[10] where his fluency in German stood him in good stead. He relates a

---

5. Minutes of the College Committee, 18 November 1914.

6. On 17 March 1915, the College Committee recorded that "the surplus of the money received by the military authorities for the use of the college premises, over and above what was required to repair the damage done to the property, should be spent in providing means for the carrying on of work among the soldiers by the students and others associated with the college." These may have included the "Committee of ladies (Mrs Anderson Scott Secretary)" who were given permission by the Senatus to use the Junior Common Room each afternoon as a rest room for convalescent soldiers (Minutes of Senatus, 10 January 1917).

7. With its HQ in Trinity College, beds in Nevile's Court cloisters and the Leys school, and temporary buildings on the cricket grounds of Clare and King's colleges to the south of Burrell's Walk, there were over 1,500 beds for officers and other ranks by the end of 1915 (Addenbrooke's Hospital Archive).

8. *Presbyterian Messenger*, April 1917, 91. Until Strahan was officially appointed as hospital chaplain by the War Office with the concurrence of the PCE Chaplains' Committee, Skinner relieved him of his pastoral duties at St Columba's, where "more than 200 cadets worship every Sunday."

9. University of Cambridge. *Historical Register, Supplement 1911–20*, 200–205.

10. "Germany: Fifty Years Apart, 1. The Changed and the Unchanged," *British Weekly*, 24 January 1935. The prison visits are likely later to have involved conscientious objectors, perhaps Westminster students or others attended to by the FOR.

conversation on one such occasion with two stereotypical German doctors,[11] one from Prussia and one from the Rhineland, which throws light not only on his sympathetic observation of human nature but also on his ability to handle a potentially awkward situation. While the Rhinelander showed him round, discussing "literature and philosophy as if the war had never been heard of," the Prussian "insisted on my lunching with them in a way that could not be denied, and he exercised all the hospitality the situation afforded. But it was just when Mackensen had defeated the Russians,[12] 'There is the beginning of the end,' he shouted, 'And then what will you English think of being associated with barbarians against a cultured people like the Germans?' I said that, if we put off the discussion till the war was over, we should do it more calmly, and he laughed and turned to something else. But, while my southern friend was disturbed at what he thought a breach of hospitality, my Prussian friend glowed with the sense of having fulfilled a duty."

If we deduce that the occasion may be dated to September 1914, Oman would have had reason around then to visit Lofthouse Park Camp, near Wakefield, where, in the context of marked public suspicion of "enemy aliens" and a strong feeling in government that these presented a serious threat to national security, the Westminster student, Joseph Sinnreich[13] was interned for seven months along with many other German or Austrian students, professors and lecturers from Cambridge.[14]

War and Peace

Intellectual salvos were also being exchanged between Britain and Germany, arguably the most controversial sparked in early September by the "Appeal to Protestant Christians Abroad," signed by twenty-nine prominent German theologians, some of whom had been active in the Anglo-German friendship

---

11. "Germany: Fifty Years Apart, 1. The Changed and the Unchanged," *British Weekly*, 24 January 1935.

12. The allusion would appear to be to the Battle of Tannenberg which ended on 30 August 1914. Due largely to the superior strategic skill of the German army, the Russian army was annihilated.

13. Minutes of Senatus, 6 June 1914, 25 November 1914, Westminster College Archives. Although previous steps to secure his release were unsuccessful, it was reported (Minutes of Senatus, 20 January 1915) that he had been released at the beginning of December and would be in residence that term.

14. Walling, *Internment*, 9. Lofthouse was known as "the gentleman's camp": many men were able to pay for their upkeep. By 1918, civilians were moved out to Knockaloe to make way for POWs. https://www.wakefieldhistoricalsociety.org.uk/wakefield-history/reports-on-lectures/2544-42/.

movement and in the Edinburgh World Missionary Conference in 1910.[15] The Appeal began by repudiating the suggestion that Germany was responsible for the war. "With the deepest conviction we must attribute it to those who have long secretly and cunningly been spinning a web of conspiracy against Germany, which now they have flung over us in order to strangle us therein." If the fellowship with Christians in other lands which was the "sacred legacy" of the Edinburgh 1910 Missionary Conference was now discredited, the Appeal protested that Germany was not the guilty party.

Of several responses, the most consequential was that drafted by the Archbishop of Canterbury and endorsed by forty-two representatives of the Free Churches and the Church of England.[16] In the opinion of the signatories, Germany's liability was incontrovertible. And so the reply contained these damning lines: "There must be no mistake about our own position. Eagerly desirous of peace; foremost to the best of our power in furthering it, keen especially to promote the close fellowship of Germany and England, we have nevertheless been driven to declare that, dear to us as peace is, the principles of truth and honour are yet more dear."[17]

Neither Oman nor Skinner signed that letter. Skinner hesitated for "most of a forenoon" till he saw that "this was not the mind of Christ on the situation."[18] He responded accordingly and received a reply which "effectually cured me of any temptation to think I could go in the same boat as these men. It was an explicit denial of the claims of Christian morality to have any say in the sphere of international relations: the doctrine of von Bernhardi in fact. But I don't seem to get much 'forradder.' I am quite clear that the church ought not to pronounce a benediction on this bloody business; but how far she or the individual Christian is bound to carry the protest I do not see, every path seems to lead to an impasse."[19] So he wrote in September an explanation why the Church ought to refrain from official declarations which may be regarded as sanctioning war. When this was published in the *Presbyterian Messenger* in January 1915, Oman was one of seventeen signatories.[20]

The Church, it was argued, is bound to declare only those things that are in accord with the teaching, the example and the spirit of Jesus; the

15. For details, see Bell, *Randall Davidson*, 740–44. Signatories included Harnack, Deissmann, Hermann, and Loofs.

16. Bailey, "British Protestant Theologians," 202.

17. Bell, *Randall Davidson*, 742. The letter was dated 23 September 1914.

18. "John Skinner, an appreciation by a former student," *Reconciliation, 1925*, 205–6.

19. "John Skinner, an appreciation by a former student," *Reconciliation, 1925*, 205–6.

20. The name of the Reverend J. D. M. Rorke of Bexhill was "accidentally omitted." *Presbyterian Messenger*, February 1915, 54.

central truth of whose gospel is the kingdom which "transcends the divisions of race and nationality, uniting men of all peoples and tongues in a common brotherhood in the bond of peace and under the law of love"; the catholicity of the church forbids the identification of Christianity with any particular nation: "it is not the concern of the Church of Christ to advocate the redressing of wrong by violence, or the establishment of righteousness in the earth by other than moral and spiritual agencies." Prominent in the New Testament is the idea that evil is to be overcome by good, not by force; in a time of war as in peace, the Church ought to preach love of enemies, forgiveness of injuries and conciliation. And the letter envisages the task of healing and reconciliation at the end of the war, "to which the spirit of Christianity alone is equal."

The issue was delicate and the editor of the *Presbyterian Messenger* feared that the letter would create controversy which might rebound upon the Church or demoralize the troops. Additionally, it offered "no point of contact between Christian ideals and the present situation. In the light of the ideals so ably and clearly presented, what are we here and now to do?"[21]

Fellowship of Reconciliation

The question was particularly pertinent for one of the signatories of the letter, Richard Roberts, minister at Crouch Hill Presbyterian Church, who noted that a number of young Germans, regular members of his congregation, were missing.[22] Realizing with horror that they might soon be fighting on the opposite side to their fellow worshippers, he decided to arrange a conference on Christianity and the War[23] and consulted Skinner as to whom he might invite, raising with him the extent of Oman's pacifist sympathies. Skinner replied: "I have not pressed him as to his attitude; but I hardly think he is prepared at present to go the whole hog. In fact, I don't know if I can myself!"[24]

On 31 October 1914, however, Skinner wrote: "Oman should certainly be invited. I am not sure that he will come; but I am hopeful that he . . might see it to be his duty to do so."[25]

---

21. *Presbyterian Messenger*, January 1915, 4.
22. Norman, *Grace Unfailing*, 5.
23. Wallis, *Valiant for Peace*, 5.
24. Letter to Richard Roberts, 25 September 1914, United Church of Canada Archives, Richard Roberts fonds, file 38.
25. Letter to Richard Roberts, United Church of Canada Archives, Richard Roberts Fonds, file 38.

At the end of December 1914 the conference was held in Cambridge with the assistance of Ebenezer Cunningham, a fellow of St John's,[26] a deacon of Emmanuel Congregational Church and an uncompromising pacifist. "Somewhat daringly"[27] he had gained permission from the Vice Chancellor to use the Arts Theatre as a venue and the Fellowship of Reconciliation was born. Oman and Skinner along with three Westminster students, Farmer, Hawkridge and MacLachlan, were among the first supporters.[28] They saw themselves as "a company of people who seek, individually and corporately, to take their part in the 'Ministry of Reconciliation' between man and man, class and class, nation and nation, believing all true reconciliation between men to be based upon a reconciliation between Man and God."[29] Love as revealed and interpreted in Jesus Christ was the framework by which members viewed the world. With regard to war, it was for the individual conscience to decide how best to proceed.

Among those "who had offered to speak or write," and whom Lucy Gardner the secretary was to approach, was Oman.[30] But Oman still felt a need "to think out [his] own relations to the present crisis."[31]

The War and Its Issues

The War and Its Issues originated in an address Oman gave in 1915 to students of Queen's College, who were having to make up their minds about how to engage with the war effort. Because Oman still needed to tease out his own thoughts, he expanded his paper for his own benefit "without thought of a public." But he agreed to publication in March that year in the hope that "in the present great perplexity" the little book would be "a gift to help towards a better solution,"[32] recognizing that "any great upheaval which

---

26. A mathematician, he is remembered for his work on special relativity.

27. Quoted in Ferguson, "Fellowship of Reconciliation."

28. So too was C. J. Cadoux, tutor in Hebrew at Mansfield College, who was to become increasingly involved with the Fellowship (Kaye, *Cadoux*, 49). Skinner was appointed to the Committee. FOR General Committee minutes, 7th Committee Meeting, 11 March 1915, London School of Economics Archives, FOR 1/1.

29. FOR General Committee minutes, first Meeting after Cambridge conference, 13 January 1915. London School of Economics Archives, FOR 1/1.

30. FOR General Committee minutes, fifth Committee Meeting, 17 February 1915. London School of Economics Archives, FOR 1/1.

31. Oman, *War and Its Issues*, preface.

32. Oman, *War and Its Issues*, preface. Published by the Cambridge University Press on a profit-sharing basis; the Syndics bought the rights from Oman on 1 January 1932. Thompson, "Oman and the University," 81.

shakes men's trust in material well-being and forces them to ask what remains when earthly succour fails, may do more to make clear the true spiritual issues of life than ages of meditation in ease and quiet."[33] Although what appears to have been a hasty expansion of Oman's original paper gives rise to an occasional unevenness in presentation, this is a remarkable little book and one of the few publications where he applies his thinking directly to concrete issues. As we shall see, that thinking was radically counter-cultural.

This is an exercise in moral philosophy. The book is divided into two main sections, "A Christian Judgment" and "The Moral Issues." Oman raises questions about the good life and consequent questions of obligation. And within this framework, he presents a balanced attitude to the "irreconcilable perplexities" raised by the war.

"A Christian Judgment"

In contrast to the stridently jingoistic views of many contemporary clergy, Oman conceives of the possibility of conscientious objection, evaluating his belief that "the strong thing in the end is not violence but the sacrifice and service of love."[34] However, does it make a difference if the war is "just"?[35] As the soldier knows, war is hell, but "can anyone so dissociate himself from the struggle of his people in so generous a conflict for human freedom?"[36] And ultimately, "where loyalty and faith and sacrifice and victory over the fear of death are found, religion cannot be out of place."[37] While then not excluding Christian engagement in war, Oman claims that, for a Christian, war can never be anything more than "a stern negative necessity." That Christianity must seek to overcome war is undeniable but "how does it set to work on that task?"[38]

33. Oman, *War and Its Issues*, 3.
34. Oman, *War and Its Issues*, 18.
35. The concept of "holy war" was part of the religious rhetoric of combatant nations within weeks of the outbreak of war. The significance of this has only recently been recognized. (MacDonald, "Holy War and the Great War," 135.) In a letter to Cairns, Oman compares attitudes to the war in Scotland and England, instancing a presbytery meeting in Scotland at which he had spoken in 1916 where "the war was treated as a purely holy thing. I spoke very mildly of the things you say, and it was as if I had in sheer wickedness poured cold water down their spines. Selbie says he is no pacifist but he found himself in an atmosphere at Glasgow University which was sheer paganism in its feeling about the war." (John Oman to D. S. Cairns, January 30, no year, from Mansfield College. Special Collections, University of Aberdeen.)
36. Oman, *War and Its Issues*, 19.
37. Oman, *War and Its Issues*, 21.
38. Oman, *War and Its Issues*, 27.

Oman is clear that pacifism is not enough. There are prior issues. A Christian attitude to war has to be seen in the context of a wider Christian witness against a capitalist social and economic system. So long as our social and economic system is exploitative, "all who live for position, money or any kind of material power, are involved in the tyranny of immoral force as much as if they were fighting in an unjust and predatory war."[39] The fact that Christians are members "of a society which represents the kingdom of God ... a rule not established by force"[40] does not absolve them from responsibility for the earthly kingdom. The church has a key role to play in the fight for social justice. Where the church's members are not seen to be in pursuit of the common good, its integrity may be questioned.

If this line of thought "exemplifies the method of Christianity, militant pacifism cannot be what is meant by not resisting evil."[41] Yet certain ideals of non-resistance may be influential: "We should never accept war as eternally necessary." "We must never consent to fight merely for a material triumph" but for "the creation of a juster and purer society worthy of the sacrifice of human lives." "We can have no part in any gospel of hate, as if at the present time the Germans were merely fiends in human shape." "A peace to be abiding must be established in righteousness and a sense of mutual benefit and good-will. That may not be hindered by a fair conflict."

However Oman realizes that these convictions on their own are insufficient; they do not help with the issue which confronted him when he addressed Westminster College on the first Friday of Lent term 1915 about the claims of National Service: How does the Christian "answer the call that is made upon his manhood."?[42] No record survives of that address, nor indeed of the paper which he presented to the students at Queen's College which was the nucleus of *War and its Issues*; but he is likely to have indicated as he does here that each individual is given "the spirit by which he can adequately deal with his own interests according to his own sense of duty."[43]

The emphasis on spiritual intuition implies a freedom to discern right and wrong, distinct from coercive discipline. But intellectual permissiveness is guarded against by the prayerful dependence of one's innermost being on God. "With regard to our vocation . . . our guiding principle shall not be

---

39. Oman, *War and Its Issues*, 29. It is interesting to observe that in 1917, Oman convened the PCE committee "On Spiritual Independence and Safeguarding the Church's Property" and was still a member of the committee in 1924. (Official Handbook of the Presbyterian Church of England, 1917, Westminster College Archives.)

40. Oman, *War and Its Issues*, 33.

41. Oman, *War and Its Issues*, 39.

42. Oman, *War and Its Issues*, 41.

43. Oman, *War and Its Issues*, 46.

personal ease, honour or gain, but God's will, and it assures us of guidance in discerning what our talents, time and circumstances require our vocation to be, if we seek that guidance in humility and freedom from anxiety."[44] Many a young person "has fought out the battle for himself, and has come out a wiser and a better man for determining yea or nay on no other ground than his own conception of his duty."[45] There are, Oman maintains, implications here for the church. First, it has to give such a person the freedom to decide on the right way forward. Any attempt to impose his duty upon him in an authoritarian manner "is a denial of the significance of Christ for every individual's direct relation to God."[46] Consequently, the church has an obligation to teach the meaning of the Cross in the spirit of love and prayer, showing "an unwavering respect for the individual's judgment of his own duty, with the one requirement that it be wholly sincere."[47] The value Oman attaches to sincerity, that quality which Lionel Trilling memorably describes as "a congruence between feeling and avowal,"[48] is of supreme importance for the moral life. It chimes with the Romantic desire for a purer form of life than the secular notion of the self. It points to the dialogue between self and soul. It is integral to the life of prayer.

Secondly, where people are seen, not *en masse* but as individuals, that has implications for Christian faith. War teaches Christians to understand the anguish of loss in the light of God's love.

> When we learn that the boy who used to come to our house and laugh with our children is dead with a bullet through his brain, we are startled into understanding war and realise not only that a warm heart has left many hearts in sorrow, but that the world is poorer by the loss of one whose modesty, courage and worldliness might have made him a leader in a still greater warfare.[49]

Likewise to think of the Germans in abstract terms as "the enemy" is to lose sight of the personal and negates God's purposes of love.

> Those of us at least who have known the Germans as generous and warm-hearted friends, and have learned much that deserves our best gratitude from their labours, ought to be able to realise that every death among them, as among ourselves, leaves

44. Oman, *War and Its Issues*, 46.
45. Oman, *War and Its Issues*, 52.
46. Oman, *War and Its Issues*, 52.
47. Oman, *War and Its Issues*, 51.
48. Trilling, *Sincerity*, 2.
49. Oman, *War and Its Issues*, 53.

> a blank in some family circle which for some heart will never be filled again while life shall last. Yet in these days we hear with ever diminishing pain that two thousand of them have gone to the bottom or that their casualties are to be numbered in millions. Can a strife which breeds in us such a temper be rightly regarded with anything except detestation and horror?[50]

In these two quotations the significance of the person is affirmed. Oman is promoting not just a sensitivity to the universal suffering caused by war but a moral imperative to put an end to it. There will be "little place for drum-beating and glory and transference of territory and the pomp and circumstance of war, but much for securer homes, purer hearts, juster laws and any other good that can go into humble lives."[51] If the church has a contribution to make, it must show itself to be catholic, in the sense of universal. Yet "All our churches . . . have become mere national churches . . . in the sense of having no interest or charity beyond the national cause." And he concludes that if the church were truly catholic "surely a German ought to be able to pray with us in our public worship."[52]

However that day is still far ahead. The churches are not "able to speak to the present distress with any clear prophetic voice."[53]

Hampered by the prevalent anti-German attitudes, they are also hampered by a materialistic outlook.

> Even the churches wealth least frequents are largely governed by men of an arm-chair habit of body and a bank-note habit of mind, the same in type at least as those who make wars and never fight them, who demand of our churches success as worldly corporations. . . . Hence much concern about numbers, funds and organisations and little about truth and love. . . . Instead of having a gospel for the poor, for man in his nakedness and his need, the comfort is only for the already comfortable, the riches of grace only for those who already possess.[54]

Oman is clear that, as a fellowship of grace, the church must transcend a craven demand for comfort and assurance and rise above its narrow

---

50. Oman, *War and Its Issues*, 19.
51. Oman, *War and Its Issues*, 55.
52. Oman, *War and Its Issues*, 56.
53. Oman, *War and Its Issues*, 58.
54. Oman, *War and Its Issues*, 59. Oman takes up de Tocqueville's thesis that "freedom alone . . . replaces at certain critical moments [a] natural love of material welfare by a loftier, more virile ideal" (*Old Regime*, xiv). But whereas de Tocqueville identifies this ideal with one's native land, Oman substitutes the moral landscape of Christianity.

perspectives. These are dangerously misguided. The church is self-preoccupied, it tends to identify itself with the nation in its opposition to Germany, its perceived adversary. This national commitment is at the expense of theological universalism. Only as the church repents of its failings, is it in a position to exercise the ministry of reconciliation to which it is called. Only then "can we hope to discern our own duty in the strife and guard ourselves from the passion and hatred which obscure more than any smoke of battle the issues of a stable, because a righteous peace."[55]

In Germany as in Britain, the church has proved itself wanting. Germany "packs her churches with people intent on nothing but victory. Her pulpits all echo to the note of absolute right and the prayers breathe an unwavering confidence that God is her great war ally."[56] When "men who have taught the whole world the value of first principles lose sight of any principle but national interest, we have a strange sense of loss of contact with reality, almost a sense of mental alienation."[57] However, Oman observes that "duty done on calm reflection" is unaffected by "the Prussian exercise of 'frightfulness' which is only a modern version of skulls, dances and war-paint."[58] And for any who think that these attitudes are confined to Germany, he cautions: "at all times the same Berserker rage slumbers in our bosom."[59]

"The Moral Issues"

In the second section of the book, Oman's thinking, actualized by the war, turns to the future. He speaks directly to "[us] especially of the elder generation, who have supplied the fuel for this conflagration which we now must leave to the younger generation to put out" and he issues a challenge: "If we are to have any right to receive that sacrifice at all, [we] must consecrate our lives as utterly to the regeneration of the whole order of our society as our young men are doing to its preservation." The only security of peace is "a human and equitable relation to our fellow-men in the society in which God has placed us."[60]

---

55. Oman, *War and Its Issues*, 60.
56. Oman, *War and Its Issues*, 61.
57. Oman, *War and Its Issues*, 62.
58. Oman, *War and Its Issues*, 62.
59. Oman, *War and Its Issues*, 63.
60. Oman, *War and Its Issues*, 69.

What would such a peace look like? He returns first of all to the theme of social justice.[61] This is not a matter of "social reforms here and there," for "our eye cannot be single in this matter of social justice, or any other, till it is fixed on our duty not our gain."[62] Then we will discover "the austere gladness of courageous living."[63] If we allow the war to give us

> a new estimate of the worth of life by service and not by sitting at meat ... all kinds of social victories will be within our reach. ... Having suffered together in our common humanity, having been all of us reduced together to the poor hazard of our lives ... only then can we have a country with the true and enduring securities and able from that vantage point to stretch forth its hand in brotherhood to all other peoples.[64]

In fact, "on nothing less can social renovation be adequately based."[65] Oman perceived that, unless weapons were controlled or eliminated, the militarism which gave rise to armed conflict would persist.

> No victory and no guarantees exacted by it can ever by themselves give us a secure and abiding peace, but the arbitrament of arms might be left in such a position as to make all other arbitraments impossible. ... A drawn battle ... which would leave Europe a vast armed camp in which the nations glared at each other with savage suspicion and dread, is not a condition to be accepted, if any devotion on our part can deliver us. Even if we could manage to patch up some form of peace, it would be a mere armed truce, in which we should watch one another like beasts of prey, while military burdens crushed out our highest interests and the military temper grew ever more hostile to the spirit of freedom.[66]

61. The is clearly articulated in "God's Ideal and Man's Reality," in Oman, *Paradox*, 60–72.

62. Oman, *War and Its Issues*, 73.

63. Oman, *War and Its Issues*, 73.

64. Oman, *War and Its Issues*, 73. This may be an over-generalization. The prewar regular army was "recruited from the bottom of Society" but "led from the top." The result was an exemplary paternalism and a rigidly hierarchical approach to discipline. Between 1914 and 1918, some officers came to see their men as partners in adversity and showed them considerable devotion. Sheffield, "Officer-Man Relations."

65. Oman, *War and Its Issues*, 74.

66. Oman, *War and Its Issues*, 76. As a measure of his continuing concern, Oman was to attend a meeting chaired by the Archbishop of York in the Central Hall Westminster on 15 June 1931 in connection with the forthcoming disarmament conference in Geneva summoned by the League of Nations. (*The Times*, 16 June 1931.) With the withdrawal from discussions of the Nazi Regime all prospects of international disarmament disappeared.

The shrewd perception that there can be no lasting peace while the nations nurture an aggressive spirit of militarism is linked to the realization that neither Germany nor Britain is immune from this.[67]

"While we grieve for the sufferings of the German people, we grieve still more that they should accept this idol [militarism]."[68] But might Britain be in like case? "If that type of militarism was wrong for Germany, it is wrong for us . . . the danger will be with us immediately the war is over."[69]

For Britain as for Germany, the principle of freedom is at stake. Oman instances conscription, "Dead Sea fruit which we will not pluck."[70] "We are fighting to free our necks from a yoke which others would impose. . . . We must be able to say that, whatever may happen to us in body or estate, we are not ourselves going to sacrifice our freedom."[71] The Germans on the other hand, have embraced autocratic rule. They "have done like sheep what their rulers have told them."

> But if we accept obligations without knowing what they are, are we better in principle? . . . The moment . . . that we appear before our rulers, not as a free people but as an army under military compulsion, we become the tools of the Foreign Office; and our rulers are established in a position of autocracy which is neither good for them nor us.[72]

Oman foresaw that after the end of the war, "more extended military organization" would be politically challenging. Compulsory military service would mean that "effective control over our foreign affairs," even of our "subsequent disapproval" would "pass from our hands." "Our liberties at home would be in grave peril."[73] Our freedom would be threatened by "restriction of civil liberties," a need for "some measure of military dictatorship," a reinforcement "of privilege and reaction, and the exhaustion of a long, costly and weary struggle."[74]

    67. Along with a large number of pacifists and others, including Skinner, Selbie, Cairns, and Forsyth, Oman signed a widely disseminated letter of protest in 1917 against the policy of reprisal represented in the bombing of Freiburg, stating that the signatories "with all the force in our power, protest against the adoption by us of precisely that method of direct and indiscriminate attack upon non-combatants, which we have been holding up to the condemnation of mankind." *Votes for Women*, 1 June 1917.

    68. Oman, *War and Its Issues*, 77.
    69. Oman, *War and Its Issues*, 80.
    70. Oman, *War and Its Issues*, 81.
    71. Oman, *War and Its Issues*, 83.
    72. Oman, *War and Its Issues*, 84.
    73. Oman, *War and Its Issues*, 86.
    74. Oman, *War and Its Issues*, 87.

Although there may be occasions when "we were driven for a time to resort to some measure of compulsion, it ought to be in measure and duration prescribed as a dangerous medicine. . . . Compulsion is alcohol, possibly a fillip to help round a hard corner, but dangerous even for that."[75]

This raises the question of the state. Is the state the servant or the master of the individual? Here again Oman's approach is balanced. "The Germans complain that we describe their attitude as militarism because we do not realise their conception of service to the state; and apart from the necessities of self-defence, they cherish compulsory military service as the supreme instrument for teaching the individual that he is just the servant of the state."[76]

Oman thought otherwise, citing the nonconformist conscience "which embodies the protest of all serious members of the state against mere selfish state action.[77]

He reminds us that in this matter Germany began before us. Luther's courageous presentation of the individual, whose rights were "established upon his duties" meant that "when God spoke, popes and Kaisers mattered nothing."[78] However "instead of developing church and state through this moral individual," "[Germany] ended with a subordination of the church to the state and thereby of the individual to the state in a way without parallel in Western Europe."[79]

As for *Kultur*, "Germany again produced the movement's most authentic voice." This was Kant whose emphasis on "autonomy of conscience," and the

> moral person as an end in himself . . . embodied its intellectual and still more its moral ideal. For such a conception of life the state is necessarily subordinate to the moral individual and could not be right except by paying heed to his independent moral judgment. Not only does that principle alone rightly constitute

75. Oman, *War and Its Issues*, 84.

76. Oman, *War and Its Issues*, 85.

77. Oman, *War and Its Issues*, 89. Pyper, "Disconnected Dialogue," illustrates this by contrasting Adolf von Harnack and C. J. Cadoux. Harnack was well known in British theological circles; before the war, he had participated in initiatives to promote friendship between English and German churches. As a staunch Lutheran, he saw Christianity as a matter of private conscience, not as "a prescription for the behaviour of a state or a government." The Quaker Cadoux "is the heir to a distinctive tradition in British civic life which has found a place for the political expression of radical Christian obedience." The locus of authority is "the individual conscience directly illuminated by the universal word of God."

78. Oman, *War and Its Issues*, 89.

79. Oman, *War and Its Issues*, 89.

the state, it alone can embrace all states in the higher conception of the Kingdom of God and afford any natural basis for peace.[80]

Germany however followed Hegel "with his doctrine of the individual as the mere organ of the absolute and necessarily subject to the state which is the Absolute's final organ." The notion that morality did not apply to the state, that the state is judge in its own cause, meant that war was the only possible court of appeal. This "remains the Prussian ideal to this day."[81] The allusion here is to the goal of the state unified under Prussia, expressed in the writings of the Hegelian Heinrich von Treitschke (1834–96) which were a sweeping popular success. With his conception of Germany as God's chosen people, entrusted with a national mission, he had his counterparts in most European countries but his exaggerated emphasis on state power was widely criticized outside of Germany. Oman is measured in his appraisal:

> Only ignorance can afford to mock at German culture . . . [but] in religion and in philosophy Germany has produced an idea of amazing creative value and then proceeded herself to apply the opposite.[82]

Oman is under no illusion: if a new way of life were to be opened up in Germany and Britain, it would necessitate for each nation a radical new way of seeing and responding, the acting out in freedom of a new identity. This leads him to ask the classic question, "What must a person do when the state asks him to do something contrary to the moral law of God?"[83]

Oman addresses the challenge in a way that is too condensed for clarity. In his reference to "revolution" it may not be fanciful to discern echoes of Calvinist politics which saw beyond "circumspect and lawful resistance" to revolution.[84] After all, the revolutionary, like the prophet, viewed himself as an instrument of God.[85] As Walzer indicates in his classic analysis, revolution could not wait upon majorities: "Political right 'devolved' only to the godly among the people: the prophet enlisted the saints."[86] Oman returns

---

80. Oman, *War and Its Issues*, 90.
81. Oman, *War and Its Issues*, 91.
82. Oman, *War and Its Issues*, 91. W. R. Sorley argues (Sorley, *International Crisis*, 26) that while differences may be exaggerated, yet it would be instructive to compare and contrast English and German theories of the state especially as they impact on human life.
83. Cairns, *Answer to Bernhardi*. Cairns proposed that he should obey God and disobey his country.
84. Walzer, *Revolution of the Saints*, 107.
85. Walzer, *Revolution of the Saints*, 107.
86. Walzer, *Revolution of the Saints*, 109.

to the theme after the war.[87] But here I would simply make the point that Oman's apparent endorsement of the French Revolution may have been too much for many of his readers, conscious of increasing industrial militancy, of the defiant tactics of suffragettes, of a fear of communism.[88]

One of the fundamental problems of a state-based system for Oman is that the power it gives to the nation-state is at the expense of the individual; as a result, it is unable to meet the needs of a world that longs for a true, global community of persons.[89]

This leads him on to discuss international relations, where he points with foresight to the risk of further conflict.

> The war has already shaken most of the poor international safeguards of peace we have hitherto possessed. The suspicions of statesmen will be increased, and the hostility of the peoples. No settlement could be devised which will not leave in some nation the sense that it can recover its position only by a new war, and there may not even be the wish to escape such an issue, when the victor as well as the vanquished is exhausted and sore. The settlement may, therefore, be such as to disturb even our present agreements, and the embers of so great a conflagration will be in danger of breaking out again into flames.[90]

He toys with the idea of "a federation of nations."[91] He would have been aware of plans that were being developed between 1914 and 1919 in a diverse and fluid political environment by people who were determined to find new means of avoiding war in the future. In 1915 Willoughby Dickinson co-founded the League of Nations Society which, following a merger in

---

87. Chapter 10.

88. Oman, *War and Its Issues*, 93. Though here he appears to be hospitable to the possibility of social revolution along the lines of France, six years on he writes: "a crowd emotion like the Terror . . . is too like the neighbourhood of Vesuvius to be a stable foundation for any secure and lofty social structure" ("Spiritual Regeneration," 48).

89. See Domingo, "Crisis."

90. Oman, *War and Its Issues*, 96.

91. The thought was not new. William Penn, having seen the effects of the internecine warfare of the seventeenth century in Europe, brought an intense desire for peace and justice to his study of international relations, and the resulting essay, "Towards the Present and Future Peace of Europe," promoted the idea of a permanent European confederation with a Parliament to settle disputes by open debate. A century later, Kant wrote that perpetual peace was not merely a utopian ideal, but a moral principle which ought to be realized and therefore could be (*Perpetual Peace: A Philosophical Sketch*, 1795). Political facts have to be faced; only when nations cease to be independent can war be prevented. Not by despotic rule, but by a federation of free and "republican" states.

1918, formed the League of Nations Union, the main pro-League body in post-war Britain. However Dickinson came to believe that the League idea, based on the principle of international state cooperation, was insufficient. A shared international identity was required.[92]

This is in line with Oman's suggestion here that a federation of churches might be a better guarantor than states of "righteousness, freedom and a good understanding." He takes issue at some length with Richard Rothe's claim that the goal of the church was to create a Christian state, arguing that the state "even as a perfectly moralized force" is insufficient to embody the Kingdom of God. The state needs borders, in some respects these will be hostile; whereas the church has "a rule to which national boundaries are irrelevant and for which a man may be asked to forsake his nation . . . a society in which they are our mother and sister and brother who do the will of our Father."[93] Secondly, the church is not a state but a fellowship, united by faith, "by individual insight into truth," and love. In Germany, the church would appear to be "wholly swallowed up in the state and to be incapable of raising any moral issue. It has become a state church."[94] In Britain, on the other hand, "our divisions have kept us in mind of the possibility of the deeper and more spiritual bond . . . but we have a long way yet to go before any church, free or established, realizes a fellowship which is . . . truly catholic because it is prepared to stand or fall upon an appeal . . . . to each man because he is the brother of Christ and capable of seeing in Christ the truth and realizing in his cross the service of love."[95]

As to the state, although it is "the guardian of civilization" serving the social, intellectual and ethical interests of its citizens, it will always need "a society which can, by setting all man's temporal activities in the midst of eternity, turn defeat to victory."[96]

The state is empirical, material. Its relationship with the church is "work in progress"; the church has yet to realize the relationship between the visible church, the institution, and the invisible church, the one church of all times and places. As visibility and invisibility are both aspects of same church, catholicity belongs to both; unity and catholicity belong together.[97]

Ultimately nation and church both depend upon personal faith; God's order is thus seen to depend on the relationship of the individual soul to

---

92. Gorman, "Ecumenical Internationalism."
93. Oman, *War and Its Issues*, 111.
94. Oman, *War and Its Issues*, 112.
95. Oman, *War and Its Issues*, 113.
96. Oman, *War and Its Issues*, 114.
97. Blei, "Communion and Catholicity."

him.[98] "What in the last ditch of our moral nature, do we believe in?" Oman's final question takes him back to where he began as he emphasizes the idolatry of trusting "security in gain and selfish good" rather than God.

> Nothing is more appalling at this moment, nothing is more ominous for the future, than the spectacle of middle-age persons who, while the young are pouring out their lives like water, are discussing markets and using the occasion to get gain.[99]

And the book ends with the solemn observation that if war is to count only for material gain "no one of us ought to accept the sacrifice." After quoting the text of 2 Samuel 23:14–17, he asks: "Is not the one question, How shall we pour out unto the Lord this offering of the blood of the men who go in jeopardy of their lives?"[100]

Reactions

Unsurprisingly, the book had a mixed reception. "R." in the *Presbyterian Messenger* reacted vigorously to Oman's critique of the Church: "This is a statement which is so far from truth and charity that on all grounds of internal evidence it must be regarded as non-Omanic, having been inserted in the manuscript by a malicious brownie while the good professor slept."[101] The reviewer looked forward to another book about the war, which would "in a strict sense be a theological book."[102] The political content was also controversial. There was some criticism of Oman's assertions that commercialism is a contributory factor to war, and that the state should be subject to the individual; and of his belief in the fundamental goodness of heart of the German people.[103] For the *New York Times Book Review*, "The spirit of his book is much finer than its substance,"[104] while the *Cambridge Review* felt that "no fair-minded man should pass the same judgment on British and German policy."[105]

   98. Oman, *Natural and Supernatural*, 449–50.
   99. Oman, *War and Its Issues*, 129.
   100. Oman, *War and Its Issues*, 130.
   101. *Presbyterian Messenger*, July 1915, 255.
   102. He would not have had long to wait for *Grace and Personality*, published in 1917.
   103. Oman, *War and Its Issues*, preface to the 2nd ed., 1916.
   104. *New York Times Book Review*, 8 August 1915, 283.
   105. *Cambridge Review*, 1 March 1916, 238. The rival of the *Cambridge Review*, the *Cambridge Magazine*, which started publication in 1912, included a popular weekly

Oman's refusal to be drawn into hatred of Germany, his belief that German imperialism was similar to Britain's in the Victorian era, his perceptions that war was turning Britain into a military and authoritarian state, his dislike of secret diplomacy and his thoughts on the need to create a just peace—all of these were contrary to the general thrust of public opinion. But they did find an echo in the programme of the Union of Democratic Control,[106] a group of radical intellectuals who advocated democratic control over the war effort and whose first public meeting took place in Cambridge on 4 March 1915.[107] The Cambridge branch was "extraordinarily unpopular"; the secretary, G. H. Hardy, had his cat poisoned and Bertrand Russell was deprived of his college lectureship at Trinity.[108] G. Lowes Dickinson "suffered nothing in Cambridge except a complete want of sympathy." However, between 1914 and 1918 the UDC campaigned against the senselessness, brutality and hysteria of the war and Oman gave them his support.[109]

Westminster Students and the YMCA[110]

Having examined *The War and Its Issues* in some detail, we now return to Westminster College, where the Senatus agreed that Oman should address the College on the first Friday of Lent Term 1915. He should "refer to the claims of National Service in one of its many forms" and assure the students that "the case of any man who entered such service would be sympathetically considered by the college authorities."[111] Nearly all had already opted

---

review of the foreign press edited by Dorothy Roden-Buxton, designed to show that there were plenty of sane moderate people in enemy countries.

106. Hanak, "Union of Democratic Control," 177–78.

107. *Cambridge Magazine*, iv, no. 16, 6 March 1915. UDC influence on the early days of the Labour movement would be hard to exaggerate. During Ramsay MacDonald's brief government in 1924, fifteen members of the UDC entered the government, nine of whom were in the Cabinet. (Schwartz, The UDC.)

108. He was not at this time a Fellow of the college. Robbins, *Abolition of War*, 89.

109. I am indebted to Professor Charles E. Bailey for his notes of an interview with Mrs. Isabella Ballard, Oman's eldest daughter, in Cambridge, March 1979, where she gave this information. Although in September 1915 the executive of the UDC decided not to accede to FOR's request to affiliate, that did not prevent individuals from supporting both bodies; see Robbins, *Abolition of War*, 60.

110. This section is largely based on Houston, "In the Open Country." Reproduced with permission.

111. Minutes of Senatus, 20 January 1915, record the decision that "Dr. Oman . . . should *urge on* students the claim"; this is amended on 13 February 1915 to "Dr. Oman . . . should *refer to* the claim."

with alacrity to serve the YMCA in Bedford,[112] and from 26 October to the end of November 1914, arrangements had been made for them to do this in relays of four for a fortnight at a time.[113] The *Presbyterian Messenger* reported approvingly on this "admirable piece of work" : "The students run the refreshment tent and in part of it . . . hold service on Sundays and family worship on week-days."[114] Their congregation consisted mostly of Scottish regiments preparing to go to France.

In 1915, shortly after his address to the College, Oman accompanied some of these students to France to work there with the YMCA.[115] The Revd John C. Carlile of Folkestone, who had just come back from a tour of the Base Camps, wrote in May: "I have been appealing to theological colleges that tutors and students should go out to Northern France, either as Red Cross workers or in YMCA huts. My friend Dr Oman, of Cambridge, with a batch of students, is already on the other side, and others will follow. No college curriculum can provide anything like the help in the development of experience, the art of securing attention, the methods of dealing directly with men as men and witnessing for Jesus Christ, as any man may obtain in the open university of an army base, or even a remount camp."[116]

In June Oman is mentioned in the Principal's report to Synod as being "fresh from his experiences with the students in France." He had described "the work of the juniors in a YMCA tent as near the fighting line as possible and within sound of the guns." And Skinner concludes: "Dr Oman's testimony goes with that of a great many others to tell how great an opportunity these tents have—an opportunity greater than that of any chaplain I ever met."[117]

The Base Camps made good placements. In Calais, Boulogne, Le Havre, Dieppe and Rouen, thousands of men were handling shiploads of men and materials for a soldier's pay; many were irked by the restrictions imposed by military discipline and bored with the dull routines of daily work. The huts were also full of units waiting for their turn on the firing line. The YMCA kept them human in the midst of unnatural and at times

---

112. In response to an urgent invitation from the YMCA supported by Tissington Tatlow, General Secretary of the SCM. Minutes of Senatus, 26 October 1914.

113. Minutes of Senatus, 25 November 1914.

114. *Presbyterian Messenger*, December 1914, 389.

115. On 13 February 1915, the Senatus minutes record that "four students of the third year, one of the second and four of the first are likely to offer their services with YMCA tents at home and abroad."

116. John C. Carlile, "With the Troops in Northern France," YM 21 May 1915, Special Collections, University of Birmingham, YMCA/K27.

117. *Presbyterian Messenger*, June 1915, 201–2.

inhuman conditions. The huts catered for social and intellectual needs. Typically a counter at one end of the hut met a constant demand for tobacco, cigarettes, bootlaces and polishes, soap and candles, bachelors' buttons. In another slightly smaller hall, beyond, there was a billiard table, a small lending library, and free stationery. Lectures were popular as were the concert parties by Lena Ashwell[118] when "the hall was packed to the utmost, by a dense, khaki-clad crowd; every window crowded by those who could not gain admittance."[119]

The huts also catered for spiritual needs. Sunday morning services were usually held by an army chaplain; on Sunday evenings, by one of the workers, and every week-night at 8:30, there were family prayers consisting of a hymn, a passage of scripture with occasionally a few words of comment, prayer and the National Anthem. Oman cautioned the students against levity:

> When a young parson in France used to talk to men just out of the trenches as if life were a gay affair, its conflicts only a football scrimmage, with a copious use of slang, the cheaper that it was mainly the clever college article, it was somewhat of an outrage. Nevertheless, to have exchanged him for Chaucer's "full solempne man" who speaks in one deep sombre tone, as though only the sob of the wind across a grey plateau were God's voice, and never the zephyr in the smiling valley or the tempest on shining mountain-tops, would not have won a better or more sympathetic hearing, even amid a welter of mud and sudden death.[120]

They were "somewhere in France"; the conventions of censorship did not encourage greater precision. But there are clues. Oman relates how, in a street in Boulogne, he met a young lad whom he had seen only recently, full of the joy of life. "Now, a few days before, he had left three hundred of his comrades behind him at Neuve Chapelle, and his face had the haggard, dazed look of a child that had lost all its bearings in the dark."[121] From the reference to Neuve Chapelle, and the shell-shocked young man, this was likely to have been in late March 1915. Then, a month or so later, following the devastation of Hill 60, Oman was with another lad, "dying slowly . . . of a bullet through the spine, beseeching me to write his mother assuring her

---

118. "Concerts for the Army," by Miss Lena Ashwell, YM, 15 October 1915, YMCA/K27.
119. Tod, "Lights and Shadows."
120. Oman, *Concerning the Ministry*, 95.
121. "Turfing the Grave," in Oman, *Dialogue with God*, 45.

that he was all right."[122] The lad was "in a little hospital at the Forward Base." "Forward" here must mean "nearer to the Front." "A little hospital" would be an apt description of a Casualty Clearing Station, which was usually a few miles behind the lines; a patient with a severe injury to the spine would have been retained there: a move to a large base would not have been considered unless survival was likely. Amongst the places that had such medical units at the time, the most likely seem to be Poperinghe, Bailleul or Hazebrouck, all "within sound of the guns."[123]

Oman came home "with a sense of the greatness of the work of the YMCA, and the possibilities of it." But he made it clear in his report to Synod that the possibilities afforded were not simply of pastoral experience or evangelistic opportunity. He reiterated the "feeling that we are passing into a new era. If we did not realise that we are in the very heart of an enormous crisis for humanity that had in it the possibility of 'scrapping' civilisation, we would not have realised the call or the opportunity. For this reason he welcomed the opportunity which had come to the students."[124]

National Service

The students, on their return to college, had now to decide where their duty lay in respect of Lord Derby's appeal[125] and the Senatus had to decide how best to assist. The view of the Senatus was that the students' "obligation to the Church is not to be held as debarring them from responding to the call for National Service." And it expressed "its sincere sympathy with them in the difficulty of their situation."[126]

Oman's attitude was consistent:

> If a man feel his call to go forth to fight his country's battle, we have a right to require him not to be swept off his feet by the mere emotion around him, to weigh his duty prayerfully, and

122. "Turfing the Grave," in Oman, *Dialogue with God*, 45.

123. For an account of the Casualty Clearing Stations, see Bosanquet, "Health Systems in Khaki." I am also indebted to Sue Light for conversations on The Great War Forum, http://1914–1918.invasionzone.com/forums/index.php?act=idx.

124. *Presbyterian Messenger*, Synod Supplement, June 1915, 17.

125. In October 1915, this was a short-lived attempt to boost recruitment to the army. Men aged between 18 and 40 were invited to attest with an obligation to join the army at a later date. It was followed in January 1916 by the Military Service Act which authorized the conscription of single men between 18 and 41. Clergy, the medically unfit, teachers, and a few others were exempt, but many theological students felt an obligation to enlist.

126. Minutes of Senatus, 9 December 1915.

to bear it in mind, that if a Christian can fight, it may not be for mere victory in battle, but only for a greater victory of justice and right to which even his country must be subject. After that his Christianity must decide and we must respect his decision.[127]

Each had to decide for himself according to his individual conscience. We may instance this by two students who each expressed appreciation of Oman's support and were to opt for different courses of action. Kenneth Keay, one of those who went with Oman to France in 1915, was awarded honours in his exit exam in 1916, when he took up a commission with the Cameronians and was wounded on the Somme.[128] He was later to serve as one of Oman's chaplains during his moderatorial year.[129]

Percy Bernard Hawkridge was awarded a Goodman Scholarship for two years from October 1914, but requested to delay coming to Westminster until 1915 as he had joined the OTC with a view to obtaining a commission after his degree.[130] But by December 1914 he had become a pacifist. Although he did enter college in October 1915, he left after one term "for family reasons."[131] As was typical in such cases, no reference is made in the college minutes to his pacifism or to his successive tribunals. His initial application for exemption on the grounds that, as a minister, he was "engaged in work of national importance" was disallowed and he appealed, on "educational, conscientious and domestic grounds." He told his tribunal on 28 March 1916 that his "objection to combatant service was because it was under military organization. If he did not have to take the military oath he would not object to RAMC work." And he explained: "I am already pledged to serve the Lord Jesus Christ, and if the requirements of the military cross the teachings of the Lord I could not see my way to do them."[132] Percy Hawkridge made it clear that he saw the Military Oath as an abrogation of freedom.[133]

127. Oman, *War and Its Issues*, 44.

128. Fasti record, Westminster College archives.

129. *Presbyterian Messenger*, January 1932.

130. Minutes of the Board of Studies, Westminster College Archives, 18 November, 1914.

131. He was the sole support for his widowed mother, who was seriously ill, and his younger sister, with whom he lived at 22 Warwick Street, Oxford; he received a stipend of £2 a week as minister of Cowley Congregational church.

132. *Oxford Times*, 1 April 1916.

133. The Tribunal was unconvinced but granted him conditional exemption for three months "on domestic grounds" (*Oxford Times*, 15 July 1916). This exemption was duly renewed on 11 July, and at his October hearing, it was announced that "he was exempted under the Act and the case need not be proceeded with so long as he remained a minister" (*Oxford Times*, 28 October 1916). College records confirm that contact was maintained while he was in Oxford, that deferred exams were duly sat, and that in February 1919 he was readmitted.

Oman and the YMCA

Oman himself now adopted the advice he had often given his students "you will help no-one to victory if you yourself shun the battle."[134] On 5 May 1916 his war medal card testifies that he arrived in France to begin civilian service with the YMCA.[135] He went out as a lecturer in the base camps. In submitting the names of proposed lecturers for approval to the Lectures Committees of the War Office and the YMCA, Basil Yeaxlee and Gilbert Murray state: "It is obvious that men who are personally out of sympathy with the war and the national policy which it implies are hardly suitable for this work. Nor would any mere profession of orthodoxy in these matters be of much value."[136] The implications are that Oman qualified. He lectured on "the historical problems of the war."[137] The lectures typically lasted for an hour to an hour and a half with half an hour or so of questions. If the men could not get their questions in in time, they would hand them in on paper in advance of the next lecture:[138] "Have we any right to assume that God will give victory to the allies?" "What is God doing in this business? Are fatalities providence, fate or merely blind accident? What is the use of talking of conscience, when the Germans are fighting us as conscientiously as we are fighting them?" Oman was impressed by "their strong sense of what was right and just, their earnestness, fairness and courtesy in debate. . . . If their knowledge was more limited than a scholar's, it was closer to life and readier to hand than most scholars manage to keep theirs."[139]

He would have been given a copy of the YMCA "Hints to speakers."[140] The advice was crisp:

> The soldier is chary of the parson. But he honours the padre. It is decidedly advantageous for the speaker to spend some considerable time among the men during the day for personal dealing.

---

134. Oman, *Concerning the Ministry*, 42.

135. National Archives, WO/372/15. The British War Medal, authorized in 1919, was awarded to eligible service personnel and civilians. The basic requirement was that they either entered a theater of war or rendered appropriate service overseas during the War; service with the YMCA was recognized. The medal, in solid silver, has a mounted figure of St George trampling the shield of the central powers with the dates 1914 and 1918. The reverse has the coinage head of George V.

136. YMCA Lectures for the Forces in France, YMCA/K26.

137. Eddy, *With Our Soldiers*, 42.

138. Frank Adkins, MA, "Tommy in His Hours of Ease. Lecturing to the Troops in France." YM, 13 July 1915. YMCA/K27.

139. Oman, *Concerning the Ministry*, 157.

140. YMCA/K24/67.

> If he can play a good game of chess, draughts or billiards with them it will help. . . . Speakers must be prepared to address men under quite unusual conditions, especially where the meeting room is used for writing, games, and the sale of refreshments. . . . the necessity therefore, of concentrating the thoughts and attention of those willing to listen is apparent . . . speakers will probably find the atmosphere dense with smoke. . . . The singing of a solo . . . will help greatly in securing the goodwill of the audience.

As regards accommodation, "modest expectations are advisable. The beds have varying degrees of hardness. Sheets are not the rule; take one, also a towel. . . . There is much mud. . . . Leggings are better than spats. Silk hats are not de rigueur, any other kind will do better." And finally, "The cut of the coat, or collar, matters little—the man matters more." While Oman was not given to bursting out in song or to wearing a silk hat, he clearly had no difficulty in relating to the soldiers. One of his students commented:

> He is thoroughly and entirely human. During his work in France under the YMCA you would see him sitting pipe in hand, amid a crowd of soldiers, his audience as much at ease with him as he with them. . . . If anyone has the idea that Dr Oman is remote, aloof, unapproachable by simple folk, let his mind be disabused at once. I have heard him described as "just a great brotherly soul" and that is exactly what he is.[141]

He was absent in France "for some months."[142] At least some of this time was spent in the Rouen camp. His old friend David Cairns, who had come to France on 18 April, was quartered there in the Cavalry Hut and delivered to the soldiers four addresses which he had given three years before in the Cambridge Schools. In their published form Cairns records his gratitude to Oman for his "invaluable help in Cambridge and in the Rouen camp."[143]

But not all of the summer was spent giving lectures. Oman "spent a good part of that delectable period in hospitals seeing the efficiency of civilisation in abusing its powers."[144] On the southern outskirts of Rouen in 1916 there were six large General Hospitals, part of the evacuation chain manned by the RAMC; there were four smaller Stationary Hospitals and a

---

141. "Appreciation of Dr. Oman: The New Principal," by E.W.P., *Presbyterian Messenger*, July 1922, 154-55.

142. *Presbyterian Messenger*, April 1917.

143. Cairns, *Reasonableness*, vi.

144. Oman, "Mr Henry Ford's Philosophy."

convalescent Depot, a halfway house for casualties returning to the Front.[145] In these, Oman "learned to look at all kinds of physical wounds without a tremor,"[146] as he was brought face to face with the grim realities of war, both physical and spiritual.

As he had done the previous year, he went beyond the base camp and nearer the front line. He records a visit to Abancourt which was associated with a rail regulating station and an ammunition dump.[147] By 1916 the YMCA tent there had been transformed into a "first class hut and billiard room,"[148] supplying refreshments daily for up to 1,000 men on the railway station. Oman's reference is not, however to the YMCA hut but to "the labour colony." But the Abancourt Labor Camp only existed for two months in March and April 1918,[149] and there is no record of a visit by Oman to France in 1918. So it seems likely that the reference is to the military prison complex at Blargies, just south of Abancourt.[150] This was a penal unit where prisoners were regularly detailed for arduous work in laboring gangs. Amongst the thirty or forty inmates of a particular hut, several of them recidivists, Oman met a "young lad who had been brought up in the most religious kind of Congregationalist home, and had never before met anything but the most reputable people."[151] It is likely that the lad was a conscientious objector, a hypothesis that may be supported by the fact that Abancourt was used by the British Army as a base in France for non-combatants[152] and that, in May 1916, two hundred conscientious objectors arrived in France for "work behind the lines."[153] We can only speculate about the lad and his future, but it appears from questions raised in the House of Commons the following year, that seventeen men in the Second Northern Non-Combatant Corps were sentenced at Abancourt for refusing to handle military supplies, their sentence of two years' hard labor being commuted to eighty days of Field Punishment No.1, where the offender was tied usually to a wooden cross, for up to two hours daily, sometimes within range of enemy shell-fire. On

---

145. http://www.1914-1918.net/hospitals.htm.

146. Oman, *Concerning the Ministry*, 28.

147. Oman, *Concerning the Ministry*, 155-56.

148. "Memorandum of Interview with Mr. Oliver McCowen re Centres in France," 31 December 1915, YMCA/K26.

149. For this information I am indebted to Ivor Lee, The Great War Forum, http://1914-1918.invasionzone.com/forums/index.php?act=idx.

150. See Payne, "Why the British Army Did Not Mutiny."

151. Oman, *Concerning the Ministry*, 155.

152. Personal correspondence with Bill Hetherington, honorary archivist, Peace Pledge Union.

153. "News in Brief," *The Times*, 6 May 1916.

the same occasion, fourteen Seventh Day Adventists were court-martialled at Abancourt for refusing to do military work on the Sabbath and sentenced to nine months' hard labor.

Although I find no comment by Oman about the appropriateness of conscientious objectors being dealt with by military rather than civil authorities, his visit to Abancourt would appear to coincide with a concerned letter to the press[154] on the subject signed by a cross-section of churchmen and professors and a similar appeal addressed to the Prime Minister by a number of professors of Victoria University and the Nonconformist colleges in Manchester. The *Presbyterian Messenger* was less convinced: "If a man has a conscientious objection which leads him away from, rather than towards, sacrifice and suffering . . . he ought not to complain if the nation which he is refusing to help in the hour of its need is inclined to deal with him somewhat curtly."[155]

For the PCE this was a particularly sensitive issue. The view of a vocal minority was that the church was on a slippery slope if it engaged in politics. And those who did not agree with that could scarcely avoid the regular postings in the *Presbyterian Messenger* of "Losses in War" and "The Manse roll of honour." On 11 April 1916, during the Synod, "a breeze arose over the 'Conscientious Objector.'"[156] Mr. McBean, of Chorlton-cum-Hardy, and Mr. Robinson of Hartlepool, had moved a motion of respect and sympathy for their plight. The Synod Clerk, acknowledging the controversial nature of the resolution, moved that the Synod pass to the next business. "Mr McBean's motion was finally withdrawn after an appeal to that effect from Dr Oman. But the Synod greatly enjoyed a brief passage of arms between teacher and pupil. Dr Oman said the motion was not in a form that could command his support. Mr McBean retorted that his thought on the subject had been formed by Dr Oman's teaching. And the Synod found relief in an outburst of laughter from a somewhat tense situation."

In early 1917, Oman ordered his uniform.[157] This had only recently, after much debate, become a requirement for YMCA workers;[158] but

---

154. See "Conscientious Objectors," *The Times*, 25 May 1916; cf. also the representations made in the House of Commons on 10 May 1916 citing instances of the brutality of military authorities and the torture of COs: http://hansard.millbanksystems.com/commons/1916/may/non-combatant-corps.

155. *Presbyterian Messenger*, May 1916, 151.

156. *Presbyterian Messenger*, June 1916, 180.

157. Charles E. Bailey, notes of an interview with Mrs. Isabella Ballard.

158. Oliver McCowen to A. K. Yapp, 4 July 1916: "The question of uniform is practically settled: the people at GHQ are very keen on its adoption. . . . I think it will be possible to turn out the uniform so that our men will not run the danger of

Oman's action signaled clearly his intention of returning to the Front. It signaled too that he had no objection in conscience to "belonging to the show where everyone is in Khaki."[159] However, whereas up to then those clergy who went to France did so "by individual arrangement with the YMCA," in the winter of 1916–17 the chronic shortage of workers obliged the association to "approach the authorities of the principal denominations in England and Scotland."[160] The Presbytery of London North Synod of which Oman was a member, "appointed an Advisory Committee" and suggested "that any ministers contemplating such service should put themselves into communication with the Convenor of the Presbytery's Committee before they take any steps."[161] While D. S. Cairns was "set free for a year" by the United Free Church College in Aberdeen to help in the religious work of the YMCA,[162] Oman was told that he was "needed more at home."[163]

"Human Freedom" and "War"

In September 1916, Oman contributed two chapters, entitled "Human Freedom" and "War," to a collection of essays edited by Vincent Henry Stanton.[164] These originated as lectures given during the Summer Meeting held in Cambridge under the University Local Lectures scheme. The overall theme for 1916 was the difficulties for Christian Theism raised by the spectacle of conflict and suffering in the world. In that they took place after the two visits Oman made to France with the YMCA in 1915 and 1916, they provide systematic evidence of his thinking on the subject during this time.

Oman raises familiar themes but he forestalls criticism. "Repetition is not always unprofitable, for, to quote Wendell Holmes, 'What would

---

being mistaken either for officers or privates." YMCA/K27 War Work No. 14. France. By September uniformed YMCA secretaries were being routinely saluted. *The Times*, 27 September 1916.

159. 20 January 1915, letter from Oliver McCowen, YMCA/K26 War Work No. 13. France. The khaki uniform, incorporating a Red Triangle badge on the cap, shoulder straps and right sleeve, was otherwise virtually indistinguishable from that worn by officers. Snape, *Back Parts of War*, 52–53.

160. "Memorandum regarding the Interdenominational Position of the YMCA," prepared at the request of Oliver H. McCowen by E. C. Carter, December 1916, YMCA/K24/5.

161. Minutes of Presbytery of London North Synod, 9 January 1917, Westminster College Archives.

162. Letter from E. C. Carter to Oliver H. McCowen, 24 January 1917, YMCA/K27.

163. Charles E. Bailey, notes of an interview with Mrs. Isabella Ballard.

164. Oman, "Freedom," and Oman, "War."

Socrates have made out of "Know thyself," if he had said it only once, instead of going on, as people complained, always saying it?"[165] But the focus in these two essays is dissimilar to the *War and Its Issues*, for he now addresses questions of theodicy. His subject here is "the religious, not the moral aspect of war . . . God, not Germany, Providence not Pacifism."[166]

"Human Freedom"

In "Human Freedom" he revisits *The Problem of Faith and Freedom* and explores the degree to which human freedom is possible, looking at issues around individual liberty and ability, and liberty and virtue, in the context of questions raised by the war. At the root of these questions was the speculation as to whether or not the world may be said to be "merely mechanical and determined" and the degree to which this is compatible with our ability to "determine our own ideals and values." He then proceeds to examine the "scientific, philosophical and religious" challenges to our claims to be free and finds all three inadequate.

Difficulties were emphasized by the war in acutely practical ways. A tendency to fatalism was intensified by the range and seemingly random power of modern artillery.[167] People in the power of forces of destruction were dehumanized and ceased to be persons; in submission to external authority all sense of individuality was submerged; religion was apt to turn to fatalism. To quote a Scottish Presbyterian chaplain, "Almost every soldier in the line has become an Ultra-Calvinist—if not a man of faith, at least a man of fatalism. . . . I have had more talks on Predestination and God's ordering of lives with soldiers than with Christian people during all my ministry."[168] As Oman observes, "It is a great strength to believe oneself safe till 'one's number is up,'"[169] and easier to ascribe the incomprehensible evils of war to an omniscient God with a "divine plan." Confused as these arguments were, yet all of them were "dimly felt at one time and reinforcing each other."[170]

In addressing these issues, Oman set himself to determine the limits of freedom—we cannot do anything we like. We are subject to many factors over which we have no control, we are influenced by a sense of moral responsibility, and our opportunities in life are not ours to determine.

165. Oman, "War," 157.
166. Oman, "War," 157.
167. Snape, *British Soldier*, 28.
168. Snape, *British Soldier*, 28.
169. Oman, "Freedom," 60.
170. Oman, "Freedom," 60.

However, we do have flexibility to determine some things, and these can be consequential. "Thus we can accomplish nothing by trying to push around the ship, but we can bring her round by applying ourselves to the helm." And even in the case of those things that are beyond our power, we can maintain "an unconquerable soul, which may alter the significance of every event in life for us."[171]

Ultimately, questions about freedom are questions about divine power. Is our dependence on God marked by constraint or freedom? If God's power can be described as that of a Father, "because it deals with us as with children, desiring to see us directed by our own insight, our dependence may not be less, but it will be mediated otherwise than by compulsion . . . the insight to find our right relation to a free world would be the highest of all acts of freedom."[172]

The scientific objection is that there is no place for freedom in a mechanically regulated world, but Oman argues that "the new idea of the atom leaves measureless room for the possibilities of the universe,"[173] and we might even in the lowest forms of life discern the possibilities of reason and purposeful choice.

The philosophical objections stem from the misleading supposition that "determination by motive and character" is due to mechanical necessity. Oman shows how we are free both for good and evil. "What is character, if not something formed by the exercise of freedom in the teeth of our natural disposition, by doing our duty, not because we liked it, but because we ought?"[174] That deep sense of responsibility springs from an inner freedom.

As to religious objections Oman addresses the view that there is no room for freedom in a world where God is omniscient and omnipotent. If God did not have a real world, with real children, but merely a Punch and Judy show, with sensitive puppets, history would simply be "a very bad nightmare. What are we to say . . . of this war, fought out by mortal men enduring agonies of conflict and wounds and death, and women and children homeless wanderers on the earth, and mere spectacle for a Deity who has prearranged all the issues leaving nothing really dependent for ourselves or others, on the endurance of free men for righteousness' sake?"[175]

---

171. Oman, "Freedom," 61.
172. Oman, "Freedom," 62.
173. Oman, "Freedom," 64.
174. Oman, "Freedom," 70.
175. Oman, "Freedom," 72.

But if on the contrary, we can describe ourselves as God's children, then "in freedom, and not in slavery, we may in the end make truth our own and abide in a love our own hearts have chosen."

> If all freedom stands not by parliaments and other safeguards, but by the faithfulness of those who have discerned that freedom is greater than life, then we can see in all our struggles . . . the creation of God's final order. As something not imposed upon us, but as a truth accepted by our own insight and a love embraced by our own hearts. Then we may see that freedom is not of mere hard resolution, but is the end towards which all God's appointments for us are directed.[176]

"War"

In his second essay, Oman observes that "the problem of God" was evident in peace as well as war. While people lived easy comfortable lives, it was easy to imagine that the world was supported by a benevolent deity, but it was equally easy to see such a world as self-sufficient with no need for a God hypothesis. "Neither view was of much help when the present distress came upon us. A true faith, however . . . blazes up highest when the storm is strongest."[177]

War, he maintains "knocks the spectacles of custom off our eyes," forcing us to confront evil and ask whether the goal of life could be found in the pursuit of pleasure and possessions. All sides in war suffer a common human agony. Only as we face up to this reality are we in a position to confront the question of redemption, not "a mere discovery that the world is evil," but "a discerning of its true meaning and purpose."

That meaning will elude us unless "we find something in our present experience which enables us to face all its evil in the assurance that this is God's world and we are God's children."[178] This is more than a vision of hope; it is fed and inspired by the courage and understanding of our predecessors: "we are founded upon the Apostles and Prophets, with Jesus Christ as the chief corner-stone."[179] We should never undervalue "those who never shrank from evil, yet never doubted the victory of good."[180]

---

176. Oman, "Freedom," 73.
177. Oman, "War," 158.
178. Oman, "War," 160.
179. Oman, "War," 161.
180. Oman, "War," 162.

War raises special problems. First, the cause of the war. There is the issue of sin. "We are left in amazement at the kind of government of the world which allows such calamitous might to one wicked human will."[181] Oman here is reflecting the popular view that the Kaiser was the embodiment of all evils emanating from imperial Germany.[182] But his second observation is more pertinent—that we cannot avoid responsibility for the corporate nature and cumulative power of evil. "War is met by war, organised destruction by organised destruction. . . . We dreamt of a good-will extending beyond the bounds of states, to include at least all civilised peoples in a republic of letters, science, art, labour. Suddenly we found our morning vision of the dawn turned to the black and lightning-riven thunder-cloud of brutal violence and national hatreds."[183] And third, the problem of the suffering of the innocent. In this particular war, all have suffered, including those responsible for the war. "Yet . . . they probably never will suffer like the humble laborious people whom they have used for their own purposes; and still less have they suffered like their homeless, destitute victims."[184]

Faced with these problems, how are we to understand the liberty of the children of God? Unless tremendous issues really depend upon human choice and the exercise of our responsibilities, "God is a meaningless word and should be named Fate."[185] Second, the kind of order which emerges from this liberty. "If the rule of God is to be measured by the decent smoothness of the result, nothing can at present be said for it."[186] But "if we are only free as we accept, of our own insight and consent, God's rule as our own will, only free as we are gladly bound," we will be able to discern how the misuse of human freedom gives rise to the tyranny of evil both in the individual and in the world. "Perhaps the most hopeless thing in our present outlook is . . . our determination to build again our old selfish, competitive social order, with its vast wealth and measureless poverty, its worthless and restless ambition, its lack of idealism in service and of brotherhood in fellowship."[187] In that we are all implicated to a greater or less extent we all share responsibility.

Then finally, there is God's way of establishing his rule. He does so, not by might, but in the manner of the Prodigal's father, by love. Loving our

181. Oman, "War," 162.
182. Hoover, *God, Germany and Britain*, 29.
183. Oman, "War," 163.
184. Oman, "War," 163.
185. Oman, "War," 165.
186. Oman, "War," 166.
187. Oman, "War," 169.

enemies "may require the suppression of crime, the resistance of oppression, the standing in the breach to protect the weak and the guiltless. Yet . . . the final triumph over evil lies . . . not with 'reeking tube or iron shard,'[188] but, even in war, with the readiness to suffer, with the pain and the sacrifice; and finally it can never be in war at all, but in the spirit of victorious sacrifice which alone can replace all need for arms."[189]

In conclusion Oman affirms that to raise the question of God is to raise the question of the meaning and purpose of life. "When we are reasoning about God we are considering whether, in spite of the success of wickedness, wickedness wins the final success; whether, in spite of violence, violence is the final power; whether the meaning of the world is cruelty and cunning or truth and goodness."[190]

Grace and Personality

The "thoroughness, originality and spiritual power"[191] with which Oman was to explore the answer to this question "ranked him especially," in the words of W. A. L. Elmslie, "as one of the outstanding Christian scholars of this century."[192] *Grace and Personality* was, in the eyes of F. R. Tennant, "the most striking of the series in which the thinking out of his convictions receives expression."[193]

It quickly earned a place among the great spiritual classics. "If you have no money," wrote the editor of the *Challenge*, "then sell your shirt and buy it."[194] And at the Assembly where Oman was called to the Principalship, the Reverend Roderick MacLeod, minister of Frognal Presbyterian Church, made a notable impression by telling how, when he visited the distinguished Congregationalist theologian P. T. Forsyth at Hackney College shortly before his death, he noted that a copy of *Grace and Personality* was lying on his bed. If a student were to ask him what he should read, Forsyth said, that would be it![195]

---

188. The reference is to Rudyard Kipling's poem "Recessional," composed for Queen Victoria's Diamond Jubilee. It points unreservedly to the transience of British imperial power in the light of the superior power of God.

189. Oman, "War," 170.

190. Oman, "War," 172.

191. Farmer, "Memoir of the Author," xxix.

192. Elmslie, *Westminster College*, 22.

193. Tennant, "John Wood Oman," 337.

194. "E.W.P.," "The New Principal," *Presbyterian Messenger*, July 1922, 154–55.

195. "E.W.P.," "The New Principal," *Presbyterian Messenger*, July 1922, 154–55.

While the thinking is dense and requires careful concentration, it is not abstract, and it is a measure of the book's popularity that it was reprinted numerous times, and revised editions appeared in 1919[196] and 1925, when it was also published in America.[197] The third edition expanded the text, Oman acknowledges, "to state more fully some ideas, which, because I had pondered them, so fully occupied my own mind, when the book was being written, as not to seem to require elaboration, but the presentation of which, read again after an interval of years, appeared too condensed to be easily understood; and second to putting more stepping-stones, as it were, in the path of my argument."[198] In acknowledging the possibility of "abstruseness," he continues: "I have this encouragement that the book has been read by many who have no technical knowledge—some of them working men, and that they seem to have understood what I was driving at, at least as well as some professional theologians who start by expecting what they do not find and with presuppositions I do not grant."[199] He had written:

> The work as it now stands is the effect of the War. It scattered my students, interrupted more directly historical and philosophical studies into which an appointment to the University lectureship on the Philosophy of Religion at Cambridge had led me, sent me into camps and hospitals where fundamental religious questions were constantly being discussed, and forced upon me the reconsideration of my whole religious position. Moreover the fact that such sorrow and wickedness could happen in the world, became the crucible in which my whole view of the world had to be tested.[200]

His intention being to convey "a view of the world which would include this and all other events in time, [he] sought to avoid direct references to the War which might divert the mind from that larger issue."[201] But he adds wryly:

> As, during the years in which the book was being written, I was living, at home or in France, continually among the men in the army, and saw the large company of my student friends sorrowfully dwindling, and was called with bitter frequency to mourn

---

196. Oman, *Grace and Personality*, 2nd ed.
197. Oman, *Grace and Personality*, New York.
198. Oman, *Grace and Personality*, 3rd ed., ix–x. There is a notable expansion of part 1 into ten sections.
199. Oman, *Grace and Personality*, 3rd ed., x.
200. Oman, *Grace and Personality*, v.
201. Oman, *Grace and Personality*, v.

with the companions of my youth and others near and dear, my success may not have been equal to my intention.[202]

That intention was to reveal that "the greatest need, even of our needy time, is a religion shining in its own light, and that, greater than all political securities for peace, would be a Christian valuation of men and means, souls and things."[203]

The groundwork had been prepared in a series of twelve articles which Oman contributed to the *Expositor* between 1911 and 1912 under the heading "Personality and Grace."[204] These were, Oman states, "already the outcome of many years of study and reflection."[205] But now they were "entirely rewritten," with a primary emphasis on theology suggested by the reversal of terms in the title.[206] Renewed thought on the subject confirmed him in the belief that "the main contention seems to have stood the test in a way impossible, not only for a merely sentimental faith in a beneficent Deity, but also for any doctrine that starts from the Absolute, whether as the absolute process of Reason or the absolute Divine Sovereignty."[207]

Part One: A Gracious Personal Relation

Oman treats grace, not as dogma or abstract theory, but as living experience. He contends that grace is personal, not, as in the "old dogmatic method," an irresistible force operated with overpowering might. So long as faith was understood as acceptance of infallible truth, "justification coming to terms with absolute legislation, regeneration the inpouring of efficacious grace . . . the whole dogmatic edifice stood solid and four-square."[208] But already before the outbreak of war, the edifice was beginning to crumble, and Oman observes: "If the infallibilities have been overthrown by inquiry and reason, they cannot be raised again by affirmation or even by the strongest conviction of their utility."[209] Given that this is the case, can we, in the face of

---

202. Oman, *Grace and Personality*, v.

203. Oman, *Grace and Personality*, vi.

204. Oman, "Personality and Grace."

205. Oman, *Grace and Personality*, vi.

206. Oman rearranged the substance of his articles into three main parts each with eight subsidiary chapters. The "antinomies of grace" (the heading is replaced in the 1919 edition by "Mechanical Opposites") are given a section on their own, some material is expanded and there is a new chapter on "Fellowship and the Means of Grace."

207. Oman, *Grace and Personality*, vi.

208. Oman, *Grace and Personality*, 3.

209. Oman, *Grace and Personality*, 7.

history and experience, maintain the conception of God and man which is based on infallibility?

Oman takes one of the most typical of soldiers' questions as an illustration. Why, if God's power and knowledge are infinite, does he not intervene to save us when our need is greatest?[210] He insists that to intervene with irresistible might would be completely out of God's character. And he illustrates this memorably:

> God does not conduct his rivers like arrows, to the sea. The ruler and compass are only for finite mortals who labour, by taking thought, to overcome their limitations, and are not for the Infinite mind. The expedition demanded by man's small power and short day produces the canal, but nature, with a beneficent and picturesque circumambulatory, the work of a more spacious and less precipitate mind, produces the river. Why should we assume that, in all the rest of his ways, he rejoices in the river, but in religion can use no adequate method save the canal? The defence of the infallible is the defence of the canal against the river.[211]

He observes drily that the "long sorrowful experience of the ages seems to show that the last thing God thinks of doing is to drive mankind, with resistless rein, on the highway of righteousness."[212]

If grace were "the might of omnipotence directed by omniscience," then how could this be reconciled with moral freedom?[213] To argue with Augustine that human life is to be entirely ruled by God is to negate moral personality. But, at the other extreme, Pelagian arguments which emphasize moral independence and diminish the role of grace, are "shallow and unsatisfying."

Oman contends that neither stance is satisfactory and here is the core of his argument. Only as we experience grace working in a personal way do we find God dealing with us as his children. "Help may be as irresistibly individual, as when we pick up a child, in its despite, from under a carriage wheel, yet it may be as little personal as when the child is still left struggling in the arms of a stranger, crying for its mother."[214]

God in his grace "deals with us as children . . . as those whom it can only truly bless by helping them to attain freedom."[215] The struggle for good

---

210. Oman, *Grace and Personality*, 7.
211. Oman, *Grace and Personality*, 8.
212. Oman, *Grace and Personality*, 9.
213. Oman, *Grace and Personality*, 10.
214. Oman, *Grace and Personality*, 27.
215. Oman, *Grace and Personality*, 56.

will be a real struggle, and the issues of evil, real calamities, but God is patient: "He will not have us accept his purpose save as our own, discern his righteousness save by our own insight, and learn his thought about his world save as our own blessed discovery. Then our dependence upon God is no more in conflict with our true moral independence."[216] His thought here is well summarized by Norman MacLeod: "Dependence and response together occur at every stage of the relation thus described. It is not grace now and freedom then. God is not alone cause and man alone effect. The living character of this relation we realise more in our prayers than in our theologies but to express it adequately must be the constant aim of the latter."[217]

Oman insists on the personal nature of God's dealings with human beings: God steadfastly respects the freedom and responsibility which he has himself bestowed on them as moral beings; grace is not to be thought of as a mere infusion of power over-riding the will, but only as a gracious personal relationship which seeks at any cost and with infinite patience to elicit a person's own insight and free response.

> Instead of a special administration of grace as a sort of love-philtre, we have a gracious relationship which has its whole quality and distinction from being personal on both sides. With that beginning, the task of salvation is manifestly to display God's mind towards us and elicit our minds towards him, and not merely to cleanse our souls by a grace acting as impersonally as bleaching powder whitening cotton.[218]

As God our Father deals with us personally as his children, we are blessed, "for our absolute religious dependence and our absolute moral independence are perfectly realised and perfectly made one."[219] We discover that God is not "a kind person doing his best," nor is religion an imperfectly "weather-tight individual shelter in the general storm" but a personal system designed "not to manufacture us free, but to help us win our freedom."[220]

---

216. Oman, *Grace and Personality*, 56. Oman returns here to the paradox that he addresses in *The Problem of Faith and Freedom*.

217. MacLeod, "John Oman," 351. Colin Gunton's suggestion that Oman "tends to make autonomy axiomatic and then rather lamely seek to find a place for grace" fails to acknowledge his carefully nuanced thinking here. Gunton, "The Real," 39.

218. Oman, *Grace and Personality*, 66.

219. Oman, *Grace and Personality*, 74.

220. Oman, *Grace and Personality*, 75.

Part Two: The Mode of Its Manifestations

Drawing on the Beatitudes, Oman affirms that, where religion and morals become one, "religion is then no more merely a life-belt but our atmosphere, our native buoyancy as it fills our lungs and our native strength as it nourishes our blood."[221] We are blessed.

However this perspective has implications for our social obligations; we are members of society and exercise responsibility for the fact that though this is God's world, it is not a good world. When we insist on using our lives for other ends than God's, we are at enmity with God, we need to be reconciled.

There is a relationship between activity in the public sphere and the concept of the self.[222] But here there is a paradox: "a gracious relation is only another name for God's love, yet it requires from us, not love, but faith." In consequence "a sentimental religion with tender appeals to love God" is inadequate to face "life's stern lessons and austere requirements" and commits us to "a valetudinarian anxiety about our spiritual symptoms." When we turn from God to ourselves "the usual result is a mixture of excited emotions, instigated confessions and suppressed intellectual convictions, all morally insincere and religiously unreal."

We readily succumb to insincerity, which for Oman is always to be deprecated, refusing "to allow the deep things of life to touch us, and so the one sure way of escaping the impact of God's truth."[223] Not only does that leave us in moral peril but it has implications for evangelism:

> There is only one right way of asking men to believe, which is to put before them what they ought to believe because it is true; and there is only one right way of persuading, which is to present what is true in such a way that nothing will prevent it from being seen except the desire to abide in darkness; and there is only one further way of helping them, which is to point out what they are cherishing that is opposed to faith. When all that has been done, it is still necessary to recognize that faith is God's gift, not our handiwork.[224]

---

221. Oman, *Grace and Personality*, 94.
222. Malik, "Justice," 182.
223. Oman, *Grace and Personality*, 121.
224. Oman, *Grace and Personality*, 123.

The question of how faith operates in the lives of individuals raises the question of revelation. But if we no longer rely on the infallibilities, what do we understand by revelation?[225]

"Faith in Christ"

By revelation, God enables himself to be personally understood, thereby "dealing with our ignorance and blindness and perversity."[226] The agent of revelation is the prophet, whose word continues "to interpret God's purpose for our lives and our society." It is not a purely intellectual exercise. This word is inspired, it reconciles and "makes us know that we know God." In line with the prophetic tradition, Jesus is the perfect reconciler.

> Faith in Christ is not primarily as he meets us in Scripture or in doctrine, but as he meets us in life . . . by manifesting God's love in Life's hardest appointments and sternest demands, by lifting up our sins and weaknesses into God's compassion and pardon, and so touching us with the love of God in its infinite requirements and infinite succour, and by giving us the spirit of peace in all our weary struggle against the Kingdom and power of darkness.[227]

> The final triumph of this manifestation is the Cross. . . . When persecution for righteousness, even to shame and agony, stirs only pardon and supplication for his oppressors, it is turned from being an evidence of God's indifference into the triumph of his love.[228]

The grace of Christ is "the supreme revelation" of the love of God and the fellowship of the Spirit, enabling us to overcome our misunderstandings and our alienation and be reconciled in freedom.

"The Fellowship and Means of Grace"

Even churches that appear on the surface to be poles apart may have similarly cirumscribed views on grace. Oman observes that the "extremest

---

225. The section on "Faith in Christ" (126–40) restates and clarifies the exposition of "Jesus Christ" in "Personality and Grace" (*Expositor*, eighth series, 3, 57–60).

226. Oman, *Grace and Personality*, 128.

227. Oman, *Grace and Personality*, 136.

228. Oman, *Grace and Personality*, 140.

Catholicism" is akin to the "extremest Evangelicalism" in that each depends on "the same conception of grace as arbitrary acts of omnipotence." Both play on the emotions either by ritualism or revivalism, with the aim of overriding the moral personality. Neither attaches meaning to the "liberty of the children of God." We have to look elsewhere if we wish to find a fellowship "which would express the relationship of a personal God to us as moral persons, so that he is gracious in our experience."[229]

First, this would "have no frontiers," being a society which operates under historical conditions but also positively asserts "a blessed dependence on an absolutely gracious God which cannot be realised except in freedom and moral independence."[230]

Secondly, its only means of grace are those which appeal "by truth alone to the common human conscience"; and manifest "God's gracious personal relation to his children." The sacraments show us "the miracle of a gracious God manifesting himself in goodness," and the Lord's Supper connects this with the Cross, "forbids us to rule out any part of our experience, and teaches us to find in agony and shame and death the manifold wisdom and measureless love of God."[231] This is the sacrament of life. In partaking we accept the world as belonging to God and his rule of love and are assured that God is not parted from us because of our sin.

Thirdly, these "special rites of the special fellowship" are distinctively sacred in that they "teach men . . . to make all things sacred," and so abolish the distinction between sacred and secular. Righteousness is then removed "from the sphere of sacred observances into the sphere of our common relations in the common life, through faith in the Father exercised amid our daily tasks and trials."[232] Then finally there is the relation of the fellowship to the rule of God. This is not in any sense to be identified merely with human moral progress. Our trust is in God not in our own merit. Yet paradoxically all God's dealings with us concern our freedom, "not indeed as if we were free, but always to make us free." And Oman observes:

> Finally, hence also the need why we should be founded on the apostles and prophets and have Jesus Christ as the chief cornerstone of our lives, to be built upon not in slavish subjection to the past, but in the freedom of God's children, who are also in themselves apostles and prophets.[233]

229. Oman, *Grace and Personality*, 156.
230. Oman, *Grace and Personality*, 157.
231. Oman, *Grace and Personality*, 160.
232. Oman, *Grace and Personality*, 160.
233. Oman, *Grace and Personality*, 163.

Part Three: The Way of Its Working

Every doctrine of grace starts with the contradiction between God's gracious will and our moral independence. The task of theology, Oman suggests, is

> not to effect some kind of working compromise between the two tubes of the binocular, but to find their proper adjustment to one clear field of vision, so that we shall not be moral and religious, but shall so depend upon God as to have in all things moral independence, till our religion becomes morality and our morality religion.[234]

When that occurs, we find that acts of grace and will, contrary as they may seem, "are the essential expression of our fellowship" with God.

"Penitence"

The paradox that "grace is grace precisely because though wholly concerned with moral goodness it does not at all depend on how moral we are"[235] is central. Penitence requires moral sincerity, "to see ourselves as we are in the real moral world." Anything else is hypocrisy. We cannot repent on demand. Repentance is an integral part of faith. "That living union of repentance and faith is what finds itself succoured in Jesus Christ, who alone perfectly sets our failure in the light of our possibilities as children of God."[236]

"Justification"

Having dealt at length with various legalistic attempts to break the vicious circle of sin and hypocrisy, Oman writes that "we are justified because by faith we enter the world of a gracious God, out of which the old hard legal requirements, with the old hard boundaries of our personality and the old self-regarding claim of rights, have disappeared, a world which is the household of our Father where love is order and power and ultimate reality."[237]

In that world

> atonement is a veritable experience and not a legal fiction. . . . There the sacrifice and service of Jesus Christ are no longer the moral absurdity of taking so absolutely personal a thing as guilt

---

234. Oman, *Grace and Personality*, 171.
235. Oman, *Grace and Personality*, 177.
236. Oman, *Grace and Personality*, 182.
237. Oman, *Grace and Personality*, 194.

and transferring it to the shoulders of another, an innocent person, but are the manifestation of our deepest and holiest relation both to God and man in a world, the meaning of which, in spite of everything, is love.[238]

Reminding us that the sole moral requirement is sincerity, Oman returns to the parable of the Prodigal Son: "The Father must say by his whole bearing towards us, My son, let us share the sorrow and live down the shame together. And that is the meaning of the Cross."[239]

Though he was prepared to believe that the doctrine of substitutionary atonement had "brought peace to burdened souls," Oman saw that:

> The true reason is that the Cross of Christ has, in spite of the theory, interpreted and displayed to religious souls the new world in which hard legal conditions do not obtain but where these legal frontiers of our moral personality have been lost in a deeper moral fellowship with our father and our brethren wherein we realise that the bearing of each other's burdens, whether of sorrow or of sin, is the surest of all realities, and that the bearing of sin in particular is the very heart of God's gracious relation to us which is love.[240]

"The Consequences of Sin"

But how can we face up to the consequences of sin? God enables us to accept the sorrow and the shame and life becomes a "sacrament of redeeming love," expressed in the sacrament of communion, where "the most awful demands of actual defeat, desertion, contempt, despair and agony and death [are] all included in the gracious dealing of the Father with His children for victory over all the consequences of sin, without and within."[241] As God's co-workers we share in the sacrifice and service by which sin and all its consequences are finally obliterated.

---

238. Oman, *Grace and Personality*, 194.
239. Oman, *Grace and Personality*, 198.
240. Oman, *Grace and Personality*, 199.
241. Oman, *Grace and Personality*, 208.

"The Will of God"

This chapter gives a finely argued analysis of the ways in which grace, while concerned with the worth of our moral selves, seeks nonetheless to direct attention from ourselves and our achievements to God. Rather than "sunning ourselves in our own righteousness," "our task is to concern ourselves about doing good, and never about being good, and we must do good for the sake of the good itself and never for our own moral improvement."[242] As we do, we realize that we are to "serve God by loving our brethren as our brethren in Christ." In this moral sense, such love is not sentiment of emotion, but "esteem for every individual according to his value to himself and his Heavenly Father."[243] And so we are delivered from "mere moral stress into the joy of God which is strength as well as peace. . . . By forgetting ourselves in service, we shall thus find ourselves again in the love that requires it, and humbly yet joyfully know that it values, not what we do, but what we are."[244]

And so he resolves the disjunction with which he began between absolute dependence on God and our own absolute independence.

> We serve God as we are true to our own souls, and we are true to our own souls only as we serve God. Neither is possible without the other, for what are our own consciousness of truth, our own moral ideals, our own personal resolve and consecration save in a world, the ultimate reality of which is to be sought in personal moral relations; and how shall that be known except as we find the liberty of the children of God by means of it?[245]

"The Communion of Saints"

If the secret of true liberty is God's will of love, we "advance in freedom through the fellowship in which love is manifested,"[246] and we need not be too concerned about its precise boundaries. There are however wrong ways of belonging to the Communion of Saints. We may so lean on the past that it "makes void God's living word."[247] For example, if we were to see Jesus as

---

242. Oman, *Grace and Personality*, 211.
243. Oman, *Grace and Personality*, 225.
244. Oman, *Grace and Personality*, 229.
245. Oman, *Grace and Personality*, 231.
246. Oman, *Grace and Personality*, 234.
247. Oman, *Grace and Personality*, 235.

"a mere pattern to be copied . . . he would fall into the rank of mere human teachers, whose authority fades as they move into the past."[248] Christ's influence is "to inspire and succour the faith which sees love to be life's final meaning and last word of power, and so to enable us to discern for ourselves its guidance and to set our hope unwaveringly on its victory."[249]

The second wrong way of belonging to the Communion of Saints is what he describes as "mystical." Although the use of this term is ambiguous and leaves Oman exposed to criticism, he does make it explicit that in this connection he is using it to signify "the seeking of an acosmic absorption into the deity and not in the sense of the awed apprehension of the infinite depth and mystery of God's being and of the world He has created and sustains."[250]

With these two caveats Oman affirms that we relate to the Communion of Saints because "persons are the only store-houses of God's purpose which do not pass away . . . and inspire in us ever deeper devotion to the personal values which are life's meaning and goal, and the only unchanging end of this ceaselessly changing world."[251]

"The Kingdom of God"

For Oman, the Rule of God is a question of how the world is made and governed. Paradoxically, "the Rule of God is an order which is outside of us, but which cannot be imposed from without. . . . It cannot operate except as it is received as our own rule."[252] But if God's kingdom "imposes itself from within," in what sense is it "a reality which makes any practical difference in the world?" Oman concludes that the problem of God's Rule in an evil world is moral not metaphysical, and can only be solved by prophetic "insight into the nature of reality."[253]

The world is sunk in calamity, hatred of good, crime and idolatry. The prophetic hope is in a "Day of the Lord," which is "always connected with an actual experience or well-grounded anticipation of great conflict or distress."[254] A mixture of boundless terror and boundless hope, the suffering of the righteous is an agonizing mystery giving rise to the discovery that

248. Oman, *Grace and Personality*, 237.
249. Oman, *Grace and Personality*, 241.
250. Farmer, "Theologians of Our Time," 185.
251. Oman, *Grace and Personality*, 246.
252. Oman, *Grace and Personality*, 249.
253. Oman, *Grace and Personality*, 251.
254. Oman, *Grace and Personality*, 261.

here is love's highest victory. What seems disaster may be only winnowing. Apocalyptic moments are times of vision and courage—when the mists clear and truth and beauty are most real: "God's Kingdom is always at hand . . . the equinoctial gales are the herald of spring and the sowing of its seed in the bitter March weather is cheerful with the promise of summer and harvest."[255]

"Eternal Life"

In his final chapter, Oman makes plain the insufficiency of throwing into the future the justification of the world order, affirming that if life's "ultimate meaning is a moral order which is love, it is absurd to say that it could be valid though the final order were death." A world in which we can live as moral persons, attain moral independence and enjoy the blessedness of God's children may be justified despite the presence of evil. So we have "victory over mortal terrors, [and] a right to be assured of victory over the last enemy, death." And he summarizes memorably: "We rightly and religiously believe in another life, because we are serving the purpose of a love for which this life is too small."[256] Here finally is the significance of grace as a gracious personal relationship: "without the possession of eternal life, we can have no right relation to ourselves, to our neighbour, or to God."[257]

One of the most remarkable features of this section as of the book as a whole is the way in which Oman handles the idea of the limitation of God's omnipotence, not by inferring some essential finitude in God but by reference to relations between God who is personal and human beings who are persons. Perhaps inevitably he was open to be misunderstood.

Reactions

Oman defends his method in the preface to the revised edition of 1919:

> As one, with four years' habit of military metaphor, expresses it, "It means going over the top and not caring a hang what is to happen." It means that for action as well as for thought: and for both inseparably. But till discovery is made that no final victory, either for truth or righteousness, ever can be won, except in the open country of the spirit, that venture is mere bravado. So long

---

255. Oman, *Grace and Personality*, 272.
256. Oman, *Grace and Personality*, 281.
257. Oman, *Grace and Personality*, 282.

> as the business of religion is thought to be with traditional faiths and accepted customs, and the business of theology to erect sandbags of learning upon their parapet, it will even seem the essence of unbelief in what God has done, and everything said on the presupposition that it is the essence of faith in what God is doing, can be accepted only as it is misconceived. Nor is the case much better, when it is thought possible both to remain in the entrenchments of outward authority and be in the open country of action and inquiry at the same time.[258]

Oman's courageous presentation of what he deemed to be the truly Christian view of the relation of God to the world met with trenchant criticism from Evangelical scholars especially in the United States, who failed, or did not wish, to recognize the force of his finely nuanced argument. Fuel was added to the fire by Nolan R. Best's exaggerated claim in his introduction to the American edition that "in essence, Dr Oman is as Calvinistic as Calvin himself."[259]

The *Princeton Theological Review* found that Oman was "seldom fair in any doctrinal discussion . . . perhaps the saddest chapter in the book is the chapter on justification." And the reviewer concludes: "The worst feature of this book is that its author claims to be a Calvinist. It is passing strange to find a competent scholar . . . devoting an elaborate volume to the refutation of one of its cardinal doctrines."[260]

The Reverend Wm. Childs Robinson of Columbia Theological Seminary judged Oman heretical. He found *Grace and Personality* to be "the most conspicuous actual example" of Presbyterian Pelagianism[261] and saw Oman's theology as "hopelessly Ritschlian": repeatedly, it was alleged, "he sides with Kant. . . . Neither Augustine nor Calvin would regard the Kantians as disciples."[262] Here it must be borne in mind that the American edition of *Grace and Personality* was published barely a year after the Auburn Affirmation which successfully challenged the right of General Assembly to impose on ordinands "Five Fundamentals" as a test of orthodoxy.[263] This challenge to entrenched conservative attitudes was a turning point in the

---

258. Oman, *Grace and Personality*, 2nd ed., viii.
259. Oman, *Grace and Personality*, New York 1925, x.
260. Clark, review of Oman, *Grace and Personality*.
261. Robinson, "Presbyterian Pelagianism."
262. Robinson, "Presbyterian Pelagianism." Oman did not accept Ritschl's thought wholesale; he criticized Ritschl as making will fundamental in religion; for Oman, we have the kingdom in the world but not of our striving.
263. The inerrancy of Scripture, the Virgin Birth, Substitutionary Atonement, the bodily resurrection of Jesus, the authenticity of Christ's miracles.

history of American Presbyterianism and the culmination of the Fundamentalist/Modernist controversy.

The question as to whether Oman's conception of grace was Calvinist is intriguing. Though he was always aware of underlying religious issues, he did not concern himself with abstract problems of Christology. He found it sufficient that "God was in the world reconciling the world to himself" and "to devote his thought to exploring this reconciling vocation of Christ, 'the mode of its manifestation' and the 'way of its working' in the souls of men and in the life of the church down the ages."[264] This may be seen notably in his approach to Justification and also, as Farmer points out, to the formula of the Trinity. This was not an invitation to speculate on the being of the Godhead but a summing up of the Christian experience of reconciliation and "therefore of a specifically Christian monotheism. This is," Farmer writes, "one of the most illuminating lines of thought in Oman's teaching."[265]

Oman had come to see that the churches of the Reformation had not got to the root of the matter of the standing of individual human beings before God. As he wrote elsewhere, "What was great in Calvin was his belief that all trust in man is a broken reed and that there is no security save in God. What was wrong in Calvin was not this faith but the direct way in which it was realized and the finality of creed as well as organization expected from it."[266] For Calvin, as for Augustine, grace was an infallible force which generated an absolute dependence. Justification, whether delivered by way of the Church, or more directly to the individual, was "a judgment arbitrarily attached to faith by absolute divine fiat."[267] Oman observes that the debate between Calvin and Arminius turned partly on questions of grace and freedom, but the discussion did not go far enough. It was left to the Enlightenment to raise the issue in terms of authoritarianism and rationalism. A fresh insight into the nature of moral personality required a radical reconstruction of the doctrine of grace, and freedom to bring together an utter dependence on God with utter moral independence. This is arguably Oman's greatest theological achievement.

In a letter to D. S. Cairns shortly after his retirement in 1935, Oman wrote:

> My contention is that because God deals with us as his children, with manifold wisdom, to the end of making us sons of God not mere chattels of his power, does not make us less his work than

264. Farmer, "Theologians of Our Time," 184.
265. Farmer, "Theologians of Our Time," 184.
266. Oman, *Honest Religion*, 38.
267. Oman, *Grace and Personality*, 21.

with Calvin's more direct way. When I came to England, if you had asked me if I was a Calvinist, I would have said in no way. But Methodism with its way of salvation largely an emotional affair . . . made me see that there was something in the piety I had known which whether for the temporal or the eternal account fell back on God not man's striving which I had not valued as I ought, and in a sense I am a Calvinist by another road than John's.[268]

Yet there is more to be said. In Farmer's words, "it should be added that Grace and Personality . . . is not only great and profound theology; it is also a great religious book . . . many have found in it, despite the demand it makes for unwavering attention and strenuous thought, a source of nourishment in their personal life amid the pressures and challenges of these days, to which they return again and again."[269] While the book is far from "the realm of light literature, which he who runs may read,"[270] with its "austerely pure conception of religion and noble ethical principles," it could be described, as F. R. Tennant recognized, as "one of the greater treasures of theological literature."[271]

Its impact on one non-combatant may be judged by the words of John Hick who relates how he read *Grace and Personality* for the first time during a lull in the fighting in 1944, when he was serving with the Friends' Ambulance Unit in Italy. He writes: "It affected me profoundly, still immersed as I was in a highly conservative Calvinist theology. It taught me that God is not primarily omnipotence and judgment but personal grace and love."[272]

The Army and Religion

In Oman's experience hundreds of the men in the camps and trenches "spent long days and nights in independent thinking which blinked no facts but faced them with a new and intense realisation of the serious issues of life and death."[273] In contrast to the thousands whose army experience meant "merely an abeyance of all thinking and a suppression of all individuality," they "fought for their own personal independence of thought and action

---

268. Letter, John Oman to D. S. Cairns, 16 October [1935]. Cairns Archive, Special Collections, University of Aberdeen.
269. Farmer, "Theologians of Our Time," 184.
270. Oman, *Grace and Personality*, 3rd ed., x.
271. Tennant, "John Wood Oman."
272. Hick, "Voyage Round John Oman," 163.
273. John Oman, "Spiritual Regeneration," 20.

amid the vast mass opinion and custom which surrounded them."[274] Such men, found in all ranks, would, in Oman's eyes, have a vital contribution to make to a reconstructed world after the war. But were the churches ready for the challenge?

This was the question which led the YMCA to appoint Cairns "to consider and interpret what was being revealed under war conditions" about the religious life of the nation and to present that result to the churches.[275] Funding was provided by the YMCA who, in line with a desire to act as "the handmaid of the Church,"[276] gave Cairns liberty "to associate with him such Leaders from the Churches as he thinks most fitted to help him in the matter."[277] He appointed a distinguished steering committee representing a cross-section of British Christianity, amongst whom was John Oman. While the ensuing publication has not been without its critics,[278] it was a herculean task for Cairns who accepted the task of draftsman. The committee had three residential meetings between August 1917 and autumn 1918 and there were also several day meetings where it considered nearly three hundred printed memoranda from "men of all ranks."[279] These were based on three topics: "what the men are thinking about Religion, Morality, and Society," "The Changes made by the War," "The Relation of the Men to the Churches." The resulting "beguiling and grandiose manifesto for church reform" shrugged off the evidence of the War Roll as "the stress of abnormal conditions,"[280] and was dismissive of the popularity of Gypsy Smith. Evidence suggests that its conclusions were predetermined.[281] Oman, however, was less inclined to discount the positive influence of evangelism. In an unpublished essay he affirmed that as, during the war, "there were moments when men were highly responsive to emotional appeal," evangelistic methods "often succeeded. In France, in particular, it was done with real simplicity and brotherly feeling, and the immediate result was often extended and apparently effective." But he added that "many of those who had been longest

---

274. John Oman, "Spiritual Regeneration," 20.

275. Cairns, *Army and Religion*, v.

276. "Memorandum Regarding the Interdenominational Position of the YMCA," YMCA/K24/5.

277. Snape, *Back Parts*, 87; for the complete list of committee members, see Cairns, *Army and Religion*, xi, xii.

278. Snape, *Back Parts*, 87–88, considers the report to be "deeply flawed." Rich Schweitzer sees all contemporary accounts as "misleading or incomplete." "Cross and Trenches," 33.

279. Cairns, *Army and Religion*, vi.

280. Cairns, *Army and Religion*, 399.

281. Cairns, *Army and Religion*, 88.

in the field found little trace of lasting change."[282] He would have agreed, however, with the report's conclusions about the challenges presented to the church by the war and its seeming inadequacy to meet the particular spiritual requirements of soldiers or their families.

As we may judge from a letter Oman sent to Cairns from Mansfield College, an invitation to contribute came at an inopportune time:

> I have been a long time in replying to you. My only excuse is that I have been occupied with much serving, in a way that is not becoming of a Christian man, for I am painfully aware that when one does many things it is never much in any vital sense. I had promised to come here for a kind of mission, which is going on and I had to make some kind of preparation and at the same time there were no end of jobs in Cambridge. I have managed, however, to write something, not what I would have wished, and if it is not what you wish, you have my most hearty consent to suppress it.[283]

Birmingham

Meanwhile, with depleted resources and a dwindling number of students, the Senatus of Westminster College had to decide on the way ahead. On 20 June 1916, Skinner reported to the College Committee that, following consultation with the Convenor of the Committee, "he had permitted the students' quarters of the college to be used for domiciling about seventy Refugee boys during the summer" and the Committee gave the arrangement its "cordial approval." This was as practical assistance to the Serbian Relief Fund which had been set up in September 1914 to ease the humanitarian crisis in Serbia, expanding its efforts from sending out medical aid to assisting Serbian refugees and prisoners of war, and later on, Serbian boy refugees, in the hope that they would ultimately return to rebuild their country. Despite public fears that the children would be unsuitable for life in Britain and a drain on public resources, through the determined activism of Dr. Seton Watson, hon. secretary of the SRF, and Mrs. Carrington Wilde, "some hundred and fifty Serbian boys, destitute through the invasion of their country, were brought to Cambridge and lodged at Westminster and Cheshunt colleges."[284] By the start of the new term in October, Skinner

282. Oman, "Spiritual Regeneration."

283. John Oman to D. S. Cairns, January 30, no year, from Mansfield College. Special Collections, University of Aberdeen.

284. Subsequently some were dispersed, some attended local schools and eventually

was able to report that the Serbian Refugee Boys, who had left the College premises on 9 September, "had been good tenants and amenable to discipline." They had also "expressed appreciation of the privilege of using the Library."[285]

In the meantime, with the imminent removal of the exemption from military service that had previously been granted to theological students, exams were held in March 1917 to allow those who were nearing the end of their course to complete it.[286]

In May that year, the Synod empowered the College Committee and the Board of Studies "to suspend next session if the outlook seemed to require it, to confer with the Professors with regard to the best way in which their services might be used, and to provide that the College buildings shall be cared for as economically as possible." At the same Synod a petition was received from the Presbytery of Birmingham for guidance and help at a time when many ministers had volunteered as forces chaplains. The Synod referred the matter to the Home Mission and Ministerial Support Committees with the suggestion that Oman should be approached with a view to taking up the work and making Birmingham his home during the session. This suggestion was made "without Oman's knowledge or consent,"[287] but it was received enthusiastically by those present. In the words of the proposer of the motion, "there is no-one more filled with Home Mission enthusiasm, or with a more far-sighted vision of what might be and ought to be. And in days when so little is doing at our College, the Church might well recognize that here is a strong man for such a heavy and urgent task as this."[288]

This seemed to solve two problems in one. The remaining Westminster students could continue to study in Birmingham while assisting local congregations who were without a minister. Further details were left to the college. The Board of Studies "approved heartily" of the scheme and Oman

---

over a dozen became members of the University, the various colleges to which they were admitted waiving fees either entirely or in part. University of Cambridge, *Historical Register*, Supplement, 200–205. With a lack of resources combined with the negative attitude of the Government, the fund was wound up in December 1920.

285. Minutes of the College Committee, 17 October 1917. The Committee noted (20 March 1918) that as the Serbian Relief Committee had received a government grant for their education work, they were "continuing their occupancy of the College buildings; but that they were liable to leave on being given a month's notice."

286. Minutes of Senatus 1917.

287. *Presbyterian Messenger*, June 1917, 152.

288. *Presbyterian Messenger*, June 1917, 152.

agreed to serve as Director of Studies, assisted from time to time by Skinner and Scott.[289]

On 17 October Skinner reported to the College Committee that the six remaining students, who had been rejected by the army for medical reasons, had taken up their residence at the Woodbrooke Settlement in Selly Oak. Oman, who had in the meantime moved nearby for the session to "Penzance," Bristol Road, gave details of the active involvement of students in "preaching and pastoral visitation in several vacant congregations as well as regular visitation of wounded soldiers." These activities were carefully circumscribed in order not to interfere with study:[290] "1. no student is to prepare more than two sermons each month; 2. Pastoral work and hospital visitation should be confined to two evenings per week except in urgent cases; 3. Two days each week as well as forenoons are to be reserved for study as far as possible."[291]

In response to questions he "accepted complete responsibility" for the decision to house the students at Woodbrooke and "explained fully his reasons" to an uneasy College Committee.[292] After some discussion "it was understood that the work of Westminster College is being carried on in Birmingham as a separate work bearing entirely on preparation for our ministry."

To put this into perspective, this seems a suitable point to take a closer look at the Settlement.

Woodbrooke

In 1903 George and Elizabeth Cadbury gifted and endowed their house and grounds for the foundation of a Quaker residential settlement for religious and social study. This grey-stone, square-cut nineteenth-century mansion[293] overlooked a secluded garden covering around ten acres, with lawns sloping

289. Minutes of the Board of Studies, 19 June 1917. As there were no first year students, no course of Church History was required. Carnegie Simpson was requested to continue assisting the congregation of St John's Wood until the end of the year, to give one Sunday each month to "one of the weaker congregations and to devote the first three months of 1918 to the congregations in Bristol and Cardiff." From March 1918 he combined the role of Interim Moderator of St Columba's Cambridge with oversight of Presbyterian troops resident in Cambridge (Minutes of the College Committee, 20 March 1918)

290. The curriculum had a significant emphasis on Dogmatics, with Hebrew up to January 1918 and New Testament from January to June 1918.

291. Minutes of the Board of Studies, 19 June 1917.

292. Minutes of the College Committee, 17 October 1917.

293. Built in 1830 on the site of a dairy farm for Josiah Mason, a founder of Birmingham University, and bought in 1881 by George Cadbury.

down to a large pool and beech, elm and oak trees lining the drive from Bristol Road. For residents, then as now, it was a "nourishing landscape."[294]

The college was intended to promote the ideals of the Bible summer-school movement which had begun in 1897 under the inspiration of John Rowntree and offered facilities for teachers, Adult School leaders, Sunday School teachers, and Home and Foreign missionaries; its ethos would have been in tune with Oman's endorsement of "workers' education" and his support of summer schools, and given the close association of the Settlement with mission, both at home and overseas, he would have welcomed the opportunity for the students to have personal contact with those in the field.

By 1917, when the Westminster students came into residence, earlier Quaker uncertainties about the purpose and organization of the Settlement were largely resolved, although lingering doubts as to whether this was to be seen as a Quaker institution or a centre of scholarship,[295] and the association in study and recreation of young men and women may have contributed to the uncertainty of the Westminster College Committee. So too might the association of the Friends with pacifism.[296] Although opinions amongst the Woodbrooke staff on the matter were divided, with the introduction of conscription in 1916, courses were provided for pacifists and Conscientious Objectors who were waiting for their Tribunals.[297]

The unease of the Committee might have been intensified by the awareness that some at least of the students were conscientious objectors, amongst them Herbert Farmer and Reginald Fenn. Given Oman's experience of camps and prisons, and his own earlier encounters with the petty sessions in Alnwick, it is likely that he was seen by his Senatus colleagues as the most suitable person to mentor such students.

These two cases illustrate how, with no clearly defined rules for the conduct of a Tribunal, no guarantee that any of its members were accustomed to weigh evidence, the power of the Military Representative and the speed with which the work had to be conducted, different decisions on similar cases were likely to be given.[298]

---

294. See "A Walk in the Garden," booklet for visitors produced by Woodbrooke Quaker Study Centre, n.d.

295. These were in part caused by the mercurial temperament of the first "Dictator of Studies," Rendel Harris. Falcetta, *James Rendel Harris*, 231–36. In 1924, Woodbrooke dropped the designation "settlement" for "college."

296. The elder son of the most uncertain member of the Committee, Dr. Voelcker, had "been killed in the great advance." Minutes of the Presbytery of London North, 19 September 1916.

297. Scott, *Herbert G. Wood*, 54.

298. "The Local Tribunals," *Oxford Times*, 4 March 1916.

Farmer's case would appear to be the more straightforward. After a brilliant undergraduate career at Peterhouse, he matriculated at Westminster college in 1914, and three years later, exited with distinction in New Testament and Theology. By then, however, he was liable for military service and on refusal, would have been sanctioned by a Tribunal. He had already in 1914 done "agricultural work in Histon" and the Minutes of the Board of Studies record the "hope" of the Senatus that he and Fenn might find work in food production near Birmingham to keep in touch with the College.[299] The proposed "food production" assignment near Birmingham may have been at Cadbury's in Bournville, a model village south-west of Birmingham built for employees of the Cadbury factory. As a Quaker firm, Cadbury's did provide some "exceptional employment" for conscientious objectors by arrangement with the Home Office, who sometimes in such cases permitted them to live in private lodgings. The proximity of Woodbrooke would have enabled the two men to sustain contact with Oman and their fellow students.[300] Farmer's affection and regard for Oman is unmistakable. In 1935, he refers in the preface to *The World and God*,[301] to "the inspiring and shaping influence on my thought . . . of my revered teacher, Dr John Oman," whom he had by then succeeded as professor of Systematic Theology and Apologetics, and to whom the book is dedicated.

Fenn's experience was harsh.[302] Having entered Westminster College in October 1915, he completed two years of study with some distinction and was confirmed in his tenure of scholarships on 5 April 1917. Being then liable for military service, he accepted a medical examination before appearing before his local tribunal. The tribunal exempted him; the military representative appealed and the county appeal tribunal withdrew the exemption on the grounds that Fenn's acceptance of a medical examination showed that he was not a sincere conscientious objector.[303] With the withdrawal of his exemption and subject to sanction, he was sentenced to 112 days hard labor in Wormwood Scrubs in November 1917.[304]

299. 20 March 1918.

300. According to Healey, Farmer "worked as a gardener in Selly Oak." Healey, *Prospect for Theology*, 31.

301. Farmer, *The World and God*, x.

302. In a personal communication, George Hood told me how for two years he spent four days each week lodging with Reg Fenn and his wife in Welwyn Garden City; but that Fenn would never speak of his war-time experiences and George deduced that he "had had a very difficult time."

303. I am indebted to Bill Hetherington, of the Peace Pledge Union, for this information from the *Tribune*, 12 July 1917.

304. Listed under "imprisoned members," FOR Newssheet, 1 November 1917.

On 20 March 1918 the Senatus "deferred consideration of his case until June," when it was hoped that he and Farmer might be assigned exceptional employment near Birmingham. He appears to have joined Oman and his student contemporaries at Woodbrooke and with Farmer served his turn on the preaching rota at Erdington. On completion of his course at Westminster College, he was ordained in July 1920, and went as a missionary to the Hakka Field in China.[305]

On 20 March 1918 Skinner was able to announce that the Woodbrooke experiment had proved a success and was worth repeating. Oman said "the men had got a good deal which could not be got in any other way." Anderson Scott "bore testimony to the cheerful way in which the students had faced the many difficult duties which had been assigned them." And the Reverend W. V. Crerar on behalf of the Birmingham Presbytery spoke of the "valuable work done by Professors and students for the congregations within the Presbytery. They were regarded by us all as helpers and have done all which could be done."

Four of the students, R. H. Halford, J. F. Marquis, E. O. Samuel, and W. K. Williamson, passed the College exit exam that August. As the arrangement with the Birmingham Presbytery[306] held good until the New Year, Oman continued there for another session[307] with the two remaining Westminster students, D. J. Wallace and R. E. Fenn.

Finally at the Senatus meeting on 22 April 1919 the Principal tabled a resolution from the Presbytery of Birmingham regarding Oman's work within the bounds and on 17 June the Synod offered "cordial thanks to Professor John Oman for his ceaselessly self-sacrificing activities during his sojourn with the theological students in Birmingham."

Oman himself took a different view of these activities. In October 1917 he wrote to Mr. Waller at Cambridge University Press: "At present I am exercising somewhat episcopal functions here in the Midlands. I have always had a suspicion that Solo Episcope did not stand for much self-denial. Now I am sure. It is a monotonous business of dull letters and troublesome people. How anyone who knows anything about it, should imagine it the foundation of religion is more a mystery to me than ever."[308]

305. Fasti file, Westminster College archives.

306. The estimated cost per student per annum in Birmingham was £100, of which £50 was contributed by the Birmingham Presbytery. The remainder was made up from scholarships and the Barbour Fund.

307. Anderson Scott, who by now was Interim Moderator of the Cheltenham congregation, was given leave of absence to act as Institute Professor, Vanderbilt University, Nashville, Tennessee.

308. 1 October 1917, from Penzance, Bristol Road, Selly Oak, Birmingham. Cambridge University Archives, PRAO, 96 12 ii.

He had oversight of three church extension projects, each of them challenging in different respects. There was the church in Chantry Road, Moseley, which was faced in 1917 with an accumulated debt, and, after acrimonious discussions, the resignation of their minister, John Reid; the disappearance of nearly a year's Session Minutes is suggestive. Oman was nominated by the Presbytery to guide the church into the next phase, which came to a satisfactory conclusion with the induction of the Reverend Norman L. Robinson on 31 January 1919.[309]

The Weoley Hill congregation had grown out of a small Presbyterian fellowship which met around four times a year at the house of Robert Aytoun, who was a tutor at Woodbrooke. In June 1918, it was able to rent Chetwynd Hall, a small disused lecture room, where weekly services were held with Aytoun as minister in charge. Two years later, it was recognized as a preaching station with a provisional session of six Moseley elders. Oman was a member of the organizing committee and on Aytoun's premature death, assumed oversight of the congregation from April 1920 to December 1921, until he was relieved of the responsibility by the appointment of his "close friend"[310] Fearon Halliday, lecturer in Philosophy of Religion and Systematic and Pastoral Theology at Selly Oak.[311]

And there was Erdington, Holly Lane. Westminster College had been involved with Erdington from the time it was established in July 1910 as a preaching station and services were held in a photographic studio at the bottom of a garden. One of Oman's closest friends, Benjamin Mein, was appointed minister-in-charge of the new congregation in the following January,[312] and Oman himself was one of several distinguished preachers to conduct worship from a platform described by the first session clerk as "a most rude affair, literally scraped together by the local committee, nailed into a feasible resemblance and covered by a square of carpet which one member supplied and which was later stolen."[313] By July 1914 enough money had been raised to buy a site for a church and hall, students of Westminster College having contributed £230. Though building plans were halted by the war, the hall was completed and the congregation met there for services. In

---

309. Price, *Moseley Presbyterian Church.*

310. Micklem, *Box and Puppets*, 63.

311. Glen and Bartlett, *Weoley Hill*. In 1929, Weoley Hill was designated a sanctioned charge, independent of Moseley and able to call a minister.

312. The appointment was confirmed from one Presbytery meeting to another until March 1913, when Mein was appointed for six months.

313. H.A., "Fifty Years of Presbyterianism in Erdington." Jubilee pamphlet, October 1965.

October 1915, Erdington was declared a "sanctioned charge" and Oman led worship there on the first Sunday.

Mein left for Moffat that year to cover for the minister of Well Road UF Church, who was on chaplaincy duty in France, and two years later, he was inducted to the charge. As his successor only lasted "till the end of the year," Oman was to serve as Interim Moderator from July 1915 to September 1918, when he was succeeded by Herbert Farmer. In his report for 1918 William Sinclair, session clerk, paid high tribute to the services of Oman and those Westminster College students who filled the breach between 1915 and 1919: "Revs Osbourne, Halford, Marquis, Williamson, H. H. Farmer, and Messrs Evans, Wallace, Fenn, B. J. Farmer."

These were joined on the preaching rota on at least one occasion by Charles Freer Andrews, who returned to Birmingham from India to visit his parents. In him, the Westminster College evacuees would have met a man described by his close friend, the Bengali poet Rabindranath Tagore, as exhibiting an "extraordinary love for India" and "endless kindness to the outcastes of this land. . . . His love for Indians was part of that love of all humanity which he accepted as the Law of Christ."[314] He attempted consciously to live out the precepts of the Sermon on the Mount. This is certain to have given pause for thought at a time when increasing government censorship led to a declaration in the House of Commons that printing of the Sermon on the Mount was an indictable offence under the Defence of the Realm Act.[315]

It will have been noted that while Oman's most intensive involvement with the Birmingham churches was during the two sessions he spent at Woodbrooke, he was already in July 1915 acting as Interim Moderator at Erdington, and for eighteen months from April 1920, he combined similar duties at Weoley Hill with his work in Cambridge. This was consistent with the efforts of the Synod's Special Committee on Birmingham Presbytery in 1915 to "commend the work of the Birmingham area to the special remembrance and sympathy of the Church,"[316] and with Oman's persuasion that it was the duty of the church to prioritize congregations in difficult social contexts.

The months at Woodbrooke also fostered a warm association between Oman and the Warden, Herbert George Wood, who had recently succeeded Rendel Harris as Director of Studies. They shared a keen interest in adult education as imparting to men and women "that love of truth which was the basis

---

314. In Andrews, *Sermon on the Mount*, ix. A friend also of Mahatma Gandhi, he was identified with India's struggle for independence.

315. Wallis, *Valiant for Peace*, 30. Vigorous protests were to no avail.

316. "Special Committee on the Birmingham Presbytery 1915, XIII D *Presbytery Matters*, Westminster College Archive.

and inspiration of all true science and art, of religion and of living."[317] And both were alive to the challenge to the churches of rebuilding after the war.

Wood's biographer suggests that "when John Oman brought a group of his students from Westminster College to share for a while in the life of Woodbrooke and to enter into the free range of discussion possible there at a time when many minds were closed against a future in which Germany could have a place, his presence must have been a strength and a solace to the Wardens."[318] In his turn, Oman would have appreciated the opportunities Woodbrooke afforded for discussion of religious, political and social issues in an atmosphere of intellectual freedom.[319] The course of study in International Relations which Wood inaugurated proved increasingly popular, and was viewed with special favour by the Fellowship of Reconciliation.[320]

The two men shared a desire to awaken the churches to a sense of responsibility for the nature of post-war reconstruction. To that end, Wood called a meeting of Birmingham clergy[321] at the Midland Hotel on 25 June 1917 and in his opening address stressed that the passionate conviction of the British people in the righteousness of their cause exposed them to grave dangers. Challenging though this would have been for many, a resolution was passed calling for a national Christian conference to discuss these matters and to consider how best to promote an international conference on just and lasting peace. A second meeting was arranged for 23 July at Queen's College, Birmingham. Here, the promotion of an international peace conference was discussed, affirming "the duty of Christians in the belligerent countries at least to attempt to arrive at a common understanding by joint conference and prayer."[322]

Although there was insufficient support from the churches to make this a viable proposition, it did inspire collaboration in the "After the War" campaign arranged by the Birmingham and District Free Church Council.[323] However, in May that year, the London Yearly Meeting of the Society of Friends expressed a similar concern for an international Christian

---

317. Scott, *Herbert G. Wood*, 92.

318. Scott, *Herbert G. Wood*, 54.

319. The "Woodbrooke spirit" attracted students from Britain and abroad with a significant influx from Norway. Falcetta, *James Rendel Harris*, 247.

320. By January 1917 there was a full quota of students and classes were being arranged in London. Minutes of the FOR General Committee, 10–11 September 1916, 15–17 January 1917. LSE Archives, FOR 1/1–1/4 Coll MISC 456.

321. Of the 480 invitations sent out, only 50 were accepted. Scott, *Herbert G. Wood*, 56.

322. Scott, *Herbert G. Wood*, 60.

323. It was in connection with this that Oman gave his lecture on "Traditions."

conference which would apply Christian principles to contemporary social and economic problems and sent an exhortation on the subject to every minister in the UK.[324] In April 1924, around 1,500 representatives of the churches (including the Roman Catholic Church), missionary societies, theological colleges, the scouting movement, with some government officials and "leaders of industry" met in Birmingham for the Conference on Christian Politics, Economics and Citizenship chaired by William Temple, then Bishop of Manchester. There were many international delegates, including Nathan Söderblom, Archbishop of Uppsala,[325] and, significantly, representation from Germany. Conference rose as a heartening message from the King was read out; then sat to receive a lukewarm communication from the Archbishop of Canterbury, followed by encouraging letters from Ramsay MacDonald, Stanley Baldwin, and Herbert Asquith. Wood edited the Conference Handbook and he and Oman were members of the Commission[326] which prepared the introductory report on "The Nature of God and His Purpose for the World."

The conference was a landmark event. As it sought to apply Christian principles to "actual existing conditions," it presented a rooted, carefully thought-out vision of what a better society could look like.[327] Colleagues "discovered an unexpected agreement, and a sense of fellowship so strong

---

324. Marian Ellis, the chief Quaker spokesperson, had discussed the matter with Wood on one or two occasions. Scott, *Herbert G. Wood*, 60.

325. Söderblom was inspired. And although vexed when some of COPEC's leaders were unable to attend his Life and Work meeting in Stockholm in 1925, he came to rely largely on the COPEC secretary, the Quaker Lucy Gardner, for his contacts with Britain. (Sundkler, *Nathan Söderblom*, 350–53.) She was not slow in pointing out to him the basic difference between the Birmingham conference, based on people with expertise and experience, and the Stockholm conference, involving appointees of the Archbishop.

326. Alongside D. S. Cairns and thirteen others. A. F. Day, SJ, signed the report with a statutory "note of reservation." In appreciation of its vital importance, "it would be exceedingly mortifying for me after having collaborated most pleasantly with men and women of great ability and evident sincerity to stand aloof."

327. The organization was impressive. A council was formed in 1919 which, following Edinburgh 1910, divided up the subject matter into twelve sections, covering a comprehensive range of social and political issues. It then assembled a group of students and "workers" who had devoted their lives to these topics to compose questionnaires which were discussed by hundreds of groups throughout the country. The findings were submitted to HQ who then set up twelve commissions consisting of men and women, Christians with expert knowledge or wide practical experience of the subject. The ensuing reports, a unique social library, were debated at the conference. See Rev. G. K. MacBean, *Advertiser*, Adelaide, Saturday, 5 April 1924.

as to make fundamental divergences, when they appeared, matters not for dispute but for frank and sympathetic discussion."[328]

---

328. *Nature of God*, vi.

10

A New Age

"Watchman" records how, towards the end of August 1914, he met Oman, with mutual friends from Newcastle, on the shore at Warkworth in Northumberland. "Almost before greeting me, he said, 'Well?' and later: 'Chaos has come again!' He proceeded, 'I feel that never will you and I look upon a world recognisably like anything we have known!'"[1]

Oman foresaw that the end of the war would mark a severance with the past when "those of us who are not prepared to reconsider all our judgments and help to build a new heaven and a new earth will not be able to retain the old but will only wander in the new time as shadowy ghosts of a vanished past."[2]

Church Reunion

As we have seen, Oman had not hesitated to "reconsider all [his] judgments" during the war. In what other ways was he to "help to build a new heaven and new earth"? A perception that the church had a key role to play in postwar reconstruction intensified his belief that the best way of proceeding was together. For a start, having spent "half [his] life in close contact with all forms of religious life in England with an interest which has never flagged,"[3]

---

1. *British Weekly*, 25 May 1939.
2. Oman, *The War and Its Issues*, 4.
3. Oman, "The Presbyterian Churches," 57.

he was persuaded that, when it came to Church union, "there was nothing to prevent the Presbyterians and Congregationalists starting at once."[4]

This was already evident in 1911 when the principal of Mansfield College Oxford,[5] W. B. Selbie, fresh from attending the Edinburgh missionary conference the previous year, organized a series of public lectures at Mansfield. Oman accepted the invitation to speak on "The Presbyterian Churches."[6] He was one of seven lecturers from different Protestant traditions who were persuaded that "living faith in Christ as all-sufficient mediator of God's grace" was determinative both for the individual and the Church, rather than the sacramental and institutional aspects of Christianity.[7] The standpoint of the series was "positive and fraternal" in the face of growing realization by those "who are painfully alive to the shame and mischief of the present situation, and who see clearly that the Church of Christ must achieve some kind of unity amid diversity if she is ever to do her proper work or meet the needs of the present age."[8] Encouragingly, the lectures were attended by an invited audience which included "a certain number of High Churchmen, especially senior men in the University, e.g., the Principal of Pusey House."[9]

Oman made it clear from the outset that he intended to treat Presbyterianism "as it ought to be," a living tradition. So he took four typical features—Calvinistic doctrine, Puritan worship, national religion, government by elders—and explored how far these had been modified over the years, enabling closer eventual collaboration with other churches.

He sketches out a dynamic approach to the Westminster Confession, where, thanks to an accompanying commentary in nearly every Presbyterian church, an extreme doctrine of election was excluded, while the ground of piety was maintained. "We have come to realise that in a relation so personal as man's dependence upon God the last words are love and patience, and that is far too great a matter to be expressed in any formula." His remarks on the degeneracy of Puritanism are characteristically incisive. "Are we not in architecture much like our neighbours, limited in display only by lack of means, and, alas! not always by that? Have we not acres of stained glass, mediaeval in everything but quality? What hymn books

---

4. Address to Calvinistic Methodist students in Aberystwyth. *Liverpool Daily Post*, Monday, 29 June 1914. This ambition was finally achieved with the formation of the United Reformed Church in 1972.

5. Where most of the students were in training for the Congregational ministry.

6. Oman, "The Presbyterian Churches."

7. Selbie, *Evangelical Christianity*, v.

8. Selbie, *Evangelical Christianity*, viii.

9. Mansfield College Annual Report, 1910–11, 12.

contain more elaborate music? Are not good organs more common among us than good organists? . . . Have not various Presbyterian Churches published forms of worship which are not more widely used only because they do not deserve to be?"[10] Where the fervour of Puritanism had cooled, its asceticism and self-discipline were applied to "the business of succeeding in life." Many Presbyterians had "mainly through education and self-denial, prospered in the world. The result is a highly respectable and in many ways most admirable person whose position in our churches, however, is apt to be determined more by his purse than by his piety."[11] And Oman pursues a familiar trope: when such a person typically desires to upgrade his church buildings, this is liable to be "mere display and upholstery . . . which every right instinct should regard as an abomination in the sight of God. . . . It is at [best] some training in generosity."[12] However at the heart of Puritanism there remains the view that "the Church is not the edifice, but the communion of saints; that its glory is not in any outward splendour, but in the souls it calls into fellowship with Christ; that the test of its success is not ritual, but humble, patient, steadfast lives; that its task is not to exalt itself at all, but to serve the community, and that it must ever be ready to decrease if thereby Christ increase."[13] As the idea of the fellowship of the elect was to serve the civil community there was no need for the Church to be "under the tutelage of the state." However in that the Church "has responsibility for the nation's poorest and most degraded," the rationale of Presbyterian organization is "its efficacy for national service."[14] Oman then turns to elders, indicating ways in which in practice, despite their "sincerity and wisdom and weight of character," their spiritual responsibilities were often not observed. And yet, he continues: "when I think of the unfailing help I received from my own, I scarce realise how a congregation is carried on without them."[15]

As Congregationalism also had changed over the years, had the point been reached "where the watchwords of Congregationalism and Presbyterianism should no longer divide us"?[16] We accept responsibility for past failures and inherit the gains of the past, yet "we may not seek to cut ourselves off from the influences of our time, intellectual, social or political, for it is in

---

10. Oman, "The Presbyterian Churches," 60.
11. Oman, "The Presbyterian Churches," 61.
12. Oman, "The Presbyterian Churches," 62.
13. Oman, "The Presbyterian Churches," 63.
14. Oman, "The Presbyterian Churches," 65.
15. Oman, "The Presbyterian Churches," 69.
16. Oman, "The Presbyterian Churches," 75.

this age God has placed us, and it is this age we are to serve."[17] If we serve in our own denomination for the sake of the whole, "we shall surmount our divisions by something more inspiring than ecclesiastical compromise, something more apostolic than the averaging of our individuality, whether in belief or organisation."[18]

How to Surmount Division?

In the light of all this, it is perhaps unsurprising that, post war, Oman was less interested in the careful parrying of doctrinal argument than in the personal and relational, according to which Christians are called to union, not for the sake of the Church, but for the world. A letter which he wrote to Professor A. C. Headlam is revealing:

> It is no doubt important that we should face each other and say what we mean on the points you raise. But the difficulty does not concern arguments. On points say like ordination different people live in a different universe of discourse. For that reason I do not feel any burning enthusiasm to open on any of the points. But if you would ask "upon what tasks should we, in spite of our divisions, unite our fellowship and our effort at this moment?" I would lead or follow or play any part. Besides any re-union worth having will come in that way and not by the most diligent ecclesiastical carpentry.[19]

While the letter is undated, we might assume that Oman here is turning down an invitation to participate in the conference of Free Church scholars at Christ Church, Oxford convened by Headlam in June 1920 to explore further the issues around reunion that had emerged during the Mansfield Conferences of January 1918, 1919 and 1920,[20] in preparation for the Lambeth Conference. Although Anderson Scott participated in at least one of these Mansfield conferences, involving representatives of the Free Churches and

17. Oman, "The Presbyterian Churches," 78.

18. Oman, "The Presbyterian Churches," 79. The theme was important for Oman and Selbie. In 1921, it was reported on 5 October by the *Western Daily Press* that Oman "opened discussion at a meeting of the 79th Autumnal Assembly of the Christian Union of England and Wales on the theme of Catholicism and Catholicity. The Rev. Dr W. B. Selbie, principal of Mansfield College Oxford, presided."

19. Oman to Headlam, 1, Westminster College Bounds, 21 May, MS 2628 Lambeth Palace Library, f50 recto and verso.

20. An additional conference was held for Free Church representatives at Mansfield College in June 1921, to formulate an official statement on the Lambeth proposals for reunion. *Reports, Mansfield College*, 1917–18, 1918–19, 1919–20, 1920–21.

the Church of England, and Carnegie Simpson was much engaged in the aftermath, I find no sign of Oman's participation.[21]

He did, however, at the end of January 1920, address an "interdenominational mission" in Oxford with Church of England, Roman Catholic and Free Church leaders, organized by the Reverend Neville Talbot of Balliol, "a daring and unconventional advocate of Christian unity and church reform."[22] For a week they met each evening with large numbers of students to discuss the relationship of Christianity to modern life under the presidency of the Bishop of Oxford, Hubert Murray Burge. The "mission,"[23] Oman wrote, seemed to be "on the whole a success in the best sense of the word. Lord Hugh Cecil delivered a really Christian speech to a matter of 1,000 students. I had a shot at a matter of 700. Micklem said the students seem fairly agreed, but the old dons looked. I am hanged if I see how this is wrong but it would be jolly risky business to set it right."[24] What precisely Oman is referring to here is tantalizingly unclear but he was evidently in tune with his younger hearers. The *Oxford Chronicle* comments approvingly: "The last thing to be desired is that the Conference should pass away in tepid conventionalities. . . . It is a welcome if belated sign that the leaders of great Christian churches should discover that at the root of the matter they have much in common." For Oman, "it was a less wasteful way of spending one's time than descending upon either Ebor or Winton."[25]

It would be to misjudge Oman however, to suggest that he regarded doctrinal conversations as unimportant. They had their place. In a book review, published in 1927, he remarks:

> We have travelled some considerable distance in the last fifty years. In very practical fellowship we have realised that we can have real unity of spirit with great difference of opinion; and now we have to realise that it need not be hindered by great diversity of organisation. Episcopal and Free Church leaders may be anxious not to give their principles away; but, after all, they

21. Carlyle et al., *Towards Reunion*.
22. *Oxford Chronicle* 23 January 1920.
23. *Oxford Chronicle* 23 January 1920.
24. Letter, Oman to Cairns, headed "Mansfield College, Oxford, January 30th." Cecil gave a talk on "Christianity and International Affairs." "Special services at the University Church with special addresses" were given by Temple, Oman and Selbie. *Oxford Chronicle*, 23 January 1920.
25. Letter, Oman to Cairns, Mansfield College, Oxford, January 30. The Archbishop of York, Cosmo Gordon Lang, chaired the large committee on reunion at the Lambeth Conference and presented the *Appeal to All Christian People*. Bell, *Randall Davidson*, 1011, 1014.

do meet together and discuss in friendliness their differences as they could not have done not many years ago. . . . The great matter is that we have a vision of what cannot be shaken, when all that can be shaken falls into decay.[26]

Westminster College After the War

At this point, it might be appropriate to pause and consider developments at Westminster College. The Senatus decided to open the college on 4 February 1919 to "all students available and as the Serbian Committee had possession of the college till 2nd March, to provide lodgings in town for the students— at the terminal fee of £15."[27] Lectures were to be held in the Senatus Room. Such students were to be admitted "as soon as they were demobilized, even if for one term only." Nine materialized immediately, with the prospect of "some twenty names or more."[28] This was taken to be a heartening indication of personal vocation at a time when the minimum stipend for ministers was meagre, and the assumed inadequacy of the church as an institution was being trumpeted.[29]

There were developments in the curriculum: the offer of Dr. Crichton in 1919 to give a course of lectures in Psychology was accepted with twelve guineas travelling expenses.[30] Women began to attend lectures. On 6 October 1919, permission was granted to "Miss Dorothy Steven of Newnham College and Miss M. R. Eley of Union Theological Seminary, New York . . . to attend lectures this and the following terms."[31] And on 23 December, "The Principal read a letter from Miss Marjorie C. [Bunnan] enquiring as to the possibility of her being admitted for study in the college next October."[32] Westminster was let to Swedish students from 21 June to 27 July 1920, and Commemoration Day with George Adam Smith as lecturer was twice postponed due to the Coal Strike.[33] On 27 October 1921, "when Cambridge was clad in the russet tints of Autumn," the new chapel, given by Sir William

---

26. Oman, review of Sheppard, *The Impatience of a Parson*.
27. Minutes, Board of Studies, 14 January 1919.
28. "The Wants of Westminster College," *Presbyterian Messenger*, March 1919.
29. Fyffe, "Brighter Prospects."
30. Minutes of Senatus, 5 July 1919.
31. Minutes of Senatus, 6 October 1919.
32. Minutes of Senatus, 23 December 1920.
33. Minutes of Senatus, 4 November 1920 and 20 May 1921.

Noble and Lady Noble in memory of their son, was dedicated.[34] And most significant of all, while the Senatus meeting on 2 June 1922 was presided over by John Skinner, the minute was signed by John Oman, Principal.

The New Principal

When Skinner retired in 1921, the chair of Old Testament and the principalship both fell vacant. A crammed and tensely excited Assembly met on 4 May 1922 to decide on his successors. The decision on the Old Testament chair was the more straightforward; by a standing vote, the House unanimously elected the sole remaining nominee, the Reverend W. A. L. Elmslie, to the post. As if to allay any doubts, it was made clear by his sponsor that Elmslie's brilliant academic career was not a mark of "barren erudition": his "apprenticeship for a chair had included a strenuous London ministry" at St John's Church, Kensington.[35] Election to the Principalship was a lengthier business. The three remaining members of Senatus were all nominated. For nearly two hours, the merits of the nominees, friends and colleagues, were debated, before tellers were called and the result announced. Oman received twelve votes more than Simpson. Simpson and Scott's proposers both moved that the election be unanimous, and so Oman was elected to the Principalship. Oman commented, on being received, that "the Principal is only *primus inter pares*; henceforth the *primus* will be writ very small, and the *pares* be large as ever. I don't need to ask for the backing of my colleagues, for I know I have that already. It is said that a man is known by his friends. If that be so, there is no job in Britain that I couldn't undertake!"[36]

In his inaugural address as principal[37] there are some recurring themes. "The most important matter in any seminary of learning is teaching, not organizing. The real business of a theological college is being done, if men come out of it knowing how to see truth for themselves; whereas, without it, the most efficient organisation may only be an elaborate device for wasting youth's precious years. The office I would magnify is still my old calling of a teacher of theology, and did this office make it secondary, it would be very Irish promotion." To that end, open-ended enquiry was vital: "Theology is bankrupt the moment there is any suspicion that it sees something else than

---

34. "Westminster College Chapel," *Presbyterian Messenger*, 1 December 1921. On the same occasion, the bust of Skinner by George Wyon was accepted on behalf of the college by Oman and placed in the old chapel at the end of the library.
35. "An Assembly Diary," *Presbyterian Messenger*, June 1922, 129.
36. "An Assembly Diary," *Presbyterian Messenger*, June 1922, 131.
37. Oman, "Method in Theology."

truth." The lifelong impact of the Robertson Smith affair confirmed his notion that "the greatest of all hindrances to religious appeal at the present time, is that religious people are more concerned about what is correct than what is true, and that ecclesiastical leaders, in particular, are more exercised about unanimity than veracity." Students and working men alike felt that the Church was "a kind of trade-union to impose upon mankind merely traditional beliefs." This, he observed from his war-time experience, led to a "sapping of the foundations." Neither science, philosophy, religion or history could come up with an adequate response. But with a strong personal faith, rooted in reality, the problem might be overcome: "a true theology leaves out nothing of the concrete varied world that is within the grasp of our finite minds, in the hope of seeing the things unseen manifested in the things which do appear." From then on, this vision is to be the basis of his theological exploration.

The office of Principal entailed a move of house. John, Mary, and their three younger daughters[38] moved from 1 The Bounds, with its sunny, spacious rooms overlooking the tennis lawn, and a bath large enough for Mary to bathe the four children all together,[39] to the Principal's Lodge, integrated with the College. It was a hard time to assume the responsibilities of principalship: for Oman personally, there were complex inheritance issues arising from his brother James's recent death in Morandava, Madagascar,[40] and the college's finances were precarious. Oman comments: "As I had never occupied myself very much with finance, either public or private, this added greatly to my sense of burden in being appointed Principal."[41] The cost of wages, lighting, heating, food had doubled and taxes more than doubled during the war. But with good management, the use of reserves, a very generous endowment and donations, the deficit was reduced to £3,000, accumulated since the war. If this were to be met by local churches, Oman felt it might also increase awareness of the other major need, students for the ministry.

Given the college's financial situation and the fact that candidates for the ministry were in short supply, questions were being raised as to how desirable it was it to continue to insist on a university course before three years of theological study. Applicants were dealt with on their own merits.

38. On 1 November 1921, their eldest daughter, Isabella Gertrude, had married the Reverend Frank Hewitt Ballard, minister of Victoria Road Congregational Church, Cambridge. John Skinner officiated, assisted by the Reverend Innes Logan, minister of St Columba's Church.

39. Personal conversation with Ia (Isabella) Ballard.

40. On 22 November 1921, although news may not have reached the family for a few weeks. See above, 16.

41. Oman, "Our College."

Some had had their studies interrupted by the War, other "special cases" like "Mr A. P. Webb," who had no university training, were to be admitted on probation to study for Entrance, and he and others were excused Latin and Hebrew. But the Senatus and Board of Studies were challenged by the fact that "in recent years these special cases have become numerous, and there appears to be no ground for supposing that there will be a speedy return to the conditions which prevailed formerly."[42] Oman wrote in 1923 that, whereas before the War, "no Church in England or Scotland was getting better material," and many students achieved academic distinction, "since the War . . . this has entirely changed."[43] Were it not for the number of students from other churches, chiefly from Scotland and Ireland, the college would have had to abandon its demand for a prior university course. In case of any misunderstanding, he makes it clear that "the reason for sending men to the University before entering in special theological study is not, primarily, knowledge of books, but contact with men and the habit of living with an open mind in face of all knowledge and even all opinion."[44] This experience was enhanced by the invitations to "friends" to "help in widening [their] spiritual horizon,"[45] and the ready response they had from business men and others to broaden the students' horizons by spending a weekend at a time in college. The apparent difficulty in recruiting ministers was a matter not so much for the college as the whole Church. "Were the churches becoming more independent of a professional ministry, the falling-off of students might be no cause for anxiety."[46]

Unity in Diversity

In following developments at Westminster College, we have temporarily neglected Oman's ecumenical perspectives, to which we now return. In *The Church and the Divine Order*, he had already argued that "if the distinctive

---

42. "Memorandum concerning the student pastor scheme," amended 14 February 1922 by Rev W. A. L. Elmslie and the Convenor. It was agreed that a student pastor scheme might be applicable where students "were of proven ability in preaching," willing to study for a degree, and be likely to gain one. An experiment was to be made with "Mr Robertson, of Edinburgh," who wished to enter the College after working with the YMCA.

43. Oman, "Our College."

44. Oman, "Our College."

45. On 30 May 1922, for example, two sessions at Westminster College were addressed by Mrs. Booth Clibborn, otherwise known as the Maréchale, the eldest daughter of General William Booth of the Salvation Army. Mann, "Fifty Years Ago."

46. Oman, "Our College."

principle of the church consists in its relation to a divine order of love for which all human history is a discipline and a preparation . . . the question of unity must ever be fundamental,"[47] and he had consistently argued since then that Church reunion should be based on fellowship in truth, love and service. In an extended essay on the theme "Spiritual Regeneration as the Basis of World Reconstruction,"[48] Oman develops his vision of "a society which shall be one in truth only because all its members see the same reality, one in love only because all have drunk of the same spirit, and one in service only because all are subjects of the same Rule of God." Because

> [our Lord] is wholly adequate for the manifestation of truth and the inspiration of love, we need no other guide or bond, but amid all human differences, we may maintain a spirit which is not really divided, and which ultimately will perfect us into one. All reunion which naturally followed the increase of this true Church would, therefore, be a sign of progress. But mere ecclesiastical union might neither spring from it, nor forward it.

"The true message is the good news that God is in Christ reconciling the world to Himself, removing every barrier to our friendship." Finally, we should all be united "to create, as a soul for the body of international amity a real living fellowship in which there is neither English nor German, Austrian nor French." The references here are to the foremost causes of international civil society between the wars: the League of Nations and the nascent Christian ecumenical movement, which between them created "a diverse and fluid international political environment."[49] The League of Nations had been canvassed successfully before the end of the war as a multilateral organization for maintaining peace but it nonetheless assumed the continued existence of national sovereignty and empire.[50] Was this adequate to prevent war?[51] Oman's perception of the urgent need to transcend national bound-

47. Oman, *Church and Divine Order*, 307.

48. University of St Andrews Special Collections. Essays were invited on this topic for competition under the auspices of the Walker Trust. In February 1921 it was announced that the first prize of £200 had been awarded to Henry T. Hodgkin of the Friends Foreign Mission Association, and "honoraria of £25 each given to F. W. Freitag, Potsdam; Edward Landsbery Grear, Norwich, Revd. John Murphy B.D., Hamilton, and Dr Oman, Westminster College, Cambridge."

49. Gorman, "Ecumenical Internationalism," 52.

50. Article 10 authorized the League to take action against states which violated the sovereignty of other states. Article 16 identified these actions: economic sanctions and the prohibition of contact between nationals of the offending state and nationals of all other states.

51. Future events were to cast doubt on this, notably the League's inability in 1931 to deal with the Japanese invasion of Manchuria.

aries and create "a real living fellowship" "as a soul for the body" bolstered his belief that the churches together could open up space for international cooperation and animate the League as a force for peace.

This is in the spirit of the irenic encyclical letter sent in 1920 by the Holy Synod of the Ecumenical Patriarchate in Constantinople "Unto all the Churches of Christ Wheresoever They Be,"[52] which was indissolubly linked with the idea of a League of Churches along the lines of the League of Nations.[53] Prepared by a group of theologians headed by Metropolitan Germanos of Thyateira,[54] it begins with the exhortation: "love one another earnestly from the heart,"[55] and claims

> that rapprochement between the various Christian churches and fellowship between them is not excluded by the doctrinal differences which exist between them. It would be useful in many ways for the real interest of each particular church and of the whole Christian body, and also for the preparation and advancement of that blessed union which will be completed in the future in accordance with the will of God.

The World Alliance for Promoting International Friendship Through the Churches

Might the World Alliance lead the way? The *Presbyterian Messenger* seemed to think so. In November 1922, we read these words: "If there were a British Council of the Alliance, such a body could do great service to educating public opinion, in labouring for the removal of the courses of friction and bitterness that make for war, and in ratifying the influence of the Church in favour of the League of Nations, which in its present or in an amended form, furnishes the best security against future wars."[56] As, for Oman, the Alliance was important at different levels, we may now briefly consider its history. It originated in 1909 in a reciprocal visit by church representatives from England to Germany.[57] On the deck of a Potsdam steamboat, Sir Wil-

---

52. January 1920. Bell, *Documents on Christian Unity*, 17–21.

53. Nathan Söderblom was to refer to it in his acceptance speech for the Nobel peace prize in 1930.

54. Metropolitan Germanos contributed actively to the founding of the WCC in 1937, and at the first General Assembly in Amsterdam in 1948, he was elected one of the six presidents.

55. 1 Peter 1:22.

56. Ramsay, "International Fellowship."

57. See Clements, "Anglo-German Churches' Exchange."

loughby Dickinson and Dr. Friedrich Siegmund-Schultze sketched out a plan to apply principles of Christian friendship to international relations.[58] Thanks to their efforts, and those of the Quaker J. Allen Baker, the founding conference of the World Alliance was held at Constance, 2–5 August, 1914.[59] As, with dramatic irony, war broke out all around, delegates left after one day and got home as best they could. But first they sturdily passed resolutions which made their object clear:

> Inasmuch as the work of conciliation and the promotion of amity is essentially a Christian task, it is expedient that the Churches in all lands should use their influence . . . to bring about good and friendly relations between the nations, so that, along the path of peaceful civilisation, they may reach that universal goodwill which Christianity has taught mankind to aspire after.[60]

Religious support for political causes was scarcely new, and although the World Alliance was certainly influenced by nineteenth-century moral campaigns such as the campaign against slavery[61] its main thrust was not to respond to international ills, but to prevent or ameliorate future international problems.[62]

Over the next few years associated councils were established in fifteen countries. The carnage of war gave the World Alliance renewed purpose, and when it convened its first postwar meeting at Oud Wassenaar hotel, The Hague, from 26 September to 3 October 1919, there were fifty-one delegates from fourteen countries,[63] including belligerents and neutrals, although the French had refused to attend because the Germans were present.[64] But the significant decision was taken to organize an international ecumenical conference on a formal basis. This conference, ultimately held in Stockholm

58. "Our German Guests. A Romance of Christian Fellowship," *Christian World*, 28 June 1928.

59. The date was chosen to mark the five-hundredth anniversary of the Council of Constance which had been convened by the German Emperor Sigismund to repair the papal schism. The conference was subsidized by the Church Peace Union in the USA with a significant benefaction by Andrew Carnegie.

60. These were published as regular reminders on the inside back page of the journal *Goodwill*.

61. It is noteworthy that one of the longest serving representatives of the PCE on the British Council was Mr. Travers Buxton, secretary (1898–1934) of the British and Foreign Anti-Slavery and Aborigines' Protection Society.

62. Gorman, "Ecumenical Internationalism."

63. "Speech delivered by Sir W. Dickinson at the meeting of the British Council of the World Alliance," 5 December 1928, London Metropolitan Archives F/DCK/038/018.

64. Bell, *Randall Davidson*, 1036.

in 1925,[65] was vigorously promoted by the Archbishop of Uppsala, Nathan Söderblom, chair of the Swedish Council of the World Alliance.[66] It would deal with "some well-defined urgent practical aims."[67] However, although the resolution was passed, it did not meet with universal favor. The Archbishop of Canterbury, Randall Davidson, left Söderblom in no doubt as to where he stood in the matter.[68] In his view, his fellow archbishop was "a churchman in a hurry, full of hazy plans which in the end did not amount to very much."[69] For his part, Söderblom saw Davidson as being "more political and cautious than whole-hearted."[70]

On 29 September 1922 the executive of the British Council of the Alliance discussed a memorandum that argued for "a permanent body of the most representative Church leaders in England . . . expressing the voice and conscience of Christianity in Great Britain."[71] They acted quickly. At the sixth Annual Meeting on 13 December 1922 new structures were accepted,[72] and the inaugural meeting of the newly constituted British Council was held at Church House, Westminster on 12-14 June 1923. Members were officially appointed by all the mainstream traditions in England, Scotland, and Wales. The PCE had three representatives, one of whom was Oman.[73] He was present at the opening service in Westminster Abbey where the Archbishop of Canterbury preached the sermon. It was their hope, Davidson said, "to breathe into the League of Nations a living soul"; not "to handle politically . . . those great issues which the League had to deal with," but "to make public opinion so powerful on Christ's side that the monstrous arbitrament of war should not be used again."[74]

65. Söderblom was awarded the Nobel Peace Prize in 1930 in recognition of his achievement. See Söderblom, "The Role of the Church in Promoting Peace."
66. Sundkler, *Nathan Söderblom*, 228-30.
67. Sundkler, *Nathan Söderblom*, 230.
68. Sundkler, *Nathan Söderblom*, 223-33. Bell gives an amusing account of how on 15 April 1921, Davidson was visited by Nathan Söderblom and his wife at Lambeth. Söderblom wanted to engage Davidson's support for the conference in Stockholm, but the Archbishop stalled, "unwilling to give himself away, either for or against." When the conference took place in 1925, the Archbishop of Canterbury was represented by the Bishop of Winchester. Bell, *Randall Davidson*, 1048-51.
69. Sundkler, *Nathan Söderblom*, 234.
70. Sundkler, *Nathan Söderblom*, 235.
71. Minutes of Executive 29 September 1922 WAIF/2/1/3. It was felt that the existing British Council, inaugurated on 6 February 1911, was not adequately rooted in church structures nor sufficiently representative of the traditions.
72. Minutes of sixth Annual Meeting 13 December 1922 WAIF/2/1/3.
73. The other two were Dr. Gillie and Mr. Travers Buxton.
74. *The Times*, 13 June 1923.

A Visit to the Ruhr and the Rhineland[75]

Almost immediately it was evident that there would be some issues where the "League of Churches" would be on its own. When the Ruhr was occupied by France and Belgium in response to Germany's defaulting on its reparation payments, the British Council of the Alliance was seriously concerned. As the invasion was technically legal in terms of the Treaty of Versailles, no action was taken by the League of Nations. Faced with a rapidly deteriorating situation, how was the Alliance to provide a moral impetus for peace?

An initiative was not long in coming. On 3 August 1923, three men met in Düsseldorf. Two were Lutheran pastors from Sweden: Sam Stadener and Alfred Wihlborg. The third, and most senior of the three, was Oman. Their stated aim was to visit the French prisons in the Ruhr occupied zone in order to "take consolation and religious support to the German prisoners."[76] The visit seems to have originated in an approach made to Nathan Söderblom by Maître Coulet, Professor in Law and attorney at the Swedish embassy in Paris who had offered to accompany him on a visit to the Ruhr.[77] The suggestion was not unprecedented. Six years before, Söderblom had responded to the plea from Siegmund-Schultze, echoed by the American YMCA, that the welfare of prisoners of war had to be investigated, and promptly sent Herman Neander to look into the matter.[78] Now, in 1923, he commended Stadener, his successor as embassy chaplain in Paris, then pastor of Ystad and a proven diplomat, as being "plus capable que moi pour une telle tâche."[79] And so Stadener and Wihlborg, secretary to the group, were commissioned by the Swedish Committee of the World Alliance. This was entirely in keeping with Söderblom's use of special envoys from Sweden whom he sent out as occasion demanded on international errands of special importance.[80] Bur this errand was different. For this time, uniquely, the Swedish envoys were accompanied by a non-Swede, John Oman.

---

75. For an earlier version of this material, see Houston, "A Visit," reproduced with permission.

76. Stadener et al., "Report of a Visit."

77. Letter to M. Delavaud, French minister at Stockholm, undated and in 2012, uncatalogued. N. Söderbloms samling, Uppsala University Library. The report dates the reply, giving permission to "the Swedish delegation" as 24 July 1923.

78. Sundkler, *Nathan Söderblom*, 183.

79. Letter to M. Delavaud. Söderblom "sought Stadener's services for difficult tasks where diplomatic skill and a knowledge of France and the French were particularly needed." (Sundkler, *Nathan Söderblom*, 171.)

80. Sundkler, *Nathan Söderblom*, 172.

A NEW AGE

Why might Söderblom have wished to widen the membership of this particular legation? There are two possibilities. First, the letter from the Swedish bishops sent on 1 February 1923 over Söderblom's signature to "our fellow Christians in all countries and to responsible statesmen, particularly to President Harding" was sharply critical of France's invasion of the Ruhr; it was approved in Germany and vehemently criticized in France. Prime Minister Poincaré, Wilfred Monod, chair of the French Council of the World Alliance, and the Roman Catholic Archbishop of Paris were highly indignant. Matters were not helped by the realization that the English and German versions of the letter were more pointed in their condemnation than the French.[81] Söderblom's attempt to salvage the situation by pleading that the translator had proved inadequate fell on deaf ears.[82]

Secondly, he would have been aware of the widely held view in Sweden that friendship between Sweden and Germany was "so solidly anchored that it can be regarded as a constant factor in [their] foreign policies."[83] That had not always been the case. Sweden was generally francophile up to the twentieth century. Swedish soldiers fought in the ranks of the French army, the royal family was French in origin and French language and culture were dominant in Swedish society. But the situation changed gradually as Sweden became the chief supplier of iron ore and timber for German industry. With the Ruhr occupation, the German purchase of ore came to a standstill and relationships between the two countries could no longer be based on trade. But there was in Sweden a chorus of sympathy for Germany following reports of the sufferings endured by the Ruhr population. The common shared history of the Church of Sweden and the Protestant church in Germany gave rise to a sense of family obligation. Swedish church congregations collected "such considerable sums for the church institutions in Germany that a proportion of the latter has been supported directly by Swedes."[84]

With this in mind, Söderblom might have considered that a visit by Swedes to German prisoners in the Ruhr would look partisan. A British delegate, however, might redress the balance. Söderblom admired what he

---

81. Weiße, "Irenic Mediator for Unity." References to the fact that the occupation led to "sexual degradation" and that troops had "torn large pieces of territory from their unarmed neighbours" did not feature in the French version. (Sundkler, *Nathan Söderblom*, 334.)

82. Söderblom, in *Die Eiche*, 1923, 200; quoted in Sundkler, *Nathan Söderblom*, 334.

83. Memorandum on the relationship of Sweden to Germany from Nadolny to Foreign Office, Berlin, 19 May 1923. *Akten zur Deutschen auswärtigen Politik*, Band VII.

84. Memorandum on the relationship of Sweden to Germany from Nadolny to Foreign Office, Berlin, 19 May 1923. *Akten zur Deutschen auswärtigen Politik*, Band VII.

had read of the British Council,[85] some of whom he had met in 1921 in the House of Lords.[86] But how did the decision to send Oman come about?

On 22 June, Nathan Söderblom, Fru Söderblom, Miss and Mr. Söderblom stayed overnight at Lambeth Palace. George Bell, then Davidson's chaplain, notes in his diary: "He specially wanted Archbishop to send a delegate to visit German prisons in the Ruhr. I had a long talk with him at night."[87] Bell makes no further reference to Söderblom's request and this is not mentioned in Davidson's papers.[88] Nor, for that matter, is Oman.

There is no indication that Davidson knew Oman particularly well. But he had contacts with people who did and whose judgment he trusted. Carnegie Simpson had chaired the committee which produced the Free Church response to the Lambeth Appeal of 1920, and was co-convenor of the subsequent "long and important series of meetings"[89] between Anglicans and the Free Churches. Davidson was "a sympathetic observer"[90] throughout, and formed a long-standing friendship with Simpson. More than once Simpson was invited to stay at Lambeth.[91]

However the invitation came about, it appears that Oman joined the group at short notice.[92] The political circumstances were fraught. Since 11 January when five French divisions and one Belgian division marched into the Ruhr, relations between France and Germany were tense. France was determined to hold the Ruhr, laying claim as her due to coking coal and dyestuffs and seizing money from banks and factories, in lieu of German reparation

85. See Söderblom, "Nobel Lecture."

86. On 25 April. The meeting was arranged by Lord and Lady Parmoor. (Minutes of the fifth Annual Meeting of the British Council of the World Alliance for Promoting International Friendship through the Churches WAIF/2/1/3.)

87. G. K. A. Bell, diary 1923-25, papers 257, Lambeth Palace archive. Söderblom admired Bell, who had worked with him during the war on the exchange of prisoners of war and whom he came to recognize as one of his closest lifelong friends. With Bell, Söderblom discussed his plans for ecumenical conferences and his hopes for peace. Is it not likely that the "long talk" on the evening of the 22 June was as least in part taken up with the situation in the Ruhr?

88. Davidson merely notes in his diary on 12 August 1923 that he had received an "interesting" visit during the past year from "Söderblom from Upsala and his family." Bell, *Randall Davidson*, 1172; Söderblom refers to "important and delightful hours spent with You in Lambeth." Letter to Randall Davidson, 29 August 1923, N. Söderbloms samling, Uppsala.

89. Simpson, *Recollections*, 76. There were 22 meetings between 1921 and 1925; see Bell, *Randall Davidson*, 1116.

90. Bell, *Randall Davidson*, 1117.

91. Simpson, *Recollections*, 82.

92. The two letters on 24 July to request a laissez-passer, from Söderblom to M. Delavaud and to General Degoutte, mention only Stadener and Wihlborg.

debts under the Treaty of Versailles. As a result, the French were faced with a campaign of passive resistance by Ruhr industrialists, mine workers and railway men. Britain remained aloof. But on the day the three churchmen met in Düsseldorf, the British Foreign Secretary, Lord Curzon, finally made it clear that Britain was not prepared to protect Germany's interests against France and that the campaign of passive resistance had to stop.[93] The German government, however, insisted that abandonment of passive resistance could only be considered when the military presence in the Ruhr was removed.[94] Frenzied diplomatic activity had come to a head.[95]

Many of the prisoners whom the three men were to meet had been implicated in passive resistance. Directors of works were held responsible for the behavior of their employees and regularly arrested. Other prisoners had been sentenced for acts of sabotage. Following the explosion of a bomb in a Belgian leave train near Duisberg, resulting in several deaths,[96] ordinances by General Degoutte proclaimed the death penalty for sabotage of railways or telephone lines and the eviction of all those who lived in the neighborhood of the accused.[97] By the end of July, eleven Germans were under sentence of death for acts of sabotage.

Travel in the Rhineland, then also under French occupation, was extremely difficult. The railway system had broken down; there were neither signals nor points, only a man with a red flag.[98] During most of July a strict blockade was imposed on the Ruhr. Movement between the occupied and unoccupied territory was prohibited and travelers were stranded.[99] By 3 August "the population was in extreme tension" and fears were growing of a Communist inspired crisis.[100]

This was the context of the visit to the prisons. Permission had not been easy to obtain. The French minister in Stockholm, Delavaud, made a condition that the delegates "were not to make any political comments

93. *The Times*, 3 August 1923.

94. *The Times*, 22 July 1923.

95. See telegrams to and from the Foreign Office in Berlin (*Akten zur deutschen auswärtigen Politik*, Serie A, Band VIII); O'Riordan, *Britain and the Ruhr Crisis*, gives a persuasive account of the hardening of stances between France and Germany and of Britain's indecisiveness.

96. *The Times*, 24 June 1923; 1 July 1923.

97. *The Times*, 1 July 1923.

98. *The Times*, 5 July 1923.

99. *The Times*, 15 July 1923.

100. *The Times*, 16 and 23 July 1923; fears were exacerbated by Karl Radek's public eulogy of Schlageter, a Krupp employee executed in May for involvement in an act of sabotage.

either during the trip or as a result of it, and agree to adhere to French regulations."[101] Hesitant military authorities in Düsseldorf finally granted them leave to visit all prisons under French administration in the Ruhr and the three men were escorted by the Protestant army chaplain, pasteur Patry.[102] They visited seven prisons, in Düsseldorf, Dortmund, Bochum, Werden, and Witten.[103] Although some of these were housed in buildings which were still partly under the administration of German authorities as civil prisons, this did not appear to be cause for friction. The number of prisoners varied, from 184 in Düsseldorf to 40 in Witten, as did the number of men per cell.[104]

The French authorities had divided the prisoners up into categories. There were the ordinary criminals. Then there were the political prisoners, amongst them prefects and mayors, post office and police officials as well as a great number of manufacturing and business people. There was a range of local leaders who had been imprisoned for offences against the French regulations, committed not by them but by offenders who had not been caught. And finally there was a group of prisoners on remand who were "sous secret" and for them the delegates had great sympathy. Suspected of having committed acts of sabotage, they were in solitary confinement, permitted neither to send nor receive letters, nor speak with a priest or lawyer without permission. This was usually refused.

In general, the prisons looked clean and prisoners seemed in reasonably good health. Provision for exercise in the fresh air varied from prison to prison. Soldiers and prisoners ate the same food, except for political prisoners whose meals were provided by the German Red Cross.

In noting all this, the report reminds us that the stated purpose of the delegation was pastoral: to see what religious provision was available in the prisons and to offer ministry, although unsupervised conversation with the prisoners was not allowed. In Düsseldorf they attended the Catholic Mass and the Protestant service and joined with gusto in singing a hymn about courage.

101. Report in Swedish, Evangelisches Zentralarchiv in Berlin, Ref: EZA 51/E ll d1.

102. Poincaré said "the French had nothing to hide." *The Times*, 6 July 1923; *British Weekly*, 31 January 1935.

103. They had no time to visit Recklinghausen, a smaller prison in the north of the Ruhr zone. They also sought entry to Duisberg prison but were unsuccessful as their papers did not permit them to visit the area occupied by Belgium.

104. In general there was one prisoner in each cell but in Dortmund there were two or three. In Witten there were medium-sized rooms accommodating three to six prisoners. The prison in Werden was in a former monastery with dormitories for about fifty beds; this was particularly popular with the prisoners.

While they were in the Ruhr, the delegates found that many prisoners, especially those who were serving longer sentences, had been transferred to prisons in the Rhineland. They felt duty-bound to visit these as well. The French Prime Minister gave permission and they were received cordially by the French authorities in Coblenz. They visited further prisons in Coblenz, Trier, Zweibrucken and Mainz, seven in all. These varied. The two prisons in Coblenz were relatively small and catered for political prisoners whose food was provided by the German Red Cross. Trier Windstrasse was larger, with 91 political prisoners, 52 remand prisoners and six held "sous secret." The régime there was harsher. As for the second prison in Trier, thanks to the hostile officiousness of the Prison Governor, time ran out before the delegation could visit. But they knew that 72 political prisoners were detained there. The situation in Zweibrucken, however, was satisfactory. This visit took place on a Sunday and the chapel was filled to overflowing for the Protestant service which Wihlborg was permitted to lead.

Oman had to leave before they reached Mainz but conditions there were particularly harsh. There were about 200 ordinary prisoners, a further twenty saboteurs from the Ruhr, a small number of political prisoners and seven on death row. Outdoor exercise was severely limited, the prison was unclean and there were "bad smells." The food was not nourishing and religious services had been suspended.

In Britain, few people seem to have known about the delegation.[105] Even the British Council, nominally responsible for sending Oman, did not appear to have known about the visit in advance, despite the lengthy discussions they had been holding all year about the Ruhr crisis. At the meeting of the Executive on 10 October 1923, which Oman attended by invitation, "Canon Barnes explained the circumstances which had led to Dr Oman's visit," though these are not elaborated. Oman gave a verbal account which aroused keen interest in the Committee, who asked for his "interesting report" to be circulated before the next meeting in November. "Dr Oman requested that a letter of thanks might be sent to the Archbishop of Uppsala at whose instigation and through whom the tour had been arranged—also to Dr Stadener, for the very valuable work which he had done." At the meeting on 14 November, "the Committee accepted Dr Oman's report which had been circulated and warmly approved of the suggestion that some part of it

---

105. George Alexander refers obliquely in this context to "a report, which, I think, was private." Alexander, "Memoir of the Author," xxiii. This may be contrasted with the reports of other visits to the Ruhr by the Scottish and English Labour Parties, the Co-operative Party, and the Quakers, all of which were immediately published in full in *The Times*.

should be inserted into the next number of *Goodwill*."[106] And it was agreed to pay his expenses for the trip which came to fifteen pounds.

A comparison between the extensive extract published in *Goodwill* and the report in Swedish[107] signed by the three men and dated Zweibrucken and Frankfurt, 12 and 14 August, is suggestive. The reports are clearly the same; there is word for word correspondence throughout. The opening sections, however, differ. There is no mention in *Goodwill* of the agency of the British Council or the Archbishop of Canterbury. Davidson was not of course, chair of the British Council—that was the Bishop of Oxford. But, as we have seen, he was involved in the appointment. Is it far-fetched to see this omission as evidence of Davidson's legendary personal caution?[108]

A further factor in the apparent secrecy might have been Davidson's habitual deference to the Foreign Secretary, Lord Curzon, over his church colleagues. This is illustrated particularly well by his response to the letter about the Ruhr prisons dated 12 November 1923 and delivered in person by Dr. Spiecker, chair of the German Council. After expressing "heartfelt thanks that you, dear Lord Archbishop, were involved in the despatch of the ministers to the prisoners, through which you contributed to the relief of the lot of the prisoners," he draws on the report of the visit to indicate that the lot of the political prisoners is still very hard. Even after the ending of passive resistance great numbers of people are still being kept prisoner. He begs the Archbishop to exert his influence on behalf of the World Alliance to secure their release.[109] Davidson referred the matter to Dickinson, secretary of the British Council, on 23 November. In reply, Dickinson advises Davidson to write to Wilfred Monod to suggest that the French Council might take some steps to secure the release of the remaining German prisoners. Davidson then indicates that "I do not think I could appropriately do this unless it were with the knowledge and general approval of the Foreign Office. . . . They might possibly see objection to such a letter from me as being likely to be twisted into some kind of secret political influence behind the back of the Government." On 13 December, Davidson asks Lord Curzon's advice. Curzon "looked up the papers on the subject of French deportations

---

106. WAIF/2/1/4.

107. I am indebted to the Reverend Camilla Veitch for her assistance in translating the report into English.

108. Cf. Randall Davidson to Nathan Söderblom, 15 August 1923: "[the memorandum about Riga] must be described simply as a document coming from Sweden, and the intimate knowledge it shows of what has happened will be its own justification. But I am sure that it must not go to the world as from me." (N. Söderbloms samling, Uppsala.)

109. Papers of Archbishop Davidson, 231–49.

from the Ruhr" and found that these had "resulted in the infliction of serious hardship." However it was his view that it was better at present to "avoid raising any issue of a controversial nature which might be calculated to jeopardise" diplomatic efforts. Davidson, "completely persuaded" that Curzon was right, suggested to Dickinson that it would be "very unwise" to intervene. Dr. Spiecker received a bland acknowledgment.

So what did the mission achieve? Dr. Spiecker's letter implies that there had been some amelioration in the situation of the prisoners. This is corroborated by Oman's warm letter of thanks to Söderblom "for the trouble you took to make our visit a success."[110] He observes: "It served a more useful purpose than I had expected. Mr Wihlborg was ready with all the arrangements and spoke at services for edification. But such success as we had was more due to Mr Stadener than to any of us, especially to his clearness and courage when some further consideration was asked for the prisoners." Requests were made of the French authorities, for example: that the prisoners should be allowed to be more out in the open air; where several prisoners share a cell, that opportunity be given them for "emptying the vessels more than once a day"; that prisoners be permitted to receive gifts freely from friends and from the Red Cross; that prisoners might talk to their relatives in a visitor's room rather than in the corridor; that they might have fresh water daily; that Roman Catholic and Protestant pastors should be given time alone with their people. And there is every indication that these requests were viewed favorably.[111] But political prisoners were often treated inhumanely, usually by NCOs. At Trier in particular, relations were very bad and prisoners were verbally abused. Although Oman addressed the issue with the High Commissioner, the implications were that little could be done.[112]

It is clear too from the report that the prisoners did benefit from the moral and spiritual support given by the visit both in services and in conversation. Oman was "regarded somewhat as Noah's dove." He observes: "Being less clerically adorned than the others, I think the prisoners spoke more freely to me. In no case had I the least difficulty in entering into conversation at once."[113] He "talked freely with all kinds of prisoners, from Baron Krupp to a small boy taken up for stealing."[114] "Usually I was met with

110. 26 October 1923. N. Söderbloms samling, Uppsala.

111. The brief report in French addressed to General Degoutte and headed Düsseldorf, 8 August 1923, is a masterpiece of diplomacy. It confines itself to a request that chaplains be allowed unsupervised access to prisoners, including those held sous secret.

112. Stadener et al., "Report of a Visit."

113. Stadener et al., "Report of a Visit."

114. Oman, "Germany: Fifty Years Apart," 31 January 1935.

the warmest sympathy. Some said they had no hope except in working for Christian principles. Some even thought that military dominance was a danger in itself." But not all were so inclined. "A Burgomaster said, 'I don't know what I am here for, but if I live to be a hundred, I will preach this to my children's children.' A police officer said, 'The minister spoke of love, I would have preferred that he had spoken of hate.'"

Oman's approachability also enabled conversation with non-prisoners. He records conversations with the French High Commissioner and the second in command and also with interpreters and privates. He spoke with many Germans outside the prisons, "especially a Superintendent and a Professor of Fine Arts" who both gave him what he found to be exact and unbiased information. Yet it is, he concludes to Söderblom,[115] "a seemingly hopeless situation. The French talk like reason and moderation incarnate, but France is for them the universe. Germany is being thrown back on force as the sole remedy. It is the old story of Athens and Sparta—every Athenian a liar, every Spartan a brute. 'Our policy may have been wrong, but it is patriotism not to admit it.'"

Even as Oman and his two colleagues faced considerable challenges in their visit to the prisons of the Ruhr and the Rhineland, there were positive outcomes. The improvements in prisoners' welfare should not be underestimated. And at times they were able to facilitate a better understanding of the value that faith has in people's lives. The long-term effect of this cannot be predicated on the immediate impact it has on an individual or community.[116] This may have been in Oman's mind as, two years later, he chaired a debate on The Church and the New Age:

> Perhaps I am as pessimistic as anyone here about the immediate outlook. We are going to pass through times of great tribulation. But I am not doubtful that we shall find in it a purpose of God, and that, when it has tested our heritage, we shall find even in the civilisation of our time, that God has been forwarding it, not merely in spite of the problems raised for us, but in them.[117]

---

115. 26 October 1923. N. Söderbloms samling, Uppsala.

116. The point is well made by Maleiha Malik, who bases her discussion of faith, politics and justice on observations made by Oman in *Grace and Personality*. Malik, "Justice," 182, 202.

117. June/July 1925. Twelfth General Council of the Alliance of the Reformed Churches holding the Presbyterian System, 387–88.

Promotion of International Christian Fellowship

At the second meeting of the British Council of the Alliance, on 21 and 22 November 1923, Sir Willoughby Dickinson commented on "the serious danger of France and England, not only failing to co-operate but becoming antagonistic," and it was decided to accept the invitation of the French Council to a conference in Lille on 15 to 16 January 1924 between the French, Belgian and British Councils "on the understanding that the policy laid down by the Management Committee of the Alliance at Zurich in April 1923, shall be the basis of the discussion as to the methods by which reconciliation may be brought about."[118] Oman was one of the British delegates.[119] On 23 January, the chair of the executive

> wished to express his satisfaction at the success which had evidently attended the Conference (Lille) and at the Resolutions which had been passed. Sir Willoughby Dickinson then gave a brief report of the proceedings at Lille. The question arose as to how the practical suggestion at the end of resolution 2, with regard to an interchange of speakers between the three countries, could best be carried into effect. The Executive agreed that the Secretary should be asked to communicate with the French Committee and find out what might be done between the two countries.[120]

Although the crisis in European diplomacy was to be resolved later that year by the implementation of the Dawes plan which provided for the end to French/Belgian occupation of the Ruhr and a staggered payment plan for German reparations, the legacy of bitterness remained.

From then until 1931 when he resigned from the British Council committee, Oman contributed actively to discussions about the Alliance's principles, practice and procedure; he gave talks, he facilitated meetings in Cambridge of the British Council and of the World Alliance, he addressed theological students about the work of the Alliance. "Dr Oman," the *British Weekly* reports, "is very enthusiastic about the work and knows a great deal about it."[121] By December that year, however, his enthusiasm is muted.

---

118. There appeared to be strong differences of opinion as to the extent to which the Alliance should be involved in politics and in particular as to whether disarmament should be enforced. Council Minutes 21 and 22 November 1923, WAIF/3/1/1.

119. Along with Bishop Hamilton Baynes, the Reverend Canon MacCulloch, the Reverend Canon Poole-Hughes, Miss Ruth Rouse, Rear-Admiral Drury-Lowe, the Reverend H. T. Taylor, the Reverend R. Nicol Cross, the Reverend Dr. Patrick, with Willoughby Dickinson and Alexander Ramsay in attendance.

120. Minutes of the Executive of the British Council, 23 January 1924, WAIF/2/1/4.

121. *British Weekly*, 28 May 1925. This was on the occasion of an address to the Joint Anglican and Free Church Fraternal at Cheshunt College, Cambridge.

Confined to the house with a bad cold, he writes to Cairns to thank him for his newly published biography of A. R. MacEwen, before turning to the meeting of the Alliance which he had attended during the week. He says: "I came away rather depressed. The only idea seems to me to rush in with political resolutions. There is no idea that the Alliance might represent the true catholic spirit and that its business is [held] up to the true Church Universal. Garvie is solemnly stodgy and Burroughs is very light weight and those who might count on the Council don't come."[122]

He returns to the theme two years later:

> There are a good few of us who, while loyal to our denominations, no longer dream of them as hindrances to friendship and co-operation with any kind of Christian. Out of this no doubt corporate unity will increase in time.... A spirit cannot do without forms. But the form we need is an expression of this view of the Church Catholic, and not a compromise with the other Catholic view that we should be one as Christ and the Father is one by having only one creed and one organization. With unity Christianity begins and does not end. The Alliance to promote friendship among all Churches is a faint beginning: and the pity is that it has not yet seen its vision or found its own soul. But all beginnings are difficult and it is something just to begin.[123]

He attended as a visitor the Eighth International Conference of the Alliance held in Cambridge, September 1 to 5 1931, where the list of three hundred delegates from thirty countries includes amongst the youth representatives Privatdozent Lic. Bonhoeffer.[124]

Christianity in a New Age

Oman expands his view of the catholicity of the church in his introduction to volume three of the ambitious project in five volumes, edited by A. S. Peake and R. G. Parsons, entitled *An Outline of Christianity: The Story of Our Civilisation*.[125] "The purpose of an introduction" he suggests promisingly, "is to shorten for the reader the long road which the author himself

---

122. John Oman to D. S. Cairns, 19 December 1925, Papers of D. S. Cairns, Aberdeen University archives.

123. Oman, review of Sheppard, *Impatience*.

124. Record of Proceedings, WAIF/3/1/1/1. 375/EMT.

125. Oman, introduction to *An Outline*. With around one hundred contributors, these volumes attempted to address comprehensively the implications of Christianity up to the present.

has had to travel, to a point of view from which the whole can be surveyed," in all its complexity. But there remains the problem of authorial perspective, and the difficulty of maintaining an objective stance when much of what one is discussing is within one's own experience.

With this caveat, he lays his cards on the table. "I can make nothing of God's doings in the world on the hypothesis that His first purpose is a well-ordered household." If his intention was that the Church be "one visible corporation, infallibly taught and directed," then the Great Schism followed by the Reformation, had to be evidence that God was "a good enough general for a division or two, but of no use at handling an army."[126] The only escape from this is to see that God "requires also man's own discernment of what is true, his own love of the graces of life and the spirit, and his own decision and steadfast purpose in following righteousness and holiness." This may entail "exploring blind alleys of error to the end, and returning wiser and stronger from the enterprise" and Oman pushes his argument to deduce that "even the painful discipline of division may have the purpose of manifesting God's Church of his free children as a higher good than God's State for his submissive subjects." From this he derives two principles that would enable some assessment of religious history to be made, the first being the form of freedom, the necessity of independence, and the second, the substance of freedom, the fullness of God's purpose. And on this basis he discusses the differences between Catholicism and Protestantism, teasing out ways in which each tradition manifested the Church as an authoritarian state.[127] "As the means of imposing faith and duty have vanished," it became vitally important that authoritarianism be replaced by faith and conscientiousness.

A comparison of the Rationalist Movement with the Evangelical Revival revealed different forms of achieving freedom; independence in intellectual and moral judgments on the one hand and "insight and feeling and inward regeneration on the other." The "Rationalist form working in the Evangelical substance showed the whole scope of our freedom." Yet the Evangelical Movement spawned idiosyncratic sects, inimical to any idea of Church unity, and causing Roman Catholics to react by advocating "the Inquisition and the Index [as] the only benevolent protection of the faithful."

Oman now turns to the future and speculates as to what might be needed to achieve "fellowship in freedom." Although "we may still have many turnings on the path before us," he concludes that

---

126. Oman, introduction to *An Outline*, xv.

127. Calvinism, for instance, created free societies, yet this was "on the security of the doctrine of predestination."

the great movement of history towards the form as well as the substance of freedom is more than the doings of individuals, however much they may have influenced its course. That the world will ever again return to the old sacerdotal hierarchy to receive from it in pupilage its beliefs and directions is not even a reasonable dream, for there can be no question of such a harbour, if we have been launched on the wide ocean and cannot put back.

What is needed to replace this is another

> Catholicism of a heart large enough to embrace differences.... It is a tribal and not a Christian idea to demand that all be like ourselves before we can have fellowship with them. This Catholicism would regard the form of freedom as well as the substance. It would seek the fulness of the truth in Jesus Christ, even all the beauty and graciousness and service of his kingdom, but it would never forget that the distinctive quality of this kingdom is that we can only enter it as we ourselves choose it freely, and are in it made free.
>
> This Church Universal may seem a long way off. But a great deal has been done in these recent years to increase understanding and cooperation.... And, if we could learn to seek fellowship in freedom, if it do not give us ecclesiastical union, it may give us a unity of the spirit, which may be better.[128]

It may be indicative of Oman's search for something more apostolic that he accepted to write a chapter in the volume *Why I am and Why I am not a Catholic*,[129] the only Presbyterian among ten authors.[130] The editors are unknown, but the book was cleared by the magisterium for consumption by the general reader. Here he addresses his assigned subject, "The Roman Catholic Hierarchy," setting out his critique clearly but "without rancour or apology," and with the "strength, insight and sympathy"[131] of one who from his student days in the UP Hall, had learned to appreciate devout Roman Catholics as fellow members of the communion of saints. Affirming his belief "in the direct witness of truth and goodness" as against "the Roman claim to control faith and direct conscience"[132] Oman sets out a vision of

---

128. Oman, introduction to *An Outline*, xxii.

129. Oman, "Hierarchy."

130. A. Goodier, R. Knox, C. C. Martindale, Hilaire Belloc, Sheila Kaye-Smith, A. C. Headlam, A. E. Taylor, H. L. Goudge, W. E. Orchard.

131. *Review and Expositor*, 28 (1931) 83–84.

132. Oman, "Hierarchy," 240.

mutual recognition by Christians as followers of Christ, leading to authentic communion between them.

> That Jesus ever conceived of his Church as being one by political method or by any employment of physical force and visible authority is inconceivable. . . . The essential unity, therefore, is not by ecclesiastical supremacy, but by surmounting or even ignoring difference and regarding all faithful followers of Christ as our brethren. But if unity depends on this spirit, and not on outward forms, we must begin with it, and not wait until we have converted the pope or the pope converted us; and the Church Universal is not one organization, but one fellowship.[133]

One of Oman's fellow contributors is W. E. Orchard who describes himself as "[accepting] so much of the Roman Catholic position and yet [remaining] a non-Roman."[134] In his review of Orchard's book *The Present Crisis of Religion*, Oman acknowledges that his own emphasis on the priority of fellowship over doctrinal union might be considered to be "hopelessly vague."

> Yet the dawning light has always much chiaroscuro, and in it the promise lies, though this will not so appear to us unless it seems to us far more important that God Himself is seeking those who seek Him than the immediate form of their creed about Him. Moreover, we must think the purpose He has in events far more important than what man purposes.[135]

"The Prophet of Westminster"[136]

This is an appropriate point to consider briefly the designation of Oman by his students as "the prophet of Westminster," a man who, from time to time "uttered things which were hard to understand."

As we saw earlier,[137] he understood his calling to ministry in terms of the pre-Christian prophets, subscribing to the Romantic idea promoted by German scholars, notably Adolf von Harnack, that these were men of profound spiritual insight who communed with God and were often at odds with their

---

133. Oman, "Hierarchy," 248.

134. Orchard, "Why I Should Find It Difficult," 204. However, he did eventually become one!

135. Oman, review of Orchard, *The Present Crisis*.

136. Robson, *Our Professors*, 14–15.

137. Above, 75.

contemporaries. As individuals, they "could stand alone because of God's call and commission to their own hearts and consciences,"[138] enabling them to confront "political rulers" and "religious dignitaries" in "faith in a universal order of truth, righteousness and mercy, which should direct all men and be served by all."[139] Following the standard historical-critical assessment of the day that "the Hebrew prophets were the first true monotheists,"[140] Oman then defined that in his own way. "God's order is thus seen to depend on the relation of the individual soul to him.... By this sense of being directly taught of God, they could affirm the responsibility of each individual for his own conscience and opportunity."[141] This independence of thought aligns the prophet with the poet as a person of exceptional sensibility.

Writing in the shadow of the first World War in awareness of the potential for future catastrophe, Oman reflects: "It is possible that we are facing the same situation as the prophets, a moral laxity which saps the national vigour, a material greed which undermines social righteousness, an international menace which threatens chaos. We might even have to look forward, as they did, to the ultimate fall of our civilisation."[142] But he reminds his readers:

> The prophets did not say: Ask for the old paths, but seek the right way and walk therein . . . they looked forward to the day when no one should need to say to his brother, know the Lord, for all should know Him, and when there would need to be no outward authority, for God would write his law in men's hearts. This high hope it was which gave them faith to believe that even the worst calamities could be blessings. That day may still seem far away, but is it not in this faith that we should work and hope?[143]

Oman came to see that the particular locus for the revelation of God's meaning and purpose was "the holy remnant," those who themselves incarnated the prophetic message. With Skinner,[144] Oman points forward from the prophet to the remnant to Christ and then to "his immediate followers who through Him also lived in this prophetic order, as appears from the

---

138. Oman, *Natural and Supernatural*, 450. See Oman, "Individual"; Oman, *Faith and Freedom*, 415.

139. Oman, *Natural and Supernatural*, 451.

140. Oman, *Natural and Supernatural*, 448; cf. Houston, "Prophecy and Religion Revisited."

141. Oman, *Natural and Supernatural*, 450; Oman, "Individual."

142. Oman, review of Orchard, *The Present Crisis*.

143. Oman, review of Orchard, *The Present Crisis*.

144. Skinner, *Prophecy and Religion*, 224.

emphasis they place on a right relation to God by faith in his meaning and purpose."[145]

Oman articulated a theology of the remnant based on appreciation of students he met not only in Cambridge and Oxford, but also at meetings of the Presbyterian Students' Fellowship and at SCM conferences. The SCM, described by the *Presbyterian Messenger* in 1915 as "one of the greatest missionary agencies in the world," was "one of the great movements of the Spirit of God in our time" giving "new hope for the coming of the Kingdom of Christ."[146] Oman remarks:

> No doubt [these] are the most thoughtful and the most religious, but they are of all kinds, pursuing a great variety of studies.... Whatever evil the war has done, it has left the new generation with more courage, not only to live their lives, but to stake them on higher interests. And I am greatly impressed by their sincere purpose to know what is true and to do what is right. They may not be a very large company, but the influence which leavens the world has always been from the few, and one cannot be in contact with them without feeling that they may be prophets of a better day.[147]

Oman appears to have seen these young people as a contemporary incarnation of Isaiah's "holy remnant." The meaning of Isaiah's remnant was increasingly debated by scholars: Skinner, in his *Commentary on Isaiah*,[148] takes the view that here we have the ideal Israel as opposed to the Israel of experience. Oman, however, saw the "holy seed" in empirical terms as having the potential to bring new life to the world. He was clear that those "who themselves incarnated the prophetic message . . . might be a very few, but, as there was no condition except the recognition of the truth itself, their fellowship was, in principle, universal." They revealed "faith in a universal order of truth, righteousness and mercy, which should direct all men and be served by all."[149]

He expands on the theme in a sermon entitled "A Dying Civilisation," where he states: "As of old, salvation can only come through the holy

---

145. Oman, *Natural and Supernatural*, 447.
146. Scott, "The SCM."
147. Oman, review of Orchard, *The Present Crisis*.
148. Skinner, *Isaiah 1–39*; Skinner, *Isaiah 40–66*.
149. Oman, *Natural and Supernatural*, 451. In *Vision and Authority*, Oman saw the prophetic task as demonstrating that our environment is reasonable, just and good, reflecting the unity of God. But in 1902 this calm vision was as yet untested. Oman, *Vision and Authority*, 78.

remnant. To it we belong as we do not bow the knee to the Baal of worldly success and lust of pleasure or power, but worship the Father in spirit and in truth by reverencing only what is spiritual and true."[150]

> Our first task is to save what we can of our present world by the call to sincere penitence and simple faith.... Then our value for rebuilding our waste civilisation to the true glory of God and the real good of man will depend ... in our unfaltering faith that God does not fail and is not discouraged, and in our possession of the prophetic vision which sees through all the night of darkness and distress "the new heavens and the new earth wherein dwelleth righteousness."[151]

Murtle Lecture

In his Murtle lecture at the University of Aberdeen, Oman returns to the theme, defining the remnant in terms of "the early doctrine of the Church"[152] as being both redeemed and redeeming, following their Lord in seeking and saving the lost. Denounced in a material world as dreamers who hold back progress, and faced with vehement denials that the final order of the world is freedom, the remnant is "in a very practical sense already in the Kingdom of God."[153] It is right, he maintains, "to cherish the hope that our civilisation will gradually regenerate itself, and to work to this end, as the prophets did in their time."[154] But this is also to acknowledge from historical experience, that such regeneration is normally achieved by way of catastrophe. How then can the remnant fulfil their task of redeeming "the world into this one and only secure Rule"?[155] Not by "labouring to build a better world by violent reforms and rigid organisations"[156] for this is to expect that "the kingdoms of the world may be theirs, if they will fall down and worship its ideal of greatness and its way of might," but by being

---

150. Oman, *Paradox of the World*, 28.
151. Oman, *Paradox of the World*, 29.
152. Oman, "In Spirit and in Truth."
153. Oman, "In Spirit and in Truth," 285.
154. Oman, "In Spirit and in Truth," 290.
155. Oman, "In Spirit and in Truth," 290.
156. Oman, "In Spirit and in Truth," 290. There may be an indirect reference here to Calvin's Geneva. For Calvin too saints were responsible for their world and for its continual reformation. But the saints of Geneva were a tightly disciplined group subject to social enforcement in God's name. They were not, in Oman's terms, free.

reconciled to God in the duty He requires, as well as in the discipline we have to undergo. Yet this duty is neither for the end we see or the powers we can apply but for an end beyond our seeing and by might beyond our working, in which righteousness, and not human schemes and prudences, is our guide. There is a widespread belief, as in earlier time, that our present form of civilisation is passing. There may be some vagueness about what the new order to which the old is to yield is to be. One thing, however, is clear. It is man not God who is to fulfil himself in many ways. It is the old story, the bricks have fallen, but we will build again with hewn stones.[157]

The calling is ethical, with a nod to Schweitzer's interim ethic, "it is not being in accord with any order that exists, but for one that ought to be."[158] Yet Oman leaves his hearers in no doubt that "to be in Christ is not the almost material mystical thing Schweitzer makes it, but to be in this spiritual order, is to be in a very practical sense already in the Kingdom of God."[159] The lecture strikes a note of optimism, already evident in Oman's New Year Message as moderator[160] that year.

We have won through, from the idea that the universe is a box of banging marbles, to the sense that it is so wonderful physically that it may well be still more wonderful spiritually. We have not yet settled all the historical questions about Scripture, but we are more ready to hear what it says to us now, whatever its origin. Few of us could give a rounded theory of Jesus Christ, but there is a much more practical and living sense that in Him we have to do with what may be vital both for our souls and our civilisation.

And this optimism extends also in some measure to the Church. During the war a large number of men turned aside from the ministry. Some of them I talked with: and I always got the same story. They believed that their religion was more real than before, but they had no longer any use for the church.

"Today" however, most of them realize the need of a "spiritual organisation" and see that

it is the members of the Churches who are found bearing the burden and the heat of the day in religious and social service,

---

157. Oman, "In Spirit and in Truth," 290.
158. Oman, "In Spirit and in Truth," 292.
159. Oman, "In Spirit and in Truth," 284. He draws attention to the Lord's Prayer as the best expression of this line of thought.
160. "The Moderator's New Year Message," *Presbyterian Messenger*, January 1932.

and with less thought of themselves or their place in it. And the younger generation are still more sympathetic. One mark is the greater number and different type of candidates for the ministry, for it follows a change which has taken place in the whole student community, a change of interest from the material to the spiritual, taking that word in a very wide sense. . . . There is still no lack of criticism of the Church, but it is because of the sense that a more spiritually effective society is the first of the world's needs. And among Churches, it is possible to speak hopefully of our own.

And he concludes: God's elect are "called in Christ for the fulfilment of His purpose, which is not merely a better but a new world. We know what a handful of poor people so inspired did in the Apostle's time: and there is no measuring what we could do, had we a like imagination."

To see this lecture against the background of the "rough words" with which Oman had in previous years castigated the Church in reports, speeches and writings, is to see a shift in emphasis from recrimination to encouragement, reinforced by the use of the inclusive first person plural. As Assembly moderator, the "prophetic word" he proclaims to the church is a vision of hope.

11

Moderator

Moderator

IN MAY 1931, THE *Presbyterian Messenger* affirmed that in the choice of Oman as its moderator designate the church had chosen "its most profound and massive thinker" and expressed pride in the fact that "the quality of a Church which has the good fortune to possess one ['a massive thinker'] can be justly assessed by the estimation in which it holds him."[1] The choice was all the more remarkable for the fact that Oman had on occasion shown himself to be such a fierce critic of the church which he served so faithfully. However, as N.L.R. states,

> John Oman has slowly but steadily grown into the confidence and affection of the Church. . . . He has never cared a straw about popularity. . . . He has always been content to declare truth and leave truth to do its own work; indeed, he would ask no higher dignity than to be a fellow-worker with the truth. Yet, in spite of this disregard of appearances and indifference to all that makes for popularity on his part, the Church is growing alive to the fact that in John Oman it has a great gift of God—that its college has as its Principal one, the value of whose penetrating thinking is recognised not only in Cambridge, but in the whole theological world, one, moreover, who is sending into the ministry of our

---

1. "The Moderator Designate," *Presbyterian Messenger*, May 1931.

Church men imbued with something of his own passion for the truth as it is in Jesus.[2]

Having chosen him in 1907 for the chair of Systematic Theology, and in 1922 as principal of the college,

> our Church has shown once and again that it can recognise weight of learning and weight of character, and all who love the Church will give thanks for this gift of discernment.... But while we sit at the feet of the thinker, we also admire and love the man.... He can make himself at home in any circle of men, a bunch of students round the fire, a circle of working people, a crowd of "Tommies" during the war. Pipe in mouth, he will be the centre of the circle, quite in his element.

His teaching

> deals sincerely and fearlessly with life as a whole. Men who have really got it in their bones can go out anywhere with it, to China, the East End of London, or a country charge, and find it essentially adequate to interpret experience and meet the needs of men.... The men who swear by Oman's theology swear by it as a theology whose keynote is reality.

Although Oman had suffered recently from a "grave illness [which] made the hearts of his friends tremble,"[3] he was now "restored to health and vigour again," and "when the assembly meets in May, all who know the new Moderator well, and, most of all, his old Westminster students, will gather with pride to hear again a truly prophetic word from their old friend and teacher."[4]

And so on the evening of 4 May 1931, we may imagine that we are seated with more than 700 delegates in Egremont church, Wallasey, a fine

---

2. "The Moderator Designate," *Presbyterian Messenger*, May 1931.

3. There is no indication as to the nature of Oman's illness. Up to then, he seems generally to have enjoyed robust good health apart from occasional colds with loss of voice. He records how he was once reduced to using a typewriter "having sprained [his] thumb diving in shallower water than [he] expected." Oman, *Concerning the Ministry*, 185. When in 1907 he "preached with considerable energy" at his final service at Clayport, he was "just recovering from a trying operation." "The Departure of Dr Oman from Alnwick," Northumberland Archives UR/p28/2/1/2/3. And in 1929, he "was taken ill while preaching at Penrith Presbyterian Church on Sunday (he preached in the morning and the afternoon though obviously ill)—and was sent to a Carlisle nursing home in a motor ambulance and operated on for appendicitis." Press clipping, 11 July 1929, Westminster College Archives.

4. "The Moderator Designate," *Presbyterian Messenger*, May 1931.

mixture of Arts and Crafts and Gothic Revival in style, and sizeable.[5] Facing us is the communion table with the pulpit on the left and the font to the right. The moderator is seated at the table in his robes of office, flanked by two assistants. There are two other tables, one occupied by the clerk of assembly "almost hidden behind an array of tomes and documents, which produce a feeling akin to awe,"[6] the other for the chair of the business committee. Dr. Lewis Robertson, retiring moderator, conducts opening worship, and then with acclaim, Principal Oman is escorted to the chair where he is received by Dr. Robertson in the name of the assembly. He then ascends the pulpit to give his moderatorial address.

His theme, "The Westminster Confession of Faith"[7] was a bold choice. Not only was this intimately associated with his theology of grace, a bone of contention for religious conservatives, but subscription to the Confession by ministers and elders had been the subject of unresolved debate in the PCE from 1883 onwards.[8] Predictably Oman's address was to rouse the ire of the Bible Standards League who were preparing to challenge him on his moderatorial visit to the PCI General Assembly the following month.[9] But on that occasion, when Oman spoke on behalf of the corresponding members[10] of the PCE, it was about the supply of ministry and the role of Presbyterians in furthering church reunion, and the assembly moderator gave a warm vote of thanks, concluding that "they felt glad as a church to have the presence of Principal Oman, and asked him to carry to the Church in England their good wishes and a message of their esteem."[11]

In his moderatorial address, Oman gets to the root of the matter immediately: whereas the Confession "plentifully corrects what it takes to be error . . . it cannot be said to have stopped controversy, wrought unity, or been the simplest vehicle of the Christian faith to the young and ignorant."

5. In 1908 when it was opened for worship, it was the largest Presbyterian church in England.

6. "The Assembly Day by Day," *Presbyterian Messenger*, 4 May 1931, 34. Oman's prefatory remark that he "had never refused to do anything the church has asked of [him]" is, strictly speaking, incorrect. Three times, in 1908, 1913 and 1928, he had turned down nomination to the eldership of St Columba's Cambridge, because "he felt that he could not do justice to the office along with his other duties." Knox, *St. Columba's Church Cambridge*, 19.

7. "The Moderator's Address," *Presbyterian Messenger*, June 1931, 48–50. (chapter 5)

8. Above, 141–42

9. *Belfast Newsletter*, 27 May 1931.

10. Members of a sister church who are guests of the Assembly without voting rights.

11. *Belfast Newsletter*, 3 June 1931.

But, given "that our faith is in God, not man . . . the question is, whether it is really the substance or only the form with which there is disagreement." There are few documents, he suggests, where these two are more in conflict. The Confession appears to have been taken over from the Roman Catholic church, but without the authority of infallibility. In consequence, things are falling apart: discipline is no longer upheld by minister or magistrate; no working of God in the individual is expected to keep the faith uniform or the fellowship one, and the Bible as the ground of all authority is subject to the same criticism as other books. "If a mechanically guaranteed authority is the true foundation of faith, we are all alike fighting a losing cause."

Yet there is another way. "We have to work out our freedom through the old forms, and until we have done so, we do not see that the forms are old." And accordingly Oman tells the parable of the Prodigal Son in terms of these forms. The point is well made. But while the forms are outdated, "the change wrought by this true evangelical faith is constantly in evidence." It is to be regulated by "Christian wisdom and regard to the situation." And Oman comments dryly: "This may be inconsistent with much of the doctrine of election but inconsistency is often to be counted for righteousness." Because salvation is not prescribed in detail, "we have a new evangelical freedom. The really great religious parts of the Confession, are concerned with faith, repentance, prayer, joy and peace. The fundamental truth is that God was in Christ reconciling the world to Himself, and our abiding commission is to beseech men in Christ's stead to be reconciled." So we live in the fellowship of the family of God.

The inescapable conclusion is that "this means an end of the old forms of the doctrine. A personal relation in which God cannot make known His truth till man sees it, or give his grace till man receives it, or fulfil His will in earth as in heaven till it is done from the heart, is an end to the old forms. But do we find the true substance?"

The challenge is to recognize that faith comes from the revelation of God's love. "By our reconciliation to God as His children, the sovereignty of God is no longer a concern of predetermination of anything." The last word is still "our hope and confidence in God's working and not man's striving." As to the covenant of grace, mechanical as it might seem, "we stand in intimate relation to our human heritage of good and ill; we have a task of handing on a better heritage." "There is something here far deeper and truer than the cheap, emotional, purely individualistic evangelism which has often taken its place." And he closes his address with a description of the church as "the fellowship of those who are one in the Father through Jesus Christ, and for the advancement of His rule in exalting all human beings to the fullness of the Divine purpose."

At the close of business, Oman expressed "his sense of the extraordinary buoyancy of spirit with which the Church is facing the difficulties of the present conditions" and personal gratitude to his six chaplains, an unusually large number, but who reflected in their persons the range of the PCE.[12]

In brief, Henry Martin, minister of St Andrew's Upper Norwood, had "spent part of his life in a shipping office as a Clerk dreaming of the days when he might become a minister." James Scott, minister of St James Alnwick, was "a licentiate of the Irish Presbyterian Church." George Burnet and David Brown were alumni of New College, Edinburgh. Burnet was recently inducted to St Stephen's Leicester, while Brown was serving at Fisher Street, Carlisle. The remaining two had been students of Oman at Westminster; Kenneth Keay went to France with the YMCA in 1915, was licensed while on active service with the Cameronians the following year, and in 1931 was ministering in Huddersfield. Lewis MacLachlan, a stalwart pacifist of the Fellowship of Reconciliation, was ordained for missionary work at Changpu, an area of huge social deprivation in North China. By 1931 he was a popular minister in Southend, from where he was shortly to move to Byker, which was described as "one of the hardest jobs in the Newcastle Presbytery."

And so, as Assembly came to an end, blessed by the singing of the last three verses of Psalm 122, the congregation filed past Oman "to receive and give the right hand of fellowship, symbolic of our unity, goodwill, and affection."[13]

During his moderatorial year, Oman had a full programme. He preached in many congregations, he attended the General Assemblies of the Church of Scotland in May and the PCI in June. There was the meeting of the Newcastle Presbytery in July, and in October, at the opening of the new church of St Columba in Coventry, he preached and Mary opened the door with a silver key. In a representative capacity he signed in June a call to prayer for the success of the World Disarmament Conference, and he accepted nomination as one of six vice-presidents of the Boys Brigade.

He might have envisaged retiring as principal in 1931 on reaching the statutory age limit, but the previous Assembly had unanimously decided that he should be reappointed for another year. The convenor of the College Committee said "the prestige of the College, which was never higher than it was now, was very largely due to the reputation, character, and scholarship

---

12. For details see Fasti records, Westminster College archives.
13. *Presbyterian Messenger*, May 1931, 45.

of its distinguished Principal," and the "whole heart of the Church and the gratitude of the Church" supported the recommendation.[14]

As retiring moderator Oman responded to a vote of thanks during the opening session of the 1932 Assembly. He had got through the year, he said, by remembering the advice of an old friend, "Be not Moderator overmuch." He "was less discouraged than he expected to be by the difficulties of the things seen and temporal, but declared that they drove him back to the realities of the unseen and the eternal." And he mentioned that the call to be moderator had come when he was "in the midst of preparing a book 'not sprightly, but laborious.'"[15]

The Natural and the Supernatural[16]

"This is a remarkable book. It is not easy to review. It is at once so comprehensive and so original. It is impossible in the space of a review to reproduce the main argument, and yet the book will not go into any pigeon-hole. It is the most original and illuminating philosophical book I have read for a long while."[17] There was widespread agreement with A. D. Lindsay's estimate of Oman's "great book"[18] although "some prospective readers have over-hastily assumed that the book had something to do with 'spiritualism.'"[19]

It had been many years in gestation, covering the span of Oman's university lectureships in philosophy of religion, supplemented by his own wide reading and the books in French and German as well as English which he reviewed for the *Journal of Theological Studies*. In an appendix on "The Holy" he gives a rare account of how these typically influenced his thought processes.[20] A general interest in the relationship between the awesome and the moral in religion had drawn his attention to the views of Kattenbusch on the Christian creeds, which he discusses in *The Church and the Divine Order*.[21] Shortly after, he read the essay by Wilhelm Windelband,

14. *Orkney Herald*, 14 May 1930. The resolution was reaffirmed twice until he finally retired in 1935.

15. *Presbyterian Messenger*, May 1932, 34. The preface to *The Natural and the Supernatural* is dated May 1931.

16. Oman, *Natural and Supernatural*, published simultaneously in Britain and the USA. See Healey, *Religion and Reality*, 12.

17. Lindsay, review of Oman, *Natural and Supernatural*.

18. "Principal Oman's Great Book," by an old student, *Presbyterian Messenger*, January 1932.

19. Knox, review of Healey, "Religion and Reality."

20. Oman, *Natural and Supernatural*, appendix A, 474.

21. Kattenbusch, *Das Apostolische Symbol*; Oman, *Church and Divine Order*, 121–23.

"Das Heilige,"[22] which reformulated Kant's transcendental approach into a philosophy of values and prompted Oman to articulate in his University lectures his own differences from the theses that were being promoted. Finally, soon after the war, he read *Das Heilige* by Rudolf Otto, which, when translated, he reviewed at length in the *Journal of Theological Studies*.[23] "I learned better," he comments, "though mainly by disagreeing with him, both how to distinguish and to relate the awesome and the ethical, the material and the spiritual."[24]

In general Oman tends to dispense with references. "I should willingly acknowledge my obligations were it possible after a somewhat extended life spent in reading and thinking on the subject; . . . to attempt to distinguish what I might claim as my own from what is due to the suggestions of others would at this time of day be a hopeless task."[25] He wishes too to avoid the tendency of specialists in religion as elsewhere, to be dull. "Religion is every man's business and nothing human should be alien to it. For the study of religion, therefore, to blear one's eyes with the dust of books may be a dehumanising process of a specially disqualifying kind."[26] George Grant observes additionally how easily a thinker can be turned into "a slave of his inheritance. In Oman's case such a danger must be avoided at all costs. For there is in him that prophetic autonomy which transcends inheritance and moulds it by judging it."[27]

He is, to quote the Hegelian scholar, T. M. Knox, "a master of style. Very few philosophers in the last thirty years in this country have been able to write so well."[28] His illustrations are particularly memorable. As an example I need only cite his unforgettable distinction between awareness, apprehension, comprehension and explanation, by the perception "when walking in a dreamy mood along a country road"[29] of a man riding a bicycle.

Scope and Method

Oman chisels out his quest for truth with profound and fearless rigor, leaving the reader with a remarkable impression of intellectual range and power.

22. Windelband, "Das Heilige."
23. Oman, review of Otto, *The Idea of the Holy*.
24. Oman, *Natural and Supernatural*, 474.
25. Oman, *Natural and Supernatural*, v.
26. Oman, *Natural and Supernatural*, 12.
27. Grant, *Concept*, 178.
28. Knox, review of *Religion and Reality*.
29. Oman, *Natural and Supernatural*, 120–23.

Over 500 pages of sometimes very abstract thought, he charts our human response to an environment in which the Natural and the Supernatural are inseparably blended, one being incomplete without the other. He is able to meet on their own terms "those who deny the existence of any other environment than the natural" with "a large-minded appreciation of any genuine contribution they have made" and "a deadly penetration into the limitations under which they labour."[30] He is dismissive of what he calls "bad religion," marked by moral and intellectual insincerity. Sincerity of feeling is "'the only gateway to reality'" and, as his old student recognizes, "it is in a supremely high degree the quality that distinguishes this book."[31]

This is primarily a philosophy of religion. Oman's whole argument assumes in his reader some sense of a supernatural environment and he makes no attempt to prove the reality of this on non-religious grounds. He assumes also that life holds absolute values and that to shun these is to reject all that is human. His enquiry is divided into four main sections, with ten appendices. In part one, he outlines the scope and method of his exploration: "As our study concerns the Natural as well as the Supernatural, no problem life raises may be totally ignored."[32] He settles for three significant areas of enquiry, and these form the substance of the remaining three sections.

He defines his terms. The Supernatural in this context is understood to be "the world which manifests more than natural values, the world which has values which stir the sense of the holy and demand to be esteemed as sacred."[33] And he continues: "the question is not that it exists, but how it exists in its relation to us and our relation to it."[34] In this context, his distinction between our experience of "the holy" and "the sacred" is particularly illuminating. On the premise that the "holy" is "the direct sense or feeling of the Supernatural"[35] and the "sacred," "its valuation as of absolute worth" he takes Rudolf Otto as his conversation partner, elaborating on his own previous study of "The Idea of the Holy."[36]

---

30. Knox, review of *Religion and Reality*.

31. "Principal Oman's Great Book," by an old student, *Presbyterian Messenger*, January 1932.

32. Oman, *Natural and Supernatural*, 110.

33. Oman, *Natural and Supernatural*, 71.

34. Oman, *Natural and Supernatural*, 72.

35. Oman, *Natural and Supernatural*, 59.

36. Oman, review of Otto, "The Idea of the Holy."

Knowing and Knowledge

In part II, Oman addresses the question "how do we know this supernatural reality?" He begins "with the largest problem, the question of our whole world and our whole experience, or in other words the problem of mind and environment, or, in technical language, of Knowing and Being." This section still impresses by its originality.

For A. D. Lindsay, Oman's account is "far the best account of Knowing I have ever read. He distinguishes four types of Knowing: awareness, apprehension, comprehension, explanation. The originality of what he has to say lies mainly in his description of the first two types, consistently neglected by philosophers who are themselves so taken up with comprehension and explanation that they simply cannot see the other forms."[37]

Yet, as Oman shows, all of these are involved in knowing. He is not content with clarifying the distinction between different processes of reasoning, explanation and comprehension on the one hand and awareness and apprehension on the other; he accomplishes the major feat of bringing them together. Following a careful analysis of Kant's distinction between the discursive and the intuitive and Hegel's dissatisfaction with such dualism, he considers Schleiermacher's "religion of aesthetic mysticism," and argues that knowledge includes intelligence, will and feeling. He is well aware, however, that theories of perception are "often the merest dry bones of what we know by perceiving" and that "one of the impoverishments of religion has been that its world is not sufficiently the poet's world, but one seen too much with eyes bleared and blinkered by theory." The poet or the child knows in a different way from the typical scientist or philosopher. Oman takes Shakespeare as the prime illustration of the poet who "works so entirely with perception, and expresses everything in forms of awareness and apprehension, he can make the common simple person see and feel what the thinker could not make him even understand."[38] In this context, his description of the poet's gifts of perception and those of the child are particularly telling.[39] His evocation of a child's direct apprehension of reality and the kind of "aesthetic knowledge" which results in a sure apprehension of other minds are memorable.[40] So too is his allusion to landscape in personal terms as

---

37. Lindsay, review of Oman, *Natural and Supernatural*.
38. Oman, *Natural and Supernatural*, 129.
39. See chapter 1.
40. Oman, *Natural and Supernatural*, 113.

a friend,[41] while his illustration of a child's experience of infinity[42] is an unforgettable expression of a personal apprehension of time and space.

Oman argues that knowledge of the supernatural environment is by "direct, unmediated intuition."[43] Like Schleiermacher, he often names this intuition, "feeling." According to F. R. Tennant, even psychologists who might dispute the validity of Oman's premises could not fail to see in the elaborately constructed argument presented in *The Natural and the Supernatural* "the signs of first-hand observation, reflection and synthesis such as prove its author to be one of the most original, independent, and impressive theologians of his generation and of his country."[44]

Necessity and Freedom

This section is in Tennant's eyes, "the most valuable part of the book."[45] It is particularly significant for ethics.[46] The concepts of necessity and freedom had been at the core of much of Oman's work to date and "though they have been more sharply divided than the two aspects of our last problem"[47] he succeeds finally in reconciling them. It is impossible to give this issue sustained attention without giving some consideration to the relationship of Science and Religion; and at the time Oman wrote this was notably the case, for the Theory of Relativity, Quantum Theory and the Theory of Evolution had altered dramatically people's views of the world. Oman had already begun to write on the topic. In 1922, he contributed five articles to the *Student Movement*, which contain the germ of his later work,[48] and three years later, along with nine other distinguished contributors from a variety of disciplines,[49] he contributed a chapter to *Science, Religion and Reality*, edited by Joseph Needham.[50] Needham was motivated by the philosopher R. G. Collingwood's sense that overspecialization would hold back scientific

41. Oman, *Natural and Supernatural*, 135.
42. Oman, *Natural and Supernatural*, 136.
43. Tennant, "John Wood Oman," 334.
44. Tennant, "John Wood Oman," 335.
45. Tennant, review of Oman, *Natural and Supernatural*.
46. Knox, review of *Religion and Reality*.
47. Oman, *Natural and Supernatural*, 218.
48. Oman, articles in the *Student Movement*.
49. It would be reasonable to suppose that the contribution of his fellow author, Bronislaw Malinowski, stimulated Oman's thought on "religions" which had already been aroused during his time at Woodbrooke.
50. Oman, "The Sphere of Religion."

progress[51] and by his argument that one could only become a "perfectly rounded character" by having some experience of religion, science, history, philosophy, and artistic creation, and the collection of essays was intended to facilitate this. This is entirely in tune with Oman's holistic approach. John MacLeod writes:

> Oman had at one point a high respect for Rationalism, insofar as Rationalism meant respect for the spirit of inquiry, willingness to be open to the voice of the actual, humility to wait for reality's witness. . . . Religion claims to deal with a real world, therefore it must never be else than open, hospitable to investigation. But now, continues Oman, the bane of the rationalistic mind is that it would measure every kind of reality in terms of one witness-pattern. Indeed, as he argues in his great chapter on Awareness in *The Natural and the Supernatural*, naturalism however intellectual has only part of natural fact.[52]

Oman shows an easy familiarity with the two major twentieth-century transformations in physics: Einstein's theory of relativity and quantum theory. With these, Newton's framework of matter and impact, which had for nearly two centuries provided fixity and intellectual guidance to science, were outgrown. Although "all this the non-mathematical inquirer only sees in a glass darkly,"[53] Oman argues persuasively that from then on the impulse to fresh departures in theoretical physics could only come from the facts of experience, which is "always new." It is in experience that meaning is revealed and, in meaning, the Supernatural.

Then there was the explosive impact of *The Origin of Species*. Five years after the cause célèbre of the "evolution trial" in Tennessee, Oman devotes two chapters to an exploration of the theory of evolution, showing the inadequacy of a purely naturalistic account of the evolution of human life and questioning the popular theory that what we have here is "the result of endless throws of blind chance, out of which selection is made by some equally blind principle of survival."[54] Responding to a skepticism which asks whether we can ever know the reality behind appearances, he distinguishes Darwin from Darwinism, seeing the originality of Darwin's account in the theory of variation and the elimination of the unfit through the will to live of the living creature. "In this insistence on the development of the

---

51. Whitworth, *Einstein's Wake*, 32. While Collingwood rejected the label "Idealist" there is a resemblance here to the views of Edward Caird. (See above, 64-65.)

52. MacLeod, "John Oman as Theologian."

53. Oman, *Natural and Supernatural*, 249.

54. Oman, article in the *Student Movement*, "The Evolutionary Historical Process."

individual frontier in the struggle for survival, Darwin has made a great contribution to our view of the universe but it is in the direction of freedom and not of process."

Accordingly, once we get away from the idea of process, we see the vital importance of what is individual in real progress. And so evolution raises the issue of evil; "the victory of freedom has such appalling casualties" that it is "hard to see how it could ever compensate for the loss and pain and evil which it at least allows, if it does not cause."[55] Oman does not evade the issue. And he responds in terms of moral choice: "However we may explain it, we can only live rightly in the Supernatural by a character won by a freedom which is free to be false and base and corrupt as well as true and gracious and good."[56] With a passing allusion to Calvin's predestinarianism being "as ghastly as it is dull,"[57] he affirms that what is at stake is "a failure to be worthy of our highest environment" which may be described as "sin." This is more than just transgression; it is radical evil. In the spiritual and physical environment, there are potentially dangerous choices to be made. But "what we ought to be never presents itself as something we merely ourselves manufacture, but is always there waiting to be realised."[58] That highest environment is "the perpetual challenge in front which makes evolution possible."[59]

> Whether we consider the matter positively or negatively, therefore, we see that, if we are to speak of evolution as organic, whether we conceive this as physical or metaphysical, it is not just development of a structure out of a universe which is merely a potency behind it, but that the emphasis is on function with a challenge before it. The vital significance is the relation of the individual to environment, as freedom in respect of the Supernatural as much as of the Natural.[60]

It has been suggested that Oman was not rigorous enough in attacking the skeptics, that a certain ambiguity in his ground work resulted from a failure to analyze his concepts; he "takes his reader straight into his brilliant use

---

55. Oman, *Natural and Supernatural*, 290.

56. Oman, *Natural and Supernatural*, 291. This is part of the approach later developed by John Hick in *Evil and the God of Love*. He writes: "Again and again I find in re-reading Oman that I have been following his footsteps."

57. Oman, *Natural and Supernatural*, 290. Hick, "A Voyage," 166.

58. Oman, *Natural and Supernatural*, 294.

59. Oman, *Natural and Supernatural*, 294.

60. Oman, *Natural and Supernatural*, 297.

of them."[61] However, Oman is not concerned in the *Natural and the Supernatural* with a systematic clarification of his own position. His approach is by means of what Farmer calls "exploratory validation."[62] What he says emerges slowly from a preliminary rejection of a multitude of errors. To quote George Grant again, "often what he himself asserts is described in a few cryptic sentences after a detailed and lucid criticism of other positions. ... *The Natural and the Supernatural* must be considered a classic condemnation and refutation of these fallacies."[63]

The Evanescent and the Eternal

In the fourth part of the book, the knowledge of the Supernatural in experience points to a world order that is "in some true sense personal."[64] A world which matters and in which we too matter. Oman decides "to use the religions because they are the concrete and illuminating presentation of the problems"[65] he is working with, in particular the relation of the Natural and the Supernatural. Oman argues that religion is presupposed in natural knowledge and is determinative of the progress of human culture. And in this respect "what we might too easily call the savage state compares favourably with the highest civilisation. There are baser and more degrading civilised idolatries than fetishism; there are among us economic injustices more unjust and in the end more brutal than among the head-hunters; savage promiscuity is not as vile a market of human beings as civilised prostitution."[66] He classifies "the religions" according to their attitudes towards the natural and their conceptions of the supernatural.

> To this central significance for any faith in the Supernatural in the way it is won and held in the face of the natural the whole history of the religions bears witness. Nor does it concern merely the manner in which the Natural and Supernatural are related, because the way they are distinguished is equally characteristic. When the Supernatural is merged in the Natural we have idolatry; when the Natural is submerged in the Supernatural, we have pantheism; when they are set sharply apart, we have deism;

61. Grant, *Concept*, 169.
62. Farmer, "Theologians of Our Time."
63. Grant, *Concept*, 195–96.
64. Oman, *Natural and Supernatural*, 340–41; Bevans, *John Oman*, 76–81; Langford, "Theological Methodology," 232–34.
65. Oman, *Natural and Supernatural*, v.
66. Oman, *Natural and Supernatural*, 359.

when they are related by some kind of moral victory, we have at least some kind of theism.

While George Grant argues that there is a danger that Oman's demonstration would, for some readers, minimize his reaction against secular rationalism, leaving him exposed unfairly to accusations of having rationalist pretensions,[67] this may be seen in the words of John Hick, as "one of the first attempts by a major Christian theologian to take systematic account of other world religions, with Oman's division into the primitive, the polytheistic, the mystical, the ceremonial-legal, and the prophetic."[68] Acknowledging that there are inadequacies in Oman's account of Buddhism, Hick concedes that "less was known about Buddhism in the West in Oman's time than today."[69]

In the final section of part IV, dealing with "The Prophetic," Oman begins "in the assurance that the world is all God's by reconciliation to his meaning in it and his purpose beyond it. This is what is meant here by a religion of reconciliation, which is also prophetic religion."[70] He elaborates at some length on what he means here, concluding that the prophets

> were able to face physical evil as real and terrible, and moral evil as calamitous and perverse, and yet say that, by his own meaning in them and his purpose beyond them, the Lord God omnipotent reigneth. This confidence that no evil could hinder life from being one moral sphere, and experience from being one triumph of faith, was the essential victory of the prophetic monotheism, and is the sole ground still of any real confidence of one God being in all and above all.[71]

He devotes several pages to prophetic witness in hope to the righteous order of the world, "the foundation for the faith to which Jesus gave the final expression, that God is not the God of the dead but of the living."[72] And this leads him to develop an interpretation of the hope of personal immortality, "a hope which includes the concrete individual with all the experience and

---

67. Grant, *Concept*, 175.
68. Hick, "A Voyage."
69. Hick, "A Voyage," 166. A more nuanced account of Hinduism may have resulted from Oman's personal contacts in Birmingham with C. F. Andrews and H. G. Wood, and his daughter Jean's close friendship while an "out-student" of Newnham College with Marjorie Sykes, the future biographer of Rabindranath Tagore. Dart, *Marjorie Sykes*.
70. Oman, *Natural and Supernatural*, 447.
71. Oman, *Natural and Supernatural*, 449.
72. Oman, *Natural and Supernatural*, 463.

character which has become truly himself. . . . This hope was not won by meditation on another life, but by proving in this life that the victory over necessity is freedom and the spirit that is made free, and that the reality of the evanescent is the revelation of things eternal as the spirit's inalienable and abiding possession."[73] In other words, "God's final order in the future [is] continuous with its realisation in the present."[74]

So he returns to the motif which permeates his theological work. For where we truly experience freedom, we experience God, God who respects our freedom like the prodigal's father, patiently waiting till we come to ourselves and ready to welcome us home. And he sums up his argument as follows:

> If we would have any content in the eternal, it is from dealing whole-heartedly with the evanescent; if we would have any content in freedom it is by victory both without and within over the necessary; if we would have any content in mind and spirit we must know aright by valuing aright. If so, religion must be a large experience in which we grow in knowledge as we grow in humility and courage, in which we deal with life and not abstractions, and with God as the environment in which we live and move and have our being and not as an ecclesiastical formula. This we realise, as environment is only to be realised, by rightly living in it. . . . Denying the world does not mean that we do not possess it in courageous use of all possibilities, but only that we do not allow it to possess us.[75]

An "old student," presumably then engaged in active ministry, forestalls any charges of irrelevance:

> It may seem a far cry from the metaphysical profundities of this volume to the Gospel that our congregations gather Sunday by Sunday to hear, and which it is our task to preach. But, as Dr. Oman has himself reminded us elsewhere, those who deal in the current coin of religious truth are dependent in the last issue on the delvers who penetrate into the deep mines where the ore is quarried amid stress of thought as well as action, and face to face with the conflicting ideas of philosophy and science. It is in the interests of truth and of the religion which has at its centre a God of Truth that Dr. Oman has girt himself to this his greatest task, bringing to it all those resources of exact knowledge,

---

73. Oman, *Natural and Supernatural*, 465.
74. Oman, *Natural and Supernatural*, 466.
75. Oman, *Natural and Supernatural*, 471.

penetrating insight, spiritual judgment, and broad sympathetic humanity with which we knew him to be so richly gifted.[76]

Poetic Intelligence

Oman had been thinking about the relationship between prophecy and religion long before the publication of *The Natural and the Supernatural*. And it is instructive to see how he had already expressed particular interest in the ways prophetic insight is apprehended and articulated with poetic intelligence. In his inaugural address as principal, he had challenged the church to articulate more faithfully the language of imagination in speaking of God. Religion "alone reaches out to what eye hath not seen and ear not heard, as it were to life's poetry and prophecy. Religion believes that the world, except as the possibility of this, is without meaning."[77] And he continues:

> Theology, as the study of religion ought, therefore, to be of the nature of prophecy. As its interest is the goal, it necessarily works on the frontiers of intuition and anticipation; and it asks what relation to the present reality best manifests what is beyond it.[78]

It is unsurprising, perhaps, that around the same time, he should have been drawn to considering the Revelation of St. John, for no book in the Bible uses symbolic language and imagery to the same extent to convey prophetic insight. Additionally, as George Caird observes,[79] "if we make adequate allowance for vast technological change, the times John lived in were astonishingly like our own." If we were able to hear what the Spirit was saying to the churches at the end of the first century AD, we might "be the better able to hear what the Spirit is saying to the churches of our own day."

It was this that motivated Oman, at a time when he must already have been contemplating his *magnum opus*, to launch into Biblical criticism.[80] He had been attending Professor Burkitt's university seminar on the Apocalypse, "not," as he says, "through any particular interest in the subject, but to a vague idea that, to think about religion, without knowing a little about its documents, is not much more use than to be a pundit on

---

76. "Principal Oman's Great Book," by an old student, *Presbyterian Messenger*, January 1932.
77. Oman, "Method in Theology," 91.
78. Oman, "Method in Theology," 91.
79. Caird, *Revelation*, v.
80. Oman, *Book of Revelation*.

its documents, without doing a little thinking about religion."[81] He was faced with a challenge: no method of interpretation to date appeared to give the text any reasonable meaning. "This did not increase my interest in the book," he comments, "but it stirred my antagonism to being baffled by a problem: so, having some leisure in a Christmas vacation, I set myself to a serious reading of the original."[82]

Revelation is indeed a puzzling book. The writer of a review of Oman's commentary in the *British Weekly* mused in 1924 that "the rocks of Patmos have sunk the ships of many adventurers."[83] Interpreters have, over the years, tried to find meaning in its structure, but whereas in some chapters the structure seems quite clear, in others there is apparent confusion.[84] Oman rose to the challenge. He had previously shown some interest in numerical systems in his detailed measurement of the Stones of Stenness where "in chains all the distances are multiples of seven . . . a sacred number in many nations from the earliest time."[85] The number seven featured regularly in the text of *Revelation*. So he began by examining the Greek texts for himself. He got to grips with the "vast erudition" of R. H. Charles.[86] And he accepted to a limited extent Charles's theory that the work of the original author had been revised by a bungling editor with barbarous Greek. The text, Oman thought, would be easier to interpret if he were able to screen out the editor's ideas. These appeared to be largely expressed in glosses. Once these were removed, however, Oman found that there was still some serious displacement of the text. So he re-arranged the book to make a more consecutive flow of thought. Then he made the discovery that the sections which it seemed necessary to rearrange were all of practically the same length. And he came to the ingenious conclusion that his proposed new subdivision into 27 sections could be explained "on the hypothesis of seven quires of double sheets, with the last sheet left blank as a cover and protection for the writing, so that the last quire consists of three and the others of four sections. In such a codex one sheet was laid above another, then both were folded, then all the quires were sewn together through the fold. That the quires should be seven adds

---

81. Oman, *Book of Revelation*, vii.

82. Oman, *Book of Revelation*, vii. He shows analogous interest in textual hypotheses in his detailed examination of "The Scripture Chronology in the Assyrian Period," which he sent for comment to George Adam Smith shortly before his visit to America in 1907. Letter from Oman to Smith, Alnwick, 10 January 1907, New College Archives, University of Edinburgh.

83. "The Apocalypse Re-Arranged," *British Weekly*, 10 April 1924.

84. Boxall, *Revelation*, 9.

85. Oman, "The Orkneys."

86. Charles, *Revelation*.

an element of probability, because while the author is not obsessed by the number seven as the editor is, he uses it with sufficient frequency to show that it is his usual unit of reckoning.[87]

Oman sought the critical support of his colleagues. Anderson Scott made fruitful suggestions; "the acute, learned and critical mind of Dr Skinner . . . also helped to guard [him] against being satisfied with too easy solutions"; T. W. Manson "from the first, found the general theory beyond dubiety."[88]

But in general Oman's theory had a reception from scholars that was at best lukewarm, at worst dismissive. As F. R. Tennant put it rather delicately, "his adventure in the field of textual criticism is not deemed by expert students to have been as successful as his researches in other departments of theology."[89] For A. E. Brooke, "brilliant and suggestive as it is, it is not convincing."[90] The post-millennialist Joseph Agar Beet was particularly severe, and Oman was provoked to publish a riposte in the *Expositor*, December 1925. "As a matter of fact, he writes, I have found a great many more mistakes than Dr Beet has discovered." For instance much of the material Oman had taken to be glosses could in fact be said to be doublets. "I suppose," he writes wryly, "that I am not the first person, who, when working with a mass of detail, could not see the wood for the trees."[91] However, "Dr Beet does scant justice"[92] to the project.

Undeterred by such criticism, with dogged determination, Oman decided to "start afresh" and published a revised theory in 1928. While he stuck to his overall scheme of twenty-seven subdivisions, one paragraph at least was returned to its original place, and one final alteration was made after the book was in proof. "This work, he writes, has been more like the solving of a Chinese puzzle than orthodox higher criticism."[93]

While scholars scoffed, it was a literary artist who first realized the originality of Oman's work. In April 1924 a review of *Book of Revelation* was published in the Adelphi magazine under the name of L. H. Davison. Under this pseudonym, D. H. Lawrence welcomed Oman's rearrangement of the text and his exposition which

87. Oman, *Book of Revelation*, 20.
88. Oman, *Book of Revelation*, ix.
89. Tennant, "John Wood Oman," 338.
90. Brooke, "The Apocalypse."
91. Oman, "The Apocalypse," 442.
92. Oman, "The Apocalypse," 438. This response was published after Beet's death in 1924. Beet had endured censure by the Wesleyan Methodist Conference between 1897 and 1905 for his unorthodox views on eschatology.
93. Oman, *Text of Revelation*, 26.

> gives one a good deal of satisfaction. The main drift we can surely accept. John's passionate and mystic hatred of the civilisation of his day, a hatred so intense only because he knew that the living realities of men's being were displaced by it, is something to which the soul answers now again. His fierce new usage of the symbols of the four Prophets of the Old Testament gives one a feeling of relief, of release into passionate actuality after the tight pettiness of modern intellect. Yet we cannot agree that Dr Oman's explanation of the *Apocalypse* is exhaustive . . . old symbols have many meanings, and we can only define one meaning in order to leave another undefined. So with the meaning of the book of *Revelation*. Hence the inexhaustibility of its attraction.[94]

Lawrence's interest in Oman is illuminated by his growing personal interest in the book of *Revelation*. Its images, symbols and myths fascinated him and stimulated his imagination. Although he claimed he was "not a scholar of any sort," he read extensively on the subject and acknowledged how much he owed to scholars, implicitly including Oman, for helping him to escape from the "all-too-moral chapel meaning of the book to another wider, older, more magnificent meaning."[95] Lawrence's last work, *Apocalypse*, was published posthumously. Here, to quote T. R. Wright, "he brings to an already difficult text a range of mediating theories, disentangling its conflicting strands of love and power. In the process he not only argues but demonstrates that to read the Bible fully requires not the one-dimensional passivity thrust upon him in childhood, but a critical engagement involving all the knowledge and imaginative insight it had taken a life-time to acquire."[96]

Lawrence perceived something in Oman's account that others had not. Even as Oman was forced to admit defeat in his attempt to rearrange the text to his satisfaction, he was developing in his commentary a coherent theory of the book as prophetic inspiration in literary form. He discerned that we do not have here "as Dr Charles says, a mixture of vision and reflexion, but simply reflexion in the form of vision,"[97] what might be called poetic intelligence. Oman continues: "Visions in what is written in obedience to a call and according to a plan must be in essence literary form, not ecstasy." John's visions unveil heavenly mysteries. As the seer is enabled to view life on earth from a divine perspective, he offers direct disclosure of the things of God.

---

94. Lawrence, *Apocalypse*, 41.
95. Lawrence, *Apocalypse*, 55.
96. Wright, *Lawrence and the Bible*, 244.
97. Oman, *Book of Revelation*, 27.

The prophet, Oman realized, was not compiling a problem book to be solved by intellectual sleight of hand. He had a message to convey and had to be understood. Poetry was his chosen vehicle. Long before Farrer[98] or Caird,[99] Oman perceived that *Revelation* was written by a supreme literary artist.

He himself read poetry, old and new,[100] a lifelong interest in Milton, Browning, Coleridge, Carlyle and Shakespeare being fostered in his student days in Edinburgh by Professor Masson.[101] He quoted Shakespeare regularly in his lectures[102] and wrote more than 100 poems.[103] "Writing poetry," he told his students, "is the severest discipline . . . but if you feel like trying, and can lift it above doggerel, it is worth while persisting."[104] Although dismissive of his own efforts, telling his students that "on the subject of poetry in particular my limitations may be most evident,"[105] he invites them to consider what constitutes great poetry, considerations which he applies to Revelation. First he acknowledges that "it is possible to read the poets for other reasons than their poetry," instancing his own enjoyment of Masefield's *Dauber*, which appealed to him as poetry, "but still more so because it speaks of my knowledge of the sea and my love for struggling humanity."[106] But then, "a poet stands or falls by his poetry . . . and the test of it is that it makes the thoughts move harmoniously. . . . The great poet is more apt to seek freedom in accepted forms than freedom from them."[107] Finally "The essential quality of the poet is not to dissect things in his intellect but to see them whole in his imagination. He is of imagination all compact, which primarily is a way of seeing."[108]

---

98. Farrer, *Revelation*.

99. Caird, *Revelation*.

100. Oman, *Concerning the Ministry*, 169–72.

101. Above, 54.

102. Healey, *Religion and Reality*, 167.

103. Bevans, *John Oman*, 124n66, records that Oman's private papers, including "over one hundred poems," were destroyed after his death.

104. Oman, *Concerning the Ministry*, 184. At least one of his students followed his advice: I am grateful to David Hawkridge for the gift of an anthology of poems by his father, formerly Moderator of the Presbyterian Church of Southern Africa: Hawkridge, *Epiphany*.

105. Oman, *Concerning the Ministry*, 169.

106. Oman, *Concerning the Ministry*, 170. He might have added a sense of the Romantic genius, set apart from an uncomprehending world, at whose hands he suffers.

107. Oman, *Concerning the Ministry*, 170.

108. Oman, *Concerning the Ministry*, 171.

In Revelation, he maintained, the clarity brought by his rearrangement of the disordered text "sheds light on the early development of Christianity by bringing into prominence the ideas which Primitive Christianity opposed to the imperial rule, and making it easier to understand how they were changed by annexing something of the idea of power from the might to which they had first been opposed."[109]

The theme is transmitted through prophetic vision which appeals to an imaginative understanding. Oman recognized that "when [prophecy] freed itself from the excitement of ecstasy and settled down . . . it retained the form of vision . . . [and] vision was constantly on the verge of poetic form."[110] The Greek used by John of Patmos may be unusual, "but it is terse, rapid, vivid, full of colour and movement."[111] The imagery is fluid, polyvalent, a kaleidoscope of symbolism, drawn from the Old Testament prophetic books and constantly forming new meanings. It requires a flexing of the imagination. "In the author of *Revelation*," he writes, "we have a mind for which such embodiment of his thought was as the breath of his nostrils and for which he was supremely endowed."[112]

For Oman, there were several strata in this poetic intelligence. First of all there was that awareness of the power and richness of symbol and metaphor which had attracted Lawrence to Oman's work. Then there was an understanding which we might call metaphysical. For a fuller development of this theme we have to return to *The Natural and the Supernatural* which almost certainly overlapped with his work on Revelation. In this context, the section on Awareness and Apprehension is particularly important. For here Oman maintains that where awareness and apprehension are reduced to comprehension and explanation, our perception is impoverished. We do not turn "to the scientist or the philosopher as authorities on what is known by awareness and apprehension . . . but to the poet . . . whose gifts are for perceiving and not for explaining."[113] Chief amongst such "keen perceivers" is Shakespeare.[114] "Just because Shakespeare works so entirely with perception, and expresses everything in forms of awareness and apprehension, he can make the common simple person see and feel what the thinker could not even make him understand."[115] He might have said the same of John of Patmos.

109. Oman, *Book of Revelation*, xi.
110. Oman, *Book of Revelation*, 23.
111. Oman, *Book of Revelation*, 13.
112. Oman, *Book of Revelation*, 25.
113. Oman, *Natural and Supernatural*, 125.
114. Oman, *Natural and Supernatural*, 124–32.
115. Oman, *Natural and Supernatural*, 129.

A third component of poetic intelligence comes with what Schleiermacher called the "art of understanding," hermeneutics.[116] Oman saw that the book of Revelation was spoken to be written and written to be heard. The hearer is enabled to enter into the drama of the story with its symbolic world in much the same way as "the Celt, whose religious oratory seeks in its ideas rather sublimity and spaciousness than precision and definiteness of plain fact and mere statement of truth."[117] As hearers flex their imaginative muscles, their understanding of truth is gradually unveiled and they gain new insight into the world.

Oman saw that an apocalyptic awareness was vital to the ongoing life of the church. Despite the difficulties he faced in attempting to rearrange the text, he was able to show in his commentary on Revelation that the truth which God speaks through his prophet may be apprehended by poetic intelligence.

Further Pursuits

Oman's "great book" was written during his years as college principal, when much of his time was taken up with routine matters such as teaching, student welfare, college finances and the recruitment of new students. While textual investigation of *Revelation* provided a diversion, he found himself engaged in a scholarly pursuit of a quite different nature.

On 26 March 1926, a peaceful spring day, Agnes Smith Lewis died at her home, Castlebrae, Cambridge. Her sister, Margaret Dunlop Gibson, had predeceased her by six years. I can only comment briefly here on the remarkable achievements of the twin sisters, so intimately associated with Westminster College,[118] who attained international distinction as Biblical and Semitic scholars, who assembled on their travels a uniquely important collection of palimpsests and whose pioneering work in the field of Christian Palestinian Aramaic has inspired scholars to the present day.[119] As Oman, who conducted the funeral service in St Columba's church, Cambridge, reminded the congregation, "Mrs Lewis's pursuits were inspired by

116. Building upon Schleiermacher, Oman grasps intuitively the link between hermeneutics and textuality which was subsequently to be developed by Gadamer and Ricoeur and most recently by Francis Watson.

117. Oman, *Book of Revelation*, 26.

118. It was mainly thanks to their generosity and decisive action that the college was built (above, 216). Cornick and Binfield, *From Cambridge to Sinai*; Soskice, *Sisters of Sinai*; Price, *Ladies of Castlebrae*.

119. Above the front door of Castlebrae was carved on the instruction of the twins, the motto *Lampada Tradam* (I shall hand on the torch). Price, *Ladies of Castlebrae*, 232.

a real religious love of the Scriptures, and were in turn an inspiration for all other kinds of Christian service."[120] They were "personally concerned with the struggling and poor" through the church Mission, to such an extent that even though they had between them received honorary doctorates from four universities and other distinguished awards, those who knew them well felt that "their simple goodness far outshone it [i.e., their academic distinction] in their admiration."[121]

Mrs. Lewis's Will

Mrs. Lewis left a substantial inheritance, with a "hotch-potch type of will,"[122] a Trust to fund three-year scholarships tenable at Westminster College, whose terms were ambiguous, and the quandary of a significant palimpsest which had been loaned for an exhibition in Leipzig and gone missing as war broke out. For the next few years, Oman, one of three trustees,[123] was actively engaged in the resolution of complex issues. We need not here concern ourselves with the niceties of deciding what was meant by "the Church" or "the Oxford church" or even "the Presbyterian church," except to remind ourselves that Oman enjoyed addressing a challenge, as may be illustrated graphically by the ending of a letter he wrote to Elmslie on Trust affairs in 1929: "I have just finished laying a parquet flooring in my drawing room, and I can assure you that it beats any other game that I have ever played. I have housemaid's knee, knuckles like Mowgli. Try it, it will reveal to you depths in the imprecatory Psalms of which you have never dreamed."[124]

There were matters of procedure. An immediate issue arose from the fact that the will, which had been drawn up in 1904, made no personal provision for "Miss Connell," who had run the household at Castlebrae for over six years. Taking into consideration the value attached to service by Mrs. Lewis before she lost her memory, Oman's suggestion that Jean Connell be paid an annuity out of the estate was warmly received by the Trustees and the College Committee. However, as Oman realized, consent was required of the residuary legatee, the General Assembly of the PCE, and the money

---

120. *Press and News*, Friday, 2 April 1926.

121. *Press and News*, Friday, 2 April 1926.

122. Letter from J. MacKay, Pendleton, to Percy Graham, 12 October 1926, Westminster College archives, WP1/3.

123. The others were George Barclay, minister of St Columba's Cambridge, and Alexander Wood, Fellow and Tutor of Emmanuel College, and bursar of Westminster College.

124. Oman to Elmslie, 28 January 1929, Westminster College archives, WP1/4.

would probably have to come out of the substantial amount left for scholarships. Ultimately, the matter was resolved with the assistance of the PCE legal advisor, to whom Oman commented characteristically: "The Trustees wish to be equitable as well as legal."[125]

Correspondence multiplied on another matter: according to the terms of the will, college professors were to receive a "retirement allowance." Oman urged with some determination that his allowance might cover "a settlement on his wife." If the company with which he was insured would pay a Joint Life Annuity to him, or to Mary if she survived, might premiums be met from the Lewis legacy income? The definitive answer was that "we must adhere strictly to the terms of the Will"[126] and Oman gave up the idea.

Once property in Edinburgh was sold and the niceties of Scots law and tax resolved, it was technically possible to proceed with the Lewis-Gibson scholarships. However, these were "explicitly declared in the Trust to be available only for students who are studying 'for the ministry of some branch of the Presbyterian Church not established by the State.'" The electors to the scholarships[127] asked bluntly: "Is the Church of Scotland in the eyes of the law 'a Church established by the State?' We need not say that we have the most cordial feelings towards the Church of Scotland, now so happily united, and we should rejoice if its students are eligible to participate in these scholarships. But obviously we must administer the Trust according to its terms . . . What is the view of the Church of Scotland of its own position in this respect?"[128]

The issue was sensitive. In October 1929, the union had taken place in Scotland between the Church of Scotland and the United Free Church, following twenty years of patient and thorough negotiation. It was "a complete vindication of the historic claim of the Scottish Kirk to spiritual freedom."[129] Yet it would still be easy to fan dissent by incautious expression of opinion south of the border. A provocative letter by Lord Wolmer and "certain

---

125. Letter from Oman to Lyell, of Gard Lyell and Company Solicitors, 5 July 1926, Westminster College archives, WP1/3.

126. Letter from J. H. Wishart to Rev. A. Alexander, 18 January, 1927, Westminster College archives, WP1/3.

127. These were the members of Senatus along with the chair and secretary of the Board of Studies.

128. Letter sent on behalf of the electors, under the signatures of Oman as chair, and W. A. L. Elmslie as secretary, to the Moderator of the Church of Scotland, John White, and copied to William Chree Esq. K. C., Procurator of the Church of Scotland, 26 April 1930, Westminster College archives, WP1/5.

129. Simpson, *Recollections*, 93. In May 1930, Simpson drafted a seven-page memorandum entitled "Is the Church of Scotland an 'Established Church'?" Westminster College Archives, WP1/5.

members of the Church Self-government League" to the *Manchester Guardian* had prompted a letter in response from Cairns, as principal of what was still then Christ's College, Aberdeen. Under the terms of the new constitution, Cairns wrote, "for the first time, the state has been persuaded in principle to admit that the Christian Church as such, is a living, growing, changing, social organism, which as such has the right to be recognised by the state, and to hold property as such. . . . Instead of Establishment, what we have now in Scotland is recognition, which is a very different thing . . . freedom from state control and the equality of all Churches before the law."[130] The words "Establishment" and "Disestablishment" were no longer applicable.

The Procurator replied to Oman that he was "unable to assist [him] in the matter."[131] The Moderator was more helpful.

> It is not easy to say what "established" means and in our negotiations we avoided the word altogether. The UFC took opinion of Counsel, and as a result passed an Act of Assembly on 24 May 1929, with reference to the consistency of the UF Church of Scotland and the principles thereof, and the relations of the Church of Scotland to the State. It should provide you with material to answer the question you ask. The Church of Scotland is not created a national Church by the State. It is national de facto and is recognised by the State for what it is. It is recognised also as possessing complete spiritual autonomy.[132]

This was evidently sufficient to satisfy the electors that applicants for a Lewis and Gibson scholarship from the Church of Scotland would be eligible under the terms of the Trust, although as a precaution these were advised to become members of the PCE for their three years of training before proceeding to the licentiate of the Church of Scotland.[133]

The Missing Manuscript

What then about the missing manuscript? On Mrs. Lewis's death, Oman made an inventory of manuscripts and discovered to his consternation that one rare manuscript that had been bequeathed to the University Library

---

130. D. S. Cairns, Letter to the Editor, *Manchester Guardian*, on "Church Establishment," 15 June 1929.

131. 10 May 1930, Chree to Oman, Westminster College archives, WP1/5.

132. 1 May 1930, White to Elmslie, Westminster College archives, WP1/5.

133. Secretary of the electors to William Kerr, 17 June 1931, WP1/4. The first Lewis and Gibson scholar was Francis G. Healey (Knox, *Westminster College*, 31).

was missing.[134] He was aware that on 1 April 1914, Mrs. Lewis and Mrs. Gibson had received a letter from Dr. Weise in Leipzig, asking whether they would be prepared to lend exhibits for the great Leipzig Book Exhibition which was to open in Leipzig on the 6 May.[135] Mrs. Lewis had agreed on condition that she personally deliver the most precious texts and she was assured that similar arrangements would be made for their return.

But the war intervened and Mrs. Lewis's memory began to fail. It would appear that no-one at Westminster College could read and distinguish the various texts in her bequests and Oman could not identify what had been lent with any certainty. He cites in a letter to Professor Brockelmann, "an MS of the Qur'an, a Syriac palimpsest and another Syriac manuscript."[136] Not until December 29 1927, on receipt of a communication from the oriental scholar, Professor Paul Kahle in Bonn,[137] did Oman know exactly which MSS had been lent: the MS of the Qur'an, a small booklet containing the text of the Lewis lectionary, some folios of the Codex Climaci Rescriptus, and a fragment of a Geniza text with Hebrew letters and Syriac (Christian Palestinian Aramaic) underneath. All of these had by then been returned to the college, including the unspecified one mentioned by Price,[138] all that is except for the MS of the Qur'an which had been bequeathed to the University Library, and Oman was to embark on an extraordinary detective trail, involving unscrupulous professors, shady specialist antiquarian booksellers, librarians and a dishonest museum director, with rumors that in August or September 1914, there had been "an attempted thievery, supposedly by an Englishman" and that in November of that year, "two Turks" fell under suspicion.[139]

134. In 1895, Mrs. Lewis bought this palimpsest from an antiquarian dealer on her way to Suez. Its provenance was unknown. In 1902, she published a monograph on the Syriac section (Lewis, *Apocrypha Syriaca*); in 1914 Alphonse Mingana produced an analysis of the Qur'an fragment. (Lewis and Mingana, *Leaves from Three Ancient Qur'ans*.) This turned out to be an exceedingly rare text from the first century of the Hijra which became known as the Mingana Palimpsest. George, *Le Palimpseste Lewis-Mingana*.

135. Die Weltausstellung fur Buchgewerbe und Graphik ended in 1924. It was the first and last of its kind.

136. Oman to Brockelmann, 8 October 1926, Westminster College archives, WT5/6/1.

137. Kahle to Oman, 29 December 1927, Westminster College archives, WT5/6/1. Oman considered Kahle to be utterly trustworthy. Oman to Richard Brandt, 31 May 1935, Westminster College archives, WT5/6/1.

138. Price, *Ladies of Castlebrae*, 224–25.

139. Brandt to Oman, 28 May 1935, Westminster College archives, WT5/6/1. See also "p.s." at WT5/6/1/15.

He established that the military had invaded the exhibition to make hospital space.[140] There had been scarcely any time to pack up the exhibits and store them in trunks and boxes. Perhaps in the general confusion it had been stored somewhere else?[141] However although Professor Kahle saw the items on display "some time before July 17,"[142] there is no reference to Mrs. Lewis or Westminster college in the main Exhibition index, only book publishers and companies. In the catalogue of the British section, there is no mention of manuscripts, only books, bindings and graphics.[143]

When Oman embarked in 1931 on his moderatorial year, having recovered from "a serious illness,"[144] the manuscript had still to be found; but assistance was on its way. Richard Brandt, a young American student who had spent the previous three years at Westminster College, spent a final year in Tübingen from 1934 to 1935.[145] His help was enlisted. With the willing assistance of Professor Kahle and Professor von Hüne who "thinks it a matter of national honour that the MSS [sic] be restored,"[146] a personal meeting was arranged with the person who had been responsible for the packing who had "a number of other things to tell that could not be conveyed by letter" and the manuscript was finally tracked down.[147] It was brought back to Westminster College in 1936 for onward transport to the University Library. The Foreign Office, who had liaised with von Hüne with the help of the Leipzig consul after Brandt's return to America,[148] pronounced itself "very satisfied" and requested of Oman that expenses be paid of £2. 5s. 7d to cover second-class rail fare (return) from Leipzig to Berlin and a cab fare at either end.[149]

---

140. Brandt to Oman, 8 February 1935, Westminster College archives, WT5/6/1/14/2.

141. Brandt to Oman, 8 February 1935, Westminster College archives, WT5/6/1.

142. Brandt to Oman, 28 May 1935, Westminster College archives, WT5/6/1.

143. I wish to record my gratitude to Dr Christa Kessler for her helpful advice about the Lewis-Gibson manuscripts and her diligent search in the British Library for catalogues of the Leipzig exhibition.

144. Above, 334.

145. Elmslie to Mingana, 15 September 1936, Westminster College archives, WT5/6/1.

146. Brandt to Oman, 29 April 1935 and 12 June 1935, Westminster College archives, WT5/6/1.

147. Brandt to Oman, 8 February 1935; 30 June 1935, Westminster College archives, WT5/6/1.

148. Brandt to Oman, 12 June 1935, Westminster College archives, WT5/6/1.

149. Stephen Gazelee to Elmslie, 27 April 1936, Westminster College archives, WT5/6/1.

The discovery of the MS, if not the attendant travail, was confirmed in a letter of 22 July 1957 by G. Meredith-Owen, Dept. Of Oriental Printed Books and Manuscripts, the British Museum:

> One of two MSS which had been lent for exhibition in Germany in 1914 was ultimately traced and recovered in 1936 and handed over to the University Library in Cambridge in accord with Mrs Lewis's will. This MS was a palimpsest of the Qur'an which was edited in 1914 by the late Professor A. Mingana of Birmingham.

12

Last Years

Germany 1934

IN SEPTEMBER 1934, AROUND the time Richard Brandt began his year at Tübingen University, Oman visited Germany for a family holiday with Mary and one of their daughters.[1] On this occasion, they did not travel in north Germany[2] but visited Oman's old haunts in Erlangen and Heidelberg and the countryside in between, allowing Oman to gain insight into the current situation in politics, the University, and the church. We see from the series of articles he wrote on his return for the *British Weekly* that he engaged in discussion with a variety of people, including University lecturers and professors, and was able to have long conversations in the evenings with a doctor of Jurisprudence with whom they lodged for a few days.[3]

Many things, he found, had not changed over the previous fifty years. The people were "as kind and friendly and frank as ever; as fond of beer and roast veal and the spectacles of abstract thought."[4] England's war mind was "still a common assumption."[5] Though Nuremberg had succumbed to

---

1. Oman, "Germany: Fifty Years Apart," I.
2. Oman had conversed with many exiles from north Germany in Cambridge. Oman, "Germany: Fifty Years Apart," I.
3. Oman, "Germany: Fifty Years Apart," II.
4. Oman, "Germany: Fifty Years Apart," I.
5. Oman, "Germany: Fifty Years Apart," I.

"villadom" with a rapidly expanding population, it was "in general, the same open, handsome, pleasant city."[6]

There were some changes. Farming was "more skilful and prosperous."[7] The "cult of the strong woman"[8] was much in evidence. But the greatest change of all he noted in Heidelberg. Student numbers had increased from 1,500 to 4,000. The old building was now devoted to the Nazi reorganization of student life in Germany. The fine university buildings were closed, as it was vacation, but he was told that the old class corps and the various unions, "over the departure of which no tears need to be shed,"[9] had been abolished. The *Exerzierplatz* was now the site of a large public building.

He formed the general impression that "the Germans seemed . . . to be a far freer people than they were fifty years ago."[10] In spite of the suppression of news and criticism, "the educated German is much better informed than might be expected in the circumstances."[11] Thanks to the liberating influence of the Republic, South Germany was no longer "official ridden as before";[12] no other period had "done so much for truly uniting the German peoples."[13] Equally striking was the fact that the army was less in evidence. Oman "never saw a single person bearing arms."[14] Because "only the public spectacle of the army could nourish military minds in young Germans,"[15] if Hitler entertained any ideas about war, "it would be an insanity, though he'd probably be quite pleased to give the impression that he could if he would."[16] Education was "effectively drilled and made an able people."[17] But while the cultivation of the military mind fostered "organised research production" and enabled "masses of knowledge" to be drilled into order, yet the inferiority complex sustained by Germany after the war arose in Oman's eyes from its submission to training for the winning of the war and the docility towards ideas that were imposed on it. "In my recent talks with

6. Oman, "Germany: Fifty Years Apart," I.
7. Oman, "Germany: Fifty Years Apart," I.
8. Oman, "Germany: Fifty Years Apart," I.
9. Oman, "Germany: Fifty Years Apart," I.
10. Oman, "Germany: Fifty Years Apart," I.
11. Oman, "Germany: Fifty Years Apart," II.
12. Oman, "Germany: Fifty Years Apart," II.
13. Oman, "Germany: Fifty Years Apart," II.
14. Oman, "Germany: Fifty Years Apart," II.
15. Oman, "Germany: Fifty Years Apart," II.
16. Oman, "Germany: Fifty Years Apart," II.
17. Oman, "Germany: Fifty Years Apart," II.

many Germans the army has never been mentioned in conversations except by one person who thought it still a heavy handicap on the nation's recovery, whereas, in the old days, it was the most familiar of all subjects."[18]

Were these apparent changes towards greater freedom "more than counterbalanced by the present autocratic rule"?[19] Oman knew the facts, even if the "interiority" of the situation eluded him.

> That Hitler has become leader as well as chancellor; that he has identified loyalty to the state with loyalty to himself; that he and his self-chosen friends exercise military law . . . that they have executed people on the mere charge of treason and rigged law-courts to their own fancy; that they have glorified race-prejudice into a religious creed and done things that are a scandal to righteousness . . . that they have removed many worthy people from office and condemned them to poverty, not only without trial, but without any charge which any reasonable persons would regard as offence; and that, without the formality of any accusation, they have put not a few into prison and concentration camps, which from all accounts are little better.[20]

"What I know most of," he writes, "is the dismissal of professors."[21] On 5 April 1933, an order had been issued by the Bavarian ministry of the Interior "to suspend for the time being those who belong to the Jewish race."[22] And two days later, under the "Law for the Restoration of the Professional Civil Service," the government obliged universities to dismiss those "who are not of Aryan descent," and any "who because of their present political activity do not offer a guarantee that they would support the national state."[23] Each

---

18. Oman, "Germany: Fifty Years Apart," II. See above, 111.

19. Oman, "Germany: Fifty Years Apart," III.

20. Oman, "Germany: Fifty Years Apart," III. On at least one occasion, Oman met in Britain with Dr. Adolf Keller, Swiss Protestant theologian and Secretary-General of the European Central Office for Ecclesiastical Aid. At the Annual Assembly of the National Council of the Evangelical Free Churches in Llandrindod Wells, from 11 to 12 March 1926, they were paired, Oman to talk on "The Positive Meaning of Protestantism," and Keller on "European Protestantism," *Western Mail*, 22 March 1926. According to the reporter for the *Nottingham and Midland Catholic News*, 3 April 1926, Oman "only lacked a mitre and staff to give us the best imitation and study of what a Protestant Pope would like to do."

21. Oman, "Germany: Fifty Years Apart," III.

22. Krabusch, "Zeittafel zur Geschichte der Universität Heidelberg." Nachtrag. (Supplementary sheet).

23. Krabusch, "Zeittafel zur Geschichte der Universität Heidelberg." Nachtrag. (Supplementary sheet).

of these decrees was implemented in Heidelberg. The first of many further restrictive measures was imposed on the universities in July 1934.

Oman instances a professor whom he knew, who was dismissed from his post and "denied any other means of livelihood,"[24] though he had a wife and five children, simply because he had written an article on Schleiermacher as an educationalist, "saying that, while he was the greatest of patriots, it never entered his head that a university was for anything but general culture." Many were similarly deposed, and those who remained to whom Oman spoke felt themselves "a living lie."[25] As the situation of the professors, as outlined by Gerhard Besier,[26] was precarious, Oman was obviously trusted. We may note one or two significant ecumenists amongst the Heidelberg theologians, notably Martin Dibelius and Walter Köhler, and we may note too that Robert Jelke, Dean of the Faculty of Theology between 1933 and 1935, was aligned with the *Deutsche Christen*,[27] and a member of the German National People's Party from 1919 to 1932. With the encouragement of Wilhelm Groh, the first Nazi Rektor from 1933 to 1936, Jelke used his position to blacken the reputations of colleagues, especially Dibelius.

The Omans were in Heidelberg while the sixth Nazi Congress was taking place in Nuremberg.[28] In a shop in the High Street, a loudspeaker was set up to broadcast Hitler's speech. Oman remarks that "Hitler was speaking, shouting out phrases in a carrying, if not specially pleasant voice, with a rather marked accent. But we were the only people who stayed any time to listen and there were never more than three or four at any one time." There was a more powerful loudspeaker in the University Square, "but if there were a score present, that was all."[29] Reflecting that one of the reasons for Hitler's success was his use of slogans, Oman instances *National-Sozialismus* as "a very admirable slogan, with ideals of mutual help and equality of service

24. Oman, "Germany: Fifty Years Apart," III.
25. Oman, "Germany: Fifty Years Apart," III.
26. Besier, "Die Theologische Fakultät," 173–260.
27. The "German Christians" were an anti-Semitic, nationalist Protestant grouping who formed the religious wing of the National Socialist Party.
28. 5 to 10 September 1934. The Congress ended with a rally where Hitler gave the closing address. Hitler's style of delivery is evident in the propaganda film by Leni Riefenstal, *Der Triumph des Willens* (The Triumph of the Will), 1935, which chronicles the rally of 1934.
29. Oman, "Germany: Fifty Years Apart," III. This may be contrasted with the crowded streets in Munich in March 1935 following Hitler's announcement of compulsory conscription in his "Proclamation to the German Volk." Brandt observes: "So it seems he has retained his popularity there. However, I think a lot of them take it very soberly, and they are very anxious to see what the reaction will be." Brandt to Oman, Westminster College archives, WT5/6/1/17/2.

for national ends."[30] It appealed to young people in the apparent promise of a new heaven and a new earth, and it appealed to working people "as a wiser, more effective, more practical Socialism." However "when people weigh them up, slogans do not tend to increase faith either in themselves or in those who utter them."[31] They are often a sign of "slipping back into the old era of the tyrannos, without the fear that its original meaning of autocrat may change to its later significance of despot."[32] Acknowledging that the immediate situation in the world was "not encouraging," and that "democratic institutions are all around us going by the board,"[33] he affirms his belief that "liberty in the end depends not on parliaments, but on those to whom it is dearer than life: and whether they are to be found or not is the final question."[34]

The Church Conflict

What then of the church? In the old days, the German Church was "the most submissively Erastian form of Christianity."[35] But it had been destabilised and liberated by the Republic. Oman returns to a point he had made previously: where people recognised what "true religion" was, they looked for the regeneration of the Church, turning away from large theological speculations "to the real business of practical faith and right living and right service to all men and all things."[36] Barely three months before the family visit to Germany, 139 representatives of Reformed, Lutheran and United Churches, including ordained ministers, church members and six university professors, had met in the Gemarke church, Wuppertal, declaring their desire to stand firm against the accommodation of the *Deutsche Christen* with National Socialism.[37] The result was the Barmen Declaration, which signalled the beginning of the Confessing Church. It proclaimed the Church's freedom in Jesus Christ, and its obedience to him as God's one and only Word, who determines its order, ministry, and relationship to the state.

30. Oman, "Germany: Fifty Years Apart," III.
31. Oman, "Germany: Fifty Years Apart," IV.
32. Oman, "Germany: Fifty Years Apart," IV.
33. Oman, "Germany: Fifty Years Apart," IV.
34. Oman, "Germany: Fifty Years Apart," IV.
35. Oman, "Germany: Fifty Years Apart," IV.
36. Oman, "Germany: Fifty Years Apart," III.
37. 29 to 31 May 1934.

Although Oman envisaged that Hitler might yet succeed in enforcing outward conformity, he alluded to the emergence of the Confessing Church in terms of remnant theology.

> The revolt has taken place, and there will still be a remnant according to election who will maintain the conflict, and, in all the ages, they alone have been the pioneers of progress, and, in the end, the victory has seldom failed to be theirs.[38]

Expressing "admiration for their courage and a hearty desire for their success," Oman is aware that "what will count for most is the presence or absence of a general atmosphere of sympathy with their purpose."[39]

The Barmen Declaration was controversial in Germany and in Britain. It challenged the ideology of the *Deutsche Christen*, who took the union of Christianity, nationalism, and militarism for granted, and promoted Hitler as God's will for Germany. Pastors were mostly loyal Nazis and a large section of Protestants were uninterested in the fate of the Jews.[40] In Britain, opinion was divided. For some, there could be no lasting friendship with the *Deutsche Christen* while they condoned Nazi persecution. But not all agreed with the Barmen theology, and there was much concern about the church conflict at a time when it was felt that Christians should work together in the interests of peace. In her important unpublished doctoral thesis,[41] Daphne Hampson indicates how some took the view that protest should be avoided, understanding Germany's fanatical nationalism as a reaction to its harsh treatment in 1918 and wishing to keep church issues separate from those raised by the Third Reich. She shows how the English churches, fearing the spread of communism and bolshevism, were initially influenced by overtures by the German Foreign Office, and that, in the period between autumn 1934 and summer 1935, there were ecumenical attempts, largely unsuccessful, to find a modus vivendi with Protestants in Germany. Bonhoeffer addressed the Life and Work conference at Fanø in the summer of 1934, but Präses Karl Koch, head of the Confessional Movement, reluctantly refused George Bell's invitation to attend, in fear that he might be regarded in Germany as a traitor;[42] Henry Hodgson sought to correct a bias towards the *Deutsche Christen* in Faith and Order by inviting Bonhoeffer to attend

---

38. Oman, "Germany: Fifty Years Apart," III.
39. Oman, "Germany: Fifty Years Apart," III.
40. Dorothy Buxton and Charles Roden Buxton spent two weeks in Germany in spring 1935 in a vain attempt to arouse awareness in church leaders of what was going on. Hampson, "British Responses," 152.
41. Hampson, "British Responses."
42. Hampson, "British Responses," 67.

its summer conference in 1935, and Bonhoeffer made it clear that he was unable to accept the invitation.[43]

Large issues of truth and freedom were at stake, and so I quote at some length what Oman writes:

> Probably I have myself written as much about freedom as any of my contemporaries and based the whole interpretation of life and history upon the hope of a freedom which shall be ordered wholly by insight and loyalty. Unless it is somehow of supreme importance that mankind should not only hold right views but hold them by seeing them to be true, and not only do right deeds but do them by discerning that they are right, I at least can discover nothing of providential order in the long, weary, contentious struggle of human history. . . . The only ultimate order we know is in seeing eye to eye in truth and directing our ways among men by the mutual deference and esteem and regard for each other's highest welfare, which we call love, and ought it not to be our faith that God will not be satisfied with less? Even if we have to measure progress towards it by His measure, with Whom a thousand days are as one day, we can see that, however at times the tide may seem to recede, it has been advancing, and that freedom, in spite of all disloyalties to it, is a more assured possession of mankind. Yet we have to recognise that, not once, but many times men have faltered in the arduous and long task and have been put back under outward law as a propaedeutic for a larger freedom, and the question is whether the present is only such a time of discipline for this end, or a sign of final failure.[44]

Reflecting that that question could only be addressed adequately with historical insight, he continues:

> The day will come when it will be seen that the Republic did not lose the war but maintained a marvellous degree of order in the chaos which followed, and that it, for the first time, made Germany one people. Nor, in spite of much failure . . . and that the immediate hope of its success died with Stresemann, will the

---

43. Bonhoeffer was at odds with the Faith and Order Movement even before 1933, and its political and theological presuppositions were not shared by the Confessing Church. The Bishop of Gloucester, A. C. Headlam, openly derided the Confessing Church and Niemöller in particular. Hampson, "British Responses to the German Church Struggle," 164 and 172. Clements, *Faith on the Frontier*, 300.

44. Oman, "Germany: Fifty Years Apart," IV.

freedom enjoyed by the people for the first time in their history, ever be forgotten.[45]

As to Hitler, "he has probably pulled down the old order even more than he knows, and we can only wish him all success in building a new, which though the nation may receive in submission, they will discover can only be made secure in liberty."[46]

Oman concludes his series of articles with the comment: "this may seem to be rather comparing the present with fifty years forward than fifty years backward, but what is the use of studying the past if not to help us anticipate the future?"[47]

Germany 1935

For the Jews, at least, the future did not look promising. From 10 to 16 September 1935, the seventh Party Congress took place in Nuremberg, where an estimated 700,000 people gathered in the medieval town, with blaring Wagnerian overtures, goose-stepping formations, and enormous flags, to hear the announcement by the Führer of the notorious Nuremberg race laws. In December, as Oman prepared to return to Germany, there was a "particularly violent outbreak of persecution."[48] He gave a paper to the Fifth European Theological Students' conference, meeting between 28 December 1935 and 3 January 1936 at the Evangelische Johannesstift, Berlin-Spandau. About fifty to sixty theological students were present from France, Germany, Britain, Holland, Hungary, Norway, Sweden, and Switzerland, and the subject of the conference, "The Church and the Confessions" was judged particularly pertinent for the fact that the meeting was held in Germany.[49] Oman spoke of "The Task of Theology." The student journalist reports:

> After criticising all forms of traditional authority, he pointed out that if our theology is to have any value it must have value for us; it must be the presentation of the highest we can see and aspire after, and it can only be accepted as it is manifested to spiritual discernment and willingness to do God's will.[50]

45. Oman, "Germany: Fifty Years Apart," IV.
46. Oman, "Germany: Fifty Years Apart," IV.
47. Oman, "Germany: Fifty Years Apart," IV.
48. Hampson, "British Responses to the German Church Struggle," 178.
49. *Student Movement*, 38 (1936), 136.
50. *Student Movement*, 38 (1936), 136.

George Alexander informs us that while the paper was read for Oman by "Mr Mackie,"[51] Oman "answered questions and took part in the discussions for two hours in German. Amongst others, he met Niemöller."[52] He would have been heartened by the reporter's perception that, despite "deep differences in theological approach and conviction . . . there was so much for which to be thankful: the common determination to take theology seriously; the desire on the part of all for mutual understanding; the spiritual solidarity which came from the sense of the common task before the Church in every land; the fellowship which was given to those who shared in these days together."[53] From Berlin, according to Healey, "he went on to Holland for what he described as a 'conference of pundits,' and there met, among others, Emil Brunner and Karl Heim."[54] While we have no other record of Oman's participation in this meeting, it has to be seen against the background of the internal strife that had beset the Confessing Church, following the worsening of state policies, between those, like Dibelius, who advocated non-cooperation with the Reich, and those who preferred to pursue compromise.[55] Karl Barth, chief drafter of the Barmen Declaration, was convinced that profound theological issues were at stake and that many of his colleagues had betrayed Barmen theology by acquiescing with the Nazis.[56] He attributed the religious syncretism and support of antisemitism of the *Deutsche Christen* to natural theology, which he saw as a perversion of Christianity. In 1934, he famously rejected Emil Brunner's account in *Natur und Gnade* with the response, *Nein!*,[57] disparaging Brunner's emphasis on faith as personal encounter with God who speaks and draws near in grace, in favour of acceptance of abstract credal propositions.[58]

Might this "conference of pundits" have been associated in some way with the new alliance that was in formation between the student body and the ecumenical movement?[59] In the summer of 1930, a small meeting of

51. Probably Robert Mackie, General Secretary of the British SCM.

52. Alexander, "Memoir of the Author," xxiii. Neither Alexander nor Healey mentions the prior visit in 1934.

53. *Student Movement*, 38 (1936), 136.

54. Healey, *Religion and Reality*, 13.

55. Begbie, "The Confessing Church," 120–21.

56. He was deprived of his chair in Bonn University in 1935 for refusing to take the statutory oath of allegiance to Hitler.

57. After the end of the war, Barth developed his own form of natural theology at the end of *Church Dogmatics* (CD IV/3.1) under the heading "Secular Parables of the Truth."

58. Clements, *Faith on the Frontier*, 272.

59. Clements, *Faith on the Frontier*, 278–79.

student and ecumenical representatives was held at Zuylen in Holland, under the chairmanship of Visser 't Hooft, to discover what the two bodies could say together. In October that year, Heim and Brunner met in Basel, with a clutch of continental theologians, to discuss the "Message."[60] Was Oman possibly attending a subsequent meeting of the "Brunner Group" in Holland?

Retirement

We now have to retrace our steps a few months. For on Commemoration Day, June 1935, Oman finally retired as principal and professor of Westminster College.[61] "His own mood was genial and cheerful as usual ... yet it was natural that the general satisfaction at the present prosperity and happy prospects of the College should be tempered by the sorrow that belongs to life's changes and farewells."[62]

T. W. Manson, Professor of New Testament Greek and Exegesis at Mansfield College, and a former student of Oman, wrote on Oman's retirement that the recognition of the College by the University was "no mere matter of courtesy," but "a real acceptance based on the knowledge that such men as Dr Oman were maintaining there the highest standards of study and teaching in the highest and most exacting of subjects."[63]

> It has meant that the library of theology has been "enriched by a series of works of outstanding value, all marked by the same qualities of deep religious insight, sure faith, and determined honesty in facing theological problems.... They are difficult books because they deal profoundly with the profoundest things in human experience; and they can only be properly appreciated by those who will give to the reading of them something of the same quality of heart and mind that went to their making....
>
> "Those qualities of heart and mind have been placed unstintingly at the service of successive generations of students for the ministry.... There are many men in the ranks of the ministry today who are able to face the difficulties and perplexities of our time with some sort of inner serenity and courage because

---

60. Clements, *Faith on the Frontier*, 272.

61. He had exercised an active ministry in the PCE of forty-six years: eighteen at Clayport, and twenty-eight at Westminster College. W. A. Leslie Elmslie followed him as principal, and he was succeeded in the Barbour Chair of Systematic Theology by H.H. Farmer.

62. Armstrong, "Westminster College Cambridge Commemoration Day."

63. T. W. Manson, "Dr John Oman," *Presbyterian Messenger*, July 1935.

they once sat at the feet of a real hero of faith, one who never shirks a difficulty, is never content merely to defeat the opposition in argument, one who all through has striven for a unified vision of God, man and the world, and wrought for nothing less than that whole truth that makes us free.

"Add to that that to be a pupil of Dr. Oman is to be his friend . . . and twenty-eight generations of students are very grateful and inordinately proud about it."

Over lunch, following the service, it was announced that Oman had been elected as Honorary Fellow of Jesus College, Cambridge, in recognition of his scholarly achievement and influence in the University, and appreciative speeches were made by representatives of Church and University. He was then presented with a smaller version of the portrait, also executed by Hugh Riviere, and tickets for a two week cruise to the fjords of Norway for himself and Mary.[64] The expedition, at the end of June,[65] gave him considerable pleasure.[66] They took some time to decide where they might live once Oman retired: according to George Alexander, they "looked around for a year [but] Cambridge drew them back." Oman wrote to Brandt on 31 May: "I have no address so far, but Westminster College will find me. We are all fairly fit except Maisie who is in the Southern General[67] Hospital with scarlet fever. However it is getting on all right."[68] Five months later, he is grappling with the upheaval of moving to 11 Hills Road, Cambridge, "an upstairs downstairs type of large Victorian house with the kitchen in the basement."[69] He writes to Cairns in October: "I have been very busy getting settled here, and only now see some kind of order evolve out of chaos. Even yet my study is not a place for quiet meditation, so that I have been unable to consider your questions, and I am not sure where the note of the passages you give me have gone to."[70] It would appear that it was not long before order was restored, for in December he signed a contract with SCM for *Concerning the Ministry*,[71] and, around three weeks later, he presented his

64. J. L. Cottle and A. S. Cooper, "Westminster College Bulletin," *Presbyterian Messenger*, August 1935.

65. Brandt to Oman, 30 June, 1935.

66. See above, 239. Healey, *Religion and Reality*, 13, 159n15.

67. The word is illegible.

68. Oman to Brandt, 31 May 1935.

69. Family recollection. An additional attraction for Oman was the large garden where he cultivated vegetables.

70. Oman to Cairns, 16 October 1935. Letters and papers of D. S. Cairns, Aberdeen University archives.

71. Oman, *Concerning the Ministry*. The Memorandum of Agreement" between Oman and the SCM Press was signed on 9 December 1935.

paper to the SCM conference in Berlin. In the summer, he gave an address at the baptism of a McConnell granddaughter, called after her grandmother.[72] For a few months, he and Mary had "every prospect of a pleasant retirement among old friends."[73] Then, after a short illness, Mary died on 17 December.

The news was received by many "with the greatest grief."[74] Generations of students associated the College with her warm hospitality and friendly welcome to the principal's Lodge. Alexander records that "it was here . . . that Mrs Oman came into her kingdom. Her interest in the men was natural and unaffected. They could talk to her freely and her memory was of the order to call forth some kindly recollection of a student years after, if his name cropped up."[75] The depths of Oman's grief may be inferred. He had dedicated *The Paradox of the Word* to Mary with three words in Greek, *soi, gnésia súzuge*, "to you, my loyal companion," and, as Alexander observed, "no three words he ever penned, albeit a quotation,[76] conveyed a great wealth of meaning or more of himself."[77] Consciously or unconsciously, in one of the sermons in the book he uses similar language about Ezekiel's wife.[78] She was "the desire of his eyes," "a true helpmate. . . . His mission still made no progress, his message stirred no less hatred, the opposition was no less bitter, but all was changed when at home he had the sunshine of perfect sympathy and perfect understanding."[79] Oman's commentary may be an over-interpretation of the biblical text, but it is surely animated by his relationship with Mary.

He wrote a heart-broken reply to Mrs. Elmslie's letter of condolence:

> The knowledge that there was serious illness came suddenly and that it was hopeless only after an operation. Then we did not know if it was kindness or merely selfish to encourage her to put up a fight for life. . . . I never knew how much her interest in people meant to them till now, and she never guessed, because she never went out to do good but only to be herself. Thank you

---

72. His insistence that we matter to a gracious God is summed up here in the statement: "None of us are very 'important' to God, but we're all very dear." Bevans, *John Oman*, 81.

73. Alexander, "Memoir of the Author," xxiv.

74. "Mrs John Oman," *British Weekly*, 24 December 1936.

75. Alexander, "Memoir of the author," xxii.

76. The reference, altered to address Mary directly, is from Phil 4:3.

77. Alexander, "Memoir of the author," xxiii.

78. Oman, "A Ministry of Sorrow," 236–46. The text is Ezek 24:16.

79. Oman, "A Ministry of Sorrow," 239.

very much for your invitation and some day when I have picked up the torn threads of my life a little, I hope to accept it.[80]

A weariness crept into Oman's life following Mary's death, though he always spoke appreciatively of family support.[81] He responded to a letter of condolence from Lesslie Newbigin: "There is not much to say about us, except that I am still here at the above address with Maisie and a sister who is a widow. We are the only two left now, and she has no children. But write me a long letter and tell me about things."[82] In the ensuing correspondence, they discuss briefly Schweitzer, Newbigin's "book," and, in January 1938, Oman mentions that he has been enjoying Dryden "neither for his poetry nor his theology but for his resoundingly [delicious] prose." His health, however, was declining. He mentions in an aside to Newbigin, "I am up again and keeping busy."[83] By July 1938, he was obviously unwell, and hesitated at first to accept the Fellowship of the British Academy on the grounds that he was "no longer able to do anything more 'to support the honour.'"[84] When Adam Welch gave the Schweich lectures on Biblical Archaeology the same year, "only reasons of health prevented Oman from being present."[85] He finished *Honest Religion*, parcelled it up for the Press and wrote Healey: "I have finished the present opus. . . . It helped me, but whether it is new enough to help any other I do not know. . . . After a bit I may be able to say myself."[86] Shortly after, on 17 May 1939, although "he was not thought to be in any immediate danger," he died "with startling suddenness"[87] as he was writing a letter to George Alexander.[88]

---

80. Oman to Mrs Elmslie, Westminster College archives. The letter must have been written on 4 January, not 4 December as stated.

81. Alexander, "Memoir of the Author," xxiv.

82. Oman to Lesslie Newbigin, 23 April 1937, University of Birmingham, Cadbury Research Library, DA29/1/1/105. The sister is Isabella, who had come to Cambridge to look after him. Thomas had died in Manchester in 1832 and Simon in South Africa in 1935. See chapter 1.[x-ref]

83. Oman to Lesslie Newbigin, 6 January 1938, University of Birmingham, Cadbury Research Library, DA29/1/1/97.

84. Alexander, "Memoir of the Author," xxiv.

85. Alexander, "Memoir of the Author," xxiv.

86. Healey, *Religion and Reality*, 159n16.

87. Alexander, "Memoir of the Author," xxv.

88. Recollection by Maisie Oman. Woodfin, "John Wood Oman (1860–1939)," 34. According to Watchman, *British Weekly*, 25 May 1939, the very last words he put on paper were "and so he died."

Honest Religion

This book may literally be described as Oman's legacy. It is a brave and frank attempt to accept the divine invitation, "Come let us reason together," untrammeled by custom or convention. He sets out briefly the views of the various German schools of thought about the Gospels, indicating that, while these "have had great value for raising the essential questions," he was "far from being persuaded of the value of their answers."[89] Each of these movements "drilled life and history into accord with some intellectual abstraction used as a battle-cry, and saw only with the spectacles of the particular theory. This also seems another challenge to one's liberty."[90] "My general purpose," Oman writes, "is to ask what a true response would mean, or, in other words, what bearing and attitude would be entire honesty in making life a continual reasoning with God in the sense of laying our minds alongside of His and open to His persuasion."[91] As Oman's son-in-law, Frank Ballard, suggests, "it is full of ripe wisdom and mature religious faith. All Oman's distinctive teaching is here, but perhaps more than in any other publication (with the single exception of the book on the Christian ministry) the man himself appears with his large knowledge of life and his sympathy with the troubles of the human heart."[92] The pursuit of truth in religion had spurred Oman to candidate for the ministry;[93] and he had pursued the quest in his published work from *Vision and Authority* and *Faith and Freedom* to *Grace and Personality* and *The Natural and the Supernatural*. But *Honest Religion* is primarily a work of Christian spirituality, a "waiting upon God," which Oman defines as "reasoning together with Him to clear our minds and understand His, it is neither arguing with Him nor about Him."[94]

Twenty chapters, based largely on "various addresses given in Cambridge,"[95] are loosely linked in a self-reflective consciousness, evoking, not the "thunderclaps"[96] of Paul, but Job, as he answers God's voice from the

---

89. Oman, *Honest Religion*, xxxiii.
90. Oman, *Honest Religion*, xxxiv.
91. Oman, *Honest Religion*, 1.
92. Frank H. Ballard, introduction to Oman, *Honest Religion*, xii.
93. See above, chapter 3.
94. Oman, *Honest Religion*, 23.
95. Frank H. Ballard, introduction to Oman, *Honest Religion*, xii.
96. Nathaniel Micklem, on learning of Oman's death, quotes Jerome's commendation of Paul, *Quem quoties lego non verba mihi videor audire sed tonitrua* ("Whenever I read him, I seem to hear, not words, but thunderclaps"). Micklem, *The Box and the Puppets*, 104.

whirlwind, humbled and satisfied. And they culminate in the fine section, "Yea and Amen."

We might single out memorable illustrations of the main theme. In the "Parable of the Spade," he claims that honest religion "concerns not merely honesty about religion, but . . . honesty within it, the vital concern not being about having religion, but about the kind of religion we have."[97] A spade can be a spade, a shovel, an implement. While "the treasures of thought, character and loyalty have been as much dug out of the earth as coal or iron . . . the world has often been cultivated with very bloody shovels, with human sacrifices and the scaffold and stake. And also with soft, sentimental, magically impressive horticultural instruments."[98] Dishonest religion may be categorised in terms of the shovel and the instrument.

Then, alluding to the "quiet association of kindred spirits and human friendliness, rightly to be called fellowship," he refers to them as keeping step, "each hearing for himself a music which has a common beat, though a double source, which we may call the music of the spheres and the low sad music of humanity, being thus of the spirit both of God and man."[99] He continues, "we catch, amid the changing notes, the melody of the eternal."[100]

Perhaps most evocative of all, Oman tells of an outing to Suffolk, in perfect weather and through lovely scenery. It culminated in a visit to Flatford Mill, where, in Taylor's terms, Oman experienced "a naturalist epiphany.[101] "I looked out of the unglazed window . . . and there, framed in it, what, after all that I had seen, seemed rather commonplace. But it was the scene of the *Hay Wain*: and Constable had done nothing to it except see it with an artist's eyes, which, however had transformed it into perfect beauty and inspired meaning." And he concludes: "Perhaps all we need for blessedness is for life's meaning so to unveil itself."[102]

As we experience ordinary things in a way which manifests their true meaning, life's wonder and mystery are revealed, till we discover that all life is revelation.[103]

There are few places in Oman's published work which are so revealing of his personal spirituality as the book's final chapter. Oman writes as one facing death, to readers who are aware of their own mortality. There is an

---

97. Oman, *Honest Religion*, 44.
98. Oman, *Honest Religion*, 47.
99. Oman, *Honest Religion*, 140.
100. Oman, *Honest Religion*, 141.
101. Taylor, *Sources of the Self*, 433.
102. Oman, *Honest Religion*, 194.
103. Bevans, "Seeing with a Prophet's Eye," 136; Oman, *Vision and Authority*, 59.

unmistakable pastoral emphasis. And familiar concerns are given a fresh context: an emphasis on the personal, sincerity and freedom, the individual conscience, God's gracious love revealed in Jesus. Oman begins with a general maxim:

> Our honesty has to face the fact that the greatest certainty in life is death, through fear of which many are subject to bondage, and that there may be the still more overshadowing fear of disaster and failure in life while it lasts. Nor is it less certain than death itself that our powers fail, our plans are frustrated, our names are a breath, our ambitions dust, and that disappointment as well as evanescence is our inescapable destiny. Wherefore freedom, if it is to be ours, must be won through this bondage as well as over it, by the urgency of the fleeting and the pathos of the mortal, while we are still enabled to live as if we were immortal and to do our work as though its fruits were to be everlasting.[104]

While many people keep themselves from facing the reality of death, "this is just what honesty does not permit." We must face death alone, but "to stand alone is so far from standing aloof, that it is then we stand most undistracted in the presence of God and are most sensitive to the needs and sorrows and evanescence of men."[105] To feel alone is, Oman suggests, a familiar experience: there are times when "the support of tradition, institution and kinship fail us and the heart knows its own bitterness to which our dearest friend is a stranger, but no situation is rightly met except alone with our own conscience and responsibility, not following the mass even if led by the wisest or supported by institutions even the most august."[106] Then we will "pay heed to the counsel of God, which leads to life indeed."

> It is the light on life's opportunity not death's shadow over its close that is to inspire and guide; and the problem for us, especially as life goes on and the horizon narrows around us, is how to live in the power of an endless life, with courage not damped and vision not darkened, interests not diminished and tasks still done as though they and we were eternal.[107]

Realistically, however, "when our honesty faces life's distresses and disappointments, and searches our own heart's timidities and hesitations . . . with the best and bravest of us does not life continually waver between

---

104. Oman, *Honest Religion*, 187.
105. Oman, *Honest Religion*, 187.
106. Oman, *Honest Religion*, 187.
107. Oman, *Honest Religion*, 188.

Yea and Nay?"[108] Yet it is at such times when "the glory of life is very dim to us and of the life to come very far away," that we become aware of "the need of Jesus Christ to affirm God's glory in life," and are able

> to say Amen even with an attitude of trust and patience, which, while giving full place in our affections to their evanescence and in our labours to their futility, will enable us to carry on to the end with ever growing assurance that what we do not see God does.[109]

We cannot do without such help "if we are to accept life's limitations in the spirit of hope and its distresses in the spirit of faith, and its conflicts in the spirit of love, with some sense of the joy set before us. And where can we find help to say it if not with One who for the joy set before Him endured the agony of the Cross and despised the shame?"[110]

The Yea "is both direct and complete. . . . From the first we were saved by hope. . . . Yet the hope springs just from reaching out beyond our limitations. It is not a dream of Elysium, but the hope to see face to face what now we know only in broken reflexion, to know as we are known what we see now in part and guess in riddle."[111]

Oman elaborates further: "This is no expectation of omniscience. The passage concludes the great lyric on love, and it is love's rule which is our concern, how nothing shall intervene in our vision of it and all be seen included in its rule. . . . Not as we retire from life and become remote from men do we rise to it, but as we pursue truth till we know that our knowledge ends with what is most worth knowing."[112] What we see in Christ Jesus are "glimpses of its deep and all-embracing dominion, enough to help us to live in the power of the hope that when the night passes and the day dawns it will be the same, yet all will be changed."[113]

He concludes:

> Here in imagination we may range in the infinite, but the real infinity of meaning and value is in the common folks around, could we love and serve them better, and in the common joys and sorrows, could we respond better, and in the common tasks, were they freed from imperfections of motive and purpose. And

---

108. Oman, *Honest Religion*, 190.
109. Oman, *Honest Religion*, 190.
110. Oman, *Honest Religion*, 192.
111. Oman, *Honest Religion*, 193.
112. Oman, *Honest Religion*, 193.
113. Oman, *Honest Religion*, 194.

if there be any works that follow us, will they not be the simple things in which our souls have been most open and sincerely honest and what we learned of the depths of God's wisdom and mercy, not the things of high notoriety?[114]

---

114. Oman, *Honest Religion*, 194.

13

"A Truly Prophetic Word"[1]

THE LARGE ASSEMBLY AT St Columba's church Cambridge for Oman's funeral service on 22 May reflected the love and esteem in which he was held by his family and friends,[2] by town and gown,[3] by the church, national, regional and local,[4] by his colleagues and by generations of past and present students at Westminster College.[5]

In his address, Carnegie Simpson paid tribute to "an honoured teacher and friend," recognising in his former colleague "a man whose mind was thralled to truth, whose soul was sure of God and whose heart was human." Amongst the numerous subsequent obituaries and testimonials, one of the

1. "The Assembly Day by Day," *Presbyterian Messenger*, 6 May 1931, 34.

2. These were Isabella and Frank Ballard, Mary, Jean and Frank McConnell, Helen; Oman's grandson, John Oman Ballard, with Oman and Hunter Blair nephews. Isabella, his sister, sent apologies. George Alexander and Buchanan Gray were listed as "family."

3. The Mayor of Cambridge was represented. Also present were: the President of Queen's (representing the Vice-Chancellor), the Master of Gonville and Caius, the Censor of Fitzwilliam House, a representative of the Master of Jesus College, the Master of Selwyn, the Principals of Westcott House and Ridley Hall, and the Mistress and Secretary of Girton College. The Faculty of Theology was well represented.

4. The moderator of the PCE, James Fraser, was one of the officiating clergy, alongside Ralph Morton, minister of St Columba's, Principal Elmslie, and Carnegie Simpson. The Board of Studies at Westminster College was represented and there were representatives of the Presbyteries of Bristol, London and Liverpool; C. H. Dodd was there to represent Mansfield College, Oxford; Henry Carter attended with others from Emmanuel Congregational Church, Cambridge, and there were many mourners from the congregation of St Columba's, Cambridge.

5. For a detailed account, see *Cambridge Daily News*, Wednesday, 24 May 1939.

simplest and most heartfelt was from his grandson, his namesake: "I was sorry when he died."[6]

As this book can claim to have shown, the quest for truth which first propelled Oman into ministry was radical and dynamic. It found expression in his career as minister, writer, teacher, and college principal; it was bound up with the life of faith and the mission of the church. It led him into the "open country of action and enquiry."[7] His world-view was tested by the "sorrow and wickedness" of war and it stood the test.[8] Distinctively, "his passionate quest for truth and for the corroborations of truth was rooted in a humble but determined faith that truth is there, and that we know enough of it to proceed."[9] His impact on his contemporaries, within and without Westminster College, was considerable. Farmer, Oman's successor in the Barbour chair, records how "to look out across the world of religion and theology, with him no longer there, is as though one were to look one morning upon a familiar landscape and find that a great headland or peak has vanished overnight."[10] Two successive principals of Mansfield College signalled their appreciation of Oman's influence. Selbie wrote "He leaves behind him a host of followers who loved him not only for his work's sake but because he was the wisest of counsellors and the most loyal of friends."[11] And Nathaniel Micklem reminisced how "when I try to think as a philosopher or theologian, I am conscious of Oman's influence at every turn."[12] But how may we discern his influence over succeeding generations? How well have the principles he maintained stood the test of time? Does the freedom which he sought still offer human and spiritual emancipation?

In the inter-war years the theological dogmatism of Karl Barth's *Römerbrief*[13] was in the ascendant in Britain, as was A. J. Ayer's metaphysical scepticism. Barth contributed to the creation of a boundary between philosophy and theology, arguing that the truths of theology had to be based on the witness of Scripture to divine revelation, not on religious sentiment, ethical experience or philosophical exploration. The ensuing "rather baleful"[14] mid-century debate resulted, chiefly in England, in a marginalising

---

6. Personal communication from John Oman Ballard.
7. Oman, *Grace and Personality*, 2nd ed., ix.
8. Oman, *Grace and Personality*, v.
9. Watchman, "John Oman."
10. Farmer, "Death of Dr. John Oman."
11. Selbie, "John Oman."
12. Micklem, *The Box and the Puppets*, 134.
13. 1st ed., 1919; 2nd ed., 1921; translated into English 1933.
14. Fergusson, *Scottish Philosophical Theology*, 23.

of religious concerns. Despite this, there were those like T. M. Knox who maintained that

> to read the *Natural and the Supernatural* is to be reinforced in the conviction that linguistic analysis as the sum and substance of philosophy is no more than ingenious trifling. When I read *Honest Religion* and find myself at home in its persuasive unorthodoxy, Barth seems to me to speak with a voice of centuries long past. I quote Oman himself from *Vision and Authority*: "The old external dogmatic attitude of the Church cannot be maintained." (pp. 94, 182).[15]

Oman was aware of the danger of reducing a complex world to what was intellectually manageable and of treating an intellectual representation of reality as if it alone were reality.[16] For conceptual wholeness, intellectual understanding had to be fused with the power of perception, the perception of a child, a poet, an artist. The enterprise was intellectually resilient and existentially satisfying. Its success depended largely on a careful use of language.

Language matters; words are more than statement of fact.[17] They are bound up with our relationship to the world. They are a vehicle of truth and meaning, which technical language can obscure. Oman was a master of style. He took pains to convey complex ideas in ordinary language. He enters into theological debate without using any of the "-ologies" he counsels his students to avoid. His stories and sermons are finely honed. He conveys meaning by an imaginative use of metaphor. And so our contemporary conception of creative imagination and of the realities to which it gives us access is transformed; our views are altered about alternatives to disengaged reason.[18] Oman's enthusiasm for the early work of Whitehead, for example, was dashed when he reviewed *Process and Reality*, which he found to be "more of an achievement in technical jargon than Hegel."[19]

Yet any supposition that Oman "had little to contribute to contemporary philosophical analysis of religious language" was given the lie by A. D. Galloway, who points out that

---

15. Knox, review of Healey, *Religion and Reality*, 549.

16. Oman, *Natural and Supernatural*, 120–43.

17. Oman, *Natural and Supernatural*, 168–84. At Edinburgh University, literature was judged to be integral to the study of philosophy; Shakespeare was held up as a model (above, 53-54).

18. Taylor, *Sources of the Self*, 498.

19. Oman, review of Whitehead, *Process and Reality*. Cf. Oman, review of Whitehead, *Religion in the Making*.

his critical epistemology, his account of the part "interest" plays in the formation of words and concepts, of the relation of judgment to language, and of the relation of language to the contextual structure in which it is used are all directly and often disconcertingly relevant. . . . He can use analysis to clarify without doing abuse to the synthetic character of language as a cultural achievement. It may be that he is a man who lived before his time and will only now begin to come into his own.[20]

Oman's profound vision of personal love was also out of tune with the dominant view among moral philosophers in the forties that nothing was objectively good or bad, right or wrong, important or unimportant. These were allegedly projections which we impose on a valueless world. Values were held to be subjective opinions, expressions of bias, and this was widely supposed to be the only acceptably modern thing to think. However, as Philippa Foot discovered, this perspective was not adequate to speak to the horror of Buchenwald and Bergen-Belsen.[21] And with Iris Murdoch, Elizabeth Anscombe, and Mary Midgley, she was to develop a system of ethics that was value-laden, giving rise to the biggest change in moral philosophy for over a century, replacing arid scholasticism with rich discussions of goodness, virtue, character. In similar spirit, Charles Taylor, who has a claim to be one of the most significant of contemporary moral philosophers, argues that a utilitarian value outlook is "entrenched in institutions of commercial and capitalist mode of existence, and tends to empty life of richness, depth, or meaning." An "instrumental society" characterised by consumerism and mass media makes a deeper meaning hard to discern. With "a loss of passion, of sense of purpose, there is no more room for things that are worth dying for."[22]

Many subsequent theological or philosophical developments were already seminally present in Oman. Before Martin Buber published *Ich und Du* in 1923[23] Oman was thinking about modes of conscious interaction and being; at least six years before Rudolph Otto published *Die Heilige* in 1917,[24] he was at work on the meaning of the "sacred."[25] In the great chapter of *The Natural and the Supernatural* which deals with epistemology, he was a forerunner of Gadamer, Derrida, and Ricoeur. And he had a role in shaping

20. Galloway, review of Healey, *Religion and Reality*, 429.
21. Lipscomb, *The Women*, 4.
22. Taylor, *Sources of the Self*, 500. There are significant echoes here of Oman.
23. Buber, *I and Thou*.
24. Otto, *The Idea of the Holy*. Oman, "The Idea of the Holy."
25. Oman, *Natural and Supernatural*, appendix A, 474.

Michael Polanyi's transition from scientific research to a broader reflection on religion and culture. Joe Oldham, secretary of the International Missionary Council from 1921 to 1938, is said to have given Polanyi "his first book on theology, a work by John Oman, the first specialist theologian whom Polanyi studied."[26]

Henry Chadwick, twenty-five years after Oman's death, commented in his Gifford lectures that "among the philosophical theologians of Liberal Protestantism the figure of John Oman towers above all others for originality and power . . . [He] is totally free of either the itch for heterodoxy or the aroma of bourgeois donnishness that hangs about too much of the Liberalism of the Edwardian age. He looked for contemporary authority in religious belief not in councils or popes, nor even in learned teachers of theology, but only in saints and all those whose moral vision remains unclouded by worldliness and compromise."[27] That Oman's thought was original is unquestionable. Recognising "the duty of untrammelled investigation . . . laid upon us by personal freedom in God,"[28] he did not subscribe to any school of theology. He was a "voice" and not an "echo."[29] Although his sturdy independence of thought was sometimes met by his contemporaries with uncomprehending exasperation,[30] it is consistent with Oman's claim that truth is not true for you until you see it for yourself.

His work was characterised by a fusion of philosophical acumen and theological depth, stimulated by voracious reading in theology, ethics and metaphysics. We can see from his *JTS* book reviews how he interrogated the works of leading theologians and philosophers, regularly before they were translated from German or French into English, often finding those with which he most disagreed to be the most productive.[31] As he illustrates in *The Problem of Faith and Freedom*, he took the view that the perspective of any given author is likely to coexist with those which have arisen later in reaction to them and that these will go on influencing and shaping each other in the present and future. The toing and froing between Oman's own thinking and that in particular of Kant, Schleiermacher, Hegel, and Ritschl

---

26. The title of Oman's book is not recorded. Scott and Moleski, *Michael Polanyi*, 213.

27. Chadwick, "Authority in Liberal Protestantism."

28. Oman, *Faith and Freedom*, 395.

29. Above, 136. In this he was making his own the "common purpose or tendency" of Scottish Idealists as identified by Edward Caird (above, 64–65).

30. Tennant, "John Wood Oman."

31. Oman, *Natural and Supernatural*.

shaped a dynamically integrated and coherent system of thought, open to dialogue with future perspectives.[32]

Oman's own thought was to be caught up most immediately in the teaching of H. H. Farmer who attempted to bring the insights of his "revered teacher"[33] into closer relationship with later emphases, notably on the historical revelation of Jesus Christ.[34] In the opinion of one of Farmer's most notable students, he was "a good deal more orthodox than Oman."[35] Reflecting on one of his own most significant works, *Evil and the God of Love*, John Hick (1922–2012) writes, "Again and again I find in re-reading Oman that I have been following in his foot-steps." Hick appreciated Oman's relative lack of interest in the historic church creeds and his perception that these were not central to true religion, understood to be a matter of knowing the limitless grace of God and living in response to it.[36] "And so, from the point of view of a 'radical' Christian of the twenty-first century, John Oman was one of the comparatively few theologians of the past who is still relevant today."[37]

Oman relied neither on doctrinal formulations, nor on purely rational speculation. He was committed to the fact that theology had to speak truly in the contemporary world and for that it had to be rooted in experience.[38] In the Festschrift for Nicholas Lash, Maleiha Malik nuances further Oman's notion of experience in her examination of the role of faith perspectives in the public sphere.[39] In this significant analysis, she engages creatively with two key ideas expressed in *Grace and Personality*, the appropriateness of theological or religious perspectives for contemporary politics and Oman's suggestion that there is a connection between such activity and the concept

---

32. Charles Taylor likewise maintains that not everyone is living by perspectives which have evolved recently, citing the student revolt in Paris in May 1968 with its strong overtones of Schiller undergirding the borrowings from Dada and Surrealism, to indicate how Romantic themes were still alive despite being sometimes masked. Taylor, *Sources of the Self*, 497.

33. Farmer, *The World and God*, 2nd ed., xi.

34. Langford, "Theological Methodology," 230.

35. Hick, "A Voyage Round John Oman," 164.

36. Oman held that the Westminster Confession had to be interpreted in order to enhance the insights of faith which it conveyed. (Above, 335–36.) In 2003, Adam Hood illustrates how for Baillie, Oman, and MacMurray, Christianity is best understood in cognitive and practical terms as responding to the problems of everyday life. This experiential approach, he suggests, is consistent with religious and cultural pluralism. Hood, *Baillie, Oman and MacMurray*.

37. Hick, "A Voyage Round John Oman," 170.

38. Bevans, "Seeing with a Prophet's Eye."

39. Malik, "Justice."

of the self. She also finds Oman's recognition of history and experience as limiting factors to be "a most attractive framework for analysis."[40]

George Grant (1918–1988) has a just claim to be regarded as Canada's greatest political philosopher, whose emphasis on social justice and individual responsibility continues to stimulate, challenge and inspire today. "At Oxford," he writes, "I found the teaching of philosophy dominated by the narrowest tradition of linguistic analysis—people such as [Gilbert] Ryle and A. J. Ayer. They simply saw philosophy as the errand boy of natural science and modern secularism. They were uninterested in the important things I wanted to think about."[41] He wasn't interested in the "minor logical twitterings which dominated Oxford philosophy"[42] at the time. He was looking for the kind of philosophy that could comprehend the "whole"—including the mystery of God, the affliction of human beings, and the ongoing search for wisdom, and he had a strong interest in the contemporary secular world. He found what he was searching for in Oman. With the encouragement of A. D. Lindsay, Master of Balliol, he embarked on doctoral studies, and was awarded DPhil in 1950 for a thesis on "The Concept of Nature and Supernature in the Theology of John Oman."

In similar vein, the distinguished missiologist Stephen Bevans writes "how much my study of and love for the work of John Oman has influenced my own missiological thinking, and I hope my missiological practise."[43] No longer do we "speak of mission as a crusade, working for Christ's victory in the world, fighting for justice, developing tactics for conversion. . . . Mission is understood much more in terms of dialogue—prophetic dialogue, yes, but dialogue nonetheless."[44]

In *Honest Religion*, Oman articulates experience as "a dialogue whereby we learn as we ask the right questions and appreciate the right answers; and this means being both humble and alert."[45] A theology of dialogue will take care to honour God as the supreme personal reality whose way of working respects the personal both in himself and in his creatures, allowing them, in the power of his love, a great deal of freedom.

Oman's theology was rooted in the realities of relationship. Oman liked people, and he was interested in the world around, intent on grasping truth over a wide range of human experience and knowledge. So he was

40. Malik, "Justice," 182.
41. Schmidt, *George Grant*, 62.
42. Schmidt, *George Grant*, 62.
43. Bevans, "Oman's Doctrine," 189.
44. Bevans, "Oman's Doctrine," 189.
45. Oman, *Honest Religion*, 30.

able to relate easily to Tommy Colligan, light-weight boxer, to Baron Krupp, languishing in prison; he was on easy terms with artists of distinction, with soldiers in YMCA camps, with students and professors in Britain and Germany. This was a person who could "discuss with fruit-growers the best soil and manure for this or that species of apple, or with organ-builders the best alloy for organ pipes." He "read everything and forgot nothing."[46] With all of these he was a fellow traveller. In the depth of his thought and faith he was and still is able to speak to the human condition.

Grace and Personality and *Honest Religion* do not shirk from confronting the challenges of living. They articulate Oman's belief that in dealing with the world, God respects and loves people in the circumstances of their lives. God does not intervene to prevent sin or fires or floods. God works through those who have caught the vision of divine order, often a small group of people, who in freedom will work towards the liberation of the world from oppression. That involves prophetic dialogue with the world and with the church.

A conscientious and lively Christian, Oman could, as we have seen, be a fierce critic of the church, asking searching and critical questions about its materialism, its complacency, its disregard of its calling to witness to things of faith to those "outside" its walls. He perceived that, as agents of truth the churches, both in Britain and in Germany, had to be more self-aware; a post-war need for reconstruction depended, in Oman's view, on spiritual regeneration, on fellowship in freedom, catholicity of heart and unity of spirit. Yet, despite his dedication to ecumenism, his primary loyalty was to the PCE which he served conscientiously as minister, professor, college principal, moderator. In its college, he set high standards for himself and expected the same of students, supportive of those who were trying their best, trenchantly critical of those who were not. In ministry, he made it plain, "spiritual cant"[47] was to be eschewed, this was dishonesty, untruth, a lack of integrity. His informal "causeries" with students, published as *Concerning the Ministry*, are notable for their simplicity of language, their wisdom and humour, and in their distilled experience have much to offer of value not only for today's ordinands but for all those who are seeking authentically to minister the gospel.

Oman's single-minded devotion to truth was founded on profound religious faith. At the heart of it was a belief that God is personal and that people matter to God; God deals with the sorrow and sin of the world as

---

46. Farmer, "Death of Dr. John Oman."

47. Arthur MacArthur, quoted in "Great Theologian Is Remembered," *Orcadian*, October 1960.

Father: "the end of all reasoning with Him is the discovery of a patient pardoning love that makes sins that may be as scarlet, white as snow."[48] In this "the unique significance of the life and death of Jesus while we were yet sinners most appears."[49] Oman used the resources of his powerful intellect and his considerable pastoral gifts to show how the purpose of life was to find in freedom that this world was really the Father's world; God is not parted from us because of our sins; the Father's rule of love prevails. For Oman, the ultimate issue was never in doubt. The bedrock of all hopes was his belief in the grace of God.

48. *Honest Religion*, 83.
49. *Honest Religion*, 83.

Bibliography

Note: the bibliography does not in general include newspaper or archival references.

Adams, John Quincy. *A History of Auburn Theological Seminary, 1818–1918*. Auburn, NY: Auburn Seminary Press, 1918.
Akten zur Deutschen auswärtigen Politik. Göttingen: Vandenhoeck und Ruprecht, 1989.
Alexander, George. "Memoir of the Author." In Oman, *Honest Religion*, xv–xxv.
Alphabetical List of Graduates of the University of Edinburgh from 1859–1888. Edinburgh: James Thin, 1889.
Andrews, C. F. *The Sermon on the Mount*. London: Allen & Unwin, 1942.
Armstrong, F. W. "Westminster College Cambridge Commemoration Day." *British Weekly*, 20 June 1935.
Bailey, Charles E. "The British Protestant Theologians in the First World War." *HTR* 77 (1984) 195–221.
Barrie, J. M. *An Edinburgh Eleven*. London: Hodder & Stoughton, 1926.
Barth, Karl. *Protestant Theology in the Nineteenth Century: Its Background and History*. London: SCM 1972 (original 1946).
Bebbington, D. W. *Evangelicalism in Modern Britain: A History from the 1730s to the 1980s*. London: Unwin and Hyman, 1989.
———. *The Nonconformist Conscience: Chapel and Politics, 1870–1914*. London: Allen & Unwin, 1982.
Begbie, Jeremy. "The Confessing Church and the Nazis: A Struggle for Theological Truth." *Anvil* 2.2 (1985) 117–30.
Bell, G. K. A. *Documents on Christian Unity, 1920–1930*. London: Oxford University Press, 1955.
———. *Randall Davidson: Archbishop of Canterbury*. 3rd ed. London: Oxford University Press, 1952.
Berlin, Isaiah. "Two Concepts of Liberty." In *Four Essays on Liberty*, 121–31. Oxford: Oxford University Press, 1969.
Bernofsky, Susan. "Schleiermacher's Translation Theory and Varieties of Foreignization: Auguste Wilhelm Schlegel vs. Johann Heinrich Voss." *Translator* 3.2 (1997) 175–92.
Besier, Gerhard. "Die Theologische Fakultät." In *Die Universität Heidelberg im Nationalsozialismus*, edited by W. U. Eckart, V. Sellin, and E. Wolgast, 173–260. Berlin: Springer, 2006.

Bevans, Stephen. *John Oman and His Doctrine of God*. Cambridge: Cambridge University Press, 1992.
———. "Oman's Doctrine of a Personal God." In Hood, *John Oman: New Perspectives*, 175–89.
———. "Seeing with a Prophet's Eye: John Oman's Experiential Method." In Hood, *John Oman: New Perspectives*, 117–39.
Biddington, Ralph. "Rationalism and Its Opposition to a Degree in Divinity at the University of Melbourne, 1905–1910." *History of Education Review* 33 (2004) 28–43.
Binfield, Clyde. *Pastors and People: The Biography of a Baptist Church, Queen's Road, Coventry*. Coventry: Sutton, 1984.
Black, John Sutherland, and George Chrystal. *The Life of William Robertson Smith*. London: Black, 1912.
Blei, Karel. "Communion and Catholicity: Reformed Perspectives on Ecclesiology." *Reformed World* 55 (2005) 369–79.
Bornkamm, Heinrich. "Die theologische Fakultät Heidelberg." In *Aus der Geschichte der Universität Heidelberg und ihrer Fakultäten*, edited by Gerhard Hinz, 135–62. Heidelberg: University of Heidelberg, 1961.
Bosanquet, Nick. "Health Systems in Khaki: The British and American Medical Experience." In *Facing Armageddon*, edited by Hugh Cecil and Peter H. Liddle, 451–65. London: Cooper, 1996.
Boucher, David, ed. *The Scottish Idealists: Selected Philosophical Writings*. Exeter: Imprint Academic, 2004.
Boxall, Ian. *Revelation: Vision and Insight*. London: SPCK, 2002.
Brooke, A. E. "The Apocalypse." Review of *Book of Revelation*, by John Oman. *JTS* 25 (1924) 303–7.
Brown, James. *The Life of a Scottish Probationer, being a Memoir of Thomas Davidson with his poems and extracts from his letters*. 3rd ed. Glasgow: Maclehose, 1889 (originally 1876).
Buber, Martin. *I and Thou*. Translated by Ronald Gregor Smith. Edinburgh: T. & T. Clark, 1937.
Caird, G. B. *A Commentary on the Revelation of St. John the Divine*. London: Black, 1966.
Cairns, David S. *An Answer to Bernhardi*. London: Oxford University Press, 1914.
———, ed. *The Army and Religion: An Inquiry and Its Bearing upon the Religious Life of the Nation*. Preface by the Bishop of Winchester. New York: Association, 1920.
———. *Christianity in the Modern World*. London: Hodder & Stoughton, 1906.
———. *David Cairns: An Autobiography . . . Edited by his Son and Daughter, with a Memoir by Professor D. M. Baillie*. London: SCM, 1950.
———. *Life and Times of Alexander Robertson MacEwen, D.D.* London: Hodder & Stoughton, 1925.
———. *The Reasonableness of the Christian Faith*. London: Hodder & Stoughton, 1918.
Cairns, John. *Principal Cairns*. Edinburgh: Oliphant, Anderson & Ferrier, 1903.
Calderwood, Henry. *Handbook of Moral Philosophy*. London: MacMillan, 1872.
Calderwood, William Leadbetter. *The Life of Henry Calderwood, LLD, FRSE by his son and the Rev David Woodside BD with a special chapter on his philosophical works by A. Seth Pringle-Pattison LLD*. London: Hodder & Stoughton, 1900.
Campbell, Gwyn. *An Economic History of Imperial Madagascar, 1750–1895: The Rise and Fall of an Island Empire*. Cambridge: Cambridge University Press, 2005.

Carlyle, A. J., et al., eds. *Towards Reunion, being contributions to mutual understanding by Church of England and Free Church writers*. London: Macmillan, 1919.

Carroll, Robert P. "The Biblical Prophets as Apologists for the Christian Religion: Reading William Robertson Smith's *The Prophets of Israel* Today." In Johnstone, *William Robertson Smith*, 148–57.

Carruthers, S. W., ed. *Digest of the Proceedings of the Synods of the Presbyterian Church of England, 1876–1905*. London: Presbyterian Church of England, 1907.

Chadwick, Henry. "Authority in Liberal Protestantism." *The Times*, 9 April 1964.

Chambers, Robert, and Thomas Thomson, eds. *A Biographical Dictionary of Eminent Scotsmen: Supplement Abercrombie-Wood*. Glasgow: Blackie, 1845.

Charles, R. H. *A Critical and Exegetical Commentary on the Revelation of St. John*. 2 vols. Edinburgh: T. & T. Clark, 1920.

Cheyne, Alec C. "Bible and Confession in Scotland: The Background to the Robertson Smith Case." In Johnstone, *William Robertson Smith*, 24–40.

Clark, David S. Review of *Grace and Personality*, by John Oman. *Princeton University Review* 25 (1927) 149–56.

Class, G. *Ideale und Güter: Untersuchungen zur Ethik*. Erlangen: Deichert, 1886.

Clayton, John. Review of *On Religion: Speeches to Its Cultured Despisers*, by Friedrich Schleiermacher, edited and translated by Richard Crouter. *JTS* 41 (1990) 761–62.

Clements, Keith. *Faith on the Frontier*. Edinburgh: T. & T. Clark and World Council of Churches, 1999.

———. "A Notable Ecumenical Anniversary: The Anglo-German Churches' Exchange Visits of 1908–9." *Ecumenical Review* 59 (2007) 257–83.

Clouston, J. Storer. *Orkney and the Archer Guards*. Proceedings of the Orkney Antiquarian Society 15. Kirkwall, Scotland: Kirkwall Press, 1937.

Cornick, David. "Cambridge and Reluctant Dissent." In *From Cambridge to Sinai: The Worlds of Agnes Smith Lewis and Margaret Dunlop Gibson*, edited by David Cornick and Clyde Binfield, 117–43. London: URC History Society and United Reformed Church, 2006.

Cornick, David, and Clyde Binfield, eds. *From Cambridge to Sinai: The Worlds of Agnes Smith Lewis and Margaret Dunlop Gibson*. London: URC History Society and the United Reformed Church, 2006.

Corts, Thomas E., ed. *Henry Drummond, a Perpetual Benediction*. Edinburgh: T. & T. Clark, 1999.

Daglish, N. "Planning the Education Bill of 1896." *History of Education* 16 (1987) 91–104.

Dart, Martha. *Marjorie Sykes: Quaker-Gandhian*. 1993. https://www.arvindguptatoys.com/arvindgupta/marjorie.pdf.

Dixon, David Dippie. *Upper Coquetdale Northumberland: Its Traditions, Folk-Lore and Scenery*. Newcastle: Redpath, 1903.

Domingo, Raphael. "The Crisis of International Law." *Vanderbilt Law Review* 42 (2021) 1543.

Drummond, Andrew L., and James Bulloch. *The Church in Late Victorian Scotland, 1874–1900*. Edinburgh: Saint Andrew Press, 1978.

Dunbar, Janet. *J. M. Barrie: The Man Behind the Image*. Boston: Houghton Mifflin, 1970.

Eddy, Sherwood. *With Our Soldiers in France*. New York: Association, 1917.

Elliott, Donald. *Trinity Camden: A Brief History*. London: Trinity Church, n.d. https://www.trinity-camden-urc.org.uk/a-brief-history-chapter-4.

Ellis, Ieuan. "Schleiermacher in Britain." *SJT* 33 (1980) 417–52.
Elmslie, W. A. L. *Westminster College Cambridge, 1899–1949*. London: Presbyterian Church of England, 1949.
Falcetta, Alessandro. *A Biography of James Rendel Harris, 1852–1941*. London: T. & T. Clark, 2018.
Farmer, H. H. "Death of Dr. John Oman: An Appreciation." *Christian World*, 25 May 1939.
———. "Memoir of the Author." In *Honest Religion*, by John Oman, xxvi–xxxii. Cambridge: Cambridge University Press, 1941.
———. "Theologians of Our Time III, John Wood Oman." *ET* 74 (1963) 132–35.
———. *The World and God: A Study of Prayer, Providence and Miracle in Christian Experience*. London: Nisbet, 1935.
Farrer, Austin. *The Revelation of St. John the Divine*. Oxford: Oxford University Press, 1964.
Ferguson, John. "The Fellowship of Reconciliation." *Cambridge Review*, December 1984.
Fergusson, David, ed. *Scottish Philosophical Theology 1700–2000*. Exeter: Imprint Academic, 2007.
Fergusson, David, and Mark W. Elliott, eds. *History of Scottish Theology*. 3 vols. Oxford: Oxford University Press, 2019.
Forbes-Leith, William. *The Scots Men-at-Arms and Life-Guards in France, from Their Formation until Their Final Dissolution*. 2 vols. Edinburgh: Paterson, 1882.
Forsyth, Peter Taylor. *The Principle of Authority in Relation to Certainty, Sanctity and Society*. London: Independent Press, 1912.
Fraser, Alexander Campbell. *Biographia Philosophica: A Retrospect*. Edinburgh: Blackwood, 1904.
———. *Philosophy of Theism*. Edinburgh: Blackwood, 1899.
Fyffe, David. "Brighter Prospects at Westminster College." *Presbyterian Messenger*, November 1919.
Galloway, A. D. Review of *Religion and Reality*, by F. G. Healey. *Religious Studies* 3 (1967) 428–29.
George, M. Alain. *Le palimpseste Lewis-Mingana de Cambridge, témoin ancien de l'histoire du Coran*. Paris: Boccard, 2011.
Glen, Margaret, and John Bartlett. *Weoley Hill United Reformed Church, Birmingham, History, 1915–1983*. Birmingham: Weoley Hill URC, 1983.
Gorman, Daniel. "Ecumenical Internationalism: Willoughby Dickinson, the League of Nations and the World Alliance for Promoting International Friendship through the Churches." *Journal of Contemporary History* 45 (2010) 51–73.
Grant, George. *The Concept of Nature and Supernature in the Theology of John Oman*. In *Collected Works of George Grant*, vol. 1, *1933–50*, edited by Arthur Davis and Peter C. Emberley, 157–401. Toronto: University of Toronto Press, 2000.
Grosvenor Square Presbyterian Church. *Faithful as David: Thomas Oman. . . .* Manchester: Grosvenor Square Presbyterian Church, 1932.
Gunton, Colin. *Enlightenment and Alienation*. London: Marshall, Morgan and Scott, 1985.
———. "The Real as the Redemptive." In *Justice the True and Only Mercy*, edited by Trevor Hart, 37–58. Edinburgh: T. & T. Clark, 1995.
Hamilton, Ian. *The Erosion of Calvinist Orthodoxy*. Fearn: Christian Focus, 2010.

Hampson, M. D[aphne]. "The British Responses to the German Church Struggle, 1933–1939." D. Phil. diss., University of Oxford, 1973.
Hanak, H. "The Union of Democratic Control during the First World War." *Historical Research* 36 (1963) 168–80.
Hastings, James, ed. *Dictionary of Christ and the Gospels*. Edinburgh: T. & T. Clark, 1906.
Hausrath, Adolf. *David Friedrich Strauss und die Theologie seiner Zeit*. Heidelberg: Bassermann, 1878.
Hawkridge, P. B. *Epiphany and Other Verses*. Lovedale, 1967.
Healey, F. G., ed. *Prospect for Theology: Essays in Honour of H. H. Farmer*. Digswell Place: Nisbet, 1966.
———. *Religion and Reality: The Theology of John Oman*. Edinburgh: Oliver & Boyd, 1965.
Hick, John. "A Voyage Round John Oman." In Hood, *John Oman: New Perspectives*, 163–71.
Hinz, Gerhard, ed. *Aus der Geschichte der Universität Heidelberg und ihrer Fakultäten, aus Anlaß des 575jährigen Bestehens der Ruprecht-Karl-Universität Heidelberg (Ruperto-Carola* Sonderband). Heidelberg: Brausdruck, 1961.
Hood, Adam. *Baillie, Oman and MacMurray: Experience and Religious Belief*. Farnham: Ashgate, 2003.
———. "God's All-Conquering Love: Oman's Preaching, Its Style and Content." In Hood, *John Oman: New Perspectives*, 140–62.
———. *John Oman: New Perspectives*. Milton Keynes: Paternoster, 2012.
Hoover, A. J. *God, Germany, and Britain in the Great War. A Study in Clerical Nationalism*. New York: Praeger, 1989.
Houston, Fleur. "Freedom as Authorization." In *Contextuality in Reformed Europe: The Mission of the Church in the Transformation of European Culture*, edited by Christine Lienemann-Perrin, H. M. Vroom, and M. Weinrich, 261–74. New York: Rodopi, 2004.
———. "In the Open Country of Action and Enquiry: John Oman and the Great War." *JURCHS* 9.1 (2012) 22–41.
———. "A Visit to the Prisons of the Ruhr and the Rhineland: An Exercise in Church Diplomacy." *JURCHS* 9.6 (2015) 371–81.
Houston, Walter. "*Prophecy and Religion* Revisited: John Skinner and Evangelical Biblical Criticism." *Religions* 12 (2021) 935. https://doi.org/10.3390/rel12110935.
Johnstone, William, ed. *William Robertson Smith: Essays in Reassessment*. Sheffield: Sheffield Academic, 1995.
Jones, Michael. "Notions of Udal Law in Orkney and Shetland: From Medieval Norse Law to Contested Vestiges of Autonomous Rights within Scots Law." In *Legislation and State Formation: Norway and Its Neighbours in the Late Middle Ages*, edited by Steinar Imsen, 133–289. Trondheim: Akademika, 2013.
Kattenbusch, Ferdinand. *Das Apostolische Symbol: Seine Entstehung, sein geschichtliche Sinn usw.* 2 vols. Leipzig: Hinrichs, 1894, 1900.
Kaye, Elaine. *C. J. Cadoux: Theologian, Scholar and Pacifist*. Edinburgh: Edinburgh University Press, 1988.
Ker, John. *Lectures on the History of Preaching*, edited by A. R. MacEwen. London: Hodder & Stoughton, 1888.
Ker, William Paton. "The Philosophy of Art." In *Essays in Philosophical Criticism*, edited by Andrew Seth and R. B. Haldane. London: Longmans, Green, 1883.

Knox, R. B[uick]. "The Bible in English Presbyterianism." *ET* 94 (1983) 166–70.

———. "Professor John Gibb and Westminster College Cambridge." *JURCHS* 3.8 (1986) 328–37.

———. "The Relationship between English and Scottish Presbyterianism, 1836–1876." *Records of the Scottish Church History Society* 21 (1981) 43–66.

———. *St. Columba's Church Cambridge, 1879–1979*. Cambridge: St Columba's Presbyterian Church, 1979.

———. *Westminster College: Its Background and History*. 2nd ed. Cambridge: Westminster College, 2007 [1972].

Knox, T. M. Review of *Religion and Reality*, by F. G. Healey. *JTS* 17 (1966) 546–50.

Krabusch, Hans. *Zeittafel zur Geschichte der Universität Heidelberg: Nachtrag*. Tipped-in sheet in Hinz, *Aus der Geschichte der Universität Heidelberg*.

Lachman, David C. *The Marrow Controversy, 1718–1732: An Historical and Theological Analysis*. Edinburgh: Rutherford House, 1988.

Landreth, P[eter]. *Presbyterian Divinity Hall: In its Changes and Enlargements for One Hundred and Forty Years*. Edinburgh: Oliphant, 1876.

Landry, Stan M[ichael]. "That All May Be One? Church Unity and the German National Idea, 1866–1883." *Church History* 80 (2011) 281–301.

———. "That All May Be One? Church Unity, Luther Memory and Ideas of the German Nation, 1817–1883." PhD diss., University of Arizona, 2010.

Langford, Thomas A. "The Theological Methodology of John Oman and H. H. Farmer." *Religious Studies* 1 (1966) 229–40.

Lawrence, D. H. *Apocalypse*. London: Penguin, 1995 (originally 1931).

Leith, Peter, and Susan Leonard. *The Kirk and Parish of Stenness*. Kirkwall: Orcadian, 2007.

Lincicum, David. "Fighting Germans with Germans: Victorian Theological Translations between Anxiety and Influence." *Journal for the History of Modern Theology* 24 (2017) 153–201.

Lindsay, A. D. Review of *Natural and Supernatural*, by John Oman. *JTS* 33 (1932) 385–88.

Lipscomb, Benjamin J. B. *The Women Are Up to Something: How Elizabeth Anscombe, Philippa Foot, Mary Midgley, and Iris Murdoch Revolutionized Ethics*. Oxford: Oxford University Press, 2022.

Little, Fergus G. "A Scottish Border Baptist Church, Kelso." *Baptist Quarterly* 21 (1965) 132–37.

MacArthur, Arthur. *Setting Up Signs: Memories of an Ecumenical Pilgrim*. London: United Reformed Church, 1997.

MacDonald, Nathan. "Holy War and the Great War in German Protestant Scholarship on the Old Testament." In *The First World War and the Mobilization of Biblical Scholarship*, edited by Andrew Mein, Nathan MacDonald and Matthew A. Collins, 135–61. London: T. & T. Clark, 2019.

MacEwen, Alexander R. *The Life and Letters of John Cairns*. London: Hodder & Stoughton, 1898.

MacLean, Neil N. *Life at a Northern University*. Aberdeen: Rosemount, 1874.

MacLeod, John. "John Oman as Theologian." *Hibbert Journal* 48 (1950) 348–53.

Maier, Bernhard. *William Robertson Smith*. Tübingen: Mohr Siebeck, 2009.

Malik, Maleiha. "Justice." In *Fields of Faith*, edited by David F. Ford, Ben Quash, and Janet Martin Soskice, 182–202. Cambridge: Cambridge University Press, 2005.

Mander, W. J. *British Idealism: A History.* Oxford Scholarship on Line, 2011.
Mann, A. Montgomery. "Fifty Years Ago—Reminiscences by A. Montgomery Mann." *Bulletin, Friends of Westminster College,* April 1969.
McCrie, C. G., ed. *The Marrow of Modern Divinity.* Glasgow: Boyce, 1902.
McDermid, Jane. "Gender, National Identity and the Royal (Argyll) Commission of Enquiry into Scottish Education (1864-1867)." *Journal of Educational Administration and History* 38 (2006) 249–62.
McIntosh, J. B. *The Presbytery of Kelso Against the Rev. Philip Bainbridge, Minister of Makerstoun.* Edinburgh: Neill, 1886.
McKimmon, Eric G. *John Oman: Orkney's Theologian. A Contextual Study of John Oman's Theology with Reference to Personal Freedom as the Unifying Principle.* PhD diss., University of Edinburgh, 2012. http://hdl.handle.net/1842/6292.
———. "The Secession and United Presbyterian Churches." In *The History of Scottish Theology,* edited by David Fergusson and Mark W. Elliott, 2:376–89. Oxford: Oxford University Press, 2019.
McLeod, Hugh. *Religion and the Working Class in Nineteenth Century Britain.* London: MacMillan, 1984.
Micklem, Nathaniel. *The Box and the Puppets.* London: Geoffrey Bles, 1957.
Middleton, Roy. *Introduction to the Works of Ralph Erskine.* Glasgow: Free Presbyterian Publications, 1991.
Muirhead, Andrew T. N. "The United Presbyterian Church Divinity Hall: History to 1860." Dissenting Academies online: Database and Encyclopedia: Dr. Williams's Centre for Dissenting Studies, November 2011.
Munson, James. *The Nonconformists: In Search of a Lost Culture.* London: SPCK, 1991.
The Nature of God and His Purpose for the World. London: Longmans, Green, 1924.
The New Statistical Account of Scotland by Ministers of the Respective Parishes. 15 vols. Edinburgh: Blackwood, 1845. https://archive.org/details/b21365805_0001.
Newbigin, Lesslie. *Unfinished Agenda.* London: SPCK, 1985.
Nicoll, W. Robertson. *"Ian MacLaren": The Life of the Rev. John Watson D.D.* London: Hodder & Stoughton, 1908.
Norman, Gwen R. P. *Grace Unfailing: The Radical Mind and the Beloved Community of Richard Roberts.* Etobicoke, Ontario: United Church Publishing, 1988.
Oman, John. "The Apocalypse." *Expositor,* 9th series, 4 (1925) 437–52.
———. Articles in *The Student Movement* 1922: "Looking round our Position," February, 98–100; "The Mathematical Mechanical Order," March, 124–25; "The Evolutionary Historical Process," April, 153–55; "Mind as the Measure of the Universe," May, 171–73; "The Sacred as the Measure of Man," June, 194–95.
———. *Book of Revelation: Theory of Text, Rearranged Text and Translation, Commentary.* Cambridge: Cambridge University Press, 1923.
———. "Christianity in a New Age." In Peake and Parsons, *An Outline of Christianity,* 3:xiii–xxii.
———. *The Church and the Divine Order.* London: Hodder & Stoughton, 1911.
———. *Concerning the Ministry.* London: SCM Press, 1936.
———. *A Dialogue with God and Other Sermons and Addresses.* London: Clarke, 1950.
———. "Germany: Fifty Years Apart. I, The Changed and the Unchanged." *British Weekly,* 24 January 1935.
———. "Germany: Fifty Years Apart. II, Officials and Military." *British Weekly,* 31 January 1935.

---. "Germany: Fifty Years Apart. III, Temper and Outlook." *British Weekly*, 7 February 1935.
---. "Germany: Fifty Years Apart. IV, The Twilight of Democracy." *British Weekly*, 14 February 1935.
---. *Grace and Personality*. Cambridge: Cambridge University Press, 1917. [Oman, *Grace and Personality*, refers here unless another edition is indicated.]
---. *Grace and Personality*. 2nd ed. Cambridge: Cambridge University Press, 1919.
---. *Grace and Personality*. 3rd ed. Cambridge: Cambridge University Press, 1925.
---. *Grace and Personality*. With an introduction by Nolan R. Best. New York: Macmillan, 1925.
---. *Honest Religion*. Cambridge: Cambridge University Press, 1941.
---. "Human Freedom." In Stanton, *Elements of Pain and Conflict*, 57–73.
---. "Individual." In Hastings, *A Dictionary of Christ and the Gospels*, 1:814–16.
---. "Individualism." In Hastings, *A Dictionary of Christ and the Gospels*, 1:816–19.
---. "Individuality." In Hastings, *A Dictionary of Christ and the Gospels*, 1:819–21.
---. "In Spirit and in Truth: The Abiding Significance of Apocalyptic." *Churchman* 46 (1932) 276–93.
---. *Lectures in Systematic Theology*, n.d. Westminster College archives.
---. "Method in Theology, an Inaugural Lecture." *Expositor* 26 (August 1923) 81–93.
---. "The Ministry of the Nonconformist Churches." In *The Problem of a Career Solved by 36 Men of Distinction*, edited by J. A. R. Cairns, 127–32. Bristol: Arrowsmith, 1926.
---."The Moderator's New Year Message." *Presbyterian Messenger,* January 1932.
---. "Mr Henry Ford's Philosophy of Industry." *British Weekly*, 20 June 1929.
---. *The Natural and the Supernatural*. Cambridge: Cambridge University Press, 1931.
---. "Notes on German Student Life." Unpublished typescript, n.d. Westminster College archives.
---. *The Office of the Ministry*. London: SCM, 1928.
---. *The Orkneys*. Typescript, undated, possibly around 1899. Westminster College archives.
---. "Our College and Its Problems." *Presbyterian Messenger,* January 1923.
---. "Personality and Grace." *Expositor*, 8th series, 2 (July–December 1911) 353–67, 456–63, 528–34; 3 (January–June 1912) 171–78, 236–42, 468–75, 528–34; 4 (July–December 1912) 57–60, 138–42, 252–62, 354–62, 526–38.
---. "The Presbyterian Churches." In *Evangelical Christianity: Its History and Witness*, edited by W. B. Selbie, 57–79. London: Hodder & Stoughton, 1911.
---. *The Problem of Faith and Freedom in the Last Two Centuries*. London: Hodder & Stoughton, 1906.
---. *Rationalism and Romanticism: A Study of Kant's "Religion Within the Limits of Reason Alone" and Schleiermacher's "Speeches on Religion."* PhD diss., University of Edinburgh, 1904.
---. "Reminiscences." In *Victoria Street United Free Church Centenary Memorial*, 1906, 31–39.
---. "Reminiscences of Continental Travel." Unpublished typescript, n.d. Westminster College archives.
---. Review of *De Kant à Ritschl: Une siècle d'histoire de la pensée chrétienne*, by H. Dubois. In *JTS* 28 (1927) 187–88.

———. Review of *The Idea of the Holy*, by Rudolf Otto. *JTS* 25 (1924) 275–86.
———. Review of *The Impatience of a Parson*, by H. R. L. Sheppard. *British Weekly*, 27 October 1927.
———. Review of *La Liberté Chrétienne: Etude sur le Principe de la Piété chez Luther*, by Robert Will. *JTS* 24 (1923) 211–14.
———. Review of *The Present Crisis in Religion*, by W. E. Orchard. *British Weekly*, 11 April 1929.
———. Review of *Process and Reality*, by A. N. Whitehead. *JTS* 33 (1931) 48–54.
———. Review of *Religion in the Making*, by A. N. Whitehead. *JTS* 28 (1927) 296–304.
———. "Ritschlianism." *JTS* 11 (1910) 469–76.
———. "The Roman Sacerdotal Hierarchy." In *Why I Am and Why I Am Not a Catholic*, 230–56. London: Cassell, 1931.
———. "Schleiermacher." *JTS* 30 (1929) 401–5.
———. "The Sphere of Religion." In *Science, Religion and Reality*, edited by Joseph Needham, 259–99. London: Sheldon, 1926.
———. "Spiritual Regeneration as the Basis of World Reconstruction." Unpublished prize-winning essay, Walker Trust, 1921. University of St Andrews Special Collections.
———. *The Text of Revelation: A Revised Theory*. Cambridge: Cambridge University Press, 1928.
———. *Vision and Authority; or, The Throne of St. Peter*. London: Hodder & Stoughton, 1902. [Oman, *Vision and Authority*, refers here unless otherwise indicated.]
———. *Vision and Authority; or, The Throne of St. Peter*. 2nd ed. London: Hodder & Stoughton, 1928.
———. *Vision and Authority; or, The Throne of St. Peter*. 8th ed. Introduction by T. W. Manson. London: Hodder & Stoughton, 1948.
———. "A Visit to America." Unpublished manuscript, Westminster College Archives.
———. "War." In Stanton, *Elements of Pain and Conflict*, 157–72.
———. *The War and Its Issues: An Attempt at a Christian Judgment*. Cambridge: Cambridge University Press, 1915.
Orchard, W. E. "Why I Should Find It Difficult to Become a Roman Catholic." In *Why I Am and Why I Am Not a Catholic*, by Hilaire Belloc et al., 204–29. London: Cassell, 1931.
Ordnance Survey Name Books. Vol. 21: *Orkney*. London: Ordnance Survey, 1879–80.
O'Riordan, Elspeth Y. *Britain and the Ruhr Crisis*. Basingstoke: Palgrave, 2001.
Otto, Rudolph. *The Idea of the Holy: An Inquiry into the Non-rational Factors in the Idea of the Divine and Its Relation to the Rational*. Translated by John W. Harvey. Oxford: Oxford University Press, 1923.
Paisley Pamphlets, 1739–1893. Renfrewshire Heritage Centre, Paisley.
Payne, David. "Why the British Army Did Not Mutiny En Masse on the Western Front in the Great War." 22 May 2008. https://www.westernfrontassociation.com/world-war-i-articles/why-the-british-army-did-not-mutiny-en-masse-on-the-western-front-during-the-first-world-war/.
Peake, A. S., and R. G. Parsons, eds. *An Outline of Christianity: The Story of Our Civilisation*. 5 vols. London: Waverley, 1926–27.
Petersen, Gotfred. *Seks år på Madagaskar: Erindringer og oplevelser*. 1904. Mission and Diakonia Archives. VID Specialized University, Stavanger.
Pevsner, Nikolaus, and Ian A. Richmond. *The Buildings of England: Northumberland*. Harmondsworth: Penguin, 1957.

Price, A. Whigham. *The Ladies of Castlebrae*. Gloucester: Sutton, 1985.

Price, Fred. *Moseley Presbyterian Church: A Candid History*. Birmingham: Moseley Local History Society, 1991.

Pyper, Hugh S. "A Disconnected Dialogue: Adolf von Harnack, C. J. Cadoux and the Biblical Case for Peace at the Outbreak of the First World War." In *The First World War and the Mobilization of Biblical Scholarship*, edited by Andrew Mein, Nathan MacDonald, and Matthew A. Collins, 241–56. London: T. & T. Clark, 2019.

Railton, Nicholas M. *No North Sea: The Anglo-German Evangelical Network in the Middle of the Nineteenth Century*. Leiden: Brill, 2000.

Ramsay, Alexander. "International Fellowship through the Churches." *Presbyterian Messenger*, November 1922.

Raven, C. E. "Social Justice." In Peake and Parsons, *An Outline of Christianity*, 4:139.

Ritschl, Albrecht. *Die christliche Lehre von der Rechtfertigung und Versöhnung*. 3 vols. Bonn: Marcus, 1870–74.

Robbins, Keith. *The Abolition of War: The "Peace Movement" in Britain, 1914–1919*. Cardiff: University of Wales Press, 1976.

Robinson, William Childs. "Presbyterian Pelagianism." *Christianity Today* 3.6 (mid-October 1932).

Robson, R. S. *Our Professors*. Edited by S. W. Carruthers. London: Presbyterian Historical Society of England, 1956.

Rogerson, J. W. *The Bible and Criticism in Victorian Britain*. Sheffield: Sheffield Academic, 1995.

Rowley, H. H. *The Servant of the Lord*. London: Lutterworth, 1952.

Schleiermacher, Friedrich. *Brief Outline of the Study of Theology*. Translated by William Farrar. Edinburgh: T. & T. Clark, 1850.

———. *The Christian Faith*. English translation from the 2nd German ed. Edited by H. R. Macintosh and J. S. Stewart. Edinburgh: T. & T. Clark, 1928.

———. *Christmas Eve: A Dialogue on the Celebration of Christmas*. Translated by William Hastie. Edinburgh: T. & T. Clark, 1890.

———. *A Critical Essay on the Gospel of St Luke*. Translated by Connop Thirlwall. London: John Taylor, 1825.

———. *Kritische Gesamtausgabe*. Edited by Hans-Joachim Birkner et al. Berlin: de Gruyter, 1985–99.

———. *On Religion: Speeches to Its Cultured Despisers* (1st ed., 1799). Edited and translated by Richard Crouter. Cambridge: Cambridge University Press, 1988.

———. *On Religion: Speeches to Its Cultured Despisers* (3rd ed., 1821). Translated by John Oman. London: Kegan Paul, Trench, Trübner, 1893 [References to Schleiermacher, *On Religion*, refer here unless otherwise indicated.]

———. "On the Different Methods of Translating." Lecture before the Academy of Berlin, 24 June 1813 (excerpts). Translated by Waltraud Bartstadt. In *Theories of Translation: An Anthology of Essays from Dryden to Derrida*, edited by Raine Schulte and John Biguenet, 36–54. Chicago: University of Chicago Press, 1992.

———. *Schleiermacher: Selected Sermons*. Translated by Mary F. Wilson, FBL. London: Hodder & Stoughton, 1890.

———. "Schleiermacher's Religious Views." *Biblical Review* 6 (1849) 239–61.

Schmidt, Larry, ed. *George Grant in Process: Essays and Conversations*. Toronto: Anansi, 1978.

Schwartz, Marvin. *The UDC in British Politics during the First World War*. Oxford: Clarendon, 1971.

Schweitzer, Rich. "The Cross and the Trenches: Religious Faith and Doubt among Some British Soldiers on the Western Front." *War and Society* 16 (1998) 33–57.

Scorgie, Glen G. *A Call for Continuity: The Theological Contribution of James Orr.* Vancouver: Regent College Publishing, 2004. (First published by Mercer University Press, Macon, GA, 1988.)

Scott, J. Hope. "The Student Christian Movement." *Presbyterian Messenger*, February 1915, 53.

Scott, Richenda C. *Herbert G. Wood: A Memoir of His Life and Thought.* London: Friends Home Service Committee, 1967.

Scott, William Taussig, and Martin X. Moleski. *Michael Polanyi: Scientist and Philosopher.* Oxford: Oxford University Press, 2005.

Selbie, W. B., ed. *Evangelical Christianity: Its History and Witness.* London: Hodder & Stoughton, 1911.

———. "John Oman." *Congregational Quarterly* 17 (1939) 281.

Sell, Alan P. F. "Living in the Half-Lights: John Oman in Context." In Hood, *John Oman: New Perspectives*, 3–63.

———. "Ritschl Appraised: Then and Now." *Reformed Theological Review* 38 (1979) 33–41.

Seth, Andrew, and R. B. Haldane, eds. *Essays in Philosophical Criticism.* London: Longmans, Green, 1883.

Sheffield, Gary. "Officer-Man Relations, Discipline and Morale in the British Army of the Great War." In *Facing Armageddon*, edited by Hugh Cecil and Peter H. Liddle, 413–24. Barnsley: Pen and Sword, 1996.

Simpson, P. Carnegie, *The Life of Principal Rainy*. London: Hodder & Stoughton, 1909.

———. *Recollections.* London: Nisbet, 1943.

Sinclair, Hugh. "Living Voices: Professor Oman." *Presbyterian Messenger*, December 1915, 429–30.

Sinclair, John, ed. *The Statistical Account of Scotland*. 21 vols. Edinburgh: Creech, 1791–99. https://catalog.hathitrust.org/Record/000153475.

Skinner, John. *The Book of the Prophet Isaiah, Chapters I–XXXIX* (Cambridge Bible for Schools and Colleges). Cambridge: Cambridge University Press, 1909 (1896).

———. *The Book of the Prophet Isaiah, Chapters XL–LXVI* (Cambridge Bible for Schools and Colleges). Cambridge: Cambridge University Press, 1910 (1898).

———. *Prophecy and Religion: Studies in the Life of Jeremiah*. Cambridge: Cambridge University Press, 1922.

———. *Some Observations on Theological Education*. Cambridge: Westminster College, 1918.

Small, Robert. *History of the Congregations of the United Presbyterian Church 1733–1900*. 2 vols. Edinburgh: Small, 1904.

Smith, George Adam. *The Life of Henry Drummond*. 2nd ed. London: Hodder & Stoughton, 1899 (1st ed., 1898).

Smith, P. J. "The Rehousing/Relocation Issue in an Early Slum Clearance Scheme: Edinburgh 1865–1885." *Urban Studies* 26 (1989) 100–114.

Smith, William Robertson. *Answer to the Form of Libel now before the Free Church Presbytery of Aberdeen*. Edinburgh: Douglas, 1878.

———. *Lectures and Essays*. Edited by J. S. Black and G. Chrystal. London: Black, 1912.

———. *The Prophets of Israel and Their Place in History*. Introduction by Robert Alun Jones. New Brunswick: Transaction, 2002. Reprint of the 1902 edition by Adam and Charles Black.

Smith-Lewis, A. [Agnes Smith Lewis], and A. Mingana. *Leaves from Three Ancient Qur'ans, possibly pre-'Othmanic, with a list of their variants*. Cambridge: Cambridge University Press, 1914.
Snape, Michael. *The Back Parts of War: The YMCA Memoirs and Letters of Barclay Baron, 1915–1919*. Woodridge: Boydell, 2009.
———. *God and the British Soldier*. London: Routledge, 2005.
Söderblom, Nathan. "The Role of the Church in Promoting Peace." Nobel Lecture, 11 December 1930. https://www.nobelprize.org/prizes/peace/1930/soderblom/lecture/.
Sorley, W. R. *The International Crisis: The Theory of the State*. London: Oxford University Press, 1916.
Soskice, Janet. *Sisters of Sinai*. London: Chatto & Windus, 2009.
Spencer, Heath A. "Kulturprotestantismus and 'Positive Christianity': A Case for Discontinuity." *Kirchliche Zeitgeschichte* 22.2 (2009) 519–49.
Stadener, Sam, John Oman, and A. Wihlborg. "Report of a Visit to the French Prisons in Germany." *Goodwill* 6.2 (December 1923).
Stanton, V. H., ed. *The Elements of Pain and Conflict in Human Life, Considered from a Christian Point of View*. Cambridge: Cambridge University Press, 1916.
Statham, Todd Reagan, *Dogma and History in Victorian Scotland*. PhD diss., McGill University, Montreal, 2011.
———. "'Landlouping Students of Divinity': Scots Presbyterians in German Theology Faculties, c. 1840 to 1914." *Zeitschrift für Kirchengeschichte* 121 (2010) 42–67.
Statter, Chris. "Managing the Disruptions: The Ministry of J. Oswald Dykes." *JURCHS* 10.2 (2018) 59–72.
Straker, Jane. *A History of St James' United Reformed Church: Incorporating Lisburn Street ad Clayport Street Presbyterian Churches*. Alnwick: St James's URC, 1989.
Strauss, David Friedrich. *Das Leben Jesu kritisch bearbeitet*. Tübingen: Osiander, 1836. Translated from the 4th ed. (1840) [by Marian Evans (George Eliot)] as *The Life of Jesus, Critically Examined*. 3 vols. London: Chapman, 1846.
Sundkler, Bengt. *Nathan Söderblom*. Lund: Gleerups, 1968.
Sutherland, Douglas. *Against the Wind*. London: Heinemann, 1968.
Svenson, Leif. "A Theology for the Bildungsbürgertum: Ritschl in Context." ThD diss., Umeå University, Sweden, 2018.
Tait, James. *Two Centuries of Border Life*. Kelso: Rutherfurd, 1889.
Taylor, Charles. *Sources of the Self: The Making of the Modern Identity*. Cambridge, MA: Harvard University Press, 1989.
T.B.M. *Slum Life in Edinburgh; or, Scenes in Its Darkest Places*. Edinburgh: Thin, 1881.
Tennant, F. R. "John Wood Oman." *Proceedings of the British Academy* 25 (1939) 332–38.
———. Review of *The Natural and the Supernatural*, by John Oman. *Mind* 41 (1932) 212–18.
Testimonials in favour of James Seth M.A. Edinburgh, candidate for the chair of Logic and Metaphysic in the University of Toronto. [1889.] Microfiche, University of Toronto. https://archive.org/stream/cihm_93533/cihm_93533_djvu.text.
Thompson, David M. "Oman and the University of Cambridge." In Hood, *John Oman: New Perspectives*, 75–94.
Thompson, Noel. "Thomas Kirkup." In *Dictionary of National Biography*, published online 11 October 2018. https://doi.org/10.1093/odnb/9780198614128.013.107247.

Titley, E. Brian. *Church, State, and the Control of Schooling in Ireland, 1900–1944*. Montreal: McGill Queen's University Press, 1983.
Tocqueville, Alexis de. *The Old Regime and the Revolution*. Garden City, NY: Doubleday, 1955.
Tod, Marcus N. "Lights and Shadows of War-Time, V. Some Experiences of Work with the YMCA." *Presbyterian Messenger*, May 1916, 155–56.
Trilling, Lionel. *Sincerity and Authenticity*. Cambridge, MA: Harvard University Press, 1972.
United Presbyterian Church Clayport Street Alnwick. Minutes of session 1853–97. Northumberland Archives UR/P28/2/1/2/2.
———. Minutes of session 1898–1923. Northumberland Archives UR/P28/2/1/2/3.
United Reformed Church. "Statement Concerning the Nature, Faith and Order of the United Reformed Church." https://urc.org.uk/images/Free-Ebooks/What_is_the_URC_Statement.pdf.
University of Cambridge. *The Historical Register*. Supplement vol. 1911–20. Cambridge: Cambridge University Press, 1920.
University of Edinburgh. Calendar, 1882–1883. Edinburgh: James Thin.
Walling, John. *The Internment and Treatment of German Nationals during the First World War*. Great Grimsby: Riparian, 2005.
Wallis, Jill. *Valiant for Peace: A History of the Fellowship of Reconciliation, 1914 to 1989*. London: Fellowship of Reconciliation, 1991.
Walzer, Michael. *The Revolution of the Saints*. Cambridge, MA: Harvard University Press, 1965.
Ward, Pamela. *The First Two Hundred Years—a History of Thropton Presbyterian Church, 1799–1999*. Thropton, Northumberland: Thropton United Reformed Church, 1999.
Warfield, Benjamin B. "The Presbyterian Churches and the Westminster Confession." *Presbyterian Review* 9 (1889) 646–57.
Watchman. "John Oman: In Memoriam." *British Weekly*, 25 May 1939.
Wawn, Andrew. *The Vikings and the Victorians*. Cambridge: Brewer, 2002.
Weiße, Wolfram. "Irenic Mediator for Unity—Partisan Advocate for Truth: Nathan Söderblom's Initiatives for Peace and Justice." In *Nathan Söderblom as a European*, edited by Sam Dahlgren, 15–42. Tro & Tanke 7. Uppsala: Svenska Kyrkans forskringsråd, 1993.
Whitehorn, Michael. *Roy Whitehorn: "A Servant of the Word," 1891–1976*. Self-published, 1991.
Whitworth, Michael H. *Einstein's Wake: Relativity, Metaphor and Modernist Literature*. Oxford: Oxford University Press, 2001.
Wilkinson, Alan. *The Church of England and the First World War*. London: SPCK, 1928.
Windelband, Wilhelm. "Das Heilige." In *Präludien: Aufsätze und Reden zur Philosophie und ihrer Geschichte*, 2:295–332. Tübingen: Mohr, 1915.
Woodfin, Yandall. "John Wood Oman (1860–1939): A Critical Study of His Contribution to Theology." PhD diss., University of Edinburgh, 1962.
Woodside, David. *The Soul of a Scottish Church; or, The Contribution of the United Presbyterian Church to Scottish Life and Religion*. Edinburgh: United Free Church of Scotland Press, 1917.
Wright, T. R. *D. H. Lawrence and the Bible*. Cambridge: Cambridge University Press, 2000.

Index of Subjects

adult education, 297
    Chautauqua Scientific and Literary
        Society, 149–50
    Christian Evidence Society, 231
    correspondence college, 231
    public lectures, 148–49
    YMCA lectures, 264
"Appeal to Protestant Christians
    Abroad," 243–44
Army and Religion, The, 288–90
Associate Church, 19
Atonement, 58, 85, 140, 163, 176, 205,
    281, 282, 286n263
    controversies, 139–40
Auburn Declaration, 207
    see also Westminster Confession
Auburn Theological Seminary, 202–5
authority
    creeds, 8, 162–63
    ecclesiastical authority, 161
    organisation, 78, 162–63, 164, 308
    personal, 160–62
    social/economic, 164–66, 230
    Vision and Authority, **158–67**
    see also conscription
awareness and apprehension, 26–29, 31,
    341, 343, 353, 354
    see also knowing and knowledge

Barmen Declaration, 365, 366, 369
Biggings, 2, 4, 5, 6,7, 14, 15, 16, 18, 21,
    26, 30, 151, 237

Book of Revelation, The (Oman), **348–53**
Brunner Group, 369–70
Burgess Oath, 19

call to ministry, 73–78
    call, Clayport, 132–34
    call, Westminster College, 212
    see also probationer
Calvinism
    grace, 286–88
    predestination, 85, 200, 269–70,
        272–73, 302
    providence of God, 31–32, 74, 174,
        264, 269
    revolution, 255
    see also Atonement controversies;
        Grace and Personality;
        Westminster Confession
Cambridge University
    Faculty of Divinity, 371
    Honorary Fellowship of Jesus
        College, 371
    Stanton lectures in philosophy of
        religion, 220
    University lectures in comparative
        religion, 220
chairs, nominations
    Aberdeen, UF College, 199
    Edinburgh University, 198–99
    Glasgow, UF College, 199–200,
        239–40

chairs, offers
    Auburn theological seminary, 202
    Chicago, Congregational Theological
        Seminary, 154, 197–98
    Melbourne, Ormond College, 201
chaplains, 337
Church and State, 106, 157, 201, 226,
        257, 303, 325, 356, 357
    Established Church, 3, 19, 35, 127,
        140, 187, 188, 356–57
    see also German church conflict
Church extension projects, Birmingham
    Chantry Road, Moseley, 296
    Holly Lane, Erdington, 52, 295,
        296–97
    Weoley Hill, 296
Church reunion, 301, 304, 305, 306
    encyclical, Ecumenical Patriarchate,
        311
    interdenominational mission,
        Oxford (1920), 277
    Mansfield conferences (1918, 1919,
        1920), 304
    Mansfield public lectures (1911), 302
    "Spiritual Regeneration as the Basis
        for World Reconstruction," 310
Church
    critique of, 130, 248, 250, 257,
        331–32, 386
    Church and Divine Order, The, 25,
        235–37, 309–10
    instrument of social reform, 56,
        164–67
    see also communion of saints;
        Church reunion; Church and
        state; missionary obligation
Common Sense philosophy, 59
communion of saints, 283–84, 303,
        326–27, 331–32
    see also Church
Concerning the Ministry, 18, 33, 55, 68,
        85, 86, 87, 88, 155–56, 227, **229**,
        264, 266, 321, 334, 352, **386**
Conference on Christian Politics,
    Economics and Citizenship,
    299–300
Confessing Church, 365, 366, 367, 369

conscientious objectors, 266–67
    Abancourt military prison
        (Blargies), 266
    Field Punishment No.1, 266
    see also pacifism; passive resistance;
        Fellowship of Reconciliation;
        Woodbrooke
conscription, 253

Declaratory Act, 70, 140, 141–42, 200n70
Defence of the Realm Act, 297
Deutsche Christen, 364, 365, 366, 369

Edinburgh slums, 82, 94, 95
    colony developments, 95, 98
    student mission, north Merchiston,
        96–97
Education Act 1870, 186
Education Act 1902, 49, 192–96, 201
    civil disobedience, 188–96
    stance on, Westminster College, 217
Education Act (Scotland) 1872, 10
Education Bill 1896, concerns, 186–88
Erlangen University
    classes in theology 109
    "Erlangen School," 102
    militarism, 111, 113
    students, 110–11
    system of study 108
    see also *Verein*
Essays in Philosophical Criticism,
    preface, 64–65
    influence of, 64, 169, 182

Faith and Freedom, 8, **168–83**, 374, 383
    lectures in America, 207–10, 212
    see also freedom; "Human Freedom"
Fellowship of Reconciliation, 242n10,
        245, 246
First Eastern Hospital, Cambridge, 242
Free Church Case, 132, 149, 200–201
Free Church Councils, 188, 190, 194,
        219, 222, 298
Free Church, 10, 13, 59, 69, 71, 76, 78–
        79, 81, 98, 127, 137, 138, 141,
        142, 146, 168, 200, 218, 237
Free Churches, 189, 195, 219, 231, 244,
        304

INDEX OF SUBJECTS

freedom
and necessity, 342–45
from oppression 192–93, 362–63
"Human Freedom," **269–71**
in Christ, 181
spiritual freedom, 225–26, 248–49, 347, 367–68
see also Faith and Freedom
funeral, 379–80

German Church Conflict, 365–68
see also *Deutsche Christen*; Barmen Declaration; Confessing Church
German scholarship, influence, 63, 72, 102, 155
grace
faith and morality, 162, 164, 140, 177, 178, 180
revealed in Christ, 120, 139, 159, 163, 170, 218, 302, 336
universal, 19, 25, 91, 142, 387
unmerited, 233, 234
see also Grace and Personality
Grace and Personality, 31, 66, 123, 142, 181, 183, **273–88**, 380, 384, 386
Green Batt meeting house, 143, 146n104, 151

Heidelberg University
dismissal of professors, 363–64; see also Nazi Congress; Nuremberg race laws
lectures, 118
militarism, 115
heresy trials
Fergus Ferguson and David Macrae, 139–40
James Morison, 140n78
George Adam Smith, 71n27
William Robertson Smith, 68, 70, 94
Higher Criticism, 69–70, 72, 78n66, 350
believing criticism, 71
see also heresy trials
holy, 30, 91, 106, 172, 187, 247n35, 329, 338, 339, 340, 382
remnant, 328

honest religion, 86
see also *Honest Religion*; sincerity; truth
Honest Religion, 31, 373, **374–78**
Hudson Bay Company, 15

Idealist Philosophy, 57, 64, 169
see also *Essays in Philosophical Criticism*, preface
individual
conscience, 196, 248, 376
individualism, 122, 181, 235
individuality, 27–28
liberty, 160, 161, 162, 269
philanthropy, 164
worth, 177, 180, 181
see also state; prophet
insincerity, 228, 278, 386

Kerr lectures, 8, 50, 161, 168, 168, 201, 206
Martin lectures, Westminster, 167, 217
knowing and knowledge, 341

League of Nations, 252n66, 310, 311, 313, 314
League of Nations Society, 256
League of Nations Union, 257
Leipzig Book Exhibition, 358
see also Mingana palimpsest
Lewis-Gibson scholarship, 356
Lutheran pastors, 314, 365
Lutheran theology, 102, 119, 122

Madagascar, 6n28, 16, 308
Madras school, 11, 12
marriage, 150–51
Marrow controversy, 18–19
see also Atonement; Westminster Confession; Calvinism
"Method in Theology," 307
Mingana palimpsest, 358–60
missionary obligation of church, 218, 232–34
see also Edinburgh slums

national service, 248, 259–60, 262–63
  Lord Derby's Appeal, 262
Natural and the Supernatural, The,
  27–29, 75, 116, 123, 328–29,
  338–48, 353, 381, 383; *see also*
  holy, nature, religion(s)
nature, sensibility to
  Alps, Swiss, 117
  Heidelberg, 116
  Hudson and Mohawk valleys, 204
  Lehigh valley, 204
  Niagara Falls, 204–5
Nazi congress, 368
Nazism 118, 364
Neuchâtel, 116
Norway, cruise, 238–39, 371
Nuremberg Race Laws, 368

On Religion: Speeches to its Cultured Despisers, **154–58**
ordination and induction, Clayport Church Alnwick, 132–37
Orkney and Shetland Association
  Edinburgh University, 237
  Glasgow reunion, 238
  see also Viking Club; Norway cruise

pacifism, 248, 263, 269
  see also conscientious objectors; passive resistance; Fellowship of Reconciliation, Woodbrooke settlement
Passive Resistance Association, PCE, 195
passive resistance, 190, 192–96, 317–20
portrait, 1
post-war, 252, 298–300, 301, 309, 328
Presbyterian Church of England, 1, 51, 81, 125, 137–38, 143, 386
  see also Presbyterian College, London; Passive Resistance Association, PCE
Presbyterian College, London, 137n62, 138n66, 215–16, 218
prison camps, 243
  Lofthouse Park Camp, Wakefield, 243
probationer, 124–26
  Makerstoun, 126–28

Paisley, St James' UP Church, 128–32
prophecy
  and poetry, 53, 348, 352–54
  and religion, 348
prophet
  instrument of God, 196, 255
  persecution of, 78
  prophet of Westminster, 48, 327–28
  prophets and apostles, 24, 271, 280
prophetic
  autonomy, 339
  dialogue, 385, 386
  hope, 284
  ideal 237
  inspiration, 351
  vocation, 75
  witness, 157, 161, 250, 346
  word, 332, 334
  see also prophetic remnant; prophecy
prophetic remnant, 236, 328–30, 366

ragged school, Alnwick, 184–85
religion(s), 180, 227, 345–46, 348, 349
Revelation (Apocalypse of St John), 348, 349, 351, 352, 353, 354
revelation
  in Bible, 72, 120, 380
  in history, 72, 120, 123
  in Jesus, 8, 75, 178, 179, 183, 208, 209, 279, 328, 336, 384
  mystery of, 171, 375, 347
revolution, 34, 173, 174, 255–56
Robertson Smith affair, 69, 77, 78, 102, 107, 158, 219, 308
Ruhr and Rhineland, 314–17

SCM conference, Berlin, 368–69
  see also Brunner Group
Secession, 9, 18, 19, 25, 51, 70, 81, 85, 86, 137, 138, 140, 141
Serbian boy refugees, 290, 291
Shakespeare, 28, 44, 54, 341, 352, 353, 381
sincerity, 91, 104n14, 222, 228, 249, 281, 282, 303, 340, 376
  see also insincerity; truth

social inequality, 181
  in America, 210–11
  social justice, 248, 252
  see also missionary obligation of church
socialism, 182, 235, 365
state
  abuse of powers, 79
  national state, 105, 363
  state and individual, 253, 254, 255, 256
  welfare provision, 98, 181
  see also Church and State
Stenness, 2, 4, 6, 7, 10, 11, 12, 13, 16, 20, 22, 151, 238
  stones of, 29–30, 349
Stromness, 2, 3, 5, 7, 10, 12, 13, 14, 15, 20, 21, 128, 134, 237
  Victoria Street UP Church, 9, 18, 21n98, 22, 24, 25
  Victoria Street UF Church, 19n93, 23
Syracuse University, 206

translation, 155–56
tribunals, 263, 293–94
Trinity Presbyterian Church, Camden, 232
truth, 120, 135, 158, 161, 172, 175, 182, 237, 275, 381, 383, 385
  Christian life and, 210, 245, 280, 283, 310, 326, 333, 367
  disregard of, 62, 76, 78, 79, 174, 228, 258
  divine, 9, 32, 72, 74, 91, 163, 278, 336, 347, 371
  love of, 57, 59, 76, 78, 180, 193, 297, 250, 271, 334, 379, 386
  openness to, 170, 171, 174, 222, 257, 273, 307, 354
  search for, 41, 71, 75–78, 80, 86, 91, 136, 180, 160, 162, 168, 226, 339. 374, 377, 380
  stance for, 101, 244, 285, 328, 329
  see also freedom; sincerity
"Tübingen School," 131n40, 175–77

Udal law, 6

Union of Democratic Control, 259
United Free Church, 19n93, 52, 149, 199, 200, 219, 268, 357
United Presbyterian Church, 9, 19n93, 25, 56, 69, 70, 71, 81, 84, 85, 86, 87, 125, 138n63, 140, 200
  see also Declaratory Act
United Presbyterian Church Divinity Hall, 80–83
  curriculum, 82–84
  placements, 93
  practical work, 93
  preaching, 84–89
  student missionary society, 93–94
University of Edinburgh, 34–36
  arts course, 36–38
  Philosophical Society, 46n44, 63–64, 66
  students, 38–42
  UP Students' Society, 39, 42–45, 100
  women students, 40, 42

Verein, 112
  duels, 113–14
  walking tour, 112–13
Viking Club, 238–39
Vision and Authority, **158–67**

Walker Trust, 310
war, 241–42, 244–45, 274, 358, 361
  holy war, 247
  War and its Issues, The, **246–59**
  "War," **271–73**
  see also "Human Freedom"; *Army and Religion*; post-war
Western Front
  Casualty Clearing Stations, 262
  General Hospitals, 265–66
  Hill 60, 261
  Neuve Chapelle, 261
Westminster College
  Barbour chair, 212, 216, 370n61
  curriculum, 199–200, 223–24
  elocution, 221–22
  placements, 223–25
  student pastor scheme, 309
  see also Serbian boy refugees

Westminster Confession, 8, 9, 138,
139-43, 302
  Moderator's address, 143, 335-36
  See also Declaratory Act; Auburn
Declaration
Whaling, 4-5, 15
Woodbrooke, 292-93, 294, 295, 296,
297, 298
World Alliance for Promoting
International Friendship
Through the Churches, 311-14
  British Council, 311-12, 313-14,
316, 319-20, 323
  prison visits, 317-19
  Lille conference, 324

YMCA
  base camps, 260-61; huts 261
  Bedford camp, 241, 260;
  lectures in base camps, 264-65, 365
  uniform, 267

Index of Names

Adamson, Robert, 63
Alexander, George William, 38, 44, 48, 52, 67, 101, 112, 196, 229, 319, 369, 371, 372, 373, 379n2
Andrews, Charles Freer, 297, 346n69
Anscombe, Elizabeth, 382
Ayer, A.J., 380, 385

Bailey, Charles E., 259n109, 267n157, 268n163
Baker, J. Allen, 312
Ballard, Frank H., 374, 379
Balmbra, John, 135, 145, 147, 197, 202, 203n82, 212, 213
Barrie, J.M., 38, 39, 40, 54, 59, 61
Barth, Karl, 119n80, 122n95, 181n158, 369, 380, 381
Bartsch, Karl, 117
Baur, Ferdinand Christian, 118n72, 174, 175, 176, 177
Bebbington, David, 187, 98
Beet, Joseph Agar, 320, 321, 350
Begg, James, 98
Bell, Andrew, 11
Bell, George, 244, 313n68, 316, 366
Berlin, Isaiah, 179n149
Besier, Gerhard, 364
Bevans, Stephen, 7n33, 53n72, 68n5, 88n116, 345n64, 352n103, 372n72, 375n103, 384n38, 385
Binfield, Clyde, 189n19
Bismarck, Otto von, 105n20, 111
Blackie, John Stuart, 39

Blair, Henry Hunter, 151–52
Bonhoeffer, Dietrich, 324, 366, 367
Booth-Clibborn, Catherine (la Maréchale), 309n45
Brandt, Richard, 358n139, 359, 361, 364n29, 370
Brooke, A.E., 350
Brown, James, 83, 88, 124, 126, 128, 134
Brunner, Emil, 369, 370
Buber, Martin, 382
Butler, Joseph, 171, 178–79, 226
Buxton, Dorothy, 259, 366n40
Buxton, Travers, 312n61, 313n73, 366n40

Cadbury, George, 292n293
Cadoux, C.J., 246n28, 254n77
Caird, Edward, 53, 64–65, 343n51, 383n29
Caird, George, 352
Cairns, David S., 106, 125, 128, 179, 197, 199n67, 212n119, 231, 232, 265, 268, 287, 289
Cairns, John, 9n45, 72n31, 80, 83, 84, 89–92, 106, 125, 138, 140–41
Calderwood, Henry, 39–42, 43, 55–59, 63, 70, 92, 100, 106, 139–40, 154, 227
Calvin, John, 286, 287
Campbell, John McLeod, 176, 205
Candlish, James, 71
Cecil, Hugh, 305
Chadwick, Henry, 383

Chivers, 241n4
Chrystal, George, 40
Class, Gustav, 118
Clements, Keith, 367n43, 369, 370
Coats, Peter, 130
Collingwood, R.G., 342
Corner, Alexander, 37
Corner, Philip, 10–11, 37
Cunningham, Ebenezer, 246
Curzon, George, 320

Darwin, Charles, 111, 343, 344
Davidson, Andrew Brice, 70, 71, 71n24
Davidson, Randall, 219, 244, 313, 320, 321
Day, A.F., 299n326
Deissmann, Gustav Adolf, 244n15
Denney, James, 168, 198n60
Derrida, Jacques, 382
Dibelius, Martin, 364, 369
Dickinson, G. Lowes, 259
Dickinson, Willoughby, 233, 256, 323, 312, 320
Drummond, Henry, 56
Duff, David, 129
Dykes, J. Oswald, 138, 141, 198, 203, 217

Einstein, Albert, 343
Ellis, Marian, 299n324
Elmslie, W.A. Leslie, 242, 273, 307, 309n42, 356n128, 370n61, 379n4
Erskine, Ebenezer, 18, 19, 85
Erskine, Ralph, 18, 19, 85
Fairbairn, Andrew Martin, 198, 217
Farmer, H. H., 87, 159, 177, 228, 241, 246, 273, 287, 288, 293, 294, 295, 297, 345, 380, 384
Farrer, Austin, 352
Fenn, Reginald, 293, 294, 295, 297
Ferguson, Fergus, 139–40
Ferrier, James Frederick, 59n100
Fischer, Kuno, 117
Foot, Philippa, 382
Forsyth, P. T., 166n77, 253n67, 273
Frank, Franz Hermann Reinhold, 109, 110, 118, 119, 121, 177

Fraser, Alexander Campbell, 34–35, 55, 59–63
Fraser, James, 223, 224, 379n4

Gadamer, Hans-Georg, 120, 382
Galloway, A.D., 381–82
Gardner, James, 102
Gardner, Lucy, 246, 299n325
Garvie, A.E., 141n81, 324
Germanos, Metropolitan of Thyateira, 311
Gibb, John, 218
Gibson, John Monro, 188, 217
Gibson, Margaret Dunlop, 216, 354
Gillie, R.C., 239, 313n73
Gowans, James, 95
Grant, George, 339, 345, 346, 385
Groh, Wilhelm, 364

Haldane, R.B., 63, 64, 65n120
Halliday, Fearon, 296
Hamilton, William, 56–57, 59, 72n31
Hampson, Daphne, 366, 367
Hardy, G.H., 259
Hare, Henry, 216
Harnack, Adolf von, 72n31, 244n15, 254n77, 327
Harris, Rendel, 293n295, 297
Hausrath, Adolf, 118–19
Hawkridge, Percy B., 246, 263
Headlam, A.C., 367n43, 304, 326n130
Healey, Francis, 14n71, 88n116, 89n118, 154n1, 157n21, 168n87, 239n113, 294n300, 352n102, 357n133, 369, 373
Hegel, Georg Wilhelm Friedrich, 57, 62, 63, 64, 65, 118, 341, 381, 383
Heidegger, Martin, 120
Heim, Karl, 369, 370
Hetherington, Bill, 266n152, 294n303
Hick, John, 288, 344n56, 346, 384
Hitler, Adolf, 362, 363, 364, 366, 368
Hodgkin, Henry, 310n48
Hodgson, Henry, 366–67
Hofmann, Johann von, 119, 120, 121, 122
Hood, Adam, 88, 125, 384n36
Hood, George, 294n302

INDEX OF NAMES

Houston, Fleur, 179n150, 259n110, 314n75
Houston, Walter, 328n140
Hulbert, Henry Harper, 221
Hüne, Friedrich von, 359

Jelke, Robert, 364

Kahle, Paul, 358, 358
Kant, Immanuel, 2, 8, 37, 57, 59, 63, 64, 65, 66, 122, 154, 168, 171, 172, 173, 177, 178, 179, 254, 256n91, 339, 341, 383
Kattenbusch, Ferdinand, 338
Keller, Adolf, 363n20
Ker, John, 72n31, 80, 83, 84–85, 96, 97, 132n44, 143, 197
Kipling, Rudyard, 273n188
Kirkup, Thomas, 181–82n160
Kirkwood, Thomas, 9, 15, 22, 23, 24, 25n114, 68, 128, 134, 135
Knox, R. Buick, 137, 138, 215, 216, 218
Knox, T.M., 339, 381
Koch, Karl, 366
Köhler, Walter, 364
Krupp, Gustav von Bohlen und Halbach, 321

Lagarde, Paul, 123
Lang, Cosmo Gordon, 305n25
Lawrence, D.H. (L. H. Davison), 350, 351, 353
Lewis, Agnes Smith, 216, 354
Limont, William, 132, 133, 134, 135, 144, 152, 153, 184
Lindsay, A.D., 338, 341, 385
Luther, Martin, 34, 101, 103, 104, 105, 106, 107, 116, 122, 123, 169, 181n158, 254

MacArthur, Arthur, 133n50, 386
Macintosh, Hugh R., 198, 199
MacLeod, John, 343
Macrae, David, 58n94, 118, 139–40
Maier, Bernard, 18, 39, 53, 71, 72, 75n46&47, 79n70, 114n52
Malik, Maleiha, 278, 322n116, 384
Malinowski, Bronislaw, 342n49

Mander, W.J., 65
Manson, T.W., 77, 86, 159, 350, 370
Masson, David M., 53–55, 352
McConnell, Frank, 379
Mein, Benjamin, 48, 50, 51, 52, 102, 134, 193, 296–97
Micklem, Nathaniel, 1, n.1, 296, 374n96, 380
Midgley, Mary, 382
Monod, Wilfred, 320
Moody, Dwight L. and Sankey, Ira D., 56, 71, 91, 146
Moody, Dwight L., 125, 91
Munson, James, 189n19
Murdoch, Iris, 382

Neander, Herman, 84, 155n6, 314
Needham, Joseph, 342
Newbigin, J. E. Lesslie, 227, 229, 373
Newbigin, J. Lesslie, 143, 151
Newman, John Henry, 173, 174, 176
Newton, Isaac, 343
Nicoll, William Robertson, 189
Niemöller, Martin, 367n43, 369
Noble, William, 306–7

Oliver, Ernest Henry, 190, 191, 194
Oman (née Blair), Mary Hannah, 150, 153, 213, 229–30, 372
Oman (née Rendall), Isabella, 2–4, 134
Oman, Helen Dixon, 153n131, 379n2
Oman, Isabella Gertrude (Ia), 6n28, 68n5, 153, 259, 308n38, 379n2
Oman, Isabella, 11, 12, 15, 16–17, 373
Oman, James, 6n28, 7, 13n65, 14, 16, 308
Oman, Jean Wood, 153n131, 346n69, 379n2
Oman, Mary Blair (Maisie), 153n131, 371, 373, 379n2
Oman, Simon Rust (Captain Oman), 2, 3, 4–10, 11, 134, 151
Oman, Simon, 15, 17, 150, 238
Oman, Thomas, 15, 17–18
Orr, James, 71, 122n95
Otto, Rudolf, 30, 226, 339, 340, 382
Otty, John Elgar Sugden, 190, 191, 194
Oud Wasenaar, 312

INDEX OF NAMES

Pascal, Blaise, 170-71, 206
Penn, William, 256n91
Petersen, Gotfred, 16
Polanyi, Michael, 383
Pyper, Hugh, 254n77

Radek, Karl, 317n100
Rainy, Robert, 68n8, 71n27, 78-80, 119n75, 201
Reid, Thomas, 59
Rendall, Magnus, 3
Ricoeur, Paul, 120, 382
Riddoch, Alexander, 13-14
Riefenstal, Leni, 364n28
Ritchie, D.G., 63,
Ritschl, Albrecht, 72, 118, 119, 121-23, 175, 176, 177, 178, 179, 182, 206, 211, 383
Riviere, Hugh Goldwin, 1-2, 371
Roberts, Richard, 245
Robertson, David, 97
Robertson, Margaret (neé Oman), 7n34, 12, 14, 15, 17
Rorke, J.D.M., 18, 195, 244n20
Rothe, Richard, 72, 118, 257
Rowntree, Joseph, 293
Russell, Bertrand, 259

Schleiermacher, Friedrich, 83, 118, 119, 120, 121, 154, 155, 156, 157, 158, 164, 172, 173, 177, 180, 226, 341, 342, 354, 364, 383
Schweitzer, Albert, 331
Scott, Charles Archibald Anderson, 216, 219, 242, 250, 295, 304, 350
Selbie, W. B., 181n159, 217n18, 247n35, 253n67, 302, 304n18, 305n24, 380
Seth, Andrew, 64
Seth, James, 37, 42, 63, 64, 198
Siegmund-Schultze, Friedrich, 312, 314
Simpson, Patrick Carnegie, 70, 73, 212n119, 219, 292n289, 305, 307, 316, 356n129, 379
Sinnreich, Joseph, 241, 243
Skinner, John, 217, 218, 219, 221, 222, 225, 230, 231, 232, 244, 245,
246, 253n67, 260, 290, 292, 295, 307, 328-29, 350
Small, Robert, 20n94, 51n61, 96, 97n145&146, 123, 127n22, 129n30, 134n52,
Smith, George Adam, 50n59, 71, 202, 306, 349
Smith, Norman Kemp, 160
Smith, William Robertson, 53, 58, 68, 70, 71, 74-76, 78-79, 98
Snape, Michael, 268n159, 289n278
Söderblom, Nathan, 299, 311n53, 313, 314, 315, 316, 320n108, 321, 322
Sorley, W.R., 63, 255n82
Spence, Magnus, 13, 13n.61, 30, 238
Stadener, Sam, 314, 316n92, 319, 321
Stanton, Vincent Henry, 268
Stewart, George Black, 204, 205, 207
Stobbs, William, 20, 21-22
Strauss, David F., 119
Sundkler, Bengt, 313, 314, 315

Tagore, Rabindranath, 297
Tait, Peter Guthrie, 40, 52-53
Talbot, Neville, 305
Tatlow, Tissington, 260n112
Taylor, Charles, 158, 165, 166, 375, 381, 382, 384n32
Tennant, F.R., 51n60, 273, 288, 342, 350, 383n30
Tocqueville, Alexis de, 250n54
Treitschke, Heinrich von, 105n20, 118n70, 255
Trilling, Lionel, 249

Visser 't Hooft, Willem Rudolf, 370

Walzer, Michael, 255
Watson, John (Ian MacLaren), 161, 203, 204n86, 216, 217
Welch, Adam Cleghorn, 38, 48, 50, 52, 199, 373
Wellhausen, Julius, 72
Whitehead, A.N., 381
Whitehorn, Roy, 1n2, 229-30
Whitehouse, Owen Charles, 220
Wihlborg, Alfred, 314, 316n92, 319, 321
Wilson, Woodrow, 211, 223

Windelband, Wilhelm, 338–39
Wood, Herbert G., 297, 298, 299, 346n69
Wood, Isabella, 3
Woodfin, Yandall, 7n33, 373n88
Woodside, David, 67, 69, 82, 84, 85, 86, 93, 94, 134, 136

Wright, T.R., 351
Wylie, Andrew, 20, 24n110
Wyon, Allan G., 225

Zahn, Theodor, 118